This unique anthology of nonfiction writing was conceived as a companion to the enduringly popular Mentor volume *Points of View: An Anthology of Short Stories*, edited by James Moffett and Kenneth R. McElheny. As readable and as thoughtfully selected as its predecessor, *Points of Departure* extends the previous volume's exploration of the craft of writing to the world of nonfiction. James Moffett's lucid and informative notes introduce each section in the context of the wide range of prose techniques this collection represents.

JAMES MOFFETT is the author of the influential ACTIVE VOICE: A WRITING PROGRAM ACROSS THE CURRICULUM and several other books on writing and the language arts. He has been ⬚⬚⬚⬚⬚⬚⬚⬚⬚⬚ Phillips Exeter Academy ⬚⬚⬚⬚⬚⬚⬚⬚⬚⬚ ⬚rnia at Berkeley, Sa⬚⬚⬚⬚⬚⬚⬚⬚⬚⬚⬚⬚⬚ ⬚lebury College Brea⬚⬚⬚⬚⬚⬚⬚⬚⬚⬚⬚⬚⬚ ⬚shops with teachers ⬚⬚⬚⬚⬚⬚⬚⬚⬚⬚⬚⬚⬚ insti-tutes in the N⬚

MENTOR

MERIDIAN

MENTOR

Anthologies You'll Want to Read

POINTS
OF
DEPARTURE

AN ANTHOLOGY
OF NONFICTION

James Moffett
EDITOR

A MENTOR BOOK

MENTOR

Published by the Penguin Group

Penguin Books USA Inc., 375 Hudson Street,
New York, New York 10014, U.S.A.
Penguin Books Ltd, 27 Wrights Lane,
London W8 5TZ, England
Penguin Books Australia Ltd, Ringwood,
Victoria, Australia
Penguin Books Canada Ltd, 10 Alcorn Avenue,
Toronto, Ontario, Canada M4V 3B2
Penguin Books (N.Z.) Ltd, 182–190 Wairau Road,
Auckland 10, New Zealand

Penguin Books Ltd, Registered Offices:
Harmondsworth, Middlesex, England

Published by Mentor, an imprint of Dutton Signet,
a division of Penguin Books USA Inc.

First Printing, March, 1985
12 11 10 9 8 7 6

Acknowledgment is made to the publishers and authors of the following books and articles for permission to quote material:

"The Coca-Cola/Grove Press Letters," vol. 14 of *Evergreen Review*. Permission granted by Irene Scheider.

Holmes letters, Harvard University Press. Reprinted by permission.

"My Dungeon Shook: Letter to My Nephew," from *The Fire Next Time*. Copyright © 1962 by James Baldwin. A Dial Press book reprinted by permission of Doubleday & Company, Inc.

"Life in London of the 1660s,." from *Everybody's Pepys: The Diary of Samuel Pepys 1660–1669*, edited by O.S. Morshead. Reprinted by permission of the Publisher, G. Bell and Sons, London.

Journal of Anais Nin. Vol. 2., edited by Gunther Stuhlman, published by Peter Owen, London.

"My Name is Margaret," from *I Know Why the Caged Bird Sings* by Maya Angelou. Random House, Inc.

(The following page constitutes an extension of this copyright page.)

REGISTERED TRADEMARK—MARCA REGISTRADA

Library of Congress Catalog Card Number: 84-62339

Printed in the United States of America

BOOKS ARE AVAILABLE AT QUANTITY DISCOUNTS WHEN USED TO PROMOTE PRODUCTS OR SERVICES. FOR INFORMATION PLEASE WRITE TO PREMIUM MARKETING DIVISION, PENGUIN BOOKS USA INC., 375 HUDSON STREET, NEW YORK, NEW YORK 10014.

Contents

RECOLLECTION 95

INVESTIGATION 163

COGITATION 371

POINTS OF DEPARTURE

Introduction

WHATEVER OTHER PURPOSE an anthology may serve, it should be a good book to read. The following assortment of correspondence and journal, autobiography and memoir, biography and history, case and profile, article and essay, has been compiled to entertain and stimulate at the same time that it arrays in a roughly significant order some instances of the various kinds of writing that comprise the world of nonfiction prose.

Actually, it's a shame to refer to this rich diversity by such a negative and nondescript term as "nonfiction." I would like here to display it in its own right and to do this from the writer's point of view. These types of writing are not a disjointed and accidental miscellany but a continuous process of symbolizing experience—when viewed as *what the writer does*. I trust that while illustrating the stances a writer may take, this arrangement of selections will also increase the pleasure of reading each. The book is a sampler for that inner author in everyone who is constantly fashioning knowledge from firsthand and secondhand experience and who at any moment can go to paper, as did those whose efforts we are about to read.

The arrangement here is not traditional but may incidentally clarify some traditional terms and concepts, such as "reportage," "exposition," "informal essay," "argumentation," and the like, that are used to talk about the reading and writing of nonfiction. I based the following categories and sequence of selections on what the author does in order to turn up and work up the material of the subject. First, does the author look within or without? If within, is the author basically recollecting or reflecting? If recollecting, is the author recalling events of yesterday or long ago, events the author keenly participated in or observed distantly?

1

If focusing outside, does the author go and look, go and ask, or go look up? And so on. These are questions about what the author actually does in order to come by and compose some subject matter. And of course to these different choices of authorial actions there correspond different purposes and audiences. Content is a factor of intent.

Whether amateur or professional, a prose writer does one of four things to generate the material of a composition. You recollect, investigate, invent, or cogitate. That is, you look back, look into, think up, or think over. These involve the faculties of sensation, memory, imagination, and reason. They are different ways of learning and knowing and of course work together and feed into each other. (Intuition is a holistic mode of knowing, cutting across and integrating faculties.)

Very roughly, these organs of knowledge-making form a progression. The senses make information according to their own lights, and memory stores this according to its own filing system. Imagination and reason go to work on this accumulated knowledge by shuffling it all up and recombining it to construct new connections, concatenations, and constellations. Imagination does this by private association, reason by public logic. But the progression is circular. The frames of reference already established by imagination and reason act downward to direct how sensation should perceive and memory should store.

Interestingly, it turns out that in arraying finished pieces of writing according to the inner and outer actions of the author one finds oneself dealing with relationships in time and space, with physical distance between those old grammatical persons of speaker, audience, and subject. This physical distance among first, second, and third persons corresponds to psychological distances among the writer, written-to, and written-about that define many aspects of composition and stake out the universe of discourse.

Since these distances vary, moreover, from one type of writing to another, one may sequence writing samples in ways that bring out these graduations of increasing distance in certain relationships among the three persons. Such scaling shows in a practical way how differences in kinds of writing relate to different decisions or necessities about the author's relation to some material and to some audience.

Scaling makes apparent also how the distancing among the trinity of persons connects with another basic feature of grammar—the tense of the verb. In discourse, time distance concerns when events occur in relation to when they are told about. As a shift of focus from first to third person indicates increasing distance between the author and the sources of information, so a shift in tense signals the abstracting of infomation to a "higher" level or more encompassing scope. It shifts from *what happened* to *what happens*, from the past tense of fact to the present tense of generalization. The hinge between narrative and generalization may be the most crucial point in the thinking process, because it is then that the mind moves from once-upon-a-time to the time-lessness of "recurring" events, from token to type.

But of course all writing is idea writing, not just essay. Narrative embodies and embeds ideas. It differs from essay and article not in lacking ideas but in *implying* or *demonstrating* ideas. So another progression takes us from implicit to explicit expression, which parallels a movement from concrete to abstract (small to large compass in time and space).

I will define abstraction, then, as expansion across time and space, involving grammatical persons and tenses, that corresponds in a measure with expansion of consciousness. But we must not think that abstracter is of itself better; though we grow by expanding mentally across time and space, this means only that we *should be able* to abstract at a high level of synopsis, not that we *should*. What is important is to be able to play over the whole abstactive spectrum according to need and wish. Considering higher abstaction within a spectrum keeps it related to the concreter realms from which it is formulated so that one can see its provenance and offset the curse of abstraction, which is its very removal from the familiar reality of the sensuous world.

All this needs illustrating, and that is precisely what the samples will do, for one thing, but we can summarize here by saying that a curious connection exists between the pragmatic issue of how various kinds of writing get done and the more broadly theoretical matter of how human beings *make* sense, that is, distill experience into symbols that may be applied to further experience. Actually, all of this is quite practical inasmuch as we need to distill from life some sort of wisdom for guidance. This entails abstacting particulars into generalities—a risky but useful and sometimes beautiful business.

But the writer does not merely abstact *from* some sources but *for* a certain audience. The abstacting process crosses the author-subject relation with the author-audience relation. The shift in abstractive attitude from first to third person is only part of what makes for different kinds of discourse. Another critical progression occurs as distance increases between the speaker and the spoken-to. But the shifts in this relation occur more noticeably in speech. Just as the speaker and spoken-about differentiate increasingly into two separate persons—an author writing about an other—so the speaker and spoken-to begin, in children, as the same person and gradually diverge as young people allow more and more for their audience and address increasingly remote audiences. Writing itself begins when speaker and listener are not in the same place at the same time. The kind of writing that captures this momentous separation of first and second persons is correspondence.

And that is where this book begins. Up to that point discourse is all oral. The opening selections here are exchanges of letters, a kind of dialog at a distance, and thus represent a transition from speech to writing. As a farewell to the interactive, collaborative discourse of dialog, letters represent a kind of matrix that will differentiate itself into all the other kinds of writing, which are monological. This opening section is called Interaction.

If letters serve as the threshold between oral and written discourse, diaries and journals make the transition from private to public audience. They constitute writing at its closest to ongoing verbalization of *what is happening*. For this reason and because diaries and journals so often serve as notes for later compositions I will call them Notation. Typically, the diarist, like the correspondent, is writing from within the events and not from the vantage point of their conclusion. In fact, a "conclusion" is a compositional decision made by an author as part of writing an autobiography or memoir. Thus letters and diaries lead from oral speech and sensory registration into Recollection and the rest of the sequence of this book.

After Interaction and Notation selections go from Recollection to Investigation to Cogitation. The participant *I* of the autobiographer and memoirist shifts to the observer *I* of the reporter-researcher. Then as the investigator's knowledge becomes secondhand the *I* dissolves into *he, she, it,* and *they*. As sources shift from first- to secondhand, the grammatical person shifts from first to third—a most important correlation. Next the investigator becomes cogitator as emphasis shifts from facts to ideas about the facts—reflection, Thinking Over and Thinking Through. The *I* reappears for a while as personal essayist—for the progression is cyclical—but assumes now a more synoptic or synthesizing role, no longer a narrator but a philosopher.

The fact that correspondence and journal-keeping preview the other kinds of nonfiction but under rudimentary conditions typifies the cyclical character of this book's progression. It is not a single, linear continuum like the color spectrum but a recursive spectrum that contains miniatures of itself. Thus the progressive divergence from each other of speaker, audience, and subject that spans the book translates into somewhat different terms and circumstances within each of the five divisions—Interaction, Notation, Recollection, Investigation, and Cogitation. For example, selections in Recollection shift from focus on the author to focus on other, whereas in Cogitation they move from emphasis on the personal context that prompted a certain general reflection to an emphasis on some generalization disembedded from any circumstances of the author that stimulated it. In other words, the sequence of selections spirals, passes the same points but on different planes.

This was the approach I used with Kenneth McElheny in compiling *Points of View: An Anthology of Short Stories* (New American Library, Mentor). In fact, the present collection may serve as a companion volume to that army of fictional techniques, which, as we said there, imitates the ways people report events in real life—as letters and diaries, autobiographies and memoirs, biographies and chronicles. Thus the narrative range of nonfiction provides the model documents that various first- and third-person fiction purports to be. And the principles by which we arrayed short stories so as to form a spectrum of fictional techniques will serve well in ordering the present collection, because the differentiations underlying our concepts of "point of view" apply beyond storytelling, being in fact features of the more general process of absbacting experience into knowledge.

In *Active Voice: A Writing Program Across the Curriculum* (Boynton/Cook), I cast the kinds of nonfiction writing into the form of brief assignment directions such as might be given to the apprentice writer to produce his or her own samples like those of the professionals arrayed here. That book also contains suggestions for how members of a writing workshop may help each other work up material and respond usefully to each other's drafts of each particular sort of writing. Some reading selections are listed there for each type, and the interrelationships of types to one another are pointed out somewhat as here. *Active Voices* 1–4 (Boynton/Cook) are anthologies of writing by students in elementary school, junior high, senior high, and college respectively that parallel, as much as is appropriate for the age, the samples of professional fiction in *Points of View* and the samples of nonfiction in this present volume. The teaching and learning of composition surely proceed best when apprentices go about writing as nearly as possible the way professionals do.

The selections themselves will fill in the picture, with guidance from some headnotes. It is sufficient for the moment to know the general rationale of the table of contents so that the sequence and juxtaposition of selections may have significance. Theory and practice are put in a position to illuminate each other. But read first of course for what each piece has to say for itself. Reading in order is just one kind of itinerary for these highly individual ports of call.

INTERACTION

LETTERS are the only kind of writing that retain the give-and-take of dialog. They may contain questions, commands, requests, threats, advice, or seduction, because receivers are responders. The audience is the smallest and closest a writer can have, and a correspondent writes under the influence of that audience and of the relationship that motivates the exchange. The term "correspondence" catches, in the idea of co-responding, the collaborative feature that is unique.

Because it aims so precisely to get a certain effect on a certain receiver, a letter perhaps manifests most clearly the rhetorical dimension of all writing—the abstracting *for* someone from some content to realize an intent. This is native art, the instinctive rhetoric of the amateur using language as only one instrument of the will. Though the professional writer may bring wrought art to correspondence, letters mainly do not aim at publication, which even for the professional comes usually from a later decision, often made by others. So in the private, impromptu, and colloquial spirit of letters we find writing of the kind anyone may practice, at its closest to conversation itself.

But within the dialog of correspondence the monologuist develops. Because they are not together, letter writers must each in turn hold forth longer alone than in conversation. Separation in space slows down the exchange in time. In the rapid turn-around of dialog, utterances are short and collaborative prompting tight. But without immediate response the correspondent must spin out a longer continuity without knowing if it is having the desired effect. This naturally causes one to select and order words and ideas more deliberately than in conversation. So in compensating for the loss of face-to-face vocal advantages, letter-writing advances composition beyond the more improvisational stage of oral speech. *Any* monologuing develops composition, because the more sustained a continuity the more selecting and ordering and self-revising have to be done.

To permit appreciation of both the dialogical and monological traits of correspondence, the following samples begin with exchanges of letters, move to one-way series, and end with the single letter. In shifting emphasis from the *I-you* relation to the *I-it* relation, this arrangement previews the movement of the whole book. But however anonymous or diffused may become the rhetorical relation of speaker to audience, even in the most formal treatise, the intent of the writer always works its effect on the reader. Only the mode changes.

Two-Way Exchange of Letters

Coca-Cola—Grove Press Letters

This complete interaction between two corporate executives takes the classic form of stimulus-and-response.

March 25, 1970

Mr. R. W. Seaver
Executive Vice President
Grove Press, Inc.
214 Mercer Street
New York, New York 10012

Dear Mr. Seaver:

Several people have called to our attention your advertisement for *Diary of a Harlem Schoolteacher* by Jim Haskins, which appeared in the *New York Times* March 3, 1970. The theme of the ad is "This book is like a weapon . . . it's the real thing."

Since our company has made use of "It's the Real Thing" to advertise Coca-Cola long prior to the publication of the book, we are writing to ask you to stop using this theme or slogan in connection with the book.

We believe you will agree that it is undesirable for our companies to make simultaneous use of "the real thing" in connection with our respective products. There will always be likelihood of confusion as to the source or sponsorship of the goods, and the use by such prominent companies would dilute the distinctiveness of the trade slogan and diminish its effectiveness and value as an advertising and merchandising tool.

"It's the Real Thing" was first used in advertising for Coca-Cola over twenty-seven years ago to refer to our product. We first used it in print advertising in 1942 and extended it to outdoor advertising, including painted walls—some of which are still displayed throughout the country. The line has appeared in advertising for Coca-Cola during succeeding years. For example, in 1954 we used "There's this about Coke— You Can't Beat the Real Thing" in national advertising. We resumed national use of "It's the Real Thing" in the summer of 1969 and it is our main thrust for 1970.

Please excuse my writing so fully, but I wanted to explain why we feel it necessary to ask you and your associates to use another line to advertise Mr. Haskins' book.

We appreciate your cooperation and your assurance that you will discontinue the use of "It's the real thing."

Sincerely,
Ira C. Herbert

March 31, 1970

Mr. Ira C. Herbert
Coca-Cola USA
P.O. Drawer 1734
Atlanta, Georgia 30301

Dear Mr. Herbert:

Thank you for your letter of March 25th, which has just reached me, doubtless because of the mail strike.

We note with sympathy your feeling that you have a proprietary interest in the phrase "It's the real thing," and I can fully understand that the public might be confused by our use of the expression, and mistake a book by a Harlem schoolteacher for a six-pack of Coca-Cola. Accordingly, we have instructed all our salesmen to notify bookstores that whenever a customer comes in and asks for a copy of *Diary of a Harlem Schoolteacher* they should request the sales personnel to make sure that what the customer wants is the book, rather than a Coke. This, we think, should protect your interest and in no way harm ours.

We would certainly not want to dilute the distinctiveness of your trade slogan nor diminish its effectiveness as an advertising and merchandising tool, but it did occur to us that since the slogan is so closely identified with your product, those who read our ad may well tend to go out and buy a Coke rather than our book. We have discussed this problem in an executive committee meeting, and by a vote of seven to six decided that, even if this were the case, we would be happy to give Coke the residual benefit of our advertising.

Problems not unsimilar to the ones you raise in your letter have occurred to us in the past. You may recall that we published *Games People Play* which became one of the biggest nonfiction best-sellers of all time, and spawned conscious imitations (*Games Children Play*, *Games Psychiatrists Play*, *Games Ministers Play*, etc.). I am sure you will agree that this posed a far more direct and deadly threat to both the author and ourselves than our use of "It's the real thing." Further, *Games People Play* has become part of our language, and one sees it constantly in advertising, as a newspaper headline, etc. The same is true of another book which we published six or seven years ago, *One Hundred Dollar Misunderstanding*.

Given our strong sentiments concerning the First Amendment, we will defend to the death your right to use "It's the real thing" in any advertising you care to. We would hope you would do the same for us, especially when no one here or in our advertising agency, I am sorry to say, realized that you owned the phrase. We were merely quoting in our ads Peter S. Prescott's review of *Diary of a Harlem Schoolteacher* in *Look* which begins "*Diary of a Harlem Schoolteacher* is the real thing, a short, spare, honest book which will, I suspect, be read a generation hence as a classic. . . ."

With all best wishes,

Sincerely yours,
Richard Seaver

Meeting of Minds
from *Holmes-Laski Letters, 1916–1935*

By contrast with such a swift and simple exchange, the correspondence begun in 1916 between U.S. Supreme Court Justice Oliver Wendell Holmes, then in his seventies, and British politi-

cal science prodigy Harold Laski, then in his twenties, lasted from their first meeting until Holmes's death in 1935 and not only played over numberless topics but also ranged across a rich register of personal feeling and anecdote, gossip, commendation and advice, erudition, wit, and intellectual interaction. A contributor to the New Republic, *Laski was in 1919 teaching government at Harvard, where conservative elements were making it hot for this outspoken radical as they were for young Felix Frankfurter at the Harvard Law School, whose very dean, Roscoe Pound, was threatened as fearful reaction to post–World War I hardships and to socialist revolution gripped the nation. Abbott Lowell was president of Harvard and Woodrow Wilson of the U.S. A liberal interpreter of the Constitution, the internationally acclaimed Holmes frequently dissented from the conservative majority of the Supreme Court, along with fellow justice Louis Brandeis.*

Notes by editor Mark DeWolfe Howe explain some of the myriad allusions naturally made by two correspondents so learned and so involved in the events of their time. This exchange previews, in its dense textual mixture, several varieties of writing to be later singled out in this book as separate kinds of composition.

Cambridge, May 11, 1919

My dear Justice:

I seem to have been drowned in committees this last week—the more irritating because they did not in the result commit. But I am full of ideas as to the methods of organising discussion in small groups and in the summer I badly want you to tell me (if you will) how you organise the conferences of the Supreme Court and how far they are effective as an instrument of thought. If I had a really first-rate student I would put him on to studying the standing-orders of parliamentary assemblies to discover their efficacy in this regard.

What you say of poetry [that it does not produce the great truths] seems to me exactly just. I can see that at an epoch of crisis a poem (Lilliburlero, etc.) will have value for the mass of men; and I can see that normally any poem is individually priceless if you happen to feel that way about it. What I can't see is that the poetic exposition of experience is *per se* more valid than any other summary—that catching the glint of sunlight on a rose, or hearing the whirr of wild bird's sunstreaked wings, or remarking that the morning is ivory-fingered means that the poet has deeper insights than other men or that I should learn more from Wordsworth's *Prelude* (which I can't read) than I should from *Tom Jones*. I like Shelley and Keats and Browning, but I don't think their remarks justify or refute my beliefs, and that makes me suspect current emotions about the vital splendor of new poetic experiments or older assertions like that of Fletcher of Saltoun.[1]

Meanwhile I have been doing some jolly reading. Next week I have to lecture on the political theories of early socialism in England and France. I've been at the old books (which are the best books) with mingled feelings of contempt and admiration. Sismondi I put far higher than I had done in my Oxford days, and I thought that Saint-Simon and Fourier owed more to him than they admit. But the fellows I thought really superb were Hodgskin, Thompson[2] and Bray[3]—the early English socialists. Not, of course, in the fundamental surplus-value theory, but in their incidental remarks on the substantial content of the machine-technology, and I'm going, somehow, to get the money to reprint them or bust.

I understand your hesitation about writing to Hale and I am glad to have your remark on Perkins's attitude to Felix. The real truth is that there's a great fight on as to the future of the School and the older Tories are eager to make the place unbearable by Pound. He is a very great Dean and the students worship him and sooner or later the Law School Alumni Association has to step in and tell the world what Pound is counting for in scholarship and prevent this idle insistence on a *status quo* which has already lost its status. But I will tell you the inwardness of this when we meet.

Are you for a novel? Joseph Conrad's *Arrow of Gold* is superb. And please tell Mrs. Holmes that her friend Basil King has just published the worst novel ever written on this hemisphere.

---

1. Andrew Fletcher (1655–1716) of Saltoun was the Scottish politician and scholar who had observed in his *Account of a Conversation Concerning a Right Regulation of Government* (1704) that he believed that "if a man were permitted to make all the ballads, he need not care who should make the laws of a nation."
2. William Thompson (1783–1833); Irish economist and socialist, who passed from Benthamite Utilitarianism to Owenite socialism; author of *Principles of the Distribution of Wealth* (1824).
3. John Francis Bray (1809–1895); American-born socialist and friend of labor; author of *Labor's Wrongs and Labor's Remedy: or the Age of Might and the Age of Right* (1839).

I am eager to hear if you read Freund in the *New Republic* of May 3rd and if you were at all influenced by his analysis.[4]

My love to you both.   Yours ever affectionately, H. J. L.

On behalf of the Harvard Law School Association, of which Holmes had been made honorary head, a lawyer named Grinnell had asked Holmes how Pound might be helped, and Holmes had solicited Laski's advice, which was to get the Association to put its support of Pound on record.

Washington, D. C., May 18, 1919

Dear Laski:

Following your suggestion I have just written this note to Grinnell. "Your letter invites suggestion and I venture one. I have a very strong conviction of the value and importance of Pound who I think has done much to maintain the superlative reputation of the School. If it were possible to pass a resolution expressing our appreciation of the way in which he has kept the School going during the war, or giving him encouragement in such form as is deemed best I should be much gratified. Perhaps you will call this to the attention of the meeting." I shall post the letter along with this. As I shall not be present I did not put it as a motion made by me.

Talking with Brandeis yesterday (a big chap) he drove a harpoon into my midriff by saying that it would be for the good of my soul to devote my next leisure to the study of some domain of fact—suggesting the textile industry, which after reading many reports &c, I could make living to myself by a visit to Lawrence. My last visit was as an undergraduate when I joined a picnic of the factory hands and on a visit to the factory next day with my classmate and host found that we were suspected to be responsible for the non-appearance of a girl that morning. I believe we convinced them of our innocence of any escapade.

---

4. "The Debs Case and Freedom of Speech," by Ernst Freund, 19 *New Republic* 13 (May 3, 1919). The article was critical of the decision and of Holmes's opinion in the *Debs* case, protesting that it allowed implied, rather than direct, provocation as justification for a conviction for speech-making, and criticizing as inappropriate the analogy of crying "Fire" in a crowded theater. Freund also criticized the Espionage Act for the power which it appeared to confer upon juries to make arbitrary, nonreviewable findings that there is a psychological nexus between words and deeds.

Well—I hate facts—and partly because of that am impressed by Brandeis's suggestion. It was good for me that instead of philosophy I was shoved into the law. I suppose it would be good for me to get into actualities touching spindles—immigration—God knows what—but I would rather meditate on the initial push and the following spin—(whatever the true translation) of ἴυγξ ἕλχε τὺ τῆνον ἐμὸν ποτὶ δῶμα τὸν ανθρα.[5] (Think not that I pretend to have been able to quote this without the book.) Meantime I have received at last *The Century of Hope* to which (at your recommendation) I turn from you.

Affectionately yours,
O. W. Holmes

Cambridge, May 20, 1919

My dear Justice:

That is a most generous letter of yours about Pound and on his account, as well as my own, I am very grateful. It will give exactly the kind of help that is needed. It raises the whole question in simple and direct form, and it makes the members realise that they must give support to a great adventure. I can't tell you how moved I am by your generosity.

Brandeis's remark to you is very interesting. Somewhere in Harnack[6] there is a sentence on the early nominalists to the effect that they were tired of abstractions and demanded contact with the hard and concrete facts. What you said the other day of socialism brings that vividly to my mind. I don't think anyone can read Thomas Hodgskin or William Thompson without a sense that their case against capitalism must be answered and that it is not easy to answer. If I may say so, you come into contact with men of property on their very best side—the lawyer of ability appealing to your intellect, the great business man describing some fine achievement, the wife of a millionaire asking you to share some deeply-felt aesthetic enjoyment, Paul Warburg making marvellously simple some vast technical complexity. You don't see the obvious evils that one gets contact with among the trade unions—the blindness to pain, the hard obstinacy, the relentless pressure, the unwillingness to experiment with the prospects of human nature. If you saw that Law-

. Theocritus, Idyll II, "The Sorceress": "Turn, magic wheel, draw homeward him I love" (Calverley, tr.).

. Adolf von Harnack (1851–1930), church historian and theologian; author of *History of Dogma* (7 vols., tr. 1896–97).

rence strike at first hand you would say (as I do) that almost any system must be better than one which gives some men economic power over others. I am not a socialist in a Marxian sense; but I am against the inheritance of great fortunes, against the refusal to allow labor a share in the control of business (an increasing share), the unwillingness to establish proper human conditions in the factory. I believe there is a real class-war and that progress towards a fuller development of human capacity comes out of the growing strength of the workers. What mainly impresses me under present industrial organisation is the wastage of capacity, which for me is the worst sin. And we try to remedy by the second sin which is social reform—a name for multiplying the number of clerks and teachers and dethroning spontaneity for paternalism. The fact is that books like G. Wallas's *Francis Place* (I am sending it to you with my love) and Hammond[7] and Miss Hutchins on the factory system[8] destroy the hypothesis of a spirit for good in what, for want of a better phrase—one calls the master-class. You talk for an hour with Furuseth[9] of the seamen or Hillman[10] of the garment workers and you will realise how little we have done to use the brains at our disposal. But this is matter for talk and I leave it to prick you later on.

I have only one week's lecturing and then four months of freedom. So I have been preparing the ground for action by reading one or two tid-bits I had reserved for easy hours. First Grote on Plato which I thought grand stuff in the grand manner. Then Benn's *Greek Philosophers* which has even Grote beaten by a mile. Then, to read a Ph.D. thesis, some early economic fellows, mainly French. I thought them, (Jean Baptiste Say,[11] Dunoyer,[12] etc.) rather poor stuff and the thesis poorer still, but I

7. J. L. and Barbara Hammond, *The Skilled Labourer* (1919); *The Village Labourer, 1760–1832* (1911); *The Town Labourer, 1760–1832* (1919).
8. B. L. Hutchins and A. Harrison, *A History of Factory Legislation* (1903).
9. Andrew Furuseth (1854–1938); President of the International Seaman's Union of America, and effective spokesman for American seamen.
10. Sidney Hillman (1887–1946), energetic President of Amalgamated Clothing Workers of America and frequent representative of labor on governmental commissions.
11. Jean-Baptiste Say (1767–1832); French economist who in accepting Adam Smith's principles contributed some new insights—particularly in the formulation of the "law of markets" and in the appreciation of the role of the *entrepreneur*.
12. Charles Dunoyer (1786–1863); conservative French economist, whose principal work, *De la liberté du travail* (3 vols., 1845), developed the thesis that government should do little for anyone, and even less than that for promoting the interests of labor.

did not prevail. I must not forget to tell you that I had them stick on the politics paper, "Discuss the view that 'the Fourteenth Amendment does not enact Mr. H. S. *Social Statics*,' " and that of fourteen who took it twelve knew who said it and three wrote clear, sensible and interesting stuff. Of such is the kingdom of heaven.

Old Haldane wrote me a most kindly letter about my *Law Review* article which pleased me much and asked very sweetly after you. He is a generous-hearted fellow.

I wish to God that fellow Hawker had got across[13] It makes one feel mean to know that men will risk their lives in adventure and end in the pathos of a lone obscurity.

My love to you both. It is good to know you are alive.

Ever yours affectionately,
H. J. L.

Washington, D. C., May 24, 1919[14]

Dear Laski:

While waiting for proof of an opinion in a case which the Chief asked me to take a few days ago although it is by no means certain that I can get a majority, your book, just arrived, and your letter call for my first activities. The book entices me because of the mention of Place, unknown to me before, in *The Century of Hope*. That I purchased, according to your directions, and am half through. I haven't had much time yet. I like to read an optimistic, hazardously generalizing book of that sort. Even though I can't follow it with entire belief, it stimulated hope. I rather like too the attitude toward man as a being of vast spiritual significance, which of course he must be for us, while I surmise that cosmically he is a case of animal like the rest. But I turn to your letter. What you say to explain my opinions, while it confirms what I have long said, fails to hit me. For a quarter of a century I have said that the real foundations of discontent were emotional not economic, and that if the socialists would face the facts and put the case on that ground I should listen to them with respect. I used to tell my wife or she used to tell me, it was a joint opinion, that the manner of the Beacon Street women toward their servants and employees did more than the women

---

13. On May 18, Henry G. Hawker, and Lt. Com. McKenzie Grieve, of the British navy, started their unsuccessful transatlantic flight, by land plane, from Newfoundland. The plane came down at sea, and they were rescued on the 19th.

14. A brief note from Laski, dated May 22, 1919, is omitted.

were worth to upset the existing order. My opinion, however, is based on the effort to think quantitatively not dramatically. I won't go over the old ground, but to my mind the notion that any rearrangement of property, while any part of the world propagates freely, will prevent civilization from killing its weaker members, is absurd. I think that the crowd now has substantially all there is—and that every mitigation of the lot of any body of men has to be paid for by some other or the same body of men—and I don't think that cutting off the luxuries of the few would make an appreciable difference in the situation. On the other hand I think that the ideals of men like Veblen besides cherishing illusions are ugly. No doubt I, like everyone, am influenced in my aesthetic preferences by my environment past and present—but I have intended to be detached. However, as the question at bottom is what kind of a world do you want, I, for whatever reason, do so far sympathize with the strug-for *lifeurs,* as the French put it, that in the ultimate necessary self-preference, I desire a world in which art and philosophy, in their use*less* aspect, may have a place. I say useless, to mark the point that they are ends in themselves. Of course I think them useful even in Veblen's world.——The proof has come, been corrected, and gone. Citations verified at Department of Justice. Now I am vacuous and can [illegible] before the robber. The moment work is done my natural bodily languor inclines me to stretch at full length and soon, *non obstant* literature, I snooze. I even have said that one should be able to go to bed at 11 a.m. to recover from the fatigue of getting up. I will try to read a little more of your optimist (Marvin) while waiting for the corrected opinion to return for distribution. There is a slight feeling of unreality in him as with others of the upward and onward—but as I have said he gives me pleasure. In the summer, if not before, you must remind me of Hodgskin and Thompson for I want to read whatever is thought best on that side. As I said those who have talked economics and whom I have read I think show yawning fallacies. I am glad that you heard from Haldane—I have had early and late encouragement from him but have not heard from him or known much of his doings for a long time. Also I have eaten good victuals at this house.

Affectionately yours,
O. W. Holmes

Cambridge, May 26, 1919

My dear Justice:

This is to introduce Mr. H. W. Massingham, the editor of the London *Nation*. It would be insolent in me to praise him; but I want to say on paper that he represents for me all that is best and most generous in English life. And it is because I want him to see what I care for most deeply in America that I send him to you.

> My love to you,
> Ever affectionately yours,
> Harold J. Laski

Cambridge, May 30, 1919

My dear Justice:

I have just been reading—as it is fitting I should read—not for the first time nor the last, your Memorial Day speech.[15] It made me even more proud of you than I am, for it has in it a beauty which this war has made thrice beautiful. The men of whom you write were my friends also and it matters nothing that they rest at Loos and Givenchy, on the Somme and at Vimy Ridge instead of Fredericksburg and Ball's Bluff and Antietam. I wish their mothers could read it and know from your warm yet moderate appraisal how they stand in our hearts also.

And I have been reading a very great book which shall be yours for the summer—if, by chance, it has escaped you. It is Benn's *History of Rationalism in the Nineteenth Century*. It's fine not only for its fine historic perspective but also because it gives one the courage that can come only from the historic demonstration that unreason contains the seeds of its own dissolution. I read also Maine on *Popular Government*—some clever predictions but the rest the typical product of a mind warped by Anglo-Indian experience. And that led me to a book which is, I think, the best I ever read on India. It's by William Archer[16] and on matters such as the supposed profundity of Indian philosophy, its supposed magnificent art, its bewildering pride in its genius for intuition, I think it is conclusive. I'd like you to read it and then, if you agree with me, to give it to Brandeis to read. It convinced me that metaphysical results, like those of science, are simply the result of dirt and sweat and that the idea that there's a royal road to truth through the intuition of a genie traveling on a lonely hillside is not merely nonsense but

---

15. *Speeches*, p. 1.
16. Presumably William Archer, *India and the Future* (1912).

also dangerous nonsense. Which made me reread friend Aristotle's *Ethics* with the conviction that no man ever lived more sane than he. I wouldn't exchange one book of it for all the volumes of all the Eastern philosophers there ever were.

I'm glad you liked *The Living Past*.[17] I've been trying it on my students to good advantage. Its mistake I think is to identify material advance with spiritual enrichment which is, I take it, the hang-over from Comtian days. I see a greater humanitarianism in these days than in the past and I value the determination that there shall be no avoidable pain. But for the rest I think the argument for progress is as yet unmade. I think there *can* be improvement. Education can make a bundle of sensual impulses into a man. But *that* education is too narrowly confined for us yet to boast of its influence. Marvin, I would argue, continually mistakes aspiration for accomplishment.

I hope you will have the chance of real talk with Massingham, whom I ventured to send to you. He is the greatest of English editors. Fearless, honest, uncompromising, with fine perception and flawless taste. Perhaps a little too much the silent Englishman, but full of knowledge of events. He can tell you of Haldane, Asquith, Morley *et al* and he knows all about you. In other words we dined together.

My love happily to you both,

Ever affectionately yours,
H. J. L.

Washington, D. C., June 1, 1919

Dear Laski:

. . . The Chief has suggested that I write a case of his and has done it in such a kind hesitating way that even if I could [have] hesitated otherwise, which I shouldn't have done, I can't now.[18] Hence I shan't be happy till I get (at) it—but your letter just arrived imperatively demands a word of agreement right off. It is apropos of Oriental insights. What I have been in the habit of saying is this. For fifty years it has been my business to know the movement of thought in one of its great expressions—the law—and my pleasure to try to know something of its movement in philosophy, and if anything is plain it is that during the period that counts—from Pericles to now—there has been a gradual

---

17. Laski evidently interpreted Holmes's reference to F. S. Marvin's *The Century of Hope* (1919), *supra*, as a reference to the same author's *The Living Past* (1913).

18. The case has not been identified.

advance and that our view of life today is more manifold and more profound than it ever has been before. When the Europe and Asia man said Europe has given us the steam engine, Asia every religion that ever commanded the reverence of mankind—I answered I bet on the steam engine. For the steam engine means science and science is the root from which comes the flower of our thought. When I have seen clever women who have read all their lives go off into enthusiasm over some oriental, pseudo-oriental, or spiritualistic fad it has struck me that all their reading seems to have given them no point of view—no *praejudicia*—or preliminary bets as to the probability that the sign turn to the left will lead to a *cul de sac*. If I follow Brandeis's suggestion I shall have little time for other things—but as my bet, on the strength of what I do know, is with Archer—bar reservations for the Taj Mahal, etc. that will keep.

I turn to another matter. I had a dear little letter from Pound expressing satisfaction at what I wrote to Grinnell but also saying that people there want to push Frankfurter out of the school. He says nothing about himself but I have been led to fear that the push extends to Pound. Two days ago I asked Brandeis if he thought it would be well for me to write to Lowell—he rather inclined yes. I still hesitate but probably should be writing to him were I not writing to you. If the school should lose Pound and Frankfurter it would lose its soul, it seems to me. I hesitate because I know no details, but my conviction is strong. So far as Pound is concerned it is also disinterested, for I don't know his opinions except through his writings and so far as I know I never have come in for much credit in them. But there can be no doubt that he is a real focus of spiritual energy—and even if his presence has prevented subscriptions to the Law School I can't but believe that the spark of inspiration is worth more than dollars. By Jove, I think I'll say that to Lowell. I am worried—and all the more that without any foreknowledge I was put in as President of the Law School Association—of course merely as a figurehead—but I hate to feel King Log. With which I shut up as the barber is due to cut my hair. Does the movement threaten you? I am full of helpless anxiety.

Affectionately yours,
O. W. Holmes

One-Way Series of Letters

Jane Austen to Fanny Knight

Often the letters of only one of the correspondents have come down to us, but in some such cases we can feel the presence of the omitted correspondent in the half that remains, as we do here in the closeness of Jane Austen to her beloved niece. Our effort as outsider to grasp allusions and piece together details reminds us that most correspondence is written for a private audience. In keeping with the flitting dates of correspondence, between her letters here Jane Austen changes her mind on a subject that was often the subject of her novels.

To Fanny Knight

Chawton Nov: 18.—Friday [1814]

I feel quite as doubtful as you could be my dearest Fanny as to *when* my Letter may be finished, for I can command very little quiet time at present, but yet I must begin, for I know you will be glad to hear as soon as possible, & I really am impatient myself to be writing something on so very interesting a subject, though I have no hope of writing anything to the purpose. I shall do very little more I dare say than say over again, what you have said before.—I was certainly a good deal surprised *at first*—as I had no suspicion of any change in your feelings, and I have no scruple in saying that you cannot be in Love. My dear Fanny, I am ready to laugh at the idea—and yet it is no laughing matter to have had you so mistaken as to your own feelings—And with all my heart I wish I had cautioned you on that point when first you spoke to me;—but tho' I did not think you then so *much* in love as you thought yourself, I did consider you as being attached in a degree—quite sufficiently for happiness, as I had no doubt it would increase with opportunity.—And from the time of our being in London together, I thought you really very much in love—But you certainly are not at all—there is no concealing it.—What strange creatures we are!—It seems as if your being secure of him (as you say yourself) had made you Indifferent. —There was a little disgust I suspect, at the Races—& I do not wonder at it. His expressions there would not do for one who had rather more Acuteness, Penetration & Taste, than Love, which was your case. And yet, after all, I *am* surprised that the change in your feelings should be so great.—He is, just what he ever was, only more evidently & uniformly devoted to *you*. This is all the difference.—How shall we account for it?—My dearest Fanny, I am writing what will not be of the smallest use to you. I am feeling differently every moment, & shall not be able to suggest a single thing that can assist your Mind.—I could lament in one sentence & laugh in the next, but as to Opinion or Counsel I am sure none will ⟨be⟩ extracted worth having from this Letter.—I read yours through the very even^g I received it— getting away by myself—I could not bear to leave off, when I had once begun.—I was full of curiosity & concern. Luckily your Aunt C. dined at the other house, therefore I had not to manœuvre away from *her*;—& as to anybody else, I do not care.—Poor dear Mr. J. P.! [John Plumtre]—Oh! dear Fanny, your mistake has been one that thousands of women fall into. He was the *first* young Man who attached himself to you. That was the charm, & most powerful it is.—Among the multitudes how- ever that make the same mistake with yourself, there can be few indeed who have so little reason to regret it;—*his* Character and *his* attachment leave you nothing to be ashamed of.—Upon the whole, what is to be done? You certainly *have* encouraged him to such a point as to make him feel almost secure of you—you have no inclination for any other person—His situation in life, family, friends, & above all his character—his uncommonly amiable mind, strict principles, just notions, good habits—*all* that *you* know so well how to value, *All* that really is of the first importance—everything of this nature pleads his cause most strongly.—You have no doubt of his having superior Abilities—he has proved it at the University—he is I dare say such a scholar as your agreeable, idle Brothers would ill bear a comparison with.—Oh! my dear Fanny, the more I write about him, the warmer my feelings become, the more strongly I feel the sterling worth of such a young Man & the desirableness of your growing in love with him again. I recommend this most thoroughly. —There *are* such beings in the World perhaps, one in a Thousand, as the Creature You and I should think perfection, Where Grace & Spirit are united to Worth, where the Manners are equal to the Heart & Understanding, but such a person may not come in your way, or if he does, he may not be the eldest son of a Man of Fortune, the Brother of your particular friend, & belonging to your own County.—Think of all this Fanny. Mr. J. P.—has advantages which do not often meet in one person. His only fault indeed seems Modesty. If he were less modest, he would be more agreeable, speak louder & look Impudenter; —and is not it a fine Character of which Modesty is the only defect?—I have no doubt that he will get more lively & more like yourselves as he is more with you;—he will catch your ways if he belongs to you. And as to there being any objection from his *Goodness,* from the danger of his becoming even Evangelical, I cannot admit *that.* I am by no means convinced that we ought not tell all to be Evangelicals, & am at least persuaded that they who are so from Reason and Feeling, must be happiest & safest.—Do not be frightened from the connection by your Brothers having most wit. Wisdom is better than Wit, & in the long run will certainly have the laugh of her side; & don't be frightened by the idea of his acting more strictly up to the precepts of the New Testament than others.—And now, my dear Fanny, having written so much on one side of the question, I shall turn round & entreat you not to commit yourself farther, & not to think of accepting him unless you really do like him. Anything is to be preferred or endured rather than marrying without Affection; and if his deficiencies of Manner &c &c strike you more than all his good qualities, if you continue to think strongly of them, give him up at once.—Things are now in such a state, that you must resolve upon one or the other, either to allow him to go on as he has done, or whenever you are together behave with a coldness which may convince him that he has been deceiving himself.—I have no doubt of his suffering a good deal for a time, a great deal, when he feels that he must give you up;—but it is no creed of mine, as you must be well aware, that such sort of Disappointments kill anybody.—Your sending the Music was an admirable Device, it made everything easy, & I do not know how I could have accounted for the parcel otherwise; for tho' your dear Papa most conscientiously hunted about till he found me alone in the Din^g-parlour, your Aunt C. had seen that he *had* a parcel to deliver.—As it was however, I do not think anything was suspected.—We have heard nothing fresh from Anna. I trust she is very comfortable in her new home. Her Letters have been very sensible & satisfactory, with no *parade* of happiness, which I liked them the better for.—I have often known young married Women write in a way I did not like, in that respect.

You will be glad to hear that the first Edit: of M. P. is all sold.—Your Uncle Henry is rather wanting me to come to Town, to settle about a 2^d Edit:—but as I could not very conveniently leave home now, I have written him my Will and pleasure, & unless he still urges it, shall not go.—I am very greedy & want to make the most of it;—but as you are much above caring about money, I shall not plague you with any particulars.—The pleasures of Vanity are more within your comprehension, & you will enter into mine, at receiving the *praise* which every now & then comes to me, through some channel or other. . . .

Yours very affec^ly
J. Austen

Your trying to excite your own feelings by a visit to his room amused me excessively.—The dirty Shaving Rag was exquisite! —Such a circumstance ought to be in print. Much too good to be lost.—Remember me particularly to Fanny C.—I thought you w^d like to hear from me, while you were with her.

To Fanny Knight

23 Hans Place, Wednesday Nov: 30 [1814]

I am very much obliged to you my dear Fanny for your letter, & I hope you will write again soon that I may know you to be all safe & happy at home.—Our visit to Hendon will interest you I am sure, but I need not enter into the particulars of it, as your Papa will be able to answer *almost* every question. I certainly could describe her bed-room, & her Drawers & her Closet better than he can, but I do not feel that I can stop to do it.—I was rather sorry to hear that she *is* to have an Instrument; it seems throwing money away. They will wish the 24 Gs. in the shape of Sheets & Towels six months hence;—and as to her playing, it never can be anything. —Her purple Pelisse rather surprised me.—I thought we had known all Paraphernalia of that sort. I do not mean to blame her, it looked very well & I dare say she wanted it. I suspect nothing worse than it's being got in secret, & not owned to anybody.—She is capable of that you know.—I received a very kind note from her yesterday, to ask me to come again & stay a night with them I cannot do it, but I was pleased to find that she had the *power* of doing so right a thing. My going was to give them *both* Pleasure very properly.—I just saw Mr. Hayter at the Play, & think his face would please me on acquaintance. I was sorry he did not dine here.—It seemed rather odd to me to be in the Theatre, with nobody to *watch* for. I was quite composed myself, at leisure for all the agitation Isabella could raise.

Now my dearest Fanny, I will begin a subject which comes in very naturally.—You frighten me out of my wits by your reference. Your affection gives me the highest pleasure, but indeed you must not let anything depend on my opinion. Your own feelings & none but your own, should determine such an important point.—So far however as answering your question, I have no scruple.—I am perfectly convinced that your present feelings supposing you were to marry *now*, would be sufficient for his happiness;—but when I think how very, very far it is from a *Now*, & take everything that *may be,* into consideration, I dare not say, 'Determine to accept him.' The risk is too great for *you*, unless your own Sentiments prompt it.—You will think me perverse perhaps; in my last letter I was urging everything in his favour, & now I am inclining the other way; but I cannot help it; I am at present more impressed with the possible Evil that may arise to *you* from engaging yourself to him—in word or mind— than with anything else.—When I consider how few young Men you have yet seen much of—how capable you are (yes, I do still think you *very* capable) of being really in love—and how full of temptation the next 6 or 7 years of your Life will probably be—(it is the very period of Life for the *strongest* attachments to be formed)—I cannot wish you with your present very cool feelings to devote yourself in honour to him. It is very true that you never may attach another Man, his equal altogether, but if that other Man has the power of attaching you *more*, he will be in your eyes the most perfect.—I shall be glad if you *can* revive past feelings, & from your unbiassed self resolve to go on as you have done, but this I do not expect, and without it I cannot wish you to be fettered. I should not be afraid of your *marrying* him;—with all his worth, you would soon love him enough for the happiness of both; but I should dread the continuance of this sort of tacit engagement, with such an uncertainty as there is, of *when* it may be completed.—Years may pass, before he is Independant.—You like him well enough to marry, but not well enough to wait.—The unpleasantness of appearing fickle is certainly great—but if you think you want Punishment for past Illusions, there it is—and nothing can be compared to the misery of being bound *without* Love, bound to one, & preferring another. *That* is a Punishment which you do *not* deserve.—I know you did not meet—or rather will not meet today—as he called here yesterday—& I am glad of it.—It does not seem very likely at least that he sh^d be in time for a Dinner visit 60 miles off. We did not see him, only found his card when we came home at 4.—Your Uncle H. merely observed that he was a day after the Fair.—He asked your Brother on Monday, (when Mr. Hayter was talked of) why he did not invite *him* too?—saying, 'I know he is in Town, for I met him the other day in Bond St.—'Edward answered that he did not know where he was to be found. —'Don't you know his chambers?—' 'No.'—I shall be most glad to hear from you again my dearest Fanny, but it must not be later than Saturday, as we shall be off on Monday long before the Letters are delivered—and write *something* that may do to be read or told. I am to take the Miss Moores back on Saturday, & when I return I shall hope to find your pleasant, little, flowing scrawl on the Table.—It will be a releif to me after playing at Ma'ams—for though I like Miss H. M. as much as one can at my time of Life after a day's acquaintance, it is uphill work to be talking to those whom one knows so little. Only *one* comes back with me tomorrow, probably Miss Eliza, & I rather dread it. We shall not have two Ideas in common. She is young, pretty, chattering, & thinking cheifly (I presume) of Dress, Company, & Admiration.—Mr. Sanford is to join us at dinner, which will be a comfort, and in the even^g while your Uncle and Miss Eliza play chess, he shall tell me comical things & I will laugh at them, which will be a pleasure to both. . . .

Thank you—but it is not settled yet whether I *do* hazard a 2^d Edition. We are to see Egerton today, when it will probably be determined.—People are more ready to borrow & praise, than to buy—which I cannot wonder at;—but tho' I like praise as well as anybody, I like what Edward calls *Pewter* too.—I hope he continues careful of his eyes & finds the good effect of it.

I cannot suppose we differ in our ideas of the Christian Religion. You have given an excellent description of it. We only affix a different meaning to the Word *Evangelical*.

Yours most affec^ly
J. Austen

Life of an Argonaut
Horace C. Snow
from *Dear Charlie*

Among the forty-niners who made the rambunctious scene of the California Gold Rush were many well-bred Easterners like the young Bostonian here, who for a couple of years wrote letters from the southern node of the Mother Lode, in the Sierra Nevada foothills, to his peer Charles, also called "Little Fitz," who was struggling to write poetry back in civilization.

A one-way series of letters develops something of the longer narrative-observational continuity of a journal. Though only an unknown private citizen himself, this correspondent truly helped to make history, in the sense that he provided some of the firsthand accounts from which historians put together our picture of the past. Note in this connection that the term "correspondent" has come to designate a newspaper reporter writing back from another land.

Cabin de Snow & Co.,
Agua Frio, Dec. 31, 1854

Dear Charlie:

. . .

Now, let me speak a few words about town. One or two days after I closed my last letter to you, another *horrible murder* was committed within one half mile of our cabin. The murder was committed at a Mexican camp, one that has sprung up within a few months. The tragedy occurred at a gambling table, there being some trouble about the bets, a few words passed and one drew a bowie knife and stabbed the other in the mouth, severing the jugular vein, causing death in a few moments. The murderer made his escape, but not without getting wounded from several revolvers which were fired at him, as he was traced a long way from the blood which left him. This affair happened in the evening. This caused considerable excitement for a few days, but now is among the things that were. Murders are so common here that the people hardly enquire into them unless they happen to know one of the parties. There have been, to my knowledge since I came here, *TWELVE* murders within fifteen miles of this place. It is just so all over California. A short time ago three men up North started on a prospecting tour and had proceeded but a short distance when they were attacked by a band of fourteen robbers. The robbers rose up from behind some small bushes and fired at the miners, expecting to kill them at the first shot, but, fortunately, they only killed one and in an instant the other two drew their revolvers and commenced returning the shots, but in a few moments only one miner was standing. He, with the most cool courage and deadly aim I ever heard of, shot ten of the robbers dead on the spot, having discharged every barrel of two revolvers. The other four being out of loads also made a rush at him with their bowie knives, confident of victory at last, I suppose, but they were mistaken. The miner proved too much for them and in a few moments two more were laid low, one mortally wounded—who has since died—and the other disabled and also marked for life, having lost his nose. The second miner, who was shot down, is now in a fair way of recovery. This miner who stood the fire had his clothes pierced by over thirty balls and yet he escaped with only two or three flesh wounds. One of the robbers made a confession before he died and stated that they were a regular, organized band and had killed Chinese, Mexicans and Americans within the last few days. There seems something almost incredible about this but then it is vouched for by a large number of miners and also a coroners inquest. This is the state of society that we have in this country; especially in the extreme north and south. Everybody carries a revolver by his side or a bowie knife and most of them both. If a person is irritable or flashy and gets insulted, the first thing he does is to draw his revolver and either shoot the man through or knock him down. He doesn't stop to reason and let his better judgment dictate but gives way to the first impulse. Here we see the immorality and dangerous consequence of carrying deadly weapons. How would it look to you to go into the court house in Boston and, out of fifty men, see forty of them armed with pistols and knives? It would probably remind you of "days of Knight-errantry" instead of civilization and humanity. Judges in this country have had to shoot witnesses dead on the stand to save their own lives. This is truly a land of *chivalry* where *satisfaction* must be had. It was a curious sight to me to see two men go out in the street with nothing on but pants, shake hands in a friendly manner, and then fight just as long as they could move. Intemperance is the mother of all these crimes. You seldom see a strictly temperate man in trouble here. I think the greatest blessing that could be conferred upon this beautiful country would be to place a line of battle ships at the Golden Gate and sink every vessel bound in to Frisco with liquor aboard. Property should not be brought into account with the happiness and lives of a half million people.

By the way, the second morning when I was serving upon the *Grand Jury,* one man did not answer to his name. We reported him to the sheriff and he went in search of him and after an hour's hunt he found him, but so drunk that he couldn't walk without help. He tried to get him into the jury room, but he was perfectly hors de combat and immediately went to sleep. We let him lay there for awhile till the disgrace of some of the grand jurors being intoxicated presented itself to our minds and then we had him carried off. We then proceeded with our business till noon and appeared before His Honor to report. The roll was called and all answered but this one. The foreman passed in the bills which we had found, whereupon the Judge enquired if we had been transacting business when one of the jurors was under the state of intoxication? The foreman told him "yes." The Judge then told us that these bills were not valid and that the jurymen would have to be discharged and our work all done over again! We found about twenty bills and over two-thirds of them were from the immediate source of intemperance. But, enough of this. What I have written, grammatically, reads most horrid. This is partly because I have written so fast and partly because I am not capable of doing better.

Today, as you will observe, is the last of "54." It is now evening and I am seated in the old log cabin writing to "Little Fitz." I wonder what he is doing this eve? Probably interested in some poem or treatise. Poem, I think, for he's been very poetical of late. It is a wonder to me how he has learned so much and still so young! do people inherit talents or is their success attributable to perseverence and industry? Now, perhaps this question might admit of some discussion, but circumstances are unfavorable for that this evening, inasmuch as the rain is pouring down like fun. My soul is in arms and eager for the *Long Tom.* The boys have gone to bed whistling "Yankee Doodle" and I feel like singing anything but "Old Hundred." I went to the Post office today expecting the 5th of December mail would come in but it did not. Tuesday will probably bring it. We look forward to the arrival of the Atlantic mail with the same pleasure that little children do to Christmas or Thanksgiving. They are the bright spots in our monotonous existence. Last mail I wrote to Helen and Smith. This mail I think I shall write a line or two to Mary or Phoebe. That you may rise to five feet nine inches and a greater proportion mentally is the wish of Horace, who will not write more till the mail arrives. Adios.

Agua Frio, Cal.
February 6th, 1855

Dear Charlie:

Two weeks more have passed and with it all hopes of visiting America the coming summer. The moon has changed and brought no rain; the weather continues one beautiful, delightful, pleasant spell, not a cloud dots the sky, not a breath of air fans your brow, and not a sign is there for rain. Everything has the appearance of spring. The grass begins to look green, trees are budding, summer birds are returning, frogs have commenced peeping and we poor, rugged miners have commenced calculating—what is to become of us. If no rain should fall this spring, I shall be obliged to remain here another year. I suppose I could sell my interests here but could get nothing what they are worth. I was offered the other day $700 for about three-fourths of my thrown-up dirt, but nothing less than $1,000 would tempt me. My Brother asks $2,000 but this is rather high. However, it is acknowledged that when water comes we have the best show of any man on the creek; therefore, you can see that pecuniarily I have but little to think about. All that troubles me is how I am going to remain here another long year without seeing some of my old chums; without getting fresh papers every morning; without getting something good to eat; without enjoying some good society; and lastly, without seeing some pretty girls!! I have anticipated so much happiness in returning this summer that the idea of being disappointed is in no way agreeable. But I suppose it is all for the best, though we cannot realize it. There are a hundred men on this creek doing nothing now, half of them out of funds and considerable in debt. The most of these are Southerners who are too lazy to work an hour or two every day and pay their board, but loafing around waiting for a time when they can make money faster. This class have our heart-felt sympathy.—the *other way*. But we are going to take things as cool as we can. We are going to subscribe for ten or twelve papers pretty soon and have some news twice a month, though it be a little late. When I can get something fresh to read or as long as I can, I am very well contented but come to read the papers through twice, advertisements and all. I have a keen appetite for America. Your letter of December 30th and papers arrived the 3rd of this month and was a welcome New Year epistle. Charlie, though much I covet a letter from you every mail, yet I do not wish you, after working hard all day and particularly at writing, to sit up in the evening when you ought to be resting, to pen me a letter. I hope you do not feel under any obligation to answer all the letters I write you. Our circumstances are very different. I am busy outdoors all day and come evening it is an agreeable change for me to write, but you have to do the same thing that you were tired of at noon, when you long for some other recreation. Now, hereafter, unless you have plenty of time you will be perfectly justified in not writing me but once a month. Then I shall be your debtor should I write twice a month. I feel just as though I was the one that was benefitted and you only troubling yourself for acquaintance sake. Hereafter, take heed I shall write something every mail but can't promise it to be worth much. How I would like to be there enjoying those Mercantile Lectures with you. It must be a rare treat to listen to such men as Beecher, Benton and Houston, men who have the courage and independence to assert what they think to be right. If the Lectures are reported, I would like a copy very much.

Wednesday Eve. the 7th:

Since last night a very great change has taken place in the weather and present appearances indicate a storm. The wind is from the right direction and the clouds look watery but the change has been so sudden that but little rain can be expected. However, if between this and next Monday we should have rain sufficient to go to washing and should continue to have till the 1st day of June, my anticipations may yet be realized. I have not deferred my hope yet and shall not as long as the atmosphere forebodes lucky times.

My Brother started last Monday for a short tour up North. I could not help thinking how different he looked to what a person would in New England starting on a similar journey. He went by horseback, as all travelling is done here. He wore spurs which were an inch in length, large leather leggings and a revolver. Self-protection is all that is thought of here.

Have I ever told you anything about our currency here? If not, I will say a few words which may be interesting. In the first place, it consists of just as many denominations as there are languages spoken. The majority of the Gold coin is American but nine-tenths of the silver is foreign. There are no cents and but very few half-dimes in the country. Therefore, the smallest piece of money made use of in making change is the dime. Till within a few months all pieces of money larger than a Mexican nine pence have passed for .25 cents, but so many one-franc pieces have been exported from France for speculation that the merchants have by a concerted movement cut them down to their original value—.18 cents. In purchasing goods, anything is sold by the bit's worth—.12½ cents. One dime passes for a bit and four of them will buy just as much as a half dollar. In paying postage if there is due five cents and you hand them a quarter, you will get a dime in return. No one complains because no one stews for a bit. This is the case in the mines, though I hear at Frisco and the lower towns they are more exact. How curious it would seem to have a dozen coppers in my pocket to jingle. Change in some places in the mines is very scarce, but as all merchants buy gold dust and weigh as small sums as a bit, there is but little trouble. No news here in particular. There have been a good many murders in the country the past month, but they are so common that but little notice is taken of them. I send you a Mariposa Chronicle, the only paper printed in this county. It resembles all the other mountain papers in the State. Being very uneasy concerning the weather, I must beg "extension" until next mail.

Yours truly,
Horace.

Agua Frio, California
February 23, 1855

Dear Charlie:

. . .

News from the States seems to be very interesting this mail. Heavy failures, high prices of provisions, dull times, contagious diseases, political shenanigans, and infantile wedlocks—infantile in sense, if not in years—all come in for a share of public attention. How different are our wants in this great world. Take today, for instance; some wish credit, some beg extensions of payments, some wish food, some honor, some power, some love, and some more moderate than the rest only wish a good clear "Tom" stream of water. Yes, give some a good tom stream of water and all other things will be added. This is the case with me. From the 1st of last January to the 21st of February hardly a drop of rain fell on the banks of Agua Frio. It has been cloudy now for nearly a week, the wind blowing in all directions during the day and raining a very little during the nights. Up North the miners are lying idle because of the large quantities of snow, while down here it is too warm for comfort in the middle of the day.

24th, A.M.: No more rain this time, Charlie. This is just as beautiful a moon as ever was seen. West wind and not a cloud to be seen. Everybody now is looking forward to the next Full Moon. Old "forty-niners" bet high on rain then. Some put off the good time coming till the sun crosses the line, while others have given up expectations for rain and are preparing to realize them. I prophesy if we should have no more rain this winter that next summer or this year will exceed any other one in trouble and crime in California. The people have lost all confidence in the civil government and are taking the reins into their own hands. Woe be to the transgressor if the multitude once gets hold of him! The prosperity of the country is generally good. Large "strikes" are being made in different parts of the mines. Great excitement about the Kern River diggings, surging now and thousands of lazy loafers are winding their way there, not to mine, but to gamble and steal. It is not the pioneer in this country that reaps the reward—the greater their success, the greater their dissipation. It is the sober second-thought individuals that profit by their new discoveries. Kern River is two hundred miles exactly south of here.

In regard to Mr. P., everything is all right. My Cousin has written me, though, I think I told you this before. I think you must be very busy and pretty hard-worked in the Traveller office. I couldn't stand—especially till I became used to it—this working evenings. This is the only part of the 24 hours that I can enjoy myself. Give me plenty to read and a room by myself or a cabin and I'm all right. If I should live here another year I think I should build me another cabin and live alone.

I did not send you a paper as I intended last mail, but send you two this. There is nothing particularly interesting in them more than that they come from California. Thank you for those papers and hope to again next mail. Nothing new here. Have been very busy lately prospecting. Must close for the *firm* have been waiting for me for some time. Trouble you again next mail.

Truly yours,
Horace.

Agua Frio, California
Friday Eve., March 9th, 1855

Dear Charlie:

Your poetic epistle of January 28th came to hand yesterday and has been read with a great deal of pleasure. I was so unprepared for such a production from you that two weeks will hardly allay the surprise. Therefore, I shall have to write this illiteral this mail and try next time to show you my *Punkins* or *poetry*. However, you can't expect much from me as the muses never were known to enter an old Log Cabin—but once and that was the cabin of a young man who crossed the plains and wrote a poetical description home to his friends. I haven't the whole production, but remember a few passages, which I will quote for your benefit.

> "In the year of '51,
> I arrived in Mormondom,
> And saw the Prophet, Brigham Young."

And so the production went on, growing more beautiful and sublime, till at last he made one desperate effort and concentrated his whole genius and fiery inspiration on the following lines:

> "About the 21st of March,
> I took up my line of march
> and reached a place
> of high renown called Hang Town."

Whether the author of this is alive now, I don't know, but my impression is that he is not, for who but Jupiter could stand such a Minerva from their hand.

Having the possible fate of this man before my eyes, I shall restrain myself sufficiently to survive the effort. Therefore, when you receive it you may allow that I am not Hors de Combat.

The good rains you speak of did not arrive here till the last day of February. The accounts you saw were probably of the first week in January. It is now nearly bedtime. All this very evening I have been cleaning and dividing our past week and a half's yield of gold. We commenced washing the 1st day of March and have washed every day and one night since— Sunday included! We have only had about thirty-six hours of rain but this has made glad the heart and yellow the pocket of many a miner. You may think it strange of my working on Sunday, but circumstances were such that I thought it justifiable. The rainy season is nearly passed and all the show we have to earn our food is when it rains or when there is water, and, as our chances are few for anything more than an occasional shower, we are obliged to improve them when they come or not at all. In these nine days we have taken out over $600.00 worth of gold and this is what I have had before me all evening. There was about $40 of the gold that was just as fine as fine sand and mixed with twice its weight of finer sand. This I had to separate and it was a very tiresome job, but the sight of such a *good pile*, and knowing that part of it was mine, made the task very easy. But unless it rains very soon again, I shall hardly handle as much gold for a long ten months. There is not now a "Tom" stream in the creek and did we not catch all that sand, we could do but little. I think with plenty of water for two months and our dirt paying about the same, that I could visit America the coming summer. There is a high wind tonight but it comes from a quarter which the "oldest inhabitants" —deer excluded—never saw rain, i.e. N.W.

However, I am contented and think of the good times coming. My brother has just informed me that all letters must be in the Post office tomorrow evening or not in season for this mail. How convenient it is to live where your letters and mail matter travel the distance of two hundred and fifty miles in the unprecedented time of six short days! and also to live where the mails never come regular or deposit regular. This letter arrangement is very pleasant, for you are always being continually taken by surprise. O America! America! What a paradise. But I must close and retire. I thought I should have had until Sunday to finish this in and write considerable more but the time is not allowed me. Not having worked very hard for sometime past till within a few days, I feel very tired and lame. We have been out before sunrise and never in till after sundown; therefore, I have retired very early every night. I am getting down on cooking when I work so hard. I must have a wife as soon as convenient. Select one for me! With your letter came the papers and Almanac. Many thanks for your kindness and trouble. Enclose a dollar as a present to you for the purpose of buying peanuts to eat while you have the "Blues." So appropriate! Shall do better the next time if the weather is favorable. If you answer this, pay me in the same coin.

Yours truly,
Horace.

Single Letter

A Spot of Tea at the Colonel's
U.S. Army Memorandum

One from of the single letter is an intraorganizational missive and may be purely imperative—a directive—or purely expository—an updating of information. The world conducts much of its business in such memoranda, usually characterized by the impersonality of the sender-receiver relationship, though compared to the public at large, both parties are small and well known to each other.

A Letter Received by a Military Man When He Was Transferred to Munich

SUBJECT: Briefing for Call to Commander's Home
To: Personnel Concerned
FROM: S-1

66th MI Gp

1. The Commanding Officer desires that newly arrived officers, warrant officers and civilian personnel call at his quarters shortly after their arrival in the command. The exact time and date will be furnished to you by the S-1 office. If your wife is present in the command, the Commanding Officer expects her to accompany you when you make your call.

2. When making your call, the Commanding Officer desires that you arrive at the exact time scheduled—not before and not later. Since promptness is essential and since there might be difficulty locating the Commander's home, it would be advisable to make a "dry run" sometime before the call.

3. The Commander desires that the call last 20 minutes. Enjoy your visit, and if refreshments are offered you may accept as you desire. When it is time to leave make your excuses politely and depart. One might say, "Thank you Col. and Mrs. ——— for your hospitality, we have enjoyed the visit and we must be leaving." You may be asked by the Commanding Officer not to hurry off, but to stay. Your reply at this time is "Thank you, but we must be going." Then go without lingering.

4. When calling on the Commander, good etiquette requires that you and your wife leave calling cards. Make sure that you do and that you leave the proper number. For the call on the Commander, the officer will leave two cards and his wife will leave one card. The cards will be left in the silver tray in the hallway. Look for it upon entering. It should be obviously apparent.

5. The correct dress for the officer is a conservative dark business suit, and for his wife, a suit appropriate for the season, to include purse and gloves.

6. If you have any questions prior to making the call, consult the S-1 Officer. Remember, the call is official in nature, it is a mandatory requirement, and it should be done in the prescribed manner.

Andrew L. Lentile
LTC, MI
S-1

Columbus to San Luis Angel

In another common sort of official letter, one reports to the funding source how well one spent the funds. In 1493 as today, the report went up the chain of command. San Luis Angel was the treasurer of Aragon, who was of course expected to pass the following letter on up to King Ferdinand and Queen Isabella.

Sir:

As I know you will be rejoiced at the glorious success that our Lord has given me in my voyage, I write this to tell you how in thirty-three days I sailed to the Indies with the fleet that the illustrious King and Queen, our Sovereigns, gave me, where I discovered a great many islands, inhabited by numberless people; and of all I have taken possession for their Highnesses by proclamation and display of the Royal Standard without opposition. To the first island I discovered I gave the name of San Salvador, in commemoration of His Divine Majesty, who has wonderfully granted all this. The Indians call it Guanaham. The second I named the Island of Santa Maria de Concepcion; the third, Fernandina; the fourth, Isabella; the fifth, Juana; and thus to each one I gave a new name. When I came to Juana,[1] I followed the coast of that isle toward the west, and found it so extensive that I thought it might be the mainland, the province of Cathay;[2] and as I found no towns nor villages on the sea-coast, except a few small settlements, where it was impossible to speak to the people, because they fled at once, I continued the said route, thinking I could not fail to see some great cities or towns; and finding at the end of many leagues that nothing new appeared, and that the coast led northward, contrary to my wish, because the winter had already set in, I decided to make for the south, and as the wind also was against my proceeding, I determined not to wait there longer, and turned back to a certain harbor whence I sent two men to find out whether there was any king or large city. They explored for three days, and found countless small communities and people, without number, but with no kind of government, so they returned. . . .

At every point where I landed, and succeeded in talking to them, I gave them some of everything I had—cloth and many other things—without receiving anything in return, but they are a hopelessly timid people. It is true that since they have gained more confidence and are losing this fear, they are so unsuspicious and so generous with what they possess, that no one who had not seen it would believe it. They never refuse anything that is asked for. They even offer it themselves, and show so much love that they would give their very hearts. Whether it be anything of great or small value, with any trifle of whatever kind, they are

1. Cuba
2. China

satisfied. I forbade worthless things being given to them, such as bits of broken bowls, pieces of glass, and old straps, although they were as much pleased to get them as if they were the finest jewels in the world. One sailor was found to have got for a leathern strap, gold of the weight of two and a half castellanos, and others for even more worthless things much more; while for a new *blancas* they would give all they had, were it two or three castellanos of pure gold or an arroba or two of spun cotton. Even bits of the broken hoops of wine casks they accepted, and gave in return what they had, like fools, and it seemed wrong to me. I forbade it, and gave a thousand good and pretty things that I had to win their love, and to induce them to become Christians, and to love and serve their Highnesses and the whole Castilian nation, and help to get for us things they have in abundance, which are necessary to us. They have no religion, nor idolatry, except that they all believe power and goodness to be in heaven. They firmly believed that I, with my ships and men, came from heaven, and with this idea I have been received everywhere, since they lost fear of me. They are, however, far from being ignorant. They are most ingenious men, and navigate, these seas in a wonderful way, and describe everything well, but they never before saw people wearing clothes, nor vessels like ours. Directly I reached the Indies in the first isle I discovered, I took by force some of the natives, that from them we might gain some information of what there was in these parts; and so it was that we immediately understood each other, either by words or signs. They are still with me and still believe that I come from heaven. They were the first to declare this wherever I went, and the others ran from house to house, and to the towns around, crying out, "Come! come! and see the men from heaven!" Then all, both men and women, as soon as they were reassured about us, came both small and great, all bringing something to eat and to drink, which they presented with marvellous kindness. . . .

They are the most timid people in the world, so that only the men remaining there could destroy the whole region, and run no risk if they know how to behave themselves properly. In all these islands the men seem to be satisfied with one wife, except they allow as many as twenty to their chief or king. The women appear to me to work harder than the men, and so far as I can hear they have nothing of their own, for I think I perceived that what one had others shared, especially food. In the islands so far, I have found no monsters, as some expected, but, on the contrary, they are people of very handsome appearance. They are not black as in Guinea, though their hair is straight and coarse, as it does not grow where the sun's rays are too ardent. And in truth the sun has extreme power here, since it is within twenty-six degrees of the equinoctial line. In these islands there are mountains where the cold this winter was very severe, but the people endure it from habit, and with the aid of the meat they eat with very hot spices.

As for monsters, I have found no trace of them except at the point in the second isle as one enters the Indies, which is inhabited by a people considered in all the isles as most ferocious, who eat human flesh. They possess many canoes, with which they overrun all the isles of India, stealing and seizing all they can. They are not worse looking than the others, except that they wear their hair long like women, and use bows and arrows of the same cane, with a sharp stick at the end for want of iron, of which they have none. They are ferocious compared to these other races, who are extremely cowardly; but I only hear this from the others. They are said to make treaties of marriage with the women in the first isle to be met with coming from Spain to the Indies, where there are no men. These women have no feminine occupation, but use bows and arrows of cane like those before mentioned, and cover and arm themselves with plates of copper, of which they have a great quantity. . . .

The eternal and almighty God, our Lord, it is Who gives to all who walk in His way, victory over things apparently impossible, and in this case signally so, because although these lands had been imagined and talked of before they were seen, most men listened incredulously to what was thought to be but an idle tale. But our Redeemer has given victory to our most illustrious King and Queen, and to their kingdoms rendered famous by this glorious event, at which all Christendom should rejoice, celebrating it with great festivities and solemn Thanksgiving to the Holy Trinity, with fervent prayers for the high distinction that will accrue to them from turning so many peoples to our holy faith; and also from the temporal benefits that not only Spain but all Christian nations will obtain. Thus I record what has happened in a brief note written on board the *Caravel*, off the Canary Isles, on the 15th of February, 1493.

Yours to command,
The Admiral

Postscript within the Letter

Since writing the above, being in the Sea of Castile, so much wind arose south southeast, that I was forced to lighten the vessels, to run into this port of Lisbon today which was the most extraordinary thing in the world, from whence I resolved to write to their Highnesses. In all the Indies I always found the temperature like that of May. Where I went in thirty-three days I returned in twenty-eight, except that these gales have detained me fourteen days, knocking about in this sea. Here all seamen say that there has never been so rough a winter, nor so many vessels lost. Done the 14th day of March.

My Dungeon Shook:
Letter to My Nephew
James Baldwin
from *The Fire Next Time,* 1962

The analytic remarks on the black-white relationship in America that make up much of the following letter show just how readily epistle may become essay if the writer generalizes about some subject. But this "essay" is addressed to a very real person, Baldwin's brother's son, and achieves its passionate eloquence precisely by setting the generalization within a traditional letter of advice and admonition, where family intimacy infuses the public ideas with feelings that people of all races can resonate with.

Dear James:

I have begun this letter five times and torn it up five times. I keep seeing your face, which is also the face of your father and my brother. Like him, you are tough, dark, vulnerable, moody—with a very definite tendency to sound truculent because you want no one to think you are soft. You may be like your grandfather in this, I don't know, but your father resemble him very much p dead, he never saw you, and he had a defeated long before he died because, at th he really believed what white people said ab of the reasons that he became so holy. I am s has told you something about all that. Nei father exhibit any tendency towards holiness: another era, part of what happened when the Ne land and came into what the late E. Franklin Frazier c the cities of destruction.'' You can only be destroyed by believing that you really are what the white world calls a *nigger*. I tell you this because I love you, and please don't you forget it.

I have known both of you all your lives, have carried your Daddy in my arms and on my shoulders, kissed and spanked him and watched him learn to walk. I don't know if you've known anybody from that far back; if you've loved anybody that long, first as an infant, then as a child, then as a man, you gain a strange perspective on time and human pain and effort. Other people cannot see what I see whenever I look into your father's face, for behind your father's face as it is today are all those other faces which were his. Let him laugh and I see a cellar your father does not remember and a house he does not remember and I hear in his present laughter his laughter as a child. Let him curse and I remember him falling down the cellar steps, and howling, and I remember, with pain, his tears, which my hand or your grandmother's so easily wiped away. But no one's hand can wipe away those tears he sheds invisibly today, which one hears in his laughter and in his speech and in his songs. I know what the world has done to my brother and how narrowly he has survived it. And I know, which is much worse, and this is the crime of which I accuse my country and my countrymen, and for which neither I nor time nor history will ever forgive them, that they have destroyed and are destroying hundreds of thousands of lives and do not know it and do not want to know it. One can be, indeed one must strive to become, tough and philosophical concerning destruction and death, for this is what most of mankind has been best at since we have heard of man. (But remember: *most* of mankind is not *all* of mankind.) But it is not permissible that the authors of devastation should also be innocent. It is the innocence which constitutes the crime.

Now, my dear namesake, these innocent and well-meaning people, your countrymen, have caused you to be born under conditions not very far removed from those described for us by

in the London of more than a hundred years
the chorus of the innocents screaming, "No! This is
How *bitter* you are!"—but I am writing this letter to
try to tell you something about how to handle *them*, for
most of them do not really know that you exist. I *know* the
conditions under which you were born, for I was there. Your
countrymen were *not* there, and haven't made it yet. Your
grandmother was also there, and no one has ever accused her of
being bitter. I suggest that the innocents check with her. She
isn't hard to find. Your countrymen don't know that *she* exists,
either, though she has been working for them all their lives.)

Well, you were born, here you came, something like fourteen
years ago; and though your father and mother and grandmother,
looking about the streets through which they were carrying you,
staring at the walls into which they brought you, had every
reason to be heavy-hearted, yet they were not. For here you were,
Big James, named for me—you were a big baby, I was not—
here you were: to be loved. To be loved, baby, hard, at once,
and forever, to strengthen you against the loveless world. Remember that: I know how black it looks today, for you. It looked
bad that day, too, yes, we were trembling. We have not stopped
trembling yet, but if we had not loved each other none of us
would have survived. And now you must survive because we
love you, and for the sake of your children and your children's
children.

This innocent country set you down in a ghetto in which, in
fact, it intended that you should perish. Let me spell out precisely what I mean by that, for the heart of the matter is here,
and the root of my dispute with my country. You were born
where you were born and faced the future that you faced because
you were black and *for no other reason*. The limits of your
ambition were, thus, expected to be set forever. You were born
into a society which spelled out with brutal clarity, and in as
many ways as possible, that you were a worthless human being.
You were not expected to aspire to excellence: you were expected to make peace with mediocrity. Wherever you have turned,
James, in your short time on this earth, you have been told
where you could go and what you could do (and *how* you could
do it) and where you could live and whom you could marry. I
know your countrymen do not agree with me about this, and I
hear them saying, "You exaggerate." They do not know Harlem,
and I do. So do you. Take no one's word for anything, including
mine—but trust your experience. Know whence you came. If you
know whence you came, there is really no limit to where you can

go. The details and symbols of your life have been deliberately constructed to make you believe what white people say about you. Please try to remember that what they believe, as well as what they do and cause you to endure, does not testify to your inferiority but to their inhumanity and fear. Please try to be clear, dear James, through the storm which rages about your youthful head today, about the reality which lies behind the words *acceptance* and *integration*. There is no reason for you to try to become like white people and there is no basis whatever for their impertinent assumption that *they* must accept *you*. The really terrible thing, old buddy, is that *you* must accept *them*. And I mean that very seriously. You must accept them and accept them with love. For these innocent people have no other hope. They are, in effect, still trapped in a history which they do not understand; and until they understand it, they cannot be released from it. They have had to believe for many years, and for innumerable reasons, that black men are inferior to white men. Many of them, indeed, know better, but, as you will discover, people find it very difficult to act on what they know. To act is to be committed, and to be committed is to be in danger. In this case, the danger, in the minds of most white Americans, is the loss of their identity. Try to imagine how you would feel if you woke up one morning to find the sun shining and all the stars aflame. You would be frightened because it is out of the order of nature. Any upheaval in the universe is terrifying because it so profoundly attacks one's sense of one's own reality. Well, the black man has functioned in the white man's world as a fixed star, as an immovable pillar: and as he moves out of his place, heaven and earth are shaken to their foundations. You, don't be afraid. I said that it was intended that you should perish in the ghetto, perish by never being allowed to go behind the white man's definitions, by never being allowed to spell your proper name. You have, and many of us have, defeated this intention; and, by a terrible law, a terrible paradox, those innocents who believed that your imprisonment made them safe are losing their grasp of reality. But these men are your brothers—your lost, younger brothers. And if the word *integration* means anything, that is what it means: that we, with love, shall force our brothers to see themselves as they are, to cease fleeing from reality and begin to change it. For this is your home, my friend, do not be driven from it; great men have done great things here, and will again, and we can make America what America must become. It will be hard, James, but you come from sturdy, peasant stock, men who picked cotton and dammed rivers and built railroads, and, in the teeth of the most terrifying odds, achieved an unassailable and monumental dignity. You come from a long line of great poets, some of the greatest poets since Homer. One of them said, *The very time I thought I was lost, My dungeon shook and my chains fell off.*

You know, and I know, that the country is celebrating one hundred years of freedom one hundred years too soon. We cannot be free until they are free. God bless you, James, and Godspeed.

Your uncle,
James

NOTATION

THE imperative and interrogative modes fade away as we leave the interactive framework of correspondence. From here on the mode is only declarative.

The audience for logs, diaries, and journals is neither particular nor exactly public; it is as the writer feels it, perhaps the writer at a later date or a party too local or indefinite as yet to constitute a publication public.

The key to diaries and journals lies in their very names, which derive from words for "day." They are "daily" registrations of events or thoughts. The category Notation emphasizes this periodic registration. The keeper of a register is always writing from *within* the events or thoughts and does not, when writing, know the conclusion. The vantage point resembles that of the correspondent rather than that of the memoirist. A gain in immediacy is a loss in "perspective" or long-range assimilation.

But one may have the best of both worlds by later writing "up" these notations. Many practicing authors, in fact, keep journals in order to stay well stocked in writing material rich with the original feeling and detail. Diaries and journals kept by amateurs often serve as "source documents" for researchers. In either case they act as notes upon which subsequent writing is based.

It seems sensible to differentiate the terms "log," "diary," and "journal," so that they may help us make some worthwhile distinctions. Let's say that a log is the very barest registration of the physical events of some enterprise, as with the log of a ship, hospital, factory, or laboratory, which is often kept by different members of an organization. A diary is personal and miscellaneous, mixing events with feelings and observations. A journal may also contain thoughts and feelings but is specialized by being focused on only one activity or area of the journal-keeper's life, such as a project or trip.

Now, one could scale these from most personal to impersonal—diary to journal to log—which would go also from least to most specialized. That would bring out significant variants of Notation, but in sequencing toward the most public we would place farthest along in our progression the most physical of these, the log. If, instead, we order them from log to diary to journal, we emphasize a more important dimension of the writer's abstracting process, which is selectivity, as contrasted with either the randomness of miscellany or the rigidity of regular routines. Composition concerns choice.

Whereas in Interaction the give-and-take between correspondents exerts the overriding influence on composition, in Notation what primarily composes the text is the selectivity of the recorder's registration. By our definitions, a log permits little choice, and a diarist is content to register heterogeneity itself for the sake of impressionistic fidelity to what is going on, whereas the journal's specialized focus and purpose constitute the beginning of a selective process that will guide composition. This is roughly an order of concrete to abstract: what the log registers is most purely physical, what the diary reflects is still the original constellation of inner and outer events, and what the journal traces is a more selective version of all that might have been recorded—though not more selective, precisely, because of a restriction to the physical phenomena but because of a prior mental restriction to a subject. Thus journals most naturally lead into informative articles and essays. They accumulate the empirical fodder for the inductive process of generalization. Diaries abound in observations and introspections, retrospections and reflections, that show kinship with many kinds of writing not so abstract as thesis essays—stories, sketches, and personal essays.

Admittedly, in common parlance and even in literary discussion, one can hear the same set of chronological notes called "log" by one, "diary" by another, and "journal" by a third. Still, for purposes of our survey here it will refine our discrimination as we read on if we do not lump together various instances of Notation, however we name them. In this respect it is not how we call things but how we scale things that is important.

Log

A Week in the Life
from Sheriff's Log of Madera County, California, 1983

Though uninterpretive, a log can be very telling, as a photograph can, by the sheer physical, slice-of-life revelation. What this means is that, by being allowed in effect to compose their own record, the actions of a locale or enterprise can speak for themselves. (People's names below have all been changed.)

NOVEMBER 10

10:45 AM A suspicious person was reported to be at the Coarsegold Frostie. Upon officer's arrival, subject was inside drinking coffee, causing no problems.

4:10 PM North Fork Elementary reported a 14 year old student driving his parent's vehicles.

NOVEMBER 11

1:40 AM Ahwahnee Hills School reported a walkaway. Juvenile was later reported to be at father's home in the Bay area.

11:15 AM A Coarsegold man reported a young juvenile riding a motorcycle on his property.

12:30 PM The Narrow Gauge Inn in Fish Camp reported the theft of a sign from their driveway. $620 loss.

2:05 PM Renata Atkins, of North Fork, was the victim of burglary to her residence. $200 loss.

8:05 PM An Oakhurst man was taken into custody for public intoxication.

NOVEMBER 12

12:30 AM A 20 year old North Fork woman was charged with using a false I.D. for purchasing alcoholic beverages.

10:00 AM Ellen Winston, of Ahwahnee, reported a burglary to her residence and theft of a generator from her property.

10:00 AM Bruce Patrickson, of Coarsegold, reported malicious mischief to a residence under construction. A window was broken, but no sign of theft. $50 damage.

1:04 PM Sierra Ambulance requested assistance with a woman down call. On officer's arrival, ambulance crew had everything under control. Victim was up and around.

1:45 PM A downed aircraft was reported northeast of Bass Lake on Iron Mountain. Search and Rescue (SAR) operation organized.

9:42 PM An Oakhurst man reported a prowler at his residence. Deputy unable to locate responsible.

NOVEMBER 13

12:04 PM An Oakhurst man reported receiving threats.

1:20 PM Deputy responded to reported fire at Oak Creek Intermediate. Fire was out on officer's arrival. Apparently arson fire was set in a school locker. No damage to structure.

3:20 PM A Coarsegold woman reported a subject had slashed her tires. Responsible agreed to replace the tires. Victim wished no charges filed if he does so.

4:30 PM Loose cattle reported in area of Manzanita Drive in Bass Lake Heights. Officer escorted cattle away from homes.

6:47 PM North Fork juvenile reported theft of his bicycle from the Pizza Factory in North Fork. Value $150.

8:54 PM Suspicious person reported at Coarsegold Inn. Subject had taken refuge on the porch of the Inn waiting for rain to stop before he continued on to Fresno. No further action required.

NOVEMBER 14

11:30 AM A North Fork man reported a possible break-in to the Manuel Ramirez cabin at Bass Lake. Entry had been made, but amount of theft, if any, was not determined at time of report.

11:30 AM Officer observed that Harrison K. Elkwood cabin at Bass Lake appears to have been broken into and slept in.

12:31 PM Wreckage of missing aircraft spotted by CHP helicopter. Body of pilot, Willie S. Nestlerod, 34, of Burson located approximately 75 feet from downed plane. Search continues for possible passenger.

NOVEMBER 15

10:53 PM A 26 year old Ahwahnee man was cited for possession of marijuana.

NOVEMBER 16

9:40 AM An Oakhurst woman reported a possible prowler in the neighborhood. Deputy unable to locate.

9:45 AM Madera County Road Department was the victim of theft of barricades, a sign and gasoline. $125 loss.

11:43 AM A Bass Lake man reported an abandoned log skidder in the parking lot of the Pines Resort. Officers attempting to identify the owner.

12:02 PM A Coarsegold man reported receiving annoying phone calls.

NOVEMBER 17

11:25 AM Report received of juvenile at Yosemite High School smoking marijuana. Turned information over to Narcotics Enforcement.

12:10 PM Muriel Skedinza, 14, of Coarsegold victim of theft of gym clothes at Y.H.S.

5:38 PM Joan Kenney, of North Fork, was the victim of theft of $170 in cash, an electric blanket and towels from her residence.

7:10 PM Donald M. Hamilton, of Coarsegold, reported the theft of a shotgun from his residence.

NOVEMBER 18

SAR team members found the body of the passenger of the plane crash which was reported November 12. He has been tentatively identified as James Harvey McGilles, 32, of Bakersfield.

Diary

Life in London of the 1660s
from Everybody's Pepys: The Diary
of Samuel Pepys 1660–1669,
edited by O.S. Morshead

---

*Samuel Pepys was a London businessman who kept a diary from
1660 to 1669, when his eyesight began to fail. Far from aiming
at publication, he wrote it in a code that was not deciphered until
over a century after his death. It is spare and concrete like a log,
the style itself being abbreviated, and he rarely reflects on anything.
But even as a straight record it has the intimacy of a diary, for he
does show himself through his routines, behavior, concerns,
likes, and dislikes. And as an honest, factual account it shows us
the reality of daily life in that period, something difficult to learn
from official archives and more public chronicles. But such a
diarist does not identify people or explain references, and sometimes it takes an army of scholars to elucidate these. Mostly, the
reader must just get to know the diarist's world from living in it
a while.*

March 1663

12th. Sat late, and having done I went home, where I found
Mary Ashwell[1] come to live with us, of whom I hope well, and
pray God she may please us: which, though it cost me something,
yet will give me much content.

1. As his wife's maid.

15th. (Lord's Day.) Up and with my wife and her woman Ashwell the first time to church. . . . Dined at home, and to church again in the afternoon, and so home, and I to my office till the evening. So home to supper and talk; and Ashwell is such good company that I think we shall be very lucky in her. So to prayers and to bed.

April 1663

April 1st. Up betimes and abroad to my brother's, but they tell me that my brother is abroad, and that my father is not yet up. At which I wondered, not thinking that he was come, though I expected him, because I looked for him at my house. So I up to his bedside and staid an hour or two talking with him. Among other things he tells me how unquiett my mother is grown, that he is not able to live almost with her, if it were not for Pall. I left him in bed, being very weary, to come to my house to-night or to-morrow, when he pleases; and so I home to dinner. My wife being lazily in bed all this morning, Ashwell and I dined below together; and a pretty girl she is, and I hope will give my wife and myself good content, being very humble and active.

4th. . . . Very merry at, before, and after dinner, and the more for that my dinner was great, and most neatly dressed by our own only maid. We had a fricasee of rabbits and chickens, a leg of mutton boiled, three carps in a dish, a great dish of a side of lamb, a dish of roasted pigeons, a dish of four lobsters, three tarts, a lamprey pie (a most rare pie), a dish of anchovies, good wine of several sorts, and all things mighty noble and to my great content. After dinner to Hide Park. . . .

At the Park was the King. . . . Here about an hour, and so leaving all by the way we home and found the house as clean as if nothing had been done there to-day from top to bottom, which made us give the cook 12*d*. a piece, each of us. So to my office about writing letters by the post, one to my brother John at Brampton telling him (hoping to work a good effect by it upon my mother) how melancholy my father is, and bidding him use all means to get my mother to live peaceably and quietly, which I am sure she neither do nor I fear can ever do; but frightening her with his coming down no more, and the danger of her conition if he should die, I trust may do good. So home and to bed.

19th. (Easter Day.) Up and this day put on my close-kneed

coloured suit which, with new stockings of the colour, with belt and new gilt-handled sword, is very handsome. After supper fell in discourse of dancing, and I find that Ashwell hath a very fine carriage, which makes my wife almost ashamed of herself to see herself so outdone; but to-morrow she begins to learn to dance for a month or two. So to prayers and to bed.

23rd. St. George's day and Coronacion, the King and Court being at Windsor, at the installing of the King of Denmark by proxy, and the Duke of Monmouth. I up betimes, and with my father, having a fire made in my wife's new closet[2] above, it being a wet and cold day, we sat there all the morning looking over his country accounts ever since his going into the country. I find his spending hitherto has been (without extraordinary charges) at full £100 per annum, which troubles me, and I did let him apprehend it, so as that the poor man wept, though he did make it well appear to me that he could not have saved a farthing of it. I did tell him how things stand with us and did shew my distrust of Pall, both for her good nature and house wifery, which he was sorry for, telling me that indeed she carries herself very well and carefully; which I am glad to hear, though I doubt it was but his doting and not being able to find her miscarriages so well nowadays as he could heretofore have done. We resolve upon sending for Will Stankes up to town to give us a right understanding in all that we have in Brampton. To my office and put a few things in order, and so home to spend the evening with my father. At cards till late; and being at supper, my boy being sent for some mustard to a neat's tongue, the rogue staid half an hour in the streets, it seems at a bonfire; at which I was very angry, and resolve to beat him to-morrow.

24th. Up betimes, and with my salt eel[3] went down in the parler and there got my boy and did beat him till I was fain to take breath two or three times. Yet for all I am afeard it will make the boy never the better, he is grown so hardened in his tricks, which I am sorry for, he being capable of making a brave man, and is a boy that I and my wife love very well. So made me ready, and to my office, where all the morning, and at noon home, sending my boy to enquire after two dancing masters at our end of the town for my wife to learn, of whose names the boy brought word. After dinner all the afternoon fiddling upon my viallin[4] (which I have not done many a day) while Ashwel

2. A small private chamber for studying, praying, meditating, or the like.
3. Rope's end.
4. Violin.

danced, above in my upper best chamber, which is a rare room for musique.

25th. My wife hath begun to learn this day of Mr. Pembleton, but I fear will hardly do any great good at it, because she is conceited that she do well already, though I think no such thing. So to bed.

26th. (Lord's Day.) Lay pretty long in bed talking with my wife, and then up and set to the making up of my monthly accounts. But Tom coming, with whom I was angry for botching my camlott coat, to tell me that my father and he would dine with me, and that my father was at our church, I got me ready and had a very good sermon of a country minister upon "How blessed a thing it is for brethren to live together in unity!" So home and all to dinner. In the evening my wife, Ashwell, and the boy and I and the dogg over the water, and walked to Half-way house and beyond into the fields, gathering of cowslipps; and so to Half-way house with some cold lamb we carried with us, and there supped; and had a most pleasant walk back again, Ashwell all along telling us some parts of their mask at Chelsey School, which was very pretty; and I find she hath a most prodigious memory, remembering so much of things acted six or seven years ago. So home, and after reading my vows, being sleepy, without prayers to bed, for which God forgive me!

29th. Up betimes, and after having at my office settled some accounts for my Lord Sandwich, I went forth, and taking up my father at my brother's, took coach and towards Chelsey, 'lighting at an alehouse near the Gatehouse at Westminster to drink our morning draught; and so up again and to Chelsey, where we found my Lord all alone at a little table with one joynt of meat at dinner. We sat down and very merry talking, and mightily extolling the manner of his retirement and the goodness of his diet, which indeed is so finely dressed: the mistress of the house, Mrs. Beeke, having been a woman of good condition heretofore, a merchant's wife, and hath all things most excellently dressed; among others her cakes admirable. . . . From ordinary discourse my Lord fell to talk of other matters to me. My father staid a good while at the window and then sat down by himself while my Lord and I were thus an hour together or two after dinner discoursing; and by and by he took his leave, and told me he would stay below for me. Anon I took leave, and coming down found my father unexpectedly in great pain and desiring for God's sake to get him a bed to lie upon, which I did; and W. Howe and I staid by him, in so great pain as I never saw, poor wretch, and with that patience, crying only: "Terrible, terrible pain, God help me, God help me," with the mournful voice that made my heart ake. He desired to rest a little alone to see whether it would abate, and W. Howe and I went down and walked in the gardens, which are very fine, and a pretty fountayne with which I was finely wetted; and up to a banquetting house, with a very fine prospect. And so back to my father, who I found in such pain that I could not bear the sight of it without weeping, never thinking that I should be able to get him from thence; but at last, finding it like to continue, I got him to go to the coach, with great pain; and driving hard, he all the while in a most unsufferable torment, not staying the coach to speak with anybody, at last we got home; and all helping him we got him to bed presently, and after half an hour's lying in his naked bed (it being a rupture with which he is troubled, and has been this 20 years), he was at good ease, and so continued, and so fell to sleep; and we went down, whither W. Stankes was come with his horses. But it is very pleasant to hear how he rails at the rumbling and ado that is in London over it is in the country, that he cannot endure it. He supped with us, and very merry; and then he to his lodgings at the Inne with the horses, and so we to bed, I to my father who is very well again, and both slept very well.

30th. Up, and after drinking my morning draft with my father and W. Stankes, to my office, where till towards noon; and then to the Exchange, and back home to dinner, where Mrs. Hunt, my father, and W. Stankes. But, Lord! what a stir Stankes makes with his being crowded in the streets and wearied in walking in London, and would not be wooed by my wife and Ashwell to go to a play, nor to White Hall, or to see the lyons, though he was carried in a coach. I never could have thought there had been upon earth a man so little curious in the world as he is. At the office all the afternoon till 9 at night; so home to cards with my father, wife, and Ashwell, and so to bed.

May 1663

2nd. Being weary last night I slept till almost seven o'clock, a thing I have not done many a day. So up and to my office (being come to some angry words with my wife about neglecting the keeping of the house clean, I calling her beggar, and she me pricklouse,[5] which vexed me), and there all the morning. . . .

5. I.e., a tailor; a reference to Pepys's ancestors.

Home to dinner, and very merry and well pleased with my wife, and so to the office again.

3rd. My wife not being very well did not dress herself but staid at home all day; and so I to church in the afternoon and so home again, and up to teach Ashwell the grounds of time and other things on the tryangle,[6] and made her take out a Psalm very well, she having a good ear and hand. And so a while to my office, and then home to supper and prayers, to bed, my wife and I having a little falling out because I would not leave my discourse below with her and Ashwell to go up and talk with her alone upon something she has to say. She reproached me but I had rather talk with any body than her, by which I find I think she is jealous of my freedom with Ashwell, which I must avoid giving occasion of.

4th. The dancing-master came, whom standing by, seeing him instructing my wife, when he had done with her he would needs have me try the steps of a coranto; and what with his desire and my wife's importunity I did begin, and then was obliged to give him entry-money 10*s.*, and am become his scholler. The truth is I think it a thing very useful for a gentleman, and sometimes I may have occasion of using it; and though it cost me what I am heartily sorry it should, besides that I must by my oath give half as much more to the poor, yet I am resolved to get it up some other way; and then it will not be above a month or two in a year. So though it be against my stomach yet I will try it a little while; if I see it comes to any great inconvenience or charge I will fling it off.

8th. Took my wife and Ashwell to the Theatre Royall, being the second day of its being opened. The play was "The Humerous Lieutenant," a play that hath little good in it. . . . In the dance the tall devil's actions was very pretty. The play being done, we home by water, having been a little shamed that my wife and woman were in such a pickle, all the ladies being finer and better dressed in the pitt than they used, I think, to be. . . .

9th. To Westminster, where at Mr. Jervas's, my old barber, I did try two or three borders and perriwiggs, meaning to wear one; and yet I have no stomach for it, but that the pains of keeping my hair clean is so great. He trimmed me, and at last I parted, but my mind was almost altered from my first purpose from the trouble that I foresee I will be in wearing them also. Thence by water home and to the office, where busy late; and so home to supper and bed.

6. Probably a triangular spinet.

11th. Up betimes and by water to Woolwich, and thence on foot to Greenwich, where going I was set upon by a great dogg, who got hold of my garters and might have done me hurt; but, Lord, to see in what a maze I was, that having a sword about me I never thought of it or had the heart to make use of it, but might for want of that courage have been worried.

12th. A little angry with my wife for minding nothing now but the dancing-master, having him come twice a day, which is a folly. To my office till late.

13th. After dinner Pembleton[7] came, and I practised. But, Lord! to see how my wife will not be thought to need telling by me or Ashwell, and yet will plead that she has learnt but a month, which causes many short fallings out between us. . . .

15th. Up betimes and walked to St. James's, where Mr. Coventry being in bed I walked in the Park, discoursing with the keeper of Pell Mell, who was sweeping of it; who told me of what the earth is mixed that do floor the Mall, and that over all there is cockle-shells powdered and spread to keep it fast; which however in dry weather turns to dust and deads the ball.[8] Home, where I found my wife and the dancing-master alone above, not dancing but talking. Now so deadly full of jealousy I am that my heart and head did so cast about and fret that I could not do any business possibly, but went out to my office; and anon late home again and ready to chide at every thing, and then suddenly to bed and could hardly sleep yet durst not say anything, but was forced to say that I had bad news from the Duke as an excuse to my wife, who by my folly has too much opportunity given her with the man, who is a pretty neat black man, but married.

16th. Up with my mind disturbed and with my last night's doubts upon me, for which I deserve to be beaten if not really served as I am fearful of being; especially since God knows that I do not find honesty enough in my own mind but that upon a small temptation I could be false to her, and therefore ought not to expect more justice from her; but God pardon both my sin and my folly herein. To my office and there sitting all the morning, and at noon dined at home. After dinner comes Pembleton, and I being out of humour would not see him, pretending business. But, Lord! with what jealousy did I walk up and down my chamber listening to hear whether they danced or no, which they

---

7. The dancing master.
8. Pall Mall was so called from the game which was played along it. In the game a boxwood ball was struck with a mallet to drive it through an iron ring suspended at the end of an alley.

did, notwithstanding I afterwards knew and did then believe that Ashwell was with them. So to my office awhile; and my jealousy still reigning I went in and, not out of any pleasure but from that only reason, did go up to them to practise, and did make an end of "La Duchesse," which I think I should, with a little pains, do very well. So broke up and saw him gone.

21th. At dinner, my wife and I had high words about her dancing, to that degree that I did enter and make a vow to myself not to oppose her or say anything to dispraise or correct her therein as long as her month lasts, in pain of 2s, 6d, for every time; which, if God pleases, I will observe, for this roguish business has brought us more disquiet than anything that has happened in a great while. After dinner to my office, where late, and then home; and Pembleton being there again we fell to dance a country dance or two, and so to supper and bed. But being at supper my wife did say something that caused me to oppose her in; she used the word devil, which vexed me, and among other things I said I would not have her to use that word; upon which she took me up most scornfully, which, before Ashwell and the rest of the world, I know not now-a-days how to check as I would heretofore, for less than that would have made me strike her. So that I fear without great discretion I shall go near to lose too my command over her, and nothing do it more than giving her this occasion of dancing and other pleasures, whereby her mind is taken up from her business and finds other sweets besides pleasing of me, and so makes her that she begins not at all to take pleasure in me or study to please me as heretofore. But if this month of her dancing were but out (as my first was this night, and I paid off Pembleton for myself) I shall hope with a little pains to bring her to her old wont.

24th. (Lord's Day.) My wife telling me that there was a pretty lady come to church with Peg Pen to-day, I against my intention had a mind to go to church to see her, and did so; and she is pretty handsome. But over against our gallery I espied Pembleton, and saw him leer upon my wife all the sermon, I taking no notice of him, and my wife upon him; and I observed she made a curtsey to him at coming out without taking notice to me at all of it, which with the consideration of her being desirous these two last Lord's days to go to church both forenoon and afternoon do really make me suspect something more than ordinary, though I am loth to think the worst; but yet it put and do still keep me at a great loss in my mind, and makes me curse the time that I consented to her dancing, and more my continuing it a second month, which was more than she desired, even after I had seen too much of her carriage with him. But I must have patience and get her into the country, or at least to make an end of her learning to dance as soon as I can. So home, and read to my wife a fable or two in Ogleby's Æsop, and so to supper, and then to prayers and to bed. My wife this evening discoursing of making clothes for the country, which I seem against, pleading lack of money; but I am glad of it in some respects because of getting her out of the way from this fellow, and my own liberty to look after my business more than of late I have done. So to prayers and to bed.

25th. Sarah Kite my cozen, poor woman, came to see me and borrow 40*s.* of me, telling me she will pay it at Michaelmas again to me. I was glad it was no more, being indifferent whether she pays it me or no; but it will be a good excuse to lend her nor give her any more. So I did freely at first word do it, and give her a crown more freely to buy her child something, she being a good-natured and painful wretch, and one that I would do good for as far as I can that I might not be burdened. My wife was not ready, and she coming early did not see her, and I was glad of it.

26th. Lay long in bed talking with my wife. So up and to my office a while and then home, where I found Pembleton; and by many circumstances I am led to conclude that there is something more than ordinary between my wife and him, which do so trouble me that I know not at this very minute that I now write this almost what either I write or am doing, nor how to carry myself to my wife in it, being unwilling to speak of it to her for making of any breach and other inconveniences, nor let it pass for fear of her continuing to offend me and the matter grow worse thereby. So that I am grieved at the very heart; but I am very unwise in being so. . . .

Nothing could get the business out of my head, I fearing that this afternoon, by my wife's sending every one abroad and knowing that I must be at the office, she has appointed him to come. This is my devilish jealousy, which I pray God may be false; but it makes a very hell in my mind, which the God of heaven remove or I shall be very unhappy. So to the office, where we sat awhile. By and by my mind being in great trouble I went home to see how things were, and there I found as I doubted Mr. Pembleton with my wife, and nobody else in the house, which made me almost mad; and, going up to my chamber, after a turn or two I went out again and called somebody on pretence of business and left him in my little room at the door, telling him I would come again to him to speak with him about his business. So in great trouble and doubt to the office, and made a quick end of our business and desired leave to be gone, pretending to go to the Temple; but it was home, and so up to my chamber, and continued in my chamber vexed and angry till he went away, pretending aloud, that I might hear, that he could not stay, and Mrs. Ashwell not being within they could not dance. But I staid all the evening walking, and though anon my wife came up to me and would have spoke of business to me, yet I construed it to be but impudence, and though my heart full yet I did say nothing, being in a great doubt what to do. So at night suffered them to go all to bed, and late put myself to bed in great discontent, and so to sleep.

27th. So I waked by 3 o'clock, my mind being troubled, and so took occasion to wake my wife, and after having lain till past 4 o'clock seemed going to rise, though I did it only to see what she would do, and so going out of the bed she took hold of me and would know what ailed me, and after many kind and some cross words I began to tax her discretion in yesterday's business; but she quickly told me my own, knowing well enough that it was my old disease of jealousy, which I denied, but to no purpose. After an hour's discourse, sometimes high and sometimes kind, I found very good reason to think that her freedom with him is very great and more than was convenient, but with no evil intent; and so after awhile I caressed her and parted seeming friends, but she crying in a great discontent. So I up and by water to the Temple. Thence to Westminster Hall, where I met with my cozen Roger Pepys, and walked a good while with him; and among other discourse as a secret he hath committed to nobody but myself, he tells me that he thinks it fit to marry again, and would have me, by the help of my uncle Wight or others, to look him out a widow between thirty and forty years old, without children and with a fortune, which he will answer in any degree with a joynture fit for her future. A woman sober, and no highflyer, as he calls it.

. . . So home back as I came, to London Bridge, and so home, where I find my wife in a musty humour, and tells me before Ashwell that Pembleton had been there, and she would not have him come in unless I was there, which I was ashamed of; but however, I had rather it should be so than the other way. So to my office to put things in order there, and by and by comes Pembleton, and word is brought me from my wife thereof, that I might come home. So I sent word that I would have her go dance, and I would come presently. So being at a great loss whether I should appear to Pembleton or no, and what would most proclaim my jealousy to him, I at last resolved to go home, and there we danced country dances and single, my wife and I; and my wife paid him off for this month also, and so he is cleared. After dancing we took him down to supper and were very merry, and I made myself so, and kind to him as much as I could, to prevent his discourse, though I perceive to my trouble that he knows all, and may do me the disgrace to publish it as much as he can. Which I take very ill, and if too much provoked shall witness it to her. After supper and he gone we to bed.

June 1663

June 2nd. To-night I took occasion with the vintner's[9] man, who came by my direction to taste again my tierce of claret, to go down to the cellar with him to consult about the drawing of it; and there to my great vexation I find that the cellar door hath long been kept unlocked, and above half the wine drunk. I was deadly mad at it, and examined my people round, but nobody would confess it: but I did examine the boy, and afterwards Will, and told him of his sitting up after we were in bed with the maids; but as to that business he denies it, which I can not remedy, but I shall endeavour to know how it went. My wife did also this evening tell me a story of Ashwell stealing some new ribbon from her, a yard or two, which I am sorry to hear, and I fear my wife do take a displeasure against her, that they will hardly stay together, which I should be sorry for because I know not where to pick such another out anywhere.

3rd. In the evening to the office and did some business, then home, and, God forgive me, did from my wife's unwillingness to tell me whither she had sent the boy, presently suspect that he was gone to Pembleton's, and from that occasion grew so discontented that I could hardly speak or sleep all night.

4th. I did by a wile get out of my boy that he did not yesterday go to Pembleton's or thereabouts, but only was sent all that time for some starch, and I did see him bringing home some; and yet all this cannot make my mind quiet.

5th. . . . About 10 o'clock my wife and I, not without some discontent, abroad by coach, and I set her at her father's; but their condition is such that she will not let me see where they live, but goes by herself when I am out of sight.

9th. Up and after ordering some things towards my wife's going

9. Wine merchant's.

into the country, to the office, where I spent the morning upon my measuring rules very pleasantly till noon. . . .

11th. Spent the evening with my wife, and she and I did jangle mightily about her cushions that she wrought with worsteds the last year, which are too little for any use; but were good friends by and by again. But one thing I must confess I do observe which I did not before, which is that I cannot blame my wife to be now in a worse humour than she used to be, for I am [so] taken up in my talk with Ashwell, who is a very witty girl, that I am not so fond of her as I used and ought to be; which now I do perceive I will remedy, but I would to the Lord I had never taken any, though I cannot have a better than her. To supper and to bed. . . .

15th. Up betimes, and anon my wife rose and did give me her keys, and put other things in order and herself against going this morning into the country. I am troubled to see her forced to sit in the back of the coach, though pleased to see her company none but women and one parson; she I find is troubled at all, and I seemed to make a promise to get a horse and ride after them; and so, kissing her often, and Ashwell once, I bid them adieu. That done, to the Trinity House where among others I found my Lords Sandwich and Craven, and my cousin Roger Pepys, and Sir Wm. Wheeler. Anon we sat down to dinner, which was very great, as they always have. Great variety of talk. Sometimes they talked of handsome women, and Sir J. Minnes saying that there was no beauty like that what he sees in the country-markets (and specially at Bury, in which I will agree with him that there is a prettiest women I ever saw), my Lord replied thus: "Sir John, what do you think of your neighbour's wife?" looking upon me. "Do you not think that he hath a great beauty to his wife? Upon my word he hath." Which I was not a little proud of. Thence by barge with my Lord of Blackfriars, where we landed and I thence walked home. My head akeing with the healths I was forced to drink to-day I sent for the barber, and he having done, I up to my wife's closett and there played on my viallin a good while, and without supper anon to bed, sad for want of my wife, whom I love with all my heart, though of late she has given me some troubled thoughts.

Snow White in Prewar Paris

from *Diary of Anaïs Nin*

Here now is a full-blown diary, rich in feeling, reflection, and imagination, studded with profiles and portraits, dialogs and anecdotes. Nin's diary floats a bit in time: the interval between an event and the recording of it is often not indicated, and entry dates are vague. Her order is more of a mental order: events and thoughts get written down according to the writer's inner agenda. Not only was she writing her fiction concurrently with the diaries, which ran for decades, but she was seeing about publication of the diaries as she was writing them. So we have here a diary tending toward literary sketch and essay.

At the time of the following excerpt, Anaïs Nin was living with little money in Paris, which was then the mecca for expatriate artists and writers, the sort of people she surrounded herself with. It is not necessary to know of all the people she mentions, some of whom became famous, like painter Marcel Duchamp and poet Antonin Artaud, some of whom did not. "Henry" is novelist Henry Miller; he and his wife June were close friends of Nin. A former model, Nin had been working in New York with psychoanalyst Otto Rank, gaining a very different experience as a treatment helper.

[August, 1935]

One afternoon in Fraenkel's studio we composed a charade on the theme of Fraenkel's death. He asks us to believe in his death just as people were asked to believe in Christ's death, because he says until we believe in it he cannot be resurrected. I cannot share Fraenkel's madness as I shared and understood Artaud's, I think because in Fraenkel the madness is intellectual, and in Artaud it was rooted in real emotional pain. And besides, Artaud is a great poet.

Writing more and more to the sound of music, writing more and more like music. Sitting in my studio tonight, playing record after record, writing, music a stimulant of the highest order, far more potent than wine. In the interior monologue there is no punctuation. James Joyce was right. It flows like a river.

Henry calls me *"Schneewittchen,"* the German word for Snow White.

I wrote about a hundred pages on my father *(Winter of Artifice).* I copied the diary I wrote in New York and returned the original to the vault in a bank where I keep them. I took a taxi to the Villa Seurat and ran into Fred carrying milk for his breakfast with Fraenkel. Fraenkel invited me in and Henry joined us. Henry was in a very good mood because he received a letter from a new admirer and we all sat down to work on mailing subscription blanks for *Black Spring,* to be brought out as part of the Obelisk series. I wrote a lot of letters to arouse interest in the book. Then Fred and I marketed for lunch, and after lunch we all went back to work. Fraenkel's *femme de ménage* washes the dishes. Richard Thoma arrives. He brings me back the copy of *House of Incest* I loaned him. He has designed a dress for me.

He tells fantastic stories of voodoo curses and black magic, which are prolongations of his romantic writing. He is not a surrealist.

We all went to the Café Select. We talked of how we are all victims of obsessional patterns and themes. Fraenkel always wants the woman he cannot have, who belongs to somebody else. Henry loves the prostitute but let a whorish aspect show in June or any woman he loves, and then he becomes critical.

I cannot rest in Louveciennes. The beauty is not enough. I have to keep racing to avoid my past catching up with me and strangling me. I have to live very fast, place many people and incidents between my past and me, because it is still a burden and a ghost.

Last night a frivolous night with friends from New York. Bright lights, savory dinner at Maxim's, Cabaret aux Fleurs to watch Kiki, but it was not Kiki who seemed attractive to me, Kiki with her bangs and short tight skirt, but her aide-de-camp, a woman so humorous and alive she vivified the entire place. I told her she was wonderful, and she answered me: "Please tell that to the *patronne.*" "Where is the *patronne?*" I said. "She is there, counting the money." So I went up to the *patronne* and told her. From the Cabaret aux Fleurs we went to the Boule

Blanche. Mr. W. was very red after a month of hunting in Scotland. When the Negro hostess bent over Mr. W. to serve his drink, he stared at her so intensely that she simply pulled her breast out of her dress and offered it to him. His face was wonderful to see. If he had been riding one of his thoroughbreds, he would have fallen off.

We are sitting at the Café Select. Dorothy Murphy joins us. She never quite knows where she is. She looks at times like a Pomeranian. She recognizes certain people, certain foods, certain drinks. But the rest of the time her eyes look on the world as from a rolling ship, and without any sense of recognition. She knows where the Coupole is, but only with her nose. But once there, on her chair, she does not know why we are sitting on those chairs, talking an unfamiliar language. Whereas it is our lips which move, it is her nose which moves and twitches. To form words as we do demands a long effort on the part of her tongue and all her phrases end in a question. We should understand the language of her nose. The syllables in the form of a perpetual question are a caricature of our talk, but the twitch of her nose is truly Pomeranian. Each vein on it bears clearly the year of vintage. One can detect the blue of Beaujolais Supérieure, the sun color of Pouilly-Fuissé. Whisky has formed little craters. Rum has designed a fine grain like the seed of figs. The entire nose, though lacking in prow, is not as pointed as a submarine, but widens in imitation of what as a woman she lacks. It is a nose which testifies to drinking valor. Sitting in her café chair with the same bewildered air of a dog in a strange place, she sniffs the smell of rain on raincoats, of rain on rubber boots, of rain on umbrellas, in puddles, the indoor air of Paris, apéritif and charcoal burners, fog and gasoline, tobacco and *café au lait*, and she is silent. Her dress has not dragged in the mud, but looks as if she had slept on the sawdust, as if the starch had been boiled out of it, as if it had been pressed through a clothes wringer. Her hat drooped like cock feathers after a fight, but one feather on it remained pointing and alert. By the time I left my chair she had opened her mouth to say something. But what she says has already been said by the feather. What it says is that if instead of one feather sticking up resolutely she had none at all, her friends would not have all abandoned her. But it was this last feather, this feather posing a question, rebelling against doom, protesting, anguished, anxious, heroic, this heroic feather rising from a cemetery of crestfallen sorrows, which dismayed, haunted and estranged people. The last tower of a castle in ruins, the last cry of a turkey condemned by the cook to die, was like that outrageously arrogant feather, surviving drunkenness, proclaiming a gaudy past, the stubborn gallantry of a flag-bearer in a battle of bottles. It was this which made people turn away.

Brassai is never without his camera. His eyes protrude as if from looking too long through a camera lens. He appears not to be observing, but when his eye has caught a person or an object it is as if he became hypnotized. He continues to talk, without looking at you. (Later, Brassai, who was Hungarian, suffered much during the war. The Germans entered his workshop and went through all his files of negatives. Looking for what? They carried away many of his photos of Paris at night, many mementoes, many prints he had found on the quays, many old and irreplaceable negatives of erotic subjects.)

Marcel Duchamp sat down with us, and talked about Brancusi. He said he was "arrested." He had found his philosophy and would not budge away from it, would not be dislodged.

Marcel Duchamp thought that an artist should never crystallize, that he should remain open to change, renewal, adventure, experiment.

Yet he himself looks like a man who died long ago. He plays chess instead of painting because that is the nearest to complete immobility, the most natural pose for a man who died. His skin seems made of parchment, and his eyes of glass. A different death from Fraenkel's, not obsessional, but noble and classical.

Inside of me I feel a microbe of jazz. It entered my blood. It is neither white nor red, this microbe which causes my agitation. Rhythm. I am aware that the rhythm of New York was external, and here it is analytical and conversational. I have a feverish need of novelty, renewal.

I am now writing on the eclipse of my relationship with my father for *Winter of Artifice*.

The mysterious theme of the flavor of events. Some pale, weak, not lasting. Others so vivid. What causes the choice of memory? What causes certain events to fade, others to gain in luminousness and spice? My posing for artists at sixteen was unreal, shadowy. The writing about it sometimes brings it to life. I taste it then. My period as a debutante in Havana, no flavor. Why does this flavor sometimes appear later, while living another episode, or while telling it to someone? What revives it when it was not lived fully at the time? During my talks with my father the full flavor of my childhood came to me. The taste of everything came back to me as we talked. But not everything came back with the same vividness; many things which I described to my father I told without pleasure, without any taste in my mouth. So it was not brought to life entirely by my desire to make it interesting for him. Some portions of my life were lived as if under ether, and many others under a complete eclipse. Some of them cleared up later, that is, the fog lifted, the events became clear, nearer, more intense, and remained as unearthed for good. Why did some of them come to life, and others not? Why did some remain flavorless, and others recover a new flavor or meaning? Certain periods like the posing, which seemed very intense at the time, violent almost, have never had any taste since. I know I wept, suffered, rebelled, was humiliated, and proud too. Yet the story I presented to my father and to Henry about the posing was not devoid of color and incidents. I myself did not feel it again as I told it. It was as if it had happened to someone else, and the interest I took in its episodes was that of a writer who recognized good material. It was not an unimportant phase of my life, it was my first confrontation with the world. It was the period when I discovered I was not ugly, a very important discovery for a woman. It was a dramatic period, beginning with the show put on for the painters, when I was dressed in a Watteau costume which suited me to perfection, and received applause and immediate engagements, ending with my becoming the star model of the Model's Club, a subject for magazine covers, paintings, miniatures, statues, drawings, water colors. It cannot be said that what is lived in a condition of unreality, in a dream, or fog, disappears altogether from memory, because I remember a ride I took through the Vallée de Chevreuse many years ago, when I was unhappy, ill, indifferent, in a dream. A mood of blind remoteness and sadness and divorce from life. This ride I took with my senses asleep, I repeated almost ten years later with my senses awakened, in good health, with clear eyes, and I was surprised to see that I had not only remembered the road, but every detail of this ride which I thought I had not seen or felt at all. Even to the taste of the huge brioche we were served at a famous inn. It was as if I had been sleepwalking while another part of my body recorded and observed the presence of the sun, the whiteness of the road, the billows of heather fields, in spite of my inability to taste and to feel at the time.

Today I can see every leaf on every tree, every face in the street, and all as clear as leaves after the rain. Everything very near. It is as if before I had a period of myopia, psychological blindness, and I wonder what caused this myopia. Can a sorrow alone, an emotional shock cause emotional blindness, deafness, sleepwalking, unreality?

Everything today absolutely clear, the eyes focusing with ease, focusing on the outline and color of things as luminous and clear as they are in New York, in Switzerland under the snow. Intensity and clearness, besides the full sensual awareness.

Neurosis is like a loss of all the senses, all perception through the senses. It causes deafness, blindness, sleep, or insomnia. It may be that it is this state which causes anxiety, as it resembles death in life, and may seem like the beginning of death itself. But why do certain things come to life, and others not? Analysis, for example, reawakened my old love for my father which I had thought buried. What were the blocks of life which fell completely into oblivion? What was lived intensely sometimes disappeared because the very intensity was unbearable. But why did things which were not important return clear and washed, and suddenly embodied?

Neurosis causes a perpetual double exposure. It can only be erased by daylight, by an isolated confrontation of it, as if it were a ghost which demanded visibility and once having been pulled out into daylight it dies. The surrealists are the only ones who believed we could live by superimpositions, express it, layer upon layer, past and present, dream and actuality, because they believe we are not one dimensional, we do not exist or experience on one level alone, and that the only way to transcend the contradictions of life is to allow them to exist in such a multilateral state.

I come back to Louveciennes to read letters from my ex-patients, all swimming in life, grateful and happy.

To escape depression sometimes, I walk all through the city, I walk until I am exhausted. I call it *"La fête des yeux."* Antiques on Rue des Saints-Pères, art galleries, fashions on the Rue Saint-Honoré. Or I buy *Vogue* and live the life of *Vogue*, all luxury and aesthetics which I gave up. I could have attended the ball at which everyone went dressed as the portraits of Velásquez. I sit at the Lido, watching the rich old ladies pick up the young Argentine dancers. I go skiing or yachting as in *Vogue* pictures. I buy a transparent cigarette case and a *chapeau auréole*. I really attend the dress show of Schiaparelli which is a magnificent work of art. I can well believe she was a painter and a sculptress before she designed dresses. But I could wear none of her things at Villa Seurat, or at Louveciennes.

I never buy for duration, only for effect, as if I recognized the ephemeralness of my settings. I know they are soon to be changed to match the inner changes. Life should be fluid.

My father, on the contrary, builds for eternity. He has such a fear of life that he struggles for permanency, to defeat change. He wants the strongest, most lasting woods, closets full of medicines for possible future needs. He is pained when I send him a letter without waiting for the chronological order. The creator's love of change and mobility does not inspire human confidence. I think in all this I am motivated by such a passion for life that the idea of not moving is for me a death concept. I shiver when people boast of having been born in the same bed in which they hope they will die. The quest for fixed values seems to me a quest for immobility and stagnation. I think of museum pieces, embalmed mummies. Whatever is not alive I want to cast away, even if it is an old chair. Whatever is not playing a role in the present drama is good for the attic. The Spaniards have a ritual: once a year they burn the old objects, in the street, in a big bonfire.

I believe in avoiding constructions which are too solid and enclose you. The same with the novel, if you catalogue too completely, the freshness and the life withers.

Colette Roberts comments on *Winter of Artifice*: "Your novel touches me. It is human and real. But because it happens more deeply than the level on which people usually experience life, there seems to be glass around it, like the glass over the paintings at the Louvre. One sees the real painting, all right, one almost feels it, but there is glass."

When I was analyzing I observed clearly that the fear of death was in proportion to not-living. The less a person was in life, the greater the fear. By being alive I mean living out of all the cells, all the parts of one's self. The cells which are denied become atrophied, like a dead arm, and infect the rest of the body. People living deeply have no fear of death.

Journal

Tierra del Fuego
Charles Darwin
from *Voyage of the "Beagle"*

Though focused specifically on observations of little-known lands and peoples, plants and animals, made during a voyage undertaken for the sake of these observations, Voyage of the "Beagle" *is curiously akin to Nin's diaries in that it too was not only published itself but served as notations for other publications. As Nin's diaries supported her novels in both a practical and psychological way, the journal Darwin kept as a young man both showed him what to do for the rest of his life—develop a theory to explain how species originate and diverge—and furnished him with much of the data to do that with.*

Darwin kept the focus on his public subject, not on himself, and whether originally or in revision, explained references for a public readership. Inasmuch as he prepared his diary for publication—that is, touched it up from a later perspective—what we have here is a diary on its way to being a memoir.

To offset the problem of excerpting, however, some information is needed. Fitz Roy was captain of the Beagle *and Darwin's roommate aboard ship. On a previous voyage Fitz Roy had picked up three aborigines of Tierra del Fuego—Jemmy Button, York Minster, and Fuegia—and taken them back to England to civilize them. He is now returning them to their country to help a Mr. Matthews establish a Christian mission. Mr. Bynoe and Mr. Low are ship's officers.*

January 15th, 1833.—The *Beagle* anchored in Goeree Roads. Captain Fitz Roy having resolved to settle the Fuegians, according to their wishes, in Ponsonby Sound, four boats were equipped to carry them there through the Beagle Channel. This channel, which was discovered by Captain Fitz Roy during the last voyage, is a most remarkable feature in the geography of this, or indeed of any other country: it may be compared to the valley of Lochness in Scotland, with its chain of lakes and firths. It is about one hundred and twenty miles long, with an average breadth, not subject to any very great variation, of about two miles; and is throughout the greater part so perfectly straight, that the view, bounded on each side by a line of mountains, gradually becomes indistinct in the long distance. It crosses the southern part of Tierra del Fuego in an east and west line, and in the middle is joined at right angles on the south side by an irregular channel, which has been called Ponsonby Sound. This is the residence of Jemmy Button's tribe and family.

19th.—Three whale-boats and the yawl, with a party of twenty-eight, started under the command of Captain Fitz Roy. In the afternoon we entered the eastern mouth of the channel, and shortly afterwards found a snug little cove concealed by some surrounding islets. Here we pitched our tents and lighted our fires. Nothing could look more comfortable than this scene. The glassy water of the little harbour, with the branches of the trees hanging over the rocky beach, the boats at anchor, the tents supported by the crossed oars, and the smoke curling up the wooded valley, formed a picture of quiet retirement. The next day (20th) we smoothly glided onwards in our little fleet, and came to a more inhabited district. Few if any of these natives could ever have seen a white man; certainly nothing could exceed their astonishment at the apparition of the four boats. Fires were lighted on every point (hence the name of Tierra del Fuego, or the land of fire), both to attract our attention and to spread far and wide the news. Some of the men ran for miles along the shore. I shall never forget how wild and savage one group appeared: suddenly four or five men came to the edge of an overhanging cliff; they were absolutely naked, and their long hair streamed about their faces; they held rugged staffs in their hands, and, springing from the ground, they waved their arms round their heads, and sent forth the most hideous yells.

At dinner-time we landed among a party of Fuegians. At first they were not inclined to be friendly; for until the Captain pulled in ahead of the other boats, they kept their slings in their hands. We soon, however, delighted them by trifling presents, such as tying red tape round their heads. They liked our biscuit: but one of the savages touched with his finger some of the meat preserved in tin cases which I was eating, and feeling it soft and cold, showed us much disgust at it, as I should have done at putrid blubber. Jemmy was thoroughly ashamed of his countrymen, and declared his own tribe were quite different, in which he was wofully mistaken. It was as easy to please as it was difficult to satisfy these savages. Young and old, men and children, never ceased repeating the word "yammerschooner," which means "give me." After pointing to almost every object, one after the other, even to the buttons on our coats, and saying their favourite word in as many intonations as possible, they would then use it in a neuter sense, and vacantly repeat "yammerschooner." After yammerschoonering for any article very eagerly, they would by a simple artifice point to their young women or little children, as much as to say, "If you will not give it me, surely you will to such as these."

At night we endeavoured in vain to find an uninhabited cove; and at last were obliged to bivouac not far from a party of natives. They were very inoffensive as long as they were few in numbers, but in the morning (21st) being joined by others they showed symptoms of hostility, and we thought that we should have come to a skirmish. An European labours under great disadvantages when treating with savages like these, who have not the least idea of the power of fire-arms. In the very act of levelling his musket he appears to the savage far inferior to a man armed with a bow and arrow, a spear, or even a sling. Nor is it easy to teach them our superiority except by striking a fatal blow. Like wild beasts, they do not appear to compare numbers; for each individual, if attacked, instead of retiring, will endeavour to dash your brains out with a stone, as certainly as a tiger under similar circumstances would tear you. Captain Fitz Roy on one occasion being very anxious, from good reasons, to frighten away a small party, first flourished a cutlass near them, at which they only laughed; he then twice fired his pistol close to a native. The man both times looked astounded, and carefully but quickly rubbed his head; he then stared awhile, and gabbled to his companions, but he never seemed to think of running away. We can hardly put ourselves in the position of these savages, and understand their actions. In the case of this Fuegian, the possibility of such a sound as the report of a gun close to his ear could never have entered his mind. He perhaps literally did not for a second know whether it was a sound or a blow, and therefore very naturally rubbed his head. In a similar manner, when a savage sees a mark struck by a bullet, it may be some time before he is able at all to understand how it is effected; for the fact of a body being invisible from its velocity would perhaps be to him an idea totally inconceivable. Moreover, the extreme force of a bullet, that penetrates a hard substance without tearing it, may convince the savage that it has no force at all. Certainly I believe that many savages of the lowest grade, such as these of Tierra del Fuego, have seen objects struck, and even small animals killed by the musket, without being in the least aware how deadly an instrument it is.

22nd.—After having passed an unmolested night, in what would appear to be neutral territory between Jemmy's tribe and the people whom we saw yesterday, we sailed pleasantly along. I do not know anything which shows more clearly the hostile state of the different tribes, than these wide border or neutral tracts. Although Jemmy Button well knew the force of our party, he was, at first, unwilling to land amidst the hostile tribe nearest to his own. He often told us how the savage Oens men "when the leaf red," crossed the mountains from the eastern coast of Tierra del Fuego, and made inroads on the natives of this part of the country. It was most curious to watch him when thus talking, and see his eyes gleaming and his whole face assume a new and wild expression. As we proceeded along the Beagle Channel, the scenery assumed a peculiar and very magnificent character; but the effect was much lessened from the lowness of the point of view in a boat, and from looking along the valley, and thus losing all the beauty of a succession of ridges. The mountains were here about three thousand feet high, and terminated in sharp and jagged points. They rose in one unbroken sweep from the water's edge, and were covered to the height of fourteen or fifteen hundred feet by the dusky-coloured forest. It was most curious to observe, as far as the eye could range, how level and truly horizontal the line on the mountain side was, at which trees ceased to grow: it precisely resembled the high-water mark of drift-weed on a sea-beach.

At night we slept close to the junction of Ponsonby Sound with the Beagle Channel. A small family of Fuegians, who were living in the cove, were quiet and inoffensive, and soon joined our party round a blazing fire. We were well clothed, and though sitting close to the fire were far from too warm; yet these naked savages, though further off, were observed, to our great surprise, to be streaming with perspiration at undergoing such a roasting.

They seemed, however, very well pleased, and all joined in the chorus of the seamen's songs: but the manner in which they were invariably a little behindhand was quite ludicrous.

During the night the news had spread, and early in the morning (23rd) a fresh party arrived, belonging to the Tekenika, or Jemmy's tribe. Several of them had run so fast that their noses were bleeding, and their mouths frothed from the rapidity with which they talked; and with their naked bodies all bedaubed with black, white,[1] and red, they looked like so many demoniacs who had been fighting. We then proceeded (accompanied by twelve canoes, each holding four or five people) down Ponsonby Sound to the spot where poor Jemmy expected to find his mother and relatives. He had already heard that his father was dead; but as he had had a "dream in his head" to that effect, he did not seem to care much about it, and repeatedly comforted himself with the very natural reflection—"Me no help it." He was not able to learn any particulars regarding his father's death, as his relations would not speak about it.

Jemmy was now in a district well known to him, and guided the boats to a quiet pretty cove named Woollya, surrounded by islets, every one of which and every point had its proper native name. We found here a family of Jemmy's tribe, but not his relations: we made friends with them; and in the evening they sent a canoe to inform Jemmy's mother and brothers. The cove was bordered by some acres of good sloping land, not covered (as elsewhere) either by peat or by forest-trees. Captain Fitz Roy originally intended, as before stated, to have taken York Minster and Fuegia to their own tribe on the west coast; but as they expressed a wish to remain here, and as the spot was singularly favourable, Captain Fitz Roy determined to settle here the whole party, including Matthews, the missionary. Five days were spent in building for them three large wigwams, in landing their goods, in digging two gardens, and sowing seeds.

The next morning after our arrival (the 24th) the Fuegians

---

1. This substance, when dry, is tolerably compact, and of little specific gravity: Professor Ehrenberg has examined it: he states that it is composed of infusoria, including fourteen polygastrica, and four phytolitharia. He says that they are all inhabitants of fresh-water; this is a beautiful example of the results obtainable through Professor Ehrenberg's microscopic researches; for Jemmy Button told me that it is always collected at the bottoms of mountain-brooks. It is, moreover, a striking fact in the geographical distribution of the infusoria, which are well known to have very wide ranges, that all the species in this substance, although brought from the extreme southern point of Tierra del Fuego, are old, known forms.

began to pour in, and Jemmy's mother and brothers arrived. Jemmy recognized the stentorian voice of one of his brothers at a prodigious distance. The meeting was less interesting than that between a horse, turned out into a field, when he joins an old companion. There was no demonstration of affection; they simply stared for a short time at each other; and the mother immediately went to look after her canoe. We heard, however, through York, that the mother had been inconsolable for the loss of Jemmy, and had searched everywhere for him, thinking that he might have been left after having been taken in the boat. The women took much notice of and were very kind to Fuegia. We had already perceived that Jemmy had almost forgotten his own language. I should think there was scarcely another human being with so small a stock of language, for his English was very imperfect. It was laughable, but almost pitiable, to hear him speak to his wild brother in English, and then ask him in Spanish ("no sabe?") whether he did not understand him.

Everything went peaceably during the three next days, whilst the gardens were digging and wigwams building. We estimated the number of natives at about one hundred and twenty. The women worked hard, whilst the men lounged about all day long, watching us. They asked for everything they saw, and stole what they could. They were delighted at our dancing and singing, and were particularly interested at seeing us wash in a neighbouring brook; they did not pay much attention to anything else, not even to our boats. Of all the things which York saw, during his absence from his country, nothing seems more to have astonished him than an ostrich, near Maldonado: breathless with astonishment he came running to Mr. Bynoe, with whom he was out walking—"Oh, Mr. Bynoe, oh, bird all same horse!" Much as our white skins surprised the natives, by Mr. Low's account a negro-cook to a sealing vessel, did so more effectually; and the poor fellow was so mobbed and shouted at that he would never go on shore again. Everything went on so quietly, that some of the officers and myself took long walks in the surrounding hills and woods. Suddenly, however, on the 27th, every woman and child disappeared. We were all uneasy at this, as neither York nor Jemmy could make out the cause. It was thought by some that they had been frightened by our cleaning and firing off our muskets on the previous evening: by others, that it was owing to offence taken by an old savage, who, when told to keep further off, had coolly spit in the sentry's face, and had then, by gestures acted over a sleeping Fuegian, plainly showed, as it was said, that he should like to cut up and eat our man. Captain Fitz

Roy, to avoid the chance of an encounter, which would have been fatal to so many of the Fuegians, thought it advisable for us to sleep at a cove a few miles distant. Matthews, with his usual quiet fortitude (remarkable in a man apparently possessing little energy of character), determined to stay with the Fuegians, who evinced no alarm for themselves; and so we left them to pass their first awful night.

On our return in the morning (28th) we were delighted to find all quiet, and the men employed in their canoes spearing fish. Captain Fitz Roy determined to send the yawl and one whale-boat back to the ship; and to proceed with the two other boats, one under his own command (in which he most kindly allowed me to accompany him), and one under Mr. Hammond, to survey the western parts of the Beagle Channel, and afterwards to return and visit the settlement. The day to our astonishment was over-poweringly hot, so that our skins were scorched: with this beautiful weather, the view in the middle of the Beagle Channel was very remarkable. Looking towards either hand, no object intercepted the vanishing points of this long canal between the mountains. The circumstances of its being an arm of the sea was rendered very evident by several huge whales[2] spouting in different directions. On one occasion I saw two of these monsters, probably male and female, slowly swimming one after the other, within less than a stone's throw of the shore, over which the beech-tree extended its branches.

We sailed on till it was dark, and then pitched our tents in a quiet creek. The greatest luxury was to find for our beds a beach of pebbles, for they were dry and yielded to the body. Peaty soil is damp; rock is uneven and hard; sand gets into one's meat, when cooked and eaten boat-fashion; but when lying in our blanket-bags, on a good bed of smooth pebbles, we passed most comfortable nights.

It was my watch till one o'clock. There is something very solemn in these scenes. At no time does the consciousness in what a remote corner of the world you are then standing, come so strongly before the mind. Everything tends to this effect; the stillness of the night is interrupted only by the heavy breathing of the seamen beneath the tents, and sometimes by the cry of a

2. One day, off the East coast of Tierra del Fuego, we saw a grand sight in several spermaceti whales jumping upright quite out of the water, with the exception of their tail-fins. As they fell down sideways, they splashed the water high up, and the sound reverberated like a distant broadside.

night-bird. The occasional barking of a dog, heard in the distance, reminds one that it is the land of the savage.

January 29th.—Early in the morning we arrived at the point where the Beagle Channel divides into two arms; and we entered the northern one. The scenery here becomes even grander than before. The lofty mountains on the north side compose the granitic axis, or backbone of the country, and boldly rise to a height of between three and four thousand feet, with one peak above six thousand feet. They are covered by a wide mantle of perpetual snow, and numerous cascades pour their waters, through the woods, into the narrow channel below. In many parts, magnificent glaciers extend from the mountain side to the water's edge. It is scarcely possible to imagine any thing more beautiful than the beryl-like blue of these glaciers, and especially as contrasted with the dead white of the upper expanse of snow. The fragments which had fallen from the glacier into the water, were floating away, and the channel with its icebergs presented, for the space of a mile, a miniature likeness of the Polar Sea. The boats being hauled on shore at our dinner-hour, we were admiring from the distance of half a mile a perpendicular cliff of ice, and were wishing that some more fragments would fall. At last, down came a mass with a roaring noise, and immediately we saw the smooth outline of a wave travelling towards us. The men ran down as quickly as they could to the boats; for the chance of their being dashed to pieces was evident. One of the seamen just caught hold of the bows, as the curling breaker reached it: he was knocked over and over, but not hurt; and the boats, though thrice lifted on high and let fall again, received no damage. This was most fortunate for us, for we were a hundred miles distant from the ship, and we should have been left without provisions or fire-arms. I had previously observed that some large fragments of rock on the beach had been lately displaced; but until seeing this wave, I did not understand the cause. One side of the creek was formed by a spur of mica-slate; the head of a cliff of ice about forty feet high, and the other side by a promontory fifty feet high, built up of huge rounded fragments of granite and mica-slate, out of which old trees were growing. This promontory was evidently a moraine, heaped up at a period when the glacier had greater dimensions.

When we reached the western mouth of this northern branch of the Beagle Channel we sailed amongst many unknown desolate islands, and the weather was wretchedly bad. We met with no natives. The coast was almost everywhere so steep, that we had several times to pull many miles before we could find space enough to pitch our two tents: one night we slept on large round boulders, with putrefying sea-weed between them; and when the tide rose, we had to get up and move our blanket-bags. The farthest point westward which we reached was Stewart Island, a distance of about one hundred and fifty miles from our ship. We returned into the Beagle Channel by the southern arm, and thence proceeded, with no adventure, back to Ponsonby Sound.

February 6th.—We arrived at Woollya. Matthews gave so bad an account of the conduct of the Fuegians, that Captain Fitz Roy determined to take him back to the *Beagle;* and ultimately he was left at New Zealand, where his brother was a missionary. From the time of our leaving, a regular system of plunder commenced; fresh parties of the natives kept arriving: York and Jemmy lost many things, and Matthews almost every thing which had not been concealed underground. Every article seemed to have been torn up and divided by the natives. Matthews described the watch he was obliged always to keep as most harassing; night and day he was surrounded by the natives, who tried to tire him out by making an incessant noise close to his head. One day an old man, whom Matthews asked to leave his wigwam, immediately returned with a large stone in his hand: another day a whole party came armed with stones and stakes, and some of the younger men and Jemmy's brother were crying: Matthews met them with presents. Another party showed by signs that they wished to strip him naked and pluck all the hairs out of his face and body. I think we arrived just in time to save his life. Jemmy's relatives had been so vain and foolish, that they had showed to strangers their plunder, and their manner of obtaining it. It was quite melancholy leaving the three Fuegians with their savage countrymen; but it was a great comfort that they had no personal fears. York, being a powerful resolute man, was pretty sure to get on well, together with his wife Fuegia. Poor Jemmy looked rather disconsolate, and would then I have little doubt, have been glad to have returned with us. His own brother had stolen many things from him; and as he remarked, "what fashion call that": he abused his countrymen, "all bad men, no sabe (know) nothing," and, though I never heard him swear before, "damned fools." Our three Fuegians, though they had been only three years with civilized men, would, I am sure, have been glad to have retained their new habits; but this was obviously impossible. I fear it is more than doubtful, whether their visit will have been of any use to them.

In the evening, with Matthews on board, we made sail back to the ship, not by the Beagle Channel, but by the southern coast.

The boats were heavily laden and the sea rough, and we had a dangerous passage. By the evening of the 7th we were on board the *Beagle* after an absence of twenty days, during which time we had gone three hundred miles in the open boats. On the 11th, Captain Fitz Roy paid a visit by himself to the Fuegians and found them going on well; and that they had lost very few more things.

On the last day of February in the succeeding year (1834), the *Beagle* anchored in a beautiful little cove at the eastern entrance of the Beagle Channel. Captain Fitz Roy determined on the bold, and as it proved successful, attempt to beat against the westerly winds by the same route, which we had followed in the boats to the settlement at Woollya. We did not see many natives until we were near Ponsonby Sound, where we were followed by ten or twelve canoes. The natives did not at all understand the reason of our tacking, and, instead of meeting us at each tack, vainly strove to follow us in our zig-zag course. I was amused at finding what a difference the circumstance of being quite superior in force made, in the interest of beholding these savages. While in the boats I got to hate the very sound of their voices, so much trouble did they give us. The first and last word was "yammerschooner." When, entering some quiet little cove, we have looked round and thought to pass a quiet night, the odious word "yammerschooner" has shrilly sounded from some gloomy nook, and then the little signal-smoke has curled up to spread the news far and wide. On leaving some place we have said to each other, "Thank Heaven, we have at last fairly left these wretches!" when one more faint halloo from an all-powerful voice, heard at a prodigious distance, would reach our ears, and clearly could we distinguish—"yammerschooner." But now, the more Fuegians the merrier; and very merry work it was. Both parties laughing, wondering, gaping at each other; we pitying them, for giving us good fish and crabs for rags, &c.; they grasping at the chance of finding people so foolish as to exchange such splendid ornaments for a good supper. It was most amusing to see the undisguised smile of satisfaction with which one young woman with her face painted black, tied several bits of scarlet cloth round her head with rushes. Her husband, who enjoyed the very universal privilege in this country of possessing two wives, evidently became jealous of all the attention paid to his young wife; and, after a consultation with his naked beauties, was paddled away by them.

Some of the Fuegians plainly showed that they had a fair notion of barter. I gave one man a large nail (a most valuable present) without making any signs for a return; but he immediately picked out two fish, and handed them up on the point of his spear. If any present was designed for one canoe, and it fell near another, it was invariably given to the right owner. The Fuegian boy, whom Mr. Low had on board, showed, by going into the most violent passion, that he quite understood the reproach of being called a liar, which in truth he was. We were this time, as on all former occasions, much surprised at the little notice, or rather none whatever, which was taken of many things, the use of which must have been evident to the natives. Simple circumstances—such as the beauty of scarlet cloth or blue beads, the absence of women, our care in washing ourselves,—excited their admiration far more than any grand or complicated object, such as our ship. Bougainville has well remarked concerning these people, that they treat the "chef-d'œuvres de l'industrie humaine, comme ils traitent les loix de la nature et ses phénomènes."

On the 5th of March, we anchored in the cove at Woollya, but we saw not a soul there. We were alarmed at this, for the natives in Ponsonby Sound showed by gestures, that there had been fighting; and we afterwards heard that the dreaded Oens men had made a descent. Soon a canoe, with a little flag flying, was seen approaching, with one of the men in it washing the paint off his face. This man was poor Jemmy,—now a thin haggard savage, with long disordered hair, and naked, except a bit of a blanket round his waist. We did not recognize him till he was close to us; for he was ashamed of himself, and turned his back to the ship. We had left him plump, fat, clean, and well dressed;—I never saw so complete and grievous a change. As soon however as he was clothed, and the first flurry was over, things wore a good appearance. He dined with Captain Fitz Roy, and ate his dinner as tidily as formerly. He told us he had "too much" (meaning enough) to eat, that he was not cold, that his relations were very good people, and that he did not wish to go back to England: in the evening we found out the cause of this great change in Jemmy's feelings, in the arrival of his young and nice-looking wife. With his usual good feeling, he brought two beautiful otter-skins for two of his best friends, and some spear-heads and arrows made with his own hands for the Captain. He said he had built a canoe for himself, and he boasted that he could talk a little of his own language! But it is a most singular fact, that he appears to have taught all his tribe some English: an old man spontaneously announced "Jemmy Button's wife." Jemmy had lost all his property. He told us that York Minster had built a large canoe, and with his wife Fuegia,[3] had several months since gone to his own country, and had taken farewell by an act of consummate villainy; he persuaded Jemmy and his mother to come with him, and then on the way deserted them by night, stealing every article of their property.

Jemmy went to sleep on shore, and in the morning returned, and remained on board till the ship got under weigh, which frightened his wife, who continued crying violently till he got into his canoe. He returned loaded with valuable property. Every soul on board was heartily sorry to shake hands with him for the last time. I do not now doubt that he will be as happy as, perhaps happier than, if he had never left his own country. Every one must sincerely hope that Captain Fitz Roy's noble hope may be fulfilled, of being rewarded for the many generous sacrifices which he made for these Fuegians, by some shipwrecked sailor being protected by the descendants of Jemmy Button and his tribe! When Jemmy reached the shore, he lighted a signal fire, and the smoke curled up, bidding us a last and long farewell, as the ship stood on her course into the open sea.

The perfect equality among the individuals composing the Fuegian tribes, must for a long time retard their civilization. As we see those animals, whose instinct compels them to live in society and obey a chief, are most capable of improvement, so is it with the races of mankind. Whether we look at it as a cause or a consequence, the more civilized always have the most artificial governments. For instance, the inhabitants of Otaheite, who when first discovered, were governed by hereditary kings, had arrived at a far higher grade than another branch of the same people, the New Zealanders,—who, although benefited by being compelled to turn their attention to agriculture, were republicans in the most absolute sense. In Tierra del Fuego, until some chief shall arise with power sufficient to secure any acquired advantage such as the domesticated animals, it seems scarcely possible that the political state of the country can be improved. At present even a piece of cloth given to one is torn into shreds and distributed; and no one individual becomes richer than another

3. Captain Sulivan, who, since his voyage in the *Beagle*, has been employed on the survey of the Falkland Islands, heard from a sealer in 1842 (?), that when in the western part of the Strait of Magellan, he was astonished by a native woman coming on board, who could talk some English. Without doubt this was Fuegia Basket. She lived (I fear the term probably bears a double interpretation) some days on board.

On the other hand, it is difficult to understand how a chief can arise till there is property of some sort by which he might manifest his superiority and increase his power.

I believe, in this extreme part of South America, man exists in a lower state of improvement than in any other part of the world. The South Sea Islanders of the two races inhabiting the Pacific, are comparatively civilized. The Esquimaux, in his subterranean hut, enjoys some of the comforts of life, and in his canoe, when fully equipped, manifests much skill. Some of the tribes of Southern Africa, prowling about in search of roots, and living concealed on the wild and arid plains, are sufficiently wretched. The Australian, in the simplicity of the arts of life, comes nearest the Fuegian: he can, however, boast of his boomerang, his spear and throwing-stick, his method of climbing trees, of tracking animals, and of hunting. Although the Australian may be superior in acquirements, it by no means follows that he is likewise superior in mental capacity: indeed, from what I saw of the Fuegians when on board, and from what I have read of the Australians, I should think the case was exactly the reverse.

Writer's Notebook
from Henry David Thoreau's *Journals*

Darwin's journal featured narrative and facts, but he did make many observations, in the sense both of saying what he saw and saying what he made of what he saw. Although many of Thoreau's journals are of that sort also, the sample offered here exemplifies the journal form at its most abstract, when it is registering mostly thoughts, inner events rather than outer. At first it may seem as if we're reversing our progression of Notation by going back toward personal diary. But the thoughts are generalizations, statements to apply at large, and they are expressed in a language so public as to become aphoristic. In other words, Thoreau here is recording his distillations of experience as they occur to him, rather than some succession of events that might have become fodder for distilling later. This makes a story of the mind.

Whereas Nin's diaries ramify in different directions—into

memoir, profile, and personal essay—and Darwin's journal lays out the material for later generalization, in the sample here Thoreau is already writing fragments of generalization essay. The difference between these entries and true essays is that the thoughts remain in the time order of their occurrence rather than being re-ordered retrospectively into a logical organization. The day-to-day point of view still predominates—time order—rather than a continuity inherent in the ideas themselves, though some of the entries might stand alone as pensées or epigrams.

Friday April 9th 1841.

It would not be hard for some quiet brave man to leap into the saddle to-day—and eclipse Napoleon's career by a grander.— Show men at length the meaning of war. One reproaches himself with supineness, that he too has sat quiet in his chamber, and not treated the world to the sound of the trumpet, that the indignation which has so long rankled in his breast, does not take to horse, and to the field. The bravest warrior will have to fight his battles in his dreams—and no earthly war note can arouse him. There are those who would not run with Leonidas—only the third rate Napoleons and Alexanders does history tell of. The brave man does not mind the call of the trumpet—nor hear the idle clashing of swords—without, for the infinite din within War is but a training compared with the active service of his peace—

Is he not at war? Does he not resist the ocean swell within him—and walk as gently as the summer's sea? Would you have him parade in uniform, and maneuver men, whose equanimity is his uniform—and who is himself maneuvered?

The times have no heart. The true reform can be undertaken any morning before unbarring our doors. It calls no convention. I can do two thirds the reform of the world myself.—

When two neighbors begin to eat corn bread, who before ate wheat—then the gods smile from ear to ear, it is very pleasant. When an individual takes a sincere step, then all the gods attend, and his single deed is sweet.

Saturday April 10th 1841.

I dont know but we should make life all too tame if we had our own way, and should miss these impulses in a happier time.

How much virtue there is in simply seeing— The hero has striven in vain for any preeminency when the student over sees him. The woman who sits in the house and *sees* is a match for a stirring captain. Those still piercing eyes as faithfully exercised on their talent will keep her even with Alexander or Shakespeare. They may go to Asia with parade—or to fairy land, but not beyond her ray. We are as much as we see— Faith is sight and knowledge. The hands only serve the eyes. The farthest blue streak in the horizon I can see, I may reach before many sunsets. What I saw alters not—in my night when I wander it is still steadfast as the star which the sailor steers by. Whoever has had one thought quite lonely—and could consciously digest that in solitude, knowing that none might accept it, may rise to the height of humanity— and overlook all living men as from a pinnacle.

   Speech never made man master of men, but the eloquently refraining from it.

Sunday April 11th 1841.

A greater baldness my life seeks, as the crest of some bare hill, which towns and cities do not afford— I want a directer relation with the sun.

.   .   .

> Death cannot come too soon
> Where it can come at all,
> But always is too late
> Unless the fates it call.

Thursday April 15th 1841.

The Gods are of no sect—they side with no man. When I imagined that nature inclined rather to some few earnest and faithful souls, and specially existed for them—I go to see an obscure individual who lives under the hill letting both gods and men alone and find that strawberries and tomatos grow for him too in his garden there, and the sun lodges kindly under his hill side—and am compelled to allow the grand catholicism of nature, and the unbribable charity of the gods.

Any simple unquestioned mode of living is alluring to men. The man who picks peas steadily for a living is more than respectable.

April 16th 1841.

I have been inspecting my neighbors' farms to-day—and chaffering with the land holders—and I must confess I am startled to find everywhere the old system of things so grim and assured. Wherever I go the farms are run out, and there they lie, and the youth must buy old land and bring it to— Every where the relentless opponents of reform are a few old maids and batchelors, who sit round the kitchen fire, listening to the singing of the tea kettle, and munching cheese rinds.

Sunday April 18th 1841.

We need pine for no office for the sake of a certain culture, for all valuable experience lies in the way of a man's duty.— My necessities of late have compelled me to study nature as she is related to the farmer—as she simply satisfies a want of the body.— Some interests have got a footing on the earth which I have not made sufficient allowance for— That which built these barns—and cleared the land thus had some valor.

We take little steps, and venture small stakes, as if our actions were very fatal and irretrievable. There is no swing to our deeds. But our life is only a retired valley where we rest on our packs awhile. Between us and our end there is room for any delay. It is not a short and easy southern way—but we must go over snow-capped mountains to reach the sun.

April 20th 1841.

You can beat down your virtue—so much goodness it must have.

When a room is furnished—comfort is not furnished.

Great thoughts hallow any labor— To day I earned seventy five cents heaving manure out of a pen, and made a good bargain of it. If the ditcher muses the while how he may live uprightly, the ditching spade and turf knife, may be engraved on the coat of arms of his posterity.

There are certain current expressions—and blasphemous moods of viewing things—as when we say "he is doing a good business" —which is more prophane than cursing and swearing— There is death and sin in such words—let not the children hear them.

Thursday April 22d 1841.

There are two classes of authors— The one write the history of their times— The other their biography.

Friday April 23d 1841.

Any greatness is not to be mistaken— Who shall cavil at it? It stands once for all on a level with the heroes of history. It is not to be patronised. It goes alone.

When I hear music, I flutter, & am the scene of life, as a fleet of merchantmen when the wind rises.

April 24th 1841.

Music is the sound of the circulation in nature's veins.— It is the flux which melts nature—men dance to it—glasses ring and vibrate—and the fields seem to undulate.— The healthy ear always hears it—nearer or more remote.

It has been a cloudy drizzling day with occasional brightenings in the mist, when the trill of the tree-sparrow seemed to be ushering in sunny hours.

April 25th 1841.

A momentous silence reigns always in the woods—and their meaning seems just ripening into expression. But alas! they make no haste— The rush sparrow—nature's minstrel of serene hours—sings of an immense leisure and duration.

When I hear a robin sing at sunset—I cannot help contrasting the equanimity of nature with the bustle and impatience of man. We return from the lyceum and caucus with such stir and excitement—as if a crisis were at hand but no natural scene or sound sympathizes with us, for nature is always silent and unpretending as at the break of day. She but rubs her eye lids.

I am struck with the pleasing friendships and unanimities of nature in the woods—as when the moss on the trees takes the form of their leaves.

There is all of civilized life in the woods—their wildest scenes have an air of domesticity and homeliness, and when the flicker's cackle is heard in the clearings, the musing hunter is reminded that civilization has imported nothing into them.

The ball room is represented by the catkins of the alder at this season—which hang gracefully like a ladies ear drops.

All the discoveries of science are equally true in their deepest recesses—nature there too obeys the same laws. Fair weather and foul concern the little red bug upon a pine stump—for him the wind goes round the right way and the sun breaks through the clouds.

Monday April 26th 1841.

At R.W.E's. [Ralph Waldo Emerson's].

The charm of the Indian to me is that he stands free and unconstrained in nature—is her inhabitant—and not her guest—and wears her easily and gracefully. But the civilized man has the habits of the house. His house is a prison in which he finds himself oppressed and confined, not sheltered and protected. He walks as if he sustained the roof—he carries his arms as if the walls would fall in and crush him—and his feet remember the cellar beneath. His muscles are never relaxed— It is rare that he overcomes the house, and learns to sit at home in it—and roof and floor—and walls support themselves—as the sky—and trees—and earth.

It is a great art to saunter.

April 27th 1841.

It is only by a sort of voluntary blindness, and omitting to see that we know our selves—as when we see stars with the side of the eye. The nearest approach to discovering what we are is in dreams. It is as hard to see oneself as to look backwards without turning round. And foolish are they that look in glasses with that intent.

The porters have a hard time, but not so hard as he that carries his own shoulders— That beats the Smyrna Turks. Some men's broad shoulders are load enough. Even a light frame can stand under a great burden, if it does not have to support itself— Virtue is boyant and elastic—it stands without effort and does not feel gravity—but sin plods and shuffles— Newton needed not to wait for an apple to fall to discover the attraction of gravitation—it was implied in the fall of man.

Wednesday April 28th 1841.

We falsely attribute to men a determined character—putting together all their yesterdays—and averaging them—we presume we know them— Pity the man who has a character to support—it is worse than a large family—he is silent poor indeed.— But in fact character is never explored, nor does it get developed in time—but eternity is its development—time its envelope. In view of this distinction, a sort of divine politeness and heavenly good breeding suggests itself—to address always the enveloped character of a man. A large soul will meet you as not having known you—taking you for what you are to be, a narrow one for what you have been—for a broad and roaming soul is as uncertain—what it may say or be—as a scraggy hill side or pasture. I may hear a fox bark—or a partridge drum—or some bird new to these localities may fly up. It lies out there as old, and yet as new. The aspect of the woods varys every day—what with their growth—and the changes of the seasons—and the influence of the elements—so that the eye of the forester never twice rests upon the same prospect— Much more does a character show newly and variedly, if directly seen. It is the highest compliment to suppose that in the intervals of conversation your companion has expanded and grown— It may be a deference which he will not understand, but the nature which underlies him will understand it—and your influence will be shed as finely on him as the dust in the sun settles on our clothes. By such politeness we may educate one another to some purpose. So have I felt myself educated sometimes— I am expanded and enlarged.

April 29th 1841.

Birds and quadrupeds pass freely through nature—without prop or stilt. But man very naturally carries a stick in his hand—seeking to ally himself by many points of nature.— as a warrior stands by his horse's side with his hand on his mane. We walk the gracefuller for a cane—as the juggler uses a leaded pole to balance him when he dances on a slack wire.

Better a monosyllabic life—than a ragged and muttered one—let its report be short and round, so that it may hear its own echo in the surrounding silence.

April 30th 1841.

Where shall we look for standard English but to the words of any man who has a depth of feeling in him?—not in any smooth and leisurely essay. From the gentlemanly windows of the country seat no sincere eyes are directed upon nature—but from the peasants horn windows a true glance and greeting occasionally.——— "For summer being ended, all things," said the pilgrim, "stand in appearance with a weather-beaten face, and the whole country full of woods and thickets represented a wild and savage hue."
Compare this with the agricultural report.

Sat. May 1st 1841.

Life in gardens and parlors is unpalatable to me—it wants rudeness and necessity to give it relish— I would at least strike my spade into the earth with as good will as the woodpecker his bill into a tree.

May 2d 1841.

Wachusett

Especial—I remember thee,
Wachusett, who like me
Standest alone without society.
Thy far blue eye—
A remnant of the sky—
Seen through the clearing or the gorge,
Or from the windows of the forge,
Doth leaven all it passes by.
Nothing is true but stands
But stands tween me and you,
Thou western pioneer,
Who know'st not shame nor fear,
By venturous spirit driven
Under the eaves of heaven,
And can'st expand thee there?
And breathe enough of air?
Upholding heaven, holding down earth,
They pastime from thy birth,
Not steadied by the one nor leaning on the other,
May I approve myself thy worthy brother.

Monday May 3d 1841.

We are all pilots of the most intricate Bahama channels— Beauty may be the sky overhead—but Duty is the water underneath. When I see a man with serene countenance in the sunshine of summer—drinking in peace in the garden or parlor, it looks like a great inward leisure that he enjoys—but in reality he sails on no summer's sea, but this steady sailing comes of a heavy hand on the tiller.

We do not attend to larks and blue birds so leisurely but that conscience is as erect as the attitude of the listener. The man of principle gets never a holiday. Our true character silently under lies all our words and actions—as the granite underlies the other strata. Its steady pulse does not cease for any deed of ours—as the sap is still ascending in the stalk of the fairest flower.

Thursday May 6th 1841.

The fickle person is he that does not know what is true or right absolutely—who has not an ancient wisdom for a life time—but a new prudence for every hour. We must sail by a sort of dead reckoning on this course of life—not speak any vessel—nor spy any headland—but in spite of all phenomena come steadily to port at last. In general we must have a catholic and universal wisdom—wiser than any particular—and be prudent enough to defer to it always. We are literally wiser than we know. Men do not fail for want of knowledge—but for want of prudence to give wisdom the preference. These low weather-cocks on barns and fences show not which way the general and steady current of the wind sets—which brings fair weather or foul—but the vane on the steeple—high up in another stratum of atmosphere tells that— What we need to know in any case is very simple. I shall not mistake the direction of my life—if I but know the high land and the main—on this side the Cordilleras on that the pacific— I shall know how to run. If a ridge intervene I have but to seek or make a gap to the sea.

Sunday May 9th 1841.

The pine stands in the woods like an Indian—untamed—with a fantastic wildness about it even in the clearings. If an Indian warrior were well painted, with pines in the back ground—he would seem to blend with the trees, and make a harmonious expression.— The pitch pines are the ghosts of Philip and Massassoit— The white pine has the smoother features of the squaw.

*   *   *

The poet speaks only those thoughts that come unbidden like the wind that stirs the trees—and men cannot help but listen. He is not listened to but heard. The weather-cock might as well dally with the wind—as a man pretend to resist eloquence.— The breath that inspires the poet has traversed a whole campagna—and this new climate here indicates that other latitudes are chilled or heated.

Speak to men as to gods and you will not be insincere.

RECOLLECTION

WE'RE now in the domain of memory. Autobiography and memoir are retrospective writing. The author writes from the perspective of some completed sequence of events, often even long after the completion. Actually, the distance from diaries and journals is only relative, the distance between an interval of hours, days, or weeks, and an interval of months, years, and decades. But the key in any case is this interval separating the time events occurred and the time they were written about. How we interpret and frame events is a factor of the time distance we have on them, to the extent that time distance equates with emotional and cognitive distance. Across time, memories become increasingly assimilated into broader frames of reference constructed according to experience acquired during the interval.

The more the first person accumulates experience the more it differentiates itself into *I-now* and *I-then,* and the more perspective the person may bring to bear on the past. In fact, *I-then* becomes like another person. This helps us to identify with actual other people, whose experience one is also progressively incorporating and analogizing to one's own. *I* becomes *we.*

Because this sense of being many people, past and present, here and there, occurs from generalizing, this progression from singular to plural follows a course toward higher abstraction, expansion in time and space. To pluralize is to generalize because multiple persons occupy more time and space than one person and because what can be truly said of a group has to be more general than what can be said of an individual. "Synoptic" literally means "fused in vision." We have to blur individuals to make a whole of them.

What distinguishes autobiography from memoir is a shift in

focus from author to other. Increasingly the subject in Recollection becomes people other than the speaker. Eventually the speaker will no longer refer to himself or herself, and at that point a story is said to be "in third person," biography or chronicle. But the first person drops out because the source of information is no longer personal recollection or no longer needs to be indicated. *We* is a stage between *I* and *he*, *she*, *they*, and *it*, between first and third person. This scale from first person singular to first person plural, then third person singular to third person plural, is illustrated by a gradation in the selections to follow in this section.

Autobiography

IT IS SOMETIMES interesting to scale autobiography according to the time gap between the end of events and the telling of them. In book-length autobiography covering a lifetime, which we will of course have to omit here, the reader can in watching this gap close also witness the gradual coinciding of *I-then* with *I-now*. The first two selections here, rather, focused solidly on the author, differentiate between an *incident* and a *phase*, and then the second two, starting to focus away from the author, distinguish a small-group *we* as subject from a broader first-person plural.

My Name Is Margaret
Maya Angelou
from *I Know Why the Caged Bird Sings,* 1969

An incident happens within a very small compass of time and space and hence is very dramatizable in the sense that it is told in enough detail of action, setting, and dialog that it could easily be staged with few if any scene changes. But what shall be an incident is an interesting compositional decision about which events are significant enough to warrant such elaboration. In the panorama of a book-length autobiography it is a close-up. The incident following, a chapter from a book covering Maya Angelou's youth, occurs within what we might call an episode—her employment as a kitchen maid—a unit of action encompassing more than an incident but less than a phase.

Recently a white woman from Texas, who would quickly describe herself as a liberal, asked me about my hometown. When I told her that in Stamps my grandmother had owned the only Negro general merchandise store since the turn of the century, she exclaimed, "Why, you were a debutante." Ridiculous and even ludicrous. But Negro girls in small Southern towns, whether poverty-stricken or just munching along on a few of life's necessities, were given as extensive and irrelevant preparations for adulthood as rich white girls shown in magazines. Admittedly the training was not the same. While white girls learned to waltz and sit gracefully with a tea cup balanced on their knees, we were lagging behind, learning the mid-Victorian values with very little money to indulge them. (Come and see Edna Lomax spending the money she made picking cotton on five balls of ecru tatting thread. Her fingers are bound to snag the work and she'll have to repeat the stitches time and time again. But she knows that when she buys the thread.)

We were required to embroider and I had trunkfuls of colorful dishtowels, pillowcases, runners and handkerchiefs to my credit. I mastered the art of crocheting and tatting, and there was a lifetime's supply of dainty doilies that would never be used in sacheted dresser drawers. It went without saying that all girls could iron and wash, but the finer touches around the home, like setting a table with real silver, baking roasts and cooking vegetables without meat, had to be learned elsewhere. Usually at the source of those habits. During my tenth year, a white woman's kitchen became my finishing school.

Mrs. Viola Cullinan was a plump woman who lived in a three-bedroom house somewhere behind the post office. She was singularly unattractive until she smiled, and then the lines around her eyes and mouth which made her look perpetually dirty disappeared, and her face looked like the mask of an impish elf. She usually rested her smile until late afternoon when her women friends dropped in and Miss Glory, the cook, served them cold drinks on the closed-in porch.

The exactness of her house was inhuman. This glass went here and only here. That cup had its place and it was an act of impudent rebellion to place it anywhere else. At twelve o'clock the table was set. At 12:15 Mrs. Cullinan sat down to dinner (whether her husband had arrived or not). At 12:16 Miss Glory brought out the food.

It took me a week to learn the difference between a salad plate, a bread plate and a dessert plate.

Mrs. Cullinan kept up the tradition of her wealthy parents. She was from Virginia. Miss Glory, who was a descendant of slaves that had worked for the Cullinans, told me her history. She had married beneath her (according to Miss Glory). Her husband's family hadn't had their money very long and what they had "didn't 'mount to much."

As ugly as she was, I thought privately, she was lucky to get a husband above or beneath her station. But Miss Glory wouldn't let me say a thing against her mistress. She was very patient with me, however, over the housework. She explained the dishware, silverware and servants' bells. The large round bowl in which soup was served wasn't a soup bowl, it was a tureen. There were goblets, sherbet glasses, ice-cream glasses, wine glasses, green glass coffee cups with matching saucers, and water glasses. I had a glass to drink from, and it sat with Miss Glory's on a separate shelf from the others. Soup spoons, gravy boat, butter knives, salad forks and carving platter were additions to my vocabulary and in fact almost represented a new language. I was fascinated with the novelty, with the fluttering Mrs. Cullinan and her Alice-in-Wonderland house.

Her husband remains, in my memory, undefined. I lumped him with all the other white men that I had ever seen and tried not to see.

On our way home one evening, Miss Glory told me that Mrs. Cullinan couldn't have children. She said that she was too delicate-boned. It was hard to imagine bones at all under those layers of fat. Miss Glory went on to say that the doctor had taken out all her lady organs. I reasoned that a pig's organs included the lungs, heart and liver, so if Mrs. Cullinan was walking around without those essentials, it explained why she drank alcohol out of unmarked bottles. She was keeping herself embalmed.

When I spoke to Bailey about it, he agreed that I was right, but he also informed me that Mr. Cullinan had two daughters by a colored lady and that I knew them very well. He added that the girls were the spitting image of their father. I was unable to remember what he looked like, although I had just left him a few hours before, but I thought of the Coleman girls. They were very light-skinned and certainly didn't look very much like their mother (no one ever mentioned Mr. Coleman).

My pity for Mrs. Cullinan preceded me the next morning like the Cheshire cat's smile. Those girls, who could have been her daughters, were beautiful. They didn't have to straighten their hair. Even when they were caught in the rain, their braids still hung down straight like tamed snakes. Their mouths were pouty little cupid's bows. Mrs. Cullinan didn't know what she missed. Or maybe she did. Poor Mrs. Cullinan.

For weeks after, I arrived early, left late and tried very hard to make up for her barrenness. If she had had her own children, she wouldn't have had to ask me to run a thousand errands from her back door to the back door of her friends. Poor old Mrs. Cullinan.

Then one evening Miss Glory told me to serve the ladies on the porch. After I set the tray down and turned toward the kitchen, one of the women asked, "What's your name, girl?" It was the speckled-faced one. Mrs. Cullinan said, "She doesn't talk much. Her name's Margaret."

"Is she dumb?"

"No. As I understand it, she can talk when she wants to but she's usually quiet as a little mouse. Aren't you, Margaret?"

I smiled at her. Poor thing. No organs and couldn't even pronounce my name correctly.

"She's a sweet little thing, though."

"Well, that may be, but the name's too long. I'd never bother myself. I'd call her Mary if I was you."

I fumed into the kitchen. That horrible woman would never have the chance to call me Mary because if I was starving I'd never work for her. I decided I wouldn't pee on her if her heart was on fire. Giggles drifted in off the porch and into Miss Glory's pots. I wondered what they could be laughing about.

Whitefolks were so strange. Could they be talking about me? Everybody knew that they stuck together better than the Negroes did. It was possible that Mrs. Cullinan had friends in St. Louis who heard about a girl from Stamps being in court and wrote to tell her. Maybe she knew about Mr. Freeman.

My lunch was in my mouth a second time and I went outside and relieved myself on the bed of four-o'clocks. Miss Glory thought I might be coming down with something and told me to go on home, that Momma would give me some herb tea, and she'd explain to her mistress.

I realized how foolish I was being before I reached the pond.

Of course Mrs. Cullinan didn't know. Otherwise she wouldn't have given me the two nice dresses that Momma cut down, and she certainly wouldn't have called me a "sweet little thing." My stomach felt fine, and I didn't mention anything to Momma.

That evening I decided to write a poem on being white, fat, old and without children. It was going to be a tragic ballad. I would have to watch her carefully to capture the essence of her loneliness and pain.

The very next day, she called me by the wrong name. Miss Glory and I were washing up the lunch dishes when Mrs. Cullinan came to the doorway. "Mary?"

Miss Glory asked, "Who?"

Mrs. Cullinan, sagging a little, knew and I knew. "I want Mary to go down to Mrs. Randall's and take her some soup. She's not been feeling well for a few days."

Miss Glory's face was a wonder to see. "You mean Margaret, ma'am. Her name's Margaret."

"That's too long. She's Mary from now on. Heat that soup from last night and put it in the china tureen and, Mary, I want you to carry it carefully."

Every person I knew had a hellish horror of being "called out of his name." It was a dangerous practice to call a Negro anything that could be loosely construed as insulting because of the centuries of their having been called niggers, jigs, dinges, blackbirds, crows, boots and spooks.

Miss Glory had a fleeting second of feeling sorry for me. Then as she handed me the hot tureen she said, "Don't mind, don't pay that no mind. Sticks and stones may break your bones, but words . . . You know, I been working for her for twenty years."

She held the back door open for me. "Twenty years. I wasn't much older than you. My name used to be Hallelujah. That's what Ma named me, but my mistress give me 'Glory,' and it stuck. I likes it better too."

I was in the little path that ran behind the houses when Miss Glory shouted, "It's shorter too."

For a few seconds it was a tossup over whether I would laugh (imagine being named Hallelujah) or cry (imagine letting some white woman rename you for her convenience). My anger saved me from either outburst. I had to quit the job, but the problem was going to be how to do it. Momma wouldn't allow me to quit for just any reason.

"She's a peach. That woman is a real peach." Mrs. Randall's maid was talking as she took the soup from me, and I wondered what her name used to be and what she answered to now.

For a week I looked into Mrs. Cullinan's face as she called me Mary. She ignored my coming late and leaving early. Miss Glory was a little annoyed because I had begun to leave egg yolk on the dishes and wasn't putting much heart in polishing the silver. I hoped that she would complain to our boss, but she didn't.

Then Bailey solved my dilemma. He had me describe the contents of the cupboard and the particular plates she liked best. Her favorite piece was a casserole shaped like a fish and the green glass coffee cups. I kept his instructions in mind, so on the next day when Miss Glory was hanging out clothes and I had again been told to serve the old biddies on the porch, I dropped the empty serving tray. When I heard Mrs. Cullinan scream, ''Mary!'' I picked up the casserole and two of the green glass cups in readiness. As she rounded the kitchen door I let them fall on the tiled floor.

I could never absolutely describe to Bailey what happened next, because each time I got to the part where she fell on the floor and screwed up her ugly face to cry, we burst out laughing. She actually wobbled around on the floor and picked up shards of the cups and cried, ''Oh, Momma. Oh, dear Gawd. It's Momma's china from Virginia. Oh, Momma, I sorry.''

Miss Glory came running in from the yard and the women from the porch crowded around. Miss Glory was almost as broken up as her mistress. ''You mean to say she broke our Virginia dishes? What we gone do?''

Mrs. Cullinan cried louder, ''That clumsy nigger. Clumsy little black nigger.''

Old speckled-face leaned down and asked, ''Who did it, Viola? Was it Mary? Who did it?''

Everything was happening so fast I can't remember whether her action preceded her words, but I know that Mrs. Cullinan said, ''Her name's Margaret, goddamn it, her name's Margaret.'' And she threw a wedge of the broken plate at me. It could have been the hysteria which put her aim off, but the flying crockery caught Miss Glory right over her ear and she started screaming.

I left the front door wide open so all the neighbors could hear.

Mrs. Cullinan was right about one thing. My name wasn't Mary.

Mucho Days and Nights in Gray
Piri Thomas
from *Down These Mean Streets*, 1967

Inasmuch as a phase is a significant stage in one's life story, lasting months or years, it is defined by the autobiographer's feeling that his or her life breaks down into certain sections with their own beginnings, developments, and climaxes. This sectioning is an act of interpretation and classification that determines the compositional use of memories. Typically, a phase is as much a description of repetitive actions—like characteristic behavior—as once-upon-a-time narrative. Book-length autobiographies combine incidents, episodes, and phases according to the author's perception of how his or her life has unfolded.

Thomas was imprisoned for an armed robbery in New York City during which he had been wounded.

One of the worst feelings I can imagine is to be something or someplace and not be able to accept the fact. So it was with me—I was a con in jail, but nothing in the world could make me accept it. Not the gray clothes, not the green bars, not the bugle's measuring of time, not the blue-uniformed hacks, not the insipid food, not the new lines in my face—nothing.

I couldn't get used to it, no matter how hard I tried. It kept pounding on me. It came to me every morning and every evening and sat heavily, like death on living tissue. I hated the evenings because a whole night in prison lay before me, and I hated the mornings because I felt like Dracula returning to his coffin.

I tried to make believe that the days were shorter instead of longer, that the moon rose within half an hour of the sun. I hated the sight of a calendar. I tried not to count the days and weeks and months and years—and I found myself counting seconds and minutes. I counted the bolts and windows, the green-splashed bars, the hacks and cons; they added up to a thousand years. The reasoning that my punishment was deserved was absent. As prison blocks off your body, so it suffocates your mind.

My life became a gray mass of hatred. I hated sunny days because of the fine times I could have been enjoying at the beach with Trina, and I hated rainy days because they were depressing and made my cell, my clothes, even my insides damp. I hated the prison noises and the smell of the guards' dark-blue uniforms. I hated the other cons for reminding me that I was one of them, and I hated myself because I *was* one of them.

Man, what a fuckin' mess I've gotten my ass into. Jail gives you plenty of time to think, and I thought and thought about the outside and the block and Trina. *I wonder what she's doing now? What time is it? She must be asleep or getting ready for bed. If I strain my eyes, I can just about make you out, baby, with your hair down and curly bouncing like and your mouth in a point, pushed out like you're always mad at somebody . . . Strain harder, eyeballs . . . I can feel your body's warmth, smell you, taste you—oh, Christ, take her out of my mind . . .*

Comstock was just like Sing Sing. Every con did something; every hack was stationed just right; and above all, every bar was in the right place—over windows and doors. For school I was assigned to study brick masonry; my regular job was on the paint gang. I was paid a nickel a day, which later was raised to a dime. The money was credited to my account, and twice a month I was permitted to make a "buy" in the amount of half my monthly wages.

If you got food from home (say, canned goods) or from the buy, you ate like a king. Otherwise you ate like a con. You ate like a con, anyway, no matter what you ate, when you ate in the mess hall. It held more than a thousand people and the combined sounds of spoons brushing against tin cups full of iodine coffee, food being chewed, men talking out of hopeful throats, feet scraping, and trays banging made the meal scene like a wild dream. But it was real. If you didn't get a care package and couldn't make a buy, you made sandwiches out of bread and whatever food you got at supper. It could be anything—spaghetti, stew, cole slaw, even soup.

The food wasn't bad once you accepted it with the same readiness you accepted your prison sentence. Sunday lunch was a pretty good meal. We got roast beef or ham, gravy, bread, potatoes, dessert, and coffee. It was the same on minor holidays like Washington's Birthday. The three big holidays were Thanksgiving, Christmas, and New Year's. For Thanksgiving and Christmas we got a great big hunk of roast chicken with the works; on New Year's Day, we got a thick cut of steak, also with the works. Usually, however, the cat that sliced the meat cut it razor thin. Our favorite joke was to solemnly hold up a letter, place a slice of meat over it and begin to read the letter through the meat.

I was jail-wise in picking my friends. There is a pecking order among prisoners. At the top are the con men, the smoothies. Just beneath them are disbarred lawyers and abortionists; their brains entitle them to respect. In the middle are the heist men. Thieves and burglars rank just below them. And at the bottom are rapists, faggots, crooked cops, and junkies.

I wanted to learn all the hustles, all the arts of knowing people and their kicks. One older guy I got to know, Sam, was one of the best con men in the business. He told me how he worked. And always he ended up by saying, "But you see, kid, I made a lot of money—but here I am." My closest *amigo* was a big black Puerto Rican everyone called Young Turk, a gentle man who was doing five to fifteen for cutting a guy up in a fight.

I also was friendly with a guy who came from a good family and had gone to all the right schools. His name was Kent, and he talked English like a college professor. I listened to him and imitated him. I wanted to speak like Kent, but not all of a sudden; that would have seemed like grandstanding. So I grabbed a dictionary and slowly learned words and tried them out in our yaks. When I first did this, Kent lifted his eyebrows and smiled slightly but not superciliously. Way down he was tickled that I wanted to emulate his stick of being, and from then on he corrected me whenever I mispronounced a word, and he smiled approvingly when I spoke grammatically. One day he said to me, "Why don't you write, Piri?"

"Write what?" I replied.

"Thoughts, ideas, poetry," he said.

I laughed. "Sure, someday . . ."

I didn't write until many years later, but I did plenty of talking. Man, in prison, everyone yakked. Yak took up time, it killed time, especially on the long days like Saturday and Sunday, when we didn't work and had a lot of yard time. And we dealt for almost anything, partly out of a desire for the stuff and partly to beat the system. Goof balls, benzedrine, phenobarbitals, splits, and green money floated around regularly. At Sing Sing we had had whisky, too, but at Comstock I never saw any whisky, bonded stuff, I mean. Instead we had fermented prunes, fruit wines, and strained shellac—all homemade, of course, but they packed a kick. Some shellac killed one con with a promising career as a sax musician and blinded two others.

Splits were common. They're round white pills with a groove across the middle, some sort of tranquilizer. If you swallow one with a glass of hot water, you get a gone high that's almost like what you get with heroin. We also dealt for red capsules of phenos, two of which, with hot water, produce a forgetting high, and for cooking mace or cinnamon, a large tablespoon of which, with a glass of hot water, closes your eyelids with a way-up-and-out feeling. Sometimes the trusties or outside gang brought in wild marijuana, which we cured and dried on the electric light bulb in the cell. But splits were the kick. One guy, Clarence, a young Negro who painted beautifully, was gone on them. Clarence really loved drugs.

"That's my woman, Lady Snow," he told me once. "I sure wish I could cop some. I got some smuggled in a while back but it was just a little piece. It's hard. These hacks check everything, even take the stamps off the letters to make sure they wasn't stuck on with paste of drugs. And you get a white shirt from home and they launder it for you, just to make sure it wasn't starched with drugs."

"Forget it, Clarence," I said.

Clarence smiled at me and said, "Dig, Piri, who do you love?"

"Me," I said.

"Well, I love Lady Snow. You can't forget about you, I can't forget about Lady Snow."

A couple of days later Clarence died in his sleep. "What happened to Clarence?" I asked Young Turk.

"That damn fool, he got some splits and it's bad enough to swallow them like he does, three or four at a gulp, but he went and crushed them and copped some works, an eyedropper and a needle, and shot himself up. His heart stopped."

I had been at Comstock two years when Clarence died, and I still had three years or more to go, depending on how the parole board decided. *Jesus,* I thought, *if only the days would vary, if only one day would be fourteen hours and another three hours long, if only daylight would come at night and vice versa—anything at all to break the monotony.* But time passed as usual. Breakfast was followed by lunch and lunch by dinner, and then the cycle started again. I could feel myself growing up; the fine peach fuzz on my face becoming a heavy stubble, my chest broadening, my voice deepening, my ideas changing. Every day brought a painful awareness of the sweetness of being free and the horror of prison's years going down the toilet bowl.

Sometimes the pressure got too much to bear, as it does with all cons, who, seeking a release from the overpowering hatred against a society that makes canaries out of human beings, let out their aggressions on each other. I had been having trouble with a con named Little. He was well named, short but powerfully built. I guess he was bugged also, and when two bugged convicts meet head on, pressure gotta come out. We got into some sort of argument, not two words were needed; he looked bad at me, I looked bad at him. I said, "Man, I'm pretty fuckin' well tired of your bullshit."

"How tired, man?" he challenged me.

"Tired enough to fight your ass to the ground," I replied.

"Okay, man, let's go to the back of the paint room and we deal."

The cons nearby heard us and dug the situation, but they made no move to let on that they did. In prison you minded your business and fought your own fights or you were a punk. Besides, they didn't want to let the guards know anything was gonna pop—and furthermore, they didn't want to cheat themselves out of a fight that would give them a break from another dull, lousy day.

Little and I walked side by side, down the ramp and into the large paint room we worked in. My guts tensed and sucked air. Casey, a big, kind, friendly guard, was on duty. He was one of the few rare human beings left in my kind of world. He looked up at us and at the casually strolling cons who wanted a good look-see at this rumble, and, sensing that something was up, eased his big hard brown wooden stick into a more favorable position. But he didn't say anything. I looked at Little, who was standing close to me for a chance to reach me fast when we started throwing punches. I pushed him away and he almost tore my jaw off with a left cross. I hadn't figured him to be a southpaw. I hit the floor hard and all I knew was to get up. I scrambled and grabbed him and punched and held, and he punched and held, and damned if I didn't feel like at last here in front of me was somebody I could take out my mad steam on; and I guess he felt the same. Little actually was my friend, one of the clique—and now we were trying to mash each other. I tore into his guts with rights, lefts and elbows; he pounded away at my face. Suddenly, it was over by silent mutual consent. We just looked at each other, lips tight and bloodied. Then Casey came over quietly and said, "You guys got it out of your systems?"

Our heads shook up and down in unison. "Okay, if you guys had picked up sticks or pipes, or used anything else other than your fists, I would have wrapped this billy stick around both your heads. As it is, I've seen nothing and you've done nothing. I don't want no more of this."

I looked at Little and he at me, and we both knew we didn't want no more. Sometimes a fight between two men makes them the greatest of friends, because of the respect that is born between the swinging fists. Casey walked away. Little and I slapped skin, and I asked him in a low voice, "Little, why didn't you work my guts over in the clinches?"

"I didn't want to hit you where you got shot," he said. "I figured I might cause you bad hurt." He walked away, and damned if I didn't feel wet in my eyes.

The Scrolls, Too, Are Mortal
Elie Wiesel
from *A Jew Today*, 1979

The next two selections form a hinge between first-person singular and plural, and both, incidentally, are not excerpts but independent compositions.

Here we are back to an incident (lasting only an hour or so), but who is it about? Wiesel? One of the other two people? Both of the other two people? All three of them? All holocaust survivors? All Jews? The Scrolls? Wiesel's telescoping of different levels of the past makes the question especially interesting.

"No, it's not me," the man says, seemingly unperturbed. "I don't know whom you're looking for, but I know it isn't me. Leave me alone. I have things to do. Go away. I have urgent work to do. My wife will be home soon. Go before she comes."

Through the half-open windows we can hear the noises from the street: furiously honking cars, brawling housewives, children playing. An infant cries, and nobody is consoling it.

"Go away," says the man seated in front of the parchment

scrolls stretched over the entire length of the table. "Can't you see, I'm only a scribe. I correct, I repair, I rewrite. I replace a faded word here, a scratched letter there. What I do is neither special nor great. I'm a simple man. I don't deserve your attention. Go away. I insist."

My gaze lingers on the scrolls. The yellowed parchment looks cracked, tortured. "Where are they from," I ask.

"From Prague. Do you know it? The town of the illustrious Maharal. The Golem's mysterious city. Did you know that that is where the Germans sent all the sacred scrolls of all the occupied towns, all the ghettos? They planned to turn Prague into a Jewish museum without Jews."

In a room above us, someone is sweeping the floor. The infant continues to cry.

"Why did they desecrate the scrolls?" the man asks without looking at me. "To take revenge? Revenge for what? It hurts me to see them like this. I try to salvage them, to give them back the love they deserve."

A dozen quill pens and an inkwell stand within his reach. I would love to watch him at work, but my presence disturbs him. He will not read, he will not write as long as I remain. But I will not go, not before I know.

"The resemblance," I say, "is striking. How do you explain this extraordinary resemblance?"

He interrupts me brutally. "There is nothing to explain. *There,* all men looked alike. They ate the same bread, killed themselves at the same tasks and slept the same sleep. Only God could make a distinction; I could not."

Hunched over, he avoids my eyes, afraid of offending me. All he wants is to remain alone. I am an intruder, and he makes me feel it. Still, I cannot let go. I trust my intuition; it rarely deceives me.

"You're keeping me from my work," he says.

Mechanically he adjusts his skullcap, just as he did *there*. And he stares at the parchment, just as he stared into nothingness *there*.

"You remind me of a friend," I say. "He meant a lot to me. I admired him, I felt great affection, much tenderness for him . . ."

He turns toward me, and for a moment we look at one another silently. Does he recognize me? Or have I made a mistake? That flattened nose, those bushy eyebrows, the way he has of constantly touching his skullcap and of sniffing the air. It is he, yes, I am sure it is he.

"There was a time when I thought of you—excuse me, him—as

someone capable of saving me, of bringing me back to life . . .
A kind of Master, a kind of father . . ."

"It wasn't me," he says morosely. "A Master is he who has
students; I have none. A father is someone who has children; I
have none. How many times must I repeat to you that your
memory is leading you astray? It's playing tricks on you. Watch
it or you'll be lost. Something like this could push you into the
abyss."

He is irritated, hostile, and I am sorry. I was too fond of him
to hurt him. But already he has calmed himself. "Memory," he
says, "yes, it sometimes lets itself be devoured by imagination. I
like both, but separately." He reaches for a pen, hesitates, sets it
down again. "One must not trust memory too much; it is faithful
only to the extent that we are faithful to it."

The last sentence makes me jump: I had heard it before, long
ago. "Memory," he added then, "memory is our real kingdom."

My tension increases. "Where were you during the war?"

"In hell. Like these sacred scrolls. Like those who studied
them. Like those who revered them."

I want details: In which camp had he been? From when to
when?

He brushes aside my questions with a tired, discouraged shrug.
"Really, what is the good of talking about it? It's all far away.
In another world, another life." He straightens himself, breathes
deeply and shakes his head. "Memory," he says. "Memory,
that is the true kingdom of man."

His voice has not changed. Weary yet warm; somber yet
evocative. I want to close my eyes and see myself, see us, in an
earlier life, transfigured. I dare not. What if, when I opened
them, he were gone?

Point-blank I interrogate him: "Tell me the truth, do you
remember me?"

"A childish question, young man. No, of course I don't
remember you."

He must have seen my disappointment. He wants to reassure
me. "What do we really know about how we relate to our
memories? They're so personal, so undefinable. Where am I
more real: in my memory or in yours? Where am I more alive?"

I no longer know. In mine perhaps. He has forgotten me,
whereas I can see him still: my companion who made me dream.
I used to like to listen to him when uncertainty began to weigh
and the wait became a threat. If there are in this world thirty-six
Just Men, then he was one of them; if there are only ten, he was
one; if there is only one, then he was that one.

"This is where my life is," says the scribe as he caresses a yellowed parchment. "The Torah, that is true memory: mine, ours. My predecessor, the one who transcribed the Five Books on these scrolls, was a saint: conscientious, meticulous, fastidious. He lived inside the letters he copied. Before he wrote the name of God, he cleansed his body and his thoughts according to the rites and customs of the ancient Kabbalists. So do I. At least I try. Whenever I come across a mutilated letter, a wounded word, I fast, I concentrate, before I give it back its original splendor. This is where my destiny unfolds, here among these shreds of the Torah, a victim of man's hate as we were its victims. I need only to look at these Books to measure the suffering they endured. And I'm overwhelmed by a great compassion. I'd give anything to be able to help them, to console them."

And now he speaks to me of the love that Jews have nurtured for the Torah from the beginning. If someone drops a scroll, the entire community does penance. The presence of the Torah sanctifies; it warms the coldest of hearts. Jews never abandon it, never part from it. The scrolls are linked with the events that punctuate and enrich the life of a community. One kisses them with passion, one dances with them, one communes with them. One honors them, one protects them. Impossible to unroll them without trembling; impossible to read in them without becoming a child again. All this the enemy knew; that was why he trampled them, dragged them through the mud and the blood, exhibited them like trophies of war and victory. With every letter he retrieves, the scribe is healing living creatures, survivors.

That had been my reason for going to see him. I had heard about this solitary scribe and his half-burned, ill-treated parchments. And I had recognized him immediately. I had scrutinized his bony face, his drooping shoulders, his eyes that knew how to probe people's inner depths and find the right, soothing, consoling word. And his tears, his tears most of all. I would like to see him cry, for then I would be sure. And he would stop denying. Only, he seems to read my thoughts, for he changes the subject: he begins to speak of his work as a scribe. He speaks of it with a sadness mixed with pride.

"God gave us these words at Sinai," he says. "I should like to give them back to Him intact."

I remember him as he was then: a buffoon turned miracle-maker. I can still hear him; he cried, he was the only one to cry. The rest of us no longer could. Gnawed by hunger, choked by smoke, awaiting death, the prisoners were in a state of prostration close to lethargy. The first tear would have opened the dam and brought the end. He alone did not fear the consequences. His weeping annoyed his fellow inmates, and that amused the torturers; the more he sobbed, the harder they laughed. Sometimes they would reward him by throwing him a crust of bread, which he immediately shared. Thus, eventually his tears pleased everyone; they protected him. And us as well.

An image: One winter evening a sickly, feverish young boy incurred the wrath of Hans, the barracks chief. A cruel and hateful man, Hans struck his victims without telling them why; he never gave reasons. He was sure to go on beating them until they died. He was obstinate, that Hans, he always went on to the end. We knew it, so did the sick boy. We tried not to think of it. What good was it to experience the inevitable before it happened? Better to let go, dissolve into nothingness and not hear the bludgeon's dull thuds. Suddenly someone moved nearby; we held our breath. Who was this suicidal fool? What was this madness? When Hans was at his task, he brooked no interference. One had to take care not to be noticed. Who was foolish enough to attract his attention? To ask for death? The buffoon, his shadow behind him, came to a standstill before the brute, who went on beating his victim. The buffoon stood staring at Hans, then he came closer and closer until he forced him to look at him. As always, the buffoon was crying, and as always, Hans burst out laughing. And the boy was spared.

The man had courage. Intercessor, guardian angel, defender of the doomed. A true Just Man, a savior. Looking like a human scarecrow, he seemed to be chasing huge invisible birds. In perpetual movement, he ran up and down the camp streets halting only where his powers were needed. He belonged to the landscape. Mornings, as we left for work, we would see him standing near the main gate, following us with his gaze. Evenings when we returned, our eyes would search him out and thank him for being there.

How long did his reign last? I do not remember. One week? One month? I remember events but not their duration. I remember a buffoon who came between death and its prey; he would appear suddenly before the killer and by his sobbing make him laugh, and the murder would be suspended.

One Sunday in autumn I was alone with him in the barracks. He offered me a few spoonfuls of soup and spoke to me of his father. "He was a good man, a man of heart. A disciple of the Bratzlaver Rebbe. He spent his life in prayer and meditation. 'Nothing is as whole as a broken heart' was one of his Master's sayings he liked to repeat. He would often take my arm and say

'What can I wish you, my son? Knowledge? Thirst for knowledge is more precious, and that I have already instilled in you. Riches? True riches only God can give. Peace also. And truth as well. But to have God grant those to you, you have to ask for them. And so I want you to know how to ask. A word of advice, my son: God likes tears. Our sages say that even when all other heavenly gates are shut, the gate of tears remains open. My wish for you? May you know how to cry. Like Jeremiah, and better than he. Like our patriarchs, and better than they . . . That is what my father, a Bratzlaver Hasid, wished for me. And you see? My father's wish was granted.''

I would give much to see him cry.

A key is turning in the lock. The door creaks and opens. A woman appears; she is breathless. ''Why can't you turn on the lights, Issahar?'' Grumbling, she continues, ''Always in the dark. In the dark, always.'' As she switches on the light she notices me. In her surprise, she almost drops her purse. ''Who is this? A visitor, a visitor at last? What is happening to you, Issahar? Are you ill? And you, are you a doctor? Who sent you? Who called for you?''

Issahar has remained seated. I stand up. Confronting us, she scrutinizes me with a mixture of curiosity and hostility. ''So? I guessed right, didn't I? You are a doctor.''

''No.''

''Then, who are you? Who could you be? What do you want from my husband?''

''Nothing,'' I say. ''I knew your husband a very long time ago. He is a friend, an old friend.''

She leans toward me, examining me closely. ''My poor gentleman . . . I think it is you who need a doctor. My husband has no friends. Not here, not anywhere. In the thirty years we've been married, I've yet to meet one single friend of his. There's a reason for that: he has no friends. I am telling you, and I know. He speaks to no one and no one speaks to him. In order not to disturb the children, you understand. Even in summer he hides here in the dark, always in the dark, tucked into his rolls of parchment, incapable of finishing a job that others would seal and deliver in no time at all . . . Even the children could do it faster . . . Issahar, who is this gentleman? Is he really your friend?''

He nods as though to say: Yes or no, what difference does it make?

''Say, Issahar, if he is your friend, why do you hide him from me so long? And you, sir, how do you explain the fact that this is the first time I have met you?''

She looks at us angrily; she feels betrayed, cheated. We have plotted against her; we have excluded her, rejected her.

''I demand an explanation! I'm entitled to it, Issahar! If he is your friend, you are guilty of having concealed him from me, and if he's not, why is he lying?''

Issahar maintains a distant, resigned silence. As for me, I do not know what position to take in this domestic squabble. The woman is a shrew. One can see that right away. Small, delicate, weasel-like. Both annoyed and annoying. Horn-rimmed glasses, piercing eyes. Cheap wig. Thin lips, nasty smile.

''So, Issahar? Make up your mind. Who is this friend? Since when do you know him? And how many more like him do you have? And why does he pretend to be a doctor? Where did you meet? What do you do when I'm not with you to help you, to protect you? I slave from morning till night, I sacrifice myself for you, and you are seeing people, you lead a secret life with friends . . . Is this my reward?''

Her temper rises, she explodes. She screams, she is choking. Her rage is driving her mad, she becomes violent. In a moment she will throw herself on both of us.

''Calm down,'' says Issahar. ''I don't know who this gentleman is. He claims he met me long ago; he's wrong. He came to buy a *Sefer Torah* and suddenly he thought he recognized me as a friend of his, a dead friend. Optical illusion or a trick played by his memory. Don't pay any attention.''

''A dead friend, you say. And what if it were one of our children?''

''What children?'' I ask.

''You wouldn't understand,'' says Issahar.

The woman seems to relent. ''I see,'' she says with a grimace. ''I see, I see.''

She rests the bag she has been holding on a chair and empties its contents of groceries, stashing them in a corner of the room, which also serves as kitchen. I examine her at closer range: in her fifties, perhaps older. A surly, wrinkled face, she looks incapable of loving herself or others, incapable of silence, of rest, of living. A wave of pity comes over me. Issahar, my friend. This woman, the wife of my friend Issahar. Do they ever talk, make plans together? How and where did they meet? To my surprise, I hear myself asking them questions. My surprise changes into amazement when I hear the woman answering me.

''So, we interest you? Why?''

"Forgive my tactlessness."

"You haven't answered me. I . . . he . . . we interest you. Why? Either you are his friend, and then you're aware of what has happened to us; or you're not, and then your behavior is suspicious."

She is making me nervous; I don't know what to say. I invent. "It's been years since I've seen Issahar . . . I didn't even know his name was Issahar."

"What? And you were his friend?! You're a dirty liar, sir!"

"No."

"Then you're sick; go and see a doctor."

"I shall."

"You promise?"

"I promise."

"Tomorrow?"

"Tomorrow."

"Why not today?"

"I'm tired."

"Exactly! That's when one should go and see a doctor!"

"Very well. I'll go tonight."

At last she is satisfied. "As long as you are so agreeable, I've decided to be nice to you, too. Tell me what you'd like to know."

"Madam, I've forgotten."

"That's serious, very serious . . . You will need a great specialist. But I know of one who lives not too far from here. I hope you're rich; he is very expensive, you know."

"I'm not rich."

"Oh! Here you go again, lying! If you're not rich, how did you hope to buy a *Sefer Torah?*"

Back and forth she goes, through the room, bumping into chairs, jostling me, and all the time she is rambling on. "If, on the other hand, you really are rich, where are the presents? Friends don't visit empty-handed, as far as I know! Where are your manners, sir?"

"He didn't know," says Issahar. "When he came, he couldn't know that the scribe . . . that I was his friend."

"So you admit you're his friend!"

"I've been trying to explain to you . . ."

"Stop, Issahar. You'll end up confusing me."

Her mood changes. "Would you like something to eat? To drink? I'll make you some tea."

"No, thank you."

"Issahar, tell him it's not nice to say no."

"Really . . . I don't want anything."

"Issahar! Think of the children! We must set an example!"

"Please," says Issahar. "Have something."

His wife brings out the kettle. She finds some cups and shoves them in front of us without ever stopping her fumbling and groaning. "You must not say no, sir. My children will tell you that you must not say no if you wish to please me. And if you displease me, you will not obtain anything from him or me."

"I want nothing from you."

"Only from him, is that it? The scrolls, you want the scrolls. You want them from him, since he's the one who corrects and restores them. But I'm the one who sells them! You didn't know that, did you? It's me you must please, sir, since you want something from me . . . What a life. Everybody wants something from everybody. You have come to pay us a visit in order to take something from us: our time, our attention, our work, our love, our past. Don't deny it, it won't do you any good. But before one takes, sir, one must give; one must say yes, sir, one must shout yes. In saying yes, one gives."

While she is reeling off her speech, her husband looks at her without really listening. I know when a man listens and when he pretends. Issahar is pretending.

"Look at Issahar," says the woman. "I tell you, look at him."

She has been whirling around me for so long that I am dizzy.

"Do you see him? He never says no. Thirty years ago I proposed to him that he marry me; he didn't say no. I wanted children. In my foolishness, I dreamed of a houseful of children, while he dreamed of a world full of children. Not the same ones, sir, not the same. Mine were healthy and radiant; his were disfigured and bloody. So, you see, I gave him mine and he gave me his. And in the dark, always in the dark, we watch them play together surrounded by the charred letters of the sacred scrolls; we listen to them as they recite the beautiful stories of the Torah, we hear them laugh. Would you like to hear them laugh, sir?"

Abruptly she turns off the light. Her abruptness takes my breath away; I can feel the anguish chilling my veins.

"We are a little cramped here," says the woman as though to excuse herself. "You mustn't be annoyed with us, we are not rich. But the children love us because we love them. Nobody else does. That is why they come and play here, and study here and take refuge inside the scrolls. Do you hear them? Ssshhh don't say a word, you'll frighten them. Hey, kids, be careful

The parchment is fragile, and sick as well, do you hear me? Be careful!''

It is too dark; I see nothing. I dare neither move nor breathe. They must both be mad. And if I stay here, I shall become mad like them. I want to free myself; I have forgotten the way to the door. I am afraid of falling over a chair, of bumping into the woman or her husband, of dropping the parchment with the children. The window is on my right, I'll open it a little wider. Should I jump? At least let me breathe in some fresh air. It is hot, I am suffocating.

"Come, children," says the woman tenderly. "A friend of Issahar's would like to meet you. Come and greet him. Don't be afraid, sir; they won't bite. Jewish children are gentle. They harm no one. Dead Jewish children, how very gentle they are in their parchment refuge . . .''

I lower my gaze, my eyelids are heavy; I hold my hands over my ears. An image explodes inside me: Issahar, *there,* with the "selected" children. The buffoon had requested permission to spend their last night with them. He had told them stories, crying to cheer them up, but he had only made them cry; they had cried together until daybreak. Then he had accompanied them to their death. Finally he had returned to the yard; and when the guards saw him, they had burst out laughing. And that night the buffoon had whispered to me, "Memory is not only a kingdom, it is also a graveyard.''

"I must go," I shout. "It's late. Please turn on the lights, I beg of you. Turn on the lights!''

Where is that door? The exit? I am panic-stricken. Who is there to call for help?

"Don't you like children, sir?" says the woman, clapping her hands. "Why, they are so good, so well-behaved. Listen to them. They are repeating what God has told them. They are His memory.''

She turns on the lights. I must look terrible, for she breaks into an evil snicker.

Issahar is pale. He pulls himself out of his torpor and rises. "I'll see you to the door," he says, touching his skullcap as if to screw it onto his skull.

In the hallway, he stops and holds out his hand. "Don't judge her. I am living with my torn scrolls and she with hers. You don't understand that it is possible to live like that? Nor do I. Nor does she.''

Through the half-open door I glimpse his wife. Her elbows are resting on the table. She seems asleep.

"There are words that cannot, that must not, be pronounced," says the scribe. "My wife is sick because she hears them from morning till night, and I because I see them. My wife hears them until late into the night; they have devastated her soul and her reason. She cries, poor woman. She can do nothing but cry."

My hand rests inside his, his warmth goes through me. I dare not pull my hand away.

"Poor woman," says the scribe. "She doesn't know that tears have more effect on the enemy, more effect on the killers, than on the God of mercy."

He has let go of my hand. And gone back into his room. As for me, I stood there a long time facing his bolted door.

Besieged
Jessie Benton Frémont
Wide Awake magazine, 1888

Whereas "we" was not the grammatical person actually employed by Wiesel but rather the more or less equal focus on both author and others, in the following true story it actually appears a number of times as the author is obliged to include herself in the larger unit to which the title "Besieged" applies. In fact, as an indication of the shifting scope of her tale, she says on one page, "We were only three . . . ," and on another, "We had in California at this time. . . ." Indeed, in telling her family story properly she has to chronicle to a degree what was happening in the whole state.

As the daughter of Senator Thomas Hart Benton, Jessie had been used to the cultivated milieus of Washington and Paris. As the wife of explorer, military leader, and unsuccessful presidential candidate John Frémont, she found herself residing for two of the Gold Rush years on his property at Bear Valley in the southern Sierra foothills. A strong, talented, and intelligent woman she turned her hand to writing memoirs some time after the events of this story, when her husband's gold-mining venture failed to "pan out" owing to circumstances other than those accounting for the siege here.

Incidentally, since Bear Valley lies only a few miles from Agua Frio, from where Horace Snow wrote his "Dear Charlie" letters, these two accounts telling about the same decade afford some idea of the source documents historians correlate and synthesize in the process of abstracting the rather more dull synopses we study in school as "history." (I am indebted to the Mariposa County Library for bringing these little-known documents to my attention and to the Mariposa Historical Society for publishing the "Dear Charlie" letters itself. "Besieged" was collected in Mother Lode Narratives *by Jessie Benton Frémont, edited by Shirley Sargent.)*

"Colonel, the Hornitas League has jumped the Black Drift!"

"What does that mean?" I asked.

"Only mining work," was the answer. "You had best go to sleep again."

And in my blissful ignorance go to sleep I did. It was in the hot summer weather, that furnace-like heat of the dry season in a deep valley of the Sierras where the only touch of cooler air comes after the night has shaded the heated earth; and it was in the dim dawn of this fresher hour that the cautious, low-spoken call was made to "the Colonel."[1]

As Mr. Frémont often rode to the mines, three miles away, before the sun was over the range, it was no surprise to find on waking that he had had his coffee and gone. How early I was not told; nor was I let to know anything of the danger that was calling out the best thinking and best action of all our people.

In my ignorance, we went about our day as usual. We could drive out quite late after the sun was well behind the western range, but all the long day we had to find in-door resources. This was to the advantage of the young people, for we had found some regular occupation necessary and made it of what was around us. Our agent had left an unusually good collection of books (he had recently died) and though it was a very irregular course, yet we secured a lot of amusement as well as instruction from these. In French there were several fine histories of France illustrated from historical portraits and pictures, and good memoirs on the French Revolution. Both the young people knew Paris well and we could locate events in palaces and parks and

---

1. Richard Dana, of *Two Years Before the Mast*, made us a delightful visit in our mountains. He told us that while every man he met was a colonel who was not a judge, yet from Stockton up "*the* Colonel" meant Mr. Frémont—hence the localism repeated here.

streets they were familiar with. A superb Shakespeare, also illustrated, gave more than enough for English study, but there were also many of the English classics, and, what fascinated us, works on medical jurisprudence, and selected cases of circumstantial evidence. From these I would read ahead—I being pilotengine for my young train—and put limits for their reading on which we would talk together after.

We were only three, but our differing ages and countries made variety in thinking. An English friend had asked us to let his son, a delightful lad of seventeen, go with us for the few months we were to be absent from New York—the boy had outgrown his strength and was ordered travel and rest. My daughter was much younger, but accustomed to grown-up minds, as she had never been sent from home. These two followed eagerly and intelligently my hap-hazard lead and we all found real pleasure in it. And the tall young Douglas became steadily stronger and more boyish. I felt very responsible for the health of this precious eldest son, and we all grew attached to him for himself. I think a clean-natured, well-bred boy of a happy affectionate nature is a charming associate. All the more if he is, as a boy should be, full of healthy, bold explosive life.

This day we settled to our talk-lesson, but soon I noticed their hearts were not in it. And at luncheon their wholesome young appetites had failed them. The two little boys were also restless, for "Isaac wouldn't let them go out to play in the barn," and it was not possible for them to play out of doors during the fierce heat of the day.

It does not take long for the mind to group little things into proofs of some larger disturbance. Too soon I had to know that that early morning messenger was a herald of danger—of almost inevitable conflict and loss of life.

It is too long to explain here; but a bad local decision had lately been made by the State Court which gave to all persons the right to enter and hold any "unoccupied" mining claim or mine. This was so worded (and so intended) that the large body of those who had not bought and regularly worked such property could seize and legally hold the property of those who had, "if unoccupied." All the trouble arose from the construction of that word, "unoccupied." A smaller miner working alone would go to his dinner, and immediately men watching for the chance would seize and hold against him his lawful property.

These outsiders had organized into a League and were bound to help one another. Property-holders, surprised by such a construction, were not ready on their side with organized resistance. And the chief Judge[2] was openly in sympathy with this League.

Now Americans much prefer to live peaceably, but they will not give up their rights. If it comes to trying force you know their record as a fighting nation is made. Consequently in a brief time there were over fifty cases entered for trial where men had been killed or had to kill others in defense of their rights.

We had in California at this time a bad element of foreigners. It was believed the English authorities over the convict settlements of Australia did not "take notice" of the shiploads of escaping convicts crowding into California.

We had enough bad Americans, but they, being Americans, had not that long inheritance of want and crime known to older countries. These criminal outcasts, exulting in their escape from Botany Bay and Sydney, finding themselves in such thinly scattered and far-apart settlements without any visible officers of the law, felt free to follow every bad impulse. Many honest but misled men were at first in this League, men who believed all the lands free because we had bought the country and they were told Mexican titles were of no value and only actual settlers could hold lands and mines. To this ignorant though honest body came the elements which only cared for this legalized chance at plunder. The Arabs say "A court of law is not a court of justice": justice would settle this question properly, but the letter of this law was against justice.

On our place was a fairly orderly, industrious and prospering people in settlements of small towns and mining camps scattered over a dozen miles of mountain country, isolated in sudden emergencies. And our nearest large town and first telegraph was eighty miles away, at Stockton on the Bay of San Francisco.

The invading party numbered over a hundred. They came from Hornitas, a place of evil fame just below our mountains—a gambling nest such as Bret Harte tells of—a place "where everything that loathes the law" found congenial soil and flourished."

These men announced we should get no help from outside, for they would let no messenger go through; they had guarded every ford and pass, and had their marksmen-watchmen out everywhere. Our local sheriff actually declined to call out a posse. "No use," he said; for the "Hornitas crowd" were the terror of our neighborhood. They had bribed the night watchman to leave free to them these mines; a group of three close together on a high

2. California Chief Justice David S. Terry.—J.B.F.

spur of the mountains, which then had been carefully worked for four years, chiefly by experienced Cornish miners brought over by the Colonel.

You must know it is very dangerous to displace the "shoring" —the timbers that protect sides and roof of the long tunnels— but the Hornitas men cared nothing for the future of the mine; no picks and slow work for them. They put in shallow blasts wherever gold showed and were already ravaging the Black Drift.

In the two other mines luckily six of our men had been still at work, so that the League could not enter them even under its own unjust law. This angered them, and they determined to starve these miners out and so compel the "unoccupied" state they required in order to take possession.

Remember that this property had been bought, paid for, and worked for years under a United States patent.

These three mines opened out high up the precipitous mountainside, close together, on a small space leveled out to receive the "dump" and allow the ox-wagons to load and turn easily; they were reached only by one road (with a few turn-outs) cut into the face of the mountain. Sixteen hundred feet below was a ravine opening to the Merced River where were the mills with waterpower. The opposite mountain rose so near and so high that it was always dark down below in the deep, deep ravine with its jagged walls of rocks and stunted shrubs. Its appropriate name was Hell's Hollow. A fall into it was death. Bad ground for a fight, you see.

Yet on this confined space were gathered the men of the League; and for our side, only the Colonel and a few of our friends. Knowing how easily a word can kindle into wrath ill-meaning and unreasoning people he preferred to be almost alone. It was hard to hear the shouts and blasts in the Black Drift and know the good work of years was being endangered; but tomorrow did not exist for the spoilers, and the day was theirs. The League, baffled by the fact of six men in the other two mines (which connected) gave answering shouts, and swore they would starve out our faithful men who steadily refused to surrender the mines.

The captain of the miners was one of the six, an excellent quiet American who had a slim little bright wife from Virginia and a brood of small children who played like chamois on the sharp mountain back of their cottage near the mines. This little woman bore the waiting and the threats quietly and bravely; doing her part to "help the Colonel."

Above all Mr. Frémont wished to prevent violence—the first shot would have brought out all the delayed evil of one side, all the restrained indignation of the other. Once begun it would have been a deadly contest—not only at the mines, but followed up wherever there was plunder to find or a friend to be avenged.

He hoped that by quietly talking with them, by keeping off new sources of dispute, above all by keeping away drink from them they would, as there were Americans among them, come to a better mind and see that violence would not ultimately profit them. Our men who had rapidly held a council with him (while I was asleep!) saw this necessity for silence and forbearance and seconded him in every way. They guarded the road and the only path anything but a goat could move on, leading along from the village to the mines; the enemy had cut off communication from the mines, and our men claimed it fair play to cut off communication to the mines. So the danger from whiskey was kept back, in spite of various efforts to get it through.

An express through to Stockton to rouse good friends there to telegraph to the Governor for State aid, as the sheriff refused to do his duty, had been immediately attempted and as immediately stopped by the guards of the League. They on their side were prepared for all moves. As the Colonel had to be with his men at the mines, and no communication was allowed between them and the village or the steam-mill, he had to leave this and all else to the care of those managing the works—chiefly two very unusually well-qualified men, the book-keeper being one; a man whose silence was as proverbial as his cool courage and high honor. He was to keep a lookout for us also.

Our two brave, faithful colored men, Isaac and Lee, were our guard—this duty the Colonel trusted to them—and as strange horsemen were riding all around firing off pistols, the little boys too were not to leave the house. This arranged rapidly, in early dawn—while I slept—he was off to the mines.

When a danger is safely over, only those who were through its agony of suspense can realize what vague horrors beset the mind. The year before I had been in Paris during the time of the Indian mutiny; its hideous facts filled the public papers, and we had some English friends in such distress as can never be forgotten. In this League were some elements as evil and cruel as the Sepoys. Our men had been ordered what to do for us if, as was threatened, the house was burned and ourselves attacked. Death from a friendly hand was more kind than chances among such wild beasts as bad men become when intoxicated.

It seems unreal—impossible, that in my own country, in the

State for which my father and my husband had done so much, on our own ground and in our own home I and my young children should have to face such a condition. And have to bear it all so helplessly; without knowledge even of what was going on but three miles from us. The only certainties to give comfort were that no firing had been heard, and no whiskey allowed to get through.

Towards evening the policy of moderation and patience began to tell. Standing under a sun of over a hundred degrees, with no space to move about and no food to eat, had tamed the enemy into offering a truce for the night. Doubts and disagreements were at work among them. The better men would not join in violence, without which they now saw they could not carry out their plan of holding these mines. They proposed to "sleep on it" and begin afresh next day, demanding everything remain as they left it.

But little Mrs. Caton rose against this. She said her husband should have food. She made her way through the packed crowd, a little creature but a great heart, carrying a big basket of provisions and—a revolver. Her finger was on the trigger as she pushed forward.

"I shoot the first man that hinders me. You wouldn't like to be shot by a woman! But I'll shoot to kill. You've just got to let me carry his supper in to Caton. You have your quarrel with the Colonel about mines and lands and you can fight that out with him. But I'm a poor woman that's got only my husband—and five children for him to work for. You sha'n' take his life for your quarrels! He's only doing his duty. He's been cap'n of these mines four years and he'll stand by them till the Colonel orders him out. And I stand by Caton. So let me pass."

And with her uplifted revolver waving like a fan towards one and then another, they fell back and let her enter the mine—some laughing, some praising her, some swearing at her. She carried not only food but ammunition; and three revolvers hung from her waist under her skirts. She "stood by Caton." Then the League set their watch at the mouths of the mines and returned to the village for the night.

The rush of relief at seeing the Colonel made me realize what I had been fearing—and it was all to begin again with morning!

He had to stand by his men on the spot. He felt it already a victory to have warded off action by discussion, to have carried them through a day without violence and without drinking. All we could do was not to distress him by showing our fears but to help him to go, quietly, and refreshed by sleep and home, to another day of chances. Then to wait—to wait with a brain growing hot and benumbed with one fixed terror!

If only we could get word to the Governor.

But our expresses had all been turned back and warned that any fresh attempt would be met by a rifle ball.

Then I was told what my two young people had done.

They had had many climbing walks up the mountain back of our house—many rides all about the country-side and with good glasses had studied out future rides on the eastern face of the mountain, from which uppermost narrow level the Yosemite Falls showed glittering and seemed near, though thirty miles distant. They knew dry creek beds and thickets of manzanita and chapparal which would effectually hide a horse carefully led up to and across the summit—then the rider could mount and make as good time as night and rough, unknown, untracked mountains allowed, down to the Merced River—following the river about eight miles up to a large mining camp where Isaac knew the miners—he had hunted and "prospected" all around about us for many years, and with Isaac's name as voucher and passport, there were men there who "would see him through" to Coulterville; Coulterville being a town and mining settlement about twenty miles to the northeast, and of a steady, law-abiding character.

Douglass had been refused permission to go in the early dawn with the Colonel—his friend's son must not be risked—but stay inactive he could not while danger pressed on us, and so the two thought up this move to the northeast while all the watching was directed west and south. With Isaac abetting, the best route had been studied out, and as dusk fell the dear boy had got off, leading my daughter's sure-footed mountain-bred mare "Ayah."[3] He was already far [away] when the Colonel got home. I had not been told, for I could not have consented.

But we both felt deeply his devotion to us.

And it was another strength for Mr. Frémont, to hope that by way of Coulterville a messenger could get off without suspicion; a day's hard riding to Stockton "eighty miles away"; the brief delay for the Governor's answer—then the swift ride back with announcement of his support. Fresh horses everywhere were only a matter of money; all lay in the success of the first messenger getting away from our place and the besieging League.

The safe hours of kindly night went all too fast. With the

3. The Hindoo name for bearer or nurse: *Little Henry and his Bearer* was a Sunday-school classic in old days.—J.B.F.

rising of the sun we were again left to watch and fear; with now the added anxiety for Douglass.

From one window was a long stretch of view, past the steam-mill and up the mountain-side to where a sharp bend in the road from the mines was clearly defined, its yellowish level and the side-cut glaring out in the hot sunshine. Often, at the usual hour for the return from the mines, the little boys vied in watching that point where just one flash of the swift horse showed back against the sunset sky, and the level tawny road then was lost in the chapparal, hiding the descent into the valley; "Father's coming! I saw him first!" was the glad cry.

Now, at this window, with sight and feeling concentrated on the bend of the road, I stayed while the dreadful time moved slowly on. Isaac permitted my little men to comfort themselves by climbing into a thick-leaved oak, where they obeyed the order for silence—the hush of dread was on us all.

While we watched the mountain-road a new danger came up from the village.

A note was brought from there by a man Isaac knew to be a friend—no other would have ventured into our inclosure while he and his dog "Rowdy" kept watch and ward—and with the note was a verbal message that "the answer must be at Bates Tavern by sundown."

It was addressed to me, and informed me that at a meeting held at Bates Tavern the night before it had been "Resolved" that I should be allowed twenty-four hours to leave the place—that an escort would see me across the mountain down to the plain—that no harm should be done to us and that I could take my children and my clothes. But that if I was not gone within the twenty-four hours the house would be burned and I must "take the consequences."

This was signed: "For all prisnt"

"Dennis O'Brien,
President."

Even in the first moment I felt pleased it was not an American name signing this document.

"They mean mischief," Isaac said. "They want to entice the Colonel away from the mines."

He was sorely angered and troubled. His Indian blood boiled for revengeful action, but Indian tactics made him submit—apparently—for we were at a woeful disadvantage. Myself and my young daughter, two little boys and the two good women who had come with us from home, with only Isaac and Lee and the dogs for guards; that was the whole garrison. That revenge would be sure and wide-spread was a comfort to Isaac—but revenge cannot restore.

Isaac learned there had been decided opposition to this move against the family, but the better men had gone to the mines.

Mr. O'Brien, President, and his faction remained at the tavern, and if they should grow wild from drinking the look out for us was bad. The near chance of meeting a grizzly bear had unnerved me, but a wild animal is a simple danger compared with the complicated horrors of a man brought down to animal nature and made furious by drink.

To gain time I sent word that an answer would be given them.

Then, back to my watch.

At least the brain had been stirred, and a tide of anger had displaced the benumbing fear.

And later in the day, not from mountain or village, but from the Indian encampment back of us in the hills came our dear English boy, looking fresh and leisurely as though just in from the usual ride.

"Douglax! Douglax!" shouted the boys (what does not the small boy see!) as they caught the first glimpse of his white turbaned head. An East Indian muslin "puggaree" wound round his hat had been agreed on as the signal of victory—and he sang out a cheery "all right!" as tired "Ayah" made for her stable.

Then, horse and man refreshed, we had details; the main facts of safety and success were so good we made him wait until he had eaten. Then, Isaac in the doorway, his gun between his knees and his dog at his feet, and Lee beside him, with the little boys and the good women listening, and his fellow-plotter serenely enjoying his success, we all heard his report.

He had started as soon as dusk set in, Isaac's directions and the stars guiding, following up the ravine where overhanging bushes hid "Ayah" as she very unwillingly was led up the mountain at her regular time for rest. After the crest was turned he could mount; then along shelving slopes with steep descents, to the river; keeping to it as well as giant bowlders and steep, projecting spurs of hills with rolling-stone-faces allowed, he came, towards midnight, to the bend and little meadow where cabins and tents and a smouldering fire showed he had reached the camp, which roused at the sound of his approach; but Isaac's name was the countersign and brought out the friend asked for. Instantly the news was given it was met by heartiest sympathy and action. Only the brief halt to saddle up, to offer the unfailing coffee, and he was off again; this time cheered by friendly companionship, and sure to lose no time as the way was well known to his comrade. This miner knew who to go to; and quickly two swift riders were off on their eighty-mile stretch—eighty miles of open plain but cut by deep rivers only one of which had a bridge, the rest only rope ferries. At these there was the risk of men watching on the side of the League.

Bret Harte has peopled this country with creations "founded on fact," doubtless—men with "a single virtue and a thousand faults" (fault is good), but to me the ferries of the Stanislaus and the Tuolumne, the lonely mining camps of the Merced and the remote mining towns tell a better story; of patient courage in work, and a brotherhood for maintaining order and the law—quick as the minute-men of our Revolution in united support of the right, and with a largeness of goodhumored generosity special to our far West life.

Coulterville had this stamp. They had lately raised there and equipped a uniformed Home Guard, to prevent disturbances and maintain order, and this body volunteered to march over at once, taking the nearer stage-road.

Before sunset they would be on the ground at the mines. By sunset our express to Stockton would be there; the telegrams to and from the Governor sent and answered, and return messengers would ride through the night so that another day would open upon the arm of the law outstretched in protection over our far-away mountain home.

Our book-keepers had given Douglass blank orders for all outlays throughout—but all would have gone well even without this, for everywhere we had struck the right kind of men—"the true vein." Men, who at every risk and sacrifice, in those early days built what was best in America into the very foundations of this empire of California; not amusing to read of as the Bret Harte characters, but the men who had home traditions and guarded them, and handed them down broader and stronger from fiery trials.

How we watched now for that horse at the turn of the road! How glad came the shout from the oak-tree—how blushing, yet proud and glad, was that refined English lad as we made him tell, himself, the modest brief story of his night ride, alone, with the stars for guide—how our chief relaxed into himself in this atmosphere of home love and support—all was good, too good for words to tell.

"They also serve who wait." The difficult waiting was almost over, and still violence was kept at bay. Now, the glad news that our expresses had gone through and were already on the return was spread abroad. It was the best—the only answer to Mr. O'Brien.

[With the half mad feeling of an officer who dressed in full uniform to go into battle, I told Isaac to put to the best open wagon the carriage horses, with their blue rosettes on their harness, and himself dressed up—while my French-woman gladly went with me.

[I put off my mourning and taking out an unused French dress of white muslin with lilac ribbons in the puffings and on the dress, a little bonnet of violet velvet and white lace in place of my wide black straw hat—I opened my wide parasol and told Isaac to drive to Bates Tavern in the village where the League had Headquarters. There I drew up and called Mr. Bates, a timid sort of publican.

[To him I gave the note of Mr. O'Brien and say there is "no answer."

[That what they demanded was against the law. 'You may come and kill us—we are but women and children and it will be easy—but *you cannot kill the law*.'

[And then I told them that while they guarded the south passes, our express had gone north and got through to Coulterville and sent all dispatches. That, by express, mule wagons had been rushing all day from Stockton . . . that the Coulterville guard was since daybreak on the march . . . and that their game was up.

[And then I said, "You can drive home Isaac," but I felt cold quivers running down my spine as we turned the large circle in front of these angry men. I fully expected to be shot in the back.][4]

During the night we heard angry voices of horsemen riding around, firing pistols, and otherwise exhaling disappointment and defiance. Bur our tired chief slept, and so did Douglass; while Isaac lying on the gallery by my window would say to me in his low cautious voice: "Don't you mind 'em—they're mad—but they're afraid of us now—we are bound to win now."

As we did. The better men refused to act longer with the disorder-loving faction.

---

4. So bold, courageous, and characteristically impulsive an act is described in this bracketed passage that it demands inclusion even though it did not appear in "Besieged" as first published. Two handwritten and one typed version of these paragraphs are in the Frémont Papers at the Bancroft Library. The quote herein is that dictated to Elizabeth B. Frémont by her mother in the final years of her life. Elizabeth and her collaborator further dramatized this episode in their *Recollections*.—S.S.

"When I go running next time I'll make sure first if we are after wild-duck or tame-duck," said an Arkansas man noted and feared as a reckless leader; he came to say to the Colonel that as he saw they were in the wrong, he wanted to stay on the place and would do hauling of quartz, "and help put down the Hornitas crowd if they stay fooling around where they've no business." This alliance was a great gain, and as effective in its way as the arrival of the fine Coulterville Guard.

Soon came the expresses, tired but triumphant. The Governor had telegraphed that the Marshall of the State would start immediately with a force of five hundred men. That, if needed, he would come up himself, with all the force required to restore and maintain order. "Nye of Stockton"—Nye, whose great establishment of wagons and mules, and teamsters who could defend their convoys as well as drive their twelve- and twenty-mule teams, made the transportation before railroads—Nye was directed to send the arms and ammunition post-haste, and the troops the same. And behold our peaceful valley traversed by "prairie-schooners" filled with fighting men and munitions of war—all concentrating on our twelve-acre inclosure whose grass was sadly cut up thereby.

We had put up a big barn and a store-room my French cook always called *"le grocerie."* Supplies for months, and for undefined numbers of friendly visitors, were the necessity up there. These barrels and sacks and many tins and much glass were now piled on planks laid across barrels under the shade of oaks and giant pines (black pepper by the quart scattered on the planks to head off the ants). Our long French trunks and boxes of delicate clothing (the "clothes" I was to have safe with my children!) were just stacked under trees; the arms and ammunition were the precious things now, and had the best accommodations, while their guard bivouacked around and found the big hay loft not a bad sleeping place—three years later how many a cherished son and husband would have been thankful for such quarters!

Of course there were lingering threats and more or less disorder, but it retreated into more congenial quarters. And in a brief time all was again safely back in smooth working order; even the Black Drift. For of what use was the mine when they could not carry off or crush the ore? Not at our mills—nor in our wagons—nor on the long private road belonging with the works. So the trouble all vanished like a bad dream. But it had developed far more good than evil; and organized the good against the evil.

The heat and the nervous strain had told against me and as Mr. Frémont had to go to San Francisco on business, he took us all with him. A friend "going East" left us his house with its beautiful garden and grounds, and in that reviving sea air and with "nothing to make us afraid" I ought to have got well. Instead of that I slipped into a nervous fever—a horrid blur of bad men shouting—of children stolen—of a riderless horse tearing round the bend and bolting into the stable, and all such horrors. Poor Douglass came in to say good-by when his steamer was to leave and I could only connect it with his ride for the relief and forbid his going. He was a distinguished and important man when I saw him next, at his own charming country house in England, with wife and children about him.

As everything ends—*"tout passe"*—I got well, and refused out-and-out to stay in San Francisco. As we had to remain until the unjust law was repealed[5] and that would require a year, I went back to the mountains "to stand by Caton."

To wind up more fully, the year brought round poetical justice; for the judge whose known prejudices caused the expression of this "law" caused also his own downfall by an act of violence. "Hoist by his own petard" he had to fly for life from outraged public feeling. The new election gave us a judge who respected justice as well as law.

All the same, our three-months summer tour had to stretch into two-years residence; in a country more remote, more isolated, more without any resources familiar to me than I should have chosen, but for all that full of interest and lasting usefulness, and teaching me effectually what one can do, and what one can do without.

5. By Judge Stephen J. Field—J.B.F.

Memoir

ONCE THE FOCUS is off the author onto others, the chief question becomes how the writer got the information. Shifts from first to third person correlate with different roles the writer may play as an informant. These roles expand in time and space as the informant tries to "cover" more.

If I am at the center of what happened, as for autobiography, I presumably have access to all I need to know, since I write as insider. If I was not at the center of the experience, I write in some degree as an outsider. If I was not even a participant but only an observer, I played only an eyewitness role. That is still firsthand in one sense, but to know about the experience as a participant, I must ask a participant what it felt like. Let's call this informant role *confidant*. The participant confides the central experience to me, and I put this knowledge together with what I learned as eyewitness. This gives an inside-outside understanding.

But what about general circumstances and conditions framing or underlying the central events, ignorance of which makes full and accurate understanding impossible? To the other reporter roles we must add a final one—what I will call the *chorus* role, drawing the term from Greek drama. A chorus is the community constituting the human environment of the principals in some action. They know the background and general circumstances that form the context of the events and of the participants. They also represent the local ethos or set of values and framework of reference.

Now, these roles all apply to the time of the events, not to the time of the telling, when the reporter can resort only to some amalgamated recollection of what he or she learned through such roles. Thus the composition of Recollection is limited by the role or roles one was able to play at the time of the events as well as by how much one actually remembers of what one originally knew. The fiction writer may make up what he or she does not know, but the nonfiction writer inevitably composes with parameters set by certain informant roles and the automatic filing system of the memory. In other words, important options of composing have already been played well before starting to pen a recollection.

These roles can be usefully translated into distances in time and space or psychological vantage points. Were you the one it happened to (in the shoes of the participant)? If not, were you there at all (as eyewitness)? Were you "close" enough to the participant, in all senses, to act as confidant? Were you a member of the chorus? Answers to these questions determine whether the writer was participant or observer; the kind of writing, autobiography or memoir; the sort of information the writer could supply as memoirist.

Let's note that as the number of roles—means of coverage—increases, the memoir represents a greater abstracting job. Suppose one has total access. Eyewitness information is sensory only. Confidant adds to this the subjective account of the participant. And chorus adds to these the necessary background. Often the memoirist played only one role at the time and hence has memories by only that access—only what the bystander could see or what a principal confided or only what everyone knew in common. In filling out facts, this synthesizing of sources entails more comprehensive abstracting, since one must do justice to each of the sources one is amalgamating. (In fiction, the actual author *chooses*, according to intent, to fabricate a role for the narrator, such as a memoirist like Nick in *The Great Gatsby*, who is a member of a chorus, an occasional confidant of Gatsby, and frequent eyewitness.)

Therese Neumann,
the Catholic Stigmatist

Paramahansa Yogananda

from *Autobiography of a Yogi,* 1946

Autobiography and memoir frequently alternate in the same book, as in the one from which the following memoir is taken. The title of the excerpted chapter clearly indicates its main subject. It is for excellent reasons that a retrospective author should flick emphasis back and forth between himself and others. We are hard put to know where our own life begins and others' lives end, so close is the interplay between one individual and others. Much of any life story is made up of relationships, identities, and interactions that partake of different lives at once. Writing can only do justice to this oneness.

Yogananda was an unusual reporter and just right to do a memoir of Therese Neumann, for he could play an informant role that, alas, is too rare as yet to include in a list of reporting roles as common as eyewitness, confidant, and chorus (roles he also played in this account).

I sailed from New York on June 9, 1935, on the *Europa.* Two students accompanied me: my secretary, Mr. C. Richard Wright, and an elderly lady from Cincinnati, Miss Ettie Bletch. We enjoyed the days of ocean peace, a welcome contrast to the past hundred weeks. Our period of leisure was short-lived; the speed of modern boats has some regrettable features!

Like any other group of inquisitive tourists, we walked about the huge and ancient city of London. On the day following my arrival I was invited to address a large meeting in Caxton Hall, at which I was introduced to the London audience by Sir Francis Younghusband.

Our party spent a pleasant day as guests of Sir Harry Lauder at his estate in Scotland. A few days later our little group crossed the English Channel to the continent, for I wanted to make a pilgrimage to Bavaria. This would be my only chance, I felt, to visit the great Catholic mystic, Therese Neumann of Konnersreuth.

Years earlier I had read an amazing account of Therese. Information given in the article was as follows:

(1) Therese, born on Good Friday in 1898, was injured in an accident at the age of twenty; she became blind and paralyzed.

(2) She miraculously regained her sight in 1923 through prayers to St. Therese of Lisieux, "The Little Flower." Later Therese Neumann's limbs were instantaneously healed.

(3) From 1923 onward, Therese has abstained completely from food and drink, except for the daily swallowing of one small consecrated wafer.

(4) The stigmata, sacred wounds of Christ, appeared in 1926 on Therese's head, breast, hands, and feet. Every Friday* she experiences the Passion of Christ, suffering in her own body all his historic agonies.

(5) Knowing ordinarily only the simple German of her village, during her Friday trances Therese utters phrases which scholars have identified as ancient Aramaic. At appropriate times in her vision, she speaks Hebrew or Greek.

(6) By ecclesiastical permission, Therese has several times been under close scientific observation. Dr. Fritz Gerlick, editor of a Protestant German newspaper, went to Konnersreuth to "expose the Catholic fraud," but ended up by reverently writing her biography.

As always, whether in East or West, I was eager to meet a saint. I rejoiced as our little party entered, on July 16th, the quaint village of Konnersreuth. The Bavarian peasants exhibited lively interest in our Ford automobile (brought with us from America) and its assorted group—an American young man, an elderly lady, and an olive-hued Oriental with long hair tucked under his coat collar.

Therese's little cottage, clean and neat, with geraniums bloom-

---

*Since the war years, Therese has not experienced the Passion every Friday but only on certain holy days of the year. Books on her life are *Therese Neumann: A Stigmatist of Our Day*, and *Further Chronicles of Therese Neumann*, both by Friedrich Ritter von Lama; and *The Story of Therese Neumann*, by A. P. Schimberg (1947); all published by Bruce Pub. Co., Milwaukee, Wisconsin; and *Therese Neumann*, by Johannes Steiner, published by Alba House, Staten Island, N.Y.

ing by a primitive well, was alas! silently closed. The neighbors, and even the village postman who passed by, could give us no information. Rain began to fall; my companions suggested that we leave.

"No," I said stubbornly. "I will stay here until I find some clue leading to Therese."

Two hours later we were still sitting in our car amidst the dismal rain. "Lord," I sighed complainingly, "why didst Thou lead me here if she has disappeared?"

An English-speaking man halted beside us, politely offering his aid.

"I don't know for certain where Therese is," he said, "but she often visits at the home of Professor Franz Wutz, a teacher of foreign languages at the University of Eichstatt, eighty miles from here."

The following morning our party motored to the quiet town of Eichstatt. Dr. Wutz greeted us cordially at his home; "Yes, Therese is here." He sent her word of the visitors. A messenger soon appeared with her reply:

"Though the bishop has asked me to see no one without his permission, I will receive the man of God from India."

Deeply touched at these words, I followed Dr. Wutz upstairs to the sitting room. Therese entered immediately, radiating an aura of peace and joy. She wore a black gown and spotless white headdress. Although her age was thirty-seven at this time, she seemed much younger; possessing indeed a childlike freshness and charm. Healthy, well-formed, rosy-cheeked, and cheerful, this is the saint who does not eat!

Therese greeted me with a very gentle handshaking. We beamed in silent communion, each knowing the other to be a lover of God.

Dr. Wutz kindly offered to serve as interpreter. As we seated ourselves, I noticed that Therese was glancing at me with naive curiosity; evidently Hindus had been rare in Bavaria.

"Don't you eat anything?" I wanted to hear the answer from her own lips.

"No, except a Host* at six o'clock each morning."

"How large is the Host?"

"It is paper-thin, the size of a small coin." She added, "I take it for sacramental reasons; if it is unconsecrated, I am unable to swallow it."

*A Eucharistic flour-wafer.

"Certainly you could not have lived on that, for twelve whole years?"

"I live by God's light."

How simple her reply, how Einsteinian!

"I see you realize that energy flows to your body from the ether, sun, and the air."

A swift smile broke over her face. "I am so happy to know you understand how I live."

"Your sacred life is a daily demonstration of the truth uttered by Christ: 'Man shall not live by bread alone, but by every word that proceedeth out of the mouth of God.' "*

Again she showed joy at my explanation. "It is indeed so. One of the reasons I am here on earth today is to prove that man can live by God's invisible light, and not by food only."

"Can you teach others how to live without food?"

She appeared a trifle shocked. "I cannot do that; God does not wish it."

As my gaze fell on her strong, graceful hands, Therese showed me a square, freshly healed wound on the back of each hand. On the palm of each hand, she pointed out a smaller, crescent-shaped wound, freshly healed. Each wound went straight through the hand. The sight brought to me a distinct recollection of the large square iron nails with crescent-tipped ends that are still used in the East but that I do not recall having seen in the West.

The saint told me something of her weekly trances. "As a helpless onlooker, I observe the whole Passion of Christ." Each week, from Thursday midnight until Friday afternoon at one o'clock, her wounds open and bleed; she loses ten pounds of her ordinary 121-pound weight. Suffering intensely in her sympa-

---

Matthew 4:4. Man's body battery is not sustained by gross food (bread) alone, but by the vibratory cosmic energy (word, or *Aum*). The invisible power flows into the human body through the gate of the medulla oblongata. This sixth bodily center is located at the back of the neck at the top of the five spinal *chakras* (Sanskrit for "wheels" or centers of radiating life forcee).

The medulla, the principal entrance for the body's supply of universal life energy (*Aum*) is directly connected by polarity with the Christ Consciousness center (*Kutastha*) in the single eye between the eyebrows; the seat of man's power of will. Cosmic energy is then stored up in the seventh center, in the brain, as a reservoir of infinite potentialities (mentioned in the *Vedas* as the "thousand-petaled lotus of light"). The Bible refers to *Aum* as the Holy Ghost or invisible life force that divinely upholds all creation. "What? know ye not that your body is the temple of the Holy Ghost which is in you, which ye have of God, and ye are not your own?'"—*I Corinthians* 6:19

thetic love, Therese yet looks forward joyously to these weekly visions of her Lord.

I realized at once that her strange life is intended by God to reassure all Christians of the historical authenticity of Jesus' life and crucifixion as recorded in the New Testament, and to display dramatically the ever living bond between the Galilean Master and his devotees.

Professor Wutz related some of his experiences with the saint.

"A group of us, including Therese, often travel for days on sight-seeing trips in Germany," he told me. "It is a striking contrast—Therese eats nothing; the rest of us have three meals a day. She remains as fresh as a rose, untouched by fatigue. Whenever the rest of us get hungry and look for wayside inns, Therese laughs merrily."

The professor added some interesting physiological details: "Because Therese takes no food, her stomach has shrunk. She has no excretions, but her perspiration glands function; her skin is alwys soft and firm."

At the time of parting, I expressed to Therese my desire to be present at her trance.

"Yes, please come to Konnersreuth next Friday," she said graciously. "The bishop will give you a permit. I am very happy you sought me out in Eichstatt."

Therese shook hands gently, many times, and walked with our party to the gate. Mr. Wright turned on the automobile radio; the saint examined it with little enthusiastic chuckles. Such a large crowd of youngsters gathered that Therese retreated into the house. We saw her at a window, where she peered at us, childlike, waving her hand.

From a conversation the next day with two of Therese's brothers, very kind and amiable, we learned that the saint sleeps only one or two hours at night. In spite of the many wounds in her body, she is active and full of energy. She loves birds, looks after an aquarium of fish, and works often in her garden. Her correspondence is large; Catholic devotees write her for prayers and healing blessings. Many seekers have been cured through her of serious diseases.

Her brother Ferdinand, about twenty-three, explained that Therese has the power, through prayer, of working out on her own body the ailments of others. The saint's abstinence from food dates from a time when she prayed that the throat disease of a young man of her parish, then preparing to enter holy orders, be transferred to her own throat.

On Thursday afternoon our party drove to the home of the

bishop, who looked at my flowing locks with some surprise. He readily wrote out the necessary permit. There was no fee; the rule made by the Church is simply to protect Therese from the onrush of casual tourists, who in previous years had flocked by thousands to Konnersreuth on Fridays.

We arrived in the village on Friday morning about nine-thirty. I noticed that Therese's little cottage possesses a glass-roofed section to afford her plenty of light. We were glad to see the doors no longer closed, but wide open in hospitable cheer. We joined a line of about twenty visitors, each carrying a permit. Many had come from great distances to view the mystic trance.

Therese had passed my first test at the professor's house by her intuitive knowledge that I wanted to see her for spiritual reasons, and not just to satisfy a passing curiosity.

My second test was connected with the fact that, just before I went upstairs to her room, I put myself into a yogic trance state in order to attain telepathic and televisional rapport with her. I entered her chamber, filled with visitors; she was lying in a white robe on the bed. With Mr. Wright close behind me, I halted just inside the threshold, awestruck at a strange and most frightful spectacle.

Blood flowed thinly and continuously in an inch-wide stream from Therese's lower eyelids. Her gaze was focused upward on the spiritual eye within the central forehead. The cloth wrapped around her head was drenched in blood from the stigmata wounds of the Crown of Thorns. The white garment was redly splotched over her heart from the wound in her side at the spot where Christ's body, long ages ago, had suffered the final indignity of the soldier's spear thrust.

Therese's hands were extended in a gesture maternal, pleading; her face wore an expression both tortured and divine. She appeared thinner and was subtly changed in many inner and outer ways. Murmuring words in a foreign tongue, she spoke with slightly quivering lips to persons who were visible to her superconscious sight.

As I was in attunement with her, I began to see the scenes of her vision. She was watching Jesus as he carried the timbers of the Cross amid the jeering multitude.* Suddenly she lifted her head in consternation: the Lord had fallen under the cruel weight.

*During the hours preceding my arrival, Therese had already passed through many visions of the closing days % Christ's life. Her entrancement usually starts with scenes of the events that followed the Last Supper and ends with Jesus' death on the Cross; or, occasionally, with his entombment.

The vision disappeared. In the exhaustion of fervid pity, Therese sank heavily against her pillow.

At this moment I heard a loud thud behind me. Turning my head for a second, I saw two men carrying out a prostrate body. But because I was coming out of the deep superconscious state, I did not immediately recognize the fallen person. Again I fixed my eyes on Therese's face, deathly pale under the rivulets of blood, but now calm, radiating purity and holiness. I glanced behind me later and saw Mr. Wright standing with his hand against his cheek, from which blood was trickling.

"Dick," I inquired anxiously, "were you the one who fell?"

"Yes, I fainted at the terrifying spectacle."

"Well," I said consolingly, "you are brave to return and look upon the sight again."

Remembering the patiently waiting line of pilgrims, Mr. Wright and I silently bade farewell to Therese and left her sacred presence.*

The Singers
Ivan Turgenev
from *A Sportsman's Notebook,* 1852

We move from she *to* they. *The title again indicates the focus—in this case, on the third person plural. Throughout most of* A Sportsman's Notebook *(or* Hunter's Sketchbook*), Turgenev narrates mainly as an observer, with a remarkable fusion of factual objectivity and atmospheric poetry. A century before the New Journalism came up with "faction," Turgenev was employing in his accounts such fictional techniques as verbatim dialog and the*

---

*An INS news dispatch from Germany, dated March 26, 1948, reported: "A German peasant woman lay on her cot this Good Friday; her head, hands, and shoulders blood-marked where Christ's body had bled from the nails of the Cross and the Crown of Thorns. Thousands of awe-filled Germans and Americans filed silently past the cottage bed of Therese Neumann."

The great stigmatist died in Konnersreuth on September 18, 1962. *(Publisher's Note)*

telling descriptive detail to bring alive what he had witnessed as
a "hunter" looking for "game."

The small village of Kolotovka, which once belonged to a lady known in the neighbourhood as Fidget from her bold and spirited ways (her real name is not recorded) but is now owned by some German or other from Petersburg, lies on the slope of a bare hill, cleft from top to bottom by a fearsome ravine, which, yawning like an abyss, winds its hollow, eroded way along the very middle of the village street and, worse than any river (for a river could at least be bridged), divides the unfortunate hamlet into two. A few lean willows droop timidly along its sandy sides; at the bottom, which is dry and copper-yellow, lie huge flag-stones of shale. A cheerless sight, there's no denying—but nevertheless the road to Kolotovka is well-known to all the people of the neighbourhood: they use it frequently and as a matter of course.

Right at the top of the ravine, a few paces off the spot where it begins as a narrow crevice, stands a small square cabin, on its own, apart from the others. It is thatched with straw and has a chimney; a single window, like a watchful eye, looks towards the ravine, and on winter evenings, lit up from within, can be seen from afar through the dull frost-haze and, for many a peasant on his way, shines out like a guiding star. Over the door of the cabin is nailed a little blue board; the cabin is a pot-house, and goes by the name of the"Snug Nook." It is a pot-house where in all probability drinks are sold no cheaper than the fixed price, but it is much better attended than any other establishment of the same sort in the neighbourhood. The reason for this is the tapster, Nikolai Ivanich.

Nikolai Ivanich was once a lithe, curly-headed, ruddy peasant lad, but is now an extremely stout, already grizzled man, with a face deep in fat, eyes of a sly benevolence, and a greasy forehead criss-crossed with a web of wrinkles. He has lived at Kolotovka for more than twenty years. Nikolai is a man of sagacity and resource, as most tapsters are. Without any special amiability or talkativeness, he has the knack of attracting and holding customers, who somehow find it entertaining to sit in front of his counter, under the calm, hospitable, but watchful eye of their phlegmatic host. He has plenty of common sense; he is well acquainted with the ways of landowner, peasant and townsman; in difficult situations he can give shrewd advice, but, like the cautious egoist that he is, he prefers to stay on the sideline and goes no further than a vague hint, uttered as if without the least purpose, to guide his clients—and then only his favourite clients—in the way of truth. He knows what he is talking about on every subject of importance or interest to the Russian male: horses and cattle, timber, bricks, crockery, textiles and leather, singing and dancing. When he has no custom, he is in the habit of sitting like a sack on the ground in front of the door of his cabin, his thin legs tucked up beneath him, swapping pleasantries with every passer-by. He has seen plenty in his time, has outlived more than a dozen of the lesser gentry who used to look in on him for a drop of "distilled," knows everything that happens for a hundred versts around, never lets on, never shows so much as in his look that he knows what even the most penetrating police officer fails to suspect. He simply keeps mum, chuckles, and busies himself with the glasses. The neighbours respect him deeply: His Excellency Mr. Shcherepetenko, the leading magnate of the district, bows to him affably every time he passes his abode. Nikolai Ivanich is a man of influence: he forced a well-known horse-thief to return a horse stolen from someone of his acquaintance; he made the peasants of a neighbouring village listen to reason when they had refused to accept a new factor, and so on. Incidentally, it mustn't be supposed that he did this from love of fair play, from any zeal for his neighbours' interest; no, he is simply at pains to avert anything that might in any way disturb his own peace. Nikolai Ivanich is married and has children. His wife, a brisk, sharp-nosed, quick-eyed townswoman, has lately put on a good deal of weight, just like her husband. He relies on her absolutely, and the money is locked up in her charge. The noisily-drunk hold her in awe; she dislikes them; there is no profit from them, only a lot of noise; the silent and sullen ones are closer to her heart. Nikolai's children are still small. The first ones all died, but the survivors resemble their parents; it is a pleasure to look at these healthy children with their clever little faces.

It was an unbearably sultry July day, when I trudged slowly, accompanied by my dog, up the Kolotovka ravine in the direction of the "Snug Nook" pot-house. The sun was blazing away in the sky with a kind of fury; it was mercilessly, bakingly hot; the air was absolutely saturated with choking dust. Glossy rooks and crows, with gaping beaks, looked piteously at the passer-by, as if to beg his sympathy; only the sparrows were undistressed and, fluffing out their feathers, twittered and scuffled about the fences even more actively than usual, or flew up from the dusty road in a flock, or hovered in grey clouds over the green hemp-yards. I was tortured by thirst. There was no water at hand: at Kolotovka, as in many other steppe-villages, in the absence of springs and wells, the peasants drink a sort of liquid filth from a pond . . . But who would give the name of water to this repulsive draught? I had it in mind to ask Nikolai Ivanich for a glass of beer or kvass.

It has to be admitted that at no season of the year does Kolotovka present a cheering spectacle; but it arouses a particularly mournful emotion when the blazing sun of July rains its pitiless rays on the tumbledown brown roofs, the deep ravine, the parched, dusty common-land, on which some thin, long-legged chickens are roaming despondently, and the shack of grey aspen-wood with holes for windows, a remnant of the former manor house, grown over with nettles, weeds and wormwood, and the pond, covered with goose-feathers, black, molten-looking, fringed with half-dried mud, and the side-ways listing dam, near which, on the fine-ground, cinder-like earth, sheep, breathless and sneezing from the heat, crowd lugubriously together and with a dismal patience hang their heads as low as can be, as if waiting for the moment when the unbearable sultriness will finally pass. With exhausted steps I was at last nearing Nikolai Ivanich's place, exciting in children the usual amazement, expressed in intense and inane stares, and in dogs the usual indignation, voiced in such hoarse and savage barking that all their insides seemed to be torn loose, afterwards subsiding into a fit of coughing and choking, when suddenly, on the threshold of the pot-house, there appeared a tall man, capless, in a frieze overcoat held below the waist with a blue belt. He had the look of a house-serf; thick grey hair burst out untidily above his dry wrinkled face. He was calling somebody and making vigorous gestures with his arms, which were clearly swinging out much farther than he intended. It was evident that he had already had a drop.

"Come on, come *on!*" he stuttered, raising his thick eyebrows with an effort. "Come on, Blinker, come on! Why, man, you're simply crawling. It isn't right, man. They're waiting for you, and you're just crawling . . . Come on!"

"All right, all right," came a jarring voice, and, from behind the cabin to the right, a short, stout, lame fellow appeared. He wore quite a neat cloth coat, with only one sleeve on; a high, pointed hat, rammed straight down over his brows, gave his podgy, round face a sly, mocking look. His little yellow eyes fairly darted around; a contained, forced smile never left his thin lips, and his long sharp nose stuck jauntily out ahead like a rudder. "I'm coming, my friend," he went on, limping in the direction of the drinking establishment. "What are you calling me for? . . . Who's waiting for me?"

"What am I calling you for?" rejoined the man in the frieze coat, reproachfully. "You're a strange one, Blinker: you're called to the pot-house, and yet you ask: what for? There's all kind of good folk waiting for you: Yasha the Turk, and Wild Master, and the huckster from Zhizdra. Yasha and the huckster have made a bet: they've wagered a quart of beer to see which wins, that is, sings best . . . d'you see?"

"Yasha's going to sing?" said the man nicknamed Blinker, with animation. "You're not lying, Muddlehead?"

"I'm not," answered Muddlehead with dignity. "It's you that's the liar. Of course he's going to sing, if he's made a bet, you lady-bird, you twister, you, Blinker!"

"Well, let's go, you ninny," rejoined Blinker.

"Well, kiss me at last, joy of my heart," stammered Muddlehead, flinging his arms out wide.

"You great milk-sop," replied Blinker, contemptuously elbowing him aside, and they both stooped and went in through the low doorway. The conversation I'd heard excited my keen curiosity. More than once rumours had reached me of Yasha the Turk, as being the best singer in the neighbourhood, and now an opportunity had suddenly presented itself to hear him in competition with another master. I quickened my pace and entered the establishment.

Probably not many of my readers have had occasion to look inside a country pot-house—but we sportsmen, there's nowhere we don't go. The arrangement of these pot-houses is remarkably simple. They usually consist of a dark entrance-passage and a room divided in two by a partition, behind which none of the customers has the right to go. Cut in the partition, above a broad oak table, is a large longitudinal aperture. On this table or counter the drink is sold. Sealed flasks of different measures stand in a row on shelves immediately opposite the aperture. In the front part of the cabin, the part at the disposal of customers, are benches, two or three empty barrels, and a corner table. Country pot-houses are for the most part pretty dark and you hardly ever see on their log walls any of those brightly coloured popular prints without which the ordinary peasant's cabin is seldom complete.

When I went into the "Snug Nook" pot-house a fairly numerous company was already assembled there.

Behind the counter, suitably enough, and filling almost the

whole width of the aperture, stood Nikolai Ivanich. In a gay cotton shirt, with an indolent smile on his chubby cheeks, he was pouring out two glasses of spirits with his podgy white hand for the two friends, Blinker and Muddlehead, who had just come in; behind him, in the corner near the window, could be seen his sharp-eyed wife. In the middle of the room stood Yasha the Turk, a lean, well-built man of twenty-three, dressed in a long-skirted blue nankeen coat. He had the appearance of a dashing young mechanic and looked as if his health was nothing to boast about. His sunken cheeks, great, restless grey eyes, straight nose with its fine, mobile nostrils, his wide-domed forehead with the pale blond curls thrust back from it, his bold but handsome and expressive lips—his whole face revealed an impressionable, passionate nature. He was in great excitement, blinking, breathing irregularly, his hands trembling as if with the fever—and indeed he had a fever, that sudden trembling fever which is so familiar to all who speak or sing in public. Beside him stood a man of about forty, broad-shouldered, with broad cheek-bones, and a low forehead, narrow Tartar eyes, a short flat nose, a square chin, and black, shiny, bristle-like hair. The expression of his face, which was swarthy with a leaden undertone, and especially of his full lips, might almost have been called ferocious if it had not been so calmly reflective. He hardly stirred, just looked slowly around like an ox from below the yoke. He wore a sort of shabby frock-coat with smooth copper buttons; an old black silk handkerchief swathed his massive neck. He was nicknamed "Wild Master." Right in front of him, on the bench below the icons, sat Yasha's competitor, the huckster from Zhizdra: a short, sturdy man of about thirty, pock-marked and curly-headed, with a blunt, upturned nose, lively brown eyes and a sparse beard. He was looking briskly round, with his hands tucked up beneath him, carelessly swinging and stamping his feet, which were clad in dandified boots with trimmings. He wore a thin new overcoat of grey cloth with a velvet collar, against which a strip of scarlet shirt, buttoned up tightly round his throat, stood out sharply. At a table in the opposite corner, to the right of the door, sat a peasant in a threadbare, greyish coat with an enormous hole at the shoulder. The sunlight fell in a fine, yellowish stream through the dusty panes of the two small windows and seemed unable to dispel the normal darkness of the room: every object was sparsely and patchily illuminated. Nevertheless, it was almost cool in the room and the feeling of stuffiness and sultriness fell from my shoulders like a burden the moment I crossed the threshold.

My arrival, I could see, at first rather confused Nikolai Ivanich's guests; but, observing that he bowed to me as to an acquaintance, they set their minds at rest and paid me no more attention. I ordered some beer and sat down in the corner next to the peasant in the torn coat.

"Well, then," sang out Muddlehead all of a sudden, after drinking a glass at one gulp, and accompanying his exclamation with those strange gestures of the arms without which he evidently never uttered a word. "What are we waiting for? It's time to begin, eh, Yasha?"

"Time to begin," repeated Nikolai Ivanich with approbation.

"Let's begin, if you like," said the huckster coolly, with a self-confident smile. "I'm ready."

"So am I," pronounced Yasha excitedly.

"Well, begin, lads, begin," squeaked Blinker.

But notwithstanding this unanimously expressed wish, neither of of them did begin; the huckster did not even rise from his bench—it was as if everyone was waiting for something to happen.

"Begin," said Wild Master sharply and with displeasure.

Yasha shivered. The huckster got up, tightened his belt and cleared his throat.

"Who's to begin?" he asked, with a slight change of voice, addressing himself to Wild Master, who was still standing motionless in the middle of the room, his thick legs widely planted, his powerful arms thrust almost to the elbow into the pockets of his trousers.

"You, huckster, you," murmured Muddlehead; "you, lad."

Wild Master gave him a sidelong look. Muddlehead squeaked faintly, faltered, looked away at the ceiling, wriggled his shoulders and fell silent.

"Draw for it," pronounced Wild Master with deliberation, "and set the quart out on the counter."

Nikolai stooped, groaned, fetched up a quart jug from the floor and set it on the table.

Wild Master looked at Yasha and said: "Well!"

Yasha rummaged in his pockets, found a two-copeck piece and marked it with his teeth. The huckster brought a new leather purse out from the skirt of his coat, slowly undid the strings, poured out a lot of small change into his hand and chose a new two-copeck piece. Muddlehead held out his battered hat with its loose and crumpled peak: Yasha and the huckster threw their coins into it.

"You choose," said Wild Master to Blinker.

Blinker grinned with self-satisfaction, took the hat in both hands and began to shake it up.

For a moment deep silence reigned; the coins chinked faintly against each other. I looked round attentively: every face expressed strained anticipation; even Wild Master had screwed up his eyes; even my neighbour, the peasant in the torn coat, had stuck out his head inquisitively. Binker put his hand into the hat and drew out the huckster's coin: there was a general sigh. Yasha flushed, and the huckster passed his hand through his hair.

"I *said* it was you," exclaimed Muddlehead, "I said so."

"Now, now, don't get all of a flutter," observed Wild Master contemptuously. "Begin," he continued, nodding to the huckster.

"What shall I sing?" asked the huckster, with rising excitement.

"Whatever you like, of course," rejoined Nikolai Ivanich, slowly folding his arms on his chest. "We can't tell you what to choose. Sing what you like; only sing it well; and then we'll judge as our conscience tells us."

"That's right—as our conscience tells us," repeated Muddlehead, and he licked the rim of his empty glass.

"Just let me clear my throat," said the huckster, fingering the collar of his coat.

"Now, don't waste time—begin!" said Wild Master decisively, and he looked down.

The huckster thought for a moment, shook his head and set off. Yasha stared at him with all his eyes. . . .

But before I proceed to describe the contest itself, it may be as well to say a few words about each of the personages in my story. The ways of some of them were already known to me when I met them in the "Snug Nook" pot-house; I found out about the rest subsequently.

To begin with Muddlehead. His real name was Evgraf Ivanov; but no one in the neighbourhood ever called him anything but Muddlehead, and he used the nickname in speaking of himself, so well did it fit him. And indeed it could not have been better suited to his insignificant, perpetually-worried expression. He was an umarried, drunken house-serf, whose master had long since despaired of him and who, having no duties and receiving not a farthing's wages, nevertheless found means of making merry every day at someone else's expense. He had many acquaintances who treated him to drinks and to tea, though they couldn't have said why, because, so far from being amusing in company, he fairly disgusted everyone with his witless chatter, his unbearable importunity, his feverish movements and his ceaseless unnatural laughter. He could neither sing nor dance; from birth he had never made a clever remark nor even a sensible one; he just muddled along and told any fib that came into his head—a regular Muddlehead! And, with it all, there wasn't a single drinking party for forty versts around at which his spindle-shanked figure failed to turn up among the guests, so used to him had people become, and so tolerant of his presence, as of an unavoidable mishap. True, they treated him contemptuously, but it was Wild Master alone who could put a curb on his crazy moods.

Blinker never left Muddlehead's side. He too was well-served by his nickname, although he didn't blink more than anyone else; but it is a plain truth that the Russians are past-masters at giving nicknames. In spite of my efforts to trace his past in every detail, I found—and so, probably, did many others—that there were dark passages in his career, places which, to use a bookish expression, were veiled in a thick mist of obscurity. I discovered only that he had once been coachman to an old, childless lady, had run away with the troika entrusted to his care, disappeared for a whole year, then, doubtless convinced by experience of the drawbacks and miseries of the vagrant's life, returned, now lame, thrown himself at his mistress's feet and, having expiated his offence by several years of exemplary conduct, had gradually won his way back into her favour, had eventually earned her full confidence and been promoted to the post of clerk; that on the lady's death he had somehow or other acquired his freedom, registered as a burgess, begun leasing melon-gardens from the neighbours, grown rich and now lived in clover. He was a man of experience, with his head well screwed on, neither bad nor good, but calculating, rather; a sly dog who understood people and knew how to make use of them. He was cautious and enterprising at the same time, like a fox; chattered like an old crone, never gave himself away, made everybody else speak their mind. What is more, he never posed as a simpleton, as some of the sly ones of his kind do; indeed, pretence could not have come easily to him. I have never seen more penetrating, shrewder eyes than his tiny, cunning "peepers."[1] They never simply looked, they were always searching and spying. Sometimes Blinker would spend whole weeks reflecting on some apparently simple enterprise, then suddenly resolve on a desperately daring course, and you would think he'd break his neck

1. The people of Orel call eyes "peepers" in the same way as they call a mouth a "gobbler."—*Author.*

over it . . . you would look again—and it would have come off perfectly, smooth as a knife through butter. He was lucky, believed in his luck and in omens. In general, he was highly superstitious. He was not liked, because he was not in the least interested in others, but he was respected. His family consisted of one small son, whom he fairly adored, and who, brought up by such a father, would probably go far. "Little Blinker's the spit of his father," the old men were already saying of him in low voices, as they sat on the mounds of earth outside their cabins and gossiped on summer evenings; and they all understood what that meant, and didn't need to say more.

Of Yasha the Turk and the huckster there is not much to be said. Yasha, nicknamed the Turk, because he was indeed the offspring of a captured Turkish woman, was at heart an artist in all senses of the word, but by vocation a dipper in a merchant's paper-mill. As for the huckster, whose lot, I confess, remains unknown to me, he struck me as a smart, resourceful townsman. Of Wild Master, however, it is worth speaking in rather greater detail.

The first impression his appearance gave was one of rude, ponderous, irresistible force. He was clumsily built, "piled-on," as we say in our part of the country, but he fairly radiated irrepressible vitality, and, strangely enough, his bearish figure was not without a certain individual grace, which proceeded perhaps from a completely serene confidence in his own strength. It was difficult to determine at first glance to what condition of life this Hercules belonged. He resembled neither servant nor townsman, neither the impoverished scrivener living in retirement nor the ruined, horse-fancying, quarrel-picking member of the smaller landowning gentry. He was something absolutely special. No one knew whence he had descended on our district; it was said that he came of free-holding stock and had previously been in Government service somewhere or other, but nothing certain was known of this; and indeed there was no one to learn it from—certainly not from him himself: a more taciturn, surly fellow never existed. No one could say for sure, either, what he lived on; he plied no trade, visited no one, hardly knew anyone, and yet he had money; not much, it is true, but money, all the same. He conducted himself, not indeed with modesty—there was absolutely nothing modest about him—but quietly; he lived as if he noticed no one around him and definitely wanted nothing from anyone. Wild Master (such as his nickname; his real name was Perevlesov) enjoyed an enormous influence in the whole neighbourhood; he was obeyed instantly and eagerly, although, so far from having any right to give anyone orders, he never made the slightest claim on the obedience of people with whom he came in contact. He spoke—and was obeyed: power always claims its due. He hardly drank, had no dealings with women, and was a passionate lover of singing. There was much that was puzzling about him; it was as if some immense forces were lying, sullenly inactive, within him, as if they knew that, once aroused, once let loose, they must destroy themselves and everything they touched; and I am sadly mistaken if some such explosion had not already occurred in the man's life, so that, taught by experience, and having just escaped destruction, he was now holding himself under an inexorable, iron control. What specially struck me about him was the mixture of a certain inborn, natural ferocity with an equally inborn nobility—a mixture such as I have met in no one else.

So the huckster stepped forward, half-closed his eyes, and began to sing in a very high falsetto. His voice was quite sweet and agreeable, though somewhat husky; he played with it, twirled it about like a toy, with constant downward trills and modulations and constant returns to the top notes, which he held and prolonged with a special effort; he stopped, then suddenly took up his previous tune again with a certain rollicking, arrogant boldness. His transitions were sometimes daring, sometimes rather comical. They would have given a connoisseur great pleasure; they would have shocked a German deeply. He was a Russian *tenore di grazia* or *ténor léger*. He sang a gay dance-tune, whose words, so far as I could catch them among the endless embellishments, extra harmonies and exclamations, were as follows:

> *I'll plough a little ground, my lass,*
> *And sow it with scarlet flowers.*

He sang, and we all listened to him with close attention. He clearly felt that he had to do with experts, and so he fairly climbed out of his skin, as the saying goes. Indeed in our country we are connoisseurs of song, and it is not for nothing that the village of Sergievsk, on the Orel highway, is renowned throughout all Russia for its specially sweet and harmonious singing. The huckster sang on for quite a while, without arousing any marked sympathy in his hearers: he missed the support of a choir. At length, after one particularly successful transition, which made even Wild Master smile, Muddlehead could not contain himself and shouted out his satisfaction. Everybody jumped. Muddlehead and Blinker began taking up the tune, joining in and calling: "Smartly does it! . . . Strike it, rascal!

. . . Strike it, hold it, you snake! Hold it, go on! Hotter still, you dog, you Herod's son!'' and so on. Nikolai Ivanich, behind the counter, waved his head approvingly to right and left. At length Muddlehead began to stamp and scrape his feet and twitch his shoulder,—Yasha's eyes blazed like coals, he trembled all over like a leaf and smiled confusedly. Only Wild Master kept the same countenance and remained motionless as before; but his gaze, fixed on the huckster, softened a little, though his lips kept their contemptuous expression. Encouraged by the signs of general satisfaction, the huckster fairly whirled along and went off into such flourishes, such tongue-clickings and drummings, such wild throat-play, that at length, exhausted, pale, bathed in hot sweat, he threw himself back, let out a last dying note—and his wild outburst was answered in unison by the company. Muddlehead threw himself on his neck and began smothering him with his long bony hands; a flush came over Nikolai's greasy face, and he seemed to have grown younger; Yasha shouted like a madman, ''Bravo, bravo!''—and even my neighbour, the peasant in the torn coat, could bear it no longer and, striking his fist on the table, exclaimed: ''A-ha! good, devil take it—good!'' and he spat to one side with determination.

''Well, lad, you've given us a treat!'' cried Muddlehead, not letting the fainting huckster out of his embrace. ''A treat, and that's the truth! You've won, lad, you've won! Congratulations—the quart is yours! Yasha can't touch you . . . Not by a long chalk, I tell you . . . Believe me!'' And he again pressed the huckster to his bosom.

''Let him go: let him go, you leech . . .'' said Blinker crossly. ''Let him sit down on the bench here; he's tired, see . . . You're a fool, lad, a real fool! Why stick to him like a fly-paper?''

''Why, then, let him sit, and I'll drink his health,'' rejoined Muddlehead, going to the counter; ''you're paying, lad,'' he added, turning to the huckster.

The huckster nodded, sat down on the bench, drew a towel out of his cap and began to wipe his face. Muddlehead drank a glass in thirsty haste, groaned, and took on the sad, preoccupied look of the serious drinker.

''You sing well, lad, so you do,'' observed Nikolai Ivanich amiably. ''Now it's your turn, Yasha: don't be nervous, mind. We'll see who's best, we will . . . But the huckster sings well, by God he does.''

''Very well, so he does,'' observed Nikolai's wife, smiling at Yasha.

''So he does, too!'' said my neighbour in a low voice

"Eh, you Polesyan Thomas!"[2] sang out Muddlehead suddenly and, coming over to the peasant with the hole in the shoulder of his coat, pointed a finger at him, began to jump, and burst into a jarring laugh. "You Polesyan! What are you doing here? Come on! you doubting Thomas!" he shouted through his laughter.

The poor peasant grew embarrassed and was just about to rise and depart hurriedly, when all of a sudden came the metallic voice of Wild Master:

"What's that unbearable animal up to now?" he said, grinding his teeth.

"Nothing," muttered Muddlehead, "nothing . . . I just . . ."

"All right then, shut up!" rejoined Wild Master. "Yasha, begin!"

Yasha took his throat in his hand.

"Why, lad, there's something . . . why . . . H'm . . . I don't rightly know . . ."

"Now, that'll do, don't be shy. Shame on you! . . . What's the fuss? . . . Sing, as God tells you to."

And Wild Master looked down and waited.

Yasha said nothing, but glanced round and covered his face with his hand. The whole company stared at him with all their eyes, especially the huckster, whose face showed, through its usual self-confidence and the triumph of his success, a faint, involuntary anxiety. He leant against the wall, again tucked his hands in beneath him, but no longer swung his legs. When at last Yasha uncovered his face, it was as pale as a corpse's; his gleaming eyes hardly showed through their lowered lashes. He breathed deeply and began to sing . . . His first note was faint and uneven, and came, it seemed, not from his chest, but from somewhere far away, as if it had chanced to fly into the room. This trembling, ringing note had a strange effect on us all; we looked at one another, and Nikolai's wife stood bolt upright. This first note was followed by another, firmer and more prolonged, but still perceptibly trembling, like a string, when, after the sudden pluck of a strong finger, it wavers with a last, quickly-dying thrill: after the second came a third, and, gradually taking on warmth and breadth, the mournful song flowed on its way. *"The paths that lay across the field,"* he sang, and we all had the feeling of something sweet and unearthly. Seldom, I confess, have I heard such a voice: it was somewhat worn and had a sort of cracked ring; at first it had even a certain suggestion

2. The inhabitants of Polesya have a name for incredulity and suspicion. —*Author*.

of the morbid; but it also held a deep, unsimulated passion, and youth, and strength, and sweetness, and a deliciously detached note of melancholy. The truthful, fervent Russian soul rang and breathed in it and fairly caught at your heart, caught straight at your Russian heartstrings. The song developed, went flowing on. Yasha was clearly overcome by ecstasy: his shyness had left him, he had surrendered completely to his happiness; his voice trembled no longer—it quivered, but with the scarcely perceptible inner quivering of passion, which pierces like an arrow into the hearer's soul. His voice grew steadily in strength, firmness and breadth. One evening, I remember, at low tide, on the flat sandy shore of the sea, which was roaring away menacingly and dully in the distance, I saw a great white gull: it was sitting, motionless, its silky breast turned towards the scarlet radiance of sunset, now and then slowly stretching its long wings towards the familiar sea, towards the low, blood-red sun; I remembered it as I listened to Yasha. He sang, completely oblivious of his rival and of us all, but clearly sustained, as waves lift a strong swimmer, by our silent passionate attention. He sang, and with every note there floated out something noble and immeasurably large, like familiar steppe-country unfolding before you, stretching away into the boundless distance. I could feel tears swelling up in my heart and rising into my eyes; dull, muffled sobs suddenly fell on my ears . . . I looked round—the tapster's wife was weeping as she leant her breast against the window. Yasha threw her a quick glance and his song flowed on still more sonorously and sweetly than before. Nikolai Ivanich looked down, Blinker turned away; Muddlehead, quite overcome by emotion, stood with his mouth stupidly gaping; the little grey peasant was quietly whimpering in his corner and shaking his head and muttering away bitterly to himself; down the iron face of Wild Master, from under his deep overhanging brows, slowly rolled a heavy tear; the huckster had raised a clenched fist to his brow and never stirred. . . .I cannot imagine how this general state of heartfelt rapture would have been dispelled if Yasha had not suddenly ended on a high, extremely thin note—as if his voice had broken. No one shouted, no one even stirred; everyone seemed to be waiting in case he would sing on; but he opened his eyes, as if surprised at our silence, cast a questioning glance round at us all, and saw that victory was his. . . .

"Yasha," said Wild Master, putting a hand on his shoulder, and—said nothing more.

We all sat as though benumbed. The huckster got up quietly and went across to Yasha. "You . . . it's yours . . . you've won,'' he brought out at last with difficulty and dashed from the room. . . .

His swift decisive movement seemed to break the spell: everyone suddenly started talking loudly, joyfully. Muddlehead sprang up in the air and began to splutter and wave his arms like the sails of a windmill; Blinker stumbled over to Yasha and they began to kiss each other; Nikolai Ivanich stood up and solemnly announced that he would add another quart of beer on his own account; Wild Master laughed a good-natured laugh, such as I had certainly not expected to hear from him; the little grey peasant kept on repeating in his corner, wiping his eyes, cheeks, nose and beard on both sleeves: "Good, by God, it's good, why, take me for a son of a bitch, it's good!" and Nikolai's wife, deeply flushed, stood up quickly and went away. Yasha enjoyed his victory like a child; his whole face was transfigured; in particular his eyes simply radiated happiness. He was dragged across to the counter; he summoned over to it the little grey peasant, who had burst into tears, he sent the host's boy after the huckster, whom, however, he failed to find, and the party began. "You'll sing to us again, you'll sing to us until evening," repeated Muddlehead, raising his arms aloft.

I looked once more at Yasha and went out. I did not want to stay—for fear of spoiling my impression. But the heat was still as unbearable as before. It was as if it hung right over the earth in a thick, heavy film; in the dark blue sky, little flashing lights seemed to be astir behind the fine, almost black dust. Everything was still; there was something hopeless, something oppressive about this deep stillness of enfeebled nature. I made my way to a hayloft and lay down on the newly-mown but already almost dried-up grass. For a while I could not drowse off; for a while Yasha's irresistible voice rang in my ears . . . but, at length, heat and exhaustion claimed their due, and I fell into a death-like sleep. When I awoke, it was dark all around; the litter of grass smelt strongly and there was a touch of dampness about it; between the thin rafters of the half-open roof, pale stars flickered faintly. I went out. The sunset glow had died away long ago, and had left behind only the faintest pallor on the horizon; in the air, so glowing-hot not long before, there was still a sense of heat underneath the freshness of night, and the lungs still thirsted for a breath of cold. There was no wind, no cloud; the sky stood round, clear, darkly translucent, quietly shimmering with countless hardly-visible stars. In the village, lights twinkled; from the brightly-lit pot-house near by came a discordant and confused hubbub, in the midst of which I thought I recognized Yasha's voice. At times there were bursts of wild laughter. I went across to the window and pressed my face against the pane. I saw a sad, though lively and animated scene: everyone was drunk—everyone, starting with Yasha. He was sitting, bare-chested, on a bench, singing in the huskiest voice some dance song of the streets, and lazily plucking and pinching the strings of a guitar. Clusters of wet hair hung above his livid face. In the middle of the pothouse, Muddlehead, coatless and completely "unscrewed," was dancing and hopping away in front of the little peasant in the grey coat; the peasant, in turn, was laboriously stamping and scraping with his exhausted feet, smiling witlessly through his dishevelled beard, and occasionally waving a hand, as if to say: "Let it rip!" Nothing could have been more ludicrous than his face; however high he lifted his brows, his heavy lids refused to stay up and drooped right down over his hardly visible, bleary eyes, which were nevertheless brimming with sweetness. He was in the endearing condition of the completely tipsy, when every passer-by who looks him in the face is absolutely bound to say: "A fine state, a fine state!" Blinker, red as a lobster, nostrils blown out wide, was laughing sardonically from a corner; only Nikolai Ivanich, as befits a good tapster, had kept his imperturbable sang-froid. Many new faces had collected in the room, but there was no sign of Wild Master.

I turned away and struck off quickly down the hill on which Kolotovka stands. A broad plain spreads out at the foot of this hill; swamped as it was with the misty waves of evening haze, it seemed vaster than ever, and as if merged with the darkened sky. I was walking with great strides along the track beside the ravine, when suddenly, from far away on the plain, came a boy's ringing voice. "Antropka! Antropka-a-a! . . ." it called, in stubborn, tearful desperation, with a long dragging-out of the last syllable.

For a few moments it was silent, then began to call again. The voice carried clearly in the unmoving, lightly-sleeping air. Thirty times at least it had called Antropka's name, when suddenly, from the opposite end of the meadow, as if from a different world, came a scarcely audible reply:

"What-a-a-a-at?"

The boy's voice called at once, glad but indignant:

"Come here, you devil!"

"What fo-o-o-r?" answered the other, after a pause.

"Because father wants to be-ee-ee-eat you," called the first voice promptly.

The second voice made no further reply, and the boy again

started calling "Antropka." I could still hear his cries, growing rarer and fainter, when it had become completely dark and I was passing the bend in the wood that surrounds my village, four versts away from Kolotovka.

"Antropka-a-a," I still seemed to hear in the air, which was full of the shadows of night.

Battle Tactics
Farley Mowat
from *The Dog Who Wouldn't Be,* 1957

A nonhuman focus—it—represents a further distancing from the I than they, to the degree that people have less rapport with other creatures and things than with each other, although naturalists like Farley Mowat seem at times almost to establish a confidant relationship with the creatures they get to know. This chapter from a book entirely about his dog qualifies as memoir because the dog was a pet and hence the experience unsought, whereas most of Mowat's fine observations of animals occur during professional excursions into their habitats and would thereby belong in the section to follow, Investigation.

After several years in Saskatoon, my family moved into a new neighborhood. River Road was on the banks of the Saskatchewan River, but on the lower and more plebeian side. The community on River Road was considerably relaxed in character and there was a good deal of tolerance for individual idiosyncrasies.

Only three doors down the street from us lived a retired schoolteacher who had spent years in Alaska and who had brought with him into retirement a team of Alaskan Huskies. These were magnificent dogs that commanded respect not only from the local canine population but from the human one as well. Three of them once caught a burglar on their master's premises, and they reduced him to butcher's meat with a dispatch that we youngsters much admired.

Across the alley from us lived a barber who maintained a sort of Transient's Rest for stray mongrels. There was an unkind rumor to the effect that he encouraged these strays only in order to practice his trade upon them. The rumor gained stature from the indisputable fact that some of his oddly assorted collection of dogs sported unusual haircuts. I came to know the barber intimately during the years that followed, and he confided his secret to me. Once, many years earlier, he had seen a French poodle shaven and shorn, and he had been convinced that he could devise even more spectacular hair styles for dogs, and perhaps make a fortune and a reputation for himself. His experiments were not without artistic merit, even though some of them resulted in visits from the Humane Society inspectors.

I had no trouble fitting myself into this new community, but the adjustment was not so simple for Mutt. The canine population of River Road was enormous. Mutt had to come to terms with these dogs, and he found the going hard. His long, silken hair and his fine "feathers" tended to give him a soft and sentimental look that was misleading and that seemed to goad the roughneck local dogs into active hostility. They usually went about in packs, and the largest pack was led by a well-built bull terrier who lived next door to us. Mutt, who was never a joiner, preferred to go his way alone, and this made him particularly suspect by the other dogs. They began to lay for him.

He was not by nature the fighting kind. In all his life I never knew him to engage in battle unless there was no alternative. His was an eminently civilized attitude, but one that other dogs could seldom understand. They taunted him because of it.

His pacific attitude used to embarrass my mother when the two of them happened to encounter a belligerent strange dog while they were out walking. Mutt would waste no time in idle braggadocio. At first glimpse of the stranger he would insinuate himself under Mother's skirt and no amount of physical force, nor scathing comment, could budge him from this sanctuary. Often the strange dog would not realize that it *was* a sanctuary and this was sometimes rather hard on Mother.

Despite his repugnance toward fighting, Mutt was no coward, nor was he unable to defend himself. He had his own ideas about how to fight, ideas which were unique but formidable. Just how efficacious they actually were was demonstrated to us all within a week of our arrival at our new address.

Knowing nothing of the neighborhood, Mutt dared to go where even bulldogs feared to tread, and one morning he foolishly pursued a cat into the ex-schoolteacher's yard. He was immediately surrounded by four ravening Huskies. They were a merciless lot, and they closed in for the kill.

Mutt saw at once that this time he would have to fight. With one quick motion he flung himself over on his back and began to pedal furiously with all four feet. It looked rather as if he were riding a bicycle built for two, but upside down. He also began to sound his siren. This was a noise he made—just how, I do not know—deep in the back of his throat. It was a kind of frenzied wail. The siren rose in pitch and volume as his legs increased their r.p.m.'s, until he began to sound like a gas turbine at full throttle.

The effect of his unorthodox behavior on the four Huskies was to bring them to an abrupt halt. Their ears went forward and their tails uncurled as a look of pained bewilderment wrinkled their brows. And then slowly, and one by one, they began to back away, their eyes uneasily averted from the distressing spectacle before them. When they were ten feet from Mutt they turned as one dog and fled without dignity for their own back yard.

The mere sight of Mutt's bicycle tactics (as we referred to them) was usually sufficient to avert bloodshed, but on occasion a foolhardy dog would refuse to be intimidated. The results in these cases could be rather frightful, for Mutt's queer posture of defense was not all empty bombast.

Once when we were out hunting gophers Mutt was attacked by a farm collie who, I think, was slightly mad. He looked mad, for he had one white eye and one blue one, and the combination gave him a maniac expression. And he acted mad, for he flung himself on the inverted Mutt without the slightest hesitation.

Mutt grunted when the collie came down on top of him, and for an instant the tempo of his legs was slowed. Then he exerted himself and, as it were, put on a sprint. The collie became air-borne, bouncing up and down as a rubber ball bounces on the end of a water jet. Each time he came down he was raked fore and aft by four sets of rapidly moving claws, and when he finally fell clear he was bleeding from a dozen ugly scratches, and he had had a bellyful. He fled. Mutt did not pursue him; he was magnanimous in victory.

Had he been willing to engage deliberately in a few such duels with the neighborhood dogs, Mutt would undoubtedly have won their quick acceptance. But such was his belief in the principles of nonviolence—as these applied to other dogs, at least—that he continued to avoid combat.

The local packs, and particularly the one led by the bull terrier next door, spared no pains to bring him to battle, and for some time he was forced to stay very close to home unless he was accompanied by Mother or by myself. It was nearly a month before he found a solution to this problem.

The solution he eventually adopted was typical of him.

Almost all the back yards in Saskatoon were fenced with vertical planking nailed to horizontal two-by-fours. The upper two-by-four in each case was usually five or six feet above the ground, and about five inches below the projecting tops of the upright planks. For generations these elevated gangways had provided a safe thoroughfare for cats. One fine day Mutt decided that they could serve him too.

I was brushing my teeth after breakfast when I heard Mutt give a yelp of pain and I went at once to the window and looked out. I was in time to see him laboriously clamber up on our back fence from a garbage pail that stood by the yard gate. As I watched he wobbled a few steps along the upper two-by-four, lost his balance, and fell off. Undaunted he returned at once to the garbage pail and tried again.

I went outside and tried to reason with him, but he ignored me. When I left he was still at it, climbing up, staggering along for a few feet, then falling off again.

I mentioned this new interest of his during dinner that night, but none of us gave it much thought. We were used to Mutt's peculiarities, and we had no suspicion that there was method behind this apparent foolishness. Yet method there was, as I discovered a few evenings later.

A squad of Bengal lancers, consisting of two of my friends and myself armed with spears made from bamboo fishing rods, had spent the afternoon riding up and down the back alleys on our bicycles hunting tigers (alley cats). As suppertime approached we were slowly pedaling our way homeward along the alley behind River Road when one of my chums, who was a little in the lead, gave a startled yelp and swerved his bike so that I crashed into him, and we fell together on the sun-baked dirt. I picked myself up and saw my friend pointing at the fence ahead of us. His eyes were big with disbelief.

The cause of the accident, and of my chum's incredulity, was nonchalantly picking his way along the top of the fence not fifty yards away. Behind that fence lay the home of the Huskies, and although we could not see them, we—and most of Saskatoon—could hear them. Their frenzied howls were punctuated by dull thudding sounds as they leaped at their tormentor and fell back helplessly to earth again.

Mutt never hesitated. He ambled along his aerial route with

the leisurely insouciance of an old gentleman out for an evening stroll. The Huskies must have been wild with frustration, and I was grateful that the fence lay between them and us.

We three boys had not recovered from our initial surprise when a new canine contingent arrived upon the scene. It included six or seven of the local dogs (headed by the bull terrier) attracted to the scene by the yammering of the Huskies. They spotted Mutt, and the terrier immediately led a mass assault. He launched himself against the fence with such foolhardy violence that only a bull terrier could have survived the impact.

We were somewhat intimidated by the frenzy of all those dogs, and we lowered our spears to the "ready" position, undecided whether to attempt Mutt's rescue or not. In the event, we were not needed.

Mutt remained unperturbed, although this may have been only an illusion, resulting from the fact that he was concentrating so hard on his balancing act that he could spare no attention for his assailants. He moved along at a slow but steady pace, and having safely navigated the Huskies' fence, he jumped up to the slightly higher fence next door and stepped along it until he came to a garage. With a graceful leap he gained the garage roof, where he lay down for a few moments, ostensibly to rest, but actually—I am certain—to enjoy his triumph.

Below him there was pandemonium. I have never seen a dog so angry as that bull terrier was. Although the garage wall facing on the alley was a good eight feet high, the terrier kept hurling himself impotently against it until he must have been one large quivering bruise.

Mutt watched the performance for two or three minutes; then he stood up and with one insolent backward glance jumped down to the dividing fence between two houses, and ambled along it to the street front beyond.

The tumult in the alley subsided and the pack began to disperse. Most of the dogs must have realized that they would have to run halfway around the block to regain Mutt's trail, and by then he might be far away. Dispiritedly they began to drift off, until finally only the bull terrier remained. He was still hurling himself at the garage wall in a paroxysm of fury when I took myself home to tell of the wonders I had seen.

From that day forth the dogs of the neighborhood gave up their attempts against Mutt and came to a tacit acceptance of him—all, that is, save the bull terrier. Perhaps his handball game against the fence had addled his brain, or it may be that he was just too stubborn to give up. At any rate he continued to lurk in ambush for Mutt, and Mutt continued to avoid him easily enough, until the early winter when the terrier—by now completely unbalanced—one day attempted to cross the street in pursuit of his enemy and without bothering to look for traffic. He was run over by an old Model T.

Mutt's remarkable skill as a fence walker could have led to the leadership of the neighborhood dogs, had that been what he desired, for his unique talent gave him a considerable edge in the popular game of catch-cat; but Mutt remained a lone walker, content to be left to his own devices.

He did not give up fence walking even when the original need had passed. He took a deep pride in his accomplishment, and he kept in practice. I used to show him off to my friends, and I was not above making small bets with strange boys about the abilities of my acrobatic dog. When I won, as I always did, I would reward Mutt with candy-coated gum. This was one of his favorite confections and he would chew away at a wad of it until the last vestige of mint flavor had vanished, whereupon he would swallow the tasteless remnant. Mother thought that this was bad for him, but as far as I know, it never had any adverse effect upon his digestive system, which could absorb most things with impunity.

INVESTIGATION

"**M**EMORY, that is the true kingdom of man," we heard the scroll repairer proclaim in Elie Wiesel's memoir. It may be true that in one way or another most of our understanding rests on memory. But it is useful for the writer to distinguish between memories accumulated by chance and memories acquired by choice—unsought and sought. The writings in Recollection are compositions of memories acquired before the intention to write about them. In an important way some fundamental composing has, in the case of autobiography and memoir, already taken place within the storage and retrieval system of memory before writing—selecting, editing, juxtaposing, classifying—according to some involuntary psychological processes that are constantly assimilating experience into previously erected structures of knowledge and emotional associations peculiar to an individual and to a culture. So Recollection represents the completion of a kind of internal writing begun in the past.

By contrast, the composition here called Investigation begins with decisions about what to do to get new information. This is the domain of reportage and research. The investigator chooses new memories to acquire. A special, conscious purpose motivates investigation—to find out something one doesn't already know, that is, hasn't yet acquired memories of. Perhaps we should think of investigation as an effort to supplement recollection, to fill in by choice an area of knowledge that chance has left deficient.

True, to the extent that we will our life, we already control what memories we will acquire by deciding to live here, work there, travel somewhere else. But we may feel that others willed much of our life when we were young, or conditions determined it beyond our control. And in any case we cannot find out all we want to know just through the routines even of the life we've chosen, although many of us no doubt choose a profession because it will in fact require investigating areas we want to learn about. If only relatively, then, Investigation represents the effort to take charge of what we shall know about.

Methodologically, Investigation combines Recollection and Notation, if we construe the latter not just as consecutive recording but as the taking of notes. In keeping with the effort to take charge of knowledge-making, the investigator ensures by some memory aids that the information sought will be remembered. So we may conceive Investigation as commonly having two stages—one of note-taking at the source of the information and a later stage of recollecting with the aid of these notes. The pulling-together of the latter stage usually comes during efforts to compose some sort of summary of what we learned from the new sources.

The whole process of registration and recollection, done more externally and deliberately in Investigation, compares to the abstractive activities going on unconsciously in the sensory and memory compositions of reality. It is in this way that writing may be regarded as a more conscious form of mimicry of the neural composition that makes up our perceptual and cognitive functioning.

What do we do to investigate something? Essentially two things—go and look or go and look up. Let's call the first reportage and the second research. These cover first- and second-hand information in a way that we may easily relate to our earlier considerations of first and third persons and the various informant roles.

Reportage

THE FACT THAT memoir and reportage may look alike as finished texts, though differently derived, indicates the kinship between the roles of memoirist *at the time of the events* and the role of reporter *while investigating*. Asked of each later, the question "How did you find out about what you wrote?" would receive similar answers for similar kinds of information. Outer events: "I was there and witnessed with my own eyes." Inner life: "I was a confidant and was told." Background: "I was a member of the community and we all knew." The eyewitness role is firsthand, the confidant secondhand, and the chorus both. So we are already familiar from Recollection with the means by which the investigator finds out. The only difference is whether we play these roles by happenstance or by design.

Let's translate the roles into simple directives. Eyewitness: go and look. Confidant: go and ask. Chorus: go and join. (Go-and-look-it-up is the imperative of research, taken up later.) These correspond in turn to practical journalistic activities—visit, interview, and saturation (living with and as the subjects one is investigating). Our samples will illustrate reportage based essentially on just one technique at a time.

Visit

The General Goes Zapping Charlie Cong

Nicholas Tomalin

London *Times*, 1966

Like most firsthand newspaper accounts, this story by a British correspondent in the Vietnam war consists of practically pure eyewitnessing. Inasmuch, however, as war reporters live to some extent with and as their subjects, Tomalin's "visit" amounts to an example also of "saturation reporting."

After a light lunch last Wednesday, General James F. Hollingsworth, of Big Red One, took off in his personal helicopter and killed more Vietnamese than all the troops he commanded.

The story of the General's feat begins in the divisional office, at Ki-Na, twenty miles north of Saigon, where a Medical Corps colonel is telling me that when they collect enemy casualties they find themselves with more than four injured civilians for every wounded Viet Cong—unavoidable in this kind of war.

The General strides in, pins two medals for outstanding gallantry to the chest of one of the colonel's combat doctors. Then he strides off again to his helicopter, and spreads out a polythene-covered map to explain our afternoon's trip.

The General has a big, real American face, reminiscent of every movie general you have seen. He comes from Texas, and is 48. His present rank is Brigadier General, Assistant Division Commander, 1st Infantry Division, United States Army (which is what the big red figure one on his shoulder flash means).

"Our mission today," says the General, "is to push those goddam VCs right off Routes 13 and 16. Now you see Routes 13 and 16 running north from Saigon toward the town of Phuoc

166

Vinh, where we keep our artillery. When we got here first we prettied up those roads, and cleared Charlie Cong right out so we could run supplies up.

"I guess we've been hither and thither with all our operations since, an' the ol' VC he's reckoned he could creep back. He's been puttin' out propaganda he's goin' to interdict our right of passage along those routes. So this day we aim to zapp him, and zapp him, and zapp him again till we've zapped him right back where he came from. Yes, sir. Let's go."

The General's UH 18 helicopter carries two pilots, two 60-calibre machine-gunners, and his aide, Dennis Gillman, an apple-cheeked subaltern from California. It also carries the General's own M16 carbine (hanging on a strut), two dozen smoke-bombs, and a couple of CS anti-personnel gas-bombs, each as big as a small dustbin. Just beside the General is a radio console where he can tune in on orders issued by battalion commanders flying helicopters just beneath him, and company commanders in helicopters just below them.

Under this interlacing of helicopters lies the apparently peaceful landscape beside Routes 13 and 16, filled with farmhouses and peasants hoeing rice and paddy fields.

So far today, things haven't gone too well. Companies Alpha, Bravo and Charlie have assaulted a suspected Viet Cong HQ, found a few tunnels but no enemy.

The General sits at the helicopter's open door, knees apart, his skinny black toecaps jutting out into space, rolls a filtertip cigarette to-and-fro in his teeth, and thinks.

"Put me down at Battalion HQ," he calls to the pilot.

"There's sniper fire reported on choppers in that area, General."

"Goddam the snipers, just put me down."

Battalion HQ at the moment is a defoliated area of four acres packed with tents, personnel carriers, helicopters and milling GIs. We settle into the smell of crushed grass. The General leaps out and strides through his troops.

"Why General, excuse us, we didn't expect you here," says a sweating major.

"You killed any 'Cong yet?"

"Well no General, I guess he's just too scared of us today. Down the road a piece we've hit trouble, a bulldozer's fallen through a bridge, and trucks coming through a village knocked the canopy off a Buddhist pagoda. Saigon radioed us to repair that temple before proceeding—in the way of civic action, General. That put us back an hour . . ."

"Yeah. Well Major, you spread out your perimeter here a bit, then get to killin' VC's will you?"

Back through the crushed grass to the helicopter.

"I don't know how you think about war. The way I see it, I'm just like any other company boss, gingering up the boys all the time, except I don't make money. I just kill people, and save lives."

In the air the General chews two more filtertips and looks increasingly forlorn. No action on Route 16, and another Big Red One general has got his helicopter in to inspect the collapsed bridge before ours.

"Swing us back along again," says the General.

"Reports of fire on choppers ahead, sir. Smoke flare near spot. Strike coming in."

"Go find that smoke."

A plume of white rises in the midst of dense tropical forest, with a Bird Dog spotter plane in attendance. Route 16 is to the right; beyond it a large settlement of red-tiled houses.

"Strike coming in, sir."

Two F105 jets appear over the horizon in formation, split, then one passes over the smoke, dropping a trail of silver, fish-shaped canisters. After four seconds' silence, light orange fire explodes in patches along an area fifty yards wide by three-quarters of a mile long. Napalm.

The trees and bushes burn, pouring dark oily smoke into the sky. The second plane dives and fire covers the entire strip of dense forest.

"Aaaaah," cries the General. "Nice. Nice. Very neat. Come in low, let's see who's left down there."

"How do you know for sure the Viet Cong snipers were in that strip you burned?"

"We don't. The smoke position was a guess. That's why we zapp the whole forest."

"But what if there was someone, a civilian, walking through there?"

"Aw come son, you think there's folks just sniffing flowers in tropical vegetation like that? With a big operation on hereabouts? Anyone left down there, he's Charlie Cong all right."

I point at a paddy field full of peasants less than half a mile away.

"That's different son. We know they're genuine."

The pilot shouts: "General, half right, two running for that bush."

"I see them. Down, down, goddam you."

In one movement he yanks his M16 off the hanger, slams in a clip of cartridges and leans right out of the door, hanging on his seatbelt to fire one long burst in the general direction of the bush.

"General, there's a hole, maybe a bunker, down there."

"Smokebomb, circle, shift it."

"But General, how do you know those aren't just frightened peasants?"

"Running? Like that? Don't give me a pain. The clips, the clips, where in hell are the cartridges in this ship?"

The aide drops a smoke canister, the General finds his ammunition and the starboard machine-gunner fires rapid bursts into the bush, his tracers bouncing up off the ground round it.

We turn clockwise in even tighter, lower circles, everyone firing. A shower of spent cartridge cases leaps from the General's carbine to drop, lukewarm, on my arm.

"I . . . WANT . . . YOU . . . TO . . . SHOOT . . . RIGHT . . . UP . . . THE . . . ASS . . . OF . . . THAT . . . HOLE . . . GUNNER."

Fourth time round the tracers flow right inside the tiny sandbagged opening, tearing the bags, filling it with sand and smoke.

The General falls back off his seatbelt into his chair, suddenly relaxed, and lets out an oddly feminine, gentle laugh. "That's it," he says, and turns to me, squeezing his thumb and finger into the sign of a French chef's ecstasy.

We circle now above a single-storey building made of dried reeds. The first burst of fire tears the roof open, shatters one wall into fragments of scattered straw, and blasts the farmyard full of chickens into dismembered feathers.

"Zapp, zapp, zapp," cries the General. He is now using semi-automatic fire, the carbine bucking in his hands.

Pow, pow, pow, sounds the gun. All the noises of this war have an unaccountably Texan ring.

"Gas bomb."

Lieutenant Gillman leans his canister out of the door. As the pilot calls, he drops it. An explosion of white vapour spreads across the wood a full hundred yards downwind.

"Jesus wept, lootenant, that's no good."

Lieutenant Gillman immediately clambers across me to get the second gas bomb, pushing me sideways into his own port-side seat. In considerable panic I fumble with an unfamiliar seatbelt as the helicopter banks round at an angle of fifty degrees. The second gas bomb explodes perfectly, beside the house, covering it with vapour.

"There's nothing alive in there," says the General. "Or they'd be skedaddling. Yes there is, by golly."

For the first time I see the running figure, bobbing and sprinting across the farmyard towards a clump of trees dressed in black pyjamas. No hat. No shoes.

"Now hit the tree."

We circle five times. Branches drop off the tree, leaves fly, its trunk is enveloped with dust and tracer flares. Gillman and the General are now firing carbines side by side in the doorway. Gillman offers me his gun: No thanks.

Then a man runs from the tree, in each hand a bright red flag which he waves desperately above his head.

"Stop, stop, he's quit," shouts the General, knocking the machine-gun so tracers erupt into the sky.

"I'm going down to take him. Now watch it everyone, keep firing roundabout, this may be an ambush."

We sink swiftly into the field beside the tree, each gunner firing cautionary bursts into the bushes. The figure walks towards us.

"That's a Cong for sure," cries the General in triumph and with one deft movement grabs the man's short black hair and yanks him off his feet, inboard. The prisoner falls across Lieutenant Gillman and into the seat beside me.

The red flags I spotted from the air are his hands, bathed solidly in blood. Further blood is pouring from under his shirt, over his trousers.

Now we are safely in the air again. Our captive cannot be more than sixteen years old, his head comes just about up to the white name patch—Hollingsworth—on the General's chest. He is dazed, in shock. His eyes calmly look first at the General, then at the Lieutenant, then at me. He resembles a tiny, fine-boned wild animal. I have to keep my hand firmly pressed against his shoulder to hold him upright. He is quivering. Sometimes his left foot, from some nervous impulse, bangs hard against the helicopter wall. The Lieutenant applies a tourniquet to his right arm.

"Radio base for an ambulance. Get the information officer with a camera. I want this Commie alive till we get back . . . just stay with us till we talk to you, baby."

The General pokes with his carbine first at the prisoner's cheek to keep his head upright, then at the base of his shirt.

"Look at that now," he says, turning to me. "You still thinking about innocent peasants? Look at the weaponry."

Around the prisoner's waist is a webbing belt, with four clips of ammunition, a water bottle (without stopper), a tiny roll of bandages, and a propaganda leaflet which later turns out to be a set of Viet Cong songs, with a twenty piastre note (about 1s. 6d.) folded in it.

Lieutenant Gillman looks concerned. "It's OK, you're OK," he mouths at the prisoner, who at that moment turns to me and with a surprisingly vigorous gesture waves his arm at my seat. He wants to lie down.

By the time I have fastened myself into yet another seat we are back at the landing pad. Ambulance orderlies come aboard, administer morphine, and rip open his shirt. Obviously, a burst of fire has shattered his right arm up at the shoulder. The cut shirt now allows a large bulge of blue-red tissue to fall forward, its surface streaked with white nerve fibres and chips of bone (how did he ever manage to wave that arm in surrender?).

When the ambulance has driven off the General gets us all posed round the nose of the chopper for a group photograph like a gang of successful fishermen, then clambers up into the cabin again, at my request, for a picture to show just how he zapped those VCs. He is euphoric.

"Jeez I'm so glad you was along, that worked out just dandy. I've been written up time and time again back in the States for shootin' up VCs, but no one's been along with me like you before."

We even find a bullet hole in one of the helicopter rotor blades. "That's proof positive they was firin' at us all the time. An' firin' on us first, boy. So much for your fellers smellin' flowers."

He gives me the Viet Cong's water bottle as souvenir and proof. "That's a chicom bottle, that one. All the way from Peking."

Later that evening the General calls me to his office to tell me the prisoner had to have his arm amputated, and is now in the hands of the Vietnamese authorities, as regulations dictate. Before he went under, he told the General's interpreters that he was part of a hardcore regular VC company whose mission was to mine Route 16, cut it up, and fire at helicopters.

The General is magnanimous in his victory over my squeamish civilian worries.

"You see son, I saw rifles on that first pair of running men. Didn't tell you that at the time. And, by the way you mustn't imagine there could have been ordinary farm folk in that house, when you're as old a veteran as I am you get to know about those things by instinct. I agree there was chickens for food with them, strung up on a pole. You didn't see anything bigger, like a pig or a cow did yuh? Well then.''

The General wasn't certain whether further troops would go to the farmhouse that night to check who died, although patrols would be near there.

It wasn't safe moving along Route 16 at night, there was another big operation elsewhere the next day. Big Red One is always on the move.

''But when them VC come back harassin' that Route 16 why, we'll zapp them again. And when they come back after that we'll zapp them again.''

''Wouldn't it be easier just to stay there all the time?''

''Why, son, we haven't enough troops as it is.''

''The Koreans manage it.''

''Yeah, but they've got a smaller area to protect. Why Big Red One ranges right over—I mean up to the Cambodian Border. There ain't no place on that map we ain't been.

''I'll say perhaps your English generals wouldn't think my way of war is all that conventional, would they? Well, this is a new kind of war, flexible, quickmoving. Us generals must be on the spot to direct our troops. The helicopter adds a new dimension to battle.

''There's no better way to fight than goin' out to shoot VCs. An' there's nothing I love better than killin' 'Cong. No, sir.''

Interview

Guitar String
New Yorker "Talk of the Town," March 7, 1983

Virtually all of the information in "Guitar String" came from an interview, which was conducted on site but could almost have been done over the telephone. The art of writing up an interview lies in how to summarize and when to quote.

True daily news dates too fast to remain of interest. Much reportage appears in magazines and newspapers as "feature articles, that is, as "human interest" portraits or sketches or "sidelights" on the news itself, among which we can include indeed the Vietnam piece. The information in features generally holds good longer than news and sometimes may even remain of enduring interest because it typifies something general.

Rose Augustine's factory, situated several floors above a cuckoo-clock manufacturer in a twelve-story building on West Twenty-fifth Street, churns out thirty miles of guitar string a day. ("I used to tell people three miles, but then I refigured it and found I'd messed up a decimal place," Mrs. Augustine told us.) Which means that in just eight and a half days the lathelike machines in Mrs. Augustine's factory can produce a guitar string long enough to be held at one end by the residents of Rochester, New York, and at the other end by the citizens of Cleveland, Ohio, and strummed. Actually, the strings at Mrs. Augustine's factory are cut in lengths of between thirty-eight and forty-one inches, depending on how far up the neck of the guitar they will be tied. Still, that's a lot of string. "There are more guitar players in this world than you'd ever dream," Mrs. Augustine said happily. Once the strings are cut, they are sorted according to width and packed in plastic bags, which are then heat-sealed and packed in cardboard cartons, which are then stacked at one end of the workroom. "I can tell by looking at the height of a stack of boxes what we have enough of. When a pile gets too high, I tell them to switch to another width of string," Mrs. Augustine said.

Considering her order-of-magnitude uncertainty about the volume of her string production, and her less than scientific approach to inventory, one might be tempted to worry over Mrs. Augustine's ability to succeed in the great hurly-burly of American capitalism. If one did that, one would be wasting one's time, for Mrs. Augustine—her firm's only salesman—is an industry leader. Her Augustine Imperial ("The Superior Concert String . . Played by the Great Masters") sells and sells and sells, as well it should, for it is a direct descendant of the first guitar string of the modern era, which was designed by Mrs. Augustine's late husband, Albert—sometimes referred to as "the rescuer of the classical guitar."

"Strings used to be made of silk and gut," Mrs. Augustine explained. "But during the Second World War there was a terrible shortage, because all the warring nations were using all the top-grade silk and gut for sutures. There was almost nothing left for instruments. My husband, who was a guitarmaker, was desperate. He went down to the war-surplus stores on Canal Street, and he saw these big spools of rejected nylon. It was used then—and still is—as fishing leader. Most of the nylon on the spool would be rough, but he could usually find enough smooth sections to make some strings. Shortly afterward, he was with Andrés Segovia, the greatest guitar player. My husband saw that Segovia had a nylon string on his guitar, and learned that some man from du Pont had given it to him. But only one. Segovia told my husband he would be in seventh heaven if he could get the first three strings in nylon."

With a rebuilt binocular grinder—also procured on Canal Street— Mrs. Augustine and her husband set to work making strings. They surprised du Pont with their request for nylon; soon after the war ended, company officials had approached most of the established stringmakers, who, for reasons of professional conservatism and self-interest ("A nylon string may not last an hour before you need a new one," Mrs. Augustine said), had told du Pont that the new material wouldn't work. But work it did. "It was a godsend. It was the first real change in stringmaking in hundreds of years. My husband is credited with being one of the leaders of the guitar revolution, even though he didn't really want to make strings. He wanted to make, and always did make, guitars."

Mrs. Augustine was in on the business from the beginning, helping out in their first workshop, which was in the basement of the building they lived in, on Central Park West. ("It was strictly illegal to have a factory in a residential building, so we had all these lights rigged up to warn us if an inspector came by or anything.") As her husband's health gradually declined, Mrs. Augustine became more and more important to the business. When her husband died, in 1967, she took charge of the company, and soon thereafter she left her other work, as a science teacher in Bayside and East Harlem public schools. "When I first stopped teaching, I wanted to do social work," she told us. "But I found that all they wanted was my presence, my warm body on the spot, and not my brains. It just seemed a social-butterfly sort of thing. So I concentrated on the business." Hardnosed, but not too hardnosed ("The greatest asset has been that it's not a do-or-die thing with me. I'm not desperate about the dollars and the pennies"), Mrs. Augustine has built the business to the point where she has received more than one offer to buy it out. And still her empire grows. Mrs. Augustine sponsors a guitar-concert series at the 92nd Street Y, and she recently bought *Guitar*

Review, a classy quarterly with articles like "Aristocratic Patronage and the Spanish Guitar in the Seventeenth Century" and "The History of Apoyando."

Finally, we asked the big question.

"Do I like the guitar?" Mrs. Augustine replied, with a smile. "I hate the guitar—I told Segovia that years ago. Segovia lived with us for years, and I wouldn't let him give me lessons. I go to three or four concerts a week—it's important for the business. And I like the guitarists very much. But I don't really enjoy the concerts. I worry too much. Not about the strings breaking but about the artists, the music. The guitar is a very difficult instrument to listen to. The volume is very small. Personally, I don't believe that it should be played in large concert halls. I have an awful lot of guitar records, but I don't go much out of my way to listen to them."

Interview Plus Visit

The Camera Looking
New Yorker "Talk of the Town,"
February 14, 1983

Drawing from the same source facilitates comparison of this selection with the last. "The Camera Looking" was composed from information distilled both from what was said and what was seen. The interview had to be conducted on site so that eyewitness material could be interwoven with direct and indirect quotation. Using two sources complicates the abstracting process, which must do justice to and integrate both.

The interviews in both these samples tap someone's expertise: the first, of an unknown and idiosyncratic but in some ways representative commercial person; the second, of an especially gifted celebrity in the field. Interviewing permits us to add other people's memories and knowledge to our own and so performs the paramount function of spreading individuals' unique knowledge.

"There are at least 100 ways to get to The Cathedral Shop at St. John the Divine," reads the caption under a bus poster that shows Philippe Petit, the tightrope artist, approaching the church's roof by way of a cable stretched high above the street. Nervy undertakings of a different but related sort were in progress at St John's last week, more or less on the ground, as Merce Cunningham and his dance company prepared to film a new dance there called "Coast Zone." Cunningham, the most adventurous choreographer of our time, has been experimenting for several years with dances that he creates specifically for film or videotape. His ambition has been to make dances designed for the camera, with its benefits and its limitations kept firmly in mind. Learning that he was at work on a new one, we went up to Amsterdam Avenue and 110th Street to take a look.

The company was assembled in the great hall of the Synod House, a long, oak-panelled room in a building just south of the main cathedral. Charles Atlas, the filmmaker who collaborates with Cunningham on these projects, had found out about it after an extended search—Cunningham wanted a larger space than he has in his Westbeth studio, downtown, and the hall was big enough, with a high ceiling, and it was not too costly to rent. The company had been rehearsing and shooting there for three weeks. (It had rehearsed for three weeks before that at Westbeth. As we arrived, four of the fifteen dancers in the company were in action, bending and swooping, then running toward the far end of the hall, closely followed by a cameraman on a dolly propelled by four perspiring stagehands. Cunningham and Atlas were behind the dolly, moving with it and observing the action. A small video monitor was mounted on the dolly, just behind the cameraman, so that they could see the action two ways—live and on the screen.

When the brief sequence ended, the dancers and the camera crew came back toward our end of the room and did it again. This happened five or six times before they went on to the next sequence. Taking a quick break between the two, Cunningham came over to say hello and to sit down for a moment. He was wearing a gray sweatsuit, black dancing shoes, and thick white socks, and he looked, as he always does, friendly and quizzical and alert. "It's exhausting, all this starting and stopping," he said. "Much worse than a stage rehearsal. My idea about technology used to be that it lets you do all sorts of things at the same time, but it doesn't work out that way. You just do the same thing over and over, and wait endlessly while they adjust the camera. You have all this marvellous equipment, but you're always having to kick it along, or put masking tape on it, or find a piece of wood to use as a wedge."

For the next half hour, Cunningham and the dancers worked on two more short, fifteen-to-twenty-second dance phrases. After that, he asked for a complete run-through of the dance, without the camera. It looked immensely complex to us, with a great deal of rapid and intricate interaction among the dancers, most of whom seemed to be very young, and several of whom appeared to be having an awfully good time. Cunningham had not given himself a part in this dance. At the age of sixty-three, he does not dance as much as he used to, although the movements he makes for himself these days are as quirky and as fascinating as any he has shown us in the past. He watched the run-through from the sidelines, and when it was finished he came over again for a few minutes' conversation.

"One of the things I'm trying to do with this piece is to work in layers," he said. "We're using a lot of closeups—something we haven't done before—and mixing them with middle and long shots. The image on camera changes quite radically when you go from a distant shot to a closeup. As the camera moves toward the dancer, there is a very gradual enlargement of the image, but then, all of a sudden, it gets very big, and the arms disappear. We're using only moving cameras—no fixed angles, and no zoom-lens shots. The camera keeps moving in and out, changing the space. On that one sequence we were working on when you came in, the camera does a five-hundred-and-forty-degree turn— is that right? A complete circle and a half, anyway. It also changes speed during the turn, going faster and faster at the end."

We asked whether the new dance wasn't unusually complicated, and he agreed that it was. "Mainly because everything is moving," he said. "But nobody ever seems to be moving in the same direction as anybody else. I've had to figure out new ways to tell the dancers where to go. I can't say, 'Move downstage,' or 'Go to stage right,' because there isn't any stage. It's like objects in space, with everything moving at a different rate of speed. We make marks on the floor to help orient the dancers, but the marks tend to disappear. It's all very confusing."

What were some of the other problems of choreographing for the camera?

"It's not just the space that's different—it's the time, too," he said. "I think you see things faster on television than you do onstage. Something that lasts for five seconds onstage can be done in one second on camera, and that's sufficient. It's the same with repetition—you get the idea much faster on TV. If something repeats too often, you flip to another channel. In this dance, I've varied the movement so there is constant change, and no repetition. But space is still the main problem. When you look at a stage, you see depth—a lot of space around people. The camera flattens everything out, and we have to find ways to compensate for that. It's to get around the flattening-out problem that I'm shooting in layers, with a lot of close-ups—to differentiate the space and the way the dancers appear in it. My objection to a filmed dance performance onstage, of the kind you often see on TV, is that you lose the space. The camera can't get the whole stage in unless it's placed very far back, and then you lose the dancers. With a work onstage, you as the spectator are always referring what you see to that large space. But the camera takes in only what it is able to take in, which isn't much."

Charles Atlas came over to discuss a technical point with Cunningham, and while they were talking a crew of workmen appeared at the back door of the hall with a huge crane-and-dolly apparatus, called a tulip crane, that would be used for high-angle camerawork during the next day's shooting. One dancer wondered why it was called a tulip crane. Another suggested that it had been developed in Holland, to pick very tall, championship tulips. Atlas went to inspect it.

"There really are a lot of problems," Cunningham told us, a bit ruefully. "A proscenium theatre makes for a certain separation and formality, a distance between the audience and the performer. Television works the other way. And the camera chooses what you look at, and that's not how I've worked in the past. I just tell myself, "Well, that's the camera looking, let's see what I can do with that.""

"Coast Zone" was being shot on regular movie film and then transferred to videotape. The company distributes its own filmed and videotaped dances, mainly for rental by colleges and universities, and there is a lively demand for them. The new dance would also be given its première, live, during the company's two-week season of performances at the City Center in March. "I imagine it will look entirely different there," Cunningham said. "I don't mean better or worse. Just different. Years ago, you know, I thought a lot about Fred Astaire, how wonderful he had been, although I never saw him onstage—it was entirely a film experience. He made dancing come alive on film. So I said, "If he can do that, maybe we can. Why not?""

Saturation

Shakespeare in the Bush
Laura Bohannan
Natural History, July–August, 1966

Interviews and visits are forays the investigator makes into foreign habitats to play the eyewitness or confidant role, but they give only glimpses. What about the long-range understanding provided by the chorus role? For this the journalist saturates himself or herself in some milieu for a longer time, lives with and as the subjects. Some reporters have done time in prison to undergo something of what inmates experience and to learn from joining the community what everyone there knows. Saturation reportage has long been the stock in trade of many anthropologists, and some of the most dedicated and sophisticated journalism of today overlaps with investigation by them and ethnographers. Although much of anthropologist Laura Bohannan's account here centers on a single conversation—perhaps the world's best example of an interview that got out of hand—she had first to learn the language and to get accepted into the community before such a conversation could ever take place.

Just before I left Oxford for the Tiv in West Africa, conversation turned to the season at Stratford. "You Americans," said a friend, "often have difficulty with Shakespeare. He was, after all, a very English poet, and one can easily misinterpret the universal by misunderstanding the particular."

I protested that human nature is pretty much the same the whole world over; at least the general plot and motivation of the greater tragedies would always be clear—everywhere—although some details of custom might have to be explained and difficulties of translation might produce other slight changes. To end an argument we could not conclude, my friend gave me a copy of

Hamlet to study in the African bush: it would, he hoped, lift my mind above its primitive surroundings, and possibly I might, by prolonged meditation, achieve the grace of correct interpretation.

It was my second field trip to that African tribe, and I thought myself ready to live in one of its remote sections—an area difficult to cross even on foot. I eventually settled on the hillock of a very knowledgeable old man, the head of a homestead of some hundred and forty people, all of whom were either his close relatives or their wives and children. Like the other elders of the vicinity, the old man spent most of his time performing ceremonies seldom seen these days in the more accessible parts of the tribe. I was delighted. Soon there would be three months of enforced isolation and leisure, between the harvest that takes place just before the rising of the swamps and the clearing of new farms when the water goes down. Then, I thought, they would have even more time to perform ceremonies and explain them to me.

I was quite mistaken. Most of the ceremonies demanded the presence of elders from several homesteads. As the swamps rose, the old men found it too difficult to walk from one homestead to the next, and the ceremonies gradually ceased. As the swamps rose even higher, all activities but one came to an end. The women brewed beer from maize and millet. Men, women, and children sat on their hillocks and drank it.

People began to drink at dawn. By mid-morning the whole homestead was singing, dancing, and drumming. When it rained, people had to sit inside their huts: there they drank and sang or they drank and told stories. In any case, by noon or before, I either had to join the party or retire to my own hut and my books. "One does not discuss serious matters when there is beer. Come, drink with us." Since I lacked their capacity for the thick native beer, I spent more and more time with *Hamlet*. Before the end of the second month, grace descended on me. I was quite sure that *Hamlet* had only one possible interpretation, and that one universally obvious.

Early every morning, in the hope of having some serious talk before the beer party, I used to call on the old man at his reception hut—a circle of posts supporting a thatched roof above a low mud wall to keep out wind and rain. One day I crawled through the low doorway and found most of the men of the homestead sitting huddled in their ragged clothes on stools, low plank beds, and reclining chairs, warming themselves against the chill of the rain around a smoky fire. In the center were three pots of beer. The party had started.

The old man greeted me cordially. "Sit down and drink." I accepted a large calabash full of beer, poured some into a small drinking gourd, and tossed it down. Then I poured some more into the same gourd for the man second in seniority to my host before I handed my calabash over to a young man for further distribution. Important people shouldn't ladle beer themselves.

"It is better like this," the old man said, looking at me approvingly and plucking at the thatch that had caught in my hair. "You should sit and drink with us more often. Your servants tell me that when you are not with us, you sit inside your hut looking at a paper."

The old man was acquainted with four kinds of "papers": tax receipts, bride price receipts, court fee receipts, and letters. The messenger who brought him letters from the chief used them mainly as a badge of office, for he always knew what was in them and told the old man. Personal letters to the few who had relatives in the government or mission stations were kept until someone went to a large market where there was a letter writer and reader. Since my arrival letters were brought to me to be read. A few men also brought me bride price receipts, privately, with requests to change the figures to a higher sum. I found moral arguments were of no avail, since in-laws are fair game, and the technical hazards of forgery difficult to explain to an illiterate people. I did not wish them to think me silly enough to look at any such papers for days on end, and I hastily explained that my "paper" was one of the "things of long ago" of my country.

"Ah," said the old man. "Tell us."

I protested that I was not a storyteller. Storytelling is a skilled art among them; their standards are high, and the audiences critical—and vocal in their criticism. I protested in vain. This morning they wanted to hear a story while they drank. They threatened to tell me no more stories until I told them one of mine. Finally, the old man promised that no one would criticize my style "for we know you are struggling with our language." "But," put in one of the elders, "you must explain what we do not understand, as we do when we tell you our stories." Realizing that here was my chance to prove *Hamlet* universally intelligible, I agreed.

The old man handed me some more beer to help me on with my storytelling. Men filled their long wooden pipes and knocked coals from the fire to place in the pipe bowls; then, puffing contentedly, they sat back to listen. I began in the proper style, "Not yesterday, not yesterday, but long ago, a thing occurred. One night three men were keeping watch outside the homestead of the great chief, when suddenly they saw the former chief approach them.''

"Why was he no longer their chief?"

"He was dead," I explained. "That is why they were troubled and afraid when they saw him."

"Impossible," began one of the elders, handing his pipe to his neighbor, who interrupted, "Of course it wasn't the dead chief. It was an omen sent by a witch. Go on."

Slightly shaken, I continued. "One of these three was a man who knew things"—the closest translation for scholar, but unfortunately it also meant witch. The second elder looked triumphantly at the first. "So he spoke to the dead chief saying, 'Tell us what we must do so you may rest in your grave,' but the dead chief did not answer. He vanished, and they could see him no more. Then the man who knew things—his name was Horatio—said this event was the affair of the dead chief's son, Hamlet."

There was a general shaking of heads round the circle. "Had the dead chief no living brothers? Or was this son the chief?"

"No," I replied. "That is, he had one living brother who became the chief when the elder brother died."

The old men muttered: such omens were matters for chiefs and elders, not for youngsters; no good could come of going behind a chief's back; clearly Horatio was not a man who knew things.

"Yes, he was," I insisted, shooing a chicken away from my beer. "In our country the son is next to the father. The dead chief's younger brother had become the great chief. He had also married his elder brother's widow only about a month after the funeral."

"He did well," the old man beamed and announced to the others, "I told you that if we knew more about Europeans, we would find they really were very like us. In our country also," he added to me, "the younger brother marries the elder brother's widow and becomes the father of his children. Now, if your uncle, who married your widowed mother, is your father's full brother, then he will be a real father to you. Did Hamlet's father and uncle have one mother?"

His question barely penetrated my mind; I was too upset and thrown too far off balance by having one of the most important elements of *Hamlet* knocked straight out of the picture. Rather uncertainly I said that I thought they had the same mother, but wasn't sure—the story didn't say. The old man told me severely that these genealogical details made all the difference and that when I got home I must ask the elders about it. He shouted out the door to one of his younger wives to bring his goatskin bag.

Determined to save what I could of the mother motif, I took a deep breath and began again. "The son Hamlet was very sad because his mother had married again so quickly. There was no need for her to do so, and it is our custom for a widow not to go to her next husband until she has mourned for two years."

"Two years is too long," objected the wife, who had appeared with the old man's battered goatskin bag. "Who will hoe your farms for you while you have no husband?"

"Hamlet," I retorted without thinking, "was old enough to hoe his mother's farms himself. There was no need for her to remarry." No one looked convinced. I gave up. "His mother and the great chief told Hamlet not to be sad, for the great chief himself would be a father to Hamlet. Furthermore, Hamlet would be the next chief: therefore he must stay to learn the things of a chief. Hamlet agreed to remain, and all the rest went off to drink beer."

While I paused, perplexed at how to render Hamlet's disgusted soliloquy to an audience convinced that Claudius and Gertrude had behaved in the best possible manner, one of the younger men asked me who had married the other wives of the dead chief.

"He had no other wives," I told him.

"But a chief must have many wives! How else can he brew beer and prepare food for all his guests?"

I said firmly that in our country even chiefs had only one wife, that they had servants to do their work, and that they paid them from tax money.

It was better, they returned, for a chief to have many wives and sons who would help him hoe his farms and feed his people; then everyone loved the chief who gave much and took nothing— taxes were a bad thing.

I agreed with the last comment, but for the rest fell back on their favorite way of fobbing off my questions: "That is the way it is done, so that is how we do it."

I decided to skip the soliloquy. Even if Claudius was here thought quite right to marry his brother's widow, there remained the poison motif, and I knew they would disapprove of fratricide. More hopefully I resumed, "That night Hamlet kept watch with he three who had seen his dead father. The dead chief again appeared, and although the others were afraid, Hamlet followed is dead father off to one side. When they were alone, Hamlet's dead father spoke."

"Omens can't talk!" The old man was emphatic.

"Hamlet's dead father wasn't an omen. Seeing him might have been an omen, but he was not." My audience looked as confused as I sounded. "It *was* Hamlet's dead father. It was a thing we call a 'ghost.' " I had to use the English word, for unlike many of the neighboring tribes, these people didn't believe in the survival after death of any individuating part of the personality.

"What is a 'ghost'? An omen?"

"No, a 'ghost' is someone who is dead but who walks around and can talk, and people can hear him and see him but not touch him."

They objected. "One can touch zombis."

"No, no! It was not a dead body the witches had animated to sacrifice and eat. No one else made Hamlet's dead father walk. He did it himself."

"Dead men can't walk," protested my audience as one man.

I was quite willing to compromise. "A 'ghost' is the dead man's shadow."

But again they objected. "Dead men cast no shadows."

"They do in my country," I snapped.

The old man quelled the babble of disbelief that arose immediately and told me with that insincere, but courteous, agreement one extends to the fancies of the young, ignorant, and superstitious. "No doubt in your country the dead can also walk without being zombis." From the depths of his bag he produced a withered fragment of kola nut, bit off one end to show it wasn't poisoned and handed me the rest as a peace offering.

"Anyhow," I resumed, "Hamlet's dead father said that his own brother, the one who became chief, had poisoned him. He wanted Hamlet to avenge him. Hamlet believed this in his heart for he did not like his father's brother." I took another swallow of beer. "In the country of the great chief, living in the same homestead, for it was a very large one, was an important elder who was often with the chief to advise and help him. His name was Polonius. Hamlet was courting his daughter, but her father and her brother . . . [I cast hastily about for some tribal analogy] warned her not to let Hamlet visit her when she was alone on her farm, for he would be a great chief and so could not marry her."

"Why not?" asked the wife, who had settled down on the edge of the old man's chair. He frowned at her for asking stupid questions and growled, "They lived in the same homestead."

"That was not the reason," I informed them. "Polonius was a stranger who lived in the homestead because he helped the chief, not because he was a relative."

"They why couldn't Hamlet marry her?"

"He could have," I explained, "but Polonius didn't think he would. After all, Hamlet was a man of great importance who ought to marry a chief's daughter, for in his country a man could have only one wife. Polonius was afraid that if Hamlet made love to his daughter, then no one else would give a high price for her."

"That might be true," remarked one of the shrewder elders, "but a chief's son would give his mistress's father enough presents and patronage to more than make up the difference. Polonius sounds like a fool to me."

"Many people think he was," I agreed. "Meanwhile Polonius sent his son Laertes off to Paris to learn the things of that country, for it was the homestead of a very great chief indeed. Because he was afraid that Laertes might waste a lot of money on beer and women and gambling, or get into trouble by fighting, he sent one of his servants to Paris secretly, to spy out what Laertes was doing. One day Hamlet came upon Polonius's daughter Ophelia. He behaved so oddly he frightened her. Indeed"—I was fumbling for words to express the dubious quality of Hamlet's madness—"the chief and many others had also noticed that when Hamlet talked one could understand the words but not what they meant. Many people thought that he had become mad." My audience suddenly became much more attentive. "The great chief wanted to know what was wrong with Hamlet, so he sent for two of Hamlet's age mates [school friends would have taken long explanation] to talk to Hamlet and find out what troubled his heart. Hamlet, seeing that they had been bribed by the chief to betray him, told them nothing. Polonius, however, insisted that Hamlet was mad because he had been forbidden to see Ophelia, whom he loved."

"Why," inquired a bewildered voice, "should anyone bewitch Hamlet on that account?"

"Bewitch him?"

"Yes, only witchcraft can make anyone mad, unless, of course, one sees the beings that lurk in the forest."

I stopped being a storyteller, took out my notebook and demanded to be told more about these two causes of madness. Even while they spoke and I jotted notes, I tried to calculate the effect of this new factor on the plot. Hamlet had not been exposed to the beings that lurk in the forests. Only his relatives in the male line could bewitch him. Barring relatives not mentioned by Shakespeare, it had to be Claudius who was attempting to harm him. And, of course, it was.

For the moment I staved off questions by saying that the great chief also refused to believe that Hamlet was mad for the love of Ophelia and nothing else. "He was sure that something much more important was troubling Hamlet's heart."

"Now Hamlet's age mates," I continued, "had brought with them a famous storyteller. Hamlet decided to have this man tell the chief and all his homestead a story about a man who had poisoned his brother because he desired his brother's wife and wished to be chief himself. Hamlet was sure the great chief could not hear the story without making a sign if he was indeed guilty, and then he would discover whether his dead father had told him the truth."

The old man interrupted, with deep cunning, "Why should a father lie to his son?" he asked.

I hedged: "Hamlet wasn't sure that it really was his dead father." It was impossible to say anything, in that language, about devil-inspired visions.

"You mean," he said, "it actually was an omen, and he knew witches sometimes send false ones. Hamlet was a fool not to go to one skilled in reading omens and divining the truth in the first place. A man-who-sees-the-truth could have told him how his father died, if he really had been poisoned, and if there was witchcraft in it; then Hamlet could have called the elders to settle the matter."

The shrewd elder ventured to disagree. "Because his father's brother was a great chief, one-who-sees-the-truth might therefore have been afraid to tell it. I think it was for that reason that a friend of Hamlet's father—a witch and an elder—sent an omen so his friend's son would know. Was the omen true?"

"Yes," I said, abandoning ghosts and the devil; a witch-sent omen it would have to be. "It was true, for when the storyteller was telling his tale before all the homestead, the great chief rose in fear. Afraid that Hamlet knew his secret he planned to have him killed."

The stage set of the next bit presented some difficulties of translation. I began cautiously. "The great chief told Hamlet's mother to find out from her son what he knew. But because a woman's children are always first in her heart, he had the important elder Polonius hide behind a cloth that hung against the wall of Hamlet's mother's sleeping hut. Hamlet started to scold his mother for what she had done."

There was a shocked murmur from everyone. A man should never scold his mother.

"She called out in fear, and Polonius moved behind the cloth. Shouting, 'A rat!' Hamlet took his machete and slashed through the cloth." I paused for dramatic effect. "He had killed Polonius!"

The old men looked at each other in supreme disgust. "That Polonius truly was a fool and a man who knew nothing! What child would not know enough to shout, 'It's me!'" With a pang, I remembered that these people are ardent hunters, always armed with bow, arrow, and machete; at the first rustle in the grass an arrow is aimed and ready, and the hunter shouts "Game!" If no human voice answers immediately, the arrow speeds on its way. Like a good hunter Hamlet had shouted, "A rat!"

I rushed in to save Polonius's reputation. "Polonius did speak. Hamlet heard him. But he thought it was the chief and wished to kill him to avenge his father. He had meant to kill him earlier that evening . . ." I broke down, unable to describe to these pagans, who had no belief in individual afterlife, the difference between dying at one's prayers and dying "unhousell'd, disappointed, unaneled."

This time I had shocked my audience seriously. "For a man to raise his hand against his father's brother and the one who has become his father—that is a terrible thing. The elders ought to let such a man be bewitched."

I nibbled at my kola nut in some perplexity, then pointed out that after all the man had killed Hamlet's father.

"No," pronounced the old man, speaking less to me than to the young men sitting behind the elders. "If your father's brother has killed your father, you must appeal to your father's age mates; *they* may avenge him. No man may use violence against his senior relatives." Another thought struck him. "But if his father's brother had indeed been wicked enough to bewitch Hamlet and make him mad that would be a good story indeed, for it would be his fault that Hamlet, being mad, no longer had any sense and thus was ready to kill his father's brother."

There was a murmur of applause. *Hamlet* was again a good story to them, but it no longer seemed quite the same story to me. As I thought over the coming complications of plot and motive, I lost courage and decided to skim over dangerous ground quickly.

"The great chief," I went on, "was not sorry that Hamlet had killed Polonius. It gave him a reason to send Hamlet away, with his two treacherous age mates, with letters to a chief of a far country, saying that Hamlet should be killed. But Hamlet changed the writing on their papers, so that the chief killed his age mates instead." I encountered a reproachful glare from one of the men whom I had told undetectable forgery was not merely immoral but beyond human skill. I looked the other way.

"Before Hamlet could return, Laertes came back for his father's funeral. The great chief told him Hamlet had killed Polonius. Laertes swore to kill Hamlet because of this, and because his sister Ophelia, hearing her father had been killed by the man she loved, went mad and drowned in the river."

"Have you already forgotten what we told you?" The old man was reproachful. "One cannot take vengeance on a madman; Hamlet killed Polonius in his madness. As for the girl, she not only went mad, she was drowned. Only witches can make people drown. Water itself can't hurt anything. It is merely something one drinks and bathes in."

I began to get cross. "If you don't like the story, I'll stop."

The old man made soothing noises and himself poured me some more beer. "You tell the story well, and we are listening. But it is clear that the elders of your country have never told you what the story really means. No, don't interrupt! We believe you when you say your marriage customs are different, or your clothes and weapons. But people are the same everywhere; therefore, there are always witches and it is we, the elders, who know how witches work. We told you it was the great chief who wished to kill Hamlet, and now your own words have proved us right. Who were Ophelia's male relatives?"

"There were only her father and her brother." *Hamlet* was clearly out of my hands.

"There must have been many more; this also you must ask of your elders when you get back to your country. From what you tell us, since Polonius was dead, it must have been Laertes who killed Ophelia, although I do not see the reason for it."

We had emptied one pot of beer, and the old men argued the point with slightly tipsy interest. Finally one of them demanded of me, "What did the servant of Polonius say on his return?"

With difficulty I recollected Reynaldo and his mission. "I don't think he did return before Polonius was killed."

"Listen," said the elder, "and I will tell you how it was and how your story will go, then you may tell me if I am right. Polonius knew his son would get into trouble, and so he did. He had many fines to pay for fighting, and debts from gambling. But he had only two ways of getting money quickly. One was to marry off his sister at once, but it is difficult to find a man who will marry a woman desired by the son of a chief. For if the chief's heir commits adultery with your wife, what can you do? Only a fool calls a case against a man who will someday be his judge. Therefore Laertes had to take the second way: he killed his sister by witchcraft, drowning her so he could secretly sell her body to the witches.''

I raised an objection. "They found her body and buried it. Indeed Laertes jumped into the grave to see his sister once more—so, you see, the body was truly there. Hamlet, who had just come back, jumped in after him.''

"What did I tell you?" The elder appealed to the others. "Laertes was up to no good with his sister's body. Hamlet prevented him, because the chief's heir, like a chief, does not wish any other man to grow rich and powerful. Laertes would be angry, because he would have killed his sister without benefit to himself. In our country he would try to kill Hamlet for that reason. Is this not what happened?''

"More or less," I admitted. "When the great chief found Hamlet was still alive, he encouraged Laertes to try to kill Hamlet and arranged a fight with machetes between them. In the fight both the young men were wounded to death. Hamlet's mother drank the poisoned beer that the chief meant for Hamlet in case he won the fight. When he saw his mother die of poison, Hamlet, dying, managed to kill his father's brother with his machete.''

"You see, I was right!" exclaimed the elder.

"That was a very good story," added the old man, "and you told it with very few mistakes. There was just one more error, at the very end. The poison Hamlet's mother drank was obviously meant for the survivor of the fight, whichever it was. If Laertes had won, the great chief would have poisoned him, for no one would know that he arranged Hamlet's death. Then, too, he need not fear Laertes' witchcraft; it takes a strong heart to kill one's only sister by witchcraft.

"Sometime," concluded the old man, gathering his ragged toga about him, "you must tell us some more stories of your country. We, who are elders, will instruct you in their true meaning, so that when you return to your own land your elders will see that you have not been sitting in the bush, but among those who know things and who have taught you wisdom.''

Biography
and History

Now FOR THE other part of Investigation—looking things up. Some knowledge can never be acquired by going and looking, going and listening, or going and joining; it is beyond the knowledge pool of even a whole live community. We cannot interview everyone we want to learn from, and some are long dead. So we must read what they wrote or consult records and archives. Research means ransacking books and other documents, along with films and tapes, to gain access to *stored* knowledge, that is to say, access to other people's compositions of what they know. (Experimental research consists of setting up a situation to observe what one would not otherwise have an occasion to observe, in order to see "what happens if. . . ." It is very important but doesn't uniquely characterize a certain kind of writing, being recorded in laboratory logs, reported in state-of-the-science articles such as "I Sing the Body Electric," on page 338, and generalized in thesis essays like those at the end of this volume.)

To establish what happened in a time past the memory of contemporaries, we usually have no recourse but to documents or the expertise of someone who knows the documents. As entirely secondhand information, history is remoter than memoir or reportage. In fact, history is a compilation and synopsis of many letters, journals, memoirs, and reportage of a given era— the very firsthand kinds of writing we have been surveying. History results from a higher order of abstraction than any of these produce because it incorporates, subsumes, and digests them in order to create a more comprehensive narrative. Because it is still narrative, however, and composed basically in the order in which events happened—chronologically—the story of the past is the lowest order of abstraction to result from research—higher than the firsthand narratives it assimilates but lower than the generalization for which it in turn furnishes fodder.

Within this third-person abstraction range roughly called history we may again scale instances according to the scope of time and space over which the events of each extend. Since the time-space covered by a single life is less than that covered by a group and requires less synoptic composition to narrate, we invoke again the distinction between singular and plural person but this time for the third person. Once more, pluralization is generalization. What happened to a group cannot be so specific as what happened to an individual; idiosyncrasies and particularities must drop off for the sake of the broader coverage. Related to the pluralization is the time-space scope of the actions. Skirmish, battle, or war? A birth, a rise in births, or a pattern of birth rates? Degree of abstraction depends partly on size of theater.

To spread all these factors out for comfortable assimilation as we read on, let's interpose between biography and history an intermediate kind of third-person narrative and call it "chronicle," the account of a small group not greatly extended in time and space and bridging from present to past, from journalism to history.

Biography

As WITH AUTOBIOGRAPHY, contrasting an incident with a larger scope of time-space helps to phase our progression more clearly. Such time units should correspond to composition units one is likely to encounter in reading. The next two selections are not excerpts but complete accounts published independently. Whereas the commonly found larger time unit for autobiography is what I called a "phase," for biography it is the "life," the capsulized story of the subject's whole lifetime.

Rarely does one have reason to capsulize one's whole life in a few pages, at least for publication, though one may for job applications, etc. For *my* story I need a whole book! Because a phase carries a point, one of some value to the author and often of applicability to others, it frequently constitutes a complete short composition. But we do not hesitate to compress another's whole life into a similar length of writing. Indeed, the "vita" has been a literary form since Plutarch and Suetonius in the first century. Worth much consideration by any writer is the ratio between the time span of the events and the length of the composition that is to encompass them. Compare telling a lifetime in 200 pages with telling it in 10 or 20. Fortunately, biographies also flourish, like autobiographies, in book length as well.

The Abduction of the "Planter"
Benjamin Quarles
Civil War History, March 1958

The author briefly situates the incident within the subject's whole life and within the period in order to bring out its significance. As more blacks became historians, and as more black history was heeded, American history was adjusted to acknowledge the role both free and enslaved blacks had played in abolition and in their own liberation. Awareness of, and respect for, black source documents made much of the difference, but often it was a question of not ignoring references to blacks in recognized documents.

To the confederate capital on a spring afternoon in the second year of the war came a one-sentence dispatch addressed to General R.E. Lee: "I have just learned by telegraph that [the] steamer 'Planter,' with five guns aboard, intended for the harbor, was stolen in Charleston this morning." Dated May 13, 1862, from the Savannah headquarters of the Department of South Carolina and Georgia, the terse report concluded with a "Very respectfully," and bore the name of the commanding officer, J.C. Pemberton.

Pemberton's dispatch referred to the "abduction" by a group of slaves of a Confederate vessel, a dramatic deed which made its instigator, Robert Smalls, "an object of interest in Dupont's fleet," as Admiral David D. Porter phrased it. The spectacular escape of Smalls and his party became one of the war's oft-told stories. Requiring careful planning and brilliant execution, the feat in truth was unparalleled in audacity. "I thought," said Smalls, as he delivered the vessel to the Union Navy, "that the 'Planter' might be of some use to Uncle Abe."

A native South Carolinian, Smalls was born in Beaufort in 1839. When he was twelve his master brought him to Charleston, where, after a succession of occupations, he finally became a rigger and began to learn boating and the twisting coastal waters. When the war came, the stockily built young slave was impressed into the Confederate service, and in March, 1862, he was made a member of the crew of the "Planter."

Formerly a cotton steamer plying the Pee Dee River and capable of carrying 1,400 bales, the "Planter" had been chartered by the war government and converted into a transport running from point to point in the Charleston harbor and the neighboring waters. Built of live oak and red cedar, the boat measured 150 feet in length, had a 30 foot beam, a depth of 7 feet 10 inches, and drew 3 feet 9 inches of water. As a Confederate dispatch boat, she mounted two guns for her own use, a 32-pounder pivot gun and a 24-pounder howitzer. Attached to the engineering department at Charleston, the "Planter" carried a crew of eleven, of whom three were whites—captain, mate, and engineer—and the remainder slaves.

By far the ablest of the slave crew was Smalls. Determined to escape, Smalls hit upon the idea of making off with the "Planter." Wherever the Union Navy extended its blockade along the Southern seacoast, freedom-minded Negroes had sensed a new opportunity. By scow, oyster boat, barge, homemade canoe, or anything that would float, they made their way to the Union men-of-war. But no plan of escape was as imaginative and as daring as Smalls's.

The young wheelsman worked out the details in his mind. The escaping party would number sixteen, of whom half would be women and children, including Smalls's wife and their two young ones. The "Planter" would put out to sea casually, as though making a routine run to reconnoiter. Knowing they could expect little mercy if caught, Smalls bound the party to agree that if they were unable to make good their flight, they would blow up the vessel rather than be taken alive. Smalls's plans embraced one final but essential detail—all three white officers would have to remain ashore for the night. Such an absence would be contrary to standing general orders which stipulated that officers of light draft vessels were to remain "on board day and night" when their boat was docked at the wharf.

Finally came such a night as Smalls waited for—the night of May 12. Coincidentally, on the afternoon of that day, 200 pounds of ammunition and four guns—"a banded rifle 42, one 8-inch columbiad, one 8-inch seacoast howitzer, and one 32-pounder" —had been loaded on the "Planter" for transport to the harbor battery, Fort Ripley.

With the white officers ashore, Smalls began to put his plan into operation. The sixteen slaves got aboard in the crisp early morning, the women and children being led below deck in pin-drop quiet. Smalls broke into Captain C.J. Relyea's cabin and took the captain's hat. At 3:00 a.m. one of the fugitives struck a match and set the kindlings on fire under the boilers; twenty-five minutes later the hawsers which moored the boat to Southern Wharf were cast off. From the pilothouse Smalls sounded the wharf signal. The shore sentinel at his post some fifty yards distant noticed the ship gliding away but sensed nothing afoot; he "did not think it necessary to stop her, presuming that she was but pursuing her usual business," in the language of an official report issued later that day.

Now to run the many fortifications in the harbor. Bristling with sea defenses, the defiant city was ringed with forts and batteries on constant alert. But for the runaway slaves there was no turning back. Hoisting the ship's two flags, Confederate and Palmetto, Smalls eased into the inner channel. He geared the "Planter" to its customary pace, although not to dash at full speed required the utmost self-control.

The critical minutes of the great deception had arrived. Wearing the captain's hat and mimicking his gait, Smalls stood in the pilothouse with the cord in his hand. As the vessel passed Fort Johnson, he pulled the lanyard on the steam whistle and gave the proper salute. All went well.

Finally the abductors approached the last hurdle, historic Fort Sumter. Thirteen months ago it was here that the opposing shots of the war had been fired, and at the identical morning hour. One of the four transport guns on the "Planter" belonged originally, as Smalls well knew, to Fort Sumter, having been struck on the muzzle during the bombardment of that bastion and now having been repaired because of the Confederacy's scarcity of heavy guns.

Abreast of Sumter, Smalls sounded the private signal, three shrill whistles followed by a hissing one. "The sentinel on the parapet called for the corporal of the guard and reported the guard-boat going out," stated the official report of Major Alfred Rhett. In turn, the corporal of the guard relayed the intelligence to the officer of the day, Captain David G. Fleming. The information had been passed along in routine fashion since it was, in Major Rhett's words, "by no means unusual for the guard-boat to run out at that hour." Then came the fateful order to permit the halted vessel to go on her way; by signal Sumter answered, "All right." The "Planter" had been taken for the guard-boat and hence allowed to pass!

The slave-manned steamer moved in a southeasterly direction and entered the main ship channel, maintaining her leisurely pace until she had outdistanced the line of fire of the Confederate battery. Then she got up steam, lowered her guns, and ran up a white flag.

Not a minute too soon was the flag of truce hoisted. Off Charleston was a Union blockading fleet of ten warships, and the "Planter" had been spied by the lookout on the inside ship, "Onward." The commander, J.F. Nickels, had ordered his ship swung around so as to train the maximum gunfire on the approaching craft. Just as the "Onward" succeeded in bringing her port guns to bear on the oncoming steamer, Commander Nickels caught sight of the white flag. The gunners relaxed.

Unmolested, the harbor boat drew up alongside the armed sailing vessel. A prize crew boarded the "Planter" and greeted its crew. Down came the white flag, and up went the American ensign. Then and there in the outer harbor the ownership of the captive boat was transferred from the Confederate States of America to the Union Navy.

Later that morning the senior officer commanding the blockading squadron off Charleston, E.G. Parrott, taking advantage of the good weather, ordered the prize crew to take the "Planter" and its captors to Port Royal, and there to report the incident to Flag Officer S.F. Du Pont. No order could have pleased Smalls and his companions more, most of them having originally come from the Sea Island region.

The "Planter" made the sixty-mile trip to Port Royal by way of St. Helena Sound and Broad River, reaching her destination shortly after ten in the evening. Word awaited Smalls that he was to report directly to Du Pont, and the next morning he was ushered aboard the flagship "Wabash." There the elderly admiral, "that stately and courteous potentate, elegant as one's ideal French marquis," listened attentively as the ex-slave told his story.

Later that day, in a lengthy report to the Secretary of the

Navy, Du Pont summed up the exploit: "The bringing out of this steamer, under all the circumstances, would have done credit to anyone." The admiral also jotted down another conclusion: "This man, Robert Smalls, is superior to any who have yet come into the lines, intelligent as many of them have been."

Back in Charleston the news was received with consternation not unmingled with disbelief. In a front-page story devoted to the "extraordinary occurrence," the *Courier* reported that "our community was intensely agitated Tuesday morning by the intelligence that the steamer 'Planter' . . . had been taken possession of by her colored crew, steamed up and boldly ran [sic] out to the blockaders." Added the daily, "The news was not at first credited." Another Charleston newspaper, the *Mercury*, concluded its descriptive story of the escape by explaining that "the run to Morris Island goes out a long way past the fort, and then turns. The 'Planter' did not turn."

Voicing the general indignation of Confederate South Carolina over the negligence of the white officers of the boat, the *Columbia Guardian* expressed a fervent wish that the "recreant parties will be brought to speedy justice, and the prompt penalty of the halter rigorously enforced." From army headquarters in Richmond came a dispatch to General Pemberton stating that General Lee had received the papers relative to the "Planter's" escape and that "he very much regrets the circumstances, and hopes that necessary measures will be taken to prevent any repetition of a like misfortune."

News of Smalls's feat quickly spread throughout the North, and public sentiment became strong for awarding prize money to the "Planter's" crew. Congress responded, moving with unusual speed. Two weeks from the day of the seizure, that body passed a bill ordering the Secretary of the Navy to have the vessel appraised and "when the value thereof shall be thus ascertained to cause an equitable apportionment of one-half of such value . . . to be made between Robert Smalls and his associates who assisted in rescuing her from the enemies of the Government." Within another week Lincoln had signed the bill.

Smalls turned out to be right in believing that the "Planter" might be of some use to the North. Admirably suited to the shallow waters of the Sea Island region, she was immediately equipped with musket-proof bulwarks and converted into a navy transport, carrying upwards of seventy men. Exactly one month after the abduction, Admiral Du Pont, in acknowledging two letters from naval officer A.C. Rhind, wrote that he was "glad that the 'Planter' has proved so useful a transport, and that we have again been able so materially to aid the army, especially at a critical time, when its generals were almost helpless for want of transports."

Early in September, 1862, the "Planter" was sold to the army, which could make much better use of a wood-burner than could the sister service. The quartermaster's department welcomed the addition, "as we have comparatively no vessels of light draft." Until she was decommissioned and sold at Baltimore in September, 1866, the "Planter" remained in military service, being used mainly as a troop transport, but seeing occasional service as a supply boat.

During most of its period of use by the armed forces, the "Planter" was piloted or commanded by Smalls. Over the four months the boat remained under navy supervision, the young Negro was employed as pilot. During the year 1863 and for the first two months in 1864, the army employed him in a like capacity, paying him $50 a month until September 30, 1863, then $75 a month from October 1 to November 30, 1863, and thenceforth $150 a month. On March 1, 1864, he was made captain.

The pilot was promoted to master as a reward for bravery under fire (before the war was over, Smalls had fought in seventeen engagements), but the appointment was merited on other grounds. For the fugitive slave brought much with him. His knowledge of the coastline of South Carolina and Georgia was intimate; few men were more familiar with the sinuous windings of those waters, and no hand was more skilled in their navigation. Indeed, "the accession of Smalls is deemed of more importance than the heavy guns of the 'Planter,' " wrote a reporter for the *Philadelphia Inquirer* (May 17, 1862), "as Smalls is thoroughly acquainted with all the intricacies of navigation in that region." Smalls also brought a knowledge of where the torpedoes had been planted to destroy the Union gunboats and where the masked batteries were located.

The intelligence he furnished was so valuable that the Secretary of the Navy, in his annual report to President Lincoln, made it a point to describe them:

From information derived chiefly from the contraband Pilot, Robert Smalls, who has escaped from Charleston, Flag Officer Du Pont, after proper reconnaissance, directed Commander Marchand to cross the bar with several gun-boats and occupy Stono. The river was occupied as far as Legarville, and examinations extended further to ascertain the position of the enemy's batteries. The seizure of Stono Inlet and river secured an important base for military operations, and was virtually a turning of the forces in the Charleston harbor.

At the war's end Smalls was among the thousands who witnessed the reraising of the American flag at Fort Sumter. This event had been scheduled for April 14, four years to the day after the one on which the Union forces had been forced to hand down the colors. Present at the flag-raising ceremonies was a distinguished roster of reformers and public notables, including William Lloyd Garrison, Judge Advocate General Joseph Holt, Supreme Court Justice N. H. Swayne, Senator Henry Wilson, and the chief speaker, Henry Ward Beecher. On hand also was Robert Anderson, brought back to Sumter to raise the very shot-pierced flag which the Southerners had forced him to lower four years previously. But perhaps the most symbolic figure present was Captain Robert Smalls, who that morning had left Charleston, Sumter bound, at the helm of the "Planter," profusely decorated with the Stars and Stripes and loaded down with hundreds "of the emancipated race."

After the war Smalls had fifty years to live, many of them spent in the public eye—as a member of the South Carolina legislature, a five-term United States Congressman, and Collector of the Port at Beaufort. But no moment of his eventful life could ever match that memorable dawn when he abducted the "Planter."

Mary Wollstonecraft
Virginia Woolf
from *The Common Reader*, Second Series, 1932

To reduce someone's life to a few pages, as in the traditional vita, is surely to slant it, whether deliberately or not. The only question is whether the slant is just. The result approaches profile to the extent that the story serves to signal a couple of main traits. In Profiles in Courage, *John F. Kennedy avowedly selected personages and aspects of their lives that fit his theme of courage among statesmen. But to relate briefly all the main facts without desiccating them and to interrelate these facts without desecrating them—well, it's a fine art.*

Great wars are strangely intermittent in their effects. The French Revolution took some people and tore them asunder; others it passed over without disturbing a hair of their heads. Jane Austen, it is said, never mentioned it; Charles Lamb ignored it; Beau Brummell never gave the matter a thought. But to Wordsworth and to Godwin it was the dawn; unmistakably they saw

> *France standing on the top of golden hours,*
> *And human nature seeming born again.*

Thus it would be easy for a picturesque historian to lay side by side the most glaring contrasts—here in Chesterfield Street was Beau Brummell letting his chin fall carefully upon his cravat and discussing in a tone studiously free from vulgar emphasis the proper cut of the lapel of a coat; and here in Somers Town was a party of ill-dressed, excited young men, one with a head too big for his body and a nose too long for his face, holding forth day by day over the tea-cups upon human perfectibility, ideal unity, and the rights of man. There was also a woman present with very bright eyes and a very eager tongue, and the young men, who had middle-class names, like Barlow and Holcroft and Godwin, called her simply "Wollstonecraft," as if it did not matter whether she were married or unmarried, as if she were a young man like themselves.

Such glaring discords among intelligent people—for Charles Lamb and Godwin, Jane Austen and Mary Wollstonecraft were all highly intelligent—suggest how much influence circumstances have upon opinions. If Godwin had been brought up in the precincts of the Temple and had drunk deep of antiquity and old letters at Christ's Hospital, he might never have cared a straw for the future of man and his rights in general. If Jane Austen had lain as a child on the landing to prevent her father from thrashing her mother, her soul might have burnt with such a passion against tyranny that all her novels might have been consumed in one cry for justice.

Such had been Mary Wollstonecraft's first experience of the joys of married life. And then her sister Everina had been married miserably and had bitten her wedding ring to pieces in the coach. Her brother had been a burden on her; her father's farm had failed, and in order to start that disreputable man with the red face and the violent temper and the dirty hair in life again she had gone into bondage among the aristocracy as a governess—in short, she had never known what happiness was, and, in its default, had fabricated a creed fitted to meet the sordid misery of real human life. The staple of her doctrine was that nothing mattered save independence. "Every obligation we receive from our fellow-creatures is a new shackle, takes from our native freedom, and debases the mind." Independence was the first necessity for a woman; not grace or charm, but energy and courage and the power to put her will into effect were her necessary qualities. It was her highest boast to be able to say, "I never yet resolved to do anything of consequence that I did not adhere readily to it." Certainly Mary could say this with truth. When she was a little more than thirty she could look back upon a series of actions which she had carried out in the teeth of opposition. She had taken a house by prodigious efforts for her friend Fanny, only to find that Fanny's mind was changed and she did not want a house after all. She had started a school. She had persuaded Fanny into marrying Mr. Skeys. She had thrown up her school and gone to Lisbon alone to nurse Fanny when she died. On the voyage back she had forced the captain of the ship to rescue a wrecked French vessel by threatening to expose him if he refused. And when, overcome by a passion for Fuseli, she declared her wish to live with him and was refused flatly by his wife, she had put her principle of decisive action instantly into effect, and had gone to Paris determined to make her living by her pen.

The Revolution thus was not merely an event that had happened outside her; it was an active agent in her own blood. She had been in revolt all her life—against tyranny, against law, against convention. The reformer's love of humanity, which has so much of hatred in it as well as love, fermented within her. The outbreak of revolution in France expressed some of her deepest theories and convictions, and she dashed off in the heat of that extraordinary moment those two eloquent and daring books—the *Reply to Burke* and the *Vindication of the Rights of Women*, which are so true that they seem now to contain nothing new in them—their originality has become our commonplace. But when she was in Paris lodging by herself in a great house, and saw with her own eyes the King whom she despised driving past surrounded by National Guards and holding himself with greater dignity than she expected, then, "I can scarcely tell you why," the tears came to her eyes. "I am going to bed," the letter ended, "and, for the first time in my life, I cannot put out the candle." Things were not so simple after all. She could not understand even her own feelings. She saw the most cherished of her convictions put into practice—and her eyes filled with tears. She had won fame and independence and the right to live her own life—and she wanted something different. "I do not wish to be loved like a goddess," she wrote, "but I wish to be necessary to you." For Imlay, the fascinating American to whom her letter was addressed, had been very good to her. Indeed, she had fallen passionately in love with him. But it was one of her theories that love should be free—"that mutual affection was marriage and that the marriage tie should not bind after the death of love, if love should die." And yet at the same time that she wanted freedom she wanted certainty. "I like the word affection," she wrote, "because it signifies something habitual."

The conflict of all these contradictions shows itself in her face, at once so resolute and so dreamy, so sensual and so intelligent, and beautiful into the bargain with its great coils of hair and the large bright eyes that Southey thought the most expressive he had ever seen. The life of such a woman was bound to be tempestuous. Every day she made theories by which life should be lived; and every day she came smack against the rock of other people's prejudices. Every day too—for she was no pedant, no cold-blooded theorist—something was born in her that thrust aside her theories and forced her to model them afresh. She acted upon her theory that she had no legal claim upon Imlay; she refused to marry him; but when he left her alone week after week with the child she had borne him her agony was unendurable.

Thus distracted, thus puzzling even to herself, the plausible and treacherous Imlay cannot be altogether blamed for failing to follow the rapidity of her changes and the alternate reason and unreason of her moods. Even friends whose liking was impartial were disturbed by her discrepancies. Mary had a passionate, an exuberant, love of Nature, and yet one night when the colours in the sky were so exquisite that Madeleine Schweizer could not help saying to her, "Come, Mary—come, nature lover—and enjoy this wonderful spectacle—this constant transition from colour to colour," Mary never took her eyes off the Baron de Wolzogen. "I must confess," wrote Madame Schweizer, "that this erotic absorption made such a disagreeable impression on me, that all my pleasure vanished." But if the sentimental Swiss was disconcerted by Mary's sensuality, Imlay, the shrewd man of business, was exasperated by her intelligence. Whenever he saw her he yielded to her charm, but then her quickness, her penetration, her uncompromising idealism harassed him. She saw through his excuses; she met all his reasons; she was even capable of managing his business. There was no peace with her—he must be off again. And then her letters followed him, torturing him with their sincerity and their insight. They were so outspoken; they pleaded so passionately to be told the truth; they showed such a contempt for soap and alum and wealth and comfort; they repeated, as he suspected, so truthfully that he had only to say the word, "and you shall never hear of me more," that he could not endure it. Tickling minnows he had hooked a dolphin, and the creature rushed him through the waters till he was dizzy and only wanted to escape. After all, though he had played at theory-making too, he was a business man, he depended upon soap and alum; "the secondary pleasures of life are very necessary to my comfort." And among them was one that for ever evaded Mary's jealous scrutiny. Was it business, was it politics, was it a woman that perpetually took him away from her? He shillied and shallied; he was very charming when they met; then he disappeared again. Exasperated at last, and half insane with suspicion, she forced the truth from the cook. A little actress in a strolling company was his mistress, she learnt. True to her own creed of decisive action, Mary at once soaked her skirts so that she might sink unfailingly, and threw herself from Putney Bridge. But she was rescued; after unspeakable agony she recovered, and then her "unconquerable greatness of mind," her girlish creed of independence, asserted itself again, and she determined to make another bid for happiness and to earn her living without taking a penny from Imlay for herself or their child.

It was in this crisis that she again saw Godwin, the little man with the big head, whom she had met when the French Revolution was making the young men in Somers Town think that a new world was being born. She met him—but that is a euphemism, for in fact Mary Wollstonecraft actually visited him in his own house. Was it the effect of the French Revolution? Was it the blood she had seen spilt on the pavement and the cries of the furious crowd that had run in her ears that made it seem a matter of no importance whether she put on her cloak and went to visit Godwin in Somers Town, or waited in Judd Street West for Godwin to come to her? And what strange upheaval of human life was it that inspired that curious man, who was so queer a mixture of meanness and magnanimity, of coldness and deep feeling—for the memoir of his wife could not have been written without unusual depth of heart—to hold the view that she did right—that he respected Mary for trampling upon the idiotic convention by which women's lives were tied down? He held the most extraordinary views on many subjects, and upon the relations of the sexes in particular. He thought that reason should influence even the love between men and women. He thought that there was something spiritual in their relationship. He had written that "marriage is a law, and the worst of all laws . . . marriage is an affair of property, and the worst of all properties." He held the belief that if two people of the opposite sex like each other, they should live together without any ceremony, or, for living together is apt to blunt love, twenty doors off, say, in the same street. And he went further; he said that if another man liked your wife "this will create no difficulty. We may all enjoy her conversation, and we shall all be wise enough to consider the sensual intercourse a very trivial object." True, when he wrote those words he had never been in love; now for the first time he was to experience that sensation. It came very quietly and naturally, working "with equal advances in the mind of each" from those talks in Somers Town, from those discussions upon everything under the sun which they held so improperly alone in his rooms. "It was friendship melting into love . . .," he wrote. "When, in the course of things, the disclosure came, there was nothing in a manner for either party to disclose to the other." Certainly they were in agreement upon the most essential points; they were both of opinion, for instance, that marriage was unnecessary. They would continue to live apart. Only when Nature again intervened, and Mary found herself with child, was it worth while to lose valued friends, she asked, for the sake of a theory? She thought not, and they were married. And then that other theory—that it is best for husband and wife to live apart—was not that also incompatible with other feelings that were coming to birth in her? "A husband is a convenient part of the furniture of the house," she wrote. Indeed, she discovered that she was passionately domestic. Why not, then, revise that theory too, and share the same roof? Godwin should have a room some doors off to work in; and they should dine out separately if they liked—their work, their friends, should be separate. Thus they settled it, and the plan worked admirably. The arrangement combined "the novelty and lively sensation of a visit with the more delicious and heartfelt pleasures of domestic life." Mary admitted that she was happy; Godwin confessed that, after all one's philosophy, it was "extremely gratifying" to find that "there is some one who takes an interest in one's happiness.'' All sorts of powers and emotions were liberated in Mary by her new satisfaction. Trifles gave her an exquisite pleasure—the sight of Godwin and Imlay's child playing together; the thought of their own child who was to be born; a day's jaunt into the country. One day, meeting Imlay in the New Road, she greeted him without bitterness. But, as Godwin wrote, ''Ours is not an idle happiness, a paradise of selfish and transitory pleasures.'' No, it too was an experiment, as Mary's life had been an experiment from the start, an attempt to make human conventions conform more closely to human needs. And their marriage was only a beginning; all sorts of things were to follow after. Mary was going to have a child. She was going to write a book to be called *The Wrongs of Women*. She was going to reform education. She was going to come down to dinner the day after her child was born. She was going to employ a midwife and not a doctor at her confinement—but that experiment was her last. She died in child-birth. She whose sense of her own existence was so intense, who had cried out even in her misery, ''I cannot bear to think of being no more—of losing myself—nay, it appears to me impossible that I should cease to exist,'' died at the age of thirty-six. But she has her revenge. Many millions have died and been forgotten in the hundred and thirty years that have passed since she was buried, and yet as we read her letters and listen to her arguments and consider her experiments, above all that most fruitful experiment, her relation with Godwin, and realise the high-handed and hot-blooded manner in which she cut her way to the quick of life, one form of immortality is hers undoubtedly: she is alive and active, she argues and experiments, we hear her voice and trace her influence even now among the living.

Chronicle

A CHRONICLE is a *group* story, usually told by contemporaries or near contemporaries, and its scope is more localized than that of history. The four selections to follow graduate from present to past and expand in time and space. To get this full sweep we start back in journalistic reportage again.

The Anatomy of a Plane Crash

Tom Emch

California Living, September 26, 1971

A pluralistic story requires a pluralistic investigative technique: the information for this narrative clearly came from interviews with numerous people who underwent the experience (as well as from the plane's log, which is the cockpit tape). Multiple interviews produce a panoramic chronicle, like the popular disaster movies, that cuts among various individual viewpoints and thus pieces together as nearly whole a picture as possible. The title here implies that the story typifies something—tells not only what happened once but says what a crash is like.

Holly Hilton, stewardess, is sitting on the left side in the rear of the aircraft. She is tall, blonde and superstitious. She never sits on the right. As the plane begins to roll down the runway, she looks out the window, and her eyes widen.

Ilsa Krekels, flight director and a fourteen year veteran with Pan Am, is in the first class section, not far from the red emergency communications button she will be pressing very soon.

Joyce Cane, stewardess and a nurse, is seated forward; so is Carol Rankin, another stewardess. Neither of them is concerned about the long takeoff roll. Some pilots elect to use every inch of runway.

In the cockpit, Captain Calvin Dyer is concerned. He sees the end of the runway. Airspeed is 170 knots. Dyer hears the liftoff signal from First Officer Paul Oakes and pulls back on the controls, rotating the aircraft to twelve degrees.

The takeoff appears normal to Frank Coil in the tower, the assistant chief who assigned runway 1-R to Flight 845. But something appears wrong to Ted Soncini, a mechanic working with Roman Kocourek on an aircraft at the 19-R runup pad. They are near the end of 1-R.

Soncini sees the big plane is still not off the ground as it crosses the runway intersection. Kocourek sees the plane cross the seawall and appear to sink slightly. Then he sees flying debris and a huge spray of water.

In the tower, Coil is watching, fascinated, as the 747 uses up all the runway and then begins to lift off. He sees a sudden cloud of dust and debris. He immediately announces "Alert One" on the airport communications system. He picks up a phone and calls for the Coast Guard. San Francisco International's Disaster Plan is triggered.

George Nessel, operations coordinator, also is in the tower. While Coil is telling the Coast Guard that the 747 may be returning for a crash landing, Nessel calls the San Mateo County Sheriff's office and asks for ambulances, and for traffic control help.

Within minutes, Millbrae Police are assigned one of the entrances. California Highway Patrol is assigned to clear a way to Peninsula Hospital. San Francisco Fire Department is told to stand by at the United Hangar.

Captain Tom Ryan of the airport fire department rolls his equipment to a stand-by position. He is informed that when the plane lands it may veer right, and he makes plans to approach the plane from the left.

The Disaster Plan is working. Radio frequencies are assigned to disaster control. Nessel gets word that five doctors are in the airport.

At the airport, stretchers and tourniquets are readied. Dr. Fred Leeds of Pan American is there. A Coast Guard doctor is on the way, and the Red Cross disaster team is rolling toward the airport. Now, the emergency personnel from a dozen agencies are in position. And ready.

Earlier, at 3:01, when Flight 845 cleared the blocks and was pushed out, the airport activity was routine.

We're on time, Captain Dyer thinks to himself. At 3:11 he gets taxi clearance. At 3:14, after a taxiway detour, the aircraft rolls up to the painted threshold on runway 1-R and stops.

Captain Dyer has been switched from runway 28-L—closed for surface repairs—to 1-R, and he is still talking to Pan Am dispatcher F. R. Kiethley, getting information. He asks for and gets confirmation on the length of 1-R, on his 708,002-pound gross takeoff weight, on temperature, wind speed and direction.

He is assured that he has 9500 feet of available runway in front of him, plus 1000 feet of clearway: no obstructions to an altitude of thirty-five feet. It is agreed that Flight 845 will take off with twenty-degree flaps. The manuals are checked. And Dyer asks flight engineer, W. A. Horne, for takeoff thrust.

It is shortly after 3:15 p.m. and the aircraft is rolling, picking up speed. Holly Hilton watches the runway go by and feels secure . . . Passenger Winfred C. Barnes, a Tokyo businessman, is sitting in Row 44 with his wife, Lois. He casually picks up a magazine. His confidence in the aircraft, the crew and the captain is supreme.

But there is one disturbing fact that everyone aboard is ignorant of, one small arithmetical fact: the available runway is not 9500 feet. It is 8400 feet, because the first 1100 feet have been closed to protect men working on the blast fence.

Flight 845 will run right off the end of runway 1-R, hit the dirt, rise and crash into the landing light pier in the Bay before becoming miraculously airborne—a huge, wounded silver bird, losing its vital hydraulic fluid.

The accident happens. There is a hard bump and a vibration.

Holly Hilton hears the plane shudder; she sees the plastic cover for the emergency chute fly off. Oxygen masks drop from the ceiling and passengers grab for them. She hears someone scream. . . .

Ilsa Krekels unsnaps her seat belt, turns to the rear and sees the main landing gear pushed up into a passenger cabin. Seats are crammed against the ceiling. A man is pinned in the wreckage. She pushes the emergency communications button and is talking directly to the captain. But everyone aboard hears it.

Her report: structural damage and injured passengers. Captain Dyer hears her, hears her call for doctors. He is busy.

The wheel-well fire warning light is on. The low-pressure warning light for the hydraulic systems is on. Horne, the flight engineer, is calling out panel readings: "Losing hydraulic fluid. We're empty in One and Three. Four is down to two gallons."

Dyer now knows the body landing gear is damaged, the controls are crippled, but the aircraft is flying, somehow. First Officer Oakes is watching the panel indicators; he tells Dyer he thinks the plane can stay in the air.

Flight 845 is at 1500 feet and climbing. And in the orange section of economy class, Winfred Barnes and his wife are asked to move forward to Row 12 near first class. The stewardesses are moving all passengers away from the damaged area.

Second flight engineer R. E. Proctor enters the cabin and tells passengers the plane has crashed into something at the end of the runway and that they are proceeding to a dumping area over the ocean to jettison fuel.

Stewardess Carol Rankin is helping passengers with their life jackets. Some of them don't work and she shows passengers how to pull hard on the cords. She tells Barnes she won't lie to him: they will probably make a belly landing. Barnes thanks her for being honest.

Holly Hilton brings a piece of broken plastic, a makeshift splint, to Dr. Steven Jordan of Ft. Lauderdale. Jordan, a passenger with head injuries himself, is working on Major Don Shrader of Treasure Island. One of Schrader's arms is nearly severed; he has leg and shoulder injuries.

Joyce Cane, the stewardess-nurse, is with the other seriously injured passenger, Daisoo Lee of Los Angeles. Lee's foot has been amputated, and he is told there are no painkillers aboard.

Later, Pan American will credit Dr. Jordan and Joyce Cane with saving the lives of both Shrader and Lee.

Third pilot W. E. Sagar, the second engineer, Proctor, and Ilsa Krekels all move through the plane and reassure passengers that "we are better off than we thought; the landing will be smooth, but the plane will stop abruptly."

In the cockpit, Dyer and Oakes are going over the fuel dumping checklist. A Coast Guard helicopter is in radio contact, and Dyer asks the 'copter pilot to maneuver underneath the 747 and assess damage.

Oakes reports bad news: only half power available for right lower rudder, for left inboard and right outboard flaps. The Coast Guard pilot makes his visual report: right body gear missing, left body gear and stabilizer damage, but the wing gears are intact.

If the Number Two hydraulic system holds, the plane can land on the wing gears. If not. . . .

Flight engineer Horne commences dumping. It takes forty-five minutes to jettison 180,000 pounds of fuel and reduce the gross weight of the aircraft to a safe figure, 435,000 pounds. They keep just enough fuel for the emergency landing ahead.

Then, with a vaporous stream of fuel trailing, Captain Dyer gently turns the aircraft back toward San Francisco International, where the crippled bird has been cleared for runway 28-L, the same runway that had been denied Dyer for takeoff.

Proctor gives emergency landing instructions to the stewardesses. They are told to return to their seats at 500 feet and wait for the landing and the order to abandon ship. They are to open the emergency doors, drop the inflatable chutes and evacuate the passengers.

Holly Hilton is worried about opening her assigned door. She has done it in training, but this is different.

Carol Rankin is worried about the woman who is hysterical. She gets the woman buckled in and assigns two male passengers to sit on either side of her and calm her down.

Stewardess Rankin coolly assigns a serviceman and another passenger to drop the escape chute as soon as she opens her door, and then she takes her seat.

The plane is at 500 feet and dropping. Passengers are in the foetal position: head down toward knees and pillow in front of face.

At 200 feet, coming in past Bay Meadows, the race track's closed-circuit television camera is trained on the 747, and thousands watch the approach. There is a mechanized armada of emergency vehicles at the airport, ready to roll.

Dyer feels the controls suddenly go soft and sloppy. At fifty feet he is unable to flare the powerful jet engines.

Flight 845 touches down on runway 28-L, bounces twice. Dyer sets the speed brake and applies reverse thrust. Horne calls out that they are getting reverse thrust only on Number Four engine, and the plane begins to veer to the right. Dyer pulls the fire bottles on all four jets. The anti-skid control isn't working and almost all of the wing gear tires blow out.

Suddenly, with a jerk, the big silver wounded bird comes to a stop. Flight 845 is over.

In the passenger cabins there is a spontaneous burst of applause, and Winfred Barnes and his wife, Lois, join in. They are all glad to be back on the ground and alive.

First officer Oakes gives the ''abandon ship'' command, and the stewardesses move to their assigned emergency doors. Forward doors are opened first. Two of the chutes do not inflate. Barnes and his wife are moved forward to another door.

Stewardesses Hilton and Rankin, in the rear, open their doors and drop chutes. The evacuation begins. And at this moment the nose gear lifts twelve feet off the ground as the entire aircraft tilts backward and settles on its tail.

The nose is so far off the ground that passengers exiting from the forward chutes are going down at a sharp angle. At the rear of the plane it is only five feet to the ground, enabling some of the passengers to jump. They are the lucky ones.

More than fifteen passengers are injured before evacuation from the forward chutes is halted by first officer Oakes. The two seriously injured passengers, Lee and Shrader, are carried out of the rear door and placed on waiting stretchers.

In a matter of minutes, twenty-nine people are rushed to Peninsula Hospital. Those coming down the forward chutes have back and leg injuries, wrist injuries, abrasions. Some are in shock. Others have minor scratches; they are examined and released.

Still in the cockpit, Captain Calvin York Dyer is calmly completing the emergency landing checklist. Then he goes below and checks the aircraft for remaining passengers. He finds none and departs from the right rear chute, the last of the 212 persons aboard Flight 845 to leave.

It has not been a good flight for any of them. But remarkably, no one is dead. The aircraft has flown even though crippled beyond anything covered in the emergency manuals. It has flown beyond anyone's belief that it could, and it has landed safely.

The captain goes immediately to the Pan Am office to make his report. It will describe everything he can remember on Flight 845.

Maynard Keynes (Rhymes with Brains) and the Mandarin Revolution
John Kenneth Galbraith
Harvard Magazine, May/June, 1977

Economist Galbraith tells here a story about both a society and an individual who greatly influenced it. (History is often told as the story of key individuals.) It is transitional in a couple of other ways as well. The earlier parts of his account rely on book research, study in his specialty, but because his generation overlapped with Keynes's, making him a member of the economics chorus, and because his own work became a part of the story, making him participant as well as observer, he can tell some of the story as memoir. Thus it is part firsthand, part secondhand, and represents very well how "contemporary history" gets written, just as it did for medieval chroniclers like Froissart, Joinville, and Villehardouin.

The ideas that made revolutions did not originate with the masses, with the people who, by any reasonable calculation, had the most reason for revolt. They came from intellectuals. This was noticed by Lenin: he thought intellectuals disputatious, perverse, undisciplined. But without them, he also believed, the armies of the proletariat would dissolve in purposeless confusion.

Those who are comfortable with things as they are, conservatives in the literal sense, have often and rightly been suspicious of intellectuals and have thought them troublemakers, unable to leave well enough alone, more reprehensible by any measure than the poor or discontented whom so unnecessarily they arouse. Intellectuals have usually thought themselves disliked because others were jealous of their brains. More often it's because they make trouble.

But intellectuals can render conservative as well as radical service. Before and after World War II, their ideas did much, for a time, to save the reputation of capitalism. As the ideas of socialism did not come from the masses, those that saved capitalism did not come from businessmen, bankers, or owners of shares whose value had gone with the wind. They came principally from John Maynard Keynes. His fate was to be regarded as peculiarly dangerous by the class he rescued.

Keynes was born in 1883, the year that Karl Marx died. His mother, Florence Ada Keynes, a woman of high intelligence, was diligent in good works, a respected community leader, and, in late life, the mayor of Cambridge. His father, John Neville Keynes, was an economist, logician, and for some fifteen years the registrary, which is to say the chief administrative officer, of the University of Cambridge. Maynard, as he was always known to friends, went to Eton, where his first interest was in mathematics. Then he went to King's College, after Trinity the most prestigious of the Cambridge colleges and the one noted especially for its economists. Keynes was to add both to its prestige in economics and, as its bursar, to its wealth.

Churchill held that great men usually have unhappy childhoods. At both Eton and Cambridge, Keynes, by his own account and that of his contemporaries, was exceedingly happy. The point could be important. Keynes never sought to change the world out of any sense of personal dissatisfaction or discontent. Marx swore that the bourgeoisie would suffer for his poverty and his carbuncles. Keynes experienced neither poverty nor boils. For him the world was excellent.

While at King's, Keynes found his interest shifting from mathematics to economics. One instrument of the change was Alfred Marshall, who was not at King's but along the river in the equally beautiful precincts of St. John's, known as John's. Marshall, who combined the reputation of a prophet with the aura of a saint, presided over the world of Anglo-American economics in nearly undisputed eminence for forty years—from 1885 until his death in 1924. When he finished with Cambridge in 1905, Keynes sat for the Civil Service examinations and did badly in economics. His explanation was characteristic: "The examiners presumably knew less than I did." But this deficiency was not fatal, and he went to the India Office. Here he relieved his boredom by work on books—a technical treatise on the theory of probability and his later book on Indian currency. Neither much changed the world or economic thought; soon he returned to Cambridge on a fellowship provided personally by Alfred Marshall. It was the economics of Alfred Marshall—the notion, in particular, of a benign tendency to an equilibrium where all willing workers were employed—that Keynes would do most to make obsolete.

When the Great War came, Keynes was not attracted to the trenches. He went to the Treasury, where his job was to take British earnings from trade, proceeds from loans floated in the United States, and returns from securities conscripted and sold abroad, and make them cover all possible overseas war purchases. And he helped the French and the Russians do the same. No magic was involved, as many have since suggested. Economic skill does not extend to getting very much for nothing. But an adept and resourceful mind was useful, and this Keynes had. In the course of time Keynes received a notice to report for military service. He sent it back. When the war was over, he was a natural choice for the British delegation to the Peace Conference. That, from the official view, was an appalling mistake.

The mood in Paris in the early months of 1919 was vengeful, myopic, indifferent to economic realities, and it horrified Keynes. So did his fellow civil servants. So did the politicians. In June he resigned and came home, and, in the next two months, he composed the greatest polemical document of modern times. It was against the reparations clauses of the Treaty and, as he saw it, the Carthaginian peace.

Europe would only punish itself by exacting, or seeking to exact, more from the Germans than they had the practical capacity to pay. Restraint by the victors was not a matter of compassion but of elementary self-interest. The case was documented with figures and written with passion. In memorable passages Keynes gave his impression of the men who were writing the peace. Woodrow Wilson he called "this blind and deaf Don Quixote." Of Clemenceau he said: "He had one illusion—France; and one disillusion, mankind . . ." On Lloyd George he was rather severe:

> How can I convey to the reader, who does not know him, any just impression of this extraordinary figure of our time, this syren, this goat-footed bard, this half-human visitor to our age from the hag-ridden magic and enchanted woods of Celtic antiquity.

Alas, no man is of perfect courage. Keynes deleted this passage on Lloyd George at the last moment.

The Economic Consequences of the Peace was published before the end of 1919. The judgment of the British Establishment was rendered by The Times: "Mr. Keynes may be a 'clever' economist. He may have been a useful Treasury official. But in writing this book, he has rendered the Allies a disservice for which their enemies will, doubtless, be grateful."

It is when they are wrong that great men most resent the breaking of ranks. For the next twenty years Keynes headed an insurance company and speculated in shares, commodities, and foreign exchange, sometimes losing, more often winning. He also taught economics, wrote extensively, and applied himself to the arts, old books, and his Bloomsbury friends. But on public matters he was kept outside. He had broken the rules.

Keynes's exclusion was his good fortune. The curse of the public man is that he first accommodates his tongue and eventually his thoughts to his public position. Presently saying nothing but saying it nicely becomes a habit. On the outside one can at least have the pleasure of inflicting the truth. Also, as a freelance intellectual, Keynes could marry Lydia Lopokova, who had just enchanted London as the star of Diaghilev's ballet. My memory retains from somewhere a couplet:

Was there ever such a union of beauty and brains
As when the lovely Lopokova married John Maynard Keynes?

For a civil servant, even for a Cambridge professor, Lopokova would then have been a bit brave. As it was (according to legend), old family friends in Cambridge asked: Has Maynard married a chorus girl?

Mostly in those years Keynes wrote. Good writing in economics is suspect—and with justification. It can persuade people. It also requires clear thought. No one can express well what he does not understand. So clear writing is perceived as a threat, something deeply damaging to the numerous scholars who shelter mediocrity of mind behind obscurity of prose. Keynes was a superb writer when he chose to try. This added appreciably to the suspicion with which he was regarded.

But while Keynes was kept outside, he could not, as would a Marxist, be ignored. He was a fellow of King's. He was the chairman of the National Mutual Insurance Company. He was the director of other companies. So he was heard. It might have been better strategy to have kept him inside and under control.

The man who suffered most from Keynes's freedom from constraint was Winston Churchill. In 1925, Churchill presided over the most dramatically disastrous error by a government in modern economic history. It was Keynes who made it famous.

The mistake was the attempted return to the gold standard at the prewar gold and dollar value of the pound—123.27 fine grains of gold and 4.86 dollars to the pound. Churchill was Chancellor of the Exchequer.

Had Britain gone back to the pound at, say, 4.40 dollars, all would have been well. With sterling bought at that rate, the cost of British commodities, manufactures, or services—coal, textiles, machinery, ships, shipping—would have been pretty much in line with those of other countries, given their prices and the cost of their currencies. With pounds bought at 4.86 dollars, British prices were about 10-percent higher than those of her competitors. Ten percent is 10 percent. It was enough to send buyers to France, Germany, the Low Countries, the United States.

Why the mistake? To go back to the old rate of exchange of pounds for gold and dollars was to show that British financial management was again as solid, as reliable, as in the nineteenth century. It proved that the war had changed nothing. It was a thought to which Winston Churchill, historian and professional custodian of the British past, was highly susceptible.

The country responded well to Churchill's House of Commons announcement of the return to gold. The New York Times said in its headline that he had carried "PARLIAMENT AND NATION TO HEIGHT OF ENTHUSIASM." Keynes wrote instead to ask why Churchill did "such a silly thing."

If British exports were to continue, British prices had to come down. Prices could come down only if wages came down. And wages could come down in only one or two ways. There could be a horizontal slash, whatever the unions might say. Or there could be unemployment, enough unemployment to weaken union demands, threaten employed workers with idleness, and thus bring down wages. This Keynes foresaw.

There was, in the end, both unemployment and a horizontal wage cut. As the mines of the Ruhr came back into production after 1924, world prices of coal fell. To meet this competition with the more expensive pound, the British coal-owners proposed a three-point program: longer hours in the pits, abolition of the minimum wage, lower wages for all. A Royal Commission agreed that the lower wage was necessary. The miners refused; the owners then locked them out. On the fourth of May, 1926, the transport, printing, iron and steel, electricity and gas, and most of the building-trades unions came out in support of the miners. This, with some slight exaggeration, was called the General Strike. For quite a few workers it didn't make too much difference; they were already on the dole, for unemployment, the other remedy, was by then well advanced. In these years unemployment ranged between 10 and 12 percent of the British labor force.

The General Strike lasted only nine days. Those who had most ardently applauded the return to gold were the first to see the strike as a threat to constitutional government, a manifestation of anarchy. Churchill took an especially principled stand. The miners remained on strike through most of 1926 but were eventually defeated. Keynes's judgment was redeemed, but he was not forgiven. It had happened again: when the men of great reputation are wrong, it is the worst of personal tactics to be right.

After 1925, British prices remained stubbornly too high. Money that might have come to Britain for goods continued to go elsewhere—quite a lot to the United States and later to France. The return to gold was meant to proclaim the strength and integrity of sterling. It demonstrated its weakness and the strength of the dollar instead.

By 1927, the loss of gold to the United States was alarming. Accordingly, in that year, Montagu Norman, the head of the

Bank of England, in company with Hjalmar Horace Greeley Schact, the head of the Reichsbank (a man whose reputation for financial wizardry was supported by an exceptionally austere appearance and a notably frozen mind), sailed for New York to try and get it back. There, in company with Charles Rist of the Banque de France, they asked the Federal Reserve to lower its interest rate, expand its loans, and thus ease monetary policy. The lower interest rates would discourage the flow of money to the United States. The easier money would mean more loans, more money, higher American prices, less competition in Britain and elsewhere from American goods, and easier sales by Europeans in the United States. The Americans obliged. This was the action that is held to have helped trigger the great stock-market speculation of 1927–29. The easier money went to finance purchases of common stocks instead.

The day of reckoning was Thursday, October 24, 1929. The New York stock market had been weak on the days before. On that morning, there was a great unrestrained and unexplained headlong rush to sell. This hit the floor of the Exchange with torrential force. The machinery could not adjust to the panic. The ticker fell far behind the market. People across the country could not tell what was happening, only that they had been ruined or would soon be ruined. So they sold and were sold. Inside the Exchange the noise was deafening. Outside in Wall Street a crowd gathered. Perhaps capitalism was collapsing. Around noon the Exchange authorities closed the visitors' gallery. It was all too obscene.

About the time the gallery closed, things took a turn for the better. A little earlier that day the great New York bankers had gathered at Morgan's next door to consider the situation. A rescue operation seemed indicated. Richard Whitney, the vice president of the Exchange, who was known to all as a Morgan broker, was told to go in and buy. This, with great ostentation, he did. The amounts authorized, though unknown, seem not to have been large. But the rescue worked, and the market turned dramatically around, although later in the day it became soft again. Whitney was a hero, his achievement was widely celebrated, and he was made president of the Exchange (not long thereafter, he was off to Sing Sing for embezzlement). The following Tuesday the real crash came. This time the bankers did not intervene. According to rumor they were unloading the stock they had bought the previous Thursday. With occasional rallies, the market went on down for nearly three years.

The Crash blighted consumer spending, business investment, and the solvency of banks and business firms. After the Great Crash came the Great Depression; first the euthanasia of the rich, then of the poor. By 1933, nearly a fourth of all American workers were without jobs. Production—gross national product—was down by a third. Around nine thousand banks failed. The government reacted normally: In June 1930, things were bad and getting much worse; a delegation called on President Hoover to ask for a public-works relief program; he said, "Gentlemen, you have come sixty days too late. The depression is over."

The effects of the Great Depression spread, and they spread around the world. The richer the country, the more advanced its industry, the worse, in general, the slump. The first solution that occurred to statesmen was to propose tightening of belts, acceptance of hardship, resort to patience. This is a natural reaction. Few can believe that suffering, especially by others, is in vain. Anything that is disagreeable must surely have beneficial economic effects.

Herbert Hoover in the United States and Heinrich Brüning in Germany were the most devoted exponents of this view. Brüning's remedial action in 1931 was especially memorable. Wages were cut; prices were cut; salaries were cut; taxes were raised. All this was done at a time when around a quarter of all German industrial workers were unemployed. Not many have wanted to ask the question that some millions of German workers did ask themselves: If this is democracy, can Hitler be worse? Andrew Mellon, Hoover's Secretary of the Treasury, had a similar proposal: "Liquidate labor, liquidate stocks, liquidate the farmers . . ." After Mellon was finished, there would be no way left but up.

Many economists—Lionel Robbins in England, Joseph Schumpeter in the United States—agreed that depression had a necessary, therapeutic function; the metaphor was that it extruded poisons that had been accumulating in the economic system. Others joined in urging patience, a course of action that is easier when supported by a regular income. And many warned that affirmative measures by government would cause inflation. The practical effect in all cases was to come out for inaction. It was not a good time for economists. Britain did abandon the gold standard and free trade. Otherwise, Westminster and Whitehall reacted to the Depression by ignoring the steady flow of advice that was coming from John Maynard Keynes.

Keynes was wholly clear as to the proper action. He wanted borrowing by the government and the expenditure of the resulting funds. The borrowing ensured the increase in the money supply; what was spent was spent by the government, and would then be respent by workers and others receiving the money. The government spending and the further spending by the recipients ensured that there would be no offsetting drop in velocity. You not only created money but enforced its use.

Keynes in these years did have one notable friend. It was the "goat-footed bard," David Lloyd George. Keynes explained helpfully that he supported Lloyd George when he was right and opposed him when he was wrong. But Lloyd George was by now in the political wilderness with the other winners and losers from World War I. Gradually for Keynes there was compensation. He became a prophet with honor, except in his own country. The most successful application of his policies was, in fact, where he was all but unknown.

The Nazis were not given to books. Their reaction was to circumstance, and this served them better than the sound economists served Britain and the United States. From 1933, Hitler borrowed money and spent—and he did it liberally, as Keynes would have advised. It seemed the obvious thing to do, given the unemployment. At first, the spending was mostly for civilian works—railroads, canals, public buildings, the *Autobahnen*. Exchange control then kept frightened Germans from sending their money abroad, and those with rising incomes from spending too much of it on imports.

The results were all a Keynesian could have wished. By late 1935, unemployment was at an end in Germany. By 1936, high income was pulling up prices or making it possible to raise them. Likewise wages were beginning to rise. So a ceiling was put over both prices and wages, and this too worked. Germany, by the late Thirties, had full employment at stable prices. It was, in the industrial world, an absolutely unique achievement.

The German example was instructive but not persuasive. British and American conservatives looked at the Nazi financial heresies—the borrowing and spending—and uniformly predicted a breakdown. Only Schacht, the banker, they said, was keeping things patched together. (They did not know that Schacht, so far as he was aware of what was happening, was opposed.) And American liberals and British socialists looked at the repression, the destruction of the unions, the Brown Shirts, the Black Shirts, the concentration camps, the screaming oratory, and ignored the economics. Nothing good, not even full employment, could come from Hitler.

It was the American case that was influential. At the close of

1933, Keynes addressed a letter to Franklin D. Roosevelt, which, not seeking reticence, he published in The New York Times. A single sentence summarized his message: "I lay overwhelming emphasis on the increase of national purchasing power resulting from governmental expenditure which is financed by loans. . . ." The following year he visited FDR, but the letter had been a better means of communication. Each man was puzzled by the face-to-face encounter. The President thought Keynes some kind of "a mathematician rather than a political economist." Keynes was depressed; he had "supposed the President was more literate, economically speaking."

Keynes wanted much more vigorous borrowing and spending; he thought the Administration far too cautious. And Washington was, indeed, reluctant.

In the early Thirties the mayor of New York was James J. Walker. Defending a casual attitude toward dirty literature, as it was then called, he said he had never heard of a girl being seduced by a book. Keynes was now, after a fashion, to prove Walker wrong. Having failed by direct, practical persuasion, he proceeded to seduce Washington and the world by way of a book. Further to prove the point against Walker, it was a nearly unreadable one.

The book was *The General Theory of Employment Interest and Money.* (For some reason Keynes omitted the commas.) He at least was not in doubt about its influence. Shortly before it was published in 1936, he told George Bernard Shaw that it would "largely revolutionise . . . the way the world thinks about economic problems." So it did.

The General Theory was published long before it was finished. Like the Bible and *Das Kapital,* it is deeply ambiguous and, as in the case of the Bible and Marx, the ambiguity helped greatly to win converts. Keynes's basic conclusion, however, can be put directly. Previously it had been held that the economic system, any capitalist system, found its equilibrium at full employment. Left to itself, it was thus that it came to rest. Idle men and idle plant were an aberration, a wholly temporary failing. Keynes showed that the modern economy could as well find its equilibrium with continuing, serious unemployment. Its perfectly normal tendency was to what economists have since come to call an underemployment equilibrium.

The ultimate cause of the underemployment equilibrium lay in the effort by individuals and firms to save more from income than it was currently profitable for businessmen to invest. What is saved from income must ultimately be spent or there will be a shortage of purchasing power. For 150 years such a possibility had been excluded in the established economics. The income from producing goods was held always to be sufficient to buy the goods. Savings were always invested. Were there a surplus of savings, interest rates fell, and this ensured their use.

Keynes did not deny that all savings got invested. But he showed that this could be accomplished by a fall in output (and employment) in the economy as a whole. Such a slump reduced earnings, changed business gains into losses, reduced personal incomes, and, while it reduced investment, it reduced savings even more. It was in this way that savings were kept equal to investment. Adjustment, a benign word in economics, could be a chilling thing.

From the foregoing came the remedy. The government should borrow and invest. If it borrowed and invested enough, all savings would be offset by investment at a high, not a low, level of output and employment. *The General Theory* validated the remedy that Keynes had previously urged.

Washington, as noted, was cool to Keynes. So, with *The General Theory* as his weapon, he captured the United States by way of the universities. His principal point of entry was Harvard. It was something I was fortunate enough to see at first hand. I was living as a young tutor at Winthrop House, one of the undergraduate residence units. Resident tutors had free rooms, free meals, and as much money as they needed. It was a lovely and tranquil world; the only drawback was that things were so different just outside the university walls. Keynes had a solution without revolution. Our pleasant world would remain; the unemployment and suffering would go. It seemed a miracle. In 1936, after the publication of *The General Theory*, there were meetings several times a week to discuss this wonderful thing.

It was the young who were captured. Economists are economical, among other things, of ideas. It is still so. They make those they acquire as graduate students do for a lifetime. Change in economics comes only with the changing generations. The great economists of that day read and reviewed Keynes and uniformly found him wrong.

But so influential was Keynes among the young at Harvard that in later years an association of alumni was formed to combat his influence. They threatened to cease financial support of the university unless his ideas were repressed or expunged, although it is not clear that many had given much before. I was singled out for attack as the Crown Prince of "Keynesism." I was greatly pleased and hoped that my friends would be properly resentful.

That was Keynes. You came to him out of conservatism, your desire for peaceful change. And by urging his ideas you won a reputation for being a radical.

From Harvard the ideas of Keynes went to Washington—by train. On Thursday and Friday nights in the New Deal years, the Federal Express out of Boston to Washington would be half-filled with Harvard faculty members, old and young. All were on the way to impart wisdom to the New Deal. After *The General Theory* was published, the wisdom that the younger economists sought to impart was that of Keynes.

It was thus that we learned of the Washington reluctance. To spend public money to create jobs might be necessary. But it was not something you urged out of choice. And to urge that a budget deficit was a *good* thing in itself—the heart of the Keynesian remedy—seemed insane. Men of sound judgment were repelled. Even one's best friends, if in positions of responsibility, were cautious in the presence of such heresy. One does not overcome such caution by logic or eloquence, but almost always the opposition comes to your rescue. It came galloping in those years.

In 1937 recovery from the Great Depression was slowly under way; production and prices were rising, although unemployment was still appalling. The men of sound judgment now asserted themselves. They moved to cut spending, raise taxes, and bring the federal budget into balance. The few Keynesians protested; our voices were drowned out in the roars of orthodox applause. As the budget moved toward balance, the recovery came to a halt. Presently there was a new and ghastly slump, a recession within the Depression. It was entirely as Keynes predicted. The men of sound judgment had made our case.

Where were our allies in Washington? They were, of all places, in the Federal Reserve System. We think of a central bank as a stronghold of myopic, unyielding conservatism. It is not an extravagant view, but the Federal Reserve was then headed by Marriner Eccles, a Utah banker of highly original mind. Eccles had seen the lines of depositors form outside his own banks to get their money. He had seen men looking without hope for work. He knew the worried, broken farmers outside town. Why not have the government spend money to provide jobs and help the farmers back to solvency? His experience had caused ideas very similar to those of Keynes to pass through his mind. Roosevelt had brought him to Washington.

Eccles's principal economic aide was Lauchlin Currie, another of the notable Canadians who, in their selfish way, had come south to rescue the Republic. Previously he had been a faculty member at Harvard, and had published a book on the supply and control of money that had anticipated some of the important propositions of Keynes. This caused him to be viewed with doubt by the great economists, and he was not promoted. (In economics one should never be right too soon. The shrewd scholar always waits until the parade is passing his door and then steps bravely out in front of the band.) Eccles and Currie became the leading exponents of Keynes in Washington.

Scholars now speak of the Keynesian Revolution. Never before had a revolution captured a country by way of a bank. No one should worry that it will happen often again.

From the Federal Reserve in the late Thirties Currie went to the White House as an assistant to FDR. This was a strategic spot. When an economic post opened in the government or someone was needed for a special economic task, he would see, if possible, that someone with reliably Keynesian views was employed. Also in the latter Thirties, Keynes won his most important influential American recruit; that was Alvin Harvey Hansen, a professor first at Minnesota and then at Harvard and one of the most prestigious figures in the American economic pantheon. Hansen was no youngster whose views could be dismissed by the economic establishment. In books and articles and through his students he propagated the faith. Hansen and two other scholars—Seymour E. Harris, another diligent evangelist at Harvard, and Paul M. Samuelson, whose textbook, in face of sharp initial attack, instructed millions—made Keynes an accepted part of American economic thought.

Although the recession of 1937 made Keynes's ideas respectable in Washington, action to lift the level of employment remained half-hearted. In 1939, the year war came to Europe, nine and a half million Americans were unemployed. That was 17 percent of the labor force. Almost as many (14.6 percent) were still unemployed in 1940.

The war then brought the Keynesian remedy with a rush. Expenditures doubled and redoubled. So did the deficit. Before the end of 1942, unemployment was minimal. In many places labor was scarce.

There is another way of looking at this history. Hitler, having ended unemployment in Germany, had gone on to end it for his enemies. He was the true protagonist of the Keynesian ideas.

*   *   *

The war revealed two of the enduring features of the Keynesian Revolution. One was the moral difference between spending for welfare and spending for war. During the Depression, very modest outlays for the unemployed seemed socially debilitating, economically unsound. Now, expenditures many times greater for weapons and soldiers were perfectly safe. It's a difference that still persists.

Also as unemployment diminished, but well before it disappeared, inflation became a threat. Keynes believed himself to have a remedy and so did his followers; it was to put everything into reverse. Raise taxes to keep pace with wartime spending, thus try by all possible means to keep down the budget deficit. Keep the cost of living stable, if necessary by subsidizing the cost of food and other staples. Labor could then be asked to forgo wage increases for the duration. Some price control and rationing might be necessary; it should be applied selectively to essentials in especially short supply. Keynes set it all out in a famous series of letters to The Times. In Washington and by now in London the proposals were widely accepted. If Keynes said so, it must surely work.

I circulated a paper with a similar set of proposals in Washington. It was an inspired action, for, as a consequence, in the spring of 1941 I was put in charge of price control, one of the most powerful economic positions of the wartime years. To say I was overjoyed would be a gross understatement.

I got the news in the Blaine Mansion, a fine Victorian structure on Massachusetts Avenue at Dupont Circle and the first headquarters for wartime price control. In a few weeks we outgrew the Blaine house. Three times during the war we burst at the housing seams and had to move. We ended in a sizable acreage previously inhabited by the Census and later taken over by the F.B.I. The expansion in staff was related to the deeper discovery that, for inflation, the ideas of Keynes as adapted by Galbraith did not work. Long before all the unemployed had jobs, corporations could raise prices—and they did. This led, in turn, to wage demands and on, potentially, to a price-wage spiral. Meanwhile, taxes could not be raised fast enough to keep pace with wartime spending. The excess of purchasing power could not, as Keynes had proposed, be mopped up.

The only hope was to go in for price-fixing on a vast scale. This, in the spring of 1942, we did, and rationing followed. That policy did work; prices were kept nearly stable throughout the war.

Previously I had argued against a general ceiling on prices

with great conviction; now I argued for it with equal passion. Almost no one noticed this change of mind. No one at all criticized it. In economics it is a far, far wiser thing to be right than to be consistent.

A revisionist view, greatly favored by partisans of the free market, now holds that price increases were only bottled up to be released after the war. There was, indeed, a bulge when the controls were lifted in 1946, but it was less by far than the increase in the single peacetime year of 1974. Without the controls, prices before the war's end would have been doubling and redoubling every year.

It was while directing price control that I first met Keynes. I had gone to study under him at Cambridge—Cambridge, England, of course—in 1937-38, but it was then that he had his first heart attack, and he did not appear at the university at all that year. He came into my outer office in Washington unannounced one day to deliver a paper. My secretary brought it in and said he seemed to feel he should see me. The name, she said, was Kines. I looked at the paper; there it was, *J. M. Keynes*. The paper was a lucid condemnation of the prices we were setting on corn and hogs. He called them maize and pigs. It was as though St. Peter had dropped in on some parish priest.

With much more emphasis on rationing and less on price control, the British economic policy during the war was otherwise similar to ours. There too it worked. British wartime planning got more from less than that of any other country. As the war ended, I led a group of economists who studied German and Japanese wartime economic management. None doubted that the British management was far more rigorous.

After 1941, the economists no longer went to Washington by train. They were already there. All saw the Keynesian remedy for depression and unemployment from, as it were, the front row. The conclusion was inescapable; what would work in war would work in peace. The Keynesian victory was now assured. The failure of the Keynesian system to deal with inflation was not stressed. Inflation was surely peculiar to the war.

Meanwhile Keynes himself was completing his last crusade. At Paris he had fought the Carthaginian peace. In 1925, he had fought Churchill and the tyranny of gold. In 1944, representatives from 44 countries had assembled at Bretton Woods in New Hampshire to ensure that the errors on gold and reparations, on which Keynes had made his reputation, were not repeated. The Bretton Woods Conference was not a conference among nations. It was a conference of nations with Keynes. The result was the

Bank for International Reconstruction and Development and the International Monetary Fund. The first would guide the minds of the victorious powers to reconstruction, not punishment. The second would give a modicum of flexibility to the rule of gold. A country in trouble could win time by borrowing from the Fund.

When the war was over, Keynes also negotiated the loan—$3.75 billion—that was to see Britain through the postwar years and until exports would again pay for imports. There was now another terrible aberration of the orthodox financial mind—this time it was the Americans. Sterling had been subject to rigid exchange controls during the war. It was made a condition of the loan that it would become fully and freely convertible into dollars (and thus into gold) according to timetable in 1947. This was done. And all who had accumulated wartime hoards of inconvertible sterling—speculators, black-market currency operators, the banks—rushed joyously to change their money into dollars. The loan was used up, literally in a matter of days. In 1925, sterling had been made convertible at an unduly high rate with disastrous results. Twenty-two years later the same error was repeated with infinite precision. This time Keynes was a reluctant participant.

Keynes had always believed that men of self-confessed financial wisdom were wonderfully consistent, especially in their mistakes. He did not live to see this further proof. On April 12, 1946, he died of another heart attack.

After the fiasco of the British loan came the Marshall Plan. This took a far more practical view of the postwar world; with it Europe recovered. The Marshall Plan was a good example of the kind of concerted effort backed by money that Keynes had called for at Bretton Woods.

Germany was a full participant in the Marshall aid. This too was the legacy of Keynes. In the years after 1945, men told each other there must, on no account, be another harsh peace. Keynes's philippic against the Versailles Treaty was now the conventional wisdom. A defeated enemy was now helped, not punished.

In Europe and the United States the two decades following the Second World War will for long be remembered as a very good time, the time when capitalism really worked. Everywhere in the industrialized countries production increased. Unemployment was everywhere low. Prices were nearly stable. When production lagged and unemployment rose, governments intervened to take up the slack, as Keynes had urged. So these were good and confident years, a good time to be an economist, and economists took and were given credit for the achievement. Only the occasional, very mild recessions were still acts of nature or of God.

But these years showed the flaws in the Keynesian miracle as well, although the faults were less celebrated. After the Marshall Plan there was hope that a similar infusion of money—capital—would also rescue the poor countries from their poverty. The rich countries weren't overwhelming in their generosity. But enough was done to show the problem.

In the European countries in the years immediately following the war, capital was the missing ingredient. This could be provided and was provided by the Marshall Plan. In the poor countries, on the other hand, industrial experience, industrial skill, industrial discipline, effective public administration, transportation systems, and many other things did not exist. These could not be supplied from abroad as was the capital. Nor could anything be done from abroad about the relentless pressure of population on land. Keynes, it was learned, at least by some, was a man for the rich countries, not the poor.

And the great lesson of the war was rediscovered. The Keynesian remedy was asymmetrical; it would work against unemployment and depression but not in reverse against inflation. It was a discovery that was only very slowly and reluctantly accepted, and now, more than thirty years later, there are still some followers of the master who are reluctant to admit the fault. Unemployment, as this is written, is high—in the United States the highest in thirty years. And industrial prices are going steadily, steadily up. What is true in the United States is worse in Britain. But Keynes, once a heretic, is now the prophet of the established faith. One must believe that for his remedies to work.

Inflation can be cured by having enough unemployment. However, with this cure no Keynesian can agree; the essence of the Keynesian system is that it cures unemployment. One can stop the increase in corporate prices and trade-union wages by direct action. (I've long thought such action inescapable.) This does not leave the market system intact as Keynes, the conservative, had intended. It is a portent of radical change that not many wish to face.

There are other problems. Keynesian support to the economy has come to involve heavy spending for arms. This, we've seen, is blessed as sound while spending for welfare and the poor is always thought dangerous. With time, too, it has become evident that Keynesian progress can be an uneven thing: many automobiles, too few houses; many cigarettes, too little health care. The great cities in trouble. As these problems have obtruded, the confident years have come to an end. The Age of Keynes was for a time but not for all time.

History

The Birth of Jim Crow

Lerone Bennett, Jr.

from *Before The Mayflower:
The History of the Negro in America:
1619–1962*, 1966

All of this took place before the author's time and hence was known to him through source documents. The events end on the threshold of our own century, however, where they leave a problem still not solved today. This selection brings us to the realm of classic history but not of the broadest, most miscellaneous sort. Circumscribed to a relatively specific topic, "The Birth of Jim Crow" is to general American Negro history what a phase is to autobiography.

I have no protection at home, or resting-place abroad . . . I am an outcast from the society of my childhood, and an outlaw in the land of my birth. "I am a stranger with thee, and a sojourner as all my fathers were." Frederick Douglass

Thomas Dartmouth Rice, one of the white pioneers in comic representation of the Negro, saw James Crow somewhere in Kentucky or Ohio and immortalized him in dialect.

> Weel a-bout and turn a-bout
> And do just so
> Every time I weel a-bout
> I jump Jim Crow

Wheeling about and turning about and jumping just so, "Daddy" Rice shuffled across the stage at New York's Bowery Theatre in 1832 and gave America its first international song hit.

By 1838, Jim Crow[1] was wedged into the language as a synonym for Negro. A noun, a verb, an adjective, a "comic" way of life.

By 1839, there was an antislavery book about him: *The History of Jim Crow.*

By 1841, there was a Jim Crow railroad car—in Massachusetts of all places.

By 1901, Jim Crow was a part of the marrow of America. But he was no longer singing. He had turned mean. The song-and-dance man had become a wall, a way of separating people from people. Demagogue by demagogue, mania by mania, brick by brick, the wall was built. Interracial riding, interracial drinking and interracial dying were banned.

The cornerstones of the great wall were two taboos: interracial eating and intermarriage. Anything approaching interracial eating was proscribed. Anything which might by any stretch of the imagination lead to intermarriage was interdicted. One law led to a hundred. One fear became a nightmare. Out came the rope. Out came the signs:

WHITE	COLORED

NEGROES AND FREIGHT

Out came the rationalizations. Cole L. Blease, the South Carolina demagogue, said it. "Whenever the Constitution comes between me and the virtue of the white women of the South, I say to hell with the Constitution."

Fear. Frenzy. White Womanhood.

Brick by brick, bill by bill, fear by fear, the wall grew taller and taller. The deaf, the dumb and the blind were separated by color. White nurses were forbidden to treat Negro males. White teachers were forbidden to teach Negro students. South Carolina forbade Negro and white cotton mill workers to look out the same window. Florida required "Negro" textbooks and "white" textbooks to be separated in warehouses. Oklahoma required

1. James Crow is an unknown soldier. Some writers say he was a Cincinnati, Ohio, slave; others say that he was a Charleston, S.C. slave. Some writers say the Crow came from old Mr. Crow, the slaveowner; others say the Crow came from the simile, black as a crow.

"separate but equal" telephone booths. New Orleans segregated Negro and white prostitutes. Atlanta provided Jim Crow Bibles for Negro and white witnesses.

In the last decade of the nineteenth century and the first decades of the twentieth, the wall went higher and higher. The thrust came from fear, from economic competition and political needs, from frustration, from an obsession with the cult of White Womanhood. In only two other countries—South Africa and Nazi Germany—have men's fears driven them to such extremes.

As the years rolled by, the wall loomed so tall that men forgot that there was a time when there was no wall, a time when national law required equal treatment in inns, hotels and railroads, when whites and blacks rubbed shoulders together in streetcars, ate in the same dining rooms and drank bad gin in the same saloons.

The extraordinary thing about the wall that fear built is that it is of so recent an origin. There were no separate but equal privies in slavery time. Nor, as C. Vann Woodward has shown in his excellent book, *The Strange Career of Jim Crow*, were there separate but equal rest rooms for a considerable period thereafter. So long as Negroes were slaves, so long as they posed no threat to the political and economic supremacy of whites, men were content to live with them on terms of relative intimacy. But when the slave became a citizen, when he got a ballot in his hot hand and a wrench and pencil and paper—well, something had to be done with him.

That something was a long time working itself out. For several years after whites undermined Black Reconstruction, Negroes and whites were served in the same inns and buried in the same graveyards. There were even some communities where Negro and white children read letters out of the same spelling books in the same classrooms. As late as 1879, Vernon Wharton reports, most of the saloons in Mississippi "served whites and Negroes in the same bar. Many of the restaurants, using separate tables, served both races in the same room."

In April, 1885, when T. McCants Stewart, a Negro lawyer and reporter, made the first Freedom Ride through the South, Jim Crow was a sometimes thing. "On leaving Washington, D.C.," he reported, "I put a chip on my shoulder, and inwardly dared any man to knock it off." McCants was pleasantly surprised. He rode first class in a car in which several whites had to sit on their baggage for lack of seats. "Bold as a lion," he went into a station dining room in Virginia and was served at a table with whites. He wrote a dispatch. "Along the Atlantic Seaboard from

Canada to the Gulf of Mexico—through Delaware, Maryland, Virginia, the Carolinas, Georgia and into Florida, all the old slave States with enormous Negro populations . . . a first-class ticket is good in a first-class coach . . ." His dispatch from Columbia, South Carolina, was lyrical. "I feel about as safe here as in Providence, R.I. I can ride in first-class cars on the railroads and in the streets. I can go into saloons and get refreshments even as in New York. I can stop in and drink a glass of soda and be more politely waited upon than in some parts of New England." Stewart finally gave up: no news was good news. "For the life of [me]," he wrote, "I can't 'raise a row' in these letters. Things seem (remember I write *seem*) to move along as smoothly as in New York or Boston . . . If you should ask me, 'Watchman, tell us of the night!' . . . I would say, 'The morning light is breaking!' "

The light Stewart saw was, in fact, the coming of the moon. Things were not what they seemed. There was still room for maneuvering, but a darkness was moving in. The road, at that time, ran through a swamp and forked off. America and the South had not yet decided which fork to take.

It seemed, for a spell, that all America would take the road leading to brotherhood and democracy. Congress, in fact, seemed determined to push America down the right fork. "Never before," Milton R. Konvitz has written, "in the history of any people was there such an obsessive concern with the establishment of fundamental rights for a minority which, until then, had had no rights at all. Congress was intent on not merely passing laws giving rights to the Negroes but on the vindication and enforcement of these rights against the former masters of slaves in sixteen states."

The legal shelter Congress erected for the ex-slaves rested on three great columns.

> The Fourteenth Amendment:
> No State shall make or enforce any law which shall abridge the privileges or immunities of citizens of the United States, nor shall any State deprive any person of life, liberty or property without due process of law, nor deny to any person within its jurisdiction the equal protection of the laws.

> The Fifteenth Amendment:
> The rights of the citizens of the United States to vote shall not be denied or abridged by the United States or by any State on account of race, color, or previous condition of servitude.

The Civil Rights Bill of 1875:
All persons within the jurisdiction of the United States shall be entitled to the full and equal enjoyment of the accommodations, advantages, facilities, and privileges of inns, public conveyances on land or water, theaters, and other places of public amusement; subject only to the conditions and limitations established by law and applicable alike to citizens of every race and color, regardless of any previous condition of servitude.

The Fourteenth Amendment, the Fifteenth Amendment, and the Civil Rights Bill were words on paper. The proof of the pudding would come literally in the eating and the riding and the balloting. When the lawyers got through with the words, these things became hedged about with prickly legal arrangements. A meal in a "white" restaurant, a ticket to a "white" opera house, a seat in a "white" railroad car: these became enormously complicated legal processes involving policemen, layers on layers of lawyers and judges and the expenditure of thousands of dollars on legal fees. It got so bad that almost everybody admitted that Negroes had certain legal rights, but almost no one could tell them where to go for redress. "When we seek relief at the hands of Congress," a Negro editor in Richmond, Virginia, said, "we are informed that our plea involves a legal question, and we are referred to the Courts. When we appeal to the Courts, we are gravely told that the question is a political one, and that we must go to Congress. When Congress enacts remedial legislation, our enemies take it to the Supreme Court, which promptly declares it unconstitutional." How did this situation come about? And why?

First, the why. The status of the Negro depended, to a great extent, on three fragile props: world public opinion, American public opinion and Nine Men in Black Robes. In the third and fourth quarters of the nineteenth century, the three props collapsed and the roof caved in. Europe, at the time, was embarking on "the Rape of Africa." America was involved in adventures with "little brown brothers" in the Caribbean. Everywhere, in this age, men were taking the blessings of white civilization to the natives. Everywhere, in these decades, men were shouldering "the white man's burden" of carrying tea, coffee, tin, and sugar back to the mother country.

America, moreover, was suffering from the prolonged hangover of the Hayes Compromise of 1877 which turned the ex-slaves over to the mercies of their ex-masters. Never before had men felt such a compulsion to believe in the innate inferiority of black and brown people. Men, Western men anyway, are so constituted that they cannot do wrong on a grand scale without believing that God or history is at their back. Science and the new discipline of sociology came to the rescue. Blood, the inkstands said, would tell. White men were superior and that was all there was to that. Nothing was more foolish than to attempt to enforce laws making brown and black people the equals of white people. White people would not stand for it, sir. Their "natural" "consciousness of kind" could not be curbed by laws and judges. "Stateways," Sociologist William Graham Sumner was saying, "cannot change folkways."

The Supreme Court was inclined to agree. In 1883, the Court declared the Civil Rights Bill unconstitutional. Ruling on several cases involving denials of equal rights to Negroes in inns, hotels, railroads and places of public amusement, the Court said the Fourteenth Amendment forbade *states*, not individuals, from discriminating. In an eloquent dissent, Justice John Marshall Harlan disagreed. The Court, he said, had gutted the Fourteenth Amendment "by a subtle and ingenious verbal criticism." Railroad corporations, inns, hotels and places of public amusement, he said, are instrumentalities of the state. "It seems to me that . . . a denial, by these instrumentalities of the States, to the Citizen, because of his race, of that equality of civil rights secured to him by law, is a denial by the State, within the meaning of the Fourteenth Amendment. If it be not, then that race is left, in respect of the civil rights in question, practically at the mercy of corporations and individuals wielding power under the States."

As it turned out, Harlan was right. But this was no comfort to Negroes who had to live with the majority decision which amputated the Fourteenth Amendment and spawned an epidemic of Jim Crow laws. Tennessee had kicked off the modern segregation movement in 1881 with a Jim Crow railroad law. Now, every Southern state, beginning with Florida in 1887, enacted Jim Crow railroad legislation.

Negroes protested bitterly. After the civil rights decision, protest meetings were held from Maine to Florida. Timothy Thomas Fortune, the influential Negro editor, said Negroes felt as if they had been "baptized in ice water." The polished John Mercer Langston told a full house at Washington's Fifteenth Street Presbyterian Church that the decision was "a stab in the back."

Henry McNeal Turner, the fiery AME bishop, said the civil

rights decision was "barbarous." A former Union chaplain, he never forgave the nation for what he considered "ungrateful" treatment of the Negro. "Years later," Lawrence D. Reddick has written, "when he felt that his last days on earth were near, he deliberately dragged himself off to Canada, in order not to die on American soil."

Enter Booker T. Washington.

When Lee surrendered to Grant on Appomattox, Booker T. Washington was a nine-year-old slave in Virginia. Seven years later, at sixteen, he entered Hampton Institute. Now, at twenty-eight, he was a comer, the president of Tuskegee Institute which he had built from the ground up, an educator who had been praised by whites for his "soundness" on racial matters and his innovations in industrial education. A year after the civil rights decision, Booker T. Washington traveled to Madison, Wisconsin, to speak to the National Education Association. The educators liked what he said.

"Brains, property, and character for the Negro," he said, "will settle the question of civil rights. The best course to pursue in regard to the civil rights bill in the South is to let it alone; let it alone and it will settle itself. Good schoolteachers and plenty of money to pay them will be more potent in settling the race question than many civil rights bills and investigating committees."

Eleven years later, Booker T. Washington turned up in Atlanta with the parable of the open hand and the separate but equal fingers. It was September 18, 1895. Atlanta was packed with people waiting for the opening of the Cotton States Exposition. Far away, in Gray Gables, Massachusetts, President Grover Cleveland was waiting to send the electric spark that would start machinery at the exposition.

In the Exposition Building, a large crowd of Negroes and whites was sweating through the opening speeches. Several whites spoke and then a man introduced "Professor Booker T. Washington." The Negro educator moved to the front of the platform. James Creelman, the famous correspondent of the *New York World,* saw "a remarkable figure; tall, bony, straight as a Sioux chief, high forehead, straight nose, heavy jaws, and strong, determined mouth, with big white teeth, piercing eyes, and a commanding manner. The sinews stood out on his bronze neck, and his muscular right arm swung high in the air, with a lead-pencil grasped in the clenched brown fist. His big feet were planted squarely, with the heels together and the toes turned out. His voice rang out clear and true, and he paused impressively as he made each point. Within ten minutes, the multitude was in an uproar of enthusiasm—handkerchiefs were waved, canes were flourished, hats were tossed in the air. The fairest women of Georgia stood up and cheered."

What was all the shouting about?

Metaphors, mostly—these and words millions were yearning to hear. Washington, whatever his limitations, was a man who could make a figure of speech shimmer and dance. He was working this day with the metaphors of the open hand and the empty bucket.

"A ship lost at sea for many days," he said, "suddenly sighted a friendly vessel. From the mast of the unfortunate vessel was seen a signal. 'Water, water; we die of thirst!' The answer from the friendly vessel at once came back, 'Cast down your bucket where you are.' A second time the signal, 'Water, water; send us water!' ran up from the distressed vessel, and was answered, 'Cast down your bucket where you are.' A third and fourth signal for water was answered, 'Cast down your bucket where you are.' The captain of the distressed vessel, at last heeding the injunction, cast down his bucket, and it came up full of fresh, sparkling water from the mouth of the Amazon River. To those of my race who depend on bettering their condition in a foreign land or who underestimate the importance of cultivating friendly relations with the southern white man, who is their next-door neighbor, I would say: 'Cast down your bucket where you are. . . .' "

To whites, Washington offered the same advice. "Cast down your bucket . . . among the eight millions of Negroes . . . who have, without strikes and labor wars, tilled your fields, cleared your forests, builded your railroads and cities . . . the most patient, faithful, law-abiding, and unresentful people that the world has seen. . . ."

Suddenly Washington flung his hand aloft with the fingers held wide apart.

"In all things that are purely social," he said, "we can be as separate as the fingers, yet [he balled the fingers into a fist] one as the hand in all things essential to mutual progress."

The crowd came to its feet, yelling.

A "great wave of sound dashed itself against the wall," Creelman wrote, "and the whole audience was on its feet in a delirium of applause." When the din had subsided, Washington mentioned the unmentionable—social equality.

"The wisest among my race," he said, "understand that the agitation of questions of social equality is the extremest folly, and that progress in the enjoyment of all the privileges that will come to us must be the result of severe and constant struggle rather than of artificial forcing."

When Washington was done, waves and waves of applause dashed against the building. And the Negroes in the audience— did they applaud, too? At the end of the speech, reporter Creelman wrote in a prophetically chilling sentence, "most of the Negroes in the audience were crying, perhaps without knowing just why."

This speech, "the Atlanta Compromise," made Washington famous and set the tone for Negro leadership for some twenty years. Washington renounced social and political equality, temporarily anyway. What did he expect in return? Support for Negro education, Washingtonians say, an end to the maimings and killings and a square deal in the economic field. It didn't turn out that way.

Down went the buckets and up they came filled with brine. Economic discrimination continued. Lynchings and murders reached staggering heights. Caste lines hardened. Separate became more and more separate and less and less equal. Washington was not responsible for these things. But his "submissive philosophy," C. Vann Woodward has said, "must have appeared to some whites as an 'invitation to further aggression.'" Woodward, a white historian, added: "It is quite certain that Booker T. Washington did not intend his so-called Atlanta Compromise to constitute such an invitation. But in proposing virtual retirement of the mass of Negroes from the political life of the South and in stressing the humble and menial role that the race was to play, he would seem unwittingly to have smoothed the path to proscription." Rayford Logan, a Negro historian, hazarded "the guess" that Washington's philosophy "consoled the consciences of the judges of the Supreme Court."

One year after Washington's Atlanta address, the Supreme Court rounded the fateful fork. In the case of *Plessy v. Ferguson,* the Court wrote into American law the doctrine of racial separation and classification. State laws requiring "separate but equal" accommodations for Negroes, the Court said, were a "reasonable" use of state police power. "The object of the [Fourteenth] Amendment," the Court said, "was undoubtedly to enforce the absolute equality of the two races before the law, but in the nature of things it could not have been intended to abolish distinctions based on color, or to enforce social, as distinguished from political equality, or a commingling of the two races upon terms unsatisfactory to either."

Justice Harlan was prophetic in his dissent. Laws requiring segregation, he said, fostered ideas of caste and inferiority and would lead to additional aggression against the rights of Negroes. "It is scarcely just to say that a colored citizen should not object to occupying a public coach assigned to his own race. He does not object, nor, perhaps, would he object to separate coaches for his race, if his rights under the law were recognized. But he objects, and ought never to cease objecting to the proposition that citizens of the white and black races can be adjudged criminals because they sit, or claim the right to sit, in the same public coach on a public highway . . . in view of the Constitution, in the eye of the law, there is in this country no superior, dominant, ruling class of citizens. There is no caste here. Our Constitution is color-blind, and neither knows nor tolerates classes among citizens. . . . It is, therefore, to be regretted that this high tribunal, the final expositor of the fundamental law of the land, has reached the conclusion that it is competent for a State to regulate the enjoyment by citizens of their civil rights solely upon the basis of race. In my opinion, the judgement this day rendered will, in time, prove to be quite as pernicious as the decision made by this tribunal in the Dred Scott case."

The Plessy decision, as Justice Harlan predicted, led to additional aggression against the rights of Negroes. Only three states had required Jim Crow waiting rooms before 1899, but in the next three decades other Southern states fell into line. Only Georgia, before 1900, had required Jim Crow seating on streetcars. North Carolina and Virginia fell into line in 1901; Louisiana in 1902; Arkansas, South Carolina, and Tennessee in 1903; Mississippi and Maryland in 1904 and Florida in 1905.

A Jim Crow mania seized men. Driven by some deep, dark urge, they piled law on law. The laws came in spurts and waves. Each year brought some new twist or elaboration. Negroes and whites were forcibly separated in public transportation, sports, hospitals, orphanages, prisons, asylums, funeral homes, morgues, cemeteries. Mobile, Alabama, required Negroes to be off the streets by 10 P.M. Birmingham, Alabama, forbade Negroes and whites to play checkers together.

Unsuccessful attempts were made to create by law Negro and white residential districts and Negro and white blocks. When the Supreme Court struck down these attempts, the movement continued under the guise of restrictive covenants and gentleman's agreements.

Jim Crow sections grew up in almost every city and town— around Beale Street in Memphis and Cotton Row in Macon, Georgia. Jim Crow was busy, too, in the North. Here, the propulsive forces were the fears and phobias of poor white immigrants. Negro immigrants, in the early days, were scattered in several sections in Northern cities. Many Negroes, in fact, lived in close proximity to the rich whites they served as domestics. Gradually, the pattern shifted and predominantly-Negro sections came into being.

The founder of Chicago was Jean Baptiste Point du Sable, a Negro who got on very well with the Indians who had a saying: "The first white man to settle at Chickagou was a Negro." Later, when the whites displaced the Indians, life became a great deal more complicated. In the nineties, Drake and Cayton report, there were five thousand Negroes in Chicago and most of them were congregated "in a long, thin sliver of land, sandwiched between a well-to-do white neighborhood and that of the so-called 'shanty Irish.'"

There was a similar development in New York City. In 1890, the 23,000 Negroes in New York were clustered in several areas. Then, in 1903, a live-wire Negro real estate operator had a bright idea. He offered to fill the many vacancies in Harlem with Negro tenants. At first, James Weldon Johnson said, the whites paid little attention to their new neighbors. Then, as more Negroes moved in, a panic developed. The whites "began fleeing as from a plague. The presence of one colored family in a block, no matter how well bred and orderly, was sufficient to precipitate a flight. House after house and block after block was actually deserted." And thus, Harlem was born.

Meanwhile, in the South, Jim Crow building continued. Beginning with Mississippi in 1890, the South turned its attention to the Negro voter. How was it possible to disfranchise poor Negroes without disfranchising poor whites. The answer the South came up with was a wall with holes in it. The wall consisted of literacy and property tests and poll taxes. The holes, designed specially for illiterate, propertyless whites, were the understanding clauses and the "grandfather clauses." If a man's ancestors voted on or before a selected date in, say, 1866—a date on which unfortunately there were no Negro voters—then he could escape the other provisions. Or he could slip through the holes of "good character" and "understanding." If he could not read or write and if he were white, surely he had "good character." If the alphabet were foreign to him and if he were white, surely he could understand and explain an article of the constitution. But if he were black, the "read and write" and "understanding" clauses were jigsaw puzzles. The story is told of a Negro teacher, a graduate of Harvard, who presented himself to a Mississippi registrar. The teacher read the state constitution and several books. The registrar came up with a passage in Latin, which the teacher read, and a passage in Greek, which the teacher read, and pages in French, German and Spanish, all of which the teacher read. Finally, the registrar held up a page of Chinese characters and asked: "What does this mean?" The teacher replied: "It means you don't want me to vote."

By "grandfather clauses," literacy and understanding tests and white primaries, the Negro was excluded from the electorate. "Pitchfork" Ben Tillman, the South Carolina demagogue, said: "We have done our level best; we have scratched our heads to find out how we could eliminate the last one of them. We stuffed ballot boxes. We shot them [Negroes]. We are not ashamed of it."

These devices were extremely effective. In 1896, for example, there were 130,344 Negro voters in Louisiana. Negro voters were in the majority in twenty-six parishes. In 1900, two years after adoption of a state constitution with a "grandfather clause," the 5,320 Negro voters were a minuscule minority in every county.

The elimination of the Negro as an active element in the political life of the South coincided with an acute class conflict between poor whites and the old aristocrats. In the eighties and nineties, the long-subdued poor whites exploded in an orgy of agrarian agitation. The horde of talented, unscrupulous demagogues who came forth to do battle for them soon discovered that Negro-baiting was heady wine to millions whose sole distinction was white skin.

The uses of Negro-baiting did not go unnoticed by the aristocrats. When poor whites and poor Negroes temporarily submerged their differences and demanded basic economic reforms, aristocrats ran up the red flag of social equality and the Populist Revolt collapsed. Reunited under a flag of white supremacy Southerners of all classes made solidarity an article of faith. Crossroads rang with tremolo references to White Womanhood and "our sacred institutions." Men stood on courthouse steps— Tillman in South Carolina, a Vardaman in Mississippi, a Hoke Smith in Georgia—and gave Negroes hell. "The way to control the nigger," W. K. Vardaman told cheering crowds, "is to whip him when he does not obey without it, and another is never to pay him more wages than is actually necessary to buy food and clothing."

The crowds loved it. They whooped and hollered and slapped their thighs and the demagogues laid it on the line. And then what happened? Lynchings—naturally. In the peak years of the

Terrible Nineties, which Rayford Logan has called the low point of the Negro's status in America, a Negro was lynched somewhere every two days or so. Lynching became in C. S. Johnson's words "a hybrid of sport-vengeance," became in Myrdal's words a form of "witch-hunting," became in H. L. Mencken's words a diversion which often took "the place of the merry-go-round, the theatre, the symphony orchestra, and other diversions common to larger communities." Newspapers advertised lynchings in advance. Crowds came from afar on chartered trains.

As the decade wore on, as the Negro-baiting became more virulent, the crowds devised more tantalizing tortures. Victims were roasted over slow fires and their bodies were mutilated. And women, Negro and white women, were sometimes the victims.

Only a small percentage of the Negroes who died by the rope or in burning fires were accused of rape. Others were charged with testifying against whites in court, seeking another job, using offensive language, failing to say "Mister" to a white man, disputing over the price of blackberries, attempting to vote, accepting a job as postmaster and being too prosperous.

Pinned against the wall by lynchings, proscription and organized pogroms, with every man's hand raised against them, Negroes flopped about aimlessly, like fish caught in a net. Intolerably oppressed by conditions which they did not understand and which they could not control, they moved from here to there and back again, from one state to another, from one county to another, from the hills to the delta, from one miserable hut to another ten miles down the road. In the "Exodus of 1879," some 40,000 Negroes stampeded out of the South to the Midwest. Random movements continued throughout the period. A group left Alabama and went to Mexico and starved and came back again. Some went to Canada. Some went to Africa.

Negro leaders grasped at straws.

They organized, wrote resolutions and issued vague threats. Ida B. Wells, the intrepid woman editor who had walked the streets of Memphis with two guns strapped to her waist, organized the first effective opposition to lynching.

More than a million Negro farmers organized a Colored Farmer's Alliance and cooperated with the Populist Movement. Negro women organized the National Association of Colored Women.

The voice of Booker T. Washington was heard in the land. Work. Save. Pray. Clean up and paint up. Buy land and don't antagonize the white folk with funny talk about social and political equality.

The National Afro-American Council called for a day of fasting and prayer. E. J. Waring, the first Negro lawyer in Baltimore, called for law suits. His idea was singularly modern. "We should organize the country over. Raise funds and employ counsel. Then, if an individual is denied some right or privilege, let the race make his wrong their cause and and test the cause in law." Forty-eight years later, another Baltimore lawyer, Thurgood Marshall, would take this idea and make of it a thing of beauty.

There were some, in this age, who believed the time for talk was past. They wanted to fight fire with fire. When the Negroes of Clarksville, Tennessee, burned part of the town in retaliation for a lynching, the editor of the *Chicago Conservator* congratulated them.

There were some who wanted a Negro state. Edwin P. McCabe, the famous state auditor of Kansas, attempted to set up an all-Negro state in the Oklahoma Territory. He had an interview with President Harrison, but the project never got off the ground.

Increasingly, in this dark age, the voice of collaboration was heard. Uncle Toms, "timid, cautious, despairing men," came forward and put themselves at the disposal of the ruling classes. Sir George Campbell, the distinguished British statesman, met a collaborator in Charleston. He was a Democrat who cooperated with the white Democrats—for a price. "His story," the shrewd Englishman said, "seemed to me a little too much as if it had been rehearsed. He tells very fluently how he was a slave, and how he was educated by his mistress; and how, after emancipation his master and mistress, being reduced to poverty, he supported them both, and eventually buried them both—he lays great stress upon the *burying.*"

Fight, protest, run, organize, work, file suits, surrender—the babble of voices was stentorian. The babble continued and the Negro masses went to the wall. Here and there, a black hand reached for a straw and caught it. But for the millions, life was a shadowy nightmare of one-room huts and day-to-day danger.

To work from sun up to sun down for a whole year and to end owing "the man" $400 for the privilege of working; to do this year after year and to sink deeper and deeper into debt; to be chained to the land by bills at the plantation store; to wash away this knowledge with bad gin, to blot it out in an ecstasy of song and prayer; to sing, to pray, to cry; to bring forth a boy child and to be told one night that four thousand people are roasting him slowly over a hot fire and leisurely cutting off his fingers and toes; to be powerless and to curse one's self for cowardice; to be conditioned by dirt and fear and shame and signs; to become a part of these signs and to feel them in the deepest recess of the spirit; to be knocked down in the streets and whipped for not calling a shiftless hillbilly "Mister"; to be a plaything of judges and courts and policemen; to be black in a white fire and to believe finally in one's own unworthiness; to be without books and words and pretty pictures; to be without newspapers and radios; to be without *understanding*, without the rationalizations of psychology and sociology, without Freud and E. Franklin Frazier and *Jet*; to not know why it is happening; to not know that it had all happened before to white people and that Hitler would do it again; to not know where to go and what to do to stay the whip and the rope and the chain; to give in finally; to bow, to scrape, to grin; and to hate one's self for one's servility and weakness and blackness—all this was a Kafkaian nightmare which continued for days and nights and years.

And if a man protested, if he said enough, no more—what then? "And if any black was fantastic enough," W. J. Cash explained in *The Mind of the South*, "to run to the courthouse for redress for a beating or any other wrong, he stood a good chance (provided he was heard at all), not only of seeing his assailant go off scot-free, but of finding the onus somehow shifted to himself, of finding himself in the dock on this or some other count, and of ending by going away for a long time to the county chain gang and the mercies of persons, hand-picked for their skills in adjusting his sense of reality."

These chain gangs were real horror-houses. Sir George Campbell was told that chain gangs were often used as schools for undisciplined young Negroes who had grown up since slavery. As schools, in short, for servility. On the slightest pretext, unmanageable young Negroes were arrested, convicted and leased to private individuals and companies. In the turpentine camps and mining camps, on levees and railroad construction, manhood was worked and whipped out of them.

With chains welded to their bodies, waist deep sometimes in mud and slime, convicts toiled day in and day out. Fortunes were founded on their misery. Their quarters were unbelievably filthy. Vermin, investigators reported, crawled over their clothes and their bodies. And it was not unusual for a female prisoner and a male prisoner to be chained to a bed together at night. After a study of Southern chain gangs, Fletcher Green, a modern scholar, concluded that they had no parallel except in the persecutions of the Middle Ages and the concentration camps of Nazi Germany.

From this bitter soil came flowers. From the chain gangs and the cotton fields, from the Jim Crow sections of Memphis, New Orleans, Birmingham, Houston, and Macon, Georgia, came songs which went forth and told the world that America had at last created a new thing. Well-mannered, well-scrubbed young people went out from Fisk University and sang the old spirituals and the world sat up and took notice.

Could anything good come out of Jim Crow town?

Tattered characters in grimy clothes strummed guitars on the levees and in mean-looking bars or relieved their despair with bitter cries on the chain gang.

> If I'd a had my weight in lime
> I'd a whupped dat captain
> Till he went stone blind.

The music went back to the slave cabins and farther, back to the polyrhythmic complexity of the forgotten land—West Africa. The music was a melding of African, European, and American elements; of the spirituals and work songs; of cries and hollers; of "devil songs" and shouts and stomps; of slow drags, marches, funeral dirges, and hymns. It was a blend and yet it was new. A thing made in America by illiterate and despised Negroes. At the turn of the century, Buddy Bolden, the first great shouter, was making the bubbling notes in New Orleans. In 1900, a boy named Louis Armstrong was born and he went out into the world and played the music called Jazz. In Tennessee, a girl named Bessie Smith was born in brutal poverty and she went out into the world and sang the songs called the Blues. "Her blues," George Hoefer has written, "could be funny and boisterous and gentle and angry and bleak, but underneath all of them ran the raw bitterness of being a human being who had to think twice about which toilet she could use. You cannot hear Bessie without hearing why Martin Luther King doesn't want to wait any more."

Life behind the Jim Crow wall was more than singing and crying. Nine out of every ten Negroes lived in the South. They were living at the subsistence level, but they were making progress. There had been a dramatic rise in literacy. In 1865, when emancipation became a fact, about one in every twenty Negroes could read and write. Thirty-five years later, more than one out of every two could read and write.

There also had been a dramatic rise in the quality of Negro group life. The Negro church had become a solid and dynamic institution. Large numbers in almost every city belonged to the AME, the AMEZ, the Baptist and the CME churches. The secret fraternal orders, the Masons, Odd Fellows, Knights of Pythias and others, had laid the basis for Negro insurance companies. In

1898, S. W. Rutherford started the National Benefit Insurance Company. In the same year, C. C. Spaulding and others organized the North Carolina Mutual Benefit Insurance Company. Two years later, Booker T. Washington and others organized the National Business League. There were four Negro banks, sixty-four drugstores and at least one millionaire. Charles P. Graves, president of the Gold Leaf Consolidated Company, and the Montana and Illinois Mining Company, was reported to be worth at least a million dollars.

By 1900, Negroes had more than $500,000 invested in funeral homes. The Negro professional class had grown to more than 47,000. There were 21,267 teachers, 15,528 preachers, 1,734 doctors, 212 dentists, 310 journalists, 728 lawyers, 2,000 actors and showmen, 236 artists, 247 photographers and one Negro congressman.

George H. White, the last Negro congressman of the post-Reconstruction era, was a symbol of the shifting fortunes of the four million freedman who, by 1900, had become eight million. By 1901, almost all of the Negroes in Southern legislatures and city councils had been eliminated. Now, in 1901, White himself was at the turning of the fork. He had been elected to Congress from North Carolina in 1896 and had been re-elected in 1898. But it was clear by the middle of his second term that he would not be elected again.

When White rose in Congress on a day in 1901, men shifted in their seats to get a better look at him. For better or worse, they would not be seeing his likes again soon.

White made the most of his last opportunity. He reviewed the whole dreary story—the rise of the Negro to political power, the undermining of Reconstruction, the gutting of the Fourteenth Amendment and the birth of Jim Crow. Now, he said, the circle had come full cycle.

And so it was time for goodbyes.

"This, Mr. Chairman, is perhaps the Negroes' temporary farewell to the American Congress; but let me say, Phoenix-like he will rise up some day and come again. These parting words are in behalf of an outraged, heartbroken, bruised and bleeding, but God-fearing people, faithful, industrious, loyal, rising people—full of potential force."

> *Weel a-bout and turn a-bout*
> *And do just so*
> *Every time I weel a-bout*
> *I jump Jim Crow.*

Russia and the West
Arnold J. Toynbee
Harper's, March, 1953

Spanning many centuries and countries, this story is barely narra
tive anymore, so far does it tend toward generalization. *I*
recounts in fact a pattern *of events. Whenever we speak o*
recurring events we are analogizing, since no events physicall
recur. So this is generalized history—the perception that event
not only happened once upon a time but have "repeated"
themselves. Changes of tense mark Toynbee's shifts in abstrac
tion level. Although his predominant tense here is the complete
past, it occasionally becomes the incompleted past and some
times even the present tense of generalization. The next ste
would be theory of history.

In the encounter between the world and the West that has bee
going on by now for four or five hundred years, the world, nc
the West, is the party that, up to now, has had the significar
experience. It has not been the West that has been hit by th
world; it is the world that has been hit—and hit hard—by th
West.

A Westerner who wants to grapple with this subject must try
for a few minutes, to slip out of his native Western skin and loo
at the encounter between the world and the West through the eye
of the great non-Western majority of mankind. Different thoug
the non-Western peoples of the world may be from one anothe
in race, language, civilization, and religion, if any Wester
inquirer asks them their opinion of the West, he will hear ther
all giving him the same answer: Russians, Moslems, Hindus
Chinese, Japanese, and all the rest. The West, they will tell him
has been the arch-aggressor of modern times, and each will hav
their own experience of Western aggression to bring up agains
him. The Russians will remind him that their country has bee
invaded by Western armies overland in 1941, 1915, 1812, 1709

and 1610; the peoples of Africa and Asia will remind him that Western missionaries, traders, and soldiers from across the sea have been pushing into their countries from the coasts since the fifteenth century. The Asians will also remind him that, within the same period, the Westerners have occupied the lion's share of the world's last vacant lands in the Americas, Australia, New Zealand, and South and East Africa. The Africans will remind him that they were enslaved and deported across the Atlantic in order to serve the European colonizers of the Americas as living tools to minister to their Western masters' greed for wealth. The descendants of the aboriginal population of North America will remind him that their ancestors were swept aside to make room for the West European intruders and for their African slaves.

This indictment will surprise, shock, grieve, and perhaps even outrage most Westerners today. Dutch Westerners are conscious of having evacuated Indonesia, and British Westerners of having evacuated India, Pakistan, Burma, and Ceylon, since 1945. British Westerners have no aggressive war on their consciences since the South African War of 1899–1902, and American Westerners none since the Spanish-American War of 1898. We forget all too easily that the Germans, who attacked their neighbors, including Russia, in the first world war and again in the second world war, are Westerners too, and that the Russians, Asians, and Africans do not draw fine distinctions between different hordes of "Franks" —which is the world's common name for Westerners in the mass. "When the world passes judgment it can be sure of having the last word," according to a well-known Latin proverb. And certainly the world's judgment on the West does seem to be justified over a period of about four and a half centuries ending in 1945. In the world's experience of the West during all that time, the West has been the aggressor on the whole; and, if the tables are being turned on the West by Russia and China today, this is a new chapter of the story which did not begin until after the end of the second world war. The West's alarm and anger at recent acts of Russian and Chinese aggression at the West's expense are evidence that, for us Westerners, it is today still a strange experience to be suffering at the hands of the world what the world has been suffering at Western hands for a number of centuries past.

II

What, then, has been the world's experience of the West? Let us look at Russia's experience, for Russia is part of the world's great non-Western majority. Though the Russians have been Christians and are, many of them, Christians still, they have never been Western Christians. Russia was converted not from Rome, as England was, but from Constantinople; and, in spite of their common Christian origins, Eastern and Western Christendom have always been foreign to one another, and have often been mutually antipathic and hostile, as Russia and the West unhappily still are today, when each of them is in what one might call a "post-Christian" phase of its history.

This on the whole unhappy story of Russia's relations with the West did, though, have a happier first chapter; for, in spite of the difference between the Russian and the Western way of life, Russia and the West got on fairly well with one another in the early Middle Ages. The peoples traded, and the royal families intermarried. An English King Harold's daughter, for instance, married a Russian prince. The estrangement began in the thirteenth century, after the subjugation of Russia by the Tatars. The Tatars' domination over Russia was temporary, because the Tatars were nomads from the Steppes who could not ever make themselves at home in Russia's fields and forests. Russia's lasting losses as a result of this temporary Tatar conquest were, not to her Tatar conquerors, but to her Western neighbors; for these took advantage of Russia's prostration in order to lop off, and annex to Western Christendom, the western fringes of the Russian world in White Russia and in the western half of the Ukraine. It was not till 1945 that Russia recaptured the last piece of these huge Russian territories that were taken from her by Western powers in the thirteenth and fourteenth centuries.

These Western conquests at Russia's expense in the late Middle Ages had an effect on Russia's life at home, as well as on her relations with her Western assailants. The pressure on Russia from the West did not merely estrange Russia from the West; it was one of the hard facts of Russian life that moved the Russians to submit to the yoke of a new native Russian power at Moscow which, at the price of autocracy, imposed on Russia the political unity that she now had to have if she was to survive. It was no accident that this newfangled autocratic centralizing government of Russia should have arisen at Moscow; for Moscow stood in the fairway of the easiest line for the invasion of what was left of Russia by a Western aggressor. The Poles in 1610, the French in 1812, the Germans in 1941, all marched this way. Since an early date in the fourteenth century, autocracy and centralization have been the dominant notes of all successive Russian regimes. The Muscovite Russian political tradition has perhaps always been a disagreeable for the Russians themselves as it has certainly been distasteful and alarming to their neighbors; but unfortunately the Russians have learned to put up with it, partly perhaps out of sheer habit, but also, no doubt, because they have felt it to be a lesser evil than the alternative fate of being conquered by aggressive neighbors.

This submissive Russian attitude toward an autocratic regime that has become traditional in Russia is, of course, one of the main difficulties, as we Westerners see it, in the relations between Russia and the West today. The great majority of people in the West feel that tyranny is an intolerable social evil. At a fearful cost we have put down tyranny when it has raised its head among our Western selves in the forms of Fascism and National Socialism. We feel the same detestation and distrust of it in its Russian form, whether this calls itself Tsarism or calls itself Communism. We do not want to see this Russian brand of tyranny spread; and we are particularly concerned about this danger to Western ideals of liberty now that we Franks find ourselves thrown upon the defensive for the first time in our history since the second Turkish siege of Vienna in 1682–83. Our present anxiety about what seems to us to be a postwar threat to the West from Russia is a well-justified anxiety in our belief. At the same time, we must take care not to allow the reversal in the relation between Russia and the West since 1945 to mislead us into forgetting the past in our natural preoccupation with the present. When we look at the encounter between Russia and the West in the historian's instead of the journalist's perspective, we shall see that, over a period of several centuries ending in 1945, the Russians have had the same reason for looking askance at the West that we Westerners feel that we have for looking askance at Russia today.

During the past few centuries, this threat to Russia from the West, which has been a constant threat from the thirteenth century till 1945, has been made more serious for Russia by the outbreak, in the West, of a technological revolution which has become chronic and which does not yet show any signs of abating.

When the West adopted firearms, Russia followed suit, and in the sixteenth century she used these new weapons from the West to conquer the Tatars in the Volga valley and more primitive peoples in the Urals and in Siberia. But in 1610 the superiority of the Western armaments of the day enabled the Poles to occupy Moscow and to hold it for two years, while at about the same time the Swedes were also able to deprive Russia of her outlet on the Baltic Sea at the head of the Gulf of Finland. The Russian retort to these seventeenth-century Western acts of aggression was to adopt the technology of the West wholesale, together with as much of the Western way of life as was inseparable from Western technology.

It was characteristic of the autocratic centralizing Muscovite regime that this technological and accompanying social revolution in Russia at the turn of the seventeenth and eighteenth centuries should have been imposed upon Russia from above downward, by the fiat of one man of genius, Peter the Great. Peter is a key figure for an understanding of the world's relations with the West not only in Russia but everywhere; for Peter is the archetype of the autocratic Westernizing reformer who, during the past two and a half centuries, has saved the world from falling entirely under Western domination by forcing the world to train itself to resist Western aggression with Western weapons. Sultans Selim III and Mohammed II and President Mustafa Kemal Atatürk in Turkey, Mehemet Ali Pasha in Egypt, and "the Elder Statesmen," who made the Westernizing revolution in Japan in the eighteen-sixties, were, all of them, following in Peter the Great's footsteps consciously or unconsciously.

Peter launched Russia on a technological race with the West which Russia is still running. Russia has never yet been able to afford to rest, because the West has continually been making fresh spurts. For example, Peter and his eighteenth-century successors brought Russia close enough abreast of the Western world of the day to make Russia just able to defeat her Swedish Western invaders in 1709 and her French Western invaders in 1812; but, in the nineteenth-century Western industrial revolution, the West once more left Russia behind, so that in the first world war Russia was defeated by her German Western invaders as she had been defeated, two hundred years earlier, by the Poles and the Swedes. The present Communist autocratic government was able to supplant the Tsardom in Russia in consequence of Russia's defeat by an industrial Western technology in 1914–17; and the Communist regime then set out, from 1928 to 1941, to do for Russia, all over again, what the Tsar Peter had done for her about 230 years earlier.

For the second time in the modern chapter of her history, Russia was now put, by an autocratic ruler, through a forced march to catch up with a Western technology that had once more shot ahead of hers; and Stalin's tyrannical course of technological Westernization was eventually justified, like Peter's, through an ordeal by battle. The Communist technological revolution in

Russia defeated the German invaders in the second world war, as Peter's technological revolution had defeated the Swedish invaders in 1709 and the French invaders in 1812. And then, a few months after the completion of the liberation of Russian soil from German-Western occupation in 1945, Russia's American-Western allies dropped in Japan an atom bomb that announced the outbreak of a third Western technological revolution. So today, for the third time, Russia is having to make a forced march in an effort to catch up with a Western technology that, for the third time, has left her behind by shooting ahead. The result of this third event in the perpetual competition between Russia and the West still lies hidden in the future; but it is already clear that this renewal of the technological race is another of the very serious difficulties now besetting the relations between these two ex-Christian societies.

III

Technology is, of course, only a long Greek name for a bag of tools; and we have to ask ourselves: What are the tools that count in this competition in the use of tools as means to power? A power-loom or a locomotive is obviously a tool for this purpose, as well as a gun, an airplane, or a bomb. But all tools are not of the material kind; there are spiritual tools as well, and these are the most potent that Man has made. A creed, for instance, can be a tool; and, in the new round in the competition between Russia and the West that began in 1917, the Russians this time threw into their scale of the balances a creed that weighed as heavily against their Western competitors' material tools as, in the Roman story of the ransoming of Rome from the Gauls, the sword thrown in by Brennus weighed against the Roman gold.

Communism, then, is a weapon; and, like bombs, airplanes, and guns, this is a weapon of Western origin. If it had not been invented by a couple of nineteenth-century Westerners, Karl Marx and Friedrich Engels, who were brought up in the Rhineland and spent the best part of their working lives in London and in Manchester respectively, Communism could never have become Russia's official ideology. There was nothing in the Russian tradition that could have led the Russians to invent Communism for themselves; and it is certain that they would never have dreamed of it if it had not been lying, ready-made, here in the West, for a revolutionary Russian regime to apply in Russia in 1917.

In borrowing from the West a Western ideology, besides a

Western industrial revolution, to serve as an anti-Western weapon, the Bolsheviki in 1917 were making a great new departure in Russian history; for this was the first time that Russia had ever borrowed a creed from the West. But it was a creed particularly well suited to serve Russia as a Western weapon for waging an anti-Western spiritual warfare. In the West, where Communism had arisen, this new creed was heresy. It was a Western criticism of the West's failure to live up to her own Christian principles in the economic and social life of this professedly Christian society; and a creed of Western origin which was at the same time an indictment of Western practice was, of course, just the spiritual weapon that an adversary of the West would like to pick up and turn against its makers.

With this Western spiritual weapon in her hands, Russia could carry her war with the West into the enemy's country on the spiritual plane. Since Communism had originated as a product of uneasy Western consciences it could appeal to other uneasy Western consciences when it was radiated back into the Western world by a Russian propaganda. And so now, for the first time in the modern Western world's history since the close of the seventeenth century, when the flow of Western converts to Islam almost ceased, the West has again found itself threatened with spiritual disintegration from inside, as well as with an assault from outside. In thus threatening to undermine Western civilization's foundations on the West's own home ground, Communism has already proved itself a more effective anti-Western weapon in Russian hands than any material weapon could ever be.

Communism has also served Russia as a weapon for bringing into the Russian camp the Chinese quarter of the human race, as well as other sections of that majority of mankind that is neither Russian nor Western. We know that the outcome of the struggle to win the allegiance of these neutrals may be decisive for the outcome of the Russo-Western conflict as a whole, because this non-Western and non-Russian majority of mankind may prove to hold the casting vote in a competition between Russia and the West for world power. Now Communism can make a twofold appeal to a depressed Asian, African, and Latin American peasantry when it is the voice of Russia that is commending Communism to them.

The Russian spokesman can say to the Asian peasantry first "If you follow the Russian example, Communism will give you the strength to stand up against the West, as a Communist Russia can already stand up against the West today." The second appeal of Communism to the Asian peasantry is Communism's claim that it can, and that private enterprise neither can nor would if it could, get rid of the extreme inequality between a rich minority and a poverty-stricken majority in Asian countries. Discontented Asians, however, are not the only public for whom Communism has an appeal. Communism also has an appeal for all men, since it can claim to offer mankind the unity which is our only alternative to self-destruction in an atomic age.

It looks as if, in the encounter between Russia and the West, the spiritual initiative, though not the technological lead, has now passed, at any rate for the moment, from the Western to the Russian side. We Westerners cannot afford to resign ourselves to this, because this Western heresy—Communism—which the Russians have taken up, seems to the great majority of people in the West to be a perverse, misguided, and disastrous doctrine and way of life. A theologian might put it that our great modern Western heresiarch Karl Marx has made what is a heretic's characteristic intellectual mistake and moral aberration. In putting his finger on one point in orthodox practice in which there has been a crying need for reform, he has lost sight of all other considerations and therefore has produced a remedy that is worse than the disease.

The Russians' recent success in capturing the initiative from us Westerners by taking up this Western heresy called Communism and radiating it out into the world in a cloud of anti-Western poison gas does not, of course, mean that Communism is destined to prevail. Marx's vision seems, in non-Marxian eyes, far too narrow and too badly warped to be likely to prove permanently satisfying to human hearts and minds. All the same, Communism's success, so far as it has gone, looks like a portent of things to come. What it tells us is that the present encounter between the world and the West is now moving off the technological plane onto the spiritual plane.

Case and Profile

TELLING STORIES leads easily to telling it as it is. This is a natural part of the inductive process of thinking whereby, after seeing so many things happen alike—"repeat themselves"—one infers from this some generality. This causes a shift from past tense to the present tense of generalization as the organizing force, from narrative to essay. Various kinds of writing represent degrees of this crucial process. Cases and profiles begin to bridge from story into statement. As part of this stretching toward generality they cause the author to employ techniques of both reportage and research.

Case

"GETTING DOWN TO CASES" is getting down to instances exemplifying some generality. A case exists as a *token* of a *type*, not just as a story for its own sake. Because its particular narrative embodies some truth applicable to other happenings, it affords the specialized professionals who read and write cases an effective way to do study in their field and provides laymen a window on that field.

Early Ego Failure: Jean
Erik Erikson
from *Childhood and Society,* 1950

Of the generation following Sigmund Freud and specializing, like Anna Freud, in the psychology of the ego, Erik Erikson became one of the world's most highly respected theorists and practitioners of psychoanalysis. He pioneered in play therapy with children. In the work from which this chapter is drawn he set forth an original and influential account of psychological matura- tion that helped illuminate those arrestations of development we call neurosis and psychosis and that connected issues of growth to types of societies. He also set a standard of compassionate observation and humanistic writing style that has continued to flourish in the work of a disciple, Robert Coles, who has also presented some fine cases in Children of Crisis *and* Women of Crisis.

This is a clinician's *case and therefore based on firsthand experience with a client. While resembling memoir or reportage in being a first-person narration about someone else, the material of this story comes neither from accidental memory nor from a journalistic excursion into another's life. Erikson came by this knowledge of Jean by attempting therapy with her over a long period of time. Part of the "case" nature of this story may be seen in Erikson's efforts to connect this account to other clinical experience and to a theoretical framework.*

To come face to face with a "schizophrenic" child is one of the most awe-inspiring experiences a psychotherapist can have. It is not the bizarreness of the child's behavior which makes the encounter so immediately challenging, but rather the very con- trast of that behavior with the appeal of some of these children. Their facial features are often regular and pleasing, their eyes are "soulful" and seem to express deep and desperate experience, paired with a resignation which children should not have. The total impression first goes to the heart and immediately convinces the clinical observer, even against the better knowledge of previous experience, that the right person and the right therapeutic regime could bring the child back on the road to coherent progress. This conviction has the more or less explicit corollary that the child has been in the wrong hands and, in fact, has every reason to mistrust his ''rejecting'' parents. (We saw how far Indians and whites would go in accusing one another of doing deliberate harm to their children; our occupational prejudice is ''the rejecting mother.'')

I first saw Jean when she was almost six years old. I did not see her at her best. She had just made a train trip, and my house was strange to her. What glimpses I could catch of her (for she was frantically on the move through garden and house) showed her to be of graceful build, but tense and abrupt in her movements. She had beautiful dark eyes which seemed like peaceful islands within the anxious grimace of her face. She ran through all the rooms of the house, uncovering all the beds she could find, as if she were looking for something. The objects of this search proved to be pillows, which she hugged and talked to in a hoarse whisper and with a hollow laugh.''

Yes, Jean was ''schizophrenic.'' Her human relationships were centrifugal, away from people. I had observed this strange phenomenon of a ''centrifugal approach,'' often interpreted as mere lack of contact, years before in the behavior of another little girl who was said to ''notice nobody.''When that little girl came down a flight of stairs toward me, her glance drifted in an absent way over a series of objects, describing concentric circles around my face. She focused on me negatively, as it were. This flight is the common denominator for a variety of other symptoms, such as the preoccupation with things far away and imagined; the inability to concentrate on any task at hand; violent objection to all close contact with others unless they fit into some imaginary scheme; and immediate diffused flight from verbal communication, when it happens to become more nearly established. Meaning is quickly replaced by parrotlike repetition of stereotyped phrases, accompanied by guttural sounds of despair.

The observation that Jean, on her mad rush through my house again and again paused long enough to concentrate her attention and to lavish her affection on bed pillows seemed significant for the following reason. Her mother had told me that Jean's extreme disorientation had begun after the mother had become bedridden with tuberculosis. She was permitted to stay at home in her own room, but the child could speak to her only through the doorway of her bedroom, from the arms of a good-natured but "tough" nurse. During this period the mother had the impression that there were things which the child urgently wanted to tell her. The mother regretted at the time that, shortly before her illness, she had let Jean's original nurse, a gentle Mexican girl, leave them. Hedwig, so the mother anxiously noticed from her bed, was always in a hurry, moved the baby about with great energy, and was very emphatic in her disapprovals and warnings. Her favorite remark was, "Ah, baby, you stink!" and her holy war was her effort to keep the creeping infant off the floor so that she would not be contaminated by dirt. If the child were slightly soiled, she scrubbed her "as if she were scrubbing a deck."

When after four months of separation Jean (now thirteen months old) was permitted to re-enter the mother's room, she spoke only in a whisper. "She shrank back from the pattern of the chintz on the armchair and cried. She tried to crawl off the flowered rug and cried all the time, looking very fearful. She was terrified by a large, soft ball rolling on the floor and terrified of paper crackling." These fears spread. First, she did not dare to touch ashtrays and other dirty objects, then she avoided touching or being touched by her elder brother and gradually by most people around her. Although she learned to feed herself and to walk at the normal time, she gradually became sad and silent.

Maybe the child's frantic affection for pillows had to do with that period when she was prevented from approaching her mother's bed. Maybe, for some reason, she had not been able to take the separation, had "adjusted" to it by a permanent pattern of fleeing from all human contact, and was now expressing her affection for the bedridden mother in her love for pillows.

The mother confirmed that the child had a fetish, a small pillow or sheet which she would press over her face when going to sleep. For her part, the mother seemed desirous of making restitution to the child for what she felt she had denied her, not only during those months of illness, but by what now seemed like a general kind of neglect by default. This mother by no means lacked affection for the child, but she felt that she had not given Jean the relaxed affection she needed most *when* she needed it most.

Some such maternal estrangement may be found in every history of infantile schizophrenia. What remains debatable is whether the maternal behavior such as the mother's relative absence and the nurse's total presence could possibly be a "cause" for such a radical disturbance in a child's functioning; or whether such children, for some intrinsic and perhaps constitutional reasons, have idiosyncratic needs which no mother would understand without professional help—and professional people, until very recently, could not even spot these children when they were young enough to be (supposedly) saved with special dosages of well-planned mother love.

On the children's part, early oral traumata are often suggested in the history. Take Jean's feeding history. The mother tried to nurse her for one week but had to give up because of a breast infection. The baby vomited, cried excessively, seemed always hungry. When Jean was ten days old, she began to suffer from thrush, which remained acute for three weeks and persisted as a low-grade infection for the remainder of her first year. Drinking was often painful. At one time during the first half of the first year, an infected layer of skin was removed from the underside of her tongue. Early moving pictures of the little girl show a heavy lower lip and a protruding, hyperactive tongue. No doubt the oral trauma had been severe. It should be noted here that Jean's main fetish consisted of a sheet which she made into a ball and pressed against her mouth with one piece between her teeth. Besides these pillows, Jean loved only instruments and machines: egg-beaters, vacuum cleaners, and radiators. She smiled at them, whispered to them, and hugged them, and was impelled by their very presence to a kind of excited dancing—all this while she remained completely uninterested in people unless they invaded her preoccupations, or unless she wished to invade theirs.

In the mother's early notes there was another item which seemed of great relevance to me. She showed me the statement of a psychologist who, when testing the child at the age of four, noted his impression that "the child had turned against speech." For it seems important to understand that these children repudiate their own sense organs and vital functions as hostile and "outside." They have a defective screening system between the inner and the outer world; their sensory contacts fail to master the overpowering impressions as well as the disturbing impulses which intrude themselves upon consciousness. They therefore experience their own organs of contact and communication as enemies, as potential intruders into a self which has withdrawn "under the skin." It is for this reason that these children close their eyes and hold their hands over their ears, or hide their whole heads in blankets, in reaction to unsuccessful contacts. Thus, only carefully dosed and extraordinarily consistent application of maternal encouragement could enable the child's ego to reconquer as it were, its own organs, and with them to perceive the social environment and to make contact with it more trustingly.

When I saw Jean she had not lived with her parents for many months, but had been taken care of by a devoted professional woman. Most of the time she appeared not to care. Yet, on the previous Christmas, after attending a party at her parents' house, the child had thrown all the presents which she had received from her parents on the street outside her foster home, stamped on them, and cried wildly. Maybe she did care. I proposed that the family move together and that, for some extended time, the mother should take over Jean's care under my guidance to be given on regular trips to their home in a college town. This family-treatment plan, I felt, should precede any direct therapy with the child.

When she found herself back within her family, with her mother in untiring attendance, Jean expressed appreciation by a determined attempt to restore intimate contact. But these attempts were often too determined and too specific in their goal. She became fascinated with *parts* of people. Her shocked brothers (older and younger) found their penises grabbed—and politely withdrew their sincere wish to co-operate in the treatment plan. Her father found her an enthusiastic attendant at his showers, where she waited for opportunities to grab his genitals. He could not hide, first, his amused consternation, and then his somewhat nervous annoyance. When he was dressed she concentrated on a bump on his hand which she called a "lumpy," and on his cigarettes, which she would tear from his lips and throw out of the window. She knew where people are vulnerable; these children, so vulnerable themselves, are masters at such diagnosis.

Luckily, Jean's greatest "partialistic" interest was in her mother's breasts; luckily, because the mother could indulge this interest for a period. The child would love to sit on the mother's lap and take sly pokes at breasts and nipples. Climbing on the mother, she would say "gloimb you, gloimb you," which apparently meant "climb on you." The mother let her sit on her for hours. The "gloimb you" gradually expanded into sing-songs such as this (I quote from the mother's diary):

> Gloimb you, gloimb you, not hurt a chest—not touch a didge—not touch a ban—not touch a dage—not touch a bandage—throw away a chest—hurt a chest.

This apparently meant that the child was preoccupied with the idea that touching her mother's chest-bandage (brassière) might hurt her. The desperate intensity and repetitiveness of these phrases even made us surmise that she communicated the idea that she had hurt the mother when she developed "chest trouble" and that she had been banished from her mother's room for this reason. For her talk seemed to indicate that the "throwing away" she referred to really meant that she had been thrown away: here again, we see that most basic imagery of expulsion and atonement. It must be understood that the most difficult verbal (and maybe conceptual) feat for these children, even where they have acquired extensive vocabularies, is to differentiate between active and passive, and between "I" and "you," the basic grammar of two-ness. As the game with the mother progressed, Jean could be heard whispering to herself "spank you" or "not pick you finger off." She apparently associated her attacks on penises with those on the mother's breasts, for she would continue, "Brother has a penis. Be gentle. Don't hurt. Don't cut off your nailfingers. Bola. Jean has a bola (vulva)." Gradually she became outspokenly self-punitive and asked to be "thrown away." In solitary games she would go back to her old fears of dirt, and would act as if she were brushing away a cobweb or throwing away something disgusting.

Let us pause here to note that Jean was already describing here the basic cycle of an infantile schizophrenic conflict. There seems to be little doubt that the child, given a chance to communicate with the mother in her own way, referred back to the time five years earlier, when her mother was ill. These children have an excellent memory—in spots, in vulnerable spots—but their memory does not seem to sustain the rudiments of a sense of identity. Their sayings, like dream images, indicate what they want to talk about, but do not indicate what causal connection is to be communicated. In talking about her mother's illness, then, so we must infer, Jean alluded to the possibility that she had hurt the mother's chest, that as token of her hurt condition the mother had worn a "bandage" and that for that reason the child had been thrown away (not permitted to come and hug her mother). The confusion as to what was hurt, the child's finger or the mother's chest, we may ascribe to semantic difficulties as well as to the faulty boundary between self and other. Adults are of little help in these matters when they say, "Don't touch it, you will hurt it," and then switch to "Don't touch it, or else you will hurt your fingers." Yet one might say that the confusion of adult dicta here fits only too well that early ego stage when all pain is experienced as "outside," all pleasure as "inside," no matter where its actual source is. Jean may never have outgrown that stage; and yet, there was also the early experience of being abandoned by the mother to a nurse who was a "don't touch" zealot. In retesting the reality of that prohibition, of course, she only had to do what she did to the men in the family. With her mother she was more fortunate. But here an important item enters—namely, the immense self-punitive tendency in these driven children. Their law is "all or none"; they take the dictum, "If thine eye offend thee, pluck it out," literally and quite seriously. Thus it may happen that a little boy in a schizo-phrenic episode requests his horrified parents in all sincerity to cut off his penis because it is no good.

The mother continued to explain patiently to Jean that her illness had not been the child's fault. She let Jean sleep with her, let her sit on her lap, and, in general, gave her the attention and consideration usually awarded only to an infant. Jean seemed to begin to believe her. After several months she showed marked improvement. She became more graceful in her movements; her vocabulary increased, or, as one should say in such cases, became apparent, for it is usually there before its presence is suspected. And she began to play! She put a little black toy dog to bed and said, "Go to sleep, dog, stay under covers; shut your eyes, have to spank you, dog." Also she began to build long block trains which were "going east." During one of these games she looked her mother in the eyes with one of her rare, completely direct glances and said, "Not go on long ride on the train sometime." "No," said the mother, "we are going to stay together."

Such improvements seemed most rewarding. They were usu-ally interrupted by crises which led to emergency calls. I would visit the family and talk with all the members of the household until I had ascertained what was going on in all their lives. A whole series of difficulties arose in this one-patient sanitarium. One can live with schizophrenic thought only if one can make a profession out of understanding it. The mother had accepted this task, which demands a particular gift of empathy and at the same time the ability to keep oneself intact. Otherwise one must refute such thinking in order to be protected against it. Each member of the household, then, in being forced to take a glance into Jean's mind, characterized as it was by the alternation of naked impul-siveness and desperate self-negation, was endangered in his own equilibrium and self-esteem. This had to be pointed out repeatedly, because Jean would constantly change the direction of her provocation. And she would withdraw repeatedly for no apparent reason.

The following incident will serve to illustrate the impact of the mother's first attempts to make Jean sleep by herself. Suddenly a pathological attachment to spoons developed, and it assumed such proportions that it led to the first crisis of despair both in Jean and in her parents. Jean would insistently repeat such sentences as "not sleep in the light in Jean's room," "light in the spoon," "incinerator in the spoon," "blankets in the spoon," etc. During dinnertime she would often sit and merely look at the "light in the spoon." Unable to make herself understood, she began to withdraw and to stay in bed for hours and days. Yet she refused to go to sleep at night. The parents put in an emergency call and asked me to try to clear up the matter. When I asked Jean to show me the light in the spoon, she showed me a plug behind a bookcase. Some weeks ago she had broken off one piece of this plug and had caused a short circuit. As I went with her to her room to investigate the electrical appliances there I found that she had a dim bulb in her room with a small spoonlike shade attached to it which was intended to keep the light from shining on her bed. Was that the original "light in the spoon"? Jean indicated it was. Now it became clear. On returning home, Jean had first slept in the mother's bed. Then the mother had slept with her in her bed. Then the mother had slept in her own bed and Jean in hers, the door ajar and the hall light on. Finally the hall light had been turned off and only the light from a small bulb ("the light in the spoon") left in Jean's room. Apparently at night, then, Jean would look at this light as her last consolation—the last "part" of her mother—and endow it with the same partialistic affection and fear which she had demonstrated in relation to her mother's breast, her father's and her brother's penises, and all the fetishes before. It was at that time that she touched the plug in the living room with those problem fingers of hers, causing a short circuit and making everything dark, including the "light in the spoon." Again she had brought on catastrophe: by touching something she had caused a crisis which threatened to leave her alone in the dark.

The circumstances having been explained all around, the spoon fetish was abandoned, and the course of restoration resumed. However, one could not fail to be impressed with the persistence of the pathogenic pattern and the violence of its eruption, for Jean was now a whole year older (nearly seven). Yet she seemed to begin to feel that her fingers could do no irreparable harm and that she could not only keep them but also use them for learning and for making beautiful things.

First, she became enchanted by the finger play which says that "this little pig does this" and "that little pig does that." She made the little pigs do what she had been doing during the day, namely, "go to market," "go to ten-cent store," "go to escalator," or "cry all the way home." Thus, in referring to the coherent series of her fingers she learned to integrate time and to establish a continuity of the various selves which had done different things at different times. But she could not say, "*I* did this" and "*I* did that." Not that I consider this a problem of mere mental capacity. The ego of schizoid (as well as schizophrenic) people is dominated by the necessity of repeating the testing and integrating experience just because it provides an inadequate sense of the trustworthiness of events at the time when they happen. Jean, then, accomplished such reintegration, together with its communication, by the use of her fingers, which, now permitted, could be readmitted to the body ego. She learned the letters of the alphabet by drawing them with her fingers, after studying them with the help of the Montessori touch method. And she learned to play melodies by scratching a xylophone with her nails. The mother reported:

> Since the time when Jean began to show such a disturbing, because apparently senseless, interest in the xylophone, I have noticed that she is actually playing it with her fingernails. She does it so quietly one cannot distinguish what she is doing. Tonight, however, I discovered that she could play "Water, Water Wild Flower" all the way through. This song requires every note in the scale. I asked for it to be repeated and watched her hand travel up and down the scale. I was amazed and made a big fuss over her, saying it was wonderful. I said, "Let's go downstairs to the others and play it for them." She came down willingly, even self-consciously, and very pleased. She now played it aloud for them, and they were astounded. She then played several other things: "Rain is Falling Down," "ABCDEFG," etc. We all praised her and she ate it up. She did not want to go upstairs but seemed to want to stay and play on for the audience, a new delightful feeling.

Thus Jean "sublimated" and gained friends, but as she regained parts of herself she also made new enemies, in new ways. For she also used her fingers for poking people and came so near to hurting a visitor's eyes that she had to be energetically stopped. She especially liked to poke her father, obviously as a sequence to her penis- and cigarette-grabbing activities. When at this point, the father had to go on a trip, she regressed to whining, resumed her sheet fetish (saying "blanket is mended"), spoke only in a soft voice, and ate little, even refusing ice cream. She had again made somebody go away by touching him! She seemed particularly desperate because she had, in fact, begun to respond to her father's devoted efforts to help her.

At the height of this new crisis, Jean lay down beside her mother in bed and with desperate crying repeated over and over, "No vulva on Jean, no eggplant, take it off, take it off, no egg in the plant, not plant the seed, cut off your finger, get some scissors, cut it off." This obviously represented the old deep self-punitive reaction.

Jean's mother gave her appropriate explanations concerning her father's "disappearance." She also told Jean that it was not because she had touched herself that her "eggplant" had disappeared; in fact, she still had one of her own way inside. Jean resumed her play with her fingers. She had to work her way again through previous stages of existence by chanting: "This little girl sleeps in the refrigerator, this little girl sleeps in the vacuum cleaner," etc. Gradually her interest in animals and now also in other children reappeared, and the fingers would represent "this little boy is jumping, this little boy is running . . . is walking . . . is racing," etc. Her interest in finger skill then was applied to various forms of locomotion both of children and of animals. She learned to read and to list the names of various domestic animals and, again using her fingers, to recite the days of the week, and adding her toes, count up to twenty. At the same time her play on the xylophone began to include more difficult French folk songs, all of which she played with great ease and abandon, knowing always exactly where to find the first note. The pleasure of having the use of her fingers restored can be seen from the mother's report:

Last Sunday Jean made a painting of a little girl in a yellow dress. At night she went up to the picture on the wall silently and felt of the paint. She paused long over the hands, each of which was bigger than the whole girl, and very carefully done with five fingers each. Then she said, "The hands are nice." I agreed, repeating the words. Then in a minute she said, "The hands are pretty." Again I agreed appreciatively. She retreated to the bed without taking her eyes off the picture as she sat down on the bed, still studying it. Then she burst out loudly, "The hands are *lovely*."

During all this time, Jean had, off and on, played the xylophone and sung songs. Now the parents were fortunate enough to find a piano teacher who was willing to base her methods on Jean's auditory gift and ingenuity in imitating. At my next visit, after being taken to my room, I heard somebody practicing some phrases of Beethoven's first sonata, and innocently remarked on the strong and sensitive touch. I thought a gifted adult was playing. To find Jean at the piano was one of the surprises which are so gripping in work with these cases—and which often prove so misleading, because again and again they make one believe in the child's total progress where one is justified in believing only in isolated and too rapid advances of special faculties. This I say with feeling and conviction, for Jean's piano playing, whether it was Beethoven, Haydn, or boogie-woogie, was truly astounding—until she turned against this gift, just as she had "turned against speech," in the words of the first psychologist who had seen her.

This completes one episode in Jean's improvement: her relation to her hands. It also completes the specimen to be reported here as an illusion of the essential ego weakness which causes these children to be swayed at one time by a "drivenness" focused on a part of another person; and at another by cruel self-punitiveness and paralyzing perfectionism. It is not that they fail to be able to learn, to remember, and to excel—usually in some artistic endeavor which reflects the sensory counterpart of their essential oral fixation. It is that they cannot integrate it all: their ego is impotent.

You will want to know how Jean fared. As the child grew more mature, the discrepancy between her age and her behavior became so marked that associations with children anywhere near her age level became impossible. Other difficulties arose which made at least an interval in a special school mandatory. There she quickly lost what she had gained in the years of her mother's heroic effort. Her treatment has since been resumed under the best residential circumstances and under the guidance of one of the most devoted and most imaginative child psychiatrists in this particular field.

The role which "maternal rejection" or special circumstances of abandonment play in cases such as Jean's is still debatable. I think one should consider that these children may very early and subtly fail to return the mother's glance, smile, and touch; an initial reserve which makes the mother, in turn, unwittingly withdraw. The truism that the original problem is to be found in the mother-child relationship holds only in so far as one considers this relationship an emotional pooling which may multiply well-being in both but which will endanger both partners when the communication becomes jammed or weakened. In those cases of infantile schizophrenia which I have seen, there was a clear deficiency in "sending power" in the child.[1] Because of the very early failure of communication, however, the child may only betray in more malignant form a frailty of affective contact which already exists in the parent(s), although in them it may be compensated for—at least in other relationships—by a special character make-up or by superior intellectual endowment.

As to the procedure described in this chapter, it should be clear that Jean's mother was capable of that exceptional curative effort which is a prerequisite for all experimentation on this frontier of human trust.

The Hatchet Man
from *Case Studies in Management,* 1964
edited by Michael Ivens and Frank Broadway

Pioneered by medicine and law, the case-study approach to teaching apprentices in the field spread to business and government. A case conveys to students a realistic example of what professionals in the field deal with on the job. Usually the cases are true

1. In the First Edition, the wording was ". . . the primary deficiency in 'sending power' was in the child." This referred only to those few cases that I had seen; and such cases were rare then in psychoanalytic practise. My statement was intended to counter certain facile interpretations then in vogue which claimed that rejecting mothers could cause such malignancy in their offspring. In the meantime, my statement has been quoted out of context in support of a strictly constitutional etiology of infantile psychosis. The careful reader of Chapter 1, however, and of Jean's history, will see that in the case fragments presented in this book I am not trying to isolate first causes and therapeutic effects, but to delineate a new conceptual area encompassing both the struggles of the ego and of social organization. This approach, no doubt, bypasses details in parent-child interaction in which constitutional and environmental defects aggravate each other malignantly. But first causes can be isolated (or ruled out) only where rigorous diagnostic criteria exist and where anamneses in quantity permit comparison. Such work can be found in the growing literature of psychoanalytic child psychiatry. (E.H.E.)

and are chosen for the possibilities they provide to analyze and discuss typical issues and problems. Often the student must come up with a solution. To facilitate this practice in problem-solving, the conclusion of a case may be withheld in the casebook until students have had a go at it and discussed alternative solutions in class.

Drawn from such a textbook for the business world, "The Hatchet Man" represents this sort of unsolved case. It is told in third person because the identity of the narrator and the information sources (probably multiple) have no importance. Spotlight is on delineation of the problem posed. This anonymity characterizes folk tales too, many of which aim likewise to instruct by embodying common issues in a representative story. Most pertinently, some African tribes tell "dilemma tales" that stop where the main character faces a difficult decision and ask the listeners to finish the story.

Arthur Mold joined the Midland Counties Engineering Company to serve a graduate apprenticeship. As he liked the Company he stayed on after qualifying. At first he was employed on design work, for which he had no great talent, but he was soon given the opportunity to move into a junior management post on production and from then on his progress was rapid. He had a methodical mind and a flair for cost reduction and he was able to apply these qualities to good effect in a number of management assignments of increasing responsibility.

By the time he was 32 he was works manager at the Company's Lincolnshire factory, where a very wide range of pumps was made by small batch or "one-off" methods. Although the products enjoyed a high reputation and order books were always full, the factory was not a large profit-earner. Mold set to work to remedy this situation. He carried out a thorough reorganization of production methods, achieving substantial economies. At the same time he patiently but firmly negotiated with the sales staff to introduce measures of product standardization, which in due course cut by half the varieties of pumps manufactured. Within two years of taking up his appointment, the profits of the factory had increased by 70 per cent.

Mold was then interviewed jointly by the managing director and the production director. The works manager of the Worcester factory had died suddenly and they were considering a number of people in the Company as replacements. Though Mold thought he had made a favourable impression, he did not expect to get the job. The factory was by far the largest the Company owned, and if he were appointed manager it would be a very substantial promotion indeed—over the heads of a good many managers senior to him in both age and status. Furthermore, all Mold's management expertise had been in batch operations, whereas the Worcester factory was a mass production unit, turning out small parts and pressings on a vast scale for the car and other engineering assembly industries.

Mold was therefore very gratified when Mr. Maclaren, the production director, instructed him a week later to go to Worcester and take over the management of the factory. The most important item in his mandate was to get costs down; business was bitterly competitive and important orders were being lost through inability to quote sufficiently low prices. Maclaren warned Mold that cost reduction would not be easy, since the factory was already reckoned to be pretty efficient. Skill, determination, even ruthlessness would be called for, but Mold would have the full support of the Board in all measures that would achieve economies.

When he arrived at Worcester, Mold found that his immediate subordinates in the management of the factory were all considerably older than he, mostly in their late forties or early fifties. He gathered that a rumour had gone round that he had been appointed as "hatchet man" and there were considerable apprehensions about what was to happen. He was, in fact, treated with very marked coolness by all his immediate colleagues, with one single exception.

The exception was Walter Brearley, a red-faced, talkative, cheerful man in his early fifties. Brearley had spent his whole working life at the Worcester factory, having joined as a craft apprentice straight from school and then gradually worked his way up to become assistant works manager. In this position he was in charge of production, with a production manager, a production planning manager, and a work study section, directly responsible to him.

From the moment Mold arrived Brearley adopted a friendly attitude to him and in fact they lunched together on Mold's first day. Mold knew that Brearley had been a candidate for the job of works manager and had expected to find him disappointed, or perhaps embittered. As he liked to be straightforward with people in his relationships with them he asked Brearley over lunch if he did not in fact resent having a younger man appointed manager over his head. Brearley said, on the contrary, he was in fact relieved that he had not been given the job of works manager

He was already a member of the local Council and a J.P. and this, together with his work as assistant works manager, gave him all the responsibility he wanted. He assured Mold that he would give him all possible support.

He did, in fact, go out of his way to put Mold in the picture. He knew the work of the factory in great detail and was able to give an enormous amount of information. He was also on excellent terms with nearly all the executives and employees in the factory and seemed to make a considerable effort to break down some of the barriers between Mold and his staff. Indeed, but for Brearley, Mold would have been very lonely in his early days at the factory.

After a while, however, Mold began to feel that there were distinct disadvantages in Brearley's friendliness. His endless stream of conversation took up a great deal of time and prevented Mold getting his teeth into the matters which he regarded as urgent and important. Mold also found that not all the information which Brearley gave him was accurate—he seemed indeed consistently to put a somewhat optimistic gloss on to the numerous facts and figures he quoted. There was, however, a further thing that irked Mold about Brearley's attitude. There seemed to him to be a faint air of patronizing familiarity about the way in which Brearley treated him. This obtruded into many conversations, and it particularly appeared whenever Mold mentioned any ideas he had for improving operations or cutting costs. Brearley almost always dismissed such ideas on one of three grounds: either that the idea had been tried before and hadn't worked, or that the unions wouldn't stand for it, or that it might be all right for a batch process but it wouldn't do for mass production.

For two or three weeks Mold made no effort to adjust his relationship with Brearley, but as he found that more and more of his time was being taken up in gossip, he decided that he must give Brearley a friendly warning. He was very anxious not to hurt his feelings and he waited several days for an opportunity to suggest tactfully that Brearley should spend rather less time in inessential conversation. Then one morning, when Brearley was launched on a long account of proceedings at a Council Meeting on the previous evening, Mold said gently, "Walter, I've got a lot to do, and I'm sure you have—how about breaking it up?" Brearley simply said, "Yes, I'll be off in a minute or two," and went on with his narrative. When, a quarter-of-an-hour later, the end still did not appear to be in sight, Mold interrupted rather more harshly and said, "Look, Walter, you must have work to do, and I certainly have—now, please, go back to your office and, in future, let's confine our talks to business matters.'' Brearley flushed, and left the office at once.

From then on Brearley's attitude to Mold changed markedly. He never approached Mold except on specific points of business and avoided him whenever possible. This worried Mold, who wondered whether he should apologize to Brearley but, as he could not make up his mind, he put off taking any action and used the time left free to start a comprehensive study of the factory's operations.

He found a number of ways in which economies could be effected and he called a meeting of the senior executives to explain his ideas to them. They were received in complete silence by everyone but Brearley, who opposed every single idea that Mold put forward. In some cases Brearley's opposition was reasoned and, in one instance, he was able to point out a serious weakness in one of the plans which Mold had put forward. In general, however, Mold got the impression that Brearley was opposing him simply for the sake of being awkward, and he had a maddening habit at the meeting of prefacing what he had to say with the remark, ''Mr Chairman, I know you think I talk too much, but I must . . .''

Mold had never before experienced any serious hostility from his colleagues and he decided that he ought to seek some advice on his relations with Brearley. The next time the production director, Mr. Maclaren, visited the factory, therefore, he mentioned to him his difficulties. He was somewhat disconcerted by Maclaren's response, which seemed to be to blame him entirely for what had happened. Maclaren said that he had known Brearley for more than 20 years and he had never before heard of anyone failing to get on with him. He implied that Mold must have been very heavy-handed in his relationships to fail to win Brearley's loyalty and support. Mold was upset by this apparent rebuke and still more disconcerted when he noticed that Maclaren later in the day went to see Brearley and spent half an hour with him.

To get relief from his worries about Brearley, Mold worked still more intensively on his plans for improving the factory management. He thought the sums expended on maintenance were excessive and he instructed the chief engineer to institute a more advanced system of planned maintenance. The chief engineer cavilled at this and when, a week later, he appeared to have made no progress, Mold informed him that he considered him unsuitable for his important position and he would take steps to have him retired and replaced by a younger and more go-ahead man. The chief engineer, finding that his own protests were unavailing, came back later to see Mold with Brearley to support him. The meeting was an unpleasant one but Mold felt that he would never secure the necessary economies in maintenance costs unless the change was made, and he refused to change his judgement. The following day he telephoned Maclaren and told him that he wanted to replace the chief engineer. Though Maclaren seemed somewhat disturbed by the news he assured Mold that he would support him, as he had promised, if he felt the move was really necessary to secure more economic operation.

Mold then turned his attention to the production lines. Lines 1–16, which turned out the simpler parts made in the factory, had all been re-equipped during recent years and seemed highly efficient. Lines 17–24, however, on which much more complex parts were made, seemed to Mold to be in some need of work study and to require replacement of certain machines by more up-to-date, faster, models.

Mold, therefore, went to Brearley to ask him to arrange for the work study section, which was responsible to Brearley, to carry out an extensive study on lines 17–24. Mold took this opportunity to try to be conciliatory towards Brearley, but Brearley at once protested that extensive work study had already been done on the lines during the last year or two and that nothing could possibly be achieved by further study. Mold insisted that they should be re-studied and Brearley, with bad grace, went to fetch the head of the work study section. While he was gone, Mold slipped out of his office to attend another matter and, on his way back, he met Brearley coming along with Hornby, the work study man. Brearley and Hornby were laughing and joking together and Mold felt pretty sure that they were joking about him. He gave his instructions to Hornby who, like Brearley, expressed the view that nothing would be gained by further study.

A few days later Hornby presented his report on the study. It greatly annoyed Mold for it virtually only said that a further study had been undertaken but that there was little that could be done to improve the production lines. One or two very minor changes were suggested, offering only derisory savings. Brearley, who had brought in the report to Mold, was obviously highly pleased with it.

Mold at once got on the phone to the Company's chief work study officer in Birmingham and asked him to send down a team of specialists to study the lines. When he divulged that his own staff had already made a study the chief work study officer showed obvious reluctance to send his own specialists and Mold had to threaten that he would take the matter to Maclaren before he promised that a team would be sent. Two days later the two-man team arrived. They agreed with Mold that there seemed to be considerable scope for improvement on lines 17–24, and they set to work at once on a detailed study. Shortly afterwards Brearley burst into Mold's office and protested furiously that Mold had brought them in without consulting him. Mold told him that he had felt obliged to bring them down in view of the extremely poor showing which Brearley and Hornby had made in the matter. He also told Brearley that he was thinking of having Hornby transferred and replaced by an abler and more co-operative man. A little while later Brearley came back again, this time with two shop stewards who, he said, had come to protest to him that outside work study consultants had been brought in without prior consultation with the unions. In fact, there was an agreement between the Company and the unions providing for work study to be undertaken at the Company's discretion, and it contained no reference as to where the work study specialists were to be drawn from. Mold managed to sort the matter out after half an hour's discussion, but he was left with the inescapable impression that Brearley was deliberately stirring up trouble.

The work study specialists came to Mold with their proposals nearly two weeks later. The savings they were able to suggest were not quite as large as Mold had hoped, but they were, nevertheless, useful. Twelve men could be dispensed with and the system for bringing material to the lines was considerably improved. Mold had long discussions with Brearley and the shop stewards about the redundant men. It was not really a difficult problem because there was plenty of alternative work in the neighbourhood and the Company made quite generous compensation payments to anyone declared redundant. The talks nevertheless dragged on and Mold again had the feeling that Brearley was being deliberately unhelpful.

Before the work study team returned Mold had a long talk with them about the top management organization of his factory. He thought this was unnecessarily cumbersome and he had 11 different senior executives reporting directly to him. Barlow, the senior man of the team, promised that he would think about the matter and send Mold an alternative organization plan. When, a week later, Barlow's alternative plan arrived, Mold was both pleased and gravely disturbed. The plan was delightfully simple and had reduced to five the number of executives reporting directly to the works manager; it seemed to provide a realistic way of streamlining the organization. What disturbed Mold, however, was that it abolished the position of assistant works manager. Mold spent many hours thinking about this plan. The more he thought about it, the more he appreciated the logic that an assistant works manager was unnecessary. Brearley was nominally in charge of production, but a production manager and a production planning manager between them were able quite competently to manage operations with relatively little reference to Brearley. Indeed, the lack of any real need for an assistant works manager was exemplified by the fact that Brearley took a great deal of time off, with the Company's permission, to attend to his Council and Magistrate's duties.

Brearley was 52, too young for early retirement under the Company's pension plan. He had deep roots in the locality, which would presumably make his transfer to another factory in the Company out of the question. Nevertheless, Mold felt that it was his duty to implement the plan which Barlow had suggested, including the abolition of the office of assistant works manager. He therefore telephoned the Company's chief personnel officer and told him what he had in mind and asked what could be done about Brearley. The chief personnel officer was aghast at the whole idea and beseeched Mold to give up the plan. Mold, however, had made up his mind and insisted that he was going to raise the matter with Maclaren and simply wanted suggestions on dealing with Brearley. The chief personnel officer, clearly very disturbed, promised to think about it and telephone Mold later.

While Mold had been telephoning he had not noticed that his office door was slightly ajar. He got up to close it and found Brearley, very white-faced, standing outside. Brearley had obviously overheard what had been going on. He said at once to Mold that he was going immediately on the train to the head office to see Mr. Maclaren and complain about the vicious victimization to which Mold was subjecting him.

The Prevention of Sleeping Sickness in Nigeria

Horace Miner

from "Culture Change Under
Pressure: A Hausa Case,"
Human Organization, Fall, 1960

---

*Many cases tell a group story. Here we complete another cycle
from first person to third person plural but this time on the more
topical/typical plane of the case history. Characteristically, a* they
*story must draw on numerous sources and at the same time meld
individuals together into some account general enough to be true
for all. The case writer must direct this synopsizing process
according to what the case purports to show—distill many personal experiences into a composite group experience that becomes itself the statement the case makes.*

Included in A Casebook on Social Change, *edited by Arthur
Niehoff, the next case does not aim any more at the novice than
at the established "change agent" in underdeveloped countries.
The equivalent folk story might be the "cautionary tale" that
tries to warn us away from a mistake someone else has already
made.*

Programs of technical assistance and community development
create culture contact conditions which are particularly well suited
to the study of change. The contact situation is narrowly delim-
ited and it is easier to identify the agents of change, the pressures
for change and the results of the contact. The study here reported
in preliminary fashion is an attempt to capitalize on such a
research situation in northern Nigeria. Here, among the Hausa,
the British Colonial government instituted a program of resettlement, health improvement and economic development. The Anchau
Scheme, as it was known, was initiated in 1937 and continued

with diminishing intensity for the next decade. Since 1948 the area has received no special attention. These facts about the scheme contributed to the decision to study it, for they provided one condition frequently lacking in previous case studies. The assistance program was old enough that its ultimate effects, rather than just its immediate effects, should be evident. The price paid for the advantage of studying the end results of the contact was, of course, the necessity of reconstructing the operational phase of the program.

The disadvantages of such an approach were mitigated by two things: extensive files of the day-to-day working papers of the Scheme personnel were still available, along with all the related reports and publications. In addition, both the British and Hausa who had been most involved in the Scheme were still available as informants. While memories are notoriously selective, this fact proved to be a methodological asset. When the records and the recollections of the two groups corresponded, the facts of the case were obvious. But when they diverged, in every case the divergences were traceable to specific differences in the cultural perspectives with which the same events were viewed. Once the bases of the distortion were understood, the true nature of the events became perfectly clear.

The Anchau Scheme was originally developed to meet a specific problem—the widespread occurrence of sleeping sickness among the Hausa. Although the Scheme was ultimately expanded to include other goals, we shall limit our discussion to the measures used to control this disease.

The British instituted a special investigation of sleeping sickness in 1921, but it was not until 1928 that they discovered that the disease had reached epidemic proportions and was rapidly decimating the population. Interestingly, the epidemic was an indirect result of the advent of *Pax Britannica*. Before the conquest of northern Nigeria in 1903, the area was in a state of turbulence as a result of incessant slave raids. Towns were heavily walled and the working of fields at any distance from the towns involved considerable risk. Large areas of the countryside were uninhabited and communication was limited. Although there was an area of endemic sleeping sickness to the south and tsetse flies were prevalent all over the North at this time, the disease remained localized. With the establishment of peace, farmers moved out into the bush and mobility increased generally. The increased fly-man contact soon produced the epidemic.

Field surveys showed that in some areas up to forty percent of the people had the disease. The basic problem was that, although there were effective curative drugs, they did little good as long as reinfection from tsetse fly bites was inevitable. The government established a research station to attack the problem and Dr. T. A. M. Nash, the staff entomologist, discovered that the tsetse fly could only live in a microclimate distinctly cooler than the generally prevailing temperatures in sunlight. The fly was therefore confined to the shaded banks of streams, the rest of the country being generally open. It was at fords and water holes that the fly-man contact occurred.

Tests revealed that if the brush were cut down along the streams, the fly could not persist in the area. On the basis of these findings the Anchau Scheme was drawn up to initiate control measures in the worst affected region. The proposal was to keep the stream banks clear in an area of 700 square miles within which lived some 50,000 people. In order to accomplish this end, part of the population had to be resettled to create sufficient density to provide the manpower to keep the streams cleared. We shall limit ourselves simply to that part of the plan which involved convincing the Hausa to keep the brush cut along the streams. In order to understand the Hausa reactions to the program, we must describe those elements of Hausa culture which are immediately relevant.

Important in this regard is their political organization. The Fulani conquest of the ancient Hausa, or Habe, States at the beginning of the nineteenth century resulted in the establishment of a series of feudally organized emirates. Each was autonomous and headed by an emir descended from the Fulani conquerors. The emirates were divided into fiefs, each allocated to a Fulani, commonly a relative of the emir. The fiefs in turns were divided into village areas, each under the control of a Hausa headman, resident in the principal settlement in his area. Even the headmen held their appointments subject to the approval of the emir. The functions of this hierarchy were the maintenance of order, the organization of defensive and offensive forces, and the collection of taxes.

The emirs were all-powerful, even to the extent of interfering with the administration of Moslem justice by the cadis. The emir's position could only be jeopardized by alienating powerful groups of fiefholders. The latter were supreme within their domains as long as they kept the emir satisfied. The village headmen had the support of the fiefholder and his forces but, in the regulation of mundane affairs within the village areas, the headman's power derived directly from the support accorded him by his villagers. Being a Hausa, his traditional role depended upon his understanding and manipulation of the local culture.

Even with peers the Hausa peasant adheres to elaborate forms of politeness. The deference shown to superiors is almost oriental in flavor. In the presence of the *hakimi*, or lord of the fief, a peasant removes his sandals, prostrates himself and remains bowed to the ground, keeps his eyes lowered, speaks only when addressed, and employs highly formalized deferential phrases when he does speak. He would never think of expressing a point of view contrary to that of the *hakimi*. Village headmen, although they are peasants themselves, are treated with extreme politeness but the system permits greater freedom of expression with these arbiters of village problems. In summary we may say that Hausa society, including its overlords, is very hierarchically organized. The advent of the British did little to change this except to limit some of the excesses of the emirs and fiefholders. Indirect rule was studiously adhered to. Although British district officers were appointed to oversee colonial administration at the local level, all administrative acts were promulgated by British authorities through the emirs. If problems arose at the local level, recommendations were made upward through the Colonial channels, the emir was persuaded to act, and the directives came down the indigenous lines of power. Because of the powerful position of the British vis-à-vis the emir and because the district officer had access to top colonial officials, a district officer could, if so inclined, wield a considerable amount of derived power in his relation to a *hakimi*.

Another aspect of the Hausa power system involves the cultural devices for holding the power of the overlords within reasonable bounds. One method which the peasants employ in limiting the nominal omnipotence of their rulers is passive resistance. When a headman transmits orders from the *hakimi* which the peasants do not want to follow, they simply fail to comply. The headman can exert his influence to try to secure compliance, but his power is only as strong as his local support. General resistance to repeated orders may be continued until sanctions are applied by the *hakimi*. Such sanctions consist of fines or jail terms and the headman may be replaced if he has been sufficiently noncooperative.

In addition to the political structure, the other aspect of Hausa culture most relevant to the Anchau plan for sleeping sickness control is the native belief concerning the nature and cause of the disease. These ideas are best understood in relation to Western concepts. In its most characteristic Nigerian form, sleeping sick-

276 POINTS OF DEPARTURE

ness produces sporadic fever, headache, edema of the face and limbs, accompanied by swelling of the cervical glands and persistent weakness. The condition may continue for years but the associated lowered resistance to disease frequently results in death from other causes. Death may even result from a flareup of the toxic effects of sleeping sickness itself, without the central nervous system becoming involved so as to produce the classic condition of continued somnolence and mental disorder. The proportion of patients who show these latter symptoms is always small. This form of the disease is normally fatal and even with treatment the patient may not recover. If he does, he will still show damage to the nervous system. The more prevalent form of sleeping sickness is not easily recognized, even by doctors, unless they have had experience with the disease. On a number of occasions medical efforts sent out to investigate epidemics of what later proved to be sleeping sickness failed to diagnose the underlying sickness and reported that the people were dying of pneumonia.

The Hausa recognized only the rarely occurring sleeping and mania symptoms as characterizing the disease *ciwon barci*, a literal translation of "sleeping sickness." They did not recognize the other more prevalent symptoms as characterizing any single disease and, in fact, most of the symptoms occur separately in connection with other maladies. *Ciwon barci* was greatly feared for it was fatal and believed to be highly contagious. Any Hausa so afflicted was completely isolated, even from his family. Although he might be driven from the community, he was more usually fed by a relative who avoided any contact with the patient or his utensils. Not infrequently the mentally deranged invalid would wander off and starve before he died of his disease. When treatment was attempted, it consisted of herbal remedies or written Koranic charms.

Some of the other terms employed to identify sleeping sickness are indicative of Hausa beliefs as to its cause. The disease was also known as *kunturu*, a word which also designates a region which has a reputation of being under evil supernatural influence. *Dudduru* refers to the disease and also means a small stream with wooded banks. Both words refer to the fundamental belief that sleeping sickness is caused by *iska*, or spirits, who live in natural features such as clumps of brush along the streams. The *iska* are pre-Islamic supernaturals who have survived the conversion of the Hausa and are still actively propitiated by the Maguzawa, who are probably pagan remnants of the early Hausa still scattered through the area. Spirit possession in the form of *bori* dancing is still common to Maguzawa and Moslem Hausa alike. The Galma River, which flows to the south of Anchau, is considered to be infested with malevolent spirits and the area is actually still dangerous for sleeping sickness. Because spirits are local, the only way to escape their effects is to leave the region. Whole villages have moved when threatened with epidemic disease. Although such action might remove a population from an area badly infested with tsetse, the insects were ubiquitous and complete escape was impossible. While the Hausa thus recognized the relation between the habitat of the tsetse fly and sleeping sickness, the role of the fly in the transmission of the disease was unknown—the *iska* were the vector.

Against the background just sketched, we are in a position to consider Hausa reactions to the methods of sleeping sickness control instituted by the British. Even before the Anchau Scheme went into operation, medical officers had made an intensive survey of the population to determine the extent of sleeping sickness and to provide treatment. Clinical diagnosis followed by microscopic verification revealed large numbers of cases who showed none of the classic symptoms. Even when tests proved the presence of the infection, the Hausa were very loath to admit that they had the awful disease which previously made them outcasts. Still today, a headman may deny that there is any sleeping sickness in his village, although he knows of cases under treatment. The British interpret these facts as representing a feeling of shame concerning the disease. On the other hand, there is considerable doubt that the Hausa ever accepted the idea that what they and the British called sleeping sickness were really the same thing. None of the old fear of the disease was felt toward medically diagnosed cases which did not fit the Hausa concept of sleeping sickness. The conflicting conceptions need not be resolved now, for advanced cases have disappeared entirely.

When the Anchau Scheme went into operation, the system of indirect rule was adhered to and the necessary orders were issued through the Emir. To strengthen the native authority channel and to reinforce on-the-spot interpretations of the Emir's orders, the Emir was persuaded to send a personal representative to remain in Anchau. Through him the British personnel could put immediate pressure on the *Hakimi*, whose residence was permanently transferred to Anchau. These changes resulted in a concentration of authority previously unknown in the area. The resettlement phase of the Scheme brought together the scattered peasants so that they were under administrative scrutiny of a sort they dearly loved to avoid. The *Hakimi* found he was no longer the highest local official and even the Emir ultimately complained that, as a result of the intense British activity around Anchau, he had been deprived of part of his emirate. In short, while native channels of power were used, everyone along the line felt under unusual administrative pressure. This method of administration of the Scheme did have one very important implication for the success of the plan. The specific methods of implementation of many of its aspects were left up to the native authorities and the acculturative adjustments to the changes were as little disruptive to the local culture as they could be.

Before stream clearance was begun, the reasons for it were explained to the Hausa from the Emir to the village elders. They were told that sleeping sickness was common among them, that it was caused by little "fish-like animals" in the blood, that these animals got into the blood when a person was bitten by a tsetse fly, and that the way to get rid of the flies was to cut down the brush along the streams. As we have seen, these statements were in conflict with native beliefs and the explanation of the idea of microörganisms was entirely beyond their experience and comprehension. It is also clear that the Hausa patterns of respect toward superiors made it impossible for them to question openly what they were told. As a result, the British were effectively isolated from any knowledge of their failure to convey to the Hausa any real understanding of what was being done.

Initial stream clearance was carried out with hired native labor. In at least two instances local Hausa refused to cut certain patches of brush because these were sacred and inhabited by spirits. Finally non-Hausa natives from the French Sudan were used to cut the sacred brush. Once the streams were cleared, a plan was drawn up to provide for annual slashing thereafter. Each headman was impressed with his responsibility and the benefits which his village would derive from the elimination of the flies. On a rough average, some two weeks of part-time communal labor would be involved during a period of agricultural inactivity. Orders for the first reslashing went out from the Emir, through the *Hakimi*. The British supervisors and native foremen appeared at the villages to oversee the work but the communal laborers failed to appear. Subsequent attempts to secure cooperation produced only a handful of men and they arrived hours late. Exasperated, the British forced the Emir to stringent action. Headmen were removed from office and fines imposed on the peasants. These methods ultimately produced results. By checking the operations year after year, the pattern of annual stream clearance was finally established.

The result of the disease treatment and the eradication of the fly was the virtual elimination of sleeping sickness. The population began to increase and even migrants came to fill up the land now free from disease. For the past ten years there have been no Scheme personnel at Anchau but a thorough check of the streams showed that the annual orders of the Emir have been carried out in almost all instances and that the area is still virtually free of fly and sleeping sickness. One may well conclude that this, the major phase of the scheme, has been a success. In terms of culture change, the Hausa have for twenty years carried out a new pattern of behavior which is essential for the biological preservation of the group.

It comes as something of a shock, therefore, to discover that stream clearance cannot be said to have been adopted into the culture of the Hausa around Anchau. The basis for such a statement is an exhaustive study of the present attitudes and conceptions of village headmen regarding sleeping sickness and its control. The village leaders were asked why they cleared the streams every year. The common denominator of the responses was that the slashing was carried out because they were forced to do it. A quarter of the headmen literally had no idea why the work was done. All of the others, however, stated that clearing the brush eliminated tsetse fly, although sometimes this response was added as an afterthought to an initial statement of ignorance of any reason for the task.

Half of those who mentioned flies also stated that they transmitted sleeping sickness. But when one pursued the subject, it became clear that this was a simple repetition of what they had been told. They saw this as the British explanation, but held firmly to their old belief that sleeping sickness was caused by spirits. Elimination of the flies was rationalized by others as desirable because the bite was painful. Still others saw the clearing as a means of driving out crop-destroying monkeys or of improving pasturage for Fulani cattle. Finally, the interviews produced that rarity in social science data, unanimous concurrence. When asked if they would continue to clear the streams if they were not forced to do so, every headman replied, "No."

What we find, therefore, is that the now long-standing practice of clearance has not been integrated into local culture at all. The foregoing material points to a clear answer as to why this vital practice would be abandoned tomorrow if administrative pressure were not maintained from outside the area. We have long known that the adoption of a new culture trait involves its ability to meet some functional need in the culture. Expressed in psychological phraseology, action agencies now commonly refer to the necessity of operating in terms of a people's "felt needs." But what can be done if a people feel no need for the innovation the agency wishes to introduce? Faced with the necessity of making people accept things for which they perceive no need, the concept of "induced needs" has arisen. The Anchau evidence fully supports the role of perceived need in culture change and constitutes a warning with regard to methods of inducing change regardless of local perceptions of the innovation.

To recapitulate what happened at Anchau, it is clear that the Hausa experienced no particular need to eliminate sleeping sickness as they knew it. The new culture pattern of stream clearance was adopted and continued solely because of the need to escape administrative sanctions applied in traditional ways. The fact that the new trait was never effectively related to local problems and beliefs produced the anomaly of the adoption of an innovation without its integration into the culture. We find that coercion can produce compliance without any fundamental cultural alteration.

Hypnotherapy of two Psychosomatic Dental Problems
Milton H. Erickson

from *Journal of the American Society of Psychosomatic Dentistry*, July, 1955

Another way that the case writer approaches generalization is to collect a number of individual cases all showing the same thing. The collection as a whole forms a rudimentary sort of thesis essay in which the multiple narratives act as detailed instances supporting the thesis, which is minimally stated as a framework to make clear what the cases demonstrate in common.

Because such case collections can run to great length, the selection here consists of only two cases, enough perhaps to catch the effect. In The Wretched of the Earth, *black psychiatrist Frantz Fanon presented a fuller collection, made up of psychiatric cases he treated during Algeria's war of liberation from*

French colonial rule. The people whose stories he told became patients, he said, not because of childhood traumas but because of the current violent civil strife, a situational pathology allowed for in orthodox psychoanalytic theory.

Milton Erickson was generally acknowledged as the world's leading practitioner of medical hypnosis, which, by his patient skill and profound integrity, he made respectable. The choice of journal in which he originally published this pair of cases tells much about both him and some dental practice: he was clearly using his clinical examples to deflect dentists from cosmetic treatment that ignored deeper matters. His rare wizardry as a healer was so practically directed to the individual's particular underlying problem that, hypnosis aside, his treatment could seem unorthodox, if not comically bizarre.

In the practice of psychiatry, one frequently encounters patients whose problems center around some physical attribute with which they are dissatisfied. Too often, they seek help from those who are qualified to deal with the physical problem involved but have not had the training or experience necessary to recognize that the patient's personality, rather than his physical condition, is the primary consideration.

Consequently, efforts to alter the physical state, regardless of the technical skill employed and the excellence of the results obtained, are unappreciated since the patient's hopeful expectations exceed the possibilities of his physical realities. This is particularly true in the fields of dentistry and plastic surgery where sometimes the most skillful work fails to meet the emotional demands of the patient.

To illustrate this type of psychosomatic problem in the field of dentistry, two case histories are presented. In each instance, the patient seized upon a dental anomaly as the explanation of a definite personality maladjustment. For each, the problem of therapy was not a correction of the dental problem but a recognition of emotional needs.

Patient A

A high school girl sought psychiatric help because she was failing her second-year work and because she had barely succeeded in meeting the first year's requirements. Her reason for coming to the writer was that she knew he was a hypnotist and because she had been much impressed by an extracurricular lecture he had given at her high school. As she entered the office, she remarked that she would probably be hypnotized by a single glance from the writer and that she most likely would not even know she was in a trance. No effort was made to disillusion her.

She had come without her parents' knowledge because she felt that they would not understand her problem. Nor could she go to anybody else she knew because they would minimize her problem and reassure her "falsely."

Her chief complaint was that she was an "absolute freak" in appearance because she had only one double-sized upper incisor tooth. This had not troubled her until the development of physical maturity and a concurrent change in residence which necessitated admission to a high school where she did not know anyone.

Her reaction to this situation had been one of withdrawal, seclusiveness and the development of much wishful thinking in which her teeth were "normal." She found herself extremely self-conscious, was unwilling to eat in the school cafeteria, avoided smiling or laughing at any cost, and her enunciation of words was faulty because of voluntary rigidity of her upper lip. However, her attitude in the office was one of ease, which she explained was because she was probably hypnotized.

During the interview, it was noted that she relied almost exclusively on slang and "jive talk." Even when making serious remarks, she couched them in extravagances of slang. In the next two interviews, she was encouraged to display her extensive knowledge of, and fluency in, past and current slang. She was delighted to display her ability. She was an excellent mimic and had a remarkable command of accents which she was most ready to display. Accordingly, she was asked to demonstrate at length the "chopped" speech of the British and the "bitten off" enunciation of the Scotch. She also had an extensive knowledge of popular songs, past and present, comic strips, nursery tales, and light literature of all sorts.

The succeeding interview was devoted to an extensive discussion of the picturesqueness of slang. This conversation unnoticeably and deviously led into a discussion of such expressions as L'i Abner's "chompin' gum," "what big teeth you have, Grandmother," "Ol' Dan Tucker, who died with a toothache in his heel," "putting the bite on Daddy for more pocket money," "sinking a fang in a banana split," and various other expressions containing references to teeth or dental activity.

She was interested and pleased, but amused by the writer's effort to talk in "hep" style. She contributed greatly and readily to the discussion by calling upon her extensive knowledge of references to teeth in popular songs, nursery tales, comics and slang, without seeming to note the personal implications involved. For the next interview, she promised to "rattle the ivory" with every reference she could dig up from "China Choppers to the Elks' Club."

The following session was fascinating. In response to a request, alternating from British to Scotch pattern of speech and utilizing slang to do so, she proceeded in rapidfire fashion to give from songs, stories, ditties, doggerel, comics, fables, slang old and new, innumerable references to teeth.

When she finally began to slow down, the remark was made, "When you put the bite on a job, you really sink your fang into it; but then you've got the really hep accessory for that. Use your choppers now to chop off a bit more of the British and your fang to bite off a bit more of the Scotch."

She paused abruptly, apparently realizing suddenly the personal implications and the fact that teeth could be an interesting, amusing, and fascinating subject.

Since she also liked puns immensely, she was immediately reminded of the comic *"That's my Pop"* and told to go home, look into the mirror, smile broadly, and then say, "That's my maw." If she did not understand, she was to consult a dictionary.

At the next interview, she was full of smiles and laughter, greeting the writer with a wide grin and saying, "Yes, sir, that's my maw." Asked what she had been doing since the last interview, she replied that she had been having a good time "chewing international fat" (i.e., talking with various accents), thereby bewildering her teachers and entertaining her schoolmates. Asked if she felt she were a freak, she stated she did not, but that her instructors surely did when she "chewed the frog, the sauerkraut, or the corn pone" (French, German and Southern accents).

Subsequently, one of her high school teachers, while discussing pedagogical problems, commented on a remarkable transformation in one of his students. He had first noted her as a shy, withdrawn, and inept girl whose speech was faulty and whose recitations were unsatisfactory. Then one day, she had given a faultless recitation with a strong British accent, repeating the performance on another day with a Scotch accent. Later, he had heard her chattering to a group in the corridor with a Norwegian accent. He now regarded her as a decidedly brilliant student, though rather inexplicable in her adolescent behavior.

Still later another instructor, in discussing his Ph.D. thesis on aspects of high school behavior, cited the instance of this same girl's remarkable transformation and her amazing linguistic abilities which had rendered her a popular, well adjusted and competent student.

Patient B

A 21-year-old girl employed as a secretary for a construction firm sought therapy because "I'm too inferior to live, I think. I've got no friends, I stay by myself and I'm too homely to get married. I want a husband, a home and children, but I haven't a chance. There's nothing for me but work and being an old maid; but I thought I'd see a psychiatrist before I committed suicide. I'm going to try you for three months' time and then, if things aren't straightened out, that's the end."

She was utterly final in this attitude and consented to only two therapeutic hours a week for three months. She paid in advance and stipulated that she be discharged at the close of the 13th interview. (She had checked the calendar and counted the possible interviews.)

She was not communicative about her past history. Her parents, neither of whom had wanted her, had been unhappy as long as she could remember. They were killed in an automobile accident shortly after her graduation from high school. Since then, she had lived in rooming houses and had worked at various stenographic and secretarial jobs. She changed jobs frequently because of dissatisfaction. When questioned concerning herself and her feelings of inferiority, she listed them bitterly as follows:

1. There is an unsightly wide space between my two upper front teeth. It's horrible and I don't dare to smile. (With difficulty she was persuaded to show this: The space was about one eighth of an inch).
2. I can't talk plain (From holding her upper lip stiffly).
3. My hair is black, course, straight and too long.
4. My breasts are too small and so are my hips small.
5. My ankles are too thick.
6. My nose is hooked (Actually very slightly).
7. I'm Jewish.

8. I'm an unwanted child, always have been and always will be.

In explaining this list of defects, all emphasis was placed upon the spacing of her upper incisors. To her this was the cause of all her difficulties. She felt that she could adjust to the "other things" but this "horrible spacing" rendered any hope of adjustment impossible. After this unhappy description of herself, she sobbed and endeavored to leave, declaring, "Keep the money, I won't need it where I'm going." However, she was persuaded to adhere to her original plan of three months' therapy.

Contrary to her description, she was definitely a pretty girl, well-proportioned and decidedly attractive. She was graceful in her movements and had good posture, except for her downcast head. Her general appearance was most unattractive. Her hair was straggly, snarled and uneven in length (she cut it herself), and the parting was crooked and careless. Her blouse lacked a button, there was a small rip in the skirt, the color combination of the blouse and the skirt was wrong, her slip showed on one side, her shoes were scuffed and her shoestrings were tied in unsightly knots. She wore no makeup and while her fingernails were well-shaped, remains of fingernail polish were only on one hand. (She had started to apply fingernail polish a few days previously, but was too discouraged to complete the task or to remove the evidence of her attempt.)

During the next four sessions, she was sullen and uncooperative, insisting that the writer earn his fee by doing all the talking. However, it was learned that she was intensely attracted to a young man two years older than she who also worked at her place of employment. She usually arranged to observe him when he went to the drinking fountain down the corridor, but ignored him and never spoke to him, although he had made overtures. Inquiry disclosed that the fountain trips were rather numerous. She made it a point to go whenever he did and apparently he behaved similarly; this had been taking place for the last two months. She proved to be a rather poor hypnotic subject and only a light trance could be induced. These and subsequent interviews were conducted in the light trance.

The next four sessions were primarily devoted to building up the general idea that by a certain date she was to acquire a completely new, quiet and modest outfit of clothes and have her hair dressed at the beauty shop. Then at a date set by the writer, she was to go to work in her new clothes. (During this period of time she continues to wear the same clothes she had worn at the first interview.) The rationalization was offered her that since she was not optimistic about the future, she might as well have "one last fling."

The ensuing two sessions were spent on the subject of her "parted teeth." She was given the assignment of filling her mouth with water and squirting it out between her teeth until she acquired a practiced aim and distance. She regarded this assignment as silly and ridiculous but conscientiously practiced each evening "because it doesn't really matter what I do."

The two following sessions were devoted, first indirectly and then more and more directly, to the idea that she would make use of her newly acquired skill of squirting water as a practical joke at the expense of the desirable young man. At first she rejected the idea. Then she accepted it as a somewhat amusing but crude fantasy and finally as a possibility to be difinitely executed. The final plan evolved was that on the next Monday, dressed in her new outfit (her nails having been polished and her hair dressed the previous Saturday at the beauty shop), she would await a favorable opportunity to precede the young man to the drinking fountain. There she would wait for his approach, fill her mouth full of water and spray him. Then she was to giggle, start to run toward him, turn suddenly and "run like hell down the corridor."

As was learned later, she carried out the suggestions fully. Late in the afternoon she had seized an opportunity to execute the plan. His look of consternation and his startled exclamation, "You damn little bitch," evoked her laughter at him. When she ran, he pursued her and caught her at the end of the corridor. Upon seizing her he declared, "For that kind of trick you're going to get a good kissing," and suited his actions to his words.

The next day, rather timid and embarrassed, she warily went to the fountain for a drink. As she bent over the fountain, she found herself being sprayed with a water pistol by the young man concealed behind a telephone booth. She immediately filled her mouth with water and charged him, only to turn and run wildly as he met her charge head on; again she was caught and kissed.

The patient failed to keep her next two appointments. She then came in at the next regular time, thoroughly well-groomed in appearance. She gave the foregoing account and stated that the second episode had resulted in a dinner invitation which had been repeated two days later. Now she was considering accepting another invitation for dinner and the theater. She further explained that this outcome of the silly prank suggested by the writer had caused her to spend many thoughtful hours "taking inventory of myself." As a result she had one request to make of him: would he coldly, judiciously and honestly appraise her in detail. When this was done, she would terminate therapy. The smile with which she made this statement was most reassuring. Her request was met by discussing:

1. Her original woebegone, desperate emotional attitude.
2. Her unkempt, frumpish appearance.
3. Her unwarranted derogation of her physical self.
4. Her misconception of a dental asset as a liability.
5. Her sincerity and cooperation in therapy, however bizarre had seemed the ideas presented.
6. The readiness with which she had assumed self-responsibility in reacting to pleasurable life situations.
7. The obvious fact that she now recognized her own personal values.
8. Her need to review her objectives in life as stated in the original interview.
9. Her personal attractiveness, not only as seen by herself, but as appreciated from the masculine point of view.

She listened attentively; at the close of the interview she thanked the writer graciously and took her departure.

Several months later, a marked copy of the local newspaper containing an announcement of her engagement was received in the mail and this was followed six months later by announcement of her marriage to the young man. Fifteen months later, a letter arrived containing a snapshot of her home, the announcement of her son's birth and a newspaper clipping telling of her husband's promotion to junior member of the construction firm. No further direct word has been received, but she has referred several patients to the writer who speak glowingly of her.

Therapy for both of these patients was predicated upon the assumption that there is a strong normal tendency for the personality to adjust if given an opportunity. The simple fact that both patients had centralized their complaints upon one single item of a psychosomatic character, which was alterable if necessary, suggested that prolonged extensive probing into the experiential life of the patients and elaborate reeducation were not necessarily indicated.

The therapeutic results obtained indicate that an uncomplicated psychotherapeutic approach may be most effective in a circumscribed psychosomatic reaction. Had this method failed with these two patients, there would still have remained the possibility of a more elaborate psychotherapeutic procedure.

Profile

WE RETURN HERE to journalism but of a somewhat more abstract
kind than narrative reportage. In fact, we are now crossing
further the borderline between narrative and generalization as the
principal organization of the composition. Whether a piece of
writing is mainly a story or a statement depends on the ratio
between past-tense narrative and present-tense generalization.
But this ratio cannot be measured by the sheer quantity of sentences cast in one or the other. It is in the nature of abstracting that
statement distills a lot of stories, and so even when the chief
purpose of a composition is to assert a generalization, the documentation and illustration may take up more space in the writing
than the statement. Which tense basically structures the composition, regardless of frequency of appearance?

A profile is a sketch, a silhouette, an outline—not primarily a
story. It answers the question, ''What is he, she, they, or it
like?'' Because it often contains much dialog and description, to
illustrate the traits of the person or enterprise being drawn, a
profile may feel as concrete to the reader as a story. But the main
structure is not chronological. Characteristically, organization is
by traits, not events, and any narratives embedded within it are
just means to approach these traits, as in telling how and when
the investigator visited the subject, or in recounting episodes,
say, from the life of the subject as gleaned from interviews. A
profile definitely features generalization. If the generalizations
themselves are very concrete in content, that is because they are
about a particular person or place, relatively circumscribed subjects
after all.

In a World of Her Own: Ursula Le Guin
Nora Gallagher
Mother Jones, January, 1984

This personal profile is of a fairly typical sort appearing constantly among feature articles in magazines and newspapers. Because the person is alive at the time of writing, the reportage techniques of visit and interview are essential—often several of each, as here—but book research also becomes necessary if the person has been written about a lot elsewhere—or has published herself.

Ursula Kroeber Le Guin lives in Portland, Oregon, in an old house that looks down on the shipyards and docks of the Willamette River. The house is clean and very spare: in the upstairs bedrooms (the Le Guins have three children, all of whom have left home), each bed is covered with a simple cotton cover, each floor has a single rug. At the end of the upstairs hallway, behind a door usually kept closed, is a tiny room, once a nursery, with French windows opening out to the tops of trees—hawthorn, pear, apple, willow. Within this room, for the past 20 years, Le Guin has been inventing and constructing whole worlds of her own.

On the wall above a narrow day bed, pieces of graph paper hang from large metal clips. On one, in Le Guin's neat, penciled hand, is a map: two fingers of land interrupted by a sea. This is Northern California, the author explains, and part of Nevada with the Central Valley in between, under water. Covering this sketch, on a sheet of transparent paper, are the familiar towns of the Napa Valley—St. Helena, Calistoga, Yountville—as well as the Sierra and the lava beds in the northeast of the state. This map is only for reference so that Le Guin will not make a gross error when she describes the distances between the very unfamiliar towns—Sinshan and Wakwaha and Chumo—on a third sheet overlaying the other two. The maps are the working papers for Le Guin's book-in-progress, which takes place sometime in the near future, after earthquakes and continental shift have destroyed San Francisco, sunk Bakersfield and given the Humboldt River in Nevada an outlet to the sea.

In this book, Le Guin has come home, using as her central location the Napa Valley, where she has spent the summer of 50 of her 54 years. It has been a long homecoming. Of all her novels, this will be one of the few that takes place on earth.

Ursula Kroeber Le Guin has been writing stories ever since an older brother taught her to write. In the past 20 years, she has published 14 novels, three books of short stories, a book of essays and two books of poems; she has collaborated on two screenplays and has written a television script of her novel *The Lathe of Heaven*. She has won four Hugo awards, three Nebula awards, a Newberry Honor Book Citation and a National Book Award. She is considered by many critics and readers to be the best writer of fantasy and science fiction in America today. But science fiction, at least as we have known it and although she had often passionately defended the gentre, is not quite what Le Guin does. "I write science fiction because that is what publishers call my books," she once wrote. "Left to myself, I should call them novels."

The appeal of science fiction lies in its subject: the "Other" —the alien world, the stuff of dreams, the raw material from the unconscious. Because these things are contained in a story with a beginning, middle and end, they are less terrifying than they might be if we met them on the street or in our nightmares. But what most American science-fiction writers did before the late 1950s, when Le Guin's generation of science-fiction writers began to publish, was to present the Other and then immediately defeat it: the aliens always get theirs in the end; the lean, square-jawed space captain shot his way through the swarm of bug-eyed monsters (with the dumb blonde clinging to his muscular arm), and the whole galaxy was made safe for free enterprise. Probably more than any other writing, science fiction reflected the mood of America: if it's different, kill it.

To this world, Le Guin has brought, well, first she has brought women: a black lawyer in *The Lathe of Heaven*; a marine biologist in *The Dispossessed*; a grocery clerk in *The Beginning Place*. Her aliens tend to be bewildered; obsessive or just plain tired. In *The Lathe of Heaven* her alien lives over a bicycle repair shop in Portland and runs a tacky secondhand store that sells among other things, old Beatle records. Le Guin has also introduced themes risky in any American novel: anarchism as a social and economic alternative, socialism, feminism, Taoism, environmentalism, love and suffering. In one wonderful story, she swept up the male image of a space ship and sex-changed it: "Intracom" is about a small space vessel that finds it has an alien on board. The alien? A fetus. The ship, a pregnant woman.

In her novels, the human scale is always kept intact; all other things are measured against it. No fantastic technology takes the place of human hand or heart: "Community is the best we can hope for," Le Guin wrote in her essay "Science Fiction and Mrs. Brown," "and community for most people means *touch*: the touch of your hand against the other's hand, the job done together, the sledge hauled together, the dance danced together, the child conceived together. We have only one body apiece, and two hands."

Last summer, I spent three days in Portland talking to Le Guin: on the small deck of the house overlooking the river, over dinner at Jake's (a wood-paneled restaurant famous for its crawfish), in the middle of a demonstration on Hiroshima Day, and standing ankle-deep in the Columbia River watching the wash from a ship. We were joined often by her husband, Charles, a professor of French history at Portland State University, a generous Southern man to whom she had dedicated two of her books. "For Charles," she wrote in *The Left Hand of Darkness,* *"sine quo non"*—without whom, nothing.

Le Guin is a smallish person with large intelligent eyes, her gray hair cut into a neat cap. On the first day we talked, she was wearing a purple silk blouse, a raw silk skirt and delicate shoes. She has a slow, direct voice and while there is about her an air of grave authority, she is also likely to burst into the accents of a French professor, a Cockney maid, a Scottish cook. At a speech she gave in London, she wore a formal black velvet suit and a propeller beanie. She has described herself as "a petty-bourgeois anarchist," "an unconsistent Taoist and a consistent unChristian." What is morality? I asked her once, and she replied, "Something you grope after when a situation comes up in which it's needed."

The Left Hand of Darkness, which won both the Hugo and Nebula science-fiction awards, is set in another galaxy, but it is about two very human problems: betrayal and fidelity. (When asked once what the most constant theme in her novels was, she replied, without stopping to think twice "Marriage.")

The book grew out of Le Guin's increasing involvement in

feminism. "Along about 1967, I began to feel a certain unease, a need to step on a little farther, perhaps, on my own," she wrote in her essay. "Is Gender Necessary ?" "I began to want to define and understand the meaning of sexuality and the meaning of gender, in my life and in our society. Much had gathered in the unconscious—both personal and collective—which must either be brought up into consciousness, or else turn destructive. It was that same need, I think, that had led Beauvoir to write *The Second Sex,* and Friedan to write *The Feminine Mystique*; and that was, at the same time, leading Kate Millett and others to write their books, and to create the new feminism. But I was not a theoretician, a political thinker or activist, or a sociologist. I was and am a fiction writer. The way I did my thinking was to write a novel. That novel, *The Left Hand of Darkness*, is the record of my consciousness, the process of my thinking."

At the center of her thinking the question became: What would a planet be like if it didn't have any wars? How would the people differ from us? What would they have or lack? Over time, she began to realize that the people of her book would be neither male nor female, but both. Thus the "Gethenians" were born: sexual androgynes, bisexuals, sexual possibles. Once a month, like other animals, they enter into a kind of heat, when their bodies change and polarize, become male or female. No one knows which he/she will be. If conception occurs, the female remains female and bears a child. If not, she returns to androgyny. The mother of one child could be the father of several others.

(Le Guin says she never really knew whether this was actually physiologically possible in humans until she gave the completed manuscript to her pediatrician, a Frenchman, to read. "It is perfectly possible," he told her, "but it is disgusting.")

There is no rape on Gethen, no division of labor between "weak women" and "strong men," and since at any time one may bear and raise a child, no males quite so free as males everywhere. There are also no wars. There are skirmishes, raids, quarrels over territory, but no huge troop movements over continents. A pregnant person does not a general make.

The hero of the book, a visitor from Earth, is very uncomfortable with this arrangement, and it is his gradual, painful discovery of love between equals that forms the book's heart. Le Guin has been criticized for using a male hero, but she has an explanation: "I knew a woman would just love it. There wouldn't be any dramatic scenes; she would just settle right down. I needed this guy who hated it, who was uncomfortable and miserable in it. It's true, a woman wouldn't have done. She would have just run around saying, 'Oooh, this is wonderful.' ''

Le Guin did not know all this when she began the novel. For her, it started with a vision of two people pulling something across a lot of snow, and much of its content was "told to her" by the characters as she went along. Once she discovered something about them, she would go back over the novel, changing pieces here and there.

"The first time I ever went to a meeting where they discussed any of my books academically," she chuckled, "a Canadian scholar was going to discuss *The Left Hand of Darkness*. He didn't know that I was going to be there. When I walked in, he was appalled. He looked at me with a savage look on his face and said, 'Just don't tell me you didn't know what you were doing.' That's a basic thing, actually, between scholars and artists. I think, *Oh, is that what I was doing?* or *Is that why I did that?* and it's very revealing. But the fact is, you cannot know that while you're doing it. The dancer can't think, *Now I'm going to take a step to the left*. That ain't the way you dance.''

We ate a dinner of cold salmon from the Columbia Gorge, sitting at a picnic table on the broad porch that encircles the rear of the house, "leftovers" from a farewell dinner Le Guin had made for her daughter Caroline the night before. (Caroline was returning to Indiana, where she is starting her doctorate in Irish literature.) On the table was a small cup holding little silver spoons, very soft, very high-quality silver, commemorative pieces minted in different towns in Colorado during the great silver mining days. These were collected by Le Guin's mother, Theodora; one was from Telluride, where she grew up.

Theodora met and married Alfred Kroeber in Berkeley, where he was a professor of anthropology at the university and she was his student (he remembered her bracelets clinking together when she spoke in class). Alfred is perhaps most well known for his work and friendship with Ishi, a Stone Age man, the last of his tribe, who stumbled into the 20th century in 1911. (Ishi died of tuberculosis in 1916, when he was probably 56.) But it was Theodora Kroeber who, in her 60s, wrote the book *Ishi In Two Worlds,* which became nearly as popular as *Coming of Age in Samoa* and is considered a standard text in anthropology.

Much of Le Guin's feeling for the Other, the anthropological details in her books and her fierce devotion to a balanced way of living on the earth, can be traced to her early upbringing.

Although the name Ishi was never mentioned in the house (the subject seemed to cause Alfred Kroeber pain), Ursula heard Native American stories and myths from her father. And she remembers him sitting and talking to two of his closest friends, one a Papago and the other a Yurok, men who, unbeknownst to her then, were also her farther's anthropological informants, and who stayed with the family in the Napa Valley each summer and played croquet with Ursula and her two older brothers.

There were other guests: refugees with funny accents, other Native Americans, and a man with large ears who would "reappear" in her novel *The Dispossessed*—J. Robert Oppenheimer.

Ishi was published in 1961, a year after Alfred Kroeber's death. The book is so well written that Ursula, stricken with guilt, asked her mother if she had been unable to write earlier because of having to raise children. Her mother replied, "I did what I wanted when I wanted to. I have long thought I'd write when I wanted to." She was, said Le Guin, "a very unusual person."

Ursula went to Berkeley High School, which she hated. "I wasn't—you know, I never—my sweaters were never quite the right length or color. I never could do it right." She then went to Radcliffe, and later Columbia, where she earned an M.A. in French, figuring she would need a skill to support herself while writing. She had already submitted poems and short stories by the time she went off to college—her father volunteered to be her agent. Some of the poems got published, but all of the short stories came back. These rejections went on until she was 27, short, civil notes; the characteristic adjective used by editors at *Redbook* and *Harper's* and *The Atlantic* was "remote." But Le Guin was not particularly discouraged: "I was dogged," she says now. "I had an absolutely unfounded self-confidence, partly a temperamental thing and the way my parents brought me up. And I knew that I would get better."

She met Charles Le Guin in 1953 on the *Queen Mary* when both were sailing to France on Fulbright scholarships. After the crossing, Le Guin was "fairly sure." The two married in France and returned at the end of the year to Macon, Georgia, where Charles had grown up.

There, in the bosom of a huge Southern family ("There are hundreds and hundreds of them," says Le Guin), Charles finished his doctorate and Ursula taught freshman French. She continued writing: she wrote a novel while she was working, once, as a secretary in the physics department of Emory University;

after the children were born, she wrote at night, when she'd done the dishes.

One of her works was published in a small university quarterly, but it was not until 1962, when she was 32, that she got her first check. Le Guin had given up reading science fiction years before, because all it seemed to be about was "hardware and soldiers." But a friend encouraged her to read Harlan Ellison, Philip K. Dick and Theodore Sturgeon, and Le Guin discovered that the genre was changing. The first story she submitted to the science-fiction market was bought by a woman editor—Cele Goldsmith Lalli, then with *Fantastic* and *Amazing* magazines, both fantasy/sci-fi monthlies. For that story, "April in Paris," Le Guin got $30, which she immediately spent on a pair of brown wool pants she had seen advertised in *The New Yorker*.

She published four novels before the *The Left Hand of Darkness*. Then, in 1970, she made of her hometown, Portland, a novel. *The Lathe of Heaven* is about a small, ordinary draftsman named George, who discovers that he can change the future (and the past, retroactively) by his dreams. It is a very delicate novel, populated by ordinary people and turtlelike aliens who find themselves in the midst of environmental catastrophes. Le Guin says she was paying homage to the late Philip K. Dick, author of *Do Androids Dream of Electric Sheep?* from which the movie *Blade Runner* was made, badly in Le Guin's opinion. Dick's books are filled with small businessmen going broke. One gets by, advises an alien in *The Lathe of Heaven*, with a little help from one's friends.

Portland is a small, easy city built along the banks of the Willamette. It is a Le Guin city, as if parts of it had been invented by her. There is Powell's Books, for example, which inhabits an old car-dealership garage. In Powell's you can find anything; you can mumble at the counter clerk about that, ah, book about liberation theology and he'll reply, "*Cry of the People*—downstairs, history." There's Jake's (crawfish, Anchor Steam beer, old wooden booths) and, down by the Willamette, there's Waterfront Park, with an area dedicated to Francis J. Murnane, former president of Local 8, ILWU. Near this park, every weekend, is the Portland Saturday Market ("Rain or shine, April through Christmas"), with crafts booths and food from teriyaki to huge, flat pastries called elephant ears. When I visited the park, four children with violins were playing a Brandenburg concerto under a freeway bridge.

Portland has sensible building-height regulations—460 feet, or about 50 stories—and many parks, including one downtown that has traditionally been reserved for women. (In 1904, the women in Portland decided they wanted a place of their own. There used to be an elderly ombudsman who stood at the entrance to the women's park and gently advised men not to go in without an escort.) Over a drinking fountain near the public library is carved in stone, "Tongues in trees/Books in the running brooks/Sermons in stones/And good in everything." I stayed in a pleasant old hotel near downtown for $24 a night.

The Le Guins have lived near Forest Park for 23 years. (There tend to be a lot of trees in Le Guin's novels. She once called herself science fiction's "most arboreal writer.") When I went up to the park for a walk on Sunday morning, a couple sat on a bridge there drinking champagne out of martini glasses.

The Le Guins and I met downtown on the evening of August 6, near the women's park, for an artists' program in memory of the bombing of Hiroshima. The night before, 200 people had painted 2,000 "shadows" on the sidewalks of Portland, outlines, one of a man playing with a cat, as reminders of the way radiation from the Hiroshima bomb burned the forms of its victims onto the sides of buildings. Le Guin read a poem toward the end of the evening's program:

> We lived forever until 1945
>
> Children have time to make mistakes,
> margin for error. Carthage
> could be destroyed and sown with salt.
> Everything was always. It would be all right.
>
> Then we turned
> (so technically sweet the turning)
> the light on.
> In the desert of that dividing light we saw
> the writing on the walls of the world.

Afterward, we walked down to Waterfront Park and people launched white balloons carrying paper cranes out over the river. A small group of drunk gentlemen stood off to the side of the demonstrators and sang something like, "The queers are dying, the queers are dying" over and over again, until someone in the crowd began to sing, very softly. "All we are saying is give peace a chance." And then another person picked it up, "All we are saying . . ." and then another—and soon, the drunken men were quiet and there was a great stillness over the water above the voices.

* * *

In 1974, Le Guin published her second novel to win both the Hugo and Nebula awards, *The Dispossessed: An Ambiguous Utopia,* which took her two and a half years to write and is her most explicit political statement to date.

In the several years prior to beginning the novel, Le Guin had been reading the major anarchist thinkers, among them Peter Kropotkin and Paul Goodman. Kropotkin was a 19th-century Russian natural scientist who, after observing animal and human life in Siberia and elsewhere in Russia, took on the Social Darwinists of his time in his book, *Mutual Aid.* The point of *Mutual Aid* is that creatures of all kinds do not progress or survive by competing with one another, but instead cooperate to ensure mutual survival. A very sweet-tempered, gentle man, Kropotkin was imprisoned in Russia (for conspiracy against the czar) in 1874, escaped to Western Europe and did not return to his homeland until the middle of the revolution in 1917. Although Kropotkin was supportive of the revolution, he became more and more critical of the Bolsheviks, finally breaking with Lenin entirely in 1920. He died, in despair, a year later.

Goodman was a 20th-century American whose book on adolescent boys, *Growing Up Absurd,* became a best seller in the '60s and is his best-known work. Like Kropotkin's, Goodman's thinking spanned many disciplines: he was a poet, a novelist, a lay therapist and a social critic. His early literary career suffered because he was a pacifist during World War II and an open homosexual.

To most people, an anarchist is a bomb-throwing terrorist and anarchy means chaos. There have been violent anarchists, but much of anarchy's bad name comes from successful propaganda against it. Anarchy is a loosely organized but often very successful political philosophy. (The recent "affinity groups" used by nuclear protesters were invented by anarchists during the Spanish Civil War.) To put it simply: anarchy is based on the realistic observation that people left to themselves, without the intervention of the state, tend to cooperate and work out their differences. This process may be awkward, inefficient and punctuated by fights, but its end result is usually more satisfying to everyone than when things are done by command.

Anarchists tend to be less theoretical and more practical than most political ideologues, relying on observation to prove their points. Thus, Goodman wrote about seating arrangements, banning cars from Manhattan, why vacant lots are good for children, why snow should be allowed to pile up in cities during the winter so that people can go sledding, and why freeways are bad for bicycles and roller skates. Goodman liked messy, active, human-scale cities. He often wrote about his belief that the work of human hands should be out in the open in our cities, not concealed in factories far from downtown. Kropotkin recorded how peasants fought fires together and dealt with childbirth.

For Le Guin, reading them and other anarchists was "like breathing fresh air. They talked about everyday life. How you do it. As a concrete thinker, as a housewife, in a number of ways, they were talking my language."

To show how anarchism might work, Le Guin constructed the planet Anarres, an anarchist's utopia. A desert planet, it is a postindustrial world—there are trains, factories, even a computer—but there are no laws or money ("To make a thief, make an owner; to create crime, create laws"); no prisons, almost no personal property, no possessive pronouns.

For contrast, and to compare anarchism to capitalism, Le Guin made another planet, Urras, a bountiful, expensive, beautiful world, populated by gorgeously arrayed men and women (the women have magnets implanted under their skin to hold jewels in place) and the hidden poor. Each planet is the moon of the other.

The hero of *The Dispossessed* is Shevek, a physicist, partly modeled after J. Robert Oppenheimer. Born on Anarres, he eventually travels to Urras. Through Shevek's eyes, we see the two planets. A city on Anarres is Le Guin's tribute to Paul Goodman:

"He passed a glassworks, the workman dipping up a great molten blob as casually as a cook serves soup. Next to it was a busy yard where foamstone was cast for construction. The gang foreman, a big woman in a smock white with dust, was supervising the pouring of a cast with a loud and splendid flow of language. After that came a small wire factory, a district laundry, a luthier's where musical instruments were made and repaired, the district small-goods distributory, a theater, a tile works. The activity going on in each place was fascinating, and mostly out in full view. Children were around, some involved in the work with adults, some underfoot making mud-pies, some busy with games in the street, one sitting perched up on the roof of the learning center with her nose deep in a book. . . . No doors were locked, few shut. There were no disguises and no advertisements. It was all there, all the work, all the life of the city, open to the eye and to the hand."

On a street on Urras, Shevek goes shopping for the first time in his life:

"Saemtenevia Prospect was two miles long, and it was a solid mass of people, traffic, and things: things to buy, things for sale. Coats, dresses, gowns, robes, trousers, breeches, shirts, blouses, hats, shoes, stockings, scarves, shawls, vests, capes, umbrellas, clothes to wear while sleeping, while swimming, while playing games, while at an afternoon party, while at an evening party, while at a party in the country, while traveling, while at the theater, while riding horses, gardening, receiving guests, boating, dining, hunting—all different. . . .

"And the strangest thing about the nightmare street was that none of the millions of things for sale were made there. They were only sold there. Where were the workshops, the factories, where were the farmers, the craftsmen, the miners, the weavers, the chemists, the carvers, the dyers, the designers, the machinists, where were the hands, the people who made? Out of sight, somewhere else. Behind walls. All the people in all the shops were either buyers or sellers. They had no relation to the things but that of possession."

In an unusual move before she had completed the manuscript, Le Guin showed it to a friend, the Marxist critic Darko Suvin, who teaches at McGill University in Montreal. Le Guin believes that Marxists and anarchists are their own best critics, "the only people that seem to speak to each other's main problems." He told her, among other things, that she couldn't have 12 chapters in an anarchist book; she must have 13. And he told her that her ending was too tight, too complete. Le Guin added a chapter and made the book open-ended.

When *The Dispossessed* was finished, Le Guin was exhausted. "I sat around and was sure I never would write again. I read Jung and I consulted the *I Ching*. For 18 months, it gave me the same answer: the wise fox sits still or something."

Since 1974, when *The Dispossessed* was published, Le Guin has published three short novels, a collection of essays and two collections of short stories. (*The Compass Rose,* the most recent, includes a story about the use of electric shock on political prisoners in a country very much like Chile.) Only one of her recent stories takes place in outer space.

"Space was a metaphor for me. A beautiful, lovely, endlessly rich metaphor for me," Le Guin says looking down toward the docks, "until it ended quite abruptly after *The Dispossessed.* I had a loss of faith, I simply—I can't explain it, I don't guess I want to explain it. I don't seem to be able to do outer space anymore.

"The last outer-space story I did was in *The Compass Rose*. It's called 'The Pathways of Desire,' and it turns out to be a hoax in a sense. Apparently it's an expression of my loss of faith."

She hates the immensely popular science-fiction films of George Lucas and Steven Spielberg. "I wouldn't go to see *E.T.*, to tell you the truth, because I disliked *Close Encounters* so profoundly.

"It seemed so exploitive. I don't know, his attitude toward people is so weird. At the end of *Close Encounters* she's got that beautiful little kid back, you know. He's been lost for weeks or months, hasn't he? She's got her little kid back—*What is she doing* taking photographs? She doesn't even have her arm around the kid. It bugs me."

She pauses and then goes on. "I feel a little weird about standing aside and being snooty because it does seem like they're not—you can talk about them quite like ordinary movies or like an art form. It's almost like a ritual. People go because other people go. It's a connection thing, isn't it? It's a weird way for people to communicate. But the trouble is, in other words, in a sense it's like a religious communion, but it's so terribly low-grade, morally so cheap. *Star Wars* is really abominable: it's all violence, and there are only three women in the known universe.

"These films are working on a very low level intellectually and morally, and in their blindness perhaps they do get close to people's feelings," she continues, "because they are not only nonintellectual, they are antiintellectual and sort of deliberately stupid. But I would rather say that about *Star Wars*. I think Steven Spielberg, on the other hand, is playing a very tricky game. I think he knows. I think he deliberately exploits archetypal images in a way that I really dislike a lot."

(I ask her how she got through dinner parties when everyone was carrying on about *E.T.* "I didn't say anything," she replies, and then changes her voice to a linebacker's—"I want to be loved.")

"I did follow our space flights. The little *Voyagers*? God, those were lovely. But what we are doing now I find in itself extremely depressing—the space shuttle. I'm not happy about it the way I was happy about the other ones. It's all military-industrial. It's a bunch of crap flying around the world, just garbage in the sky. I think that did have to do with my loss of faith. My God, we could muck that up just as bad as—we're going to repeat the same . . .

"I think we're sick," she finally says. "I hate to make big pronouncements, but I don't know how you bring up a kid. There's the size of our population and people who work so hard, and no one praises them for it. We've overbred our species."

But, I point out, the saving grace for us in many of her books is the presence of others.

"But they don't have to be human others," she replied. "We live with others on all sides at all times. That's the thing about religion, about monotheism. They say we're other and better. It's a very silly and dangerous course. It also relates to feminism. Women have been treated as animals have been. If the men insist on talking about it that way, then the men and God can walk in Eden—they can walk alone there."

She gets up at 5:30 in the morning these days to work on the new book. In the little room at the end of the hall. The population in the book is very small, nearly that of the world in the late Stone Age, a few million here, a few million there and great herds of animals. There is no hero in the book; there are many, many voices and a female anthropologist named Pandora.

Before I leave, we go out to Sauvie Island to pick blueberries. Finding none to pick, we picnic on the banks of the Columbia. Ursula asks Charles if it was Debbie Reynolds who divorced Eddie Fisher because he brushed his teeth with warm water, and Charles replies no, it was Elizabeth Taylor who divorced Nicky Hilton. She rolls up her pants and stands in the shallow water, the wake of the ships moving in neat waves toward her, each wave a pattern, each one the exact same distance from the next as they stroke the shore.

Mozart heard his music all at once, she had told me earlier, then he had to write it down, to extend it into time.

Does Mildred Nelson Have an Herbal Cure for Cancer?

Peter Barry Chowka

Whole Life Times, January/February, 1984

A profile of an enterprise requires the same techniques as for one about a person—go look, go look it up. Although the next profile focuses partly on the person heading the enterprise, the real subject is the work she directs. And clearly this enterprise has been chosen because the work has been challenged. So in addition to illustrating profiles of a group or place, this sample shows how a profile may be used to explore a controversial issue.

Within sight of the border that divides the United States and Mexico, in a private clinic on a hillside high above the sprawling city of Tijuana, a unique experiment in healing is helping, and apparently curing, scores of people suffering from cancer.

For more than two decades now, the promise of non-toxic therapies, particularly the use of traditional herbs, has drawn a steady stream of people from around the world to the Bio-Medical Center, as the clinic is called. Overseeing the facility is Mildred Nelson, R.N., a feisty, no-nonsense but totally compassionate individual—a Texas native in her 37th year of working "with Hoxsey" as she describes the therapy offered at Bio-Medical.

Mildred, in fact, is a distinctive, unforgettable person—a knowledgeable, down-to-earth health care pioneer whose approach is consistently vilified by U.S. medical authorities but universally respected by her patients. During an average week she treats as many patients as Tijuana's half-dozen other cancer clinics combined.

The Hoxsey therapy combines non-toxic internal and external medicines made from a dozen or so herbs with supportive treatment that includes a special diet, vitamin and mineral supplements, and encouraging patients to assume a large degree of responsibility for their own healing. Sitting in her office, where an entire wall is given to storing thousands of patients' medical records, Mildred estimates that "in the neighborhood of 80 percent" of the people who come to Bio-Medical are helped by the therapy.

This astonishing statement is offered matter-of-factly, and independent observation suggests that it may indeed be accurate. In any case, Mildred insists that a first-time visitor "see for yourself—go talk to the patients and ask how they're doing. That's the real story." In turn, all of the patients one encounters express unequivocal satisfaction with the Hoxsey treatment: Many of them, back at Bio-Medical for their periodic checkups, say their cancers have been kept satisfactorily under control for years. After having spent a total of six weeks at Bio-Medical—interviewing dozens of patients and examining the medical records of a representative sample during four separate visits over the past three years—I can report that the stories I heard appeared to be true.

Herbal Horse Sense

The origins of the current therapy go back 150 years to a prize stallion belonging to veterinarian John Hoxsey. The horse developed cancer but supposedly cured itself by instinctively eating certain stalks, berries, roots, and herbs that grew wild in the fields. John Hoxsey, the story goes, gathered these herbs, combined them, and successfully treated other cancerous animals. Ultimately, the formulas were passed on to Hoxsey's descendants who, in time, used the preparations to treat cancer in humans.

In 1919, at the age of 18, Harry Hoxsey, John Hoxsey's great-grandson, became involved in the work. He founded the Hoxsey Cancer Clinic in Dallas, Texas, which by the 1950s was one of the largest privately-owned medical facilities in the world. It used the Hoxsey herbs and other non-toxic, unconventional approaches of the period.

Benedict FitzGerald, a noted Massachusetts attorney, was hired from the Justice Department in the early 1950s to investigate Hoxsey and other alternative cancer treatments for a U.S. Senate committee. "Harry Hoxsey," FitzGerald recalls 30 years later, "was a very colorful character. He had a tremendous knowledge of cancer. And he certainly had a following of people who claimed he had done a lot for them. He had some pretty effective results down there.''

Over time, the positive reputation of the Dallas clinic spread nationwide. But the large and powerful orthodox cancer establishment disapproved of alternative approaches. In particular, the Hoxsey treatment—inexpensive and simple compared to surgery, radiation, and drugs—became a favored target of organized medical groups. Charged repeatedly by medical authorities with practicing medicine without a license, using unapproved therapies, and other violations, Harry spent much of his time in court. Interestingly, legal proceedings were never initiated by any of his patients.

Flight from Harassment

Hoxsey was made a victim of a tactic long favored by orthodoxy: condemnation without investigation. FitzGerald observes, ''Hoxsey wasn't trying to conceal anything. In fact, he was very open to investigation, willing to prove that he had something.'' Repeatedly, Hoxsey petitioned doctors, state authorities, the National Cancer Institute, the United States Senate, and other groups to visit his clinic and test his therapy. Most of his entreaties were to no avail.

By the end of the 1950s Hoxsey was pressured out of business. Mildred, who was by then the chief nurse, tried to keep the clinic going in several other locations, always one step ahead of the authorities. In 1963, weakened by a heart condition (he died in the mid-1970s), Harry encouraged Mildred to move the therapy center to Tijuana.

A source familiar with the border operation observes, ''The Mexican government takes a very different approach to alternative therapies than we do in the States. As long as they're satisfied that what's going on in the clinics isn't harmful to the patients, they generally have a hands-off policy.''

Mildred Nelson was introduced to Hoxsey in 1946 when her mother Della Mae Nelson, suffering from cancer, decided to undergo the Hoxsey therapy. A conventionally trained nurse, Mildred believed that Hoxsey was a quack. ''So I went down to Dallas,'' she remembers, ''thinking I would talk Mother out of it. When I walked in and Harry found out I was a nurse, he said, 'Here are the patients' records, the nurses and doctors are in there working, the patients are sitting out there. Go through whatever you want, talk to anyone, ask questions.' I nearly fell over!" (Mildred's mother went on to be treated by Hoxsey and today, well into her 80s, she is alive and well.)

Later in 1946, still skeptical, she says, Mildred was hired by Harry. It was not until she had worked at the Dallas clinic for a year, however, and saw for herself patients returning with their cancers improved that she became convinced of the value of the therapy. She has been associated with it ever since.

An Open Door

Over the years Mildred has treated thousands of patients, too many for her to estimate the exact number. She carefully maintains complete medical files on all of them and can recall from memory graphic details about many people whom she has helped. Most of her patients are middle-class U.S. residents, but many are poor; wealthy and notable people have sought her help, too.

The openness of Hoxsey that impressed Mildred in 1946 characterizes the Bio-Medical Center today. Having been prepared by Establishment accounts to find seaminess and rampant exploitation, I was amazed instead during my first visit to find a serious, competent, well-run facility—informal and offering easy access to the doctors, staff, and medical records. Unlike cancer facilities in the States, the place had a discernibly cheerful and upbeat mood. The doors to all of the rooms, including treatment areas, remained open. The employees seemed highly dedicated to their work. And the patients seemed unusually eager to share their experiences.

An 81-year-old man from Santa Monica, California, said he had returned to Bio-Medical several times, satisfied that his metastasized prostate cancer that had been diagnosed in the United States several years earlier was under control. On this visit, back for a routine checkup, he said with a smile, "The doctors don't have to tell me the results, because I feel it myself—I feel good."

Another patient, a middle-aged woman from Las Vegas, said she had been diagnosed with terminal malignant melanoma two years before; after surgery at home had failed to halt the disease she refused amputation of her arm and instead came to Bio-Medical after hearing about the place from a friend. When I met her she seemed well and in good spirits; her latest diagnostic tests, she said, showed good results.

I spoke with a 69-year-old man from Utah as Mildred sooth-ingly dressed his tumor of the left ear. His doctors back home, he said, asked him a year ago to think about having an operation. "I'm still thinking about it," he joked, "but I'm here instead."

Caring for Each Other

"It's amazing," he continued, "the sense of comradeship and friendship that's built up in a place like this. One person's trouble is everybody's trouble. There's an entirely different atti-tude here—you see smiles on the patients' faces when you come in in the morning. Your attitude starts to pick up and that's nine-tenths of the battle. Back home, there's despair. But after you've been here a short time you have a sense of hope.

"It isn't all easy," he added. "There's times of pain. But then you see the results—that's the thing that does it."

Several patients volunteered, "I'd be dead now if it weren't for Mildred and Hoxsey."

"Our patients are the greatest," Mildred says. "They're free-thinking people from all walks of life. Nobody leads them around. They've studied this and made their own decisions."

Hoxsey therapy is compatible with other approaches to degen-erative illness that are described as non-toxic, holistic, or metabolic. "We consider cancer a systemic disease," Harry Hoxsey wrote in his book *You Don't Have to Die* (New York: Milestone Books, 1956). "It occurs only in the presence of a profound physiological change in the constituents of body fluids and a consequent chemical imbalance in the organism." Mildred adds, "It's very simple: Hoxsey normalizes and balances the chemistry within the body. When you get everything normalized, the abnor-mal cells—the tumor cells—cease to grow. And very slowly the tumor is absorbed and excreted, and it's gone."

If there is a weakness in this theory it is its apparent vagueness. Modern medicine, after all, requires a therapeutic intervention to be exact and reproducible; Hoxsey herbs, in contrast, have not been explained in terms of established pharmacological criteria. In her defense, Mildred observes that, like Harry, she is a clinical practitioner and an empiricist—not a research scientist. She is too preoccupied with helping patients—working sometimes 12 or more hours a day—to try to define precisely why the therapy appears to work.

New and Traditional Approaches

Still, the treatment offered today at Bio-Medical is by no means simplistic. There is advanced diagnostic equipment on the premises, the six resident Mexican M.D.s are well-qualified (and speak fluent English), patients' needs are considered individually, and there is an openness to employing other promising non-toxic measures as adjuncts. Mildred follows new developments in the field of diet and cancer, for example, and keeps up with the latest reports in conventional medical journals. In line with progressive research findings, megadoses of certain vitamins like C are prescribed. Psychology is seen as increasingly important. "Mental attitude goes a long way in healing," Mildred observes. "The patients who make it are often the ones who really want to live—so they take their medicines, stay on the diet, and do the other things they're supposed to do."

Herbs provide the basis of the therapy. The oral medicines, intended to help eliminate toxins from the body and balance the metabolism, include potassium iodide, red clover, licorice, burdock, stillingia, barberis, poke root, cascara, prickly ash bark, and buckthorn bark. The powder and paste, applied to external cancers, contain escharotic agents—caustics—commonly used to treat external malignancies before the advent of modern radiation and chemotherapy. In fact, most of the components of the Hoxsey medicines have been employed for centuries to treat cancer and other conditions.

Herbalism, of which Hoxsey therapy may be considered a branch, is the most ancient form of healing. Many modern conventional drugs are still derived from plants (for example, digitalis from foxglove). In October 1980 the Public Broadcasting System series *Nova* ("The Cancer Detectives of Lin Xian") reported that Chinese researchers have determined that a common local medicinal herb often inexplicably reverses the course of early forms of esophageal cancer.

In Canada, Essiac, an herb-based cancer therapy of Native American origin similar to Hoxsey, was in use with apparent success from 1924 through the late 1970s, when it was stopped by Canadian medical authorities. Yet herbalism continues to be denigrated in conventional medical circles. In 1968 the influential American Cancer Society (ACS) reported in its list of *Unproven*

Methods of Cancer Management (which amounts to a blacklist of alternative approaches) that it "does not have evidence that treatment used at the Bio-Medical Center, including . . . the Hoxsey method . . . is of objective benefit in the treatment of cancer." Mildred observes, and the Cancer Society confirms, however, that no representative of the ACS has ever actually visited the Bio-Medical Center nor investigated the Hoxsey approach.

No One Is Turned Away

Perhaps the most notewrothy feature of the Bio-Medical Center is the economics of its treatment. A one-time fee (currently about $1800) is asked of all patients; it guarantees a person therapy for the duration of his or her life, including return visits for examinations and unlimited supplies of the Hoxsey medicines and nutritional supplements. (The only additional charges may be for outside lab work.)

Lack of money, however, does not prevent a person from receiving treatment. The subject is not even raised until after one has undergone diagnosis and received initial therapy. "Those who don't have the money," Mildred confirms, "say that, and they pay what they can monthly or later on. The door is always open here." A patient volunteered, "Mildred drives an old pickup truck, she lives in a house-trailer, and a lot of the doctors here walk to work. I'm very well pleased with the financial aspects." "The theory behind the one-shot fee," Mildred explains, "is that it helps encourage patients to keep coming back—their only expense is travel—so they can be followed up for five years or more. It prevents them from going off the program.

"Nobody ever gets a bill from here," she continues. "I never sent a bill in my life. Patients know what they owe. Patients actually pay *more* when they don't get a bill."

Ultimately, Mildred Nelson is the central source of strength at the Bio-Medical Center. She is always available to her patients, and is never far from the two telephones which bring queries at all hours from people throughout North America and beyond. Extremely well-versed in cancer and its whole range of treatments, Mildred is an extraordinary clinician—gentle, firm, cajoling, or reassuring as the individual patient's condition demands. An associate observes, "Mildred is the clinic director, the nurse, the psychologist, and, I guess you'd have to say, the mother figure. She fits into just about all of the different categories imaginable.''

A Timeless Healer

In the past it was not uncommon for a healer to embody many of these different roles. But today medicine has fragmented into a dizzying array of competing specialties; it is a hierarchical profession, too, with nurses near the bottom in terms of influence and responsibility. Indeed, a frequent orthodox criticism of Mildred is that she is *only* a registered nurse. Because, it is alleged, she has overstepped the boundaries of her credentialed specialty, her healing abilities and favorable clinical results are denigrated or simply ignored.

A current statistic highlights the context: Although women comprise 70 percent of the medical work force today, only 7 percent of U.S. physicians are female. In *Witches, Midwives, and Nurses: A History of Women Healers* (Feminist Press, 1973), Barbara Ehrenreich and Deirdre English document the systematic suppression of female healers that began in the Middle Ages (when women using herbs and psychology were branded as witches) and continues to the present. ''Women have always been healers,'' they observe. But during the past century, ''Curing became the exclusive province of the doctor: caring was relegated to the nurse.''

Mildred rejects this stricture. ''I've been considered a rebel all of my life for being into this type of thing,'' she muses. ''I even had trouble getting through nurse's training, because if a patient needed something done, *I* did it whether or not I was supposed to. I was always in hot water.'' Yet, Mildred insists that she does not seek unnecessary controversy. ''I'm actually rather straight-laced,'' she says.

Today Mildred continues her rebellion by advocating medical self-care, insisting that patients assume complete responsibility for their own health. ''I tell people,'' she says emphatically, '' 'Find out how to take care of yourself.' But most of the American people are not disciplined—they don't *want* to take care of themselves; they want somebody else to do it for them. They don't want to give up their martini with dinner, even if it kills them; can you imagine that?''

Since 1963 Mildred has been responsible for singlehandedly carrying on the challenging work of Hoxsey. It has been a "hard, rough life," she notes, one that she might not choose a second time around.

At the end of a long day, Mildred admits that "Often you run into some of the most heartbreaking things in the world here, and it makes you wonder, 'Why in the world am I involved in this?" Quickly and emphatically, she answers her own question. "When we lose one, we don't lose 'em in the condition like they do across the border—wasting away or in pain. And there have been lots of people who have lived a full, complete life as a result of Hoxsey. That makes me feel good. It keeps me going."

Generalized
Information

SINCE TRUE STORIES are also information, we have to distinguish that kind of fact from articles like the following that present information in the present tense of generalization. When the chrono-logic of time order no longer serves to sequence the material of a composition, by what kind of logic *does* one organize? Generalized information is distilled from many individual experiences and removed beyond the particular circumstances of time, place, and investigator. For the new order one must look to the characteristics and organization of the material itself.

Directions

THE ONLY LINGERING of chronological organization occurs in our first two instances, which are sets of directions for how to make or do something. Even here, however, we find no once-upon-a-time story but merely a repeatable sequence of step-by-step actions such as comprise any set of directions. Also inherent in direction-giving is the use of the imperative mode, a throwback to dialog and correspondence, with the great difference that the one receiving the commands is a remote, generalized reader.

Typically, chronological organization mixes with logical, imperative mode with declarative, because the writer of directions usually must explain the materials and tools employed as well perhaps as the purpose of the actions. In fact, directions frequently make little sense or prove impossible to follow without considerable background, so that much of the writing consists of building a context for the actions themselves. Finally, however concrete the actions themselves may be, they must be disembedded from any overly local conditions, circumstances, and assumptions so that all sorts of different individual readers in different places may be able to apply the directions. Giving good directions is hard because it challenges very seriously our native egocentricity, the transcending of which is a factor of increasing abstractive power.

The Complete Breath
Yogi Ramacharaka
from *Science of Breath*, 1904

These are directions for how to do something rather than how to make something, which requires materials and results in a product. The sample here focuses on just the body but emphasizes reasons. How-to for health care and personal development has been around a long time but until recently was communicated by demonstration and oral directions. The instructions for the yogic "complete breath" go back probably 5,000 years. How-to magazines and manuals constitute an enormous portion of today's reading matter.

Perhaps the best way to teach you how to develop the Yogi Complete Breath would be to give you simple directions regarding the breath itself, and then follow up the same with general remarks concerning it. Right here we wish to say that this Complete Breath is not a forced or abnormal thing, but on the contrary is a going back to first principles—a return to Nature. The healthy adult savage and the healthy infant of civilization both breathe in this manner, but civilized man has adopted unnatural methods of living, clothing, etc., and has lost his birthright. And we wish to remind the reader that the Complete

Breath does not necessarily call for the complete filling of the lungs at every inhalation. One may inhale the average amount of air, using the Complete Breathing Method and distributing the air inhaled, be the quantity large or small, to all parts of the lungs. But one should inhale a series of full Complete Breaths several times a day, whenever opportunity offers, in order to keep the system in good order and condition.

The following simple exercise will give you a clear idea of what the Complete Breath is:

(1) Stand or sit erect. Breathing through the nostrils, inhale steadily, first filling the lower part of the lungs, which is accomplished by bringing into play the diaphragm, which descending exerts a gentle pressure on the abdominal organs, pushing forward the front walls of the abdomen. Then fill the middle part of the lungs, pushing out the lower ribs, breastbone and chest. Then fill the higher portion of the lungs, protruding the upper chest, thus lifting the chest, including the upper six or seven pairs of ribs. In the final movement, the lower part of the abdomen will be slightly drawn in, which movement gives the lungs a support and also helps to fill the highest part of the lungs.

At first reading it may appear that this breath consists of three distinct movements. This, however, is not the correct idea. The inhalation is continuous, the entire chest cavity from the lower diaphragm to the highest point at the chest in the region of the collar-bone, being expanded with a uniform movement. Avoid a jerky series of inhalations, and strive to attain a steady continuous action. Practice will soon overcome the tendency to divide the inhalation into three movements, and will result in a uniform continuous breath. You will be able to complete the inhalation in a couple of seconds after a little practice.

(2) Retain the breath a few seconds.

(3) Exhale quite slowly, holding the chest in a firm position, and drawing the abdomen in a little and lifting it upward slowly as the air leaves the lungs. When the air is entirely exhaled, relax the chest and abdomen. A little practice will render this part of the exercise easy, and the movement once acquired will be afterward performed almost automatically.

It will be seen that by this method of breathing all parts of the respiratory apparatus are brought into action, and all parts of the lungs, including the most remote air cells, are exercised. The chest cavity is expanded in all directions. You will find it quite a help to you if you will practice this breath before a large mirror, placing the hands lightly over the abdomen so that you may feel the movements. At the end of the inhalation, it is well to occasionally slightly elevate the shoulders, thus raising the collar-bone and allowing the air to pass freely into the small upper lobe of the right lung, which place is sometimes the breeding place of tuberculosis.

At the beginning of practice, you may have more or less trouble in acquiring the Complete Breath, but a little practice will make perfect, and when you have once acquired it you will never willingly return to the old methods.

The practice of the Complete Breath will make any man or woman immune to Consumption and other pulmonary troubles, and will do away with all liability to contract "colds," as well as bronchial and similar weaknesses. Consumption is due principally to lowered vitality attributable to an insufficient amount of air being inhaled. The impairment of vitality renders the system open to attacks from disease germs. Imperfect breathing allows a considerable part of the lungs to remain inactive, and such portions offer an inviting field for bacilli, which invading the weakened tissue soon produce havoc. Good healthy lung tissue will resist the germs, and the only way to have good healthy lung tissue is to use the lungs properly.

Consumptives are nearly all narrow-chested. What does this mean? Simply that these people were addicted to improper habits of breathing, and consequently their chests failed to develop and expand. The man who practices the Complete Breath will have a full broad chest and the narrow-chested man may develop his chest to normal proportions if he will but adopt this mode of breathing. Such people must develop their chest cavities if they value their lives. Colds may often be prevented by practicing a little vigorous Complete Breathing whenever you feel that you are being unduly exposed. When chilled, breathe vigorously a few minutes, and you will feel a glow all over your body. Most colds can be cured by Complete Breathing and partial fasting for a day.

The quality of the blood depends largely upon its proper oxygenation in the lungs, and if it is under-oxygenated it becomes poor in quality and laden with all sorts of impurities, and the system suffers from lack of nourishment, and often becomes actually poisoned by the waste products remaining uneliminated in the blood. As the entire body, every organ and every part, is dependent upon the blood for nourishment, impure blood must have a serious effect upon the entire system.

The stomach and other organs of nutrition suffer much from improper breathing. Not only are they ill nourished by reason of the lack of oxygen, but as the food must absorb oxygen from the blood and become oxygenated before it can be digested and assimilated, it is readily seen how digestion and assimilation is impaired by incorrect breathing. And when assimilation is not normal, the system receives less and less nourishment, the appetite fails, bodily vigor decreases, and energy diminishes, and the man withers and declines. All from the lack of proper breathing.

Even the nervous system suffers from improper breathing, inasmuch as the brain, the spinal cord, the nerve centers, and the nerves themselves, when improperly nourished by means of the blood, become poor and inefficient instruments for generating, storing, and transmitting the nerve currents.

The effect of the reproductive organs upon the general health is too well known to be discussed at length here, but we may be permitted to say that with the reproductive organs in a weakened condition the entire system feels the reflex action and suffers sympathetically. The Complete Breath produces a rhythm which is Nature's own plan for keeping this important part of the system in normal condition, and, from the first, it will be noticed that the reproductive functions are strengthened and vitalized, thus, by sympathetic reflex action, giving tone to the whole system.

In the practice of the Complete Breath, during inhalation, the diaphragm contracts and exerts a gentle pressure upon the liver, stomach and other organs, which in connection with the rhythm of the lungs acts as a gentle massage of these organs and stimulates their actions, and encourages normal functioning. Each inhalation aids in this internal exercise, and assists in causing a normal circulation to the organs of nutrition and elimination.

The Western world is paying much attention to Physical Culture just now, which is a good thing. But in their enthusiasm they must not forget that the exercise of the external muscles is not everything. The internal organs also need exercise, and Nature's plan for this exercise is proper breathing. The diaphragm is Nature's principal instrument for this internal exercise. Its motion vibrates the important organs of nutrition and elimination, and massages and kneads them at each inhalation and exhalation, forcing blood into them, and then squeezing it out, and imparting a general tone to the organs. Any organ or part of the body which is not exercised gradually atrophies and refuses to function properly, and lack of the internal exercise afforded by the diaphragmatic action leads to diseased organs. The Complete Breath gives the proper motion to the diaphragm, as well as exercising the middle and upper chest. It is indeed "complete" in its action.

From the standpoint of Western physiology alone, without reference to the Oriental philosophies and science, this Yogi system of Complete Breathing is of vital importance to every man, woman and child who wishes to acquire health and keep it. Its very simplicity keeps thousands from seriously considering it, while they spend fortunes in seeking health through complicated and expensive "systems." Health knocks at their door and they answer not. Verily the stone which the builders reject is the real cornerstone of the Temple of Health.

Compost Pile
John Jeavons
from *How to Grow More Vegetables*, 1974

Although the overriding purpose of this selection is to direct us how to make compost by a particular method, it represents well the sort of how-to article that surrounds the directions with so much information as almost to constitute a factual article.

In nature, living things die and their death allows life to be reborn. Both animals and plants die on forest floors and in meadows to be composted by time, water, microorganisms, sun and air to produce a soil improved in texture and nutriment. Organic agriculture follows nature's example. Leaves, grass, spiders, birds, trees and plants should be returned to the soil and reused—not thrown away. Composting is an important way to recycle such elements as carbon, nitrogen, oxygen, sulfur, calcium, iron, phosphorus, potash, trace minerals and microorganisms. These elments are all necessary to maintain the biological cycles of life that exist in nature. All too often we participate instead in agricultural stripmining.

Composting in nature occurs in at least three ways: (1) In the form of manures, which are plant and animal foods composted inside the body of an animal (including earthworms) and then further aged outside the animal by the heat of fermentation. Earthworms are especially good composters. Their castings are 5 times richer in nitrogen, 2 times richer in exchangeable calcium, 7 times richer in available phosphorus and 11 times richer in available potassium than the soil they inhabit. (2) In the form of animal and plant bodies which decay on top of the soil in nature and in compost piles. (3) In the form of roots, root hairs, and microbiotic life which remain and decay beneath the surface of the soil after harvesting. It is estimated that one rye plant in good soil grows 3 miles of roots a day, 387 miles of roots in a season and 6,603 miles of root hairs each season![1]

Compost has a dual function. It improves the structure of the soil. This means the soil will be easier to work, will have good aeration and water retention characteristics and will be resistant to erosion. Less nutriment leaches out in a soil with adequate organic matter. Compost also provides *nutriments* for plant growth, and its humic acid makes nutriments in the soil (especially insoluble ones, such as bone meal) more available to plants.

Improved texture and nourishment produce a healthy soil. A healthy soil produces healthy plants better able to resist insect and disease attacks due in part to a higher protein content in the plants. Most insects look for sick plants to eat—those plants with a relatively higher carbohydrate content. The best way to control insects and diseases in plants is with a living, healthy soil rather than with poisons which kill this life.

Compost keeps soil at maximum health with a minimum of expense. Generally, it is unnecessary to buy fertilizers in order to be able to grow with nature. At first, organic fertilizers may have to be purchased so that the soil can be brought to a satisfactory level of fertility in a short period of time. Once this has been done, the health of the soil can be maintained with compost, crop rotation, and small amounts of manure, bone meal and wood ash.

Compost is high in humus and humic acid. Humus results from the decomposing and synthesizing activities of organisms in organic matter. The importance of adding soil at various stages to your compost pile is clear. The soil contains a good starter supply of these organisms. The organisms help in several ways. Some break down complex compounds into simpler ones the plants can utilize. One soil bacterium, azotobacter, converts atmospheric nitrogen into food for plants. Other microorganisms tie up nitrogen surpluses. The surpluses are released gradually as

[1]. Helen Philbrick and Richard B. Gregg, *Companion Plants and How To Use Them*, The Devin-Adair Company, Old Greenwich, Connecticut, 1966, pp. 75–76.

the plants need nitrogen. An excessive concentration of available nitrogen in the soil (which makes plants susceptible to disease) is therefore avoided. There are predaceous fungi which attack and devour nematodes, but they are only found in large amounts in a soil with adequate humus.

The microbiotic life provides a living pulsation in the soil which preserves its vitality for the plants. The microbes tie up essential nutriments in their own body tissues as they grow, and then release them slowly as they die and decompose. In this way, they help stabilize food release to the plants. These organisms are also continuously excreting a whole range of organic compounds into the soil. Sometimes described as "soil glue," these excretions help hold the soil structure together. The organic compounds also contain disease-curing antibiotics, health producing vitamins and enzymes that are integral parts of biochemical reactions in a healthy soil.

It is important to note the difference between *fertilization* and *fertility*. There can be plenty of fertilizer in the soil and plants still may not grow well. Add compost to the soil and the humic acid it contains begins to release the hidden nutriment in a form available to the plants. This was the source of the amazing fertility of Alan Chadwick's garden at Santa Cruz.

The recipe for a biodynamic/French Intensive Method compost is *by weight: ⅓ dry vegetation, ⅓ green vegetation and kitchen wastes,* and *⅓ soil*—though we have found with our heavy clay soil that less soil produces better results. The ground underneath the pile should be loosened to a depth of 12–24 inches to expose the bottom layer of the pile to the bacteria and organisms in the soil and to provide good drainage. The materials should be added to the pile in 1–2 inch layers with the dry vegetation on the bottom, the green vegetation and kitchen wastes second and the soil third (a ¼–½ inch layer). Green vegetation is 95 percent more effective than dry vegetation as a "starter" because its higher nitrogen content helps start and maintain the fermentation process. Dry vegetation is high in carbon content. It is difficult for the compost pile to digest carbon without sufficient amounts of nitrogen. Unless you have a large household it may be necessary to save your kitchen scraps in a tight-lidded unbreakable container for several days to get enough material for the kitchen waste layer. Hold your breath when you dump them because the stronger smelling form of anaerobic decomposition process will be accelerated by the already fermenting waste. All kitchen scraps may be added to this layer except meats and sizeable amounts of oily salad scraps. Be sure to include bones, tea leaves, coffee grounds and citrus rinds.

Add the soil immediately after the kitchen waste. It contains microorganisms which speed decomposition, keeps the smell down to a minor level and prevents flies from laying eggs in the garbage. The smell will be difficult to eliminate entirely when waste from members of the cabbage family is added. In a few days, however, even this soil-minimized odor will disappear. As each layer is added, water it lightly so the pile is *evenly* moist—like a wrung-out damp towel that is entirely wet, but does not give out excess water when it is squeezed. Sufficient water is necessary for the proper heating and decomposition of the materials. Too little water results in decreased biological activity and too much simply drowns the aerobic microbiotic life. Water the pile when necessary as you water the garden. The particles in the pile should glisten. During the rainy season some shelter or covering may be needed to prevent overwatering and the less optimal anaerobic decomposition that occurs in a water-logged pile. (The conditions needed for proper functioning of a compost pile and those required for good plant growth in raised beds are similar. In both cases the proper mixture of air, soil nutriments, texture, microorganisms and water is essential.)

Compost piles can be built in a pit in the ground or in a pile above the ground. The latter is preferable, since during rainy periods a pit can fill with water. A pile can be made with or without a container. A container is not necessary, but can help shape a pile and keep the materials looking neat. The least expensive container is made of 12 foot long, 3 foot wide, 1 inch mesh, chicken wire with five 3 foot long, 1 inch by 2 inch boards and two sets of small hooks and eyes. The boards are nailed along the two 3 foot ends of the wire and at 3 foot intervals along the length of the wire. The hooks and eyes are attached to the two end boards near the top and bottom. The unit is then placed as a circle on the ground, the hooks attached to the eyes, and the compost materials placed inside. The materials hold up the circle. After the pile is built, the wire enclosure may be removed and the materials will stay in place. You may now use the enclosure to build another pile, or you may use it later to turn the first pile into, if you decide to turn it to speed the decomposition process.

There are three ways to speed up the decomposition rate in a compost pile. One way is to *increase the amount of nitrogen*. The ratio of carbon to nitrogen is critical for the breakdown rate. Materials with a high carbon to nitrogen ratio, such as wood, may take years to decompose alone since they lack sufficient nitrogen-bearing materials upon which the bacteria depend for food. Such materials are sawdust, dry leaves, wood shavings, grainstubble and straw. To boost the rate of decay in carbonaceous materials, add nitrogen-rich materials such as newly cut grass, fresh manure, vegetable wastes, green vegetation or a fertilizer such as blood or fish meal. Three to five pounds of blood or fish meal per cubic yard of compost is probably a good amount of fertilizer with which to fortify a compost pile with a high carbon content. These fertilizers are lightly sprinkled on each layer as the pile is built.

A second method is to *increase the amount of air* (aeration). Beneficial aerobic bacteria thrive in a well aerated pile. Proper layering and periodic turning of the pile will accomplish this. Third, the *surface area of the materials may be increased*. The smaller the size of the materials, the greater the amount of their exposed surface area. Broken up twigs will decompose more rapidly than when twigs are left whole. We discourage the use of shredders because nature will do the job in a relatively short time and everyone has sufficient access to materials which will compost rapidly without resorting to a shredder. The noise from these machines is quite disturbing and spoils the peace and quiet of a garden. They also consume increasingly scarce fuel.

Note that at least *three different materials of three different textures* are used in the biodynamic/French intensive method compost recipe and other recipes. The varied texture will allow good drainage and aeration in the pile. The compost will also have a more diverse nutriment content. A pile made primarily of leaves or grass cuttings makes the passage of water and air through the pile difficult because both tend to mat. Both good air and water penetration are required for proper decomposition. The layering of the materials further promotes a mixture of textures and nutriments and helps insure even decomposition.

A minimum pile size of 3 feet by 3 feet by 3 feet (1 cubic yard weighing about 1000 pounds) is recommended. Smaller piles fail to provide the insulation necessary for proper heating (up to 160 degrees) and allow the penetration of too much air. It is all right to build piles up slowly to this size as materials become available, though it is best to build an entire pile at one time. A pile will cure to ½ to ⅓ its original size, depending on the materials used. A large pile size might be 6 feet high, 6 feet wide and 12 feet long.

The best time to prepare compost is in the *spring or autumn* when biological activity is highest (Too much heat or cold slows down and even kills the microbiotic life in the pile.) The two high activity periods conveniently coincide with the maximum availability of materials in the spring, as grass and other plants begin to grow rapidly, and in the autumn, as leaves fall and other plant life begins to die. The pile should optimally be built under a deciduous oak tree. This tree's nature provides the conditions for the development of excellent soil underneath it. And compost is a kind of soil. The second best place is under another deciduous tree. As a last resort, evergreen trees may be used. The shade and windbreak provided by the trees also help keep the pile at an even moisture level. (The pile should be placed 6 feet away from the tree's trunk so it will not provide a haven for potentially harmful insects.)

Compost is ready to use when it is dark and rich looking. You should not be able to discern the original source of the materials from the texture and the materials should crumble in your hands. Mature compost even smells good—like water in a forest spring! A biodynamic/French intensive pile should be ready to use in 2½ to 3 months. Usually, no turning is needed as the materials used and their layering allow for good aeration and complete breakdown. Compost for use in flats should be passed through a sieve of ½ inch or ¼ inch wire fabric. In the garden a *minimum* maintenance dressing of ½ pound of compost per square foot should be added to the soil before each crop. Guidelines for *general* maintenance dressings are a 1 inch layer of compost or 8 cubic feet of compost per 100 square feet (about 3 pounds per square foot).

The biodynamic/French intensive method of compost making differs in particular from the biodynamic method[2] in that it is simpler to prepare, normally uses no manure and usually uses no herbal solutions to stimulate microorganism growth. Weeds, such as stinging nettle, and plants, such as fava beans, are sometimes added in the preparation of special piles, however. Special mixtures are created to meet particular pH, texture and nutriment requirements. Separate compost piles are made of small tree branches since they can take two years to decompose.

The biodynamic/French intensive method of making compost differs from the Rodale compost method[3] in the use of little or no

2. For the biodynamic method of compost preparation, see pages 37 to 51 in *The Pfeiffer Garden Book*, Alice Heckel (Ed.), Biodynamic Farming and Gardening Association, Inc., Stroudsburg, Pennsylvania, 1967.
3. For the Rodale method of compost preparation, see pages 59 to 86 in *The Basic Book of Organic Gardening*, Robert Rodale (Ed.), Ballantine Books, New York, 1971.

manure and usually no rock powder fertilizers or nitroge
supplements. As mentioned before, manure used continually an
in large amounts, is an imbalanced fertilizer, although it is
good texturizing agent because of its usual decomposed sawdus
content. When fertilizers are added to a compost pile muc
of their nutriment value can leach out by the time the pil
is ready to use. The nitrogen supplements do, however, spee
up the decomposition process. Both the biodynamic and Rodal
methods are good ones, proven by use over a long perio
of time. Chadwick's recipe seems simpler to use and equall
effective.

Some people use *sheet composting* (a process of spreadin
uncomposted organic materials over the soil and then diggin
them into the soil where they decompose). The disadvantage c
this method is that the soil should not be planted for 3 months c
so until decomposition has occurred. Soil bacteria tie up th
nitrogen during the decomposition process, thereby making
unavailable to the plants. Sheet composting is beneficial if it i
used during the winter in cold areas, because the tie-up prevent
the nitrogen from leaching out during winter rains.

Other people use *green manure composting* (the growing c
cover crops such as vetch, clover, alfalfa, bean, pea or othe
legumes until just before maturity when the plants are dug int
the soil). This is an excellent way to bring unworked soil into
reasonable condition. Cover crops are rich in nitrogen, so the
boost the nutriment quality of the soil without one's having
resort to the purchase of fertilizers. Their stems and leave
contain a lot of nitrogen and their roots support nitrogen-fixin
bacteria. These bacteria take nitrogen from the air and fix it i
nodules on the roots, which you can see when you pull the plant
up. They also help you dig. Their roots loosen the soil an
eventually turn into humus beneath the earth. Fava beans ar
exceptionally good for green manuring if you plan to plan
tomatoes, because their decomposed bodies help eradicate tc
mato wilt organisms from the soil.

Due to their high nitrogen content, cover crops decompos
rapidly. Planting can usually follow one month after the plant
are dug into the soil. The disadvantage of the green manurin
process is that the land is out of production during the period c
cover crop growth and the shorter one month period of decom
position. In some areas, the long term improvement in the soil
nutritive content and structure compensates for this limitatior

The advantage of the small-scale biodynamic/French intensive method is that composting still is feasible. Even if you decide to use their produce and not to dig cover crops in, the growing process will put nitrogen into the soil and will make it possible to grow plants such as corn and tomatoes, which are heavy feeders. And the plant residues may be used in the compost pile.

Some materials should not be used in the preparation of compost:

- Plants infected with disease or a severe insect attack where eggs could be preserved or where the insects themselves could survive in spite of the compost pile's heat.

- Poisonous plants, such as oleander, hemlock, and castor bean, which harm soil life.

- Plants which take too long to break down, such as magnolia leaves.

- Plants which have acids toxic to other plants, such as eucalyptus leaves.

- Plants which may be too acidic or contain substances that interfere with the decomposition process, such as pine needles. Pine needles are extremely acidic and contain a form of kerosene. (Special compost piles are often made of acidic materials, such as pine needles and leaves, however. This compost will lower the soil's pH and stimulate acid loving plants like strawberries.)

- Ivy and succulents, which may not be killed in the heat of the decomposition process and can regrow when the compost is placed in a planting bed.

- Pernicious weeds such as wild morning glory and bermuda grass, which will probably not be killed in the decomposition process and which will choke out other plants when they resprout after the compost is placed in a planting bed.

- Cat and dog manures, which can contain pathogens harmful to children. These pathogens are not always killed in the heat of the compost pile.

Plants infected with disease or insects and pernicious weeds should be burned to be properly destroyed. Their ash then becomes a good fertilizer. The ash will also help control harmful soil insects, such as carrot worms, which shy away from the alkalinity of ashes.

Parts of a regular compost pile, which have not broken down completely by the end of the composting period, should be placed on the bottom of a new pile. This is especially true for twigs and small branches which can use the extra protection of the pile's height to speed their decomposition in a situation of increased warmth and moisture.

Factual Articles

WHILE ALL PRESENTING generalized information, the following articles differ in how personally the facts were acquired, ranging from first-person, firsthand reportage and accumulated personal expertise to preponderantly third-person, secondhand book research. These contrasts relate in turn to some differences in organization and purpose.

TRAVELOGUE

Malta
Elizabeth Pepper and John Wilcock
from *A Guide to Magical and Mystical Sites*, 1977

This article represents a kind of heavily annotated travel guide. Since the authors wished to feed in considerable background information about the island and particular sites on it, much of the article consists of history, biography, and other book-researched information. But as a muted form of directions—recommendations—a travel guide retains some flavor of the imperative mode.

along with a spatial *organization. One moves not from event to event but from site to site. At each place, which the authors visited themselves, they insert some facts obtained secondhand. The effect is of a personally guided tour by an authority.*

Nobody has ever been able to explain the ancient temples of Malta. According to radiocarbon dating, they are the oldest free-standing stone monuments in the world and yet they seem to have no link with any other civilizations. The oldest of the temples date back to before the construction of the Egyptian pyramids. They were built by a race that left no written records, for writing was yet to be invented. And they have survived because they were buried and forgotten. Through centuries of occupation by one invader after another, they remained deep under the earth, rediscovered only in the last century.

Lying between Sicily, fifty miles to the northeast, and the North African coast, the islands of Malta have always appeared to be a strategic base for nations using the western Mediterranean, and it is hardly surprising that the Phoenicians, Carthaginians, Romans, Arabs, and Normans—to name but a few—all in turn coveted and dominated the islands. All left minor traces, although nothing as impressive as the megalith builders, but modern Malta owes little to these early conquerors. In fact no single nation ever shaped and developed the islands as much as that body known as the Knights of St. John who accepted Malta reluctantly as its headquarters (after losing a former base in Rhodes) in the sixteenth century and who did not leave until 270 years later.

The Order of St. John, like their better-known contemporaries the Knights Templars, grew out of a handful of knights who formed themselves into a protective force to succor the Crusaders. It became an international order whose predominantly upper-class members took vows of poverty, chastity, and obedience, and who owed their allegiance to the Pope. The Knights built themselves into a superb fighting force whose only major setback came when they were outnumbered by the Turks and forced out of their headquarters on Rhodes. At first reluctant to accept the grant of Malta, and for a long time unwilling to develop it, they eventually took over its administration and fortification and governed and held it superbly through the rule of twenty-eight successive Grand Masters. They left both their genetic and their cultural impress on the islands.

The capital of Malta, Valletta, named after the sixth of the Grand Masters, Jean de La Valette-Parisot who served from

1557 to 1568, is a charming town on a scale just small enough to get around on foot. Its main street, Kingsway, is a permanent pedestrian mall somewhat reminiscent of Dubrovnik, and the visitor quickly learns to relish the evening walk along it when the shops stay open, and the whole town turns out for the casual promenade.

Evenings, in fact, are when Valletta is at its best with churchbells ringing, candles flickering in windows, and the hazy air of the back streets permeated with a rich mixture of countless cooking smells. Like many Mediterranean lands, Malta lives much of its life in the open, and most places on this small island offer views of the sea. Valletta itself, dominating a hilly peninsula, offers picture-postcard views from its outer battlements, particularly over the Grand Harbour. Any number of small, inexpensive hotels line the picturesque steps of St. Ursula Street (try the friendly Grand Harbour Hotel), all looking out over this deep-water bay which has provided a storm-free shelter and an almost impregnable stronghold since the days of the Knights.

Even today, almost two full centuries after their departure, reminders of their presence abound on all sides. Before Valletta was founded, Fort St. Angelo, built by the Moors across the harbor to the east, was the center of their power. Successive Grand Masters strengthened and extended the defenses here, consolidating their power for an assault that never came, once the siege of 1565 was over. The fort is now a Royal Navy base, its formidable bastions infiltrated with all the accouterments of paranoia and panoply that a modern military establishment possesses. Visitors are unwelcome, unless they book for the regular Wednesday morning tour via the tourist office. The officer on duty has total authority to bar all others, and rumor has it that even retired admirals have been unable to gain admittance.

But Valletta, and Malta generally, is replete with ancient buildings and ancient memories: St. John's Co-Cathedral, built in the sixteenth century by the Order's chief engineer, Gerolamo Cassar, with its richly decorated walls and canvases by Mattia Preti and Caravaggio, both member-knights. In the crypt are tombs of several of the Grand Masters. Different sections of the fortifications were defended by different groups of knights, divided into "tongues" roughly representing their different nationalities. They lived in various inns around town, the best preserved of which is the charming Auberge D'Aragon, a white building with a spacious patio at the foot of Archbishop Street where it now serves as the headquarters of the Ministry of Education and Culture.

The flavor of those siege-conscious times, when every day might bring invasion, can perhaps best be recaptured by visiting the armory of the magnificent palace, in the center of town, where a vast hall is lined with pikes, guns, lances, suits of armor, and all the other trappings of battle. It isn't hard to imagine these holy knights turning themselves into superbly equipped men of war when the occasion demanded.

Many knightly artifacts can be seen in the basement of the Fine Arts Museum on South Street: more armor, a seventeenth-century robe, ancient bells, anchors, cannonballs, guns, and swords. There are stone models of the proposed additions to the St. Angelo fortifications—made by a Spanish military engineer in 1680 at the request of Grand Master Gregorio Carafa. Some indication of what these regal knights looked like can be gleaned from the plates and paintings bearing their portraits. Upstairs there are more paintings by Caravaggio, Tintoretto, and other sixteenth-century master.

A vast amount of valuable art, treasures which the Knights had been collecting for 300 years and which were distributed throughout the churches of Malta, were plundered by Napoleon in the late eighteenth century and were later lost when his fleet was sunk by Nelson during the Battle of the Nile.

Grand Master Emanuel Pinto, whose metal measuring cups are displayed in the museum as well as his portrait in an oval frame, was possibly the best known of his line, and certainly the longest in office (1741–1773). His very longevity gave credence to rumors that he and his friend Cagliostro had achieved the age-old quest for the *elixir vitae*, the secret of eternal life. In 1758 after reading his premature obituary in a French paper he is reported to have exclaimed, "Aha, it is the shadow of Pinto, not Pinto, who rules in Malta." But he continued to rule with an iron hand—"he was haughty, severe and implacable" writes Roderick Cavaliero—and in his final years set up a laboratory in which Cagliostro worked. A secretary to the subsequent Grand Master, Emanuel De Rohan Polduc, wrote that Pinto "dissipated immense sums" in his unsuccessful search for the philosopher's stone, a quest that preoccupied numerous great minds of that century and the previous one.

Although the Order's compatriots, the Knights Templars—both were founded in Jerusalem for similar purposes in the twelfth century—were heavily involved in occult practices, there are only a few tantalizing hints that the Knights of Malta shared similar interests.

During the rule of La Cassière (1572-1581) there were allegations that "heresy" was rife throughout the Order, but nobody has chronicled the specific details.

Count Cagliostro, born as Giuseppe Balsamo in Palermo, Sicily, always insisted that his real birth (i.e. spiritual *rebirth*) took place in Malta after he had been initiated into the Order. "This accession came to him through the mysteries of St. John: tradition, the esoteric language of the Apocalypse, the intuitive methods of visionaries, the revelation of the cabala, the mystique of supernatural interventions on the fringe of doctrine admitted by the Church, and the call of the sublime," is how François Ribadeau Dumas puts it in his book, *Cagliostro, Scoundrel or Saint*. Dumas adds that the Grand Master taught young Balsamo "the inner meaning of occultism: the discovery of the transcendent lying behind tangible reality, the ceaseless search for a way to control forces acting upon all mankind."

As a child in Sicily, a country where in the eighteenth century the sorcerer was as common as the priest, Cagliostro had already achieved an awesome reputation. One day while playing with friends he answered a query about where some little girl was by drawing a square on the ground, making some mysterious passes with his hands, and producing an image of the child within it.

On leaving Sicily he traveled widely, visiting Rhodes (where he sold hemp and silk), Egypt, and Rome. While in London he studied Egyptian magical rites and back in Malta at first made a precarious living selling beauty creams and elixirs for long life, before establishing a friendship with Grand Master Pinto.

His renowned "recipe for perpetual youth," which appears translated from a German treatise (published at Munich in 1919) in A. E. Waite's *Lives of Alchemistical Philosophers*, outlines a forty-day retreat to be made "once in every fifty years beginning during the full moon of May." During this period, Cagliostro explains, the participant must fast, partaking only of May dew and certain herbs. Toward the end of the forty-day period, most of which is to be spent in bed, a few grains of what he terms "the Universal Medicine" will help the hair, teeth, nails, and skin to be renewed.

At his later trials (Rome in 1790, Zurich in 1791) Cagliostro was accused not only of possessing the secret of prolonging life, but also of practicing alchemical gold-making, teaching cabalistic arts, and pretending to call up and exorcise spirits. How much of this activity he conducted while on Malta was not established. In his final years he sought asylum to live on the island, but this was denied him.

There is no doubt that the Order, and especially its all-powerful Grand Master, was in an ideal position to explore some of the arcane (and heretical) occult knowledge of the day. Rich and almost invulnerable, Malta was the total master of all it surveyed, virtually an independent island kingdom theoretically answerable only to the Pope, who maintained a representative on the island in the form of an Inquisitor. This post often marked a man for promotion and twenty-five Inquisitors later became Cardinals, two became Popes.

It may be only because of this ambitious spy in their midst that so little evidence of the Knights' secret practices has come down to us. But the evidence is undoubtedly there, possibly in some of the thousands of books and manuscripts in their decaying leather bindings which fill the cavernous, twenty-foot-high shelves in Valletta's public library, the last building to be built by the Order before its departure from Malta in 1798. There are scores of books of handwritten letters in Italian, the brown ink faded but still clearly legible, an almost-complete record of all the correspondence between Malta and the Vatican for the centuries of the Knights' rule. There is a letter from Henry VIII to Grand Master L'Isle Adam, dated November 22, 1530, and manuals of signals containing neatly-drawn flags for the use of the Knights' sea-going galleys.

Another of the *auberges,* or "inns," in which the Knights were quartered is now Valletta's National Museum on Kingsway. There is little here from "recent" times when the Order held sway, the displays being devoted mostly to the era 1650-1450 B.C. when Malta reached the highest point of its prehistoric development. Burnished pottery and giant vases from the so-called Tarxien period demonstrate the ingenuity of craftsmen whose work preceded the invention of the potter's wheel, all their products being laboriously built up from one successive coil of clay after another.

From the Tarxien temples come the "fertility symbols"—small plaster penises and breasts as well as slabs bearing representations of both. There are also casts of a bull and a sow that are easier to identify than the well-worn originals still at Tarxien itself, a few miles south of Valletta. The museum also contains the immense stone slab with its recessed "cupboard" in which a flint knife and goat's horn were found, and about which Dr. David Trump writes in the official catalog: "Romanticism must always be guarded against in archaeology, but surely here the romantic explanation must be the correct one: that the sacrificial knife, with the horn of one of its victims, was put away carefully in readiness for a later celebration which never came. What prevented it? We wish we knew."

There is nothing that explains the mystery of the temples—to whom they were built, and why—but scale models of the major ones demonstrate how similar was their design for a period of about six centuries, dating from as far before the Christian era as we have come since.

The extraordinary subterranean temple known as the Hal Saflieni and Hypogeum ("under the earth") may offer the most clues to what this early pagan religion was all about. In this intricate series of elaborately carved and decorated caves, which had lain hidden for centuries until building workers accidentally cut through the roof in 1902, mysterious oracular rites were performed. Possibly some devotees came to the temple to sleep, subsequently having their dreams interpreted by priests. One of Malta's most famous ancient relics, a terra-cotta statue of a sleeping woman lying on her side, is barely five inches long, and in the three-quarters of a century since it was found, has prompted more speculation than many a major work. What is the cause of her serenity, her apparently blissful dreams?

The descent into the Hypogeum from the street-level museum is via a spiral staircase into a small cave bearing faint traces of red paint. The temple's interior was probably painted originally and in some rooms the decorated spirals and pentagons are still visible. Ingeniously the ancient builders carved pillars and lintels out of the solid rock to form the entrance to the main hall, and indeed the whole subterranean temple closely resembles similar edifices above ground. One room leads into another, up, down and around—the whole elaborate structure going down to forty feet below ground, representing who knows how many thousands of man-hours expended with antler picks and flints by a race whose gods are no longer known.

Passing out of the Oracle's room, where a recessed niche transforms a deep, male voice into a resonant, awe-inspiring echo (particularly in the darkness or possibly dim light of an oil lamp), we come first to a decorated chamber and then to what is believed to have been the holiest room, with its five carved pillars and semicorbeled ceiling. Here animals for sacrifice may have been tethered, the rope fastened through two interconnected holes in the floor. Stone plugs capped these holes when the site was first excavated and under one of them was found a pair of sheep's horns.

"It is evident that after a burnt sacrifice a portion of the animal was stowed away in [one of] the recesses so numerous in these temples," reported Sir Themistocles Zammitt, then director of the Malta Museum who was conducting the excavations. "That a burnt sacrifice was offered before the statue of the divinity worshipped is beyond doubt, for not far from the altar the pavement is deeply eroded by the action of the fire, which has likewise reddened the stone by its intense heat."

In 1913, while Zammitt was working on the Hypogeum dig, he was approached by a farmer who said that huge blocks of stone blocked plowing beneath his field and asked the diggers to investigate. A sample trench uncovered the top of two uprights which were joined in a manner suggesting a great megalithic circle. There was no time for further exploration that year and the following year, 1914, was the beginning of World War I, so it was not until 1915 that the work began at Tarxien, now generally accepted to be the last of Malta's temples to be built and representing, therefore, the absolute flowering of this particular culture.

At Tarxien was found a huge stone statue representing the lower torso of a woman who must originally have been nine or ten feet tall. All that remains are the feet and hem of a skirt, of the same type worn by the sleeping woman and other figures. Most writers have speculated that fertility was the principle worshiped by these ancient people; they prayed that the land remain rich and productive and that the women, represented by figures with immense breasts and pregnant stomachs, would continue to give birth to workers to harvest it. Many of the figures found here, and now displayed in Valletta's National Museum, stand with one hand resting on an extended belly, the other pointing downward to the earth.

The approach to the Tarxien temple is through a garden filled with cabbage, potatoes, and flowers, but once past the perpendicular stones that form the entranceway it opens up into the series of interconnected semicircular chambers that are a familiar feature of all Malta's ancient temples. There are the usual spherical stones which appear to have been used as rollers to transport the heavy blocks around, numerous altars, and stone slabs decorated with spiral patterns. One slab, also since removed to Valletta, depicted a procession of six animals: a pig, a ram, and four animals looking a bit like Moorish goats, which don't exist on Malta today but whose horns were similar to those discovered at ancient sites. Another slab, still at the site, depicts reliefs of a sow with thirteen suckling teats and a bull. The bones of all such animals were found in niches adjoining the sacrificial altars.

Zammitt, who for an archeologist appears unusually open-minded about magic, suggests that this early Neolithic population had in addition to its artistic achievements "elaborated a religious system of a type which we usually attribute to much later generations." In his book *Prehistoric Malta*, a record of his meticulously documented excavations, he adds:

> The building of sanctuaries, the sacrificial offering of animals slaughtered and burnt before an image or symbol, the consultation of oracles in special oracular chambers, the rites of divination by incubation and interpretation of inspired dreams as suggested by the chambers and figurines of the Hal Saflieni and Hypogeum point to a high moral development and a complicated system of worship such as have never hitherto been attributed to a people who had not yet become familiar with metals and with the ideas supposed to have been introduced into Europe along with them.

He pondered on the limestone "rolling" balls and the stones shaped like cones which "must have played an important part in some magico-religious ritual" and posed an original theory to explain the 10 foot by 10 foot block of pavement inset with five deep pits. These, he suggests, might be "divination blocks" into which stones from a pile nearby were thrown: "lot-casting based on the different ways in which the ball was holed."

Other writers have explained the holes as receptacles for the blood whose life-giving properties invested it with a peculiarly important symbolism in such ceremonies. It was the practice to cover the bones of the dead with red ochre in ancient times, a symbolic reinvestiture of the bones with life, and this paint could also be found on many temple walls. Professor J. D. Evans observes that workmen who discovered some such bones lying in a partly waterlogged well tomb reported they were covered in "fresh blood."

In his book *Malta*, Evans tells of the amulets found at Tarxien which were covered with abstract signs ("probably with magical or talismanic significance"), one, a piece of greenstone with a sign like a three-legged Greek "pi" was encrusted with red stones and gold, both imports to the island. Another small figurine was penetrated all over with sharp fragments of shell while the clay was still wet—a fruitful subject for speculation ranging from sympathetic magic or black magic to some sort of acupuncture technique. Most of these little figures, Evans suggests, might be evidence of a healing cult and were deposited in temples to effect cures or to give thanks for them.

Musing about whether or not the original temples had roofs, something that has been debated inconclusively since their first discovery, he points to the absence of central pillars but also observes that signs of fire on the walls of one temple would suggest that a wooden roof was burned. As to the temples' purpose, he adds: "Collective rock cut and megalithic tombs of Western Europe . . . are all in some degree shrines where rites for propitiation of ancestor spirits were carried out." The religion, he thought, probably grew out of the cult of the dead (the Hypogeum was not only a temple but a burial ground—the bones of almost 6,000 people were found there.)

Evans pondered on whether the bulls, horns, and snakes which came to be depicted in the latter phases of Maltese prehistoric culture might have been due to influences from Crete and whether the ancient Maltese could have been known in the prehistoric world as "great magicians, healers, men of spiritual power generally." He draws no final conclusions.

A tiny museum at the entrance to both the Tarxien temples and the Hypogeum (both are within half a mile of each other in the sleepy town of Pawla, southeast of the peninsula on which stands Valletta) displays some of the flint, obsidian, and bone tools used in their construction, also necklaces of beads and fish vertebrae in use by the worshipers. Scale models give an overall grasp of the temples' shape. The model of the Hypogeum is especially revealing with its intricate honeycomb of caves, all sitting calmly under a deserted Victorian house whose florid, peeling wallpaper can still be seen.

A mile or two further southeast, in the barren, rock-strewn valley which adjoins the pretty fishing village of Marsaxlokk (good bathing) are the Ghar Dalam caves whose prehistoric mammal occupants, by comparison, make the temple worshipers seem like our contemporaries. The hippopotamuses and elephants that once lived here up to a quarter of a million years ago may have walked over on what was a continuous land bridge between Sicily and the Maltese islands, gradually becoming extinct as the land receded and left them trapped. The main cave is enormous, high enough to drive a double-decker bus into it, and stretching back for several hundred yards. In the adjoining museum are thousands of bones, tusks, and teeth of these extinct mammals as well as a few bones from much-later human cave dwellers.

What are probably the most impressive megalithic sites on Malta are also the most inaccessible because of bad roads untraveled by local buses. These are the twin temples of Hagar Qim on a cliff overlooking the sea just past the southwest town of Orendi, and the temple of Mnajdra, a few hundred yards below it and nearer to the sea.

Both these temples predate Tarxien, but what they lack in sophistication they more than compensate for with their towering majesty at this lonely site. Hagar Qim's front wall is formed from massive slabs, topped with horizontal slabs which give it the solid appearance of an impregnable fortress. But inside there are the familiar semicircular chambers, altars (some mushroom-shaped ones have a raised rim around the top—possibly to collect blood), niches, carved apertures through which oracles may or may not have spoken, and immense stones stippled with innumerable dots and grooves. It was at Hagar Qim that the famous "fat ladies" were found, statues that can now be seen in the National Museum in Valletta.

Walking around the earthen floor of this temple and inspecting the numerous interconnecting inner rooms, it is impossible to guess who may have worshiped here almost 3,000 years before the Christian era. There is nothing remotely like these temples outside the Maltese islands, in the view of Dr. David Trump, "so we cannot use foreign influence to explain them away." But there's no doubt that they were temples erected to worship some deity. The so-called oracle holes and the fact that the temples were divided into what appear to be public and inner sections would seem to imply a privileged priesthood.

"The increasing evidence [for this] could be quoted as a possible cause for internal revolt," says Dr. Trump, a former curator at Malta's National Museum whose book *Malta: An Archaeological Guide* is both fascinating and comprehensive. The excessive temple building, he says, in an attempt to explain the culture's demise, "might imply neglect of the precious soil of the fields. It could have depleted dangerously the local timber resources, again encouraging soil erosion. To the unprovable 'mights' and 'perhapses' we could add drought, plague, religious hysteria even, or foreign invasion."

Mnajdra's rooms and niches are as numerous as those of its companion temple up the hill, and just as baffling. The solid walls, towering up to fifteen feet high, have preserved the interior of this sheltered spot perhaps better than elsewhere. "In this temple, perhaps more than any other," says Trump, "we come tantalizingly close to the beliefs and rituals of its builders while remaining aware that further progress in understanding is probably impossible."

Because of the location of these temples, with an impressive view over the sea and of the tiny rocky islet of Filfa, moonlit nights make an especially impressive time to pay a visit. Until the enclosing wall is completed, both these temples are open at all times.

Margaret Murray quotes a tradition in her book *Excavations in Malta* that Hagar Qim was built solely by women, but she gives no evidence for this. At Tas-Silg, east of Marsaxlokk, she says another legend concerns the eight-foot "Saracen woman" said to be buried with a spinning wheel of solid gold. There's long been a local belief in the tale of the poor farmer who many years ago dug up a solid gold sheep with his plow and broke it into pieces before selling to the goldsmith for a pension that kept him the rest of his life.

On the cliffs in this region around Tas-Silg, in Roman times, was a temple dedicated to the Syrian goddess Astarte, known to the Greeks as Hera. This may have been the Temple of Juno (Hera's Latin name) which historians report was despoiled about 73 B.C.

The ancient walled city of Mdina, once known as Melita, is much richer in the antiquities of the Christian era than in those of prehistoric days. A Roman villa just outside the city moat (which was dug by the Arabs in the ninth century) has a remarkable tiled floor whose patterns offer the kind of eye-catching perspective still popular today. Other relics of the villa/museum are various funerary monuments "dedicated to the gods of the underworld" as well as a pedestal bearing a dedication to Apollo and the notation that local citizens contributed 110,792 sesterces for its erection.

Mdina's "modern" suburb of Rabat is also interesting but not half so fascinating as the walled town itself, with its cathedral clock noting the day, month, and year, and its excellent museum of natural history with explanatory plans of the island's geology, rock strata, and flora and fauna.

Much of Malta is monotonously barren, strewn with rock and stone-fenced fields, few bigger than the average suburban backyard, but the view from Mdina's city walls is splendid, especially to the northeast where St. Paul's Bay is supposedly the site of

Paul's landing back in first century A.D. The cave in which he is said to have lived adjoins the cathedral in Rabat.

Southwest of Rabat, on the Dingli cliffs, is one of the best examples of the mysterious "cart-ruts" which innumerable archeologists have tried to explain, leaving the inescapable conclusion that there is not only more here than meets the eye but conceivably evidence of strange magical practices, too.

The ruts are deep grooves in bare limestone rock which must have been cut while the rock was still covered with soil, for limestone hardens too much to cut when it has been long exposed to air. The tracks run in parallel lines often for long distances, sometimes up sheer slopes, and occasionally disappearing into the sea. Most historians seem to have decided that they couldn't have been made by wheels (some of the angles of turn are too sharp) and must have been made by poles, loosely tied together, with the burden resting between them.

"By themselves the cart tracks tell a story of immense activity on the part of a considerable population evidently engaged in the transport of a heavy material on hundreds of carts for hundreds of years," Dr. Zammitt writes. "There could be no idea then of road building in the Roman sense of levelling and metalling rough surfaces; the carts were evidently pushed over any rocky surface in the direction desired, whether smooth or hummocky, flat, slanting, hollowed or raised."

Dr. Trump tells us that the commonest pattern is for tracks of this nature, which are the result of wear not deliberate cutting, to climb from one cultivated valley to the next, often by the most convenient route, which is why they are so often found paralleling the roads of today. On the average the parallel tracks are about fifty-five inches apart and sometimes several inches deep. Most could be explained, he says, by regular agricultural activities.

On the Dingli cliffs, just south of Buskett Gardens, the tracks are so numerous, crisscrossing each other, that the spot has been colloquially termed "Clapham Junction" by some writers. On the face of it, there seems to be little explanation for their concentration at this point. Another good selection can be seen at the Naxxar Gap below St. Paul and Targa where ruts approach the ancient defense wall known as Victoria Lines and sweep across the Mosta Road.

The island of Gozo is smaller than Malta and less barren. Its fertile valleys have traditionally produced much of the food to feed its sister island to the south. Gozo is reached by a ferryboat that looks a bit like a Mississippi River steamer: a half-hour ride across calm waters after the pleasant drive up Malta's coast to Marfa, the embarkation point.

Getting around Gozo is very easy: the island is only about ten miles long by four or five miles wide, and buses run to most place. Victoria, the somewhat olde-worlde capital, has two movie theaters, one hotel with a good restaurant, and a main square whose thickly-foliaged trees shelter so many birds that their raucous shrieking can be heard all over town. Only unwary tourists park their cars under the trees in the square, and locals rarely walk through without a hat.

Victoria's major place of interest is the hilltop castle, part of which comprises a museum containing fertility symbols and a finely-dressed block of stone with a snake carving from the Ggantija temple a few miles to the east. There are also numerous Roman relics, such as stone-carved inscriptions and various gods, coins, and vases, many of them recovered from the wrecked Roman vessel found at Xlendi Bay. This little fishing harbor, incidentally, is a delightful hideaway, virtually deserted out of season when self-contained apartments on the harbor can be rented for next to nothing. Some of the best lace comes from Gozo and Xlendi is a good place to buy it.

Ggantija, which is among the oldest of the Maltese temples, dates back to as early as 2600 or 2800 B.C. It was first excavated in 1827, in times when excavation meant little more than uncovering the site, saving the main items and leaving everything else to the elements. Fortunately it became a popular subject for numerous artists, one of whom, the German Brocktorff, painted a series of watercolors which depict details of features long since destroyed. The pictures can be seen in the Valletta library on Malta.

In the nineteenth century few thought of such sites as prehistoric, although the first description of Ggantija to appear, published by L. Mazzara, Paris, bore the curious title of *Temple Anti-Diluvian des Geants*. The temple is very similar to the ones we have already seen on Malta itself, and although one of the earliest visitors made passing reference to a subterranean temple similar to the Hypogeum, this has never since been discovered.

Two of the problems that have troubled most archeologists since Ggantija was first uncovered (the excavations at Hagar Qim and Mnajdra came twelve years later) are, given how small the Maltese population must have been in prehistoric times, how were the temples first built and paid for? In his *The Story of*

Malta, Brian Blouet comments: "It has been suggested that Malta was a 'magic island sanctuary' with a great part of the religious paraphernalia being paid for by gifts or fees extracted from pilgrims coming from other lands." But this theory is open to objection, he says, because if such pilgrims did come to Malta they left no traces of their presence, nor have relics from this Maltese temple era been found in other lands.

In a later era Malta built up a considerable export trade in cotton and citrus fruits, but these crops were introduced during the Arab domination of the islands which lasted from A.D. 870 to 1090.

The region around Ggantija is scattered with other sites, none as impressive as the main temple, but it's worth paying a visit to nearby Xaghra (where a painted clock on the church announces a never-changing 11:47). Weird, rambling underground caves sprawl under the village, their antiquity emphasized by the Victorian houses above them. Access is usually via a carved stone staircase into what would ordinarily be a kitchen cellar—except that some of these "cellars" stretch for hundreds of feet and are filled with stalactites and stalagmites.

STATE-OF-KNOWLEDGE REPORT

I Sing the Body Electric
Kathleen McAuliffe
Omni, November, 1980

This is a state-of-the-art report on research in some applied science. It entailed interview/visits with several authorities in the field, some background reading in current periodicals, and consulting of basic science texts. This common type of reportage pulls together for the layman what is known on a certain topic at a certain time and situates historically the recent research, either updating a long-standing investigation, or, as here, signaling a new area of experimentation.

Imagine if we could speak to cells, instructing them to grow more quickly or slowly, change their shape and function, or organize themselves into new tissues to replace damaged ones. Without lifting a scalpel to flesh or injecting a chemical into the bloodstream, scientists are doing just that. They have discovered a way to tap into the body's internal communication network and transmit messages in a language that cells understand. That language consists of electrical signals—the universal code by which living organisms regulate growth, development, and repair.

We all wear an invisible garment, an electromagnetic cloak that shields us from head to toe. From the moment of conception, electrical currents began to flow in the tiny embryo, guiding the incredibly intricate process that culminates in birth. When a salamander regrows a limb, similar currents flow along the injured extremity as if reenacting a critical step of embryogenesis. Once the new organism—or limb—is fully formed, the currents abate. Yet we all retain an electromagnetic halo as a birthday suit that we carry throughout life. Disturbances in these fields portend illness. In fact, this is the basis for acupuncture diagnosis. Whenever bodily injury is sustained, our primordial currents flow strong until the wound heals over.

Bioelectricity is nothing new. As far back as the eighteenth century. Luigi Galvani discovered this source of energy in the twitching of a frog's leg strung between two pieces of metal. Only recently, however, have we realized just how pervasive a role electricity plays in governing vital cellular functions. Our enlightenment has revealed a radical new approach to medical therapy. Doctors are seeking to alter out internal currents with external ones. By applying electricity to the body, they believe, it will one day be possible to grow back the amputee's limb, repair the paraplegic's severed spinal cord, and stop the cancer victim's uncontrolled proliferation of cells.

"Electricity will become as ubiquitous in medical practice as surgery or drugs; in many instances it will supplant them," says Dr. Andrew Bassett, of Columbia-Presbyterian Medical Center, in New York City. An orthopedic surgeon, he was one of the first to use electricity to mend bone fractures that had stubbornly resisted all other treatments. Dr. Bassett's technique is to position electric coils around the injury so that a pulsating electromagnetic field induces tiny currents in the bone.

"The patients love it," Bassett says, "because they don't have to go under the knife." They don't even have to be hospitalized. Once the coils, given out only by prescription, have been specially fitted, they can be taken home in a lightweight case. If they are worn 12 hours a day, the fracture usually mends within four to six months. And the therapy is totally painless.

"You would experience almost the same field strength by standing under a fluorescent light." Bassett says, "except that the fields employed in therapy are organized in a different informational pattern."

Beyond Bone Repair

So far, bone healing is the only use of his electrical coils approved by the U.S. Food and Drug Administration, but Bassett is anxious to see the applications spread beyond the orthopedic wards. From his animal studies, for example, Bassett discovered that electricity will consistently double or triple the growth rate of peripheral nerves—those found in the limbs.

"If peripheral nerves are severed," says Bassett, "they rarely repair themselves. If an individual ruptures his sciatic nerve in a head-on collision or puts his hand through glass and cuts his median nerve, years of therapy may be required before he regains even a fraction of the normal motor control.

Although only two human patients have been tested up until now, Bassett is greatly encouraged by the results. The electromagnetic field promoted the same beneficial nerve growth seen in laboratory animals. "It's still too soon to say whether this is the panacea for peripheral nerve injuries or not." Bassett cautions. "Time will tell. But I think we have the upper edge."

It is clear Bassett believes that electricity will also give medical science the "upper edge" in repairing damage to the central nervous system. A solution to this pressing problem might benefit more than 6 million people in the United States alone, ranging from paraplegics to stroke victims.

How does electricity produce these startling effects? Cells respond to artificially induced currents just as well as to the body's own. Nature alone performs miracles, scientists merely exploit them.

Earlier in this century several investigators began to study the electrical currents produced by a variety of living organisms— from embryonic seaweed to tadpoles. Working after World War II, Dr. Robert O. Becker, of the Veterans Administration Hospital in Syracuse, New York, had one distinct advantage over his predecessors: the growth of sophisticated electronic technology. "The kinds of tools available to me right off the shelf were much more sensitive," Dr. Becker said. Although many of his colleagues see him as the supreme catalyst in the field—"the man in modern times who asked the right questions at the right moment," one puts it—Becker takes another view: "If you look at things from a historical perspective, I'm not such a smart guy. I was just plain lucky."

Becker's involvement in electrical therapy began with a pioneering study of injury currents. Immediately after an organism is wounded, damaged cells become leaky. Charged atoms, called ions, pour out of the cells forming a current. By measuring voltages generated at injury sites, Becker uncovered clues to one of nature's most baffling inequities: why the lowly salamander can regenerate as much as one third of its total body mass, while man can scarcely endure damage to a single vital organ. Moreover, his findings suggested that currents of only a few billionths of an ampere might be the key to rectifying this gross imbalance of the evolutionary scale. Using an implanted electrode, Becker stimulated a rat to regrow its amputated foreleg down to the elbow joint. The portion that grew back was not perfect, but there was clear evidence of multitissue organization, including new muscles, bone, cartilage, and nerve.

Then a researcher at the University of Kentucky Medical School, Dr. Stephen Smith, applied the same technique to regenerating the legs of frogs. A more highly evolved species than the salamander, the frog cannot normally grow back an amputated extremity. But Dr. Smith modified Becker's procedure in one important way. Electricity was introduced through an electrode that migrated down the limb as new tissue grew back. "In one instance," he reported, "a new leg formed in complete anatomical precision, right down to the individual digits of the frog's webbed feet."

For over 20 years Becker has doggedly pursued an unorthodox theory: Higher animals—whether frog, rat, or man—don't naturally regenerate limbs because they produce too little electricity to trigger the formation of a limb bud. Becker has long suspected that, given the appropriate electrical environment, the cells in our body—like those in the salamander—could still be made to differentiate into new tissues.

"It is time the medical establishment accepted the concept that a considerable amount of regenerative growth could be restored to the human," he states in his characteristically forthright manner. "This applies to almost every tissue in the body, from the brain through the spinal cord to peripheral nerves, fingers, whole limbs, and organs. If we can identify the mechanisms that stimulate and control regeneration in the salamander, I see no innate reason why man cannot be stimulated to do the same thing."

Miracles in the Marrow

If the "medical establishment" has been slow in coming round to his viewpoint, it is hardly astonishing. Until Becker's landmark experiment on the rat in 1973, many doctors considered his ideas heretical. That weak currents could transform an amputee's stump into a limb seemed more akin to witchcraft than to medicine. Furthermore, Becker's theory assumed that mammalian cells were capable of extraordinary feats, for the process of regeneration is, in its very essence, a rebirth.

When a salamander regrows a limb or an organ, red blood cells at the injury site lose their specialized function. They return to a primitive, almost prenatal state, ready to be molded anew. In fact, this cluster of amorphous cells is called a blastema, a term sometimes applied to embryonic cells. As the blastema grows in size, the undifferentiated cells become specialized again, regrouping themselves into all the complex tissues of the body part that they are to replace.

No one ever dreamed that mammalian cells could undergo such a dramatic metamorphosis. For a start, our red blood cells, unlike those of the amphibian, have no nuclei and thus do not contain genetic material. Yet when minute electrical currents were applied to the rat's forearm, a blastema formed. Becker's detective work soon solved this mystery. In mammals, the blastema appears to be derived from nucleated cells in the bone marrow.

The implications were far-reaching: We have retained our ancient ancestors' capacity to regenerate! It is only the controlling factor that has been lost over the course of evolution. All the evidence pointed to electricity as the controlling factor, but a central enigma remained. Why do some organisms generate more than others? What drives the injury current?

Acupuncturists have long been aware of electromagnetic fields surrounding the body. Eastern practitioners today commonly monitor variations in these fields to diagnose underlying disease In his effort to track down the "organic battery" that powers the injury current. Becker began to investigate these natural fields. Over a five-year period he measured stable voltages on the skin of organisms ranging from salamander to man. In all instances the fields roughly paralleled the major pathways of the nervous system.

This gave Becker an important lead, for a mysterious link between nerves and regeneration had been known since the early 1950s. Dr. Marcus Singer, at Case Western Reserve University, in Cleveland, showed that nerves must make up at least one third of the total tissue mass in an extremity before regeneration will occur spontaneously. By transplanting extra nerves to a frog's forelimb, he produced about a centimeter of new tissue growth at the amputation site. Could nerves provide the electrical signal that triggers blastema formation?

To find out for sure, Becker carried his investigation one step further. He measured electrical voltage on the outside of the nerve fibers themselves. According to standard textbook accounts, there is only one mechanism by which nerves transmit an electrical signal. That message consists of a series of brief impulses that move down the nerve fiber. Becker, however, discovered what he believes to be a second and most primitive method for the nervous system to transmit information. His measurements indicated that the cells coating the outside of peripheral nerves carry a continuously flowing current, in contrast to the short bursts of electrical activity the nerves themselves conduct. This constant current, he believes, radiates throughout the body's dense network of peripheral nerves and gives rise to the field patterns all organisms display. It seemed logical to him that disturbances in these fields, created by an injury, for example, would be detected by cells, which would then begin repair processes. If the nerve mass were large enough, the voltages generated could be sufficient to initiate complete regeneration. Otherwise, scar tissue would form.

Becker's theory clashed with the traditional concept of how the nervous system functions. "I got an awful lot of lumps on my head when I first published my report in *Nature*," he recalls. But his colleagues' initial skepticism has gradually given way to broader—although by no means universal—acceptance. Neurophysiologists, Becker reports, have been the most receptive to his ideas.

Although there are nonbelievers at a theoretical level, few

doubt the practical significance of Becker's work. A growing number of scientists are now confident—which scientists weren't only a decade ago—that regeneration of human body parts will be achieved, probably within our lifetime. And it was Becker, in conjunction with Bassett, who developed the electrical method of healing bone fractures. The treatment may earn both doctors a Nobel Prize in medicine. (It has been rumored that Becker's name appeared on the Nobel committee's list of nominees last year.)

Ion Messengers

Bone healing is one of the few examples of man's ability to regenerate an injured part spontaneously. "It is truly a regenerative process," says Becker, "because a blastema actually forms." In this instance, however, the source of electrical voltage is not the nerves alone. The bone itself becomes electrically polarized when bent or broken. As Bassett and Becker discovered, its crystalline structure converts mechanical stress into electrical energy, a finding independently made at about the same time by two Japanese doctors, Iwao Yasuda and Eiichi Fukada. These voltages in turn help to guide cellular-repair mechanisms, beginning with the appearance of a blastema at the fracture site. Unfortunately, sometimes something goes awry in the normal healing process and a troublesome nonunion develops. Electricity, they reasoned, might be the solution.

Animal studies confirmed the idea. Then by introducing direct current through an electrode at the fracture Dr. Carl Brighton and his colleagues at the University of Pennsylvania Medical School were able to cure severely crippled patients, many of whom had been scheduled for amputation because their disabled limbs had become infected. At dozens of clinics in the United States and abroad, electricity has become the preferred treatment for difficult bone nonunions. Since the first clinical experiments, however, orthopedists have varied in their approach to electrotherapy. Bassett, for example, prefers electrical coils to electrodes because they preclude surgical intervention. His procedure's success rate is 85 percent; he hopes it will eventually work in 95 to 98 percent of cases.

Relief in Space

Bassett's coils are so simple to operate that astronauts may use them in space to prevent what NASA officials commonly refer to as astro-osteoporosis. Astronauts' bones become thin and brittle owing to a loss of calcium. Over prolonged space missions, the condition worsens. When the Soviet cosmonauts first returned from their 175-day journey aboard *Salyut 6,* they were no more capable of walking than jellyfish are. Vigorous rehabilitation is required to recover from this "spaceman's disease," which for a while threatened to jeopardize the future of manned space exploration.

But astro-osteoporosis is not a disease. In fact, it is a remarkable adaptation to life in zero gravity. "The astronauts produced less bone," says Bassett, "because they didn't need big, heavy bones in the weightlessness of space. Their bone was under less mechanical stress. Hence, it did not generate the normal electrical voltages that help maintain bone formation." The coils, he believes, should counteract what would otherwise be a superior adaptation to permanent residence in space.

Like several other doctors in the forefront of electrical medicine, Bassett is now attacking the problem of repairing damage to the spinal cord—the cause of partial or total body paralysis. Earlier in his career while working with neurosurgeon James B. Campbell, he discovered a simple, nonelectrical technique to promote central-nervous-system growth. After the scientists created a defect in a cat's spinal cord, the injured area would be wrapped in a mille-pore sleeve, a type of filter material. Hundreds of thousands of nerve fibers would grow across the gap.

"Unfortunately," says Bassett, "the lower half of the cat's body remained paralyzed. By the time the nerve fibers had grown back, the motor neurons below the point of transection had formed abnormal connections with neighboring cells—what we call collateral sprouting. The switchboard was busy. There were no free circuits for the nerves to connect to.

"Now what triggers collateral sprouting in the first place is an injury current. To open the switchboard, we then inserted electrodes into the spinal cord. This drove the voltage in the opposite direction, countering the injury current. In fact, we found we could eliminate collateral sprouting in small, defined areas. To do this on a practical basis, however, we would have needed two billion electrodes, each touching an individual cell. But now we can induce currents in the spinal cord using coils. We don't have to make do with electrodes.''

Dogged Experimentation

Bassett has a commanding presence. Behind his facade of determination one senses a warm man who has much compassion for his patients. While we were sitting in his office, one of his experimental subjects—a short-haired beagle—arrived for his inspection. Surrounding its head was a fan-shaped collar, lending the animal the majestic air of an Elizabethan grande dame. The beagle, which Bassett greeted affectionately, had just undergone an experiment studying the effects of electricity on wound healing. The collar prevented the dog from licking the open sore.

"What sore?" I asked, looking over the dog's shiny pelt.

"Well, as you can see, the experiment was successful," Bassett said. "Depending upon the electrical fields we apply it is possible to modify the pattern of wound healing." Very shortly he will be launching clinical studies to see whather the same approach can be used to heal bedsores, which affllict 20 to 30 percent of all invalids.

Equally encouraging, Drs. Walter Booker and E. B. Chung, at Howard University, in Washington, D.C. have been very successful in treating burn victims with pulsed electromagnetic fields. The therapy not only accelerates healing but reduces swelling around the charred flesh. Dr. Chung says, "Patients report almost immediate relief after a single therapeutic session."

A recurrent pattern pervades the history of medicine. Often new treatments are adopted long before anyone fully understands why they work. Electricity is no exception. Becker's meticulous probing has helped to identify several important sources of bioelectricity, from the electrical voltages generated by bone to the electromagnetic fields that radiate from our nerve network. Yet there is an aura of mystery around the magical transformations that take place at the most fundamental level—that of the cell. By intercepting the electrical messages the body transmits, scientists have learned how to code signals that make sense to cells. In effect, they are practicing a form of speech through mimicry— without understanding the basis of the language itself. Wha information is encoded in the electrical signal? Why do cells alter their behavior in response to changes in their electrica environment?

Cellular Fine-Tuning

There are still many more questions than answers, but a few unifying principles have emerged. In an office adjacent to Bassett's, electrochemist Art Pilla develops and finetunes the electromagnetic pulses used in therapy. "In every single living system studied," Pilla says, "we have found that the same level of currents is required to exert cellular control. If the amplitude and frequency of the electromagnetic current do not fall within a specific range, cells fail to respond." Only when he tunes the signal into the "biological waveband" is it possible to establish a dialogue with cells.

In cellular communication, ions—not words—are the key elements. "At the right waveband," Pilla explains, "the electrical signal appears to move ions, such as sodium, magnesium, and calcium, across the selective membrane of the cell. This in turn unleashes a chain of chemical reactions within the cell itself, which may ultimately lead to the unraveling of DNA—the first step toward growth and repair." According to Pilla, the influx of ions may determine, among other things, why some genes are switched on or off. Could electricity transform a cancerous cell into a normal one? Or a bone cell into cartilage? Pilla is seeking the answers to these and other questions that are inextricably tied to genetic control.

Unlike other pioneers in this new field, Pilla did not originally train in biological science. Before he joined the research team at Columbia-Presbyterian, he worked for a battery manufacturer. Then, while flying to the West Coast to attend a conference on electrochemistry, he happened to sit beside a member of Bassett's group.

Today, almost 12 years later, Pilla is convinced that electricity is a revolutionary technique for controlling innumerable processes in the body. "I've always believed in a Morse code approach," he says. "That we could, in fact, send in heavily coded signals and modulate everything. Of course, we don't know how to do it yet!" he exclaims. "But that day is approaching."

Sitting at his computer console, working out the pulsed wave forms he uses, Pilla has the gleeful look of a young child who has just been given a new toy. His enthusiasm is contagious. Dozens of scientists consult him daily over the phone, and he is always entering research projects with them. Every time he gets his hands on a new piece of information, it sparks off yet another idea for an experiment. Working in collaboration with Smith, he has helped develop electrical pulses that will speed salamander limb regeneration by a factor of four—or stop new tissue growth altogether. "In the presence of some fields." says Pilla, "the salamander looks as if it is a nonregenerating form."

Canceling Cancer

Smith and Pilla are also studying the effects of electricity on cancer growth. "We have found certain pulses that kill lymphoma cells grown in culture," Pilla remarks. "Other fields change the cell lining of the lymphoma, transforming it into a fibroblast—a type of connective-tissue cell found throughout the body."

Both scientists caution that their research is still merely at the experimental stage. Yet they are optimistic about the results of one of the first animal studies, which Pilla conducted with William Riegelson, of the Medical College of Virginia, and Larry Norton and Laurie Tansman, of Mount Sinai School of Medicine, in New York City. At the one hundred fifty-seventh meeting of the Electrochemical Society, held in St. Louis last May, the team reported that mice injected with deadly melanoma cells lived an average of 27 days when untreated, 36 days if given chemotherapy, and 43 days when chemotherapy and electricity were combined. Though these early findings are encouraging, more research will be required before electricity's true potential in cancer therapy can be properly evaluated. Pilla notes that the electrical pulses will probably have to be refined for each individual, depending upon the type of cancer.

Cancer therapy is far from the only exciting avenue of research Pilla is now pursuing. He is equally intrigued by the possibility of using electromagnetic fields to alter brain functioning. To test his theories, he is now working with Dr. Ross Adey, president of the Veterans Administration Hospital in Los Angeles. Bassett describes Dr. Adey as "one of the most amazing individuals in biophysics today." Adey has shown that he can increase the rate of learning and memory retention in primates and cats by focusing an electromagnetic field at the animal's head while training is under way. The electrical signal is carried over a radio frequency, and Adey modulates its amplitude in the same way an

AM radio is tuned. Adey believes that neurological changes occur because the frequency of the electrical signals is within the same range as the alpha and beta waves of the brain. But Pilla emphasizes another interesting aspect of his results. He thinks Adey's findings represent a more general phenomenon. The currents he uses to enhance learning and memory just happen to be similar to those that are biologically active in other cell systems.

For the immediate future, most experts agree that electrical therapy will have the greatest impact in healing tissues that do display some regenerative capacity—skin, bone, and peripheral nerves. But as science becomes more sophisticated in controlling vital functions with electricity, infinite possibilities may open up. Conquering cancer, regrowing whole limbs and organs, and augmenting the brain's cognitive processes are just a few of the advances that electrical medicine may offer.

Earlier in this century the introduction of vaccines and antibiotics brought enormous improvements in the treatment of smallpox, scarlet fever, tuberculosis and other infectious diseases. Electricity may bring about a comparable revolution in the treatment of chronic diseases and physical impairments now thought beyond hope. "There is not a single branch of medicine that will remain unchanged as a result of this powerful tool for controlling life processes." Bassett declares.

CHARACTERIZING DESCRIPTION

Water Ouzel
John Muir
from *The Mountains of California*, 1911

Here the authority speaks for himself and gives the public the benefit of long cumulative experience. At the time that naturalist and early environmentalist John Muir published this generalized description, it was the definitive information on a creature as yet little observed by white men and thus served as a kind of encyclopedic entry on the subject (except that it was anything but dry!). His knowledge was virtually all firsthand, but this is neither a casual narrative memoir nor a journalistic sketch. It is logically organized trait by trait and conveys a full profile—not of one water ouzel but of water ouzels as a species—detailing one at a time their appearance, behavior, habitation, song, and so on. The I plays in and out, recounts illustrative anecdotes, and describes in a lively personal voice, giving us a feeling for the source of the information. So though we relapse here into some first person with a distinctive authorial presence, this is a solid, objectively presented exposition of information abstracted from myriad personal experiences into a lasting reference work. It is informal science.

The waterfalls of the Sierra are frequented by only one bird—the ouzel or water thrush (*Cinclus Mexicanus*, Sw.). He is a singularly joyous and lovable little fellow, about the size of a robin, clad in a plain waterproof suit of bluish gray, with a tinge of chocolate on the head and shoulders. In form he is about as smoothly plump and compact as a pebble that had been whirled in a pot-hole, the flowing contour of his body being interrupted only by his strong feet and bill, the crisp wing-tips, and the up-slanted wren-like tail.

Among all the countless waterfalls I have met in the course of ten years' exploration in the Sierra, whether among the icy peaks, or warm foot-hills, or in the profound yosemitic cañons of the middle region, not one was found without its ouzel. No cañon is too cold for this little bird, none too lonely, provided it be rich in falling water. Find a fall, or cascade, or rushing rapid, anywhere upon a clear stream, and there you will surely find its complementary ouzel, flitting about in the spray, diving in foaming eddies, whirling like a leaf among beaten foam-bells; ever vigorous and enthusiastic, yet self-contained, and neither seeking nor shunning your company.

If disturbed while dipping about in the margin shallows, he either sets off with a rapid whir to some other feeding-ground up or down the stream, or alights on some half-submerged rock or snag out in the current, and immediately begins to nod and curtsey like a wren, turning his head from side to side with many other odd dainty movements that never fail to fix the attention of the observer.

He is the mountain streams' own darling, the hummingbird of blooming waters, loving rocky ripple slopes and sheets of foam as a bee loves flowers, as a lark loves sunshine and meadows. Among all the mountain birds, none has cheered me so much in my lonely wanderings—none so unfailingly. For both in winter and summer he sings, sweetly, cheerily, independent alike of sunshine and of love, requiring no other inspiration than the stream on which he dwells. While water sings, so must he, in heat or cold, calm or storm, ever attuning his voice in sure accord; low in the drought of summer and the drought of winter, but never silent.

During the golden days of Indian summer, after most of the snow has been melted, and the mountain streams have become feeble—a succession of silent pools, linked together by shallow, transparent currents and strips of silvery lace-work—then the song of the ouzel is at its lowest ebb. But as soon as the winter clouds have bloomed, and the mountain treasuries are once more replenished with snow, the voices of the streams and ouzels increase in strength and richness until the flood season of early summer. Then the torrents chant their noblest anthems, and then is the flood-time of our songster's melody. As for weather, dark days and sun days are the same to him. The voices of most songbirds, however joyous, suffer a long winter eclipse; but the ouzel sings on through all the seasons and every kind of storm. Indeed, no storm can be more violent than those of the waterfalls in the midst of which he delights to dwell. However dark and boisterous the weather, snowing, blowing, or cloudy, all the same he sings, and with never a note of sadness. No need of spring sunshine to thaw *his* song, for it never freezes. Never shall you hear anything wintery from *his* warm breast; no pinched cheeping, no wavering notes between sorrow and joy; his mellow, fluty voice is ever tuned to downright gladness, as free from dejection as cock-crowing.

It is pitiful to see wee frost-pinched sparrows on cold mornings in the mountain groves shaking the snow from their feathers, and hopping about as if anxious to be cheery, then hastening back to their hidings out of the wind, puffing out their breast feathers over their toes, and subsiding among the leaves, cold and breakfastless, while the snow continues to fall, and there is no sign of clearing. But the ouzel never calls forth a single touch of pity; not because he is strong to endure, but rather because he seems to live a charmed life beyond the reach of every influence that makes endurance necessary.

One wild winter morning, when Yosemite Valley was swept its length from west to east by a cordial snowstorm, I sallied forth to see what I might learn and enjoy. A sort of gray, gloaming-like darkness filled the valley, the huge walls were out of sight, all ordinary sounds were smothered, and even the loudest booming of the falls was at times buried beneath the roar of the heavy-laden blast. The loose snow was already over five feet deep on the meadows, making extended walks impossible without the aid snowshoes. I found no great difficulty, however, in making my way to a certain ripple on the river where one of my ouzels lived. He was at home, busily gleaning his breakfast among the pebbles of a shallow portion of the margin, apparently unaware of anything extraordinary in the weather. Presently he flew out to a stone against which the icy current was beating, and turning his back to the wind, sang as delightfully as a lark in springtime.

After spending an hour or two with my favorite, I made my way across the valley, boring and wallowing through the drifts, to learn as definitely as possible how the other birds were spending their time. The Yosemite birds are easily found during the winter because all of them excepting the ouzel are restricted to the sunny north side of the valley, the south side being constantly eclipsed by the great frosty shadow of the wall. And because the Indian Cañon groves, from their peculiar exposure are the warmest, the birds congregate there, more especially in severe weather.

I found most of the robins cowering on the lee side of the larger branches where the snow could not fall upon them, while two or three of the more enterprising were making desperate efforts to reach the mistletoe berries by clinging nervously to the under side of the snow-crowned masses, back downward, like woodpeckers. Every now and then they would dislodge some of the loose fringes of the snow-crown, which would come sifting down on them and send them screaming back to camp, where they would subside among their companions with a shiver, muttering in low, querulous chatter like hungry children.

Some of the sparrows were busy at the feet of the larger trees gleaning seeds and benumbed insects, joined now and then by a robin weary of his unsuccessful attempts upon the snow-covered berries. The brave woodpeckers were clinging to the snowless sides of the larger boles and overarching branches of the camp trees, making short flights from side to side of the grove, pecking now and then at the acorns they had stored in the bark, and chattering aimlessly as if unable to keep still, yet evidently putting in the time in a very dull way, like storm-bound travelers at a country tavern. The hardy nuthatches were threading the open furrows of the trunks in their usual industrious manner, and uttering their quaint notes, evidently less distressed than their neighbors. The Steller's jays were, of course, making more noisy stir than all the other birds combined; ever coming and going with loud bluster, screaming as if each had a lump of melting sludge in his throat, and taking good care to improve the favorable opportunity afforded by the storm to steal from the acorn stores of the woodpeckers. I also noticed one solitary gray eagle braving the storm on the top of a tall Pine stump just outside the main grove. He was standing bolt upright with his back to the wind, a tuft of snow piled on his square shoulders, a monument of passive endurance. Thus every snow-bound bird seemed more or less uncomfortable if not in positive distress. The storm was reflected in every gesture, and not one cheerful note, not to say song, came from a single bill; their cowering, joyless endurance offering a striking contrast to the spontaneous, irrepressible gladness of the ouzel, who could no more help exhaling sweet song than a rose sweet fragrance. He *must* sing, though the heavens fall. I remember noticing the distress of a pair of robins during the violent earthquake of the year 1872, when the Pines of the valley, with strange movements, flapped and waved their branches, and beetling rock brows came thundering down to the meadows in tremendous avalanches. It did not occur to me in the midst of the excitement of other observations to look for the ouzels, but I doubt not they were singing straight on through it all, regarding the terrible rock thunder as fearlessly as they do the booming of the waterfalls.

What may be regarded as the separate songs of the ouzel are exceedingly difficult of description, because they are so variable and at the same time so confluent. Though I have been acquainted with my favorite ten years, and during most of this time have heard him sing nearly every day, I still detect notes and strains that seem new to me. Nearly all of his music is sweet and tender, lapsing from his round breast like water over the smooth lip of a pool, then breaking farther on into a sparkling foam of melodious notes, which glow with subdued enthusiasm, yet without expressing much of the strong, gushing ecstasy of the bobolink or skylark.

The more striking strains are perfect arabesques of melody, composed of a few full, round, mellow notes, embroidered with delicate trills which fade and melt in long slender cadences. In a general way his music is that of the streams refined and spiritualized. The deep booming notes of the falls are in it, the trills of rapids, the gurgling of margin eddies, the low whispering of level reaches, and the sweet tinkle of separate drops oozing from the ends of mosses and falling into tranquil pools.

The ouzel never sings in chorus with other birds, nor with his kind, but only with the streams. And like flowers that bloom beneath the surface of the ground, some of our favorite's best song-blossoms never rise above the surface of the heavier music of the water. I have often observed him singing in the midst of beaten spray, his music completely buried beneath the water's roar; yet I knew he was surely singing by his gestures and the movements of his bill.

His food, as far as I have noticed, consists of all kinds of water insects, which in summer are chiefly procured along shallow margins. Here he wades about ducking his head under water and deftly turning over pebbles and fallen leaves with his bill, seldom choosing to go into deep water where he has to use his wings in diving.

He seems to be especially fond of the larvae of mosquitoes, found in abundance attached to the bottom of smooth rock channels where the current is shallow. When feeding in such places he wades upstream, and often while his head is under water the swift current is deflected upward along the glossy curves of his neck and shoulders, in the form of a clear, crystalline shell, which fairly incloses him like a bell-glass, the shell being broken and re-formed as he lifts and dips his head; while ever and anon he sidles out to where the too powerful current carries him off his feet; then he dexterously rises on the wing and goes gleaning again in shallower places.

But during the winter, when the stream banks are embossed in snow, and the streams themselves are chilled nearly to the freezing-point, so that the snow falling into them in stormy weather is not wholly dissolved, but forms a thin, blue sludge, thus rendering the current opaque—then he seeks the deeper portions of the main rivers, where he may dive to clear water beneath the sludge. Or he repairs to some open lake or millpond, at the bottom of which he feeds in safety.

When thus compelled to betake himself to a lake, he does not plunge into it at once like a duck, but always alights in the first place upon some rock or fallen Pine along the shore. Then flying out thirty or forty yards, more or less, according to the character of the bottom, he alights with a dainty glint on the surface, swims about, looks down, finally makes up his mind, and disappears with a sharp stroke of his wings. After feeding for two or three minutes, he suddenly reappears, showers the water from his wings with one vigorous shake, and rises abruptly into the air as if pushed up from beneath, comes back to his perch, sings a few minutes, and goes out to dive again; thus coming and going, singing and diving at the same place for hours.

The ouzel is usually found singly; rarely in pairs, excepting during the breeding-season, and *very* rarely in threes or fours. I once observed three thus spending a winter morning in company, upon a small glacier lake, on the Upper Merced, about seventy-five hundred feet above the level of the sea. A storm had occurred during the night, but the morning sun shone unclouded, and the shadowy lake, gleaming darkly in its setting of fresh snow, lay smooth and motionless as a mirror. My camp chanced to be within a few feet of the water's edge, opposite a fallen Pine, some of the branches of which leaned out over the lake. Here my three dearly welcome visitors took up their stations, and at once began to embroider the frosty air with their delicious melody, doubly delightful to me that particular morning, as I had been somewhat apprehensive of danger in breaking my way down through the snow-choked cañons to the lowlands.

The portion of the lake bottom selected for a feeding-ground lies at a depth of fifteen or twenty feet below the surface, and is covered with a short growth of algae and other aquatic plants—facts I had previously determined while sailing over it on a raft. After alighting on the glassy surface, they occasionally indulged in a little play, chasing one another round about in small circles; then all three would suddenly dive together, and then come ashore and sing.

The ouzel seldom swims more than a few yards on the surface, for, not being web-footed, he makes rather slow progress, but by means of his strong, crisp wings he swims, or rather flies, with celerity under the surface, often to considerable distances. But it is in withstanding the force of heavy rapids that his strength of wing in this respect is most strikingly manifested. The following may be regarded as a fair illustration of his power of sub-aquatic flight. One stormy morning in winter when the Merced River was blue and green with unmelted snow, I observed one of my ouzels perched on a snag out in the midst of a swift-rushing rapid, singing cheerily, as if everything was just to his mind; and while I stood on the bank admiring him, he suddenly plunged into the sludgy current, leaving his song abruptly broken off. After feeding a minute or two at the bottom, and when one would suppose that he must inevitably be swept far downstream, he emerged just where he went down, alighted on the same snag, showered the water beads from his feathers, and continued his unfinished song, seemingly in tranquil ease as if it had suffered no interruption.

The ouzel alone of all birds dares to enter a white torrent. And though strictly terrestrial in structure, no other is so inseparably related to water, not even the duck, or the bold ocean albatross, or the stormy petrel. For ducks go ashore as soon as they finish feeding in undisturbed places, and very often make long flights overland from lake to lake or field to field. The same is true of most other aquatic birds. But the ouzel, born on the brink of a stream, or on a snag or boulder in the midst of it, seldom leaves it for a single moment. For, notwithstanding he is often on the wing, he never flies overland, but whirs with rapid, quail-like beat above the stream, tracing all its windings. Even when the stream is quite small, say from five to ten feet wide, he seldom shortens his flight by crossing a bend, however abrupt it may be; and even when disturbed by meeting some one on the bank, he prefers to fly over one's head, to dodging out over the ground. When, therefore, his flight along a crooked stream is viewed endwise, it appears most strikingly wavered—a description on the air of every curve with lightning-like rapidity.

The vertical curves and angles of the most precipitous torrents he traces with the same rigid fidelity, swooping down the inclines of cascades, dropping sheer over dizzy falls amid the spray, and ascending with the same fearlessness and ease, seldom seeking to lessen the steepness of the acclivity by beginning to ascend before reaching the base of the fall. No matter though it may be several hundred feet in height he holds straight on, as if about to dash headlong into the throng of booming rockets, then darts abruptly upward, and, after alighting at the top of the precipice to rest a moment, proceeds to feed and sing. His flight is solid and impetuous, without any intermission of wing-beats—one homogeneous buzz like that of a laden bee on its way home. And while thus buzzing freely from fall to fall, he is frequently heard giving utterance to a long outdrawn train of unmodulated notes, in no way connected with his song, but corresponding closely with his flight in sustained vigor.

Were the flights of all the ouzels in the Sierra traced on a chart, they would indicate the direction of the flow of the entire system of ancient glaciers, from about the period of the breaking up of the ice-sheet until near the close of the glacial winter; because the streams which the ouzels so rigidly follow are, with the unimportant exceptions of a few side tributaries, all flowing in channels eroded for them out of the solid flank of the range by the vanished glaciers—the streams tracing the ancient glaciers, the ouzels tracing the streams. Nor do we find so complete compliance to glacial conditions in the life of any other mountain bird, or animal of any kind. Bears frequently accept the pathways laid down by glaciers as the easiest to travel; but they often leave them and cross over from cañon to cañon. So also, most of the birds trace the moraines to some extent, because the forests are growing on them. But they wander far, crossing the cañons from grove to grove, and draw exceedingly angular and complicated courses.

The ouzel's nest is one of the most extraordinary pieces of bird architecture I ever saw, odd and novel in design, perfectly fresh and beautiful, and in every way worthy of the genius of the little builder. It is about a foot in diameter, round and bossy in outline, with a neatly arched opening near the bottom, somewhat like an old-fashioned brick oven, or Hottentot's hut. It is built almost exclusively of green and yellow mosses, chiefly the beautiful fronded hypnum that covers the rocks and old drift-logs in the vicinity of waterfalls. These are deftly interwoven, and felted together into a charming little hut; and so situated that many of the outer mosses continue to flourish as if they had not been plucked. A few fine, silky-stemmed grasses are occasionally found interwoven with the mosses, but, with the exception of a thin layer lining the floor, their presence seems accidental, as they are of a species found growing with the mosses and are probably plucked with them. The site chosen for this curious mansion is usually some little rock shelf within reach of the lighter particles of the spray of a waterfall, so that its walls are kept green and growing, at least during the time of high water.

No harsh lines are presented by any portion of the nest as seen in place, but when removed from its shelf, the back and bottom, and sometimes a portion of the top, is found quite sharply angular, because it is made to conform to the surface of the rock upon which and against which it is built, the little architect always taking advantage of slight crevices and protuberances that may chance to offer, to render his structure stable by means of a kind of gripping and dovetailing.

In choosing a building-spot, concealment does not seem to be taken into consideration; yet notwithstanding the nest is large and guilelessly exposed to view, it is far from being easily detected, chiefly because it swells forward like any other bulging moss cushion growing naturally in such situations. This is more especially the case where the nest is kept fresh by being well sprinkled. Sometimes these romantic little huts have their beauty enhanced by rock ferns and grasses that spring up around the mossy walls, or in front of the doorsill, dripping with crystal beads.

Furthermore, at certain hours of the day, when the sunshine is poured down at the required angle, the whole mass of the spray enveloping the fairy establishment is brilliantly irised; and it is through so glorious a rainbow atmosphere as this that some of our blessed ouzels obtain their first peep at the world.

Ouzels seem so completely part and parcel of the streams they inhabit, they scarce suggest any other origin than the streams themselves; and one might almost be pardoned in fancying they come direct from the living waters, like flowers from the ground. At least, from whatever cause, it never occurred to me to look for their nests until more than a year after I had made the acquaintance of the birds themselves, although I found one the very day on which I began to search. In making my way from Yosemite to the glaciers at the heads of the Merced and Tuolumne Rivers, I camped in a particularly wild and romantic portion of the Nevada cañon where in previous excursions I had never failed to enjoy the company of my favorites, who were attracted here, no doubt, by the safe nesting-places in the shelving rocks, and by the abundance of food and falling water. The river, for miles above and below, consisted of a succession of small falls from ten to sixty feet in height, connected by flat, plume-like cascades that go flashing from fall to fall, free and almost channelless, over waving folds of glacier-polished granite.

On the south side of one of the falls, that portion of the precipice bathed by the spray presents a series of little shelves and tablets caused by the development of planes of cleavage in the granite, and by the consequent fall of masses through the action of the water. "Now, here," said I, "of all places, is the most charming spot for an ouzel's nest." Then carefully scanning the fretted face of the precipice through the spray, I at length noticed a yellowish moss cushion, growing on the edge of a level tablet within five or six feet of the outer folds of the fall. But apart from the fact of its being situated where one acquainted with the lives of ouzels would fancy an ouzel's nest ought to be, there was nothing in its appearance visible at first sight, to distinguish it from other bosses of rock-moss similarly situated with reference to perennial spray; and it was not until I had scrutinized it again and again, and had removed my shoes and stockings and crept along the face of the rock within eight or ten feet of it, that I could decide certainly whether it was a nest or a natural growth.

In these moss huts three or four eggs were laid, white like foam bubbles; and well may the little birds hatched from them sing water-songs, for they hear them all their lives, and even before they are born.

I have often observed the young just out of the next making their odd gestures, and seeming in every way as much at home as their experienced parents, like young bees on their first excursions to the flower fields. No amount of familiarity with people and their ways seems to change them in the least. To all appearance their behavior is just the same on seeing a man for the first time, as when they have seen him frequently.

On the lower reaches of the rivers where mills are built, they sing on through the din of the machinery, and all the noisy confusion of dogs, cattle, and workmen. On one occasion, while a wood-chopper was at work on the river-bank, I observed one cheerily singing within reach of the flying chips. Nor does any kind of unwonted disturbance put him in bad humor, or frighten him out of calm self-possession. In passing through a narrow gorge, I once drove one ahead of me from rapid to rapid, disturbing him four times in quick succession where he could not very well fly past me on account of the narrowness of the channel. Most birds under similar circumstances fancy themselves pursued, and become suspiciously uneasy; but, instead of growing nervous about it, he made his usual dippings, and sang one of his most tranquil strains. When observed within a few yards their eyes are seen to express remarkable gentleness and intelligence; but they seldom allow so near a view unless one wears clothing of about the same color as the rocks and trees, and knows how to sit still. On one occasion, while rambling along the shore of a mountain lake, where the birds, at least those born that season, had never seen a man, I sat down to rest on a large stone close to the water's edge, upon which it seemed the ouzels and sandpipers were in the habit of alighting when they came to feed on that part of the shore, and some of the other birds also, when they came down to wash or drink. In a few minutes, along came a whirring ouzel and alighted on the stone beside me, within reach of my hand. Then suddenly observing me, he stooped nervously as if about to fly on the instant, but as I remained as motionless as the stone, he gained confidence, and looked me steadily in the face for about a minute, then flew quietly to the outlet and began to sing. Next came a sandpiper and gazed at me with much the same guileless expression of eye as the ouzel. Lastly, down with a swoop came a Steller's jay out of a Fir tree, probably with the intention of moistening his noisy throat. But instead of sitting confidingly as my other visitors had done, he rushed off at once, nearly tumbling heels over head into the lake in his suspicious confusion, and with loud screams roused the neighborhood.

Love for songbirds, with their sweet human voices, appears to be more common and unfailing than love for flowers. Every one loves flowers to some extent, at least in life's fresh morning, attracted by them as instinctively as hummingbirds and bees. Even the young Digger Indians have sufficient love for the brightest of those found growing on the mountains to gather them and braid them as decorations for the hair. And I was glad to discover, through the few Indians that could be induced to talk on the subject, that they have names for the wild rose and the lily, and other conspicuous flowers, whether available as food or otherwise. Most men, however, whether savage or civilized, become apathetic toward all plants that have no other apparent use than the use of beauty. But fortunately one's first instinctive love of songbirds is never wholly obliterated, no matter what the influences upon our lives may be. I have often been delighted to see a pure, spiritual glow come into the countenances of hard business men and old miners, when a songbird chanced to alight near them. Nevertheless, the little mouthful of meat that swells out the breasts of some songbirds is too often the cause of their death. Larks and robins in particular are brought to market in hundreds. But fortunately the ouzel has no enemy so eager to eat his little body as to follow him into the mountain solitudes. I never knew him to be chased even by hawks.

An acquaintance of mine, a sort of foot-hill mountaineer, had a pet cat, a great, dozy, overgorwn creature, about as broad-shouldered as a lynx. During the winter, while the snow lay deep, the mountaineer sat in his lonely cabin among the Pines smoking his pipe and wearing the dull time away. Tom was his sole companion, sharing his bed, and sitting beside him on a stool with much the same drowsy expression of eye as his master. The good-natured bachelor was content with his hard fare of soda bread and bacon, but Tom, the only creature in the world acknowledging dependence on him, must needs be provided with fresh meat. Accordingly he bestirred himself to contrive squirrel traps, and waded the snowy woods with his gun, making sad havoc among the few winter birds, sparing neither robin, sparrow, nor tiny nuthatch, and the pleasure of seeing Tom eat and grow fat was his great reward.

One cold afternoon, while hunting along the river-bank, he noticed a plain-feathered little bird skipping about in the shallows, and immediately raised his gun. But just then the confiding songster began to sing, and after listening to his summery melody the charmed hunter turned away, saying, "Bless your little heart, I can't shoot you, not even for Tom."

Even so far north as icy Alaska, I have found my glad singer. When I was exploring the glaciers between Mount Fairweather and the Strickeen River, one cold day in November, after trying in vain to force a way through the innumerable icebergs of Sum Dum Bay to the great glaciers at the head of it, I was weary and baffled and sat resting in my canoe convinced at last that I would have to leave this part of my work for another year. Then I began to plan my escape to open water before the young ice which was beginning to form should shut me in. While I thus lingered drifting with the bergs, in the midst of these gloomy forebodings and all the terrible glacial desolation and grandeur, I suddenly heard the well-known whir of an ouzel's wings, and, looking up saw my little comforter coming straight across the ice from the shore. In a second or two he was with me, flying three times round my head with a happy salute, as if saying, "Cheer up, old friend; you see I'm here, and all's well." Then he flew back to the shore, alighted on the topmost jag of a stranded iceberg, and began to nod and bow as though he were on one of his favorite boulders in the midst of a sunny Sierra cascade.

The species is distributed all along the mountain ranges of the Pacific Coast from Alaska to Mexico, and east to the Rocky Mountains. Nevertheless, it is as yet comparatively little known. Audubon and Wilson did not meet it. Swainson was, I believe, the first naturalist to describe a specimen from Mexico. Specimens were shortly afterward procured by Drummond near the sources of the Athabasca River, between the fifty-fourth and fifty-sixth parallels; and it has been collected by nearly all of the numerous exploring expeditions undertaken of late through our Western States and Territories; for it never fails to engage the attention of naturalists in a very particular manner.

Such then, is our little cinclus, beloved of every one who is so fortunate as to know him. Tracing on strong wing every curve of the most precipitous torrents from one extremity of the Sierra to the other; not fearing to follow them through their darkest gorges and coldest snow-tunnels; acquainted with every waterfall, echoing their divine music; and throughout the whole of their beautiful lives interpreting all that we in our unbelief call terrible in the utterances of torrents and storms, as only varied expressions of God's eternal love.

ENCYCLOPEDIC ENTRY

Mullein
Michael Moore
from *Medicinal Plants of the Mountain West*, 1979

This is an actual encyclopedic entry from a reference book entirely written by one person and in an engaging style. It is based on both personal experience and book research, highly compacted together. The description is organized trait-by-trait like "Water Ouzel" but is fitted into a format that is the same for all entries since they are all about the same type of item. Handbooks represent highly condensed information, but the subject matter in this case is very concrete and simple.

Verbascum thapsus Scrophulariaceae

OTHER NAMES: Velvet Plant, Blanket Leaf, Candlewick, Punchón, Gordolobo

APPEARANCE: Mullein is a distinctive plant wherever it is found and, like Burdock and Evening Primrose, is generally a biennial. The first year the plant forms a rosette of large basal leaves and a light-colored taproot. The second year the single thick flower stalk is formed. All parts of the plant are densely hairy and flannellike, with the yellowish sap forming small blackish splotches where it has been bruised or pierced by insects. The single phalluslike stalk is completely covered with tight little flower buds, small yellow flowers, and round tiny-seeded pods, all intermixed. Some plants may form several flowering branches if the season is long or insect attack has stunted the main stem, but such plants are an exception. The normal two-year cycle is variable in lower warm or higher cold altitudes; some individuals may be annual or survive three or four years.

HABITAT: Elsewhere Mullein is a plant of waste places, but in the West it has found a solid niche in the areas between the Juniper/Piñon and Ponderosa belts, blanketing roadsides and disturbed earth. In California it is more common in the inland ranges, forming sporadic stands in the San Bernardino Mountains and Sierra Madres, but found only infrequently in the coastal ranges and Sierra Nevada foothills, generally above 4,500 feet. Mullein is common but intermittent in the central and northern parts of Arizona and widespread in the Rockies and other ranges of the inland West.

COLLECTING: The large basal leaves of the second-year plants are preferable; they must be washed well, squeezed out, and dried. If being dried for smoking, the stems should be cut away before drying; otherwise, the leaves are dried intact and crushed for tea. The flowers and buds should be removed singly while still fresh in whatever manner seems appropriate. It is a time-consuming job and the lazier picker may treat the stalks like corncobs, slicing off the flowers, buds, and pods in a rape-and-pillage fashion. Being a trifle fussy (and purer of heart) I pluck them out singly with a pointed grapefruit spoon left over from my California years, delicately prying them out with the spoon tip and my thumb . . . a sort of Mullein-flower yoga. Although it might seem easier to simply uproot a whole plant and gut it later at a more appropriate time, this allows the plant to draw in its sap to the thick stem. Flowers and leaves subsequently removed will be substandard. Leaves should be removed in the field although the flowers may be removed from lopped off spikes within the same day. The roots are sliced and dried.

MEDICINAL USE: Mullein is an herb for the lungs and throat and can be consumed in any rational quantity needed, being basically free of toxicity. It is a mild sedative to the lungs and is especially useful in the initial stages of an infection, when there is a mild fever, a raspiness in the throat, and a hot, dry feeling in the chest. Its effect decreases when the infection is broken and an expectorant is needed. A tablespoon of the slightly disagreeable leaves, well crushed, is steeped in sweetened water and drunk slowly during the day. The flowers are far preferable for a more energetic infection, relaxing bronichial spasm and acting as a mild sedative. Boiling water is poured over five to ten of the flowers and steeped for at least ten minutes, drunk slowly, and repeated as often as needed. People with strong skin sensitivities should take the trouble to filter the tea through a fine cloth—especially the flowers, since the coarse hairs can cause irritation to the throat membranes. Most individuals find this no problem, but people with many allergies might react to the flowers; this is noticeable immediately, causing a slight reflex contraction of the throat.

The chopped leaves have been smoked for centuries to relax spasmodic coughing in chest infections, and asthma, and can be used with Lobelia or Jimson Weed for greater effect. A useful earache oil can be made from equal volumes of the fresh flowers and olive oil, steeped over the water heater for several weeks and strained. This can be warmed slightly, then several drops placed in the ear canal, which will be found especially useful for small children and pets with ear mites. The root is also a diuretic and urinary tract astringent. One-half teaspoon in one-fourth cup of water drunk before retiring will incease the tone of the triangular base of the bladder (the trigone) and aid in preventing bed-wetting or incontinence.

CULTIVATION: From the tiny ripe seeds, sown anywhere in the fall. Mullein is a useful and safe remedy but is not always common, particularly in California, so cultivation or wild sowing might be appropriate.

OTHER USES: Although not comparable in luxuriance to two-ply scented bathroom tissue, it is sort of floral designed, and may be used similarly . . . and there is no chance of confusing it with poison oak.

Myth
Mircea Eliade
from *Man, Myth, and Magic,*
an encyclopedia, 1970

One of the world's greatest authorities on comparative religion condenses into a few pages the gist of his vast knowledge of mythology but saves room to give examples of his broad generalizations, which span many centuries and many cultures.

Although such knowledge comes mainly from book research, in the case of an erudite specialist this knowledge has been individually acquired over many years and supplemented and adjusted by pertinent travels and communications with other scholars. Such a person speaks as a member of a chorus made up not only of the contemporary community of colleagues but of the past authors of the books consulted and extended today.

The compactness itself of encyclopedic entries requires great abstracting because so much material is compressed into so little space. And in the case of a subject like myth, the material itself contains abstractions in the form of folk symbols.

For the Greeks, *mythos* meant 'fable,' 'tale,' 'talk,' 'speech,' but finally came to denote 'what cannot really exist.' The earliest Greek philosophers had criticized and rejected the Homeric myths as fictions and inventions. Xenophanes (6th—5th century B.C.) rejected the immortality of the gods as described by Homer and Hesiod. He especially criticized picturing the gods in human form (anthropomorphism). 'But if cattle and horses or lions had hands, or were able to draw with their hands and do the works that man can do, horses would draw the forms of gods like horses, and cattle like cattle, and they would make their bodies such as they each had themselves.'

In these critiques of Homeric mythology may be seen an effort to free the concept of divinity from the anthropomorphic expressions of the poets. Nevertheless, the mythology of Homer and Hesiod continued to interest the elite in all parts of the Hellenistic world. But the myths were no longer taken literally; what was now sought was their 'hidden meanings.' The Stoics developed the *allegorical interpretation* of Homeric mythology and, in general, of all religious traditions. For example, when the myth says that Zeus bound Hera, the episode really signifies that the ether is the limit of the air, and so on. Another very successful interpretation was *euhemerism*, called after Euhemerus (early 3rd century B.C.): he tried to prove that gods were ancient kings who had been deified. Consequently, the myths represented the confused memory or an imaginative transfiguration of the exploits of the primitive kings. The Christian apologists borrowed this Hellenistic interpretation of mythology. For them, myths were fictional stories, full of falsehood and absurdities, to be rejected as abominations.

It is only in the past 50 years that Western scholars have

discovered the primary and true meaning of myth. But the scientific study of mythology was already popular in the second half of the 19th century, especially through the works of Max Müller, Andrew Lang and Sir James Frazer. According to Müller, mythology was a 'disease of language.' Lang asserted that myths result from a personification of natural forces or phenomena, a mental process characteristic of the animistic stage of culture. Frazer regarded myths as mistaken explanations of human or natural phenomena. At the beginning of the century, Freud and Jung gave a new impetus to the study of myths by pointing out the striking similarities between their contents and the world of the unconscious.

Myth—a True Story

But the new and positive approach to myth is greatly indebted to the results of modern ethnology. The scientific study of archaic societies—those societies in which mythology is, or was until recently, 'living'—has revealed that myth, for the 'primitive' man, means a *true story* and, beyond that, a story that is a most precious treasure because it is *sacred, exemplary* and *significant*.

This new value given the term 'myth' makes its use in contemporary parlance somehow equivocal. Today the word is employed both in the old sense, inherited from the Greeks, of 'fiction' or 'illusion,' and in the sense familiar to historians of religions, the sense of 'sacred tradition, primordial revelation, exemplary model.'

In general, one can say that in every case where we have access to a still living tradition, any myth *tells how something came into being*. The 'something' may be the world, or man, or an animal species, or a social institution. Myth, then, is always an account of a 'creation'; it relates how something was produced, began to be. Myth tells only of that which *really happened*. The actors in myths are supernatural beings. They are known principally by what they did in the times of the beginnings. Hence myths disclose their creative activity and reveal the sacredness (or simply the supernaturalness) of their works. It is this intervention of supernatural beings that made the world what it is today. The myth is regarded as a sacred story and hence a 'true-story,' because it always deals with realities. The myth which tells how the world was made is 'true' because the existence of the world is there to prove it; the myth of the origin of death is equally true because man's mortality proves it, and so on.

Because myth relates the acts of supernatural beings and the manifestation of their sacred powers, it becomes the exemplary model for all significant human activities. 'We must do what the gods did in the beginning,' proclaims a well-known Brahmanic text. 'It was thus that the (mythical) Ancestors did, and we do likewise,' declare the Kai of New Guinea.

What happened in the beginning can be repeated by the power of rites. For this reason it is essential to know the myths. By recollecting the myths, by re-enacting them, the man of archaic societies is able to repeat what the Gods, the Heroes or the Ancestors did in the times of the beginnings. To quote only one example: a certain tribe live by fishing—because in mythical times a Supernatural Being taught their ancestors to catch and cook fish. The myth *tells the story* of the first fishery, and in so doing, at once *reveals* a superhuman act, *teaches* men the way to perform it, and finally *explains why* this particular tribe *must* procure their food in this way. For archaic man, myth is a matter of primary importance, for it concerns him directly, in his existence on earth.

The Great Themes

This *existential function of myth* explains why a number of major themes are common to different mythologies. Cosmogonic myths (those describing the creation of the universe) and myths of origin, for example, are to be found everywhere. Destruction of an old world and creation of a new is likewise a largely distributed theme. Myths of the creation of mankind appear to be universal, though the story may vary: the first humans were created by Mother Earth and Father Sky, or by a bisexual deity, or were fashioned from earth or from vegetables by a creator, and so on.

But every mythical account of the *origin* of anything presupposes and continues the *cosmogony*—the story of the world's creation. The creation of the world being the preeminent instance of creation, the cosmogony becomes the exemplary model for creation of every kind. This is why the fabulous history of the dynasties in Tibet opens by rehearsing the birth of the cosmos from an egg. The Polynesian genealogical chants begin in the same way. Such ritual genealogical chants are composed by the bards when the princess is pregnant, and they are communicated to the hula dancers to be learned by heart. The dancers, men and women, dance and recite the chant continuously until the child is born. It is as if the embryological development of the future chief were accompanied by a recapitulation of the cosmogony, the history of the world and the history of the tribe. The gestation of a chief is the occasion for a symbolic re-creation of the world.

The periodic renewal of the world through a symbolic repetition of the cosmogony is found among many primitive and archaic people. In Mesopotamia the creation of the world was ritually reiterated during the New Year festival. A series of rites re-enacted the fight between Marduk and Tiamat (the dragon symbolizing the primordial ocean), the victory of the god, and his world-creating labours. The 'Poem of Creation' (*Enuma elish*) was recited in the temple. But the cosmogony was symbolically repeated also at other important or critical moments; for example (as in Egypt and Fiji) on the accession of a new sovereign.

The End of the World

Myths of cosmic cataclysms are extremely widespeard among primitives. They tell how the world was destroyed and mankind annihilated except for a single couple or a few survivors. These myths—implying as they do in clearer or darker fashion, the re-creation of a new universe—express the archaic and universal idea of the progressive degradation of a cosmos, necessitating its periodical destruction and re-creation.

The myth of the end of the world was also popular in ancient India, Mesopotamia, Persia and Greece. In Judaeo-Christian theory, the end of the world will occur only once, just as the cosmogony occurred only once. The cosmos that will reappear after the catastrophe will be the same cosmos that God created at the beginning of time, but purified, regenerated, restored to its original glory. This earthly paradise will not be destroyed again but will have no end.

Paradise Regained

Now it is especially this type of myth that admirably illustrates the relevance and significance of mythology to people today. For the myth of the end of the world is at the centre of countless prophetic movements, of which the best known are the Oceanian Cargo Cults. These movements announce that the world is about to be destroyed and that the tribe will regain a kind of paradise: the dead will rise again and there will be neither death nor sickness. But this new creation—or recovery of paradise—will be preceded by a series of cosmic catastrophes. The earth will shake, there will be rains of fire, the mountains will crumble and fill the valleys, the whites and the natives who have not joined the cult will be annihilated. Thus, in 1923 the prophet Ronovuro, of the island of Espiritu Santo (New Hebrides), predicted a flood to be followed by the return of the dead in cargo ships loaded with rice and other provision. In 1933, in the valley of Markham in New Guinea, a man named Marafi declared that the return of the dead would be preceded by a cosmic cataclysm; but the next day it would be found that the dead had already arrived, loaded with gifts, and there would be no need for the people ever again to work.

Similar phenomena occurred in the Congo when the country became independent in 1960. In some villages the inhabitants tore the roofs off their huts to give passage to the gold that their ancestors were to rain down. Elsewhere everything was allowed to go to rack and ruin, except the roads to the cemetery, by which the ancestors would make their way to the village. Even the orgiastic excesses had a meaning, for according to the myth, from the dawn of the New Age all women would be held in common by all men.

Scenario for Superman

Another example of the relevance of mythology to modern man is the extremely widespread myth of the Hero. He is abandoned immediately after his birth because of a prophecy threatening danger to his father, a king. The child is saved by animals or shepherds and is suckled by a female animal or by a humble woman. When fully grown, he embarks on extraordinary adventures (slays monsters, overcomes death, and so on). Later he finds his parents and takes revenge on his father (or uncle); finally he is recognized and achieves rank and homage. The dangers and trials of the Hero (encounters with monsters and demons, descends into hell, and the rest) have an initiatory meaning. By overcoming all these ordeals, the young man proves that he has surpassed the human condition and henceforth he belongs to a class of semi-divine beings.

Now, many epic legends and folk tales use and readapt the highly dramatic scenarios of a hero's initiation (for example, Siegfried, Arthur, Robin Hood). Furthermore, the myth of the Hero survives in the legends of many medieval kings and in the aureole of the Reformer, the Revolutionary, the political Martyr, the Party Leader. But even in contemporary Western societies one can recognize the nostalgia for Heroes and heroic deeds—for example, the 'Superman,' or the immense popularity of detective novels, with the exemplary struggle between Good and Evil, between the Hero (i.e., the Detective) and the criminal, who is the modern incarnation of the Demon.

COGITATION

ALL writing, again, is about ideas, but the emphasis of this last section falls on more *explicit* statements of ideas. Also, in moving from Investigation to Cogitation we shift from fact to thought, a distinction that can only be relative, of course, like others in this book. Eliade's generalizations about world myths are thought about fact. His essay is a summation of research, but such a summation entails considerable interpretation and inference. Thought builds on fact. Like the other sections, Cogitation incorporates those preceding it.

As writing, Cogitation covers reflection, thesis, and theory, those compositions very loosely called "essay" that are organized primarily to assert generalizations, to explain them, combine them, and argue them. These are the most abstract kinds of writing, but last is not necessarily best. The progression of this book traces the knowledge-making that underlies the varieties of nonfiction writing. It is not a scale of values. Worldly learning proceeds through the hierarchical stages of sensation, memory, and reason. If Cogitation climaxes our discursive trip, that is because the explicit formulation of generalizations presupposes prior assimilations of experience that had to be presented here first. True, higher abstraction implies higher consciousness. To compose explicitly around a proposition or set of ideas, one has to be conscious of one's own thoughts. (Of course writing often raises thought to consciousness.) What is important is not to write higher abstractions but to have a choice about whether to do so.

Cogitation consists of two fundamental ways of thinking that of necessity underlie ways of writing—induction and deduction.

By induction we infer generalities from particulars, the behavior of ants from this ant, that ant, and so on. It comprises the empirical method of scientific knowledge-making. Myriad instances of *what happened* on numerous occasions are synthesized into one generalization about *what happens* all the time. At the most abstract level of generalization these are our "universal laws." The writing we have surveyed so far has been essentially inductive, that is, has been working from registration, recollection, and conscious collection of data to their distillation into a few general truths.

Deduction starts not with data but with some previous generalization of data, now assumed to be a truth, and uses it as a tool to find out what else may, logically, be true. We may apply deduction back downward by using such a truth to interpret "raw" data, as when we apply a generalization like "opposites attract," taken from one domain, to other domains to see what turns up. Or we may logically combine one general truth with others to see what other truth syllogism may yield. If this is true, and that is true, what else do they imply together that is also true? This reasoning extapolates concreter knowledge into riskier but farther-reaching "laws." It is the part of science that bridges into mathematics.

Deduction represents a higher plane of abstraction than induction, which operates on more physical data (more localized in time and space). Induction works by analogy, determining that some things are alike and classifying them together. The logic of classes (which also underlies metaphor) is less abstract than the logic of propositions, by which generalizations are combined to extract from their joint implication a further proposition. This latter is a process of tautology or verbal equations whereby some statements are a way of saying other statements that make explicit certain heretofore buried implications. ("This is tantamount to saying. . . .")

Inasmuch as induction represents mind on matter and deduction mind on mind, deduction is a higher abstractive operation. Put another way, seeing similarities among objects (analogy or the logic of classes) has to occur first, as a prerequisite, before the seeing of equations among generalizations (tautology or the logic of propositions). What makes a hierarchy is that some kinds of processing must take place before others can go on. This is true of the abstracting of experience into knowledge and explains how kinds of nonfiction writing may be arrayed in a progression.

The samples making up this section shade between induction and deduction but not in a neat spectrum, because good cogitative writing naturally mixes the two as authors arrive at and combine generalizations in the same essay. Furthermore, our progression here recognizes other important distinctions commonly described as "informal" and "formal" or "personal" and "impersonal." Actually, these distinctions concern the degree to which the first person remains in evidence and leaves the thoughts embedded in the original circumstances that prompted them. These cause the style and organization to vary between "formal" and "informal."

Let's call the personal, informal essay Reflection and the impersonal, formal essay Thesis. These correspond to Thinking Over and Thinking Through.

Reflection

THINKING OVER is mentally reacting to some relatively fresh experience—a kind of intellectual reflex. The author writes under the impact of some incident, news, recent observation, or other stimulus that is presented to the reader along with the thoughts it stirred. Like most writing so far surveyed, this shows the source of the generalization and something of the generalizing itself. So we have first-person narrative lead-ins or frameworks, but the purpose is clearly to state ideas in a personal, concrete context that disarms, relaxes, and entertains a readership that may shy from formal essay. Story keeps statement unobtrusive even when explicit. Again, folk literature contains significant parallels. Parables and fables make statements while telling tales.

Column

Chair Chat
Jon Carroll
San Francisco Chronicle, December 19, 1983

In today's Western culture, the natural home of the personal essay is the newspaper column or magazine "department" or "corner." The chatty style, the everyman I, the almost apologetic injection of generalization are rhetorical ploys that work well with a mass audience, for whom they model a reflective stance easy to identify with that helps people to "re-run" their own experience. This sample represents reflection on a recent conversation, a common point of departure since the author may easily continue in the column monolog some issue raised in the dialog.

Here's the Scene: One of those dinner parties with more strangers than friends around the table. The wine is lovely; the pasta is impeccable. Sitting next to me, on my right, is a young man in a wheelchair. We have already spoken of the wine and pasta; we have already praised the undeniable good taste of the hostess and of the food she has prepared.

"So," I say to the guy in the wheelchair, "what happened? Why are you confined to that wheelchair?"

"Sssssssssstt." It is the woman to my left. She is hissing at me. I swivel my head.

"Huh?" I say, ever the graceful conversationalist.

"Don't, you know, mention, the, uh, don't," she says, putting her right hand out at table level, palm down, and moving it rapidly back and forth, mezzo-mezzo style. "You know, I, well . . ."

"Multiple sclerosis," says the guy in the wheelchair. "MS started about three years ago."

"Oh, God," says the woman.

"What?" I ask the woman.

"Too late," she says. "Oh, no."

The guy in the wheelchair continues his explanation. We discuss symptoms, cures, theories, difficulties. The woman to my left sinks lower and lower in her seat.

Why is it, I wondered later, that people think it's somehow in bad taste to talk to a handicapped person about his or her handicap? People in wheelchairs know they're in wheelchairs. They pay a good deal of daily attention to their ambulatory appliance. If you bring up this more-or-less central fact in their lives, they will almost certainly not be surprised.

"You mean, well, by God you're right. So I am. Never thought of it that way. Wish you hadn't brought it up. Now I'll be depressed all evening." Won't happen.

Suppose you were sitting next to an extremely tall person. Maybe you wouldn't bring up his height right away, but after an exchange of views on other topics of the day, you might ask about the thrills and agonies of unusual tallness. It is a topic on which he has some expertise, and it is a truism of social behavior that one should try to draw people out.

If you were sitting next to a known Nobel Prize winner, you might at some point ask her about Stockholm. "A very clean city, I hear. Lovely public parks, according to reports. Enjoy yourself?" You know.

And yet a surprisingly large number of people think that it's bad form to talk to handicapped people about their handicap. And, it seems to me, that reinforces the sense of shame and apartness that is one of the most terrible side-effects of physical disability.

It's almost superstitious, as though talking about it is somehow going to bring the everyday reality of crippling accident or wasting disease closer to home and hearth. Word magic, booga booga.

And if everyone at a dinner party is resolutely pretending that Guest A is not confined to a wheelchair, then Guest A is going to have a harder time believing that being confined to a wheelchair is an OK way to be, and even a hard time introducing various amusing or instructive anecdotes centering around his situation.

Worse yet, such over-polite reticence reduces the opportunity for understanding. The more opportunities that those of us who are without visible physical handicaps get to have an immediate and direct report on the nature of the experience of those who are so afflicted, the better we'll be able to understand it cleanly and work through our own fears and fantasies.

Meaning only to say: Excessive gentility results in boring and emotionally arid evenings. Stop talking about the weather and ask the questions you want to ask.

A Gift to Remember
Ellen Goodman
Boston Globe, December, 1980

This shows the writer taking the commonest, most fleeting moment and turning the spontaneous reflections on it into a compact, provocative essay whose generalization most people can apply to their own lives. This deft "common touch" owes to both the columnist's choice of experience and to the style of expression, which is colloquial and designed to slip through any anti-intellectual defenses.

The man stood in the checkout line, holding onto the new bicycle as if it were a prize horse. From time to time, he caressed the blue machine gently, stroking the handlebars, patting the seat, running his fingers across the red reflectors on the pedals.

His pleasure, his delight, finally infected me. "It's a beautiful bike," I said to him, shifting my own bundles.

The man looked up sheepishly and explained. "It's for my son." Then he paused and, because I was a stranger, added, "I always wanted a bike like this when I was a kid."

"Yes," I smiled. "I'm sure he'll love it."

The man continued absentmindedly handling his bicycle, and I looked around me in the Christmas line.

There were carts and carts full of presents. I wondered what was really in them. How many others were buying gifts they always wished for. How many of us always give what we want, or wanted, to receive?

I've done it myself, I know that. Consciously or not. I've made up for the small longings, the silly disappointments of my own childhood, with my daughter's. The doll with long, long hair, the dog, the wooden dollhouse—these were all absent from the holidays past.

I never told my parents when they missed the mark. How

many of us did? I remember, sheepishly, the tin dollhouse, the parakeet, the doll with the "wrong" kind of hair.

Like most children, I was guilty about selfishness, about disappointment. I didn't know what gap might exist between what my parents wanted to give and what they could give . . . but I thought about it.

I knew they cared and, so, even when it wasn't exactly right, I wanted to return something for my gift. I wanted to please my parents with my pleasure.

But standing in that line, I thought about what else is passed between people. Gifts that come from a warehouse of feelings rather than goods.

Maybe we assume other people want what we want, and try to deliver it. Maybe in every season, we project from our needs, we giftwrap what was lacking in our own lives.

My parents, descendants of two volatile households, wanted to give us peace. They did. But I am conscious now of also giving my child the right to be angry. In the same way, I know parents who came from rigid households and busily provide now what they needed then: freedom. They don't always feel their children's ache for "structure."

I know others who grew up in poor households and now make money as a life-offering for their families. They don't understand when it isn't valued.

There are women so full of angry memories of childhood responsibilities that they can't comprehend their children's wish to help. There are men so busy making up for their fathers' disinterest that they can't recognize their sons' plea: lay off.

Every generation finds it hard sometimes to hear what our children need, to feel what they are missing, because our own childhood is still ringing in our ears.

It isn't just parents and children who miss this connection between giving and receiving. Husbands and wives, men and women, may also give what they want to get—caretaking, security attention—and remain unsatisfied. Our most highly prized sacrifices may lie unused under family trees.

Of course there are people who truly "exchange." The lucky ones are in fine tune. The careful ones listen to each other. They trade lists. They learn to separate the "me" from the "you." They stop rubbing balm on other people to relieve their own sore spots.

Perhaps the man in line with me is lucky or careful. I saw him wheel his gift through the front door humming, smiling. For a moment, I wondered if his son hinted for a basketball or a book. This time, I hope he wanted what his father wanted for him.

America Needs Poor Soldiers
Arthur Hoppe
San Francisco Chronicle, August 16, 1971

---

*This columnist is reacting to an idea in a news statement made
by a government official. One common form of today's journalistic argument is the satiric scenario, a specialty of Hoppe and of
others like Art Buchwald. It is another concrete, folk way of
bringing out the meaning of specific events. The scenarist extrapo-
lates these original events by imagining others that in some way
logically follow from them. Thus Hoppe seizes on this news item
to show a relationship between war and unemployment that is
true for more than just the administration currently in office.*

> Housing Secretary George Romney, in a new admin-
> istration tack on unemployment, said more Ameri-
> cans are out of jobs because fewer are being killed
> in Vietnam. "One of the basic questions Americans
> are going to have to ask themselves," he said, "is,
> 'Will people be willing to have more boys killed
> in Vietnam or higher unemployment at home?' "
> —News item.

Nonsense! This just shows the administration's muddled thinking and lack of initiative when it comes to tackling the nation's
economic ills.

Despite what Mr. Romney says, killing American boys in
Vietnam isn't going to solve unemployment at home. Not in our
lifetime. Why, even during the hey-day of the war we were
killing only 200 or so Americans a week over there. At that rate
it would take close to 500 years to wipe out the country's 4.8
million jobless.

True, Mr. Nixon keeps saying he's looking for long-range
solutions to our economic troubles. But 500 years? That's
ridiculous. Surely, there are better answers than that.

Hotheads, of course, will immediately demand we launch World War III on the grounds that if Vietnam will wipe out unemployment in 500 years, World War III will wipe it out overnight. But let's hope Mr. Nixon turns a deaf ear to such drastic approaches. Why throw the baby out with the bathwater?

If we keep in mind that the logical method of eliminating unemployment is to eliminate the unemployed, then by far the most efficient, economical solution is to simply line them up and shoot them.

Unfortunately, civil libertarians and other bleeding hearts will never stand for this. "Lining up American citizens and shooting them," they will say, "is not the American way."

And that's true. The American way as Mr. Romney's statement suggests, is to conscript American citizens into uniform, send them overseas and let somebody else shoot them.

But one of the basic questions Americans are going to have to ask themselves is, "Can we afford to draft an army of 4.8 million unemployed and send them overseas to get shot?"

The answer, regretfully, is no. It cost us $30 billion a year to field an army of only a half million in Vietnam. So sending 4.8 million to fight overseas would cost close to $300 billion. Ending employment isn't worth it.

Revenge Is Sour
George Orwell
Tribune, November 9, 1945

Columnists represent the natural tendency to want to react to an event as well as report it. But one can only react to single events so long, it seems, without going further and connecting multiple events across different times and places. So as reporters become columnists, TV news anchors become commentators, and journalists become essayists. George Orwell's writings, which include a great deal of journalism, show especially clearly this relationship between gathering information and generalizing from it. In the following selection he reacts to a loaded issue of the end of

World War II by relating it to a couple of incidents he witnessed not long before as a war correspondent. While crisply stating his generality, his title also expresses Orwell's stubborn penchant for overturning the common sentiment.

Whenever I read phrases like "war guilt trials", "punishment of war criminals", and so forth, there comes back into my mind the memory of something I saw in a prisoner-of-war camp in South Germany, earlier this year.

Another correspondent and myself were being shown round the camp by a little Viennese Jew who had been enlisted in the branch of the American army which deals with the interrogation of prisoners. He was an alert, fair-haired, rather good-looking youth of about twenty-five, and politically so much more knowledgeable than the average American officer that it was a pleasure to be with him. The camp was on an airfield, and, after we had been round the cages, our guide led us to a hangar where various prisoners who were in a different category from the others were being "screened."

Up at one end of the hangar about a dozen men were lying in a row on the concrete floor. These, it was explained, were SS officers who had been segregated from the other prisoners. Among them was a man in dingy civilian clothes who was lying with his arm across his face and apparently asleep. He had strangely and horribly deformed feet. The two of them were quite symmetrical, but they were clubbed out into an extraordinary globular shape which made them more like a horse's hoof than anything human. As we approached the group the little Jew seemed to be working himself up into a state of excitement.

"That's the real swine!" he said, and suddenly he lashed out with his heavy army boot and caught the prostrate man a fearful kick right on the bulge of one of his deformed feet.

"Get up, you swine!" he shouted as the man started out of sleep, and then repeated something of the kind in German. The prisoner scrambled to his feet and stood clumsily to attention. With the same air of working himself up into a fury—indeed he was almost dancing up and down as he spoke—the Jew told us the prisoner's history. He was a "real" Nazi: his party number indicated that he had been a member since the very early days, and he had held a post corresponding to a General in the political branch of the SS. It could be taken as quite certain that he had had charge of concentration camps and had presided over tortures and hangings. In short, he represented everything that we had been fighting against during the past five years.

Meanwhile, I was studying his appearance. Quite apart from the scrubby, unfed, unshaven look that a newly captured man generally has, he was a disgusting specimen. But he did not look brutal or in any way frightening: merely neurotic and, in a low way, intellectual. His pale, shifty eyes were deformed by powerful spectacles. He could have been an unfrocked clergyman, an actor ruined by drink, or a spiritualist medium. I have seen very similar people in London common lodging houses, and also in the Reading Room of the British Museum. Quite obviously he was mentally unbalanced—indeed, only doubtfully sane, though at this moment sufficiently in his right mind to be frightened of getting another kick. And yet everything that the Jew was telling me of his history could have been true, and probably was true! So the Nazi torturer of one's imagination, the monstrous figure against whom one had struggled for so many years, dwindled to this pitiful wretch, whose obvious need was not for punishment, but for some kind of psychological treatment.

Later, there were further humiliations. Another SS officer, a large, brawny man, was ordered to strip to the waist and show the blood-group number tattooed on his under-arm; another was forced to explain to us how he had lied about being a member of the SS and attempted to pass himself off as an ordinary soldier of the Wehrmacht. I wondered whether the Jew was getting any real kick out of this new-found power that he was exercising. I concluded that he wasn't really enjoying it, and that he was merely—like a man in a brothel, or a boy smoking his first cigar, or a tourist traipsing round a picture gallery—*telling* himself that he was enjoying it, and behaving as he had planned to behave in the days when he was helpless.

It is absurd to blame any German or Austrian Jew for getting his own back on the Nazis. Heaven knows what scores this particular man may have had to wipe out; very likely his whole family had been murdered; and, after all, even a wanton kick to a prisoner is a very tiny thing compared with the outrages committed by the Hitler régime. But what this scene, and much else that I saw in Germany, brought home to me was that the whole idea of revenge and punishment is a childish day-dream. Properly speaking, there is no such thing as revenge. Revenge is an act which you want to commit when you are powerless and because you are powerless: as soon as the sense of impotence is removed, the desire evaporates also.

Who would not have jumped for joy, in 1940, at the thought of seeing SS officers kicked and humiliated? But when the thing becomes possible, it is merely pathetic and disgusting. It is said that when Mussolini's corpse was exhibited in public, an old woman drew a revolver and fired five shots into it, exclaiming, "Those are for my five sons!" It is the kind of story that the newspapers make up, but it might be true. I wonder how much satisfaction she got out of those five shots, which, doubtless, she had dreamed years earlier of firing. The condition of her being able to get near enough to Mussolini to shoot at him was that he should be a corpse.

In so far as the big public in this country is responsible for the monstrous peace settlement now being forced on Germany, it is because of a failure to see in advance that punishing an enemy brings no satisfaction. We acquiesced in crimes like the expulsion of all Germans from East Prussia—crimes which in some cases we could not prevent but might at least have protested against—because the Germans had angered and frightened us, and therefore we were certain that when they were down we should feel no pity for them. We persist in these policies, or let others persist in them on our behalf, because of a vague feeling that, having set out to punish Germany, we ought to go ahead and do it. Actually there is little acute hatred of Germany left in this country, and even less, I should expect to find, in the army of occupation. Only the minority of sadists, who must have their "atrocities" from one source or another, take a keen interest in the hunting-down of war criminals and quislings. If you ask the average man what crime Goering, Ribbentrop and the rest are to be charged with at their trial, he cannot tell you. Somehow the punishment of these monsters ceases to seem attractive when it becomes possible: indeed, once under lock and key, they almost cease to be monsters.

Unfortunately, there is often need of some concrete incident before one can discover the real state of one's feelings. Here is another memory from Germany. A few hours after Stuttgart was captured by the French army, a Belgian journalist and myself entered the town, which was still in some disorder. The Belgian had been broadcasting throughout the war for the European Service of the BBC, and, like nearly all Frenchmen or Belgians, he had a very much tougher attitude towards "the Boche" than an Englishman or an American would have. All the main bridges into the town had been blown up, and we had to enter by a small footbridge which the Germans had evidently made efforts to defend. A dead German soldier was lying supine at the foot of the steps. His face was a waxy yellow. On his breast someone had laid a bunch of the lilac which was blossoming everywhere.

The Belgian averted his face as we went past. When we were well over the bridge he confided to me that this was the first time he had seen a dead man. I suppose he was thirty-five years old, and for four years he had been doing war propaganda over the radio. For several days after this, his attitude was quite different from what it had been earlier. He looked with disgust at the bomb-wrecked town and the humiliations the Germans were undergoing, and even on one occasion intervened to prevent a particularly bad bit of looting. When he left, he gave the residue of the coffee we had brought with us to the Germans on whom we were billeted. A week earlier he would probably have been scandalised at the idea of giving coffee to a "Boche". But his feelings, he told me, had undergone a change at the sight of "ce pauvre mort" beside the bridge: it had suddenly brought home to him the meaning of war. And yet, if we had happened to enter the town by another route, he might have been spared the experience of seeing even one corpse out of the—perhaps—twenty million that the war has produced.

Personal Essay

The Hidden Teacher
Loren Eiseley
from *The Star Throwers*, 1978

Imagine a group of conversationalists taking turns telling anecdotes that all show the same thing or make the same point. This is the basic structure of Eiseley's essay. It is a more complicated way for the monologuist writer to make a statement than just telling a single story. The reader has to grasp the connection between one brief story and the next and eventually follow the thread of idea across all the instances, even though, as here, the accumulating stories complicate as well as illustrate a point.

We may regard the concept of the "hidden teacher" as a generalization arrived at by induction from such examples as those given in the essay, but of course by the time of writing the essay the generalization has been formulated enough to serve as a deductive tool to ransack experience for further examples of itself. In other words, Eiseley thinks over several experiences at once, but some of this reflection may have led to the generality and some may have been prompted by it. In any case, the high ratio of personal anecdote keeps even so philosophical a piece suspended between memoir and thesis, that is to say, in personal essay. Finally, the reader may judge whether Eiseley sequenced his stories significantly or whether if he had told them in another order he could have made his points as well.

Sometimes the best teacher teaches only once to a single child or to a grownup past hope.
—ANONYMOUS

I

The putting of formidable riddles did not arise with today's philosophers. In fact, there is a sense in which the experimental method of science might be said merely to have widened the area of man's homelessness. Over two thousand years ago, a man named Job, crouching in the Judean desert, was moved to challenge what he felt to be the injustice of his God. The voice in the whirlwind, in turn, volleyed pitiless questions upon the supplicant—questions that have, in truth, precisely the ring of modern science. For the Lord asked of Job by whose wisdom the hawk soars, and who had fathered the rain, or entered the storehouses of the snow.

A youth standing by, one Elihu, also played a role in this drama, for he ventured diffidently to his protesting elder that it was not true that God failed to manifest Himself. He may speak in one way or another, though men do not perceive it. In consequence of this remark perhaps it would be well, whatever our individual beliefs, to consider what may be called the hidden teacher, lest we become too much concerned with the formalities of only one aspect of the education by which we learn.

We think we learn from teachers, and we sometimes do. But the teachers are not always to be found in school or in great laboratories. Sometimes what we learn depends upon our own powers of insight. Moreover, our teachers may be hidden, even the greatest teacher. And it was the young man Elihu who observed that if the old are not always wise, neither can the teacher's way be ordered by the young whom he would teach.

For example, I once received an unexpected lesson from a spider.

It happened far away on a rainy morning in the West. I had come up a long gulch looking for fossils, and there, just at eye level, lurked a huge yellow-and-black orb spider, whose web was moored to the tall spears of buffalo grass at the edge of the arroyo. It was her universe, and her senses did not extend beyond the lines and spokes of the great wheel she inhabited. Her extended claws could feel every vibration throughout that delicate structure. She knew the tug of wind, the fall of a raindrop, the flutter of a trapped moth's wing. Down one spoke of the web ran a stout ribbon of gossamer on which she could hurry out to investigate her prey.

Curious, I took a pencil from my pocket and touched a strand of the web. Immediately there was a response. The web, plucked by its menacing occupant, began to vibrate until it was a blur. Anything that had brushed claw or wing against that amazing snare would be thoroughly entrapped. As the vibrations slowed, I could see the owner fingering her guidelines for signs of struggle. A pencil point was an intrusion into this universe for which no precedent existed. Spider was circumscribed by spider ideas; its universe was spider universe. All outside was irrational, extraneous, at best raw material for spider. As I proceeded on my way along the gully, like a vast impossible shadow, I realized that in the world of spider I did not exist.

Moreover, I considered, as I tramped along, that to the phagocytes, the white blood cells, clambering even now with some kind of elementary intelligence amid the thin pipes and tubing of my body—creatures without whose ministrations I could not exist—the conscious "I" of which I was aware had no significance to these amoeboid beings. I was, instead, a kind of chemical web that brought meaningful messages to them, a natural environment seemingly immortal if they could have thought about it, since generations of them had lived and perished, and would continue to so live and die, in that odd fabric which contained my intelligence—a misty light that was beginning to seem floating and tenuous even to me.

I began to see that, among the many universes in which the world of living creatures existed, some were large, some small, but that all, including man's, were in some way limited or finite.

We were creatures of many different dimensions passing through each other's lives like ghosts through doors.

In the years since, my mind has many times returned to that far moment of my encounter with the orb spider. A message has arisen only now from the misty shreds of that webbed universe. What was it that had so troubled me about the incident? Was it that spidery indifference to the human triumph?

If so, that triumph was very real and could not be denied. I saw, had many times seen, both mentally and in the seams of exposed strata, the long backward stretch of time whose recovery is one of the great feats of modern science. I saw the drifting cells of the early seas from which all life, including our own, has arisen. The salt of those ancient seas is in our blood, its lime is in our bones. Every time we walk along a beach some ancient urge disturbs us so that we find ourselves shedding shoes and garments or scavenging among seaweed and whitened timbers like the homesick refugees of a long war.

And war it has been indeed—the long war of life against its inhospitable environment, a war that has lasted for perhaps three billion years. It began with strange chemicals seething under a sky lacking in oxygen; it was waged through long ages until the first green plants learned to harness the light of the nearest star, our sun. The human brain, so frail, so perishable, so full of inexhaustible dreams and hungers, burns by the power of the leaf.

The hurrying blood cells charged with oxygen carry more of that element to the human brain than to any other part of the body. A few moments' loss of vital air and the phenomenon we know as consciousness goes down into the black night of inorganic things. The human body is a magical vessel, but its life is linked with an element it cannot produce. Only the green plant knows the secret of transforming the light that comes to us across the far reaches of space. There is no better illustration of the intricacy of man's relationship with other living things.

The student of fossil life would be forced to tell us that if we take the past into consideration the vast majority of earth's creatures—perhaps over 90 percent—have vanished. Forms that flourished for a far longer time than man has existed upon earth have become either extinct or so transformed that their descendants are scarcely recognizable. The specialized perish with the environment that created them, the tooth of the tiger fails at last, the lances of men strike down the last mammoth.

In three billion years of slow change and groping effort only one living creature has succeeded in escaping the trap of special-

ization that has led in time to so much death and wasted endeavor.
It is man, but the word should be uttered softly, for his story is
not yet done.

With the rise of the human brain, with the appearance of a
creature whose upright body enabled two limbs to be freed for
the exploration and manipulation of his environment, there had
at last emerged a creature with a specialization—the brain—that,
paradoxically, offered escape from specialization. Many animals
driven into the nooks and crannies of nature have achieved
momentary survival only at the cost of later extinction.

Was it this that troubled me and brought my mind back to a
tiny universe among the grass blades, a spider's universe concerned with spider thought?

Perhaps.

The mind that once visualized animals on a cave wall is now
engaged in a vast ramification of itself through time and space.
Man has broken through the boundaries that control all other life.
I saw, at last, the reason for my recollection of that great spider
on the arroyo's rim, fingering its universe against the sky.

The spider was a symbol of man in miniature. The wheel of
the web brought the analogy home clearly. Man, too, lies at the
heart of a web, a web extending through the starry reaches of
sidereal space, as well as backward into the dark realm of
prehistory. His great eye upon Mount Palomar looks into a
distance of millions of light-years, his radio ear hears the whisper of even more remote galaxies, he peers through the electron
microscope upon the minute particles of his own being. It is a
web no creature of earth has ever spun before. Like the orb
spider, man lies at the heart of it, listening. Knowledge has
given him the memory of earth's history beyond the time of his
emergence. Like the spider's claw, a part of him touches a world
he will never enter in the flesh. Even now, one can see him
reaching forward into time with new machines, computing,
analyzing, until elements of the shadowy future will also compose part of the invisible web he fingers.

Yet still my spider lingers in memory against the sunset sky.
Spider thoughts in a spider universe—sensitive to raindrop and
moth flutter, nothing beyond, nothing allowed for the unexpected,
the inserted pencil from the world outside.

Is man at heart any different from the spider, I wonder: man
thoughts, as limited as spider thoughts, contemplating now the
nearest star with the threat of bringing with him the fungus rot
from earth, wars, violence, the burden of a population he refuses
to control, cherishing again his dreams of the Adamic Eden he

had pursued and lost in the green forests of America. Now it beckons again like a mirage from beyond the moon. Let man spin his web, I thought further; it is his nature. But I considered also the work of the phagocytes swarming in the rivers of my body, the unresting cells in their mortal universe. What is it we are a part of that we do not see, as the spider was not gifted to discern my face, or my little probe into her world?

We are too content with our sensory extensions, with the fulfillment of that Ice Age mind that began its journey amidst the cold of vast tundras and that pauses only briefly before its leap into space. It is no longer enough to see as a man sees—even to the ends of the universe. It is not enough to hold nuclear energy in one's hand like a spear, as a man would hold it, or to see the lightning, or times past, or time to come, as a man would see it. If we continue to do this, the great brain—the human brain—will be only a new version of the old trap, and nature is full of traps for the beast that cannot learn.

It is not sufficient any longer to listen at the end of a wire to the rustlings of galaxies; it is not enough even to examine the great coil of DNA in which is coded the very alphabet of life. These are our extended perceptions. But beyond lies the great darkness of the ultimate Dreamer, who dreamed the light and the galaxies. Before act was, or substance existed, imagination grew in the dark. Man partakes of that ultimate wonder and creativeness. As we turn from the galaxies to the swarming cells of our own being, which toil for something, some entity beyond their grasp, let us remember man, the self-fabricator who came across an ice age to look into the mirrors and the magic of science. Surely he did not come to see himself or his wild visage only. He came because he is at heart a listener and a searcher for some transcendent realm beyond himself. This he has worshiped by many names, even in the dismal caves of his beginning. Man, the self-fabricator, is so by reason of gifts he had no part in devising—and so he searches as the single living cell in the beginning must have sought the ghostly creature it was to serve.

II

The young man Elihu, Job's counselor and critic, spoke simply of the "Teacher," and it is of this teacher I speak when I refer to gifts man had no part in devising. Perhaps—though it is purely a matter of emotional reactions to words—it is easier for us today to speak of this teacher as "nature," that omnipresent all which contained both the spider and my invisible intrusion into her carefully planned universe. But nature does not simply represent reality. In the shapes of life, it prepares the future; it offers alternatives. Nature teaches, though what it teaches is often hidden and obscure, just as the voice from the spinning dust cloud belittled Job's thought but gave back no answers to its own formidable interrogation.

A few months ago I encountered an amazing little creature on a windy corner of my local shopping center. It seemed, at first glance, some long-limbed, feathery spider teetering rapidly down the edge of a store front. Then it swung into the air and, as hesitantly as a spider on a thread, blew away into the parking lot. It returned in a moment on a gust of wind and ran toward me once more on its spindly legs with amazing rapidity.

With great difficulty I discovered the creature was actually a filamentous seed, seeking a hiding place and scurrying about with the uncanny surety of a conscious animal. In fact, it *did* escape me before I could secure it. Its flexible limbs were stiffer than milkweed down, and, propelled by the wind, it ran rapidly and evasively over the pavement. It was like a gnome scampering somewhere with a hidden packet—for all that I could tell, a totally new one: one of the jumbled alphabets of life.

A new one? So stable seem the years and all green leaves, a botanist might smile at my imaginings. Yet bear with me a moment. I would like to tell a tale, a genuine tale of childhood. Moreover, I was just old enough to know the average of my kind and to marvel at what I saw. And what I saw was straight from the hidden Teacher, whatever be his name.

It is told in the Orient of the Hindu god Krishna that his mother, wiping his mouth when he was a child, inadvertently peered in and beheld the universe, though the sight was mercifully and immediately veiled from her. In a sense, this is what happened to me. One day there arrived at our school a newcomer, who entered the grade above me. After some days this lad, whose look of sleepy-eyed arrogance is still before me as I write, was led into my mathematics classroom by the principal. Our class was informed severely that we should learn to work harder.

With this preliminary exhortation, great rows of figures were chalked upon the blackboard, such difficult mathematical problems as could be devised by adults. The class watched in helpless wonder. When the preparations had been completed, the young pupil sauntered forward and, with a glance of infinite boredom that swept from us to his fawning teachers, wrote the answers, as instantaneously as a modern computer, in their proper place upon the board. Then he strolled out with a carelessly exaggerated yawn.

Like some heavy-browed child at the wood's edge, clutching the last stone hand ax, I was witnessing the birth of a new type of humanity—one so beyond its teachers that it was being used for mean purposes while the intangible web of the universe in all its shimmering mathematical perfection glistened untaught in the mind of a chance little boy. The boy, by then grown self-centered and contemptuous, was being dragged from room to room to encourage us, the paleanthropes, to duplicate what, in reality, our teachers could not duplicate. He was too precious an object to be released upon the playground among us, and with reason. In a few months his parents took him away.

Long after, looking back from maturity, I realized that I had been exposed on that occasion, not to human teaching, but to the Teacher, toying with some sixteen billion nerve cells interlocked in ways past understanding. Or, if we do not like the anthropomorphism implied in the word teacher, then nature, the old voice from the whirlwind fumbling for the light. At all events, I had been the fortunate witness to life's unbounded creativity—a creativity seemingly still as unbalanced and chance-filled as in that far era when a black-scaled creature had broken from an egg and the age of the giant reptiles, the creatures of the prime, had tentatively begun.

Because form cannot be long sustained in the living, we collapse inward with age. We die. Our bodies, which were the product of a kind of hidden teaching by an alphabet we are only beginning dimly to discern, are dismissed into their elements. What is carried onward, assuming we have descendants, is the little capsule of instructions such as I encountered hastening by me in the shape of a running seed. We have learned the first biological lesson: that in each generation life passes through the eye of a needle. It exists for a time molecularly and in no recognizable semblance to its adult condition. It *instructs* its way again into man or reptile. As the ages pass, so do variants of the code. Occasionally, a species vanishes on a wind as unreturning as that which took the pterodactyls.

Or the code changes by subtle degrees through the statistical altering of individuals; until I, as the fading Neanderthals must once have done, have looked with still-living eyes upon the creature whose genotype was quite possibly to replace me. The genetic alphabets, like genuine languages, ramify and evolve along unreturning pathways.

If nature's instructions are carried through the eye of a needle, through the molecular darkness of a minute world below the field of human vision and of time's decay, the same, it might be said, is true of those monumental structures known as civilizations. They are transmitted from one generation to another in invisible puffs of air known as words—words that can also be symbolically incised on clay. As the delicate printing on the mud at the water's edge retraces a visit of autumn birds long since departed, so the little scrabbled tablets in perished cities carry the seeds of human thought across the deserts of millennia. In this instance the teacher is the social brain, but it, too, must be compressed into minute hieroglyphs, and the minds that wrought the miracle efface themselves amidst the jostling torrent of messages, which, like the genetic code, are shuffled and reshuffled as they hurry through eternity. Like a mutation, an idea may be recorded in the wrong time, to lie latent like a recessive gene and spring once more to life in an auspicious era.

Occasionally, in the moments when an archaeologist lifts the slab over a tomb that houses a great secret, a few men gain a unique glimpse through that dark portal out of which all men living have emerged, and through which messages again must pass. Here the Mexican archaeologist Ruz Lhuillier speaks of his first penetration of the great tomb hidden beneath dripping stalactites at the pyramid of Palenque: "Out of the dark shadows, rose a fairy-tale vision, a weird ethereal spectacle from another world. It was like a magician's cave carved out of ice, with walls glittering and sparkling like snow crystals." After shining his torch over hieroglyphs and sculptured figures, the explorer remarked wonderingly: "We were the first people for more than a thousand years to look at it."

Or again, one may read the tale of an unknown pharaoh who had secretly arranged that a beloved woman of his household should be buried in the tomb of the god-king—an act of compassion carrying a personal message across the millennia in defiance of all precedent.

Up to this point we have been talking of the single hidden teacher, the taunting voice out of that old Biblical whirlwind which symbolizes nature. We have seen incredible organic remembrance passed through the needle's eye of a microcosmic world hidden completely beneath the observational powers of creatures preoccupied and ensorcelled by dissolution and decay. We have seen the human mind unconsciously seize upon the principles of that very code to pass its own societal memory forward into time. The individual, the momentary living cell of the society, vanishes, but the institutional structures stand, or if they change, do so in an invisible flux not too dissimilar from that persisting in the stream of genetic continuity.

Upon this world, life is still young, not truly old as stars are measured. Therefore it comes about that we minimize the role of the synapsid reptiles, our remote forerunners, and correspondingly exalt our own intellectual achievements. We refuse to consider that in the old eye of the hurricane we may be, and doubtless are, in aggregate, a slightly more diffuse and dangerous dragon of the primal morning that still enfolds us.

Note that I say "in aggregate." For it is just here, among men, that the role of messages, and, therefore, the role of the individual teacher—or, I should say now, the hidden teachers—begin to be more plainly apparent and their instructions become more diverse. The dead pharaoh, though unintentionally, by a revealing act, had succeeded in conveying an impression of human tenderness that has outlasted the trappings of a vanished religion.

Like most modern educators I have listened to student demands to grade their teachers. I have heard the words repeated until they have become a slogan, that no man over thirty can teach the young of this generation. How would one grade a dead pharaoh, millennia gone, I wonder, one who did not intend to teach, but who, to a few perceptive minds, succeeded by the simple nobility of an act.

Many years ago, a student who was destined to become an internationally known anthropologist sat in a course in linguistics and heard his instructor, a man of no inconsiderable wisdom, describe some linguistic peculiarities of Hebrew words. At the time, the young student, at the urging of his family, was contemplating a career in theology. As the teacher warmed to his subject, the student, in the back row, ventured excitedly, "I believe I can understand that, sir. It is very similar to what exists in Mohegan."

The linguist paused and adjusted his glasses. "Young man," he said, "Mohegan is a dead language. Nothing has been recorded of it since the eighteenth century. Don't bluff."

"But sir," the young student countered hopefully, "It can't be dead so long as an old woman I know still speaks it. She is Pequot-Mohegan. I learned a bit of vocabulary from her and could speak with her myself. She took care of me when I was a child."

"Young man," said the austere, old-fashioned scholar, "be at my house for dinner at six this evening. You and I are going to look into this matter."

A few months later, under careful guidance, the young student published a paper upon Mohegan linguistics, the first of a long series of studies upon the forgotten languages and ethnology of the Indians of the northeastern forests. He had changed his vocation and turned to anthropology because of the attraction of a hidden teacher. But just who was the teacher? The young man himself, his instructor, or that solitary speaker of a dying tongue who had so yearned to hear her people's voice that she had softly babbled it to a child?

Later, this man was to become one of my professors. I absorbed much from him, though I hasten to make the reluctant confession that he was considerably beyond thirty. Most of what I learned was gathered over cups of coffee in a dingy campus restaurant. What we talked about were things some centuries older than either of us. Our common interest lay in snakes, scapulimancy, and other forgotten rites of benighted forest hunters.

I have always regarded this man as an extraordinary individual, in fact, a hidden teacher. But alas, it is all now so old-fashioned. We never protested the impracticality of his quaint subjects. We were all too ready to participate in them. He was an excellent canoeman, but he took me to places where I fully expected to drown before securing my degree. To this day, fragments of his unused wisdom remain stuffed in some back attic of my mind. Much of it I have never found the opportunity to employ, yet it has somehow colored my whole adult existence. I belong to that elderly professor in somewhat the same way that he, in turn, had become the wood child of a hidden forest mother.

There are, however, other teachers. For example, among the hunting peoples there were the animal counselors who appeared in prophetic dreams. Or, among the Greeks, the daemonic supernaturals who stood at the headboard while a man lay stark and listened—sometimes to dreadful things. "You are asleep," the messengers proclaimed over and over again, as though the man lay in a spell to hear his doom pronounced. "You, Achilles, you, son of Atreus. You are asleep, asleep," the hidden ones pronounced and vanished.

We of this modern time know other things of dreams, but we know also that they can be interior teachers and healers as well as the anticipators of disaster. It has been said that great art is the night thought of man. It may emerge without warning from the soundless depths of the unconscious, just as supernovas may blaze up suddenly in the farther reaches of void space. The critics, like astronomers, can afterward triangulate such worlds but not account for them.

A writer friend of mine with bitter memories of his youth, and estranged from his family, who, in the interim, had died, gave me this account of the matter in his middle years. He had been working, with an unusual degree of reluctance, upon a novel that contained certain autobiographical episodes. One night he dreamed; it was a very vivid and stunning dream in its detailed reality.

He found himself hurrying over creaking snow through the blackness of a winter night. He was ascending a familiar path through a long-vanished orchard. The path led to his childhood home. The house, as he drew near, appeared dark and uninhabited, but, impelled by the power of the dream, he stepped upon the porch and tried to peer through a dark window into his own old room.

"Suddenly," he told me, "I was drawn by a strange mixture of repulsion and desire to press my face against the glass. I knew intuitively they were all there waiting for me within, if I could but see them. My mother and my father. Those I had loved and those I hated. But the window was black to my gaze. I hesitated a moment and struck a match. For an instant in that freezing silence I saw my father's face glimmer wan and remote behind the glass. My mother's face was there, with the hard, distorted lines that marked her later years.

"A surge of fury overcame my cowardice. I cupped the match before me and stepped closer, closer toward that dreadful confrontation. As the match guttered down, my face was pressed almost to the glass. In some quick transformation, such as only a dream can effect, I saw that it was my own face into which I stared, just as it was reflected in the black glass. My father's haunted face was but my own. The hard lines upon my mother's aging countenance were slowly reshaping themselves upon my living face. The light burned out. I awoke sweating from the terrible psychological tension of that nightmare. I was in a far port in a distant land. It was dawn. I could hear the waves breaking on the reef."

"And how do you interpret the dream?" I asked, concealing a sympathetic shudder and sinking deeper into my chair.

"It taught me something," he said slowly, and with equal slowness a kind of beautiful transfiguration passed over his features. All the tired lines I had known so well seemed faintly to be subsiding.

"Did you ever dream it again?" I asked out of a comparable experience of my own.

"No, never," he said, and hesitated. "You see, I had learned it was just I, but more, much more, I had learned that I was they. It makes a difference. And at the last, late—much too late—it was all right. I understood. My line was dying, but I understood. I hope they understood, too." His voice trailed into silence.

"It is a thing to learn," I said. "You were seeking something and it came." He nodded, wordless. "Out of a tomb," he added after a silent moment, "my kind of tomb—the mind."

On the dark street, walking homeward, I considered my friend's experience. Man, I concluded, may have come to the end of that wild being who had mastered the fire and the lightning. He can create the web but not hold it together, not save himself except by transcending his own image. For at last, before the ultimate mystery, it is himself he shapes. Perhaps it is for this that the listening web lies open: that by knowledge we may grow beyond our past, our follies, and ever closer to what the Dreamer in the dark intended before the dust arose and walked. In the pages of an old book it has been written that we are in the hands of a Teacher, nor does it yet appear what man shall be.

Seeing

Annie Dillard

from *Pilgrim at Tinker Creek*, 1975

A remarkable combination of personal presence and of high-level generalization characterizes the preceding and following essays along with many of the best in the English language. "Seeing" is not so much organized as orchestrated, which is a fitting way of organizing perceptions that all pay about a central idea. Instead of telling several incidents that show the same thing, Dillard accumulates various firsthand experiences that show different things about the same basic phenomenon. The title indicates the theme, which Dillard develops gradually from different starting points—old memories, recent observations, passages in books.

Her essay advances in a circular way like a musical composition in which motifs once sounded are picked up and developed further later, each motif giving new meaning to the others as the whole fills out. She tightly alternates particular and general, instance and idea, playing freely up and down the abstractive scale. This draws the reader into the very inductive process of generalizing. It is like several miniature essays slowly woven into one complex one. Beneath all this one feels the naturalist's journal entries, but one feels also the careful recomposition of these into sustained continuity, the variations on a theme that builds to a climax. No doubt the practice of calling student essays "themes" recognizes that the traditional personal essay has from its inception with Montaigne—through Hazlitt and Lamb, Emerson and Thoreau—tended toward this musical structure rather than toward either chronology or logical organization.

Dillard's fresh wording and phrasing, her original connections, unexpected juxtapositions, sharp physical and mental vision, organically poetic style—these are all generated by the very effort to see that she is writing about. As a model of how to look and say, the writer as seer deserves to be part of the topic here, and this kind of self-inclusion goes well beyond mere hosting calculated to put the reader at ease with ideas.

When I was six or seven years old, growing up in Pittsburgh, I used to take a precious penny of my own and hide it for someone else to find. It was a curious compulsion; sadly, I've never been seized by it since. For some reason I always "hid" the penny along the same stretch of sidewalk up the street. I would cradle it at the roots of a sycamore, say, or in a hole left by a chipped-off piece of sidewalk. Then I would take a piece of chalk, and, starting at either end of the block, draw huge arrows leading up to the penny from both directions. After I learned to write I labeled the arrows: SURPRISE AHEAD or MONEY THIS WAY. I was greatly excited, during all this arrow-drawing, at the thought of the first lucky passer-by who would receive in this way, regardless of merit, a free gift from the universe. But I never lurked about. I would go straight home and not give the matter another thought, until, some months later, I would be gripped again by the impulse to hide another penny.

It is still the first week in January, and I've got great plans. I've been thinking about seeing. There are lots of things to see, unwrapped gifts and free surprises. The world is fairly studded and strewn with pennies cast broadside from a generous hand. But—and this is the point—who gets excited by a mere penny? If you follow one arrow, if you crouch motionless on a bank to watch a tremulous ripple thrill on the water and are rewarded by the sight of a muskrat kit paddling from its den, will you count that sight a chip of copper only, and go your rueful way? It is dire poverty indeed when a man is so malnourished and fatigued that he won't stoop to pick up a penny. But if you cultivate a healthy poverty and simplicity, so that finding a penny will literally make your day, then, since the world is in fact planted in pennies, you have with your poverty bought a lifetime of days. It is that simple. What you see is what you get.

I used to be able to see flying insects in the air. I'd look ahead and see, not the row of hemlocks across the road, but the air in front of it. My eyes would focus along that column of air, picking out flying insects. But I lost interest, I guess, for I dropped the habit. Now I can see birds. Probably some people can look at the grass at their feet and discover all the crawling creatures. I would like to know grasses and sedges—and care. Then my least journey into the world would be a field trip, a series of happy recognitions. Thoreau, in an expansive mood, exulted, "What a rich book might be made about buds, including, perhaps, sprouts!" It would be nice to think so. I cherish mental images I have of three perfectly happy people. One collects stones. Another—an Englishman, say—watches clouds. The third lives on a coast and collects drops of seawater which he examines microscopically and mounts. But I don't see what the specialist sees, and so I cut myself off, not only from the total picture, but from the various forms of happiness.

Unfortunately, nature is very much a now-you-see-it, now-you-don't affair. A fish flashes, then dissolves in the water before my eyes like so much salt. Deer apparently ascend bodily into heaven; the brightest oriole fades into leaves. These disappearances stun me into stillness and concentration; they say of nature that it conceals with a grand nonchalance, and they say of vision that it is a deliberate gift, the revelation of a dancer who for my eyes only flings away her seven veils. For nature does reveal as well as conceal: now-you-don't-see-it, now-you-do. For a week last September migrating red-winged blackbirds were feeding heavily down by the creek at the back of the house. One day I went out to investigate the racket; I walked up to a tree, an Osage orange, and a hundred birds flew away. They simply materialized out of the tree. I saw a tree, then a whisk of color, than a tree again. I walked closer and another hundred blackbirds took flight. Not a branch, not a twig budged: the birds were apparently weightless as well as invisible. Or, it was as if the leaves of the Osage orange had been freed from a spell in the form of red-winged blackbirds; they flew from the tree, caught my eye in the sky, and vanished. When I looked again at the tree the leaves had reassembled as if nothing had happened. Finally I walked directly to the trunk of the tree and a final hundred, the real diehards, appeared, spread, and vanished. How could so many hide in the tree without my seeing them? The Osage orange, unruffled, looked just as it had looked from the house, when three hundred red-winged blackbirds cried from its crown. I looked downstream where they flew, and they were gone. Searching, I couldn't spot one. I wandered downstream to force them to play their hand, but they'd crossed the creek and scattered. One show to a customer. These appearances catch at my throat; they are the free gifts, the bright coppers at the roots of trees.

It's all a matter of keeping my eyes open. Nature is like one of those line drawings of a tree that are puzzles for children: Can you find hidden in the leaves a duck, a house, a boy, a bucket, a zebra, and a boot? Specialists can find the most incredibly well-hidden things. A book I read when I was young recommended an easy way to find caterpillars to rear: you simply find some fresh caterpillar droppings, look up, and there's your caterpillar. More recently an author advised me to set my mind at ease about those piles of cut stems on the ground in grassy fields. Field mice make them; they cut the grass down by degrees to reach the seeds at the head. It seems that when the grass is tightly packed, as in a field of ripe grain, the blade won't topple at a single cut through the stem; instead, the cut stem simply drops vertically, held in the crush of grain. The mouse severs the bottom again and again, the stem keeps dropping an inch at a time, and finally the head is low enough for the mouse to reach the seeds. Meanwhile, the mouse is positively littering the field with its little piles of cut stems into which, presumably, the author of the book is constantly stumbling.

If I can't see these minutiae, I still try to keep my eyes open. I'm always on the lookout for antlion traps in sandy soil, monarch pupae near milkweed, skipper larvae in locust leaves. These things are utterly common, and I've not seen one. I bang on hollow trees near water, but so far no flying squirrels have appeared. In flat country I watch every sunset in hopes of seeing the green ray. The green ray is a seldom-seen streak of light that rises from the sun like a spurting fountain at the moment of sunset; it throbs into the sky for two seconds and disappears. One more reason to keep my eyes open. A photography professor at the University of Florida just happened to see a bird die in midflight; it jerked, died, dropped, and smashed on the ground. I squint at the wind because I read Stewart Edward White: "I have always maintained that if you looked closely enough you could *see* the wind—the dim, hardly-made-out, fine débris fleeing high in the air." White was an excellent observer, and devoted an entire chapter of *The Mountains* to the subject of seeing deer: "As soon as you can forget the naturally obvious and construct an artificial obvious, then you too will see deer."

But the artificial obvious is hard to see. My eyes account for less than one percent of the weight of my head; I'm bony and dense; I see what I expect. I once spent a full three minutes looking at a bullfrog that was so unexpectedly large I couldn't see it even though a dozen enthusiastic campers were shouting directions. Finally I asked, "What color am I looking for?" and a fellow said, "Green." When at last I picked out the frog, I saw what painters are up against: the thing wasn't green at all, but the color of wet hickory bark.

The lover can see, and the knowledgeable. I visited an aunt and uncle at a quarter-horse ranch in Cody, Wyoming. I couldn't do much of anything useful, but I could, I thought, draw. So, as we all sat around the kitchen table after supper, I produced a sheet of paper and drew a horse. "That's one lame horse," my aunt volunteered. The rest of the family joined in: "Only place to saddle that one is his neck"; "Looks like we better shoot the poor thing, on account of those terrible growths." Meekly, I slid the pencil and paper down the table. Everyone in that family, including my three young cousins, could draw a horse. Beautifully. When the paper came back it looked as though five shining, real quarter horses had been corraled by mistake with a papier-mâché moose; the real horses seemed to gaze at the monster with a steady, puzzled air. I stay away from horses now, but I can do a creditable goldfish. The point is that I just don't know what the lover knows; I just can't see the artificial obvious that those in the know construct. The herpetologist asks the native, "Are there snakes in that ravine?" "Nosir." And the herpetologist comes home with, yessir, three bags full. Are there butterflies on that mountain? Are the bluets in bloom, are there arrowheads here, or fossil shells in the shale?

Peeping through my keyhole I see within the range of only about thirty percent of the light that comes from the sun; the rest is infrared and some little ultraviolet, perfectly apparent to many animals, but invisible to me. A nightmare network of ganglia, charged and firing without my knowledge, cuts and splices what I do see, editing it for my brain. Donald E. Carr points out that the sense impressions of one-celled animals are *not* edited for the brain: "This is philosophically interesting in a rather mournful way, since it means that only the simplest animals perceive the universe as it is."

A fog that won't burn away drifts and flows across my field of vision. When you see fog move against a backdrop of deep pines, you don't see the fog itself, but streaks of clearness floating across the air in dark shreds. So I see only tatters of clearness through a pervading obscurity. I can't distinguish the fog from the overcast sky; I can't be sure if the light is direct or reflected. Everywhere darkness and the presence of the unseen appalls. We estimate now that only one atom dances alone in every cubic meter of intergalactic space. I blink and squint. What planet or power yanks Halley's Comet out of orbit? We haven't seen that force yet; it's a question of distance, density, and the pallor of reflected light. We rock, cradled in the swaddling band of darkness. Even the simple darkness of night whispers suggestions to the mind. Last summer, in August, I stayed at the creek too late.

Where Tinker Creek flows under the sycamore log bridge to the tear-shaped island, it is slow and shallow, fringed thinly in cattail marsh. At this spot an astonishing bloom of life supports vast breeding populations of insects, fish, reptiles, birds, and mammals. On windless summer evenings I stalk along the creek bank or straddle the sycamore log in absolute stillness, watching for muskrats. The night I stayed too late I was hunched on the log staring spellbound at spreading, reflected stains of lilac on the water. A cloud in the sky suddenly lighted as if turned on by a switch; its reflection just as suddenly materialized on the water upstream, flat and floating, so that I couldn't see the creek bottom, or life in the water under the cloud. Downstream, away from the cloud on the water, water turtles smooth as beans were gliding down with the current in a series of easy, weightless push-offs, as men bound on the moon. I didn't know whether to trace the progress of one turtle I was sure of, risking sticking my face in one of the bridge's spider webs made invisible by the gathering dark, or take a chance on seeing the carp, or scan the mudbank in hope of seeing a muskrat, or follow the last of the swallows who caught at my heart and trailed it after them like streamers as they appeared from directly below, under the log, flying upstream with their tails forked, so fast.

But shadows spread, and deepened, and stayed. After thousands of years we're still strangers to darkness, fearful aliens in an enemy camp with our arms crossed over our chests. I stirred. A land turtle on the bank, startled, hissed the air from its lungs and withdrew into its shell. An uneasy pink here, an unfathomable blue there, gave great suggestion of lurking beings. Things were going on. I couldn't see whether that sere rustle I heard was a distant rattlesnake, slit-eyed, or a nearby sparrow kicking in the dry flood debris slung at the foot of a willow. Tremendous action roiled the water everywhere I looked, big action, inexplicable. A tremor welled up beside a gaping muskrat burrow in the bank and I caught my breath, but no muskrat appeared. The ripples continued to fan upstream with a steady, powerful thrust. Night was knitting over my face an eyeless mask, and I still sat transfixed. A distant airplane, a delta wing out of nightmare, made a gliding shadow on the creek's bottom that looked like a stingray cruising upstream. At once a black fin slit the pink cloud on the water, shearing it in two. The two halves merged together and seemed to dissolve before my eyes. Darkness pooled in the cleft of the creek and rose, as water collects in a well. Untamed, dreaming lights flickered over the sky. I saw hints of hulking underwater shadows, two pale splashes out of the water, and round ripples rolling close together from a blackened center.

At last I stared upstream where only the deepest violet remained of the cloud, a cloud so high its underbelly still glowed feeble color reflected from a hidden sky lighted in turn by a sun halfway to China. And out of that violet, a sudden enormous black body arced over the water. I saw only a cylindrical sleekness. Head and tail, if there was a head and tail, were both submerged in cloud. I saw only one ebony fling, a headlong dive to darkness; then the waters closed, and the lights went out.

I walked home in a shivering daze, up hill and down. Later I lay open-mouthed in bed, my arms flung wide at my sides to steady the whirling darkness. At this latitude I'm spinning 836 miles an hour round the earth's axis; I often fancy I feel my sweeping fall as a breakneck arc like the dive of dolphins, and the hollow rushing of wind raises hair on my neck and the side of my face. In orbit around the sun I'm moving 64,800 miles an hour. The solar system as a whole, like a merry-go-round unhinged, spins, bobs, and blinks at the speed of 43,200 miles an hour along a course set east of Hercules. Someone has piped, and we are dancing a tarantella until the sweat pours. I open my eyes and I see dark, muscled forms curl out of water, with flapping gills and flattened eyes. I close my eyes and I see stars, deep stars giving way to deeper stars, deeper stars bowing to deepest stars at the crown of an infinite cone.

"Still," wrote van Gogh in a letter, "a great deal of light falls on everything." If we are blinded by darkness, we are also blinded by light. When too much light falls on everything, a special terror results. Peter Freuchen describes the notorious kayak sickness to which Greenland Eskimos are prone. "The Greenland fjords are peculiar for the spells of completely quiet weather, when there is not enough wind to blow out a match and the water is like a sheet of glass. The kayak hunter must sit in his boat without stirring a finger so as not to scare the shy seals away. . . . The sun, low in the sky, sends a glare into his eyes, and the landscape around moves into the realm of the unreal. The reflex from the mirrorlike water hypnotizes him, he seems to be unable to move, and all of a sudden it is as if he were floating in a bottomless void, sinking, sinking, and sinking. . . . Horror-stricken, he tries to stir, to cry out, but he cannot, he is completely paralyzed, he just falls and falls." Some hunters are especially cursed with this panic, and bring ruin and sometimes starvation to their families.

Sometimes here in Virginia at sunset low clouds on the southern or northern horizon are completely invisible in the lighted sky. I only know one is there because I can see its reflection in still water. The first time I discovered this mystery I looked from cloud to no-cloud in bewilderment, checking my bearings over and over, thinking maybe the ark of the covenant was just passing by south of Dead Man Mountain. Only much later did I read the explanation: polarized light from the sky is very much weakened by reflection, but the light in clouds isn't polarized. So invisible clouds pass among visible clouds, till all slide over the mountains; so a greater light extinguishes a lesser as though it didn't exist.

In the great meteor shower of August, the Perseid, I wail all day for the shooting stars I miss. They're out there showering down, committing hara-kiri in a flame of fatal attraction, and hissing perhaps at last into the ocean. But at dawn what looks like a blue dome clamps down over me like a lid on a pot. The stars and planets could smash and I'd never know. Only a piece of ashen moon occasionally climbs up or down the inside of the dome, and our local star without surcease explodes on our heads. We have really only that one light, one source for all power, and yet we must turn away from it by universal decree. Nobody here on the planet seems aware of this strange, powerful taboo, that we all walk about carefully averting our faces, this way and that, lest our eyes be blasted forever.

Darkness appalls and light dazzles; the scrap of visible light that doesn't hurt my eyes hurts my brain. What I see sets me swaying. Size and distance and the sudden swelling of meanings confuse me, bowl me over. I straddle the sycamore log bridge over Tinker Creek in the summer. I look at the lighted creek bottom: snail tracks tunnel the mud in quavering curves. A crayfish jerks, but by the time I absorb what has happened, he's gone in a billowing smokescreen of silt. I look at the water: minnows and shiners. If I'm thinking minnows, a carp will fill my brain till I scream. I look at the water's surface: skaters, bubbles, and leaves sliding down. Suddenly, my own face, reflected, startles me witless. Those snails have been tracking my face! Finally, with a shuddering wrench of the will, I see clouds, cirrus clouds. I'm dizzy, I fall in. This looking business is risky.

Once I stood on a humped rock on nearby Purgatory Mountain, watching through binoculars the great autumn hawk migration below, until I discovered that I was in danger of joining the hawks on a vertical migration of my own. I was used to binoculars, but not, apparently, to balancing on humped rocks while looking through them. I staggered. Everything advanced and receded by turns; the world was full of unexplained foreshortenings and depths. A distant huge tan object, a hawk the size of an elephant, turned out to be the browned bough of a nearby loblolly pine. I followed a sharp-shinned hawk against a featureless sky, rotating my head unawares as it flew, and when I lowered the glass a glimpse of my own looming shoulder sent me staggering. What prevents the men on Palomar from falling, voiceless and blinded, from their tiny, vaulted chairs?

I reel in confusion; I don't understand what I see. With the naked eye I can see two million light-years to the Andromeda galaxy. Often I slop some creek water in a jar and when I get home I dump it in a white china bowl. After the silt settles I return and see tracings of minute snails on the bottom, a planarian or two winding round the rim of water, roundworms shimmying frantically, and finally, when my eyes have adjusted to these dimensions, amoebae. At first the amoebae look like *muscae volitantes*, those curled moving spots you seem to see in your eyes when you stare at a distant wall. Then I see the amoebae as drops of water congealed, bluish, translucent, like chips of sky in the bowl. At length I choose one individual and give myself over to its idea of an evening. I see it dribble a grainy foot before it on its wet, unfathomable way. Do its unedited sense impressions include the fierce focus of my eyes? Shall I take it outside and show it Andromeda, and blow its little endoplasm? I stir the water with a finger, in case it's running out of oxygen. Maybe I should get a tropical aquarium with motorized bubblers and lights, and keep this one for a pet. Yes, it would tell its fissioned descendants, the universe is two feet by five, and if you listen closely you can hear the buzzing music of the spheres.

Oh, it's mysterious lamplit evenings, here in the galaxy, one after the other. It's one of those nights when I wander from window to window, looking for a sign. But I can't see. Terror and a beauty insoluble are a ribband of blue woven into the fringes of garments of things both great and small. No culture explains, no bivouac offers real haven or rest. But it could be that we are not seeing something. Galileo thought comets were an optical illusion. This is fertile ground: since we are certain that they're not, we can look at what our scientists have been saying with fresh hope. What if there are *really* gleaming, castellated cities hung upside-down over the desert sand? What limpid lakes and cool date palms have our caravans always passed untried? Until, one by one, by the blindest of leaps, we light on the road to these places, we must stumble in darkness and hunger. I turn from the window. I'm blind as a bat, sensing only from every direction the echo of my own thin cries.

I chanced on a wonderful book by Marius von Senden, called *Space and Sight*. When Western surgeons discovered how to perform safe cataract operations, they ranged across Europe and America operating on dozens of men and women of all ages who had been blinded by cataracts since birth. Von Senden collected accounts of such cases; the histories are fascinating. Many doctors had tested their patients' sense perceptions and ideas of space both before and after the operations. The vast majority of patients, of both sexes and all ages, had, in von Senden's opinion, no idea of space whatsoever. Form, distance, and size were so many meaningless syllables. A patient "had no idea of depth, confusing it with roundness." Before the operation a doctor would give a blind patient a cube and a sphere; the patient would tongue it or feel it with his hands, and name it correctly. After the operation the doctor would show the same objects to the patient without letting him touch them; now he had no clue whatsoever what he was seeing. One patient called lemonade "square" because it pricked on his tongue as a square shape pricked on the touch of his hands. Of another postoperative patient, the doctor writes, "I have found in her no notion of size, for example, not even within the narrow limits which she might have encompassed with the aid of touch. Thus when I asked her to show me how big her mother was, she did not stretch out her hands, but set her two index-fingers a few inches apart." Other doctors reported their patients' own statements to similar effect. "The room he was in . . . he knew to be but part of the house, yet he could not conceive that the whole house could look bigger"; "Those who are blind from birth . . . have no real conception of height or distance. A house that is a mile away is thought of as nearby, but requiring the taking of a lot of steps. . . . The elevator that whizzes him up and down gives no more sense of vertical distance than does the train of horizontal."

For the newly sighted, vision is pure sensation unencumbered by meaning: "The girl went through the experience that we all go through and forget, the moment we are born. She saw, but it did not mean anything but a lot of different kinds of brightness." Again, "I asked the patient what he could see; he answered that he saw an extensive field of light, in which everything appeared dull, confused, and in motion. He could not distinguish objects." Another patient saw "nothing but a confusion of forms and colours." When a newly sighted girl saw photographs and paintings, she asked, " 'Why do they put those dark marks all over them?' 'Those aren't dark marks,' her mother explained, 'those are shadows. That is one of the ways the eye knows that things have shape. If it were not for shadows many things would look flat.' 'Well, that's how things do look,' Joan answered. 'Everything looks flat with dark patches.' "

But it is the patients' concepts of space that are most revealing. One patient, according to his doctor, "practiced his vision in a strange fashion; thus he takes off one of his boots, throws it some way off in front of him, and then attempts to gauge the distance at which it lies; he takes a few steps towards the boot and tries to grasp it; on failing to reach it, he moves on a step or two and gropes for the boot until he finally gets hold of it."

"But even at this stage, after three weeks' experience of seeing," von Senden goes on, " 'space,' as he conceives it, ends with visual space, i.e. with colour-patches that happen to bound his view. He does not yet have the notion that a larger object (a chair) can mask a smaller one (a dog), or that the latter can still be present even though it is not directly seen."

In general the newly sighted see the world as a dazzle of color-patches. They are pleased by the sensation of color, and learn quickly to name the colors, but the rest of seeing is tormentingly difficult. Soon after his operation a patient "generally bumps into one of these colour-patches and observes them to be substantial, since they resist him as tactual objects do. In walking about it also strikes him—or can if he pays attention—that he is continually passing in between the colours he sees, that he can go past a visual object, that a part of it then steadily disappears from view; and that in spite of this, however he twists and turns—whether entering the room from the door, for example, or returning back to it—he always has a visual space in front of him. Thus he gradually comes to realize that there is also a space behind him, which he does not see."

The mental effort involved in these reasonings proves overwhelming for many patients. It oppresses them to realize, if they ever do at all, the tremendous size of the world, which they had previously conceived of as something touchingly manageable. It oppresses them to realize that they have been visible to people all along, perhaps unattractively so, without their knowledge or consent. A disheartening number of them refuse to use their new vision, continuing to go over objects with their tongues, and lapsing into apathy and despair. "The child can see, but will not make use of his sight. Only when pressed can he with difficulty be brought to look at objects in his neighbourhood; but more than a foot away it is impossible to bestir him to the necessary effort." Of a twenty-one-year-old girl, the doctor relates, "Her unfortunate father, who had hoped for so much from this operation, wrote that his daughter carefully shuts her eyes whenever she wishes to go about the house, especially when she comes to a staircase, and that she is never happier or more at ease than when, by closing her eyelids, she relapses into her former state of total blindness." A fifteen-year-old boy, who was also in love with a girl at the asylum for the blind, finally blurted out, "No, really, I can't stand it any more; I want to be sent back to the asylum again. If things aren't altered, I'll tear my eyes out."

Some do learn to see, especially the young ones. But it

changes their lives. One doctor comments on "the rapid and complete loss of that striking and wonderful serenity which is characteristic only of those who have never yet seen." A blind man who learns to see is ashamed of his old habits. He dresses up, grooms himself, and tries to make a good impression. While he was blind he was indifferent to objects unless they were edible; now, "a sifting of values sets in . . . his thoughts and wishes are mightily stirred and some few of the patients are thereby led into dissimulation, envy, theft and fraud."

On the other hand, many newly sighted people speak well of the world, and teach us how dull is our own vision. To one patient, a human hand, unrecognized, is "something bright and then holes." Shown a bunch of grapes, a boy calls out, "It is dark, blue and shiny. . . . It isn't smooth, it has bumps and hollows." A little girl visits a garden. "She is greatly astonished, and can scarcely be persuaded to answer, stands speechless in front of the tree, which she only names on taking hold of it, and then as 'the tree with the lights in it.' " Some delight in their sight and give themselves over to the visual world. Of a patient just after her bandages were removed, her doctor writes, "The first things to attract her attention were her own hands; she looked at them very closely, moved them repeatedly to and fro, bent and stretched the fingers, and seemed greatly astonished at the sight." One girl was eager to tell her blind friend that "men do not really look like trees at all," and astounded to discover that her every visitor had an utterly different face. Finally, a twenty-two-year-old girl was dazzled by the world's brightness and kept her eyes shut for two weeks. When at the end of that time she opened her eyes again, she did not recognize any objects, but, "the more she now directed her gaze upon everything about her, the more it could be seen how an expression of gratification and astonishment overspread her features; she repeatedly exclaimed: 'Oh God! How beautiful!' "

I saw color-patches for weeks after I read this wonderful book. It was summer; the peaches were ripe in the valley orchards. When I woke in the morning, color-patches wrapped round my eyes, intricately, leaving not one unfilled spot. All day long I walked among shifting color-patches that parted before me like the Red Sea and closed again in silence, transfigured, wherever I looked back. Some patches swelled and loomed, while others vanished utterly, and dark marks flitted at random over the whole dazzling sweep. But I couldn't sustain the illusion of flatness. I've been

around for too long. Form is condemned to an eternal danse
macabre with meaning: I couldn't unpeach the peaches. Nor can
I remember ever having seen without understanding; the color-
patches of infancy are lost. My brain then must have been
smooth as any balloon. I'm told I reached for the moon; many
babies do. But the color-patches of infancy swelled as meaning
filled them; they arrayed themselves in solemn ranks down distance which unrolled and stretched before me like a plain. The
moon rocketed away. I live now in a world of shadows that
shape and distance color, a world where space makes a kind of
terrible sense. What gnosticism is this, and what physics? The
fluttering patch I saw in my nursery window—silver and green
and shape-shifting blue—is gone; a row of Lombardy poplars
takes its place, mute, across the distant lawn. That humming
oblong creature pale as light that stole along the walls of my
room at night, stretching exhilaratingly around the corners, is
gone, too, gone the night I ate of the bittersweet fruit, put two
and two together and puckered forever my brain. Martin Buber
tells this tale: "Rabbi Mendel once boasted to his teacher Rabbi
Elimelekh that evenings he saw the angel who rolls away the
light before the darkness, and mornings the angel who rolls away
the darkness before the light. 'Yes,' said Rabbi Elimelekh, "in
my youth I saw that too. Later on you don't see these things any
more."

Why didn't someone hand those newly sighted people paints
and brushes from the start, when they still didn't know what
anything was? Then maybe we all could see color-patches too,
the world unraveled from reason, Eden before Adam gave names.
The scales would drop from my eyes; I'd see trees like men
walking; I'd run down the road against all orders, hallooing and
leaping.

Seeing is of course very much a matter of verbalization. Unless I
call my attention to what passes before my eyes, I simply won't
see it. It is, as Ruskin says, "not merely unnoticed, but in the
full, clear sense of the word, unseen." My eyes alone can't
solve analogy tests using figures, the ones which show, with
increasing elaborations, a big square, then a small square in a big
square, then a big triangle, and expect me to find a small triangle
in a big triangle. I have to say the words, describe what I'm
seeing. If Tinker Mountain erupted, I'd be likely to notice. But if
I want to notice the lesser cataclysms of valley life, I have to
maintain in my head a running description of the present. It's not

that I'm observant; it's just that I talk too much. Otherwise, especially in a strange place, I'll never know what's happening. Like a blind man at the ball game, I need a radio.

When I see this way I analyze and pry. I hurl over logs and roll away stones; I study the bank a square foot at a time, probing and tilting my head. Some days when a mist covers the mountains, when the muskrats won't show and the microscope's mirror shatters, I want to climb up the blank blue dome as a man would storm the inside of a circus tent, wildly, dangling, and with a steel knife claw a rent in the top, peep, and, if I must, fall.

But there is another kind of seeing that involves a letting go. When I see this way I sway transfixed and emptied. The difference between the two ways of seeing is the difference between walking with and without a camera. When I walk with a camera I walk from shot to shot, reading the light on a calibrated meter. When I walk without a camera, my own shutter opens, and the moment's light prints on my own silver gut. When I see this second way I am above all an unscrupulous observer.

It was sunny one evening last summer at Tinker Creek; the sun was low in the sky, upstream. I was sitting on the sycamore log bridge with the sunset at my back, watching the shiners the size of minnows who were feeding over the muddy sand in skittery schools. Again and again, one fish, then another, turned for a split second across the current and flash! the sun shot out from its silver side. I couldn't watch for it. It was always just happening somewhere else, and it drew my vision just as it disappeared: flash, like a sudden dazzle of the thinnest blade, a sparking over a dun and olive ground at chance intervals from every direction. Then I noticed white specks, some sort of pale petals, small, floating from under my feet on the creek's surface, very slow and steady. So I blurred my eyes and gazed towards the brim of my hat and saw a new world. I saw the pale white circles roll up, roll up, like the world's turning, mute and perfect, and I saw the linear flashes, gleaming silver, like stars being born at random down a rolling scroll of time. Something broke and something opened. I filled up like a new wineskin. I breathed an air like light; I saw a light like water. I was the lip of a fountain the creek filled forever; I was ether, the leaf in the zephyr; I was flesh-flake, feather, bone.

When I see this way I see truly. As Thoreau says, I return to my senses. I am the man who watches the baseball game in silence in an empty stadium. I see the game purely; I'm abstracted and dazed. When it's all over and the white-suited players lope off the green field to their shadowed dugouts, I leap to my feet; I cheer and cheer.

But I can't go out and try to see this way. I'll fail, I'll go mad. All I can do is try to gag the commentator, to hush the noise of useless interior babble that keeps me from seeing just as surely as a newspaper dangled before my eyes. The effort is really a discipline requiring a lifetime of dedicated struggle; it marks the literature of saints and monks of every order East and West, under every rule and no rule, discalced and shod. The world's spiritual geniuses seem to discover universally that the mind's muddy river, this ceaseless flow of trivia and trash, cannot be dammed, and that trying to dam it is a waste of effort that might lead to madness. Instead you must allow the muddy river to flow unheeded in the dim channels of consciousness; you raise your sights; you look along it, mildly, acknowledging its presence without interest and gazing beyond it into the realm of the real where subjects and objects act and rest purely, without utterance. "Launch into the deep," says Jacques Ellul, "and you shall see."

The secret of seeing is, then, the pearl of great price. If I thought he could teach me to find it and keep it forever I would stagger barefoot across a hundred deserts after any lunatic at all. But although the pearl may be found, it may not be sought. The literature of illumination reveals this above all: although it comes to those who wait for it, it is always, even to the most practiced and adept, a gift and a total surprise. I return from one walk knowing where the killdeer nests in the field by the creek and the hour the laurel blooms. I return from the same walk a day later scarcely knowing my own name. Litanies hum in my ears; my tongue flaps in my mouth Ailinon, alleluia! I cannot cause light; the most I can do is try to put myself in the path of its beam. It is possible, in deep space, to sail on solar wind. Light, be it particle or wave, has force: you rig a giant sail and go. The secret of seeing is to sail on solar wind. Hone and spread your spirit till you yourself are a sail, whetted, translucent, broadside to the merest puff.

When her doctor took her bandages off and led her into the garden, the girl who was no longer blind saw "the tree with the lights in it." It was for this tree I searched through the peach orchards of summer, in the forests of fall and down winter and spring for years. Then one day I was walking along Tinker Creek thinking of nothing at all and I saw the tree with the lights in it. I saw the backyard cedar where the mourning doves roost charged and transfigured, each cell buzzing with flame. I stood on the grass with the lights in it, grass that was wholly fire, utterly focused and utterly dreamed. It was less like seeing than like being for the first time seen, knocked breathless by a powerful glance. The flood of fire abated, but I'm still spending the power. Gradually the lights went out in the cedar, the colors died, the cells unflamed and disappeared. I was still ringing. I had been my whole life a bell, and never knew it until at that moment I was lifted and struck. I have since only very rarely seen the tree with the lights in it. The vision comes and goes, mostly goes, but I live for it, for the moment when the mountains open and a new light roars in spate through the crack, and the mountains slam.

Book Review

An Anatomy of Melancholy
Conrad Aiken
New Republic, February 7, 1923

As reflection on a recent reading experience, a book review is another sort of reactive essay, but as writing about writing it represents abstracting about an abstraction and thus falls rather high on our scale. How fast a book review becomes dated depends as much as anything else on how long the book itself endures. Here one new poet reviews a work of another new poet that became the landmark long poem of the age. If this review can still interest us, that is a tribute to the scope of both reviewer and reviewed.

Mr. T. S. Eliot is one of the most individual of contemporary poets, and at the same time, anomalously, one of the most "traditional." By individual I mean that he can be, and often is (distressingly, to some) aware in his own way; as when he observes of a woman (in "Rhapsody on a Windy Night") that the door "opens on her like a grin" and that the corner of her eye "Twists like a crooked pin." Everywhere, in the very small body of his work, is similar evidence of a delicate sensibility, somewhat shrinking, somewhat injured, and always sharply itself. But also, with this capacity or necessity for being aware in his own way, Mr. Eliot has a haunting, a tyrannous awareness that there have been many other awarenesses before; and that the extent of his own awareness, and perhaps even the nature of it, is a consequence of these. He is, more than most poets, conscious of his roots. If this consciousness had not become acute in *Prufrock* or the *Portrait of a Lady*, it was nevertheless probably there: and the roots were quite conspicuously French, and dated, say, 1870–1900. A little later, as his sense of the past had become more pressing, it seemed that he was positively redirecting his roots—urging them to draw a morbid dramatic sharpness from Webster and Donne, a faded dry gilt of cynicism and formality from the Restoration. This search of the tomb produced "Sweeney" and "Whispers of Immortality." And finally, in *The Waste Land*, Mr. Eliot's sense of the literary past has become so overmastering as almost to constitute the motive of the work. It is as if, in conjunction with the Mr. Pound of the *Cantos*, he wanted to make a "literature of literature"—a poetry actuated not more by life itself than by poetry; as if he had concluded that the characteristic awareness of a poet of the twentieth century must inevitably, or ideally, be a very complex and very literary awareness, able to speak only, or best, in terms of the literary past, the terms which had molded its tongue. This involves a kind of idolatry of literature with which it is a little difficult to sympathize. In positing, as it seems to, that there is nothing left for literature to do but become a kind of parasitic growth on literature, a sort of mistletoe, it involves, I think, a definite astigmatism—a distortion. But the theory is interesting if only because it has colored an important and brilliant piece of work.

The Waste Land is unquestionably important, unquestionably brilliant. It is important partly because its 433 lines summarize Mr. Eliot, for the moment, and demonstrate that he is an even better poet than most had thought; and partly because it embodies the theory just touched upon, the theory of the "allusive" method in poetry. *The Waste Land* is, indeed, a poem of allusion all compact. It purports to be symbolical; most of its symbols are drawn from literature or legend; and Mr. Eliot has thought it necessary to supply, in notes, a list of the many quotations, references, and translations with which it bristles. He observes candidly that the poem presents "difficulties," and requires "elucidation." This serves to raise at once, the question whether these difficulties, in which perhaps Mr. Eliot takes a little pride, are so much the result of complexity, a fine elaborateness, as of confusion. The poem has been compared, by one reviewer, to a "full-rigged ship built in a bottle," the suggestion being that it is a perfect piece of construction. But *is* it a perfect piece of construction? Is the complex material mastered, and made coherent? Or, if the poem is not successful in that way, in what way is it successful? Has it the formal and intellectual complex unity of a microscopic Divine Comedy; or is its unity—supposing it to have one—of another sort?

If we leave aside for the moment all other considerations, and read the poem solely with the intention of understanding, with the aid of the notes, the symbolism; of making out what it is that is symbolized, and how these symbolized feelings are brought into relation with each other and with the other matters in the poem; I think we must, with reservations, and with no invidiousness, conclude that the poem is not, in any formal sense, coherent. We cannot feel that all the symbolisms belong quite inevitably where they have been put; that the order of the parts is an inevitable order; that there is anything more than a rudimentary progress from one theme to another; nor that the relation between the more symbolic parts and the less is always as definite as it should be. What we feel is that Mr. Eliot has not wholly annealed the allusive matter, has left it unabsorbed, lodged in gleaming fragments amid material alien to it. Again, there is a distinct weakness consequent on the use of allusions which may have both intellectual and emotional value for Mr. Eliot, but (even with the notes) none for us. The "Waste Land" of the Grail Legend might be a good symbol, if it were something with which we were sufficiently familiar. But it can never, even when explained, be a good symbol, simply because it has no immediate associations for us. It might, of course, be a good *theme*. In that case it would be *given* us. But Mr. Eliot uses it for purposes of overtone; he refers to it; and as overtone it quite clearly fails. He gives us, superbly, a waste land—not *the* Waste Land. Why, then, refer to the latter at all—if he is not, in the poem, really going to use it? Hyacinth fails in the same way. So does the

Fisher King. So does the Hanged Man, which Mr. Eliot tells us he associates with Frazer's Hanged God—we take his word for it. But if the precise association is worth anything, it is worth *putting into the poem*; otherwise there can be no purpose in mentioning it. Why, again, Datta, Dayadhvam, Damyata? Or Shantih? Do they not say a good deal less for us than "Give: sympathize: control" or "Peace"? Of course; but Mr. Eliot replies that he wants them not merely to mean those particular things, but also to mean them in a particular way—that is, to be remembered in connection with a Upanishad. Unfortunately, we have none of us this memory, nor can he give it to us; and in the upshot he gives us only a series of agreeable sounds which might as well have been nonsense. What we get at, and I think it is important, is that in none of these particular cases does the reference, the allusion, justify itself intrinsically, make itself felt. When we are aware of these references at all (sometimes they are unidentifiable) we are aware of them simply as something unintelligible but suggestive. When they have been explained, we are aware of the material referred to, the fact, (for instance, a vegetation ceremony,) as something useless for our enjoyment or understanding of the poem, something distinctly "dragged in," and only, perhaps, of interest as having suggested a pleasantly ambiguous line. For unless an allusion is made to live identifiably, to flower where transplanted, it is otiose. We admit the beauty of the implicational or allusive method; but the key to an implication should be in the implication itself, not outside of it. We admit the value of esoteric pattern: but the pattern should disclose its secret, should not be dependent on a cypher. Mr. Eliot assumes for his allusions, and for the fact that they actually allude to something, an importance which the allusions themselves do not, as expressed, aesthetically command, nor, as explained, logically command; which is pretentious. He is a little pretentious, too, in his "plan"—*qui pourtant n'existe pas*. If it is a plan, then its principle is oddly akin to planlessness. Here and there, in the wilderness, a broken finger-post.

I enumerate these objections not, I must emphasize, in derogation of the poem, but to dispel, if possible, an illusion as to its nature. It is perhaps important to note that Mr. Eliot, with his comment on the "plan," and several critics, with their admiration of the poem's woven complexity, minister to the idea that *The Waste Land* is, precisely, a kind of epic in a walnut shell: elaborate, ordered, unfolded with a logic at every joint discernible; but it is also important to note that this idea is false. With or without the notes the poem belongs rather to that symbolical order in which one may justly say that the "meaning" is not explicitly, or exactly, worked out. Mr. Eliot's net is wide, its meshes are small; and he catches a good deal more—thank heaven—than he pretends to. If space permitted one could pick out many lines and passages and parodies and quotations which do not demonstrably, in any "logical" sense, carry forward the theme, passages which unjustifiably, but happily, "expand" beyond its purpose. Thus the poem has an emotional value far clearer and richer than its arbitrary and rather unworkable logical value. One might assume that it originally consisted of a number of separate poems which have been telescoped—given a kind of forced unity. the Waste Land conception offered itself as a generous net which would, if not unify, at any rate contain these varied elements. We are aware of a superficial "binding"—we observe the anticipation and repetition of themes, motifs; "Fear death by water" anticipates the episode of Phlebas, the cry of the nightingale is repeated; but these are pretty flimsy links, and do not genuinely bind because they do not reappear naturally, but arbitrarily. This suggests, indeed, that Mr. Eliot is perhaps attempting a kind of program music in words, endeavoring to rule out "emotional accidents" by supplying his readers, in notes, with only those associations which are correct. He himself hints at the musical analogy when he observes that "in the first part of Part V three themes are employed."

I think, therefore, that the poem must be taken—most invitingly offers itself—as a brilliant and kaleidoscopic confusion; as a series of sharp, discrete, slightly related perceptions and feelings, dramatically and lyrically presented, and violently juxtaposed, (for effect of dissonance) so as to give us an impression of an intensely modern, intensely literary consciousness which perceives itself to be not a unit but a chance correlation or conglomerate of mutually discolorative fragments. We are invited into a mind, a world, which is a "broken bundle of mirrors"; a "heap of broken images." Isn't it that Mr. Eliot, finding it "impossible to say just what he means"—to recapitulate, to enumerate all the events and discoveries and memories that make a consciousness—has emulated the "magic lantern" that throws "the nerves in pattern on a screen"? If we perceive the poem in this light, as a series of brilliant, brief, unrelated or dimly related pictures by which a consciousness empties itself of its characteristic contents, then we also perceive that, anomalously, though the dropping out of any one picture would not in the least affect the logic or "meaning" of the whole, it would seriously detract from the value of the portrait. The "plan" of the poem would not greatly suffer, one makes bold to assert, by the elimination of "April is the cruelest month," or Phlebas, or the Thames daughters, or Sosostris or "You gave me hyacinths" or "A woman drew her long black hair out tight"; nor would it matter if it did. These things are not important parts of an important or careful intellectual pattern; but they are important parts of an important emotional ensemble. The relation between Tiresias (who is said to unify the poem, in a sense, as spectator) and the Waste Land, or Mr. Eugenides, or Hyacinth, or any other fragment, is a dim and tonal one, not exact. It will not bear analysis, it is not always operating, nor can one with assurance, at any given point, say how much it is operating. In this sense *The Waste Land* is a series of separate poems or passages, not perhaps all written at one time or with one aim, to which a spurious but happy sequence has been given. This spurious sequence has a value—it creates the necessary superficial formal unity; but it need not be stressed, as the Notes stress it. Could one not wholly rely for one's unity—as Mr. Eliot *has* largely relied—simply on the dim unity of "personality" which would underlie the retailed contents of a single consciousness? Unless one is going to carry unification very far, weave and interweave very closely, it would perhaps be as well not to unify at all; to dispense, for example, with arbitrary repetitions.

We reach thus the conclusion that the poem succeeds—as it brilliantly does—by virtue of its incoherence, not of its plan; by virtue of its ambiguities, not of its explanations. Its incoherence is a virtue because its *donnée* is incoherence. Its rich, vivid, crowded use of implication is a virtue, as implication is *always* a virtue—it shimmers, it suggests, it gives the desired strangeness. But when, as often, Mr. Eliot uses an implication beautifully—conveys by means of a picture-symbol or action-symbol a feeling—we do not require to be told that he had in mind a passage in the *Encyclopedia*, or the color of his nursery wall; the information is disquieting, has a sour air of pedantry. We "accept" the poem as we would accept a powerful, melancholy tone-poem. We do not want to be told what occurs; nor is it more than mildly amusing to know what passages are, in the Straussian manner, echoes or parodies. We cannot believe that every syllable has an algebraic inevitability, nor would we wish it so. We could dispense with the French, Italian, Latin, and Hindu phrases—they are irritating. But when our reservations have all been made, we accept *The Waste Land* as one of the most moving and original poems of our time. It captures us. And we sigh, with a dubious eye on the "notes" and "plan," our bewilderment that after so fine a performance Mr. Eliot should have thought it an occasion for calling "Tullia's ape a marmosyte." Tullia's ape is good enough.

Editorial

The Burning of the Dead
Lafcadio Hearn
New Orleans *Times-Democrat,* March 30, 1884

An editorial is an expression of opinion in reaction to some public events. It is another form of journalistic essaying and stands midway between personal and impersonal essay. "Opinion" indicates that the ideas are not proven fact and are not universally shared. To the extent that the topics are localized in time and space, editorials date rapidly or seem parochial to outsiders. The very ephemerality of the asserted generalizations serves as a good index to their level of abstraction, since more summative statements apply more broadly across peoples in different places and epochs. An anthologist becomes especially aware of how rarely a writer reacting to "current events" manages to come up with reflections that can interest readers of other countries and generations. It helps if the editorialist is responding to something as broad as a trend rather than a mere event. It helps even more if the editorialist sees the universal through the local.

The strong feeling in favor of cremation both at home and abroad is a sign of the times. It is true that this feeling is by no means that of the great majority as yet; but it is the feeling of a very intelligent and imposing minority which has the power to make converts rapidly in multitude. The mind of the nineteenth century is undergoing a reaction in favor of ancient funeral rites and pagan common sense. Is this because we are growing skeptical—because the old superstitions and the Folklore of the Dead are rapidly passing away? Certainly the feeling against cremation is most strong where superstitions do most survive. But the vanishing away of certain dark forms of belief, and the tendency of the times to abandon old customs and old ideas, are themselves due to those vast economical changes which have already modified the face of the world, and broken down barriers between nations. The skepticism of the period is a cause, perhaps—but only a subordinate cause, for the open advocacy of cremation. The great primal cause is the enormous industrial progress of the period, enabling countries to maintain populations ten times larger than could have found support some centuries ago. The world's markets are becoming more colossal than was ever Babylon or Egyptian Thebes; cities of a hundred thousand people spring up every few decades in the midst of what were previously wildernesses; and towns of insignificant size receive sudden nourishment from railroads and swell to metropolitan proportions. In many American cities population doubles itself at astonishingly brief intervals; and the intervening lands are cultivated to their utmost extent by a rapidly increasing race of sturdy farmers. In Europe the increase of population is slower by far, but it is nevertheless astounding when compared with the populousness of the sixteenth and seventeenth centuries. A generation ago London had barely three millions of inhabitants; she has now almost five millions. All the great capitals are becoming more populous. Science and invention have enabled the human race to multiply extraordinarily. But with the increase of life there is the inevitable increase of disease; and the work of Death is becoming so gigantic that the living can scarcely find place for his harvests. Cemeteries are too quickly filled;—the city grows out to them and around them and beyond them; the expenses of extramural burial increase continuously; the earth is overfed with corpses until she can no longer digest them, and the air of each metropolis becomes heavy with odors of dissolution. Inhumation can no longer meet the demands of hygiene;—Science has taken the alarm, and seeks to summon Fire to the assistance of earth. Fire, the All-Producer, as personified in the sun—(*Surya*, 'The Begetter')—is also the All-Purifier. Fire, not earth, shall devour the dead in centuries to come as in centuries that have passed away. Cremation will become at last, not a choice, but a necessity. It may first be established as optional; it will then become obligatory. These are the declarations and predictions of its advocates.

Elsewhere we publish extracts from an excellent article upon that subject, which appeared in the Paris *Figaro*. The author, who is a devout Roman Catholic, admirably points out the absence of any potent religious argument against the incineration of the dead, while he also dwells upon the horrors of slow decomposition and the involuntary yet inevitable condemnation of thousands to a *living burial*. But there is also a poetical side to the sinister question, which might be dilated upon—the swift restoration of the substances of being to their primal source of light and air—the remelting of the body into the pure and luminous elements which formed them. The body soars with the rising of the flame which enwraps it, soars toward that blue to which all eyes turn at times with an indefinite longing—as though there were something of the bird in every human heart.

"The earth," poetically sang a Vedic poet, "receives the dead even as a mother wraps the fold of her robe about the weary child who sinks to slumber in her arms." The thought seems beautiful, but the words are untrue. For the earth is a cannibal; —she devours her children as hideously but infinitely more slowly than the python devours his prey—so hideously that only the bravest soldiers of Science have ever dared to peer into the processes of her digestion—as did Orfila. Perhaps it would be well if certain sentimental opponents of cremation should behold that indescribable treatise of his upon Juridical Exhumation with its frightful colored plates, whose horrors surpass the most loathsome conceptions of madness and the most appalling monstrosities of nightmare. One glance at these secrets of the tomb were enough to convert the bitterest anti-cremationist! And how slow the decay! Sometimes in five years the earth has not consumed its food. Poets may write touching pantheistic madrigals concerning the ultimate blending of all flesh with that "Universal Paste formed of the shapes that God melts down"; but has the poet ever dared to raise the coffin-lid and observe the ghastly transmutation for an instant? Could even the philosopher dare so much; —for the breath of the tomb is fatal. Death permits only the high-priests of science to study that ghastly chemistry and live! Surely the noblest works of God are wrought in fire;—in flame were born all the hosts of heaven, and of flame is the visible soul of stars;—fire is the creative force of Nature; and to fire alone rightfully belongs the task of redissolving that which it first warmed and shaped into life. Modern respect for the dead is really superficial: it stops at the surface of graves and at the entrances of vaults. To abandon the body of a friend, a child, a woman beloved, to worms and to all the frightful fermentations of the tomb, seems, when we reflect upon it, barbarous—hideous! Even the Parsee Towers of Silence, with their vultures and birds of carrion hovering in spiral flight, contain naught so frightful as do our fairest sepulchres;—better surely abandon the dead unto the birds of heaven than to the worms of earth. Death was not a nightmare to antique civilizations; it became so only when the funeral pyres had ceased to flame, and the funeral urns had ceased to be. There was nothing sinister, nothing awful about the tombs of the Greek or Roman dead—only the graceful vases containing the "pinch of scentless and delicate dust" gathered from the pyre—"the dust of the soul's own butterfly-wings," as it has been so daintily termed.

The crematories of the future will do the work better than the pyres of the ancients—much more perfectly, and much more cheaply. Incineration, if not complete, also has its horrors; —excepting a corpse in decomposition, there is nothing so goblin-like and appalling as a half-burned body. The antique process was slow, and in the intervals of feeding the fire there must have been ghastly sights. But in the strong, clear flame of the crematory-retort horror cannot endure an instant. There will be no room for such a spectacle as that described by one witness of the burning of Shelley's remains.

The desire for cremation is a sign of progress, a token of a healthier tendency of mind. Yet, it must be confessed, even cremation, as now advocated in its most scientific form, does not wholly satisfy human feeling in regard to the disposal of the dead. There are strange doubts—obscure as any Egyptian prayer— anxieties and fears. . . . If it be true that one person in every 5000 is buried alive, might not one in every 5000 also be burned alive? Where is the guarantee, since there is no assurance of death before visible decomposition sets in? Again, who knows precisely when all thought and sensation dies within the most secret chambers of the brain? When must the last spark of being fade out into utter darkness? Only a ghost might know; but the dead have no voice—even in dreams. The assurances of science do not wholly reassure; for science has scarcely yet begun to comprehend the deeper secrets of physiology and the mysteries of life. Some day revelations might be made too terrible to think of—revelations of consciousness resurrected momentarily in the midst of the material dissolution—strange flaring-up of sensations, of fancies and memories long forgotten—weird vitality of remembrances rekindled by the touch of destruction, by the combustion of death—just as characters of invisible ink are made visible by the approach of flame. Electricity alone—that holiest form of fire—may furnish ultimately some satisfactory means of answering all fearful doubt, when it shall become possible to dissolve a body instantaneously—as water is decomposed by the galvanic battery.

Ironic Proposal

A Modest Proposal
Jonathan Swift
1729

The prototype of the satiric scenario was more complex than today's journalistic brevity permits. Swift elaborated both the details of his scenario and the arguments for his proposal, which of course score serious points about the actuality of British rule in Ireland in his day. Born in Ireland, and the unorthodox dean of Saint Patrick's Cathedral in Dublin at the time of writing this, Swift was reacting to the pitiless exploitation of the Irish population by absentee British landlords. He chose to express this reaction not through denunciation but through proposal, which is, after all, a suggestion for an audience to take up—a sort of mock invitation to the English ruling class to reform their practices. As for the degree of authorial distance, it may be best expressed in scholar William Alfred Eddy's remark, "The dispassionate, business-like tone in which he unfolds the grotesque proposal is but a thin layer of cooled lava covering a pit of boiling indignation whose depth has never been sounded."

For Preventing the Children of Poor People in Ireland from Being a Burden to Their Parents or Country, and for Making Them Beneficial to the Public

It is a melancholy object to those who walk through this great town or travel in the country, when they see the streets, the roads, and cabin doors, crowded with beggars of the female sex, followed by three, four, or six children, all in rags and importuning every passenger for an alms. These mothers, instead of being able to work for their honest livelihood, are forced to employ all their time in strolling to beg sustenance for their helpless infants: who as they grow up either turn thieves for want of work, or leave their dear native country to fight for the pretender in Spain, or sell themselves to the Barbadoes.

I think it is agreed by all parties that this prodigious number of children in the arms, or on the backs, or at the heels of their mothers, and frequently of their fathers, is in the present deplorable state of the kingdom a very great additional grievance; and therefore, whoever could find out a fair, cheap, and easy method of making these children sound, useful members of the commonwealth would deserve so well of the public as to have his statue set up for a preserver of the nation.

But my intention is very far from being confined to provide only for the children of professed beggars; it is of a much greater extent, and shall take in the whole number of infants at a certain age who are born of parents in effect as little able to support them as those who demand our charity in the streets.

As to my own part, having turned my thoughts for many years upon this important subject and maturely weighed the several schemes of other projectors, I have always found them grossly mistaken in the computation. It is true, a child just dropped from its dam may be supported by her milk for a solar year, with little other nourishment; at most not above the value of 2s., which the mother may certainly get, or the value in scraps, by her lawful occupation of begging; and it is exactly at one year old that I propose to provide for them in such a manner as instead of being a charge upon their parents or the parish, or wanting food and raiment for the rest of their lives, they shall on the contrary contribute to the feeding, and partly to the clothing, of many thousands.

There is likewise another great advantage in my scheme, that it will prevent those voluntary abortions, and that horrid practice of women murdering their bastard children, alas! too frequent among us! sacrificing the poor innocent babes I doubt more to avoid the expense than the shame, which would move tears and pity in the most savage and inhuman breast.

The number of souls in this kingdom being usually reckoned one million and a half, of these I calculate there may be about two hundred thousand couples whose wives are breeders; from which number I subtract thirty thousand couples who are able to maintain their own children, although I apprehend there cannot be so many, under the present distresses of the kingdom, but this being granted, there will reman an hundred and seventy thousand breeders. I again subtract fifty thousand for those women who miscarry, or whose children die by accident or disease within the year. There only remains one hundred and twenty thousand children of poor parents annually born. The question therefore is, how this number shall be reared and provided for, which, as I have already said, under the present situation of affairs, is utterly impossible by all the methods hitherto proposed. For we can neither employ them in handicraft or agriculture; we neither build houses (I mean in the country) nor cultivate land: they can very seldom pick up a livelihood by stealing, till they arrive at six years old, except where they are of towardly parts, although I confess they learn the rudiments much earlier, during which time, they can however be properly looked upon only as probationers, as I have been informed by a principal gentleman in the county of Cavan, who protested to me that he never knew above one or two instances under the age of six, even in a part of the kingdom so renowned for the quickest proficiency in that art.

I am assured by our merchants, that a boy or a girl before twelve years old is no salable commodity; and even when they come to this age they will not yield above three pounds, or three pounds and half-a-crown at most on the exchange; which cannot turn to account either to the parents or kingdom, the charge of nutriment and rags having been at least four times that value.

I shall now therefore humbly propose my own thoughts, which I hope will not be liable to the least objection.

I have been assured by a very knowing American of my acquaintance in London, that a young healthy child well nursed is at a year old a most delicious, nourishing, and wholesome food, whether stewed, roasted, baked, or boiled; and I make no doubt that it will equally serve in a fricassee or a ragout.

I do therefore humbly offer it to public consideration that of the hundred and twenty thousand children already computed, twenty thousand may be reserved for breed, whereof only one-fourth part to be males; which is more than we allow to sheep, black cattle or swine; and my reason is, that these children are seldom the fruits of marriage, a circumstance not much regarded by our savages, therefore one male will be sufficient to serve four females. That the remaining hundred thousand may, at a year old, be offered in the sale to the persons of quality and fortune through the kingdom; always advising the mother to let them suck plentifully in the last month, so as to render them plump and fat for a good table. A child will make two dishes at an entertainment for friends; and when the family dines alone, the fore or hind quarter will make a reasonable dish, and seasoned with a little pepper or salt will be very good boiled on the fourth day, especially in winter.

I have reckoned upon a medium that a child just born will weigh 12 pounds, and in a solar year, if tolerably nursed, increaseth to 28 pounds.

I grant this food will be somewhat dear, and therefore very proper for landlords, who, as they have already devoured most of the parents, seem to have the best title to the children.

Infants' flesh will be in season throughout the year, but more plentiful in March, and a little before and after; for we are told by a grave author, an eminent French physician, that fish being a prolific diet, there are more children born in Roman Catholic countries about nine months after Lent than at any other season; therefore, reckoning a year after Lent, the markets will be more glutted than usual, because the number of popish infants is at least three to one in this kingdom: and therefore it will have one other collateral advantage, by lessening the number of papists among us.

I have already computed the charge of nursing a beggar's child (in which list I reckon all cottagers, laborers, and four-fifths of the farmers) to be about two shillings per annum, rags included; and I believe no gentleman would repine to give ten shillings for the carcass of a good fat child, which, as I have said, will make four dishes of excellent nutritive meat, when he hath only some particular friend or his own family to dine with him. Thus the squire will learn to be a good landlord, and grow popular among his tenants; the mother will have eight shillings net profit, and be fit for work till she produces another child.

Those who are more thrifty (as I must confess the times require) may flay the carcass; the skin of which artificially dressed will make admirable gloves for ladies, and summer boots for fine gentlemen.

As to our city of Dublin, shambles may be appointed for this purpose in the most convenient parts of it, and butchers we may be assured will not be wanting; although I rather recommend buying the children alive than dressing them hot from the knife as we do roasting pigs.

A very worthy person, a true lover of his country, and whose virtues I highly esteem, was lately pleased in discoursing on this matter to offer a refinement upon my scheme. He said that many gentlemen of this kingdom, having of late destroyed their deer, he conceived that the want of venison might be well supplied by the bodies of young lads and maidens, not exceeding fourteen years of age nor under twelve; so great a number of both sexes in every country being now ready to starve for want of work and service; and these to be disposed of by their parents, if alive, or otherwise by their nearest relations. But with due deference to so excellent a friend and so deserving a patriot, I cannot be altogether in his sentiments; for as to the males, my American acquaintance assured me, from frequent experience, that their flesh was generally tough and lean, like that of our school-boys by continual exercise, and their taste disagreeable; and to fatten them would not answer the charge. Then as to the females, it would, I think, with humble submission be a loss to the public, because they soon would become breeders themselves; and besides, it is not improbable that some scrupulous people might be apt to censure such a practice (although indeed very unjustly), as a little bordering upon cruelty; which, I confess, hath always been with me the strongest objection against any project, however so well intended.

But in order to justify my friend, he confessed that this expedient was put into his head by the famous Psalmanazar, a native of the island Formosa, who came from thence to London above twenty years ago, and in conversation told my friend, that in his country when any young person happened to be put to death, the executioner sold the carcass to persons of quality as a prime dainty; and that in his time the body of a plump girl of fifteen, who was crucified for an attempt to poison the emperor, was sold to his imperial majesty's prime minister of state, and other great mandarins of the court, in joints from the gibbet, at four hundred crowns. Neither indeed can I deny, that if the same use were made of several plump young girls in this town, who without one single groat to their fortunes cannot stir abroad without a chair, and appear at playhouse and assemblies in foreign fineries which they never will pay for, the kingdom would not be the worse.

Some persons of a desponding spirit are in great concern about that vast number of poor people, who are aged, diseased, or maimed, and I have been desired to employ my thoughts what course may be taken to ease the nation of so grievous an encumbrance. But I am not in the least pain upon that matter because it is very well known that they are every day dying and rotting by cold and famine, and filth and vermin, as fast as can be reasonably expected. And as to the young laborers, they are now in as hopeful a condition; they cannot get work, and consequently pine away for want of nourishment, to a degree that if at any time they are accidentally hired to common labor, they have not strength to perform it; and thus the country and themselves are happily delivered from the evils to come.

I have too long digressed, and therefore shall return to my subject. I think the advantages by the proposal which I have made are obvious and many, as well as of the highest importance.

For first, as I have already observed, it would greatly lessen the number of papists, with whom we are yearly over-run, being the principal breeders of the nation as well as our most dangerous enemies; and who stay at home on purpose with a design to deliver the kingdom to the pretender, hoping to take their advantage by the absence of so many good protestants, who have chosen rather to leave their country than stay at home and pay tithes against their conscience to an episcopal curate.

Secondly, The poorer tenants will have something valuable of their own, which by law may be made liable to distress and help to pay their landlord's rent, their corn and cattle being already seized, and money a thing unknown.

Thirdly, Whereas the maintenance of an hundred thousand children, from two years old and upward, cannot be computed at less than ten shillings a-piece per annum, the nation's stock will be thereby increased fifty thousand pounds per annum, beside the profit of a new dish introduced to the tables of all gentlemen of fortune in the kingdom who have any refinement in taste. And the money will circulate among ourselves, the goods being entirely of our own growth and manufacture.

Fourthly, The constant breeders, beside the gain of eight shillings sterling per annum by the sale of their children, will be rid of the charge of maintaining them after the first year.

Fifthly, This food would likewise bring great custom to taverns; where the vintners will certainly be so prudent as to procure the best receipts for dressing it to perfection, and consequently have their houses frequented by all the fine gentlemen, who justly value themselves upon their knowledge in good eating; and a skilful cook, who understands how to oblige his guests, will contrive to make it as expensive as they please.

Sixthly, This would be a great inducement to marriage, which all wise nations have either encouraged by rewards or enforced by laws and penalties. It would increase the care and tenderness of mothers toward their children, when they were sure of a settlement for life to the poor babes, provided in some sort by the public, to their annual profit instead of expense. We should see an honest emulation among the married women, which of them could bring the fattest child to the market. Men would become as fond of their wives during the time of their pregnancy as they are now of their mares in foal, their cows in calf, their sows when they are ready to farrow; nor offer to beat or kick them (as is too frequent a practice) for fear of a miscarriage.

Many other advantages might be enumerated. For instance, the addition of some thousand carcasses in our exportation of barreled beef, the propagation of swine's flesh, and improvement in the art of making good bacon, so much wanted among us by the great destruction of pigs, too frequent at our tables; which are no way comparable in taste or magnificence to a well-grown, fat, yearling child, which roasted whole will make a considerable figure at a lord mayor's feast or any other public entertainment. But this and many others I omit, being studious of brevity.

Supposing that one thousand families in this city would be constant customers for infants' flesh, beside others who might have it at merry-meetings, particularly weddings and christenings, I compute that Dublin would take off annually about twenty thousand carcasses; and the rest of the kingdom (where probably they will be sold somewhat cheaper) the remaining eighty thousand.

I can think of no one objection that will possibly be raised against this proposal, unless it should be urged that the number of people will be thereby much lessened in the kingdom. This I freely own, and was indeed one principal design in offering it to the world. I desire the reader will observe, that I calculate my remedy for this one individual kingdom of Ireland and for no other that ever was, is, or I think ever can be upon earth. Therefore let no man talk to me of other expedients: of taxing our absentees at five shillings a pound; of using neither clothes nor household furniture except what is of our own growth and manufacture; of utterly rejecting the materials and instruments that promote foreign luxury; of curing the expensiveness of pride, vanity, idleness, and gaming in our women; of introducing a vein of parsimony, prudence, and temperance; of learning to love our country, wherein we differ even from LAPLANDERS and the inhabitants of TOPINAMBOO; of quitting our animosities and factions, nor act any longer like the Jews, who were murdering one another at the very moment their city was taken; of being a little cautious not to sell our country and conscience for nothing; of teaching landlords to have at least one degree of mercy toward their tenants; lastly, of putting a spirit of honesty, industry, and skill into our shopkeepers; who, if a resolution could now be taken to buy only our native goods, would immediately unite to cheat and exact upon us in the price, the measure, and the goodness, nor could ever yet be brought to make one fair proposal of just dealing, though often and earnestly invited to it.

Therefore I repeat, let no man talk to me of these and the like expedients, till he hath at least some glimpse of hope that there will be ever some hearty and sincere attempt to put them in practice.

But as to myself, having been wearied out for many years with offering vain, idle, visionary thoughts, and at length utterly despairing of success I fortunately fell upon this proposal; which, as it is wholly new, so it hath something solid and real, of no expense and little trouble, full in our own power, and whereby we can incur no danger in disobliging ENGLAND. For this kind of commodity will not bear exportation, the flesh being of too tender a consistence to admit a long continuance in salt, although perhaps I could name a country which would be glad to eat up our whole nation without it.

After all, I am not so violently bent upon my own opinion as to reject any offer proposed by wise men, which shall be found equally innocent, cheap, easy, and effectual. But before something of that kind shall be advanced in contradiction to my scheme, and offering a better, I desire the author or authors will be pleased maturely to consider two points. First, as things now stand, how they will be able to find food and raiment for an hundred thousand useless mouths and backs. And secondly, there being a round million of creatures in human figure throughout this kingdom, whose whole subsistence put into a common stock would leave them in debt two millions of pounds sterling, adding those who are beggars by profession to the bulk of farmers, cottagers, and laborers, with their wives and children who are beggars in effect: I desire those politicians who dislike my overture, and may perhaps be so bold as to attempt an answer, that they will first ask the parents of these mortals, whether they would not at this day think it a great happiness to have been sold for food at a year old in the manner I prescribe, and thereby have avoided such a perpetual scene of misfortunes as they have since gone through by the oppression of landlords, the impossibility of paying rent without money or trade, the want of common sustenance, with neither house nor clothes to cover them from the inclemencies of the weather, and the most inevitable prospect of entailing the like or greater miseries upon their breed for ever.

I profess, in the sincerity of my heart that I have not the least personal interest in endeavoring to promote this necessary work, having no other motive than the public good of my country, by advancing our trade, providing for infants, relieving the poor, and giving some pleasure to the rich. I have no children by which I can propose to get a single penny; the youngest being nine years old, and my wife past child-bearing.

Speech

If We Had Left at Daybreak We Would Be There by Now
Carlos Fuentes

Harvard commencement address of June, 1983, printed in the *Harvard Gazette* of that month

---

The scope and complexity of Fuentes's argument could, on the one hand, place it far up the abstraction scale. He states several main generalizations, documents them with history, explains each, and combines them for conclusion. But this cogent argument is also a speech delivered in person to a particular audience on a particular date in reaction to "current events." These circumstances influence considerably the composition and style of the essay. As befits both vocal oratory and the assimilation of ideas by ear, he parcels his ideas out in short sentences and sentence fragments, to some extent deliberately redundant. Fuentes expostulates, praises, and admonishes his live audience, which includes, he realizes, present and future influencers of national policy. He speaks in his own person as a Latin neighbor and writer. So the very high-level I-it relation is framed by an I-you relation reminiscent of dialog or correspondence. We have only to imagine Fuentes addressing these ideas to his compatriots or to illiterates.

Mr. President, Members of the Corporation, Members of the Harvard Alumni Association, Ladies and Gentlemen:

Some time ago, I was travelling in the state of Morelos in Central Mexico, looking for the birthplace of Emiliano Zapata, the village of Anenecuilco.

I stopped on the way and asked a campesino, a laborer of the fields, how far it was to that village.

He answered me: "If you had left at daybreak, you would be there now."

This man had an internal clock which marked the time of his own personality and of his own culture.

For the clocks of all men and women, of all civilizations, of all histories, are not set at the same hour.

One of the wonders of our menaced globe is the variety of its experiences, its memories and its desires.

Any attempt to impose a uniform politics on this diversity is like a prelude to death.

Lech Walesa is a man who started out at daybreak, at the hour when the history of Poland demanded that the people of Poland act to solve the problems that a repressive government and a hollow party no longer knew how to solve.

We in Latin America who have practiced solidarity with Solidarity salute Lech Walesa today.

The honor done to me by this great center of learning, Harvard University, is augmented by the circumstances in which I receive it.

I accept this honor as a citizen of Mexico, and as a writer from Latin America.

Let me speak to you as such.

As a Mexican first:

The daybreak of a movement of social and political renewal cannot be set by calendars other than those of the people involved.

With Walesa and Solidarity, it was the internal clock of the people of Poland that struck the morning hour.

So it has always been: with the people of my country during our revolutionary experience; with the people of Central America in the hour we are all living; and with the people of Massachusetts in 1776.

The dawn of revolution reveals the total history of a community.

This is a self-knowledge that a society cannot be deprived of without grave consequences.

The Experience of Mexico

The Mexican Revolution was the object of constant harassment, pressures, menaces, boycotts and even a couple of armed interventions between 1910 and 1932.

It was extremely difficult for the United States Administrations of the time to deal with violent and rapid change on the southern border of your country.

Calvin Coolidge convened both Houses of Congress in 1927 and—talkative for once—denounced Mexico as the source of "Bolshevik" subversion in Central America.

We were the first domino.

But precisely because of its revolutionary policies favoring agrarian reform, secular education, collective bargaining and recovery of natural resources—all of them opposed by the successive governments in Washington, from Taft to Hoover—Mexico became a modern, contradictory self-knowing and self-questioning nation.

The Revolution did not make an instant democracy out of my country. But the first revolutionary government, that of Francisco I. Madero, was the most democratic regime we have ever had: Madero respected free elections, a free press and an uncontrollable Congress. Significantly, he was promptly overthrown by a conspiracy of the American Ambassador, Henry Lane Wilson, and a group of reactionary generals.

So, before becoming a democracy, Mexico first had to become a nation.

What the Revolution gave us all was the totality of our history and the possibility of a culture. "The Revolution"—wrote my compatriot, the great poet Octavio Paz—"The Revolution is a sudden immersion of Mexico in its own being. In the revolutionary explosion . . . each Mexican . . . finally recognizes, in a mortal embrace, the other Mexican."

Paz himself, Diego Rivera and Carlos Chavez, Mariano Azuela Azuela and Jose Clemento Orozco, Juan Rulfo and Rufino Tamayo: we all exist and work because of the revolutionary experience of our country. How can we stand by as this experience is denied, through ignorance and arrogance, to other people, our brothers, in Central America and the Caribbean?

A great statesman is a pragmatical idealist. Franklin D. Roosevelt had the political imagination and the diplomatic will to respect Mexico when President Lazaro Cardenas, in the culminating act of the Mexican Revolution, expropriated the nation's oil resources in 1938.

Instead of menacing, sanctioning or invading, Roosevelt negotiated.

He did not try to beat history. He joined it.

Will no one in this country imitate him today?

The lessons applicable to the current situation in Latin America are inscribed in the history—the very difficult history—of Mexican-American relations.

Why have they not been learnt?

Against Intervention

In today's world, intervention evokes a fearful symmetry.

As the United States feels itself authorized to intervene in Central America to put out a fire in your front yard—I'm delighted that we have been promoted from the traditional status of back yard—then the Soviet Union also feels authorized to play the fireman in all of its front and back yards.

Intervention damages the fabric of a nation, the chance of its resurrected history, the wholeness of its cultural identity.

I have witnessed two such examples of wholesale corruption by intervention in my lifetime.

One was in Czechoslovakia in the fall of 1968. I was there then to support my friends the writers, the students and statesmen of the Prague Spring. I heard them give thanks, at least, for their few months of freedom as night fell once more upon them: the night of Kafka, where nothing is remembered but nothing is forgiven.

The other time was in Guatemala in 1964, when the democratically elected government was overthrown by a mercenary invasion openly backed by the C.I.A. The political process of reform and self-recognition in Guatemala was brutally interrupted to no one's benefit: Guatemala was condemned to a vicious circle of repression, that continues to this day.

Intervention is defined as the action of the paramount regional power against a smaller state within its so-called "sphere of influence."

Intervention is defined by its victims. .

But the difference between Soviet actions in their "sphere of influence" and United States actions in theirs is that the Soviet regime is a tyranny and you are a democracy.

Yet more and more, over the past two years, I have heard North Americans in responsible positions speak of not caring whether the United States is loved, but whether it is feared; not whether it is admired for its cultural and political accomplishments, but respected for its material power; not whether the rights of others are respected, but its own strategic interests are defended.

These are inclinations that we have come to associate with the brutal diplomacy of the Soviet Union.

But we, the true friends of your great nation in Latin America, we the admirers of your extraordinary achievements in literature, science and the arts and of your democratic institutions, of your Congress and your courts, your universities and publishing houses and your free press—we your true friends, because we are your friends, will not permit you to conduct yourselves in Latin American affairs as the Soviet Union conducts itself in Central European and Central Asian affairs.

You are not the Soviet Union.

We shall be the custodians of your own true interests by helping you to avoid these mistakes.

We have memory on our side.

You suffer too much from historical amnesia.

You seem to have forgotten that your own Republic was born out of the barrel of a gun: the American Revolutionaries also shot their way to power.

We hope to have persuasion on our side, but also the body of international and inter-American law to help us.

We also have our own growing strategic preoccupations as to whether, under the guise of defending us from remote Soviet menaces and delirious domino effects, the United States would create one vast Latin American protectorate.

Meeting at Cancun on April 29, the Presidents of Mexico and Brazil, Miguel de la Madrid and Joao Figueiredo, agreed that "the Central American crisis has its origin in the economic and social structures prevalent in the region and [that] the efforts to overcome it must . . . avoid the tendency to define it as a chapter in East-West confrontation.''

And the Prime Minister of Spain, Felipe Gonzalez, on the eve of his visit to Washington, defined U.S. involvements in Central America as ''fundamentally harmful'' to the nations of the region and damaging to the international standing of the United States.

Yes, your alliances will crumble and your security will be endangered if you do not demonstrate that you are an enlightened, responsible power in your dealings with Latin America.

Yes, you must demonstrate your humanity and your intelligence here, in this house we share, our Hemisphere, or nowhere shall you be democratically credible.

Where are the Franklin Roosevelts, the Sumner Welleses, the George Marshalls, and the Dean Achesons demanded by the times?

Friends and Satellites

The great weakness of the Soviet Union is that it is surrounded by satellites, not by friends.

Sooner or later, the rebellion of the outlying nations in the Soviet sphere will eat, more and more deeply, into the innards of what Lord Carrington recently called ''a decaying Byzantium.''

The United States has the great strength of having friends, not satellites, on its borders.

Canada and Mexico are two independent nations that disagree on many issues with the United States.

We know that in public, as in personal life, nothing is more destructive of the self than being surrounded by sycophants.

But the same way as there are ''yes men'' in this world, there are ''yes nations.''

A ''yes nation'' harms itself as much as it harms its powerful protector: it deprives both of dignity, foresight and the sense of reality.

Nevertheless, Mexico has been chosen as a target of ''diplomatic isolation'' by the National Security Council Document on Policy in Central America and Cuba through Fiscal Year 84.

We know in Latin America that ''isolation'' can be a euphemism for destabilization.

Indeed, every time a prominent member of the Administration in Washington refers to Mexico as the ultimate domino, a prominent member of the Administration in Mexico City must stop in his tracks, offer a rebuttal and consolidate the nationalist legitimation of the Mexican government: Mexico is capable of governing itself without outside interference.

But if Mexico is a domino, then it fears being pushed from the North rather than from the South; such has been our historical experience.

This would be the ultimate accomplishment of Washington's penchant of the self-fulfilling prophecy: A Mexico destabilized by American nightmares about Mexico. We should all be warned about this.

Far from being "blind" or "complacent," Mexico is offering its friendly hand to the United States to help it avoid the repetition of costly historical mistakes which have deeply hurt us all, North Americans and Latin Americans.

Public opinion in this country shall judge whether Mexico's obvious good faith in this matter is spurned as the United States is driven into a deepening involvement in the Central American swamp.

A Vietnam all the more dangerous because of its nearness to your national territory, indeed, but not for the reasons officially invoked. The turmoil of revolution, if permitted to run its course, promptly finds its institutional channels.

But if thwarted by intervention it will plague the United States for decades to come: Central America and the Caribbean will become the Banquo of the United States: an endemic drain on your human and material resources.

The source of change in Latin America is not in Moscow or Havana: it is in history.

So, let me turn to ourselves, as Latin Americans.

Four Failures of Identification

The failure of your present hemispheric policies is due to a fourfold failure of identification.

The *first* is the failure to identify change in Latin America in its cultural context.

The second is the failure to identify nationalism as the historical bearer of change in Latin America.

The third is the failure to identify the problems of international redistribution of power as they affect Latin America.

The fourth is the failure to identify the grounds for negotiations as these issues create conflict between the United States and Latin America.

The Cultural Context of Latin America

First, the cultural context of change in Latin America.

Our societies are marked by cultural continuity and political discontinuity.

We are a Balkanized polity, yet we are deeply united by a common cultural experience.

We are and we are not of the West.

We are Indian, Black and Mediterranean.

We received the legacy of the West in an incomplete fashion, deformed by the Spanish monarchy's decision to outlaw unorthodox strains, to defeat the democratic yearnings of its own middle class and to superimpose the vertical structures of the Medieval imperium on the equally pyramidal configuration of power in the Indian civilization of the Americas.

As it embarked on its imperial dealings with men and women of different cultures—if they had left at daybreak, they would be there now—Spanish absolutism mutilated the Iberian tree of its Arab and Jewish branches, heavy with fruit.

The United States is the only major power of the West that was born beyond the Middle Ages, modern at birth.

As part of the fortress of the Counter-Reformation, Latin America has had to do constant battle with the past. We did not acquire freedom of speech, freedom of belief, freedom of enterprise as our birthrights, as you did.

We have had to fight desperately for them.

The complexity of the cultural struggles underlying our political and economic struggles has to do with unresolved tensions, sometimes as old as the conflict between pantheism and monotheism; or as recent as the conflict between tradition and modernity.

This is our cultural baggage, both heavy and rich.

The issues we are dealing with, behind the headlines, are very old.

They are finally being aired today, but they originated in colonial, sometimes in pre-Conquest situations and are embedded in the culture of Iberian Catholicism and its emphasis on dogma and hierarchy, an intellectual inclination that sometimes drives us from one church to another in search of refuge and certitude.

They are bedeviled by patrimonial confusions between private and public rights and forms of sanctified corruption that include nepotism, whim and the irrational economic decision made by the head of the clan, untrammelled by checks and balances.

They have to do with the traditions of paternalistic surrender to the Caudillo, the profound faith in ideas over facts, the strength of elitism and personalism and the weakness of the civil societies; the struggles between theocracy and political institutions, and between centralism and local government.

Since Independence in the 1820's we have been obsessed with catching up with the Joneses: the West.

We created legal countries which disguised the real countries abiding—or festering—behind the constitutional facades.

Latin America has tried to find solutions to its old problems by exhausting the successive ideologies of the West: Liberalism, Positivism and Marxism.

Today, we are on the verge of transcending this dilemma by recasting it as an opportunity, at last, to be ourselves—societies neither new nor old, but, simply, authentically, Latin American as we sort out, in the excessive glare of instant communications or in the eternal dusk of our isolated villages, the benefits and the disadvantages of a tradition that now seems richer and more acceptable than it did one hundred years of solitude ago.

But we are also forced to contemplate the benefits and disadvantages of a modernity that now seems less promising than it did before economic crisis, the tragic ambiguity of science and that barbarism of nations and philosophies that were once supposed to represent "progress," all drive us to search for the time and space of culture in ourselves.

We are true children of Spain and Portugal. We have compensated for the failures of history with the successes of art.

We are now moving to what our best novels and poems and paintings and films and dances and thoughts have announced for so long: the compensation for the failures of history with the successes of politics.

The real struggle for Latin America is then, as always, a struggle with ourselves, within ourselves.

We must solve it by ourselves.

Nobody else can truly know it: we are living through our family quarrels.

We must assimilate this conflicted past.

Sometimes we must do it—as has occurred in Mexico, Cuba, El Salvador and Nicaragua—through violent means.

We need time and culture.

We also need patience.

Both ours and yours.

Nationalism in Latin America

Second, the identification of nationalism as the legitimate bearer of change in Latin America.

The cultural conflict I have evoked includes the stubbornness of the minimal popular demands, after all these centuries, which equate freedom with bread, schools, hospitals, national independence and a sense of dignity.

If left to ourselves, we will try to solve these problems by creating national institutions to deal with them.

All we ask from you is cooperation, trade and normal diplomatic relations.

Not your absence, but your civilized presence.

We must grow with our own mistakes.

Are we to be considered your true friends, only if we are ruled by right-wing, anti-Communist despotisms?

Instability in Latin America—or anywhere in the world, for that matter—comes when societies cannot see themselves reflected in their institutions.

Democracy in Latin America

Change in our societies shall be radical in two dimensions.

Externally, it will be more radical the more the United States intervenes against it or helps to postpone it.

Internally, it will of necessity be radical in that it must one day face up to the challenges we have so far been unable to meet squarely: we must face democracy along with reform; we must face cultural integrity along with change; we must all finally face, Cubans, Salvadorans, Nicaraguans and Argentinians, Mexicans and Colombians, the questions that await us on the threshold of our true history: Are we capable, with all the instruments of our civilization, of creating free societies, societies that take care of the basic needs of health, education and labor, but without sacrificing the equally basic needs of debate, criticism and political and cultural expression?

I know that all of us, without exception, have not truly fulfilled these needs in Latin America.

I also know that the transformation of our national movements into pawns of the East-West conflict makes it impossible for us to answer this question: Are we capable of creating free national societies?

This is perhaps our severest historical test.

Rightly or wrongly, many Latin Americans have come to identify the United States with opposition to our national independence.

Some perceive in United States policies the proof that the real menace to a great power is not really the other great power, but the independence of the national states: how else to understand U.S. actions that seem meaninglessly obsessed with discrediting the national revolutions in Latin America?

Some are thankful that another great power exists, and appeal to it.

All of this also escalates and denaturalizes the issues at hand and avoids considering the third failure I want to deal with today, the failure to understand redistribution of power in the Western hemisphere.

Latin America and the Redistribution of Power

It could be debated whether the explosiveness of many Latin American societies is due less to stagnation than to growth, the quickest growth of any region in the world since 1945.

But this has been rapid growth without equally rapid distribution of the benefits of growth.

The contrast has become as explosive and understandable as it was in 1810 against Spanish colonial rule.

And it has coincided, internationally, with rapidly expanding relations between Latin America and new European and Asian partners in trade, financing, technology and political support.

Latin America is thus part and parcel of the universal trend away from bipolar to multipolar or pluralistic structures in international relations.

Given this trend, the decline of one superpower mirrors the decline of the other superpower.

This is bound to create numerous areas of conflict. As Chancellor Helmut Schmidt eloquently expressed it from this same rostrum, "We are living in an economically interdependent world of more than 150 countries—without having enough experience in managing this interdependence."

Both superpowers increasingly face a perfectly logical movement towards national self-assertion accompanied by growing multilateral relationships beyond the decaying spheres of influence.

No change comes about without tension and in Latin America this tension arises as we strive for greater wealth and independence, but also as we immediately start losing both because of internal economic injustice and external economic crisis.

The middle classes we have spawned over the past 50 years are shaken by a revolution of diminishing expectations—of Balzacian "lost illusions."

Modernity and its values are coming under critical fire while the values of nationalism are discovered to be perfectly identifiable with traditionalist, even conservative considerations.

The mistaken identification of change in Latin America as somehow manipulated by a Soviet conspiracy not only irritates the nationalism of the left. It also resurrects the nationalist fervors of the right—where, after all, Latin American nationalism was born in the early 19th century.

You have yet to feel the full force of this backlash, which reappeared in Argentina and the South Atlantic crisis last year, in places such as El Salvador and Panama, Peru and Chile, Mexico and Brazil.

A whole continent, in the name of cultural identity, nationalism and international independence, is capable of uniting against you.

This should not happen.

The chance of avoiding this continental confrontation is in the fourth and final opening I wish to deal with today: that of negotiations.

Negotiations Before It Is Too Late

Before the United States has to negotiate with extreme cultural, nationalistic and internationalist pressures of both the left and the right in the remotest nations of this hemisphere—Chile and

Argentina—in the largest nation—Brazil—and in the closest one—Mexico—it should rapidly, in its own interest as well as ours, negotiate in Central America and the Caribbean.

We consider in Mexico that each and every one of the points of conflict in the region can be solved diplomatically, through negotiations, before it is too late.

There is no fatality in politics that says: given a revolutionary movement in any country in the region, it will inevitably end up providing bases for the Soviet Union.

What happens between the daybreak of revolution in a marginal country and its imagined destiny as a Soviet base?

If nothing happens but harassment, blockades, propaganda, pressures and invasions against the revolutionary country, then that prophecy will become self-fulfilling.

But if power with historical memory and diplomacy with historical imagination come into play, we, the United States and Latin America, might end up with something very different:

A Latin America of independent states building institutions of stability, renewing the culture of national identity, diversifying our economic interdependence and wearing down the dogmas of two musty 19th-century philosophies.

And a United States giving the example of a tone in relations which is present, active, cooperative, respectful, aware of cultural differences and truly proper for a great power unafraid of ideological labels, capable of coexisting with diversity in Latin America as it has learnt to coexist with diversity in Black Africa.

Precisely 20 years ago, John F. Kennedy said at another Commencement ceremony:

"If we cannot end now our differences, at least we can help make the world safe for diversity."

This, I think, is the greatest legacy of the sacrificed statesman whose death we all mourned.

Let us understand that legacy, by which death ceased to be an enigma and became, not a lament for what might have been, but a hope for what can be.

This can be.

The longer the situation of war lasts in Central America and the Caribbean, the more difficult it shall be to assure a political solution.

The more difficult it will be for the Sandinistas to demonstrate good faith in their dealings with the issues of internal democracy now brutally interrupted by a state of emergency imposed as response to foreign pressures.

The more difficult it will be for the civilian arm of the Salvadoran rebellion to maintain political initiative over the armed factions.

The greater the irritation of Panama as it is used as a springboard for a North American war.

The greater the danger of a generalized conflict, dragging in Costa Rica and Honduras.

Everything can be negotiated in Central America and the Caribbean, before it is too late.

Non-aggression pacts between each and every state.

Border patrols.

The interdiction of passage of arms, wherever they may come from, and the interdiction of foreign military advisers, wherever they may come from.

The reduction of all the armies in the region.

The interdiction, now or ever, of Soviet bases or Soviet offensive capabilities in the area.

What would be the *quid pro quo?*

Simply this: the respect of the United States, respect for the integrity and autonomy of all the states in the region, including normalization of relations with all of them.

The countries in the region should not be forced to seek solutions to their problems outside themselves.

The problems of Cuba are Cuban and shall be so once more when the United States understands that by refusing to talk to Cuba on Cuba, it not only weakens Cuba and the United States, but strengthens the Soviet Union.

The mistake of spurning Cuba's constant offers to negotiate whatever the United States wants to discuss frustrates the forces in Cuba desiring greater internal flexibility and international independence.

Is Fidel Castro some sort of superior Machiavelli whom no gringo negotiator can meet at a bargaining table without being bamboozled by him?

Nicaragua

The problems of Nicaragua are Nicaraguan but they will cease to be so if that country is deprived of all possibility for normal survival.

Why is the United States so impatient with four years of Sandinismo, when it was so tolerant of 45 years of Somocismo?

Why is it so worried about free elections in Nicaragua, but so indifferent to free elections in Chile?

And why, if it respects democracy so much, did the United States not rush to the defence of the democratically elected President of Chile, Salvador Allende, when he was overthrown by the Southern Jaruzelski, General Augusto Pinochet?

How can we live and grow together on the basis of such hypocrisy?

Nicaragua is being attacked and invaded by forces sponsored by the United States.

It is being invaded by counter-revolutionary bands led by former commanders of Somoza's National Guard who are out to overthrow the Revolutionary government and re-instate the old tyranny.

Who will stop them from doing so if they win?

These are not freedom fighters. They are Benedict Arnolds.

El Salvador

The problems of El Salvador, finally, are Salvadoran.

The Salvadoran rebellion did not originate and is not manipulated from outside El Salvador. To believe this is akin to crediting Soviet accusations that the Solidarity Movement in Poland is somehow the creature of the United States. The passage of arms from Nicaragua to El Salvador has not been proved: no arms have been intercepted.

The conflict in El Salvador is the indigenous result of a process of political corruption and democratic impossibility that began in 1931 with the overturning of the electoral results by the Army, and culminated in the electoral fraud of 1972, which deprived the Christian Democrats and the Social Democrats of their victory and forced the sons of the middle class into armed insurrection. The Army had exhausted the electoral solution.

This Army continues to outwit everyone in El Salvador— including the United States. It announces elections after assassinating the political leadership of the opposition, then asks the opposition to come back and participate in these same hastily organized elections—as dead souls, perhaps?

This Gogolian scenario means that truly free elections cannot be held in El Salvador as long as the Army and the death squads are unrestrained and fueled by American dollars.

Nothing now assures Salvadorans that the Army and the squads can either defeat the rebels or be controlled by political institutions.

It is precisely because of the nature of the Army that a political settlement must be reached in El Salvador promptly, not only to stop the horrendous death count, not only to restrain both the Army and the armed rebels, not only to assure your young people in the Unied States that they will not be doomed to repeat the horror and futility of Vietnam, but to reconstruct a political initiative of the center-left majority that must now reflect, nevertheless, the need for a restructured Army. El Salvador cannot be governed with such a heavy burden of crime.

The only other option is to transform the war in El Salvador into an American war.

But why should a bad foreign policy be bipartisan?

Without the rebels in El Salvador, the United States would never have worried about "democracy" in El Salvador. If the rebels are denied political participation in El Salvador, how long will it be before El Salvador is totally forgotten once more?

Let us remember, let us imagine, let us reflect.

The United States can no longer go it alone in Central America and the Caribbean. It cannot, in today's world, practice the anachronistic policies of the "Big Stick."

It will only achieve, if it does so, what it cannot truly want.

Many of our countries are struggling to cease being banana republics.

They do not want to become balalaika republics.

Do not force them to choose between appealing to the Soviet Union or capitulating to the United States.

My plea is this one:

Do not practice negative overlordship in this hemisphere.

Practice positive leadership. Join the forces of change and patience and identity in Latin America.

The United States should use the new realities of redistributed world power to its advantage. All the avenues I have been dealing with come together now to form a circle of possible harmony: the United States has true friends in this hemisphere; these friends must negotiate the situations that the United States, while participating in them, cannot possibly negotiate for itself, and the negotiating parties—from Mexico and Venezuela, Panama and Colombia, tomorrow perhaps our great Portuguese speaking sister, Brazil, perhaps the new Spanish democracy, reestablishing the continuum of our Iberian heritage, and expanding the Contadora group—have the intimate knowledge of the underlying cultural problems.

And they have the imagination for assuring the inevitabl passage from the American sphere of influence, not to the Sovie sphere, but to our own Latin American authenticity in a pluralistic world.

President Bok, Ladies and Gentlemen:

My friend Milan Kundera, the Czech novelist, makes a ple for "the small cultures" from the wounded heart of Centra Europe.

I have tried to echo it today from the convulsed heart of Lati America.

Politicians will disappear.

The United States and Latin America will remain.

What sort of neighbors will you have?

What sort of neighbors will we have?

That will depend on the quality of our memory and also of ou imagination.

"If we had started out at daybreak, we would be there now."

Our times have not coincided.

Your daybreak came quickly.

Our night has been long.

But we can overcome the distance between our times if we ca both recognize that the true duration of the human heart is in th present, this present in which we remember and we desire: thi present where our past and our future are one.

Reality is not the product of an ideological phantasm.

It is the result of history.

And history is something we have created ourselves.

We are thus responsible for our history.

No one was present in the past.

But there is no living present with a dead past.

No one has been present in the future.

But there is no living present without the imagination of better world.

We both made the history of this Hemisphere.

We must both remember it.

We must both imagine it.

We need your memory and your imagination or ours sha never be complete.

You need our memory to redeem your past, and our imagina tion to complete your future.

We may be here on this hemisphere for a long time.

Let us remember one another.

Let us respect one another.

Let us walk together outside the night of repression and hunger and intervention, even if for you the sun is at high noon and for us at a quarter to twelve.

Thesis and Theory

NOW WE MOVE from Thinking Over to Thinking Through. Of course the essays we have just been reading all asserted in some way one or more generalizations, but even in the latter samples, which combined several generalizations, the elements of Thinking Over dominated or lingered—the reaction to things relatively recent, the evident first-person presence, some informality of manner and approach, and some feeling of interaction with the audience. Now, with Thesis, we see the withdrawal for better or worse of obvious authorial presence, personal context, and personal structuring of ideas. In other words, Thinking Over has now evolved completely into Thinking Through.

Samples in this concluding category disembed ideas about as fully as possible from the personality and local circumstances that gave rise to them. But an author always remains and is a person, and that person comes through most powerfully now in the terms of the subject, the third person, less evidently but necessarily in the selection, organization, style and argument—in the very nature and presentation of the idea. Rhetoric more nearly approaches logic itself as the central appeal shifts from heart to head, but a rhetoric there is, and the writer-reader relation is simply submerged in the consideration of the subject.

In fact, a possible benefit of touring from *I* to *it*, from here to there, concrete to abstract, can be that we perceive, so as never to forget, how the so-called higher discourse, in evolving from lower, assimilates, secretes within itself something of all the stages in between.

Thesis

Whiteness
Herman Melville
from *Moby Dick,* 1851

Now for the classic thesis essay stating a generalization and supporting it with examples that illustrate and prove it. Our next sample is of this sort until midway, when Melville writes, "But though without doubt this point be fixed, how is mortal man to account for it?" That is, after what he regards as abundant documentation, Melville considers the generalization about whiteness now established and turns to the question of why it is true. Giving causes for some effect is another common sort of thesis essay, since causation may be asserted as simply one other generalization. Anyone who has ever written a term paper or an essay exam will recognize these two sorts and may even have combined them in one essay as Melville has here.

What about the sources from which an author draws instances and documentation? They are precisely the various first- and secondhand sources we have been surveying up to this point. Because "Whiteness" encompasses an extraordinary range of time and space, Melville may draw widely from nature, history, and human behavior. Next to the exact formulation of the thesis generalization itself, the choice of examples makes or breaks this sort of essay. They must not only fit the thesis one has posted but also fit the audience. To judge from Melville's proliferation of examples from very different domains, it seems he democratically set his rhetoric for a very pluralistic audience indeed, accommodating both bookworm and animal lover. Along with the idiosyncratic style, this personal repertory of allusions gives away the underlying presence of the unseen I.

Though in many natural objects, whiteness refiningly enhances beauty, as if imparting some special virtue of its own, as in marbles, japonicas, and pearls; and though various nations have in some way recognised a certain royal pre-eminence in this hue; even the barbaric, grand old kings of Pegu placing the title "Lord of the White Elephants" above all their other magniloquent ascriptions of dominion; and the modern kings of Siam unfurling the same snow-white quadruped in the royal standard; and the Hanoverian flag bearing the one figure of a snow-white charger; and the great Austrian Empire, Cæsarian, heir to overlording Rome, having for the imperial colour the same imperial hue; . . . and though, besides all this, whiteness has been even made significant of gladness, for among the Romans a white stone marked a joyful day; and though in other mortal sympathies and symbolisings, this same hue is made the emblem of many touching, noble things—the innocence of brides, the benignity of age; though among the Red Men of America the giving of the white belt of wampum was the deepest pledge of honour; though in many climes, whiteness typifies the majesty of Justice in the ermine of the Judge, and contributes to the daily state of kings and queens drawn by milk-white steeds; though even in the higher mysteries of the most august religions it has been made the symbol of the divine spotlessness and power; by the Persian fire worshippers, the white forked flame being held the holiest on the altar; and in the Greek mythologies, Great Jove himself being made incarnate in a snow-white bull; and though to the noble Iroquois, the midwinter sacrifice of the sacred White Dog was by far the holiest festival of their theology, that spotless, faithful creature being held the purest envoy they could send to the Great Spirit with the annual tidings of their own fidelity; and though directly from the Latin word for white, all Christian priests derive the name of one part of their sacred vesture, the alb or tunic, worn beneath the cassock; and though among the holy pomps of the Romish faith, white is specially employed in the celebration of the Passion of our Lord; though in the Vision of St. John, white robes are given to the redeemed, and the four-and-twenty elders stand clothed in white before the great white throne, and the Holy One that sitteth there white like wool; yet for all these accumulated associations, with whatever is sweet, and honourable, and sublime, there yet lurks an elusive something in the innermost idea of this hue, which strikes more of panic to the soul than that redness which affrights in blood.

This elusive quality it is, which causes the thought of whiteness, when divorced from more kindly associations, and coupled with any object terrible in itself, to heighten that terror to the furthest bounds. Witness the white bear of the poles, and the white shark of the tropics; what but their smooth, flaky whiteness makes them the transcendent horrors they are? That ghastly whiteness it is which imparts such an abhorrent mildness, even more loathsome than terrific, to the dumb gloating of their aspect. So that not the fierce-fanged tiger in his heraldic coat can so stagger courage as the white-shrouded bear or shark.[1]

Bethink thee of the albatross, whence come those clouds of spiritual wonderment and pale dread, in which that white phantom sails in all imaginations? Not Coleridge first threw that spell; but God's great, unflattering laureate, Nature.[2]

1. With reference to the Polar bear, it may possibly be urged by him who would fain go still deeper into this matter, that it is not the whiteness, separately regarded, which heightens the intolerable hideousness of that brute; for, analysed, that heightened hideousness, it might be said, only arises from the circumstance, that the irresponsible ferociousness of the creature stands invested in the fleece of celestial innocence and love; and hence, by bringing together two such opposite emotions in our minds, the Polar bear frightens us with so unnatural a contrast. But even assuming all this to be true; yet, were it not for the whiteness, you would not have that intensified terror.

As for the white shark, the white gliding ghostliness of repose in that creature, when beheld in his ordinary moods, strangely tallies with the same quality in the Polar quadruped. This peculiarity is most vividly hit by the French in the name they bestow upon that fish. The Romish mass for the dead begins with "Requiem eternam" (eternal rest), whence *Requiem* denominating the mass itself, and any other funeral music. Now in allusion to the white, silent stillness of death in this shark, and the mild deadliness of his habits, the French call him *Requin*.

2. I remember the first albatross I ever saw. It was during a prolonged gale, in waters hard upon the Antarctic seas. From my forenoon watch below, I ascended to the overclouded deck; and there, dashed upon the main hatches, I saw a regal, feathery thing of unspotted whiteness, and with a hooked, Roman bill sublime. At intervals, it arched forth its vast archangel wings, as if to embrace some holy ark. Wonderous flutterings and throbbings shook it. Though bodily unharmed, it uttered cries, as some king's ghost in supernatural distress. Through its inexpressible, strange eyes, methought I peeped to secrets which took hold of God. As Abraham before the angels, I bowed myself; the white thing was so white, its wings so wide, and in those for ever exiled waters, I had lost the miserable warping memories of traditions and of towns. Long I gazed at that prodigy of plumage. I cannot tell, can only hint, the things that darted through me then. But at last I awoke; and turning, asked a sailor what bird was this. A goney, he replied. Goney! I never had heard that name before; is it conceivable that this glorious thing is utterly unknown to men ashore! never! But some time after, I learned that goney was some seaman's name for albatross. So that by no possibility could Coleridge's wild Rhyme have had aught to do with those mystical impressions which were mine, when I saw that bird upon our deck. For neither had

Most famous in our Western annals and Indian traditions is that of the White Steed of the Prairies; a magnificent milk-white charger, large-eyed, small-headed, bluff-chested, and with the dignity of a thousand monarchs in his lofty, overscorning carriage. He was the elected Xerxes of vast herds of wild horses, whose pastures in those days were only fenced by the Rocky Mountains and the Alleghanies. At their flaming head he westward trooped it like that chosen star which every evening leads on the hosts of light. The flashing cascade of his mane, the curving comet of his tail, invested him with housings more resplendent than gold and silver-beaters could have furnished him. A most imperial and archangelical apparition of that unfallen, western world, which to the eyes of the old trappers and hunters revived the glories of those primeval times when Adam walked majestic as a god, bluff-browed and fearless as this mighty steed. Whether marching amid his aides and marshals in the van of countless cohorts that endlessly streamed it over the plains, like an Ohio; or whether with his circumambient subjects browsing all around at the horizon, the White Steed gallopingly reviewed them with warm nostrils reddening through his cool milkiness; in whatever aspect he presented himself, always to the bravest Indians he was the object of trembling reverence and awe. Nor can it be questioned from what stands on legendary record of this noble horse, that it was his spiritual whiteness chiefly, which so clothed him with divineness; and that this divineness had that in it which, though commanding worship, at the same time enforced a certain nameless terror.

But there are other instances where this whiteness loses all that accessory and strange glory which invest it in the White Steed and Albatross.

I then read the Rhyme, nor knew the bird to be an albatross. Yet, in saying this, I do but indirectly burnish a little brighter the noble merit of the poem and the poet.

I assert, then, that in the wonderous bodily whiteness of the bird chiefly lurks the secret of the spell; a truth the more evinced in this, that by a solecism of terms there are birds called gray albatrosses; and these I have frequently seen, but never with such emotions as when I beheld the Antarctic fowl.

But how had the mystic thing been caught? Whisper it not, and I will tell; with a treacherous hook and line, as the fowl floated on the sea. At last the Captain made a postman of it; tying a lettered, leathern tally round its neck, with the ship's time and place; and then letting it escape. But I doubt not, that leathern tally, meant for man, was taken off in Heaven, when the white fowl flew to join the wing-folding, the invoking, and adoring cherubim!

What is it that in the Albino man so peculiarly repels and often shocks the eye, as that sometimes he is loathed by his own kith and kin! It is that whiteness which invests him, a thing expressed by the name he bears. The Albino is as well made as other men—has no substantive deformity—and yet this mere aspect of all-pervading whiteness makes him more strangely hideous than the ugliest abortion. Why should this be so?

Nor, in quite other aspects, does Nature in her least palpable but not the less malicious agencies, fail to enlist among her forces this crowning attribute of the terrible. From its snowy aspect, the gauntleted ghost of the Southern Seas has been denominated the White Squall. Nor, in some historic instances, has the art of human malice omitted so potent an auxiliary. How wildly it heightens the effect of that passage in Froissart, when, masked in the snowy symbol of their faction, the desperate White Hoods of Ghent murder their bailiff in the market-place!

Nor, in some things, does the common, hereditary experience of all mankind fail to bear witness to the supernaturalism of this hue. It cannot well be doubted, that the one visible quality in the aspect of the dead which most appals the gazer, is the marble pallor lingering there; as if indeed that pallor were much like the badge of consternation in the other world, as of mortal trepidation here. And from that pallor of the dead, we borrow the expressive hue of the shroud in which we wrap them. Nor even in our superstitions do we fail to throw the same snowy mantle round our phantoms; all ghosts rising in a milk-white fog.—Yea, while these terrors seize us, let us add, that even the king of terrors, when personified by the evangelist, rides on his pallid horse.

Therefore, in his other moods, symbolise whatever grand or gracious thing he will by whiteness, no man can deny that in its profoundest idealised significance it calls up a peculiar apparition of the soul.

But though without dissent this point be fixed, how is mortal man to account for it? To analyse it, would seem impossible. Can we, then, by the citation of some of those instances wherein this thing of whiteness—though for the time either wholly or in a great part stripped of all direct associations calculated to impart to it aught fearful, but, nevertheless, is found to exert over us the same sorcery, however modified;—can we thus hope to light upon some chance clue to conduct us to the hidden cause we seek?

Let us try. But in a matter like this, subtlety appeals to subtlety, and without imagination no man can follow another into these halls. And though, doubtless, some at least of the imaginative impressions about to be presented may have been shared by most men, yet few perhaps were entirely conscious of them at the time, and therefore may not be able to recall them now.

Why to the man of untutored ideality, who happens to be but loosely acquainted with the peculiar character of the day, does the bare mention of Whitsuntide marshal in the fancy such long, dreary, speechless processions of slow-pacing pilgrims, downcast and hooded with new-fallen snow? Or, to the unread, unsophisticated Protestant of the Middle American States, why does the passing mention of a White Friar or a White Nun, evoke such an eyeless statue in the soul?

Or what is there apart from the traditions of dungeoned warriors and kings (which will not wholly account for it) that makes the White Tower of London tell so much more strongly on the imagination of an untravelled American, than those other storied structures, its neighbours—the Byward Tower, or even the Bloody? And those sublimer towers, the White Mountains of New Hampshire, whence, in peculiar moods, comes that gigantic ghostliness over the soul at the bare mention of that name, while the thought of Virginia's Blue Ridge is full of a soft, dewy, distant dreaminess? Or why, irrespective of all latitudes and longitudes, does the name of the White Sea exert such a spectralness over the fancy, while that of the Yellow Sea lulls us with mortal thoughts of long lacquered mild afternoons on the waves, followed by the gaudiest and yet sleepiest of sunsets? Or, to choose a wholly unsubstantial instance, purely addressed to the fancy, why, in reading the old fairy tales of Central Europe, does "the tall pale man" of the Hartz forest, whose changeless pallor unrustlingly glides through the green of the groves—why is this phantom more terrible than all the whooping imps of the Blocksburg?

Nor is it, altogether, the remembrance of her cathedral-toppling earthquakes; nor the stampedoes of her frantic seas; nor the tearlessness of arid skies that never rain; nor the sight of her wide field of leaning spires, wrenched cope-stones, and crosses all adroop (like canted yards of anchored fleets); and her suburban avenues of house-walls lying over upon each other, as a tossed pack of cards;—it is not these things alone which make tearless Lima, the strangest, saddest city thou can'st see. For Lima has taken the white veil; and there is a higher horror in this whiteness of her woe. Old as Pizarro, this whiteness keeps her ruins forever new; admits not the cheerful greenness of complete decay; spreads over her broken ramparts the rigid pallor of an apoplexy that fixes its own distortions.

I know that, to the common apprehension, this phenomenon of whiteness is not confessed to be the prime agent in exaggerating the terror of objects otherwise terrible; nor to the unimaginative mind is there aught of terror in those appearances whose awfulness to another mind almost solely consists in this one phenomenon, especially when exhibited under any form at all approaching to muteness or universality. What I mean by these two statements may perhaps be respectively elucidated by the following examples.

First: The mariner, when drawing nigh the coasts of foreign lands, if by night he hear the roar of breakers, starts to vigilance, and feels just enough of trepidation to sharpen all his faculties; but under precisely similar circumstances, let him be called from his hammock to view his ship sailing through a midnight sea of milky whiteness—as if from encircling headlands shoals of combed white bears were swimming round him, then he feels a silent, superstitious dread; the shrouded phantom of the whitened waters is horrible to him as a real ghost; in vain the lead assures him he is still off soundings; heart and helm they both go down; he never rests till blue water is under him again. Yet where is the mariner who will tell thee, "Sir, it was not so much the fear of striking hidden rocks, as the fear of that hideous whiteness that so stirred me?"

Second: To the native Indian of Peru, the continual sight of the snow-howdahed Andes conveys naught of dread, except, perhaps, in the mere fancying of the eternal frosted desolateness reigning at such vast altitudes, and the natural conceit of what a fearfulness it would be to lose oneself in such inhuman solitudes. Much the same is it with the backwoodsman of the West, who with comparative indifference views an unbounded prairie sheeted with driven snow, no shadow of tree or twig to break the fixed trance of whiteness. Not so the sailor, beholding the scenery of the Antarctic seas; where at times, by some infernal trick of legerdemain in the powers of frost and air, he, shivering and half shipwrecked, instead of rainbows speaking hope and solace to his misery, views what seems a boundless churchyard grinning upon him with its lean ice monuments and splintered crosses.

But thou sayest, methinks this white-lead chapter about whiteness is but a white flag hung out from a craven soul; thou surrenderest to a hypo.

Tell me, why this strong young colt, foaled in some peaceful valley of Vermont, far removed from all beasts of prey—why is it that upon the sunniest day, if you but shake a fresh buffalo robe behind him, so that he cannot even see it, but only smells its wild animal muskiness—why will he start, snort, and with bursting eyes paw the ground in phrensies of affright? There is no remembrance in him of any gorings of wild creatures in his green northern home, so that the strange muskiness he smells cannot recall to him anything associated with the experience of former perils; for what knows he, this New England colt, of the black bisons of distant Oregon?

No: but here thou beholdest even in a dumb brute, the instinct of the knowledge of the demonism in the world. Though thousands of miles from Oregon, still when he smells that savage musk, the rending, goring bison herds are as present as to the deserted wild foal of the prairies, which this instant they may be trampling into dust.

Thus, then, the muffled rollings of a milky sea; the bleak rustlings of the festooned frosts of mountains; the desolate shiftings of the windrowed snows of prairies; all these are as the shaking of that buffalo robe to the frightened colt!

Though neither knows where lie the nameless things of which the mystic sign gives forth such hints; yet with me, as with the colt, somewhere those things must exist. Though in many of its aspects this visible world seems formed in love, the invisible spheres were formed in fright.

But not yet have we solved the incantation of this whiteness, and learned why it appeals with such power to the soul; and more strange and far more portentous—why, as we have seen, it is at once the most meaning symbol of spiritual things, nay, the very veil of the Christian's Deity; and yet should be as it is, the intensifying agent in things the most appalling to mankind.

Is it that by its indefiniteness it shadows forth the heartless voids and immensities of the universe, and thus stabs us from behind with the thought of annihilation, when beholding the white depths of the milky way? Or is it, that as in essence whiteness is not so much a colour as the visible absence of colour, and at the same time the concrete of all colours; is it for these reasons that there is such a dumb blankness, full of meaning, in a wide landscape of snows—a colourless, all-colour of atheism from which we shrink? And when we consider that other theory of the natural philosophers, that all other earthly hues—every stately or lovely emblazoning—the sweet tinges of sunset skies and woods; yea, and the gilded velvets of butterflies, and the butterfly cheeks of young girls; all these are but subtile deceits, not actually inherent in substance, but only laid on from without; so that all deified Nature absolutely paints like the harlot, whose allurements cover nothing but the charnel-house within; and when we proceed further, and consider that the mystical cosmetic which produces every one of her hues, the great principle of light, forever remains white or colourless in itself, and if operating without medium upon matter, would touch all objects, even tulips and roses, with its own blank tinge—pondering all this, the palsied universe lies before us a leper; and like wilful travellers in Lapland, who refuse to wear coloured and colouring glasses upon their eyes, so the wretched infidel gazes himself blind at the monumental white shroud that wraps all the prospect around him.

The Functions of War
from *Report from Iron Mountain,* 1967
edited by Leonard C. Lewin

---

*As the title indicates, the basic organization of this more imper-
sonal thesis is a list, but each function of war enumerated
constitutes a separate generalization, and these are one at a time
asserted and documented. Actually, these are subgeneralizations
to support the master thesis that war is "the principal organizing
force in most societies." This more complex composition—a
generalization at one level serving as an example at another
level—fits the hierarchical thought structures of higher abstracting,
where more synoptic generalization can be formulated only after
some prerequisite generalizations of lesser compass have been
induced from their own, concreter sources. Combining theses,
vertically and laterally, builds a theory.*

. . . The preeminence of the concept of war as the principal
organizing force in most societies has been insufficiently
appreciated. This is also true of its extensive effects throughout
the many nonmilitary activities of society. These effects are less
apparent in complex industrial societies like our own than in

primitive cultures, the activities of which can be more easily and fully comprehended.

We propose . . . to examine these nonmilitary, implied, and usually invisible functions of war, to the extent that they bear on the problems of transition to peace for our society. The military, or ostensible, function of the war system requires no elaboration; it serves simply to defend or advance the "national interest" by means of organized violence. It is often necessary for a national military establishment to create a need for its unique powers—to maintain the franchise, so to speak. And a healthy military apparatus requires regular "exercise," by whatever rationale seems expedient, to prevent its atrophy.

The nonmilitary functions of the war system are more basic. They exist not merely to justify themselves but to serve broader social purposes. If and when war is eliminated, the military functions it has served will end with it. But its nonmilitary functions will not. It is essential, therefore, that we understand their significance before we can reasonably expect to evaluate whatever institutions may be proposed to replace them.

Economic

The production of weapons of mass destruction has always been associated with economic "waste." The term is pejorative, since it implies a failure of function. But no human activity can properly be considered wasteful if it achieves its contextual objective. The phrase "wasteful but necessary," applied not only to war expenditures but to most of the "unproductive" commercial activities of our society, is a contradiction in terms. ". . . The attacks that have since the time of Samuel's criticism of King Saul been leveled against military expenditures as waste may well have concealed or misunderstood the point that some kinds of waste may have a larger social utility."[1]

In the case of military "waste," there is indeed a larger social utility. It derives from the fact that the "wastefulness" of war production is exercised entirely outside the framework of the

1. Arthur I. Waskow, *Toward the Unarmed Forces of the United States* (Washington: Institute for Policy Studies, 1966), p. 9. (This is the unabridged edition of the text of a report and proposal prepared for a seminar of strategists and Congressmen in 1965; it was later given limited distribution among other persons engaged in related projects.)

economy of supply and demand. As such, it provides the only critically large segment of the total economy that is subject to complete and arbitrary central control. If modern industrial societies can be defined as those which have developed the capacity to produce more than is required for their economic survival (regardless of the equities of distribution of goods within them), military spending can be said to furnish the only balance wheel with sufficient inertia to stabilize the advance of their economies. The fact that war is "wasteful" is what enables it to serve this function. And the faster the economy advances, the heavier this balance wheel must be.

This function is often viewed, oversimply, as a device for the control of surpluses. One writer on the subject puts it this way: "Why is war so wonderful? Because it creates artificial demand . . . the only kind of artificial demand, moreover, that does not raise any political issues: *war, and only war, solves the problem of inventory*."[2] The reference here is to shooting war, but it applies equally to the general war economy as well. "It is generally agreed," concludes, more cautiously, the report of a panel set up by the U.S. Arms Control and Disarmament Agency, "that the greatly expanded public sector since World War II, resulting from heavy defense expenditures, has provided additional protection against depressions, since this sector is not responsive to contraction in the private sector and has provided a sort of buffer or balance wheel in the economy."[3]

The *principal* economic function of war, in our view, is that it provides just such a flywheel. It is not to be confused in function with the various forms of fiscal control, none of which directly engages vast numbers of men and units of production. It is not to be confused with massive government expenditures in social welfare programs; once initiated, such programs normally become integral parts of the general economy and are no longer subject to arbitrary control.

But even in the context of the general civilian economy war cannot be considered wholly "wasteful." Without a long-established war economy, and without its frequent eruption into large-scale shooting war, most of the major industrial advances known to history, beginning with the development of iron, could never have taken place. Weapons technology structures the

2. David T. Bazelon, "The Politics of the Paper Economy," *Commentary* (November 1962), p. 409.

3. *The Economic Impact of Disarmament* (Washington: USGPO, January 1962).

economy. According to the writer cited above, "Nothing is more ironic or revealing about our society than the fact that hugely destructive war is a very progressive force in it. . . . War production is progressive because it is production that would not otherwise have taken place. (It is not so widely appreciated, for example, that the civilian standard of living *rose* during World War II.)"[4] This is not "ironic or revealing," but essentially a simple statement of fact.

It should also be noted that war production has a dependably stimulating effect outside itself. Far from constituting a "wasteful" drain on the economy, war spending, considered pragmatically, has been a consistently positive factor in the rise of gross national product and of individual productivity. A former Secretary of the Army has carefully phrased it for public consumption thus: "If there is, as I suspect there is, a direct relation between the stimulus of large defense spending and a substantially increased rate of growth of gross national product, it quite simply follows that defense spending *per se* might be countenanced on *economic grounds alone* [emphasis added] as a stimulator of the national metabolism."[5] Actually, the fundamental nonmilitary utility of war in the economy is far more widely acknowledged than the scarcity of such affirmations as that quoted above would suggest.

But *negatively* phrased public recognitions of the importance of war to the general economy abound. The most familiar example is the effect of "peace threats" on the stock market, e.g., "Wall Street was shaken yesterday by news of an apparent peace feeler from North Vietnam, but swiftly recovered its composure after about an hour of sometimes indiscriminate selling."[6] Savings banks solicit deposits with similar cautionary slogans, e.g., "If peace breaks out, will you be ready for it?" A more subtle case in point was the recent refusal of the Department of Defense to permit the West German government to substitute nonmilitary goods for unwanted armaments in its purchase commitments from the United States; the decisive consideration was that the German purchases should not affect the general (nonmilitary) economy. Other incidental examples are to be found in the

4. David T. Bazelon, "The Scarcity Makers," *Commentary* (October 1962), p. 298.

5. Frank Pace, Jr., in an address before the American Bankers' Association, September 1957.

6. A random example, taken in this case from a story by David Deitch in the *New York Herald Tribune* (9 February 1966).

pressures brought to bear on the Department when it announces plans to close down an obsolete facility (as a "wasteful" form of "waste"), and in the usual coordination of stepped-up military activities (as in Vietnam in 1965) with dangerously rising unemployment rates.

Although we do not imply that a substitute for war in the economy cannot be devised, no combination of techniques for controlling employment, production, and consumption has yet been tested that can remotely compare to it in effectiveness. It is, and has been, the essential economic stabilizer of modern societies.

Political

The political functions of war have been up to now even more critical to social stability. It is not surprising, nevertheless, that discussions of economic conversion for peace tend to fall silent on the matter of political implementation, and that disarmament scenarios, often sophisticated in their weighing of international political factors, tend to disregard the political functions of the war system within individual societies.

These functions are essentially organizational. First of all, the existence of a society as a political "nation" requires as part of its definition an attitude of relationship toward other "nations." This is what we usually call a foreign policy. But a nation's foreign policy can have no substance if it lacks the means of enforcing its attitude toward other nations. It can do this in a credible manner only if it implies the threat of maximum political organization for this purpose—which is to say that it is organized to some degree for war. War, then, as we have defined it to include all national activities that recognize the possibility of armed conflict, is itself the defining element of any nation's existence vis-à-vis any other nation. Since it is historically axiomatic that the existence of any form of weaponry insures its use, we have used the word "peace" as virtually synonymous with disarmament. By the same token, "war" is virtually synonymous with nationhood. The elimination of war implies the inevitable elimination of national sovereignty and the traditional nation-state.

The war system not only has been essential to the existence of nations as independent political entities, but has been equally indispensable to their stable internal political structure. Without it, no government has even been able to obtain acquiescence in its "legitimacy," or right to rule its society. The possibility of war provides the sense of external necessity without which no government can long remain in power. The historical record reveals one instance after another where the failure of a regime to maintain the credibility of a war threat led to its dissolution, by the forces of private interest, of reactions to social injustice, or of other disintegrative elements. The organization of a society for the possibility of war is its principal political stabilizer. It is ironic that this primary function of war has been generally recognized by historians only where it has been expressly acknowledged—in the pirate societies of the great conquerors.

The basic authority of a modern state over its people resides in its war powers. (There is, in fact, good reason to believe that codified law had its origins in the rules of conduct established by military victors for dealing with the defeated enemy, which were later adapted to apply to all subject populations.[7]) On a day-to-day basis, it is represented by the institution of police, armed organizations charged expressly with dealing with "internal enemies" in a military manner. Like the conventional "external" military, the police are also substantially exempt from many civilian legal restraints on their social behavior. In some countries, the artificial distinction between police and other military forces does not exist. On the long-term basis, a government's emergency war powers—inherent in the structure of even the most libertarian of nations—define the most significant aspect of the relation between state and citizen.

In advanced modern democratic societies, the war system has provided political leaders with another political-economic function of increasing importance: it has served as the last great safeguard against the elimination of necessary social classes. As economic productivity increases to a level further and further above that of minimum subsistence, it becomes more and more difficult for a society to maintain distribution patterns insuring the existence of "hewers of wood and drawers of water." The further progress of automation can be expected to differentiate still more sharply between "superior" workers and what Ricardo called "menials," while simultaneously aggravating the problem of maintaining an unskilled labor supply.

The arbitrary nature of war expenditures and of other military activities make them ideally suited to control these essential class relationships. Obviously, if the war system were to be discarded

---

7. *Vide* L. Gumplowicz, in *Geschichte der Staatstheorien* (Innsbruck Wagner, 1905) and earlier writings.

new political machinery would be needed at once to serve this vital subfunction. Until it is developed, the continuance of the war system must be assured, if for no other reason, among others, than to preserve whatever quality and degree of poverty a society requires as an incentive, as well as to maintain the stability of its internal organization of power.

Sociological

Under this heading, we will examine a nexus of functions served by the war system that affect human behavior in society. In general, they are broader in application and less susceptible to direct observation than the economic and political factors previously considered.

The most obvious of these functions is the time-honored use of military institutions to provide antisocial elements with an acceptable role in the social structure. The disintegrative, unstable social movements loosely described as "fascist" have traditionally taken root in societies that have lacked adequate military or paramilitary outlets to meet the needs of these elements. This function has been critical in periods of rapid change. The danger signals are easy to recognize, even though the stigmata bear different names at different times. The current euphemistic clichés—"juvenile delinquency" and "alienation"—have had their counterparts in every age. In earlier days these conditions were dealt with directly by the military without the complications of due process, usually through press gangs or outright enslavement. But it is not hard to visualize, for example, the degree of social disruption that might have taken place in the United States during the last two decades if the problem of the socially disaffected of the post–World War II period had not been foreseen and effectively met. The younger, and more dangerous, of these hostile social groupings have been kept under control by the Selective Service System.

This system and its analogues elsewhere furnish remarkably clear examples of disguised military utility. Informed persons in this country have never accepted the official rationale for a peacetime draft—military necessity, preparedness, etc.—as worthy of serious consideration. But what has gained credence among thoughtful men is the rarely voiced, less easily refuted, proposition that the institution of military service has a "patriotic" priority in our society that must be maintained for its own sake.

Ironically, the simplistic official justification for selective service comes closer to the mark, once the nonmilitary functions of military institutions are understood. As a control device over the hostile, nihilistic, and potentially unsettling elements of a society in transition, the draft can again be defended, and quite convincingly, as a "military" necessity.

Nor can it be considered a coincidence that overt military activity, and thus the level of draft calls, tend to follow the major fluctuations in the unemployment rate in the lower age groups. This rate, in turn, is a time-tested herald of social discontent. It must be noted also that the armed forces in every civilization have provided the principal state-supported haven for what we now call the "unemployable." The typical European standing army (of fifty years ago) consisted of ". . . troops unfit for employment in commerce, industry, or agriculture, led by officers unfit to practice any legitimate profession or to conduct a business enterprise."[8] This is still largely true, if less apparent. In a sense, this function of the military as the custodian of the economically or culturally deprived was the forerunner of most contemporary civilian social-welfare programs, from the W.P.A. to various forms of "socialized" medicine and social security. It is interesting that liberal sociologists currently proposing to use the Selective Service System as a medium of cultural upgrading of the poor consider this a *novel* application of military practice.

Although it cannot be said absolutely that such critical measures of social control as the draft require a military rationale, no modern society has yet been willing to risk experimentation with any other kind. Even during such periods of comparatively simple social crisis as the so-called Great Depression of the 1930s, it was deemed prudent by the government to invest minor make-work projects, like the "Civilian" Conservation Corps, with a military character, and to place the more ambitious National Recovery Administration under the direction of a professional army officer at its inception. Today, at least one small Northern European country, plagued with uncontrollable unrest among its "alienated youth," is considering the expansion of its armed forces, despite the problem of making credible the expansion of a non-existent external threat.

Sporadic efforts have been made to promote general recognition of broad national values free of military connotation, but they have been ineffective. For example, to enlist public support of even such modest programs of social adjustment as "fighting

8. K. Fischer, *Das Militär* (Zurich: Steinmetz Verlag, 1932), pp. 42–43.

inflation'' or ''maintaining physical fitness'' it has been necessary for the government to utilize a patriotic (i.e., military) incentive. It sells ''defense'' bonds and it equates health with military preparedness. This is not surprising; since the concept of ''nationhood'' implies readiness for war, a ''national'' program must do likewise.

In general, the war system provides the basic motivation for primary social organization. In so doing, it reflects on the societal level the incentives of individual human behavior. The most important of these, for social purposes, is the individual psychological rationale for allegiance to a society and its values. Allegiance requires a cause; a cause requires an enemy. This much is obvious; the critical point is that the enemy that defines the cause must seem genuinely formidable. Roughly speaking, the presumed power of the ''enemy'' sufficient to warrant an individual sense of allegiance to a society must be proportionate to the size and complexity of the society. Today, of course, that power must be one of unprecedented magnitude and frightfulness.

It follows, from the patterns of human behavior, that the credibility of a social ''enemy'' demands similarly a readiness of response in proportion to its menace. In a broad social context, ''an eye for an eye'' still characterizes the only acceptable attitude toward a presumed threat of aggression, despite contrary religious and moral precepts governing personal conduct. The remoteness of personal decision from social consequence in a modern society makes it easy for its members to maintain this attitude without being aware of it. A recent example is the war in Vietnam; a less recent one was the bombing of Hiroshima and Nagasaki.[9] In each case, the extent and gratuitousness of the slaughter were abstracted into political formulae by most Americans, once the proposition that the victims were ''enemies'' was established. The war system makes such an abstracted response possible in nonmilitary contexts as well. A conventional example of this mechanism is the inability of most people to connect, let us say, the starvation of millions in India with their own past conscious political decision-making. Yet the sequential logic linking a decision to restrict grain production in America with an eventual famine in Asia is obvious, unambiguous, and unconcealed.

9. The obverse of this phenomenon is responsible for the principal combat problem of present-day infantry officers: the unwillingness of otherwise ''trained'' troops to fire at an enemy close enough to be recognizable as an individual rather than simply as a target.

What gives the war system its preeminent role in social organization, as elsewhere, is its unmatched authority over life and death. It must be emphasized again that the war system is not a mere social extension of the presumed need for individual human violence, but itself in turn serves to rationalize most nonmilitary killing. It also provides the precedent for the collective willingness of members of a society to pay a blood price for institutions far less central to social organization than war. To take a handy example, ". . . rather than accept speed limits of twenty miles an hour we prefer to let automobiles kill forty thousand people a year."[10] A Rand analyst puts it in more general terms and less rhetorically: "I am sure that there is, in effect, a desirable level of automobile accidents—desirable, that is, from a broad point of view; in the sense that it is a necessary concomitant of things of greater value to society."[11] The point may seem too obvious for iteration, but it is essential to an understanding of the important motivational function of war as a model for collective sacrifice.

A brief look at some defunct premodern societies is instructive. One of the most noteworthy features common to the larger, more complex, and more successful of ancient civilizations was their widespread use of the blood sacrifice. If one were to limit consideration to those cultures whose regional hegemony was so complete that the prospect of "war" had become virtually inconceivable—as was the case with several of the great pre-Columbian societies of the Western Hemisphere—it would be found that some form of ritual killing occupied a position of paramount social importance in each. Invariably, the ritual was invested with mythic or religious significance; as with all religious and totemic practice, however, the ritual masked a broader and more important social function.

In these societies, the blood sacrifice served the purpose of maintaining a vestigial "earnest" of the society's capability and willingness to make war—i.e., kill and be killed—in the event that some mystical—i.e., unforeseen—circumstance were to give rise to the possibility. That the "earnest" was not an adequate substitute for genuine military organization when the unthinkable enemy, such as the Spanish conquistadores, actually appeared on the scene in no way negates the function of the ritual. It was

10. Herman Kahn, *On Thermonuclear War* (Princeton, N.J.: Princeton University Press, 1960), p. 42.

11. John D. Williams, "The Nonsense about Safe Driving," *Fortune* (September 1958).

primarily, if not exclusively, a symbolic reminder that war had once been the central organizing force of the society, and that this condition might recur.

It does not follow that a transition to total peace in modern societies would require the use of this model, even in less "barbaric" guise. But the historical analogy serves as a reminder that a viable substitute for war as a social system cannot be a mere symbolic charade. It must involve real risk of real personal destruction, and on a scale consistent with the size and complexity of modern social systems. Credibility is the key. Whether the substitute is ritual in nature or functionally substantive, unless it provides a believable life-and-death threat it will not serve the socially organizing function of war.

The existence of an accepted external menace, then, is essential to social cohesiveness as well as to the acceptance of political authority. The menace must be believable, it must be of a magnitude consistent with the complexity of the society threatened, and it must appear, at least, to affect the entire society.

Ecological

Man, like all other animals, is subject to the continuing process of adapting to the limitations of his environment. But the principal mechanism he has utilized for this purpose is unique among living creatures. To forestall the inevitable historical cycles of inadequate food supply, post-Neolithic man destroys surplus members of his own species by organized warfare.

Ethologists[12] have often observed that the organized slaughter of members of their own species is virtually unknown among other animals. Man's special propensity to kill his own kind (shared to a limited degree with rats) may be attributed to his inability to adapt anachronistic patterns of survival (like primitive hunting) to his development of "civilizations" in which these patterns cannot be effectively sublimated. It may be attributed to other causes that have been suggested, such as a maladapted "territorial instinct," etc. Nevertheless, it exists and its social expression in war constitutes a biological control of his relationship to his natural environment that is peculiar to man alone.

12. *Vide* most recently K. Lorenz, in *Das Sogenannnte Böse: zur Naturgeschichte der Aggression* (Vienna: G. Borotha-Schoeler Verlag, 1964).

War has served to help assure the *survival* of the human species. But as an evolutionary device to *improve* it, war is almost unbelievably inefficient. With few exceptions, the selective processes of other living creatures promote both specific survival *and* genetic improvement. When a conventionally adaptive animal faces one of its periodic crises of insufficiency, it is the "inferior" members of the species that normally disappear. An animal's social response to such a crisis may take the form of a mass migration, during which the weak fall by the wayside. Or it may follow the dramatic and more efficient pattern of lemming societies, in which the weaker members voluntarily disperse, leaving available food supplies for the stronger. In either case, the strong survive and the weak fall. In human societies, those who fight and die in wars for survival are in general its biologically stronger members. This is natural selection in reverse.

The regressive genetic effect of war has been often noted[13] and equally often deplored, even when it confuses biological and cultural factors.[14] The disproportionate loss of the *biologically* stronger remains inherent in traditional warfare. It serves to underscore the fact that survival of the species, rather than its improvement, is the fundamental purpose of natural selection, if it can be said to have a purpose, just as it is the basic premise of this study.

But as the polemologist Gaston Bouthoul[15] has pointed out, other institutions that were developed to serve this ecological function have proved even less satisfactory. (They include such established forms as these: infanticide, practiced chiefly in ancient and primitive societies; sexual mutilation; monasticism; forced emigration; extensive capital punishment, as in old China and eighteenth-century England; and other similar, usually localized, practices.)

Man's ability to increase his productivity of the essentials of physical life suggests that the need for protection against cyclical

13. Beginning with Herbert Spencer and his contemporaries, but largely ignored for nearly a century.

14. As in recent draft-law controversy, in which the issue of selective deferment of the culturally privileged is often carelessly equated with the preservation of the biologically "fittest."

15. G. Bouthoul, in *La Guerre* (Paris: Presses universitaires de France, 1953) and many other more detailed studies. The useful concept of "polemology," for the study of war as an independent discipline, is his, as is the notion of "demographic relaxation," the sudden temporary decline in the rate of population increase after major wars.

famine may be nearly obsolete.[16] It has thus tended to reduce the apparent importance of the basic ecological function of war, which is generally disregarded by peace theorists. Two aspects of it remain especially relevant, however. The first is obvious: current rates of population growth, compounded by environmental threat of chemical and other contaminants, may well bring about a new crisis of insufficiency. If so, it is likely to be one of unprecedented global magnitude, not merely regional or temporary. Conventional methods of warfare would almost surely prove inadequate, in this event, to reduce the consuming population to a level consistent with survival of the species.

The second relevant factor is the efficiency of modern methods of mass destruction. Even if their use is not required to meet a world population crisis, they offer, perhaps paradoxically, the first opportunity in the history of man to halt the regressive genetic effects of natural selection by war. Nuclear weapons are indiscriminate. Their application would bring to an end the disproportionate destruction of the physically stronger members of the species (the "warriors") in periods of war. Whether this prospect of genetic gain would offset the unfavorable mutations anticipated from postnuclear radioactivity we have not yet determined. What gives the question a bearing on our study is the possibility that the determination may yet have to be made.

Another secondary ecological trend bearing on projected population growth is the regressive effect of certain medical advances. Pestilence, for example, is no longer an important factor in population control. The problem of increased life expectancy has been aggravated. These advances also pose a potentially more sinister problem, in that undesirable genetic traits that were formerly self-liquidating are now medically maintained. Many diseases that were once fatal at preprocreational ages are now cured; the effect of this development is to perpetuate undesirable susceptibilities and mutations. It seems clear that a new quasi-eugenic function of war is now in process of formation that will have to be taken into account in any transition plan. For the time being, the Department of Defense appears to have recognized such factors, as has been demonstrated by the planning under way by the Rand Corporation to cope with the breakdown in the

16. This seemingly premature statement is supported by one of our own test studies. But it hypothecates both the stabilizing of world population growth and the institution of fully adequate environmental controls. Under these two conditions, the probability of the permanent elimination of involuntary global famine is 68 percent by 1976 and 95 percent by 1981.

ecological balance anticipated after a thermonuclear war. The Department has also begun to stockpile birds, for example, against the expected proliferation of radiation-resistant insects, etc.

Cultural and Scientific

The declared order of values in modern societies gives a high place to the so-called "creative" activities, and an even higher one to those associated with the advance of scientific knowledge. Widely held social values can be translated into political equivalents, which in turn may bear on the nature of a transition to peace. The attitudes of those who hold these values must be taken into account in the planning of the transition. The dependence, therefore, of cultural and scientific achievement on the war system would be an important consideration in a transition plan even if such achievement had no inherently necessary social function.

Of all the countless dichotomies invented by scholars to account for the major differences in art styles and cycles, only one has been consistently unambiguous in its application to a variety of forms and cultures. However it may be verbalized, the basic distinction is this: Is the work war-oriented or is it not? Among primitive peoples, the war dance is the most important art form. Elsewhere, literature, music, painting, sculpture, and architecture that has won lasting acceptance has invariably dealt with a theme of war, expressly or implicitly, and has expressed the centricity of war to society. The war in question may be national conflict, as in Shakespeare's plays, Beethoven's music, or Goya's paintings, or it may be reflected in the form of religious, social, or moral struggle, as in the work of Dante, Rembrandt, and Bach. Art that cannot be classified as war-oriented is usually described as "sterile," "decadent," and so on. Application of the "war standard" to works of art may often leave room for debate in individual cases, but there is no question of its role as the fundamental determinant of cultural values. Aesthetic and moral standards have a common anthropological origin, in the exaltation of bravery, the willingness to kill and risk death in tribal warfare.

It is also instructive to note that the character of a society's culture has borne a close relationship to its war-making potential, in the context of its times. It is no accident that the current "cultural explosion" in the United States is taking place during an era marked by an unusually rapid advance in weaponry. This relationship is more generally recognized than the literature on the subject would suggest. For example, many artists and writers are now beginning to express concern over the limited creative options they envisage in the warless world they think, or hope, may be soon upon us. They are currently preparing for this possibility by unprecedented experimentation with meaningless forms; their interest in recent years has been increasingly engaged by the abstract pattern, the gratuitous emotion, the random happening, and the unrelated sequence.

The relationship of war to scientific research and discovery is more explicit. War is the principal motivational force for the development of science at every level, from the abstractly conceptual to the narrowly technological. Modern society places a high value on "pure" science, but it is historically inescapable that all the significant discoveries that have been made about the natural world have been inspired by the real or imaginary military necessities of their epochs. The consequences of the discoveries have indeed gone far afield, but war has always provided the basic incentive.

Beginning with the development of iron and steel, and proceeding through the discoveries of the laws of motion and thermodynamics to the age of the atomic particle, the synthetic polymer, and the space capsule, no important scientific advance has not been at least indirectly initiated by an implicit requirement of weaponry. More prosaic examples include the transistor radio (an outgrowth of military communications requirements), the assembly line (from Civil War firearms needs), the steel-frame building (from the steel battleship), the canal lock, and so on. A typical adaptation can be seen in a device as modest as the common lawnmower; it developed from the revolving scythe devised by Leonardo da Vinci to precede a horse-powered vehicle into enemy ranks.

The most direct relationship can be found in medical technology. For example, a giant "walking machine," an amplifier of body motions invented for military use in difficult terrain, is now making it possible for many previously confined to wheelchairs to walk. The Vietnam war alone has led to spectacular improvements in amputation procedures, blood-handling techniques, and surgical logistics. It has stimulated new large-scale research on malaria and other tropical parasite diseases; it is hard to estimate how long this work would otherwise have been delayed, despite its enormous nonmilitary importance to nearly half the world's population.

Other

We have elected to omit from our discussion of the nonmilitary functions of war those we do not consider critical to a transition program. This is not to say they are unimportant, however, but only that they appear to present no special problems for the organization of a peace-oriented social system. They include the following:

War as a general social release. This is a psychosocial function, serving the same purpose for a society as do the holiday, the celebration, and the orgy for the individual—the release and redistribution of undifferentiated tensions. War provides for the periodic necessary readjustment of standards of social behavior (the "moral climate") and for the dissipation of general boredom, one of the most consistently undervalued and unrecognized of social phenomena.

War as a generational stabilizer. This psychological function, served by other behavior patterns in other animals, enables the physically deteriorating older generation to maintain its control of the younger, destroying it if necessary.

War as an ideological clarifier. The dualism that characterizes the traditional dialectic of all branches of philosophy and of stable political relationships stems from war as the prototype of conflict. Except for secondary considerations, there cannot be, to put it as simply as possible, more than two sides to a question because there cannot be more than two sides to a war.

War as the basis for inter-national understanding. Before the development of modern communications, the strategic requirements of war provided the only substantial incentive for the enrichment of one national culture with the achievements of another. Although this is still the case in many inter-national relationships, the function is obsolescent.

We have also forgone extended characterization of those functions we assume to be widely and explicitly recognized. An obvious example is the role of war as controller of the quality and degree of unemployment. This is more than an economic and political subfunction; its sociological, cultural, and ecological aspects are also important, although often teleonomic. But none affect the general problem of substitution. The same is true of certain other functions; those we have included are sufficient to define the scope of the problem.

Theory

The Dread of Woman
Karen Horney
International Journal of Psycho-Analysis, 1932

This well-regarded reviser of Freudianism writes here for a peer professional audience, as footnotes alone indicate, certainly for a much less diverse readership than do our previous two authors. But her generalization is equally far-reaching and her composition more complex. The structure includes a hierarchy of more and less abstract generalizations and cause-and-effect couplings among statements. Moreover, she assumes some other propositions without asserting or supporting them because they are premises of the theory in which she situates her own theory. Fortunately, this is a subject of universal appeal. What gives the essay a personal orientation on it are her psychoanalytic training, her second-generation perspective in the discipline, her particular clinical experience as a therapist, and her perceptions as an individual and a woman.

Observations on a Specific Difference in the Dread Felt by Men and by Women Respectively for the Opposite Sex

In his ballad of *The Diver*, Schiller tells how a squire leaps into a dangerous whirlpool in order to win a woman—at first symbolized by a goblet. Horror-struck, he describes the perils of the deep by which he is doomed to be engulfed:

Yet at length comes a lull o'er the mighty commotion,
As the whirlpool sucks into black smoothness the swell
Of the white-foaming breakers—and cleaves through the ocean
A path that seems winding in darkness to hell.
Round and round whirled the waves—deeper and deeper still driven,
Like a gorge through the mountainous main thunder-riven!

Happy they whom the rose-hues of daylight rejoice,
The air and the sky that to mortals are given!
May the horror below never more find a voice—
Nor man stretch too far the wide mercy of Heaven!
Never more—never more may he lift from the sight
The veil which is woven with Terror and Night!

Below at the foot of the precipice drear,
Spread the glowing, and purple, and pathless Obscure!
A silence of Horror that slept on the ear,
That the eye more appalled might the Horror endure!
Salamander—snake—dragon—vast reptiles that dwell
In the deep, coil'd about the grim jaws of their hell.

(TRANSLATION BY BULWER LYTTON)

The same idea is expressed, though far more pleasantly, in the Song of the Fisherboy in *Wilhelm Tell:*

The clear smiling lake woo'd to bathe in its deep,
A boy on its green shore had laid him to sleep;
Then heard he a melody
Flowing and soft,

"Die Angst vor der Frau Über einen spezifischen Unterschied in der männlichen und weiblichen Angst vor dem anderen Geschlecht," *Intern. Zeitschr. f. Psychoanal.* XVIII (1932), pp. 5–18; *Int. J. Psycho-Anal.* XIII (1932), pp. 348–60. Reprinted with the permission of *The International Journal of Psycho-Analysis.*

And sweet as when angels are singing aloft.
And as thrilling with pleasure he wakes from his rest,
The waters are murmuring over his breast;
And a voice from the deep cries,
"With me thou must go, I charm the young shepherd,
I lure him below."

(TRANSLATION BY THEODORE MARTIN)

Men have never tired of fashioning expressions for the violent force by which man feels himself drawn to the woman, and side by side with his longing, the dread that through her he might die and be undone. I will mention particularly the moving expression of this dread in Heine's poem of the legendary Lorelei, who sits high on the bank of the Rhine and ensnares the boatman with her beauty.

Here once more it is water (representing, like the other "elements," the primal element "woman") that swallows up the man who succumbs to a woman's enchantment. Ulysses had to bid his seamen bind him to the mast in order to escape the allurement and the danger of the sirens. The riddle of the Sphinx can be solved by few, and most of those who attempt it forfeit their lives. The royal palace in fairy tales is adorned with the heads of the suitors who have had the hardihood to try to solve the riddles of the king's beautiful daughter. The goddess Kali[1] dances on the corpses of slain men. Samson, whom no man could conquer, is robbed of his strength by Delilah. Judith beheads Holofernes after giving herself to him. Salome carries the head of John the Baptist on a charger. Witches are burnt because male priests fear the work of the devil in them. Wedekind's "Earth Spirit" destroys every man who succumbs to her charm, not because she is particularly evil, but simply because it is her nature to do so. The series of such instances is infinite; always, everywhere, the man strives to rid himself of his dread of women by objectifying it. "It is not," he says, "that I dread her; it is that she herself is malignant, capable of any crime, a beast of prey, a vampire, a witch, insatiable in her desires. She is the very personification of what is sinister." May not this be one of the principal roots of the whole masculine impulse to creative

---

1. See Daly's account in his article, "Hindumythologie und Kastrationskomplex," *Imago*, Bd. XIII (1927).

work—the never-ending conflict between the man's longing for the woman and his dread of her?[2]

To primitive sensibilities the woman becomes doubly sinister in the presence of the bloody manifestations of her womanhood. Contact with her during menstruation is fatal:[3] men lose their strength, the pastures wither away, the fisherman and the huntsman take nothing. Defloration involves the utmost danger to the man. As Freud shows in "The Taboo of Virginity,"[4] it is the husband in particular who dreads this act. In this work Freud, too, objectifies this anxiety, contenting himself with a reference to the castration-impulses that actually do occur in women. There are two reasons why this is not an adequate explanation of the phenomenon of the taboo itself. In the first place, women do not so universally react to defloration with castration-impulses recognizable as such; these impulses are probably confined to women with a strongly developed masculine attitude. And, secondly, even if defloration invariably aroused destructive impulses in the woman, we should still have to lay bare (as we should do in every individual analysis) the urgent impulses within the man himself which make him view the first—forcible—penetration of the vagina as so perilous an undertaking; so perilous, indeed, that it can be performed with impunity only by a man of might or by a stranger who chooses to risk his life or his manhood for a recompense.

Is it not really remarkable (we ask ourselves in amazement), when one considers the overwhelming mass of this transparent material, that so little recognition and attention are paid to the fact of men's secret dread of women? It is almost more remarkable that women themselves have so long been able to overlook it; I will discuss in detail elsewhere the reasons for their attitude in this connection (i.e., their own anxiety and the impairment of their self-respect). The man on his side has in the first place very obvious strategic reasons for keeping his dread quiet. But he also tries by every means to deny it even to himself. This is the

2. Sachs explains the impulse to artistic creation as the search for companions in guilt. In this, I think, he is right, but he does not seem to me to go deeply enough into the question, since his explanation is one-sided and takes into account only part of the whole personality, namely, the superego. (Sachs, "Gemeinsame Tagträume," *Internationaler Psychoanalytischer Verlag.*)

3. Cf. Daly, "Der Menstruationskomplex," *Imago*, Bd. XIV (1928); and Winterstein, "Die Pubertätsriten der Mädchen und ihre Spuren im Märchen," *Imago*, Bd. XIV (1928).

4. Freud, "The Taboo of Virginity" (1918), *Collected Papers*, Vol. IV.

purpose of the efforts to which we have alluded, to "objectify" it in artistic and scientific creative work. We may conjecture that even his glorification of women has its source not only in his cravings for love, but also in his desire to conceal his dread. A similar relief, however, is also sought and found in the disparagement of women that men often display ostentatiously in their attitudes. The attitude of love and adoration signifies: "There is no need for me to dread a being so wonderful, so beautiful, nay, so saintly." That of disparagement implies: "It would be too ridiculous to dread a creature who, if you take her all round, is such a poor thing."[5] This last way of allaying his anxiety has a special advantage for the man: It helps to support his masculine self-respect. The latter seems to feel itself far more threatened at its very core by the admission of a dread of women than by the admission of dread of a man (the father). The reason why the self-feeling of men is so peculiarly sensitive just in relation to women can only be understood by reference to their early development, to which I will return later.

In analysis this dread of women is revealed quite clearly. Male homosexuality has for its basis, in common indeed with all the other perversions, the desire to escape from the female genital, or to deny its very existence. Freud has shown that this is a fundamental trait in fetishism,[6] in particular; he believes it to be based, however, not on anxiety, but on a feeling of abhorrence due to the absence of the penis in women. I think, however, that even from his account we are absolutely forced to the conclusion that there is anxiety at work as well. What we actually see is dread of the vagina, thinly disguised under the abhorrence. Only *anxiety* is a strong enough motive to hold back from his goal a man whose libido is assuredly urging him on to union with the woman. But Freud's account fails to explain this anxiety. A boy's castration anxiety in relation to his father is not an adequate reason for his dread of a being to whom this punishment has already happened. Besides the dread of the father, there must be a further dread, the object of which is the woman or the female genital. Now this dread of the vagina itself appears

5. I well remember how surprised I was myself the first time I heard the above ideas asserted—by a man—in the shape of a universal proposition. The speaker was Groddeck, who obviously felt that he was stating something quite self-evident when he remarked in conversation, "Of course men are afraid of women." In his writings Groddeck has repeatedly emphasized this fear.

6. Freud, "Fetishism," *Int. J. Psycho-Anal.*, Vol IX (1928).

unmistakably not only in homosexuals and perverts, but also in the dreams of male analysands. All analysts are familiar with dreams of this sort and I need only give the merest outline of them: e.g., a motorcar is rushing along and suddenly falls into a pit and is dashed to pieces; a boat is sailing in a narrow channel and is suddenly sucked into a whirlpool; there is a cellar with uncanny, blood-stained plants and animals; one is climbing a chimney and is in danger of falling and being killed.

Dr. Baumeyer of Dresden[7] allows me to cite a series of experiments that arose out of a chance observation and illustrate this dread of the vagina. The physician was playing ball with the children at a treatment center, and after a time showed them that the ball had a slit in it. She pulled the edges of the slit apart and put her finger in, so that it was held fast by the ball. Of 28 boys whom she asked to do the same, only 6 did it without fear and 8 could not be induced to do it at all. Of 19 girls 9 put their fingers in without a trace of fear; the rest showed a slight uneasiness but none of them serious anxiety.

No doubt the dread of the vagina often conceals itself behind the dread of the father, which is also present; or in the language of the unconscious, behind the dread of the penis in the woman's vagina.[8]

There are two reasons for this. In the first place, as I have already said, masculine self-regard suffers less in this way, and secondly, the dread of the father is more tangible, less uncanny in quality. We might compare it to the difference between the fear of a real enemy and of a ghost. The prominence given to the anxiety relating to the castrating father is therefore tendentious, as Groddeck has shown, for example, in his analysis of the thumb-sucker in *Struwwelpeter*; it is a man who cuts off the thumb, but it is the mother who utters the threat, and the instrument with which it is carried out—the scissors—is a female symbol.

From all this I think it probable that the masculine dread of the woman (the mother) or of the female genital is more deep-

<hr/>

7. The experiments were conducted by Frll. Dr. Hartung at a children's clinic in Dresden.

8. Boehm, "Beiträge zur Psychologie der Homosexualität," *Intern. Zeitschr. f. Psychoanal.*, XI (1925); Melanie Klein, "Early Stages of the Œdipus Conflict," *Int. J. Psycho-Anal.*, Vol. IX (1928); "The Importance of Symbol-Formation in the Development of the Ego," *Int. J. Psycho-Anal.*, Vol. XI (1930); "Infantile Anxiety-Situations reflected in a Work of Art and in the Creative Impulse," *Int. J. Psycho-Anal.*, Vol. X (1929), p. 436.

seated, weighs more heavily, and is usually more energetically repressed than the dread of the man (father), and that the endeavor to find the penis in women represents first and foremost a convulsive attempt to deny the existence of the sinister female genital.

Is there any ontogenetic explanation of this anxiety? Or is it not rather (in human beings) an integral part of masculine existence and behavior? Is any light shed upon it by the state of lethargy—even the death—after mating, which occurs frequently in male animals?[9] Are love and death more closely bound up with one another for the male than for the female, in whom sexual union potentially produces a new life? Does the man feel, side by side with his desire to conquer, a secret longing for extinction in the act of reunion with the woman (mother)? Is it perhaps this longing that underlies the "death-instinct"? And is it his will to live that reacts to it with anxiety?

When we endeavor to understand this anxiety in psychological and ontogenetic terms, we find ourselves rather at a loss if we take our stand on Freud's notion that what distinguishes infantile from adult sexuality is precisely that the vagina remains "undiscovered" for the child. According to that view, we cannot properly speak of a genital primacy; we must rather term it a primacy of the phallus. Hence it would be better to describe the period of infantile genital organization as the "phallic phase."[10] The many recorded remarks of boys at that period of life leave no doubt of the correctness of the observations on which Freud's theory is based. But if we look more closely at the essential characteristics of this phase, we cannot help asking whether his description really sums up infantile genitality as such, in its specific manifestation, or applies only to a relatively later phase of it. Freud states that it is characteristic that the boy's interest is concentrated in a markedly narcissistic manner on his own penis: "The driving force which this male portion of his body will generate later at puberty expresses itself in childhood essentially as an impulsion to inquire into things—as sexual curiosity." A very important part is played by questions as to the existence and size of the phallus in other living beings.

But surely the essence of the phallic impulses proper, starting as they do from organ sensations, is a desire to *penetrate*. That these impulses do exist can hardly be doubted; they manifest

9. Bergmann, *Muttergeist und Erkenntnisgeist*.
10. Freud, "The Infantile Genital Organization of the Libido" (1923), *Collected Papers*, Vol. II.

themselves too plainly in children's games and in the analysis of little children. Again, it would be difficult to say what the boy's sexual wishes in relation to his mother really consisted in if not in these very impulses; or why the object of his masturbation anxiety should be the father as the castrator, were it not that masturbation was largely the autoerotic expression of heterosexual phallic impulses.

In the phallic phase the boy's psychic orientation is predominantly narcissistic; hence the period in which his genital impulses are directed toward an object must be an earlier one. The possibility that they are not directed toward a female genital, of which he instinctively divines the existence, must certainly be considered. In dreams, both of earlier and later life, as well as in symptoms and particular modes of behavior, we find, it is true, representations of coitus that are oral, anal, or sadistic without specific localization. But we cannot take this as a proof of the primacy of corresponding impulses, for we are uncertain whether, or how far, these phenomena already express a displacement from the genital goal proper. At bottom, all that they amount to is to show that a given individual is influenced by specific oral, anal, or sadistic trends. Their evidential value is the less because these representations are always associated with certain affects directed against women, so that we cannot tell whether they may not be essentially the product or the expression of these affects. For instance, the tendency to debase women may express itself in anal representations of the female genital, while oral representations may express anxiety.

But besides all this, there are various reasons why it seems to me improbable that the existence of a specific female opening should remain "undiscovered." On the one hand, of course, a boy will automatically conclude that everyone else is made like himself; but on the other hand his phallic impulses surely bid him instinctively to search for the appropriate opening in the female body—an opening, moreover, that he himself lacks, for the one sex always seeks in the other that which is complementary to it or of a nature different from its own. If we seriously accept Freud's dictum that the sexual theories formed by children are modeled on their own sexual constitution, it must surely mean in the present connection that the boy, urged on by his impulses to penetrate, pictures in fantasy a complementary female organ. And this is just what we should infer from all the material I quoted at the outset in connection with the masculine dread of the female genital.

It is not at all probable that this anxiety dates only from

puberty. At the beginning of that period the anxiety manifests itself quite clearly, if we look behind the often very exiguous façade of boyish pride that conceals it. At puberty a boy's task is obviously not merely to free himself from his incestuous attachment to his mother, but more generally, to master his dread of the whole female sex. His success is as a rule only gradual; first of all he turns his back on girls altogether, and only when his masculinity is fully awakened does it drive him over the threshold of anxiety. But we know that as a rule the conflicts of puberty do but revive, *mutatis mutandis*, conflicts belonging to the early ripening of infantile sexuality and that the course they take is often essentially a faithful copy of a series of earlier experiences. Moreover, the grotesque character of the anxiety, as we meet with it in the symbolism of dreams and literary productions, points unmistakably to the period of early infantile fantasy.

At puberty a normal boy has already acquired a conscious knowledge of the vagina, but what he fears in women is something uncanny, unfamiliar, and mysterious. If the grown man continues to regard woman as the great mystery, in whom is a secret he cannot divine, this feeling of his can only relate ultimately to one thing in her: the mystery of motherhood. Everything else is merely the residue of his dread of this.

What is the origin of this anxiety? What are its characteristics? And what are the factors that cloud the boy's early relations with his mother?

In an article on female sexuality[11] Freud has pointed out the most obvious of these factors: It is the mother who first forbids instinctual activities, because it is she who tends the child in its babyhood. Secondly, the child evidently experiences sadistic impulses against its mother's body,[12] presumably connected with the rage evoked by her prohibitions, and according to the talion principle, this anger has left behind a residue of anxiety. Finally— and this is perhaps the principal point—the specific fate of the genital impulses itself constitutes another such factor. The anatomical differences between the sexes lead to a totally different situation in girls and in boys, and really to understand both their anxiety and the diversity of their anxiety we must take into account first of all *the children's real situation* in the period of their early sexuality. The girls nature as biologically conditioned

11. *Int. J. Psycho-Anal.*, Vol. XI (1930), p. 281.
12. Cf. the work of Melanie Klein, quoted above, to which I think insufficient attention has been paid.

gives her the desire to receive, to take into herself;[13] she feels or knows that her genital is too small for her father's penis and this makes her react to her own genital wishes with direct anxiety; she dreads that if her wishes were fulfilled, she herself or her genital would be destroyed.[14]

The boy, on the other hand, feels or instinctively judges that his penis is much too small for his mother's genital and reacts with the dread of his own inadequacy, of being rejected and derided. Thus his anxiety is located in quite a different quarter from the girl's; his original dread of women is not castration anxiety at all, but a reaction to the menace to his self-respect.[15]

In order that there may be no misunderstanding, let me emphasize that I believe these processes take place purely instinctively on the basis of organ sensations and the tensions of organic needs; in other words, I hold that these reactions would occur even if the girl had never seen her father's penis or the boy his mother's genital, and neither had any sort of intellectual knowledge of the existence of these genitalia.

Because of this reaction on the part of the boy, he is affected in another way and more severely by his frustration at the hands of his mother than is the girl by her experience with her father. A blow is struck at the libidinal impulses in either case. But the girl has a certain consolation in her frustration—she preserves her physical integrity. But the boy is hit in a second sensitive spot—his sense of genital inadequacy, which has presumably accompanied his libidinal desires from the beginning. If we assume that the most general reason for violent anger is the foiling of impulses that at the moment are of vital importance, it follows that the boy's frustration by his mother must arouse a twofold fury in him: first through the thrusting back of his libido upon itself, and secondly, through the wounding of his masculine self-regard. At the same time old resentment springing from pregenital frustrations is probably also made to flare up again. The result is that his phallic impulses to penetrate merge with his anger at frustration, and the impulses take on a sadistic tinge.

Here let me emphasize a point that is often insufficiently brought out in psychoanalytical literature—namely, that we have no reason to assume that these phallic impulses are naturally

13. This is not to be equated with passivity.

14. In another paper I will discuss the girl's situation more fully.

15. I would refer here also to the points I raised in a paper entitled "Das Misstrauen zwischen den Geschlechtern," *Die psychoanalytische Bewegung* (1930).

sadistic and that therefore it is inadmissible, in the absence of specific evidence in each case, to equate "male" with "sadistic," and on similar lines "female" with "masochistic." If the admixture of destructive impulses is really considerable, the mother's genital must, according to the talion principle, become an object of direct anxiety. Thus, if it is first made distasteful to him by its association with wounded self-regard, it will by a secondary process (by way of frustration anger) become an object of castration anxiety. And probably this is very generally reinforced when the boy observes traces of menstruation.

Very often this latter anxiety in its turn leaves a lasting mark on the man's attitude to women, as we learn from the examples already given at random from very different periods and races. But I do not think that it occurs regularly in all men in any considerable degree, and certainly it is not a *distinctive* characteristic of the man's relation to the other sex. Anxiety of this sort strongly resembles, *mutatis mutandis*, anxiety we meet with in women. When in analysis we find it occurring in any noteworthy intensity, the subject is invariably a man whose whole attitude toward women has a markedly neurotic twist.

On the other hand I think that the anxiety connected with his self-respect leaves more or less distinct traces in every man and gives his general attitude toward women a particular stamp that either does not exist in women's attitude to men, or if it does, is acquired secondarily. In other words, it is no integral part of their feminine nature.

We can only grasp the general significance of this male attitude if we study more closely the development of the boy's infantile anxiety, his efforts to overcome it, and the ways in which it manifests itself.

According to my experience, the dread of being rejected and derided is a typical ingredient in the analysis of every man, no matter what his mentality or the structure of his neurosis. The analytic situation and the constant reserve of the woman analyst bring out this anxiety and sensitiveness more clearly than they appear in ordinary life, which gives men plenty of opportunity to escape from these feelings either by avoiding situations calculated to evoke them or by a process of overcompensation. The specific basis of this attitude is hard to detect, because in analysis it is generally concealed by a feminine orientation, for the most part unconscious.[16]

16. Cf. Boehm, "The Femininity Complex in Men," *Int. J. Psycho-Anal.*, Vol. XI (1930).

To judge by my own experience, this latter orientation is no less common, though (for reasons which I will give) less blatant, than the masculine attitude in women. I do not propose to discuss its various sources here; I will only say that I conjecture that the early wound to his self-regard is probably one of the factors liable to disgust the boy with his male role.

His typical reaction to that wound and to the dread of his mother that follows from it is obviously to withdraw his libido from her and to concentrate it on himself and his genital. From the economic point of view this process is doubly advantageous; it enables him to escape from the distressing or anxiety-fraught situation that has developed between himself and his mother, and it restores his masculine self-respect by reactively strengthening his phallic narcissism. The female genital no longer exists for him; the "undiscovered" vagina is a denied vagina. This stage of his development is fully identical with Freud's phallic phase.

Accordingly we must understand the inquiring attitude that dominates this phase and the specific nature of the boy's inquiries as expressing a retreat from the object followed by a narcissistically tinged anxiety.

His first reaction, then, is in the direction of a heightened phallic narcissism. The result is that to the wish to be a woman, which younger boys utter without embarrassment, he now reacts partly with renewed anxiety lest he should not be taken seriously and partly with castration anxiety. Once we realize that masculine castration anxiety is very largely the ego's response to the *wish to be a woman*, we cannot altogether share Freud's conviction that bisexuality manifests itself more clearly in the female than in the male.[17] We must leave it an open question.

A feature of the phallic phase that Freud emphasizes shows up with special clearness the narcissistic scar left by the little boy's relation with his mother: "He behaves as if he had a dim idea that this member might be and should be larger."[18] We must amplify the observation by saying that this behavior begins, indeed, in the phallic phase, but does not cease with it; on the contrary, it is displayed naïvely throughout boyhood and persists later as a deeply hidden anxiety about the size of the subject's penis or his potency, or else as a less concealed pride about them.

17. Freud, "Female Sexuality," *Inter. J. Psycho-Anal.*, Vol. XI (1930), p. 281.
18. Freud, "The Infantile Genital Organization of the Libido," *Collected Papers*, Vol. II.

Now one of the exigencies of the biological differences between the sexes is this: that the man is actually obliged to go on proving his manhood to the woman. There is no analogous necessity for her. Even if she is frigid, she can engage in sexual intercourse and conceive and bear a child. She performs her part by merely *being*, without any *doing*—a fact that has always filled men with admiration and resentment. The man on the other hand has to *do* something in order to fulfill himself. The ideal of "efficiency" is a typical masculine ideal.

This is probably the fundamental reason why, when we analyze women who dread their masculine tendencies, we always find that they unconsciously regard ambition and achievement as attributes of the male, in spite of the great enlargement of women's sphere of activity in real life.

In sexual life itself we see how the simple craving of love that drives men to women is very often overshadowed by their overwhelming inner compulsion to prove their manhood again and again to themselves and others. A man of this type in its more extreme form has therefore one interest only: to conquer. His aim is to have "possessed" many women, and the most beautiful and most sought-after women. We find a remarkable mixture of this narcissistic overcompensation and of surviving anxiety in those men who, while wanting to make conquests, are very indignant with a woman who takes their intentions too seriously, or who cherish a lifelong gratitude to her if she spares them any further proof of their manhood.

Another way of averting the soreness of the narcissistic scar is by adopting the attitude described by Freud as the propensity to debase the love object.[19] If a man does not desire any woman who is his equal or even his superior—may it not be that he is protecting his threatened self-regard in accordance with that most useful principle of sour grapes? From the prostitute or the woman of easy virtue one need fear no rejection, and no demands in the sexual, ethical, or intellectual sphere. One can feel oneself the superior.[20]

This brings us to a third way, the most important and the most

19. Freud, "Contributions to the Psychology of Love," *Collected Papers,* Vol. IV.

20. This does not detract from the importance of the other forces that drive men to prostitutes, which have been described by Freud in his "Contributions to the Psychology of Love," *Collected Papers,* Vol. IV; and by Boehm in his "Beiträge zur Psychologie der Homosexualität, *Intern. Zeitschr. f. Psychoanal.,* Bd. VI (1920) and Bd. VIII (1922).

ominous in its cultural consequences: that of diminishing the self-respect of the woman. I think that I have shown that men's disparagement of women is based upon a definite psychic trend toward disparaging them—a tendency rooted in the man's psychic reactions to certain given biological facts, as might be expected of a mental attitude so widespread and so obstinately maintained. The view that women are infantile and emotional creatures, and as such, incapable of responsibility and independence is the work of the masculine tendency to lower women's self-respect. When men justify such an attitude by pointing out that a very large number of women really do correspond to this description, we must consider whether this type of woman has not been cultivated by a systematic selection on the part of men. The important point is not that individual minds of greater or lesser caliber, from Aristotle to Moebius, have expended an astonishing amount of energy and intellectual capacity in proving the superiority of the masculine principle. What really counts is the fact that the ever-precarious self-respect of the "average man" causes him over and over again to choose a feminine type that is infantile, nonmaternal, and hysterical, and by so doing to expose each new generation to the influence of such women.

Hypothesis

The Serpent Power
John Michell
from *The New View over Atlantis*, 1969, 1983

"Theory" has a double sense in common parlance. It may mean a reasonably supported explanatory thought structure, like the theory of evolution, or it may mean just a speculation. But strictly speaking, a less proven, more speculative thesis should be called a hypothesis. Archaeologist John Michell proposes here an extremely broad hypothesis for which he adduces some evidence but which invites further proof from the many disciplines that would have to be involved. The higher the abstraction level

of a proposition the more areas of knowledge and expertise will it touch upon, and the more evidence will it require. The abstracter the speculation, the more it depends on previous abstractions that already encompass much time and space. These successive distillations of distillations increase the amount of speculation, because they become increasingly difficult to prove by tangible means. At a certain altitude, science abandons ordinary language, which is too sense-besotted and ambiguous, and resorts to the purely logical language of mathematics, which has its own hierarchy of propositions meta to each other and applying beneath themselves.

Thus, put in the most compressed way, this survey of nonfiction has covered that range of the symbolic spectrum that we call history and science and left us on the verge of mathematics. Starting on the threshold between oral and written language, dialog and monolog, we have traversed that range of discourse corresponding to knowledge-making that still refers to the physical world. Beyond lies the special discourse of language that refers only to itself.

Our final sample remains well within common discourse, but the ultimately cosmic scope of its subject, its crossing of disciplines, its combining of theses into a theory—a theory that for now remains a hypothesis—may suggest the highest reaches of knowledge-making that continue beyond the verbal spectrum.

Only within recent years, since the development of universal communications allowed us to compare the antiquities of our own countries with those of others, have we been able to see the extent of the vast ruin within which we all live. If we ignore all alterations to the landscape arising within the last three thousand years and consider the world as it must have looked in prehistoric times, the pattern that emerges is one so incompatible with our idea of civilization that it is easy entirely to miss its significance. For what we find is this.

A great scientific instrument lies sprawled over the entire surface of the globe. At some period, thousands of years ago, almost every corner of the world was visited by people with a particular task to accomplish. With the help of some remarkable power, by which they could cut and raise enormous blocks of stone, these men created vast astronomical instruments, circles of erect pillars, pyramids, underground tunnels, cyclopean stone platforms, all linked together by a network of tracks and alignments, whose course from horizon to horizon was marked by stones, mounds and earthworks. W. J. Perry, in *The Children of the Sun*, traces the progress of these people across the Pacific, pointing out as an example of their amazing achievements the number of remote, uninhabitable islands bearing the ruins of great laborious pyramids and megalithic structures. Whether this enormous surge of energy, which within a few hundred years covered the whole earth with stone circles and earthworks, was released from one group or race, or whether it flowed spontaneously as a wave of universal inspiration is not yet clear. It appears to some that while the stone circles of northern Europe were built by the native inhabitants, those of Polynesia were the work of prehistoric missionaries. Yet Stonehenge, the latest and most perfect circle in Britain, has more in common with Crete than the native tradition, while local variations in the design and operation of astronomical structures indicate that every race made its own contribution towards a universal civilization.

No one knows how the world-wide task was achieved, or why these people outside the range of written history devoted their skills and resources to the construction of a celestial pattern of stone and earthworks across the earth's surface. The key to the mystery must surely lie in the study of that great pattern itself and its relation to the subtle forces of the landscape.

When Alfred Watkins experienced his extraordinary moment of clairvoyance in which the veins of the countryside appeared to stand out across the plains and hills, he saw or gained knowledge of something beyond the range of normal vision. We know that the whole surface of the earth is washed by a flow of energy known as the magnetic field. Like all other heavenly bodies, the earth is a great magnet, the strength and direction of its currents influenced by many factors including the proximity and relative positions of the other spheres in the solar system, chiefly the sun and moon. Other influences on the strength and activity of the magnetic current derive from the composition of the ground over which it passes. Over firm, flat country it is placid and regular, while over rocky, broken land it becomes violent and disturbed, reacting with the elements to cause magnetic storms and, in northern regions, auroras and polar lights. In the neighbourhood of geological faults the magnetic flow becomes particularly agitated due to the springs of current which at these places burst through the earth's crust. Government stations all over the world measure the periodic and cyclical variations in the magnetic field chiefly to provide accurate figures for correcting the compass, and there are three such stations in Britain.

Yet although the flow of terrestrial magnetism is closely watched, and a certain amount is known about the various factors that influence its rhythm, notably the 27-day intervals of its quiet and disturbed periods, and although its relationship to the sunspot cycle and hence to meteorological conditions is an established fact, little is understood about its nature and effect. Yet all the evidence from the remote past points to the conclusion that the earth's natural magnetism was not only known to men some thousands of years ago but provided them with a source of energy and inspiration to which their whole civilization was tuned.

A map of Britain showing the distribution of prehistoric habitation is almost an exact reversal of one giving modern population density. The mountains of Scotland and Wales, the lonely islands, the rocky peninsula of Cornwall, the barren deserts of Dartmoor and the Derbyshire Peak are thick with traces of prehistoric settlement. Yet the fertile areas are little marked. The places where we now live, the plains and valleys, were less settled than the inaccessible wastes that today we find uninhabitable. The old belief, still conditioning many of our attitudes towards prehistory, was that before the Celtic migration the inhabitants of Britain were benighted savages, forced to cower on the hilltops for fear of wild beasts and predatory neighbours. The elaborate cultivation terraces that ridge the slopes of the southern hills were seen as the cramped meadows of people living in a perpetual desperate state of siege. Our recently acquired knowledge of the scientific and resourceful civilization that flourished in Britain long before the arrival of the Celtic Druids makes this picture seem absurd. Yet although the figure of the savage ancient Briton is merely a picturesque myth, the theories that depend upon it are, for lack of any better, still widely held. The sites of their magical science are usually classified as of defensive or ritual significance, a notion which is both vague and inaccurate. In the first place, it is obvious that many prehistoric earthworks were conceived as something other than military structures. Often they are so extensive that an impossibly large army would be needed to man the ramparts of what are still known as hill forts. Some are linear and enclose no fortified position. The vast scale of prehistoric engineering is not yet generally recognized. The Dorsetshire cursus is a great double earthwork over six miles long; others in Ireland stretch even further, yet their purpose is quite unknown. All over the landscape walls of earth define ancient trackways, encircle hilltops and shape mountain ridges, forming a great many of the field boundaries still in use today. Many earth rings stand outside rather than within a moat; others were never more than a foot or so in height. In neither case could they serve a military purpose. The fact that some prehistoric earthworks provided ready-made fortifications at the time of the Roman invasion has no more relevance to their true meaning than the discovery that churches are frequently adapted as strongholds during modern street warfare. In any case the existence in prehistoric times of closely linked, intercommunicating centres, engaged in the same scientific programme from one end of the country to the other, can only indicate that the various communities lived together in a state of peaceful cooperation where elaborate fortifications would be wholly unnecessary. These monuments are not then purely defensive, and the explanation that they were made for ritual purposes is merely another way of saying that their purpose and use are unknown.

Walking along the Sussex downs, or across any of the high ridges that stand above the southern plains, one has entered a world different in many ways from that which lies below it. The poetic image of the hills calling to one another across the valleys is highly evocative, and there are moments when it is impossible not to become aware of the direct truth which it expresses. Major Tyler described his impression that the site of the church at Walkhampton was in some way communicating with the rock of Brentor church visible far across Dartmoor. To stand on the hilltop at Cerne Abbas in Dorset above the head of the old naked giant, cut into the sloping turf, is to experience the definite sensation of a difference in quality between the wild elevated world of prehistoric habitation and the present village in the quiet secluded valley below with its pretty thatched cottages and mediaeval church. In the same way there is no comparison between the comfortable intimate atmosphere of a Devon village sheltering on the edge of Dartmoor and that of the elemental country high up in the moor, still thickly covered with the remains of prehistoric settlement.

We have no means of expressing, other than in aesthetic terms, what it is that makes one part of the country seem different from another. We speak vaguely of a certain spot being picturesque, powerful and stimulating, or peaceful and soothing. Yet the Chinese geomancers had a definite standard by which the quality of a place could be measured and judged. They reckoned every site in terms of the current they called the dragon force; and, from what we know of the characteristics they attributed to this current, it seems they could only have been referring to the mysterious stream of terrestrial magnetism about which we now know so little. The geomancer sets out to read the hidden character of the countryside, combining his terrestrial observations with an astrological interpretation of the prevailing celestial influences. His information, it seems, is gained by astronomy and by use of the magnetic compass; and these are precisely the means by which the earth's magnetic field is measured today.

The strength and direction of the current varies according to the certain phases of the sun and moon. The sun imposes a daily rhythm modified by other influences including that of the lunar cycle, for the moon exerts the same influence upon this invisible flow as it does on the tides. The full moon produces a marked increase in magnetic activity around noon with a quiet period just before sunset. The effects of the other bodies on the flow of current has not yet been estimated but J. A. Fleming remarks in *Terrestrial Magnetism*, 'It is but natural to infer that a similar influence emanates from the planets or from the distant stars.'

Of all the astronomical events that influence the earth's magnetic field the most dramatic is an eclipse of the sun or moon. When this takes place, the magnetic activity normally stimulated by the eclipsed body greatly diminishes, with considerable effect on the regular flow of terrestrial current. An eclipse of the moon has no apparent physical influence on the earth other than in the effect it produces on the level of terrestrial magnetism. It may well be significant therefore that the function of many of the prehistoric stone observatories of Britain and elsewhere was the accurate prediction of lunar eclipses.

The methods used were highly ingenious and evolved. Professor Fred Hoyle, who confirmed Hawkins's discovery that the Aubrey holes at Stonehenge formed a perfect eclipse predictor, remarked that until he investigated its use he was unaware that it was possible to achieve such results given only the resources of 1850 B.C. Much of the astronomical information which Stonehenge was built to gather could have had relevance only to the prediction of lunar eclipses, and the circle of Aubrey holes seems to have been constructed to mark the 56-year cycle in which these events take place. Many other stone circles were used for the most delicate lunar observation. The complicated cycles of the moon include a periodic deviation of only 0.9° from its regular course, a feature not rediscovered in modern time until observed by Tycho Brahé in the seventeenth century. This minute deviation was closely watched in Britain 4000 years ago at stone circles from which the moon crossing the horizon could be measured against the slope of a distant peak. The most perfect effects were obtained in the Hebrides and the wild parts of western Scotland where the profile of the horizon was shaped and marked to define the path of the setting moon. The extraordinary importance attached to this insignificant tremor in the moon's progress could only have arisen from the recognition that it gives warning of a possible lunar eclipse. Only when the moon is near the higher limit of its periodic deviation is it necessary to make further observations to discover whether an eclipse is imminent.

No plausible explanation has ever been put forward for the quite remarkable interest which prehistoric men showed in acquiring advance warning of an approaching eclipse. But if their science had any meaning at all, they must have had a purpose in directing so much of their effort towards this end. From the evidence of old beliefs and legends it appears that an eclipse is traditionally an event to be feared, against whose effects certain precautions should be taken. It is inconceivable that the ancient astronomers with their highly advanced observational science and cosmology could have been ignorant of the circumstances in which eclipses occur, and these familiar and predictable events could hardly have produced merely unreasoned or superstitious terror in those who understand their exact nature and cause. Yet the prehistoric dread of eclipses has survived in many parts of the world up to the present day. There must have been some good reason why, 4000 years ago, people were nervous of eclipses and took extreme care to gain warning of their approach. The only physical effect they could possibly have anticipated was the sudden interruption to the even flow of the terrestrial magnetic current, for this is the one way in which an eclipse affects proceedings on earth.

The Chinese, as we have seen, sited every building and tomb by reference to the paths taken by dragons across the face of the country, and traces of the same practice can be found in every part of the world. African missionaries are still advised by their native followers that certain sites are suitable for a church while others would be unfavourable or disastrous. There are many stories from Hawaii and Polynesia of the foolishness of the first Christian priests who insisted on building their churches at random instead of on their appropriate sites and thereby brought misfortune to themselves and their cause. The lines of dragon current, by which the natural spiritual centres can be located, are determined partly astronomically by means of standing stones and other observational devices and partly by an interpretation of the magnetic or inspirational character of the countryside. There can be no doubt that the dragon current refers to some natural flow of force, related to the earth's magnetic field.

Many of the greatest works of the megalithic builders involve the construction of a hidden chamber set deep within the earth or at the heart of some great artificial edifice. In Ireland the chambers of New Grange and Knowth are among the finest examples. The huge mounds that cover these secret rooms are not merely piles of earth heaped up at random. They are carefully and purposely constructed in a way which bears direct comparison with Wilhelm Reich's energy accumulator. The chamber itself is lined with stone covered with a layer of turf and with successive layers of clay and sod. These layers are carefully built up, different types and colours of clay being used at each stage. Finally the whole structure is buried under a great mound of earth.

Almost every megalithic site includes at least one such buried chamber. In Ireland narrow entrances to stone lined underground pits and galleries are found at the centre of ringed earthwork enclosures or raths. These artificial caverns, known as souterrains, or in Cornwall as fogous, are found with local variations in many parts of the world. Their entrances are frequently orientated towards a significant astronomical declination or aligned upon a well-marked ley. This is particularly noticeable in the case of long barrows and fogous, and the clearest example is the southern entrance to New Grange, from which extends a visible alignment of standing stone and earth mound.

The purpose of these underground structures has never been satisfactorily explained. Various suggestions have been put forward that they were used for storage, burial, refuge, religious ceremonies or habitation, but no one interpretation of their purpose holds good for them all. Yet from the similarity of the principles behind their construction it is evident that they are all in some way based on an identical plan. As is the case with stone circles, great care was exercised in the selection of particular building materials, various special types of clay and stone being transported from considerable distances across country. The bluestones, of which at Stonehenge there are three distinct types, were originally quarried in the Prescelly Mountains of South Wales over a hundred miles away. Theories have been put forward to explain how these great stones were carried from Wales to Wiltshire, but no one can say why this task was considered necessary, for there is no lack of good local stone on Salisbury Plain. Obviously the bluestones possess some quality which makes their presence essential to the ultimate purpose of Stonehenge. The use of foreign stones and clay from distant beds in the construction of the mound-covered chamber at New Grange emphasizes the importance which the megalith builders attached to the selection of their materials, presumably for some practical reason connected with their elemental science.

Australian Aborigines erect stone circles as instruments of divination, and many other of their practices indicate that they once shared with the Druids of Britain a system of natural magic derived from a great universal civilization. They still remember the mythological routes which, like the leys of Britain and the dragon paths of China, run in straight lines across their continent, linking the holy places and centres of ritual.

In 1960 Mr. Charles Mountford travelled for three hundred miles across the Central Australian deserts with a group of native men on a seasonal journey to reanimate the spirit of the sacred centres along certain lines. He found that each tribe looks after its own stretches of line, visiting the centres at the appropriate season, at each centre singing of a local episode in the history of creation. The successive rituals form what the Aboriginals call a 'line of songs', woven between the geomantic centres of their landscape. In his book *Winbaraku and the Myth of Jarapiri*, Mr. Mountford gives the reason for these seasonal journeys, 'It is an aboriginal belief that every food, plant and animal . . . has an increase centre where a performance of the proper rituals will release the life essence or *kurunba* of that particular plant or animal, and thereby bring about its increase.'

These centres, all scenes of a certain incident in the great poem that describes the creation of life, are marked by some natural feature, a hill, rock or spring. Paintings on the rock walls, continually restored, show the undulating serpent, symbol of the current of life energy; and various sacred objects hidden nearby are decorated with a plan of the serpent's route across the landscape. The aborigines say that it is not the paintings themselves that procure the release of life essence but the rock on which they are drawn. It is the energy from these rocks that creates rain and fertilizes plants and animals. The paintings and ritual songs stimulate its flow and benefit the creatures with which the current of a particular spot is associated.

Here again we find the belief that various kinds of rock have certain peculiar qualities, each creating its own distinctive form of energy. The Aborigines' rituals are but the feeble reflection of a former system of magic and natural science; yet evidently they retain something of their old power, for, where they are allowed to lapse, the Aborigines lose their ability to sustain life in the bitter deserts of their native land. The discoveries of Rudolf Steiner, particularly those which he presented in his lectures on agriculture, do much to confirm their magical view of nature and the life force. Steiner's experiments revealed the extent to which planetary influences affect not only the magnetic currents at the earth's surface, but the layers of mineral ore deep below. The minerals within their rocks are never still or inactive, but are subject to regular cycles of motion in accordance with the orbits of the particular planet to which they chiefly respond. At certain seasons they become charged with energy which they gradually release into the soil, and this allows seeds to germinate and stimulates vegetable growth. Steiner stressed the importance of planting at a time when the celestial influence is waning, so that the seed has time to settle into the earth before becoming exposed to the recurring cycle of fertilizing energy acting through the earth's minerals.

Few take seriously the Aborigines' claim that by their invocations they are encouraging the flow of life essence, for the extent to which the influence of its native human inhabitants can affect the fertility of a country is a question now hardly considered. That the healthy growth of plants can be stimulated by music is a fact proved by repeated experiments. In England, since the process of farming became mechanized and large areas of growing corn are hardly visited before the harvest, individual farmers have noticed that the crops in outlying fields are often less abundant than those near the farmhouse. Whether or not this is so, no one can have failed to notice the signs of a blight slowly covering the countryside. The disappearance of butterflies, the considerable decrease in the numbers of bees, wasps and other insects, the absence of certain once familiar birds and wild flowers, the lowered resistance to disease of trees such as oaks and elms, all these are symptoms of vital stagnation. Not only in the remote parts of Wales and Scotland is it possible to walk for miles through beautiful and once populous country now utterly deserted. Many parts of the rich agricultural land of southern England are almost equally lonely as machines replace the indigenous labourers. The seasonal feasts and dragon processions, deriving from the same primeval source as the serpent ceremonies of the Australian aborigines, are no longer held, and, though this may be taken merely as the poetic expression of a widely acknowledged phenomenon, something of the abundant spirit of the countryside has died with them, as if in consequence of a magic rite no longer performed. So many unexpected factors have been found by experiment to stimulate or inhibit growth, and so little is known about the true nature of its development, that we can hardly exclude the possibility that rituals producing vibrations of music and human magnetism may affect it to a far greater extent than is yet recognized.

The posthumous appearance of Mr. Guy Underwood's *The Pattern of the Past* has provided further clues to the nature of the mysterious earth currents, which inspired the former civilization. Mr. Underwood was both an archaeologist and a dowser. Through the use of a sensitive divining rod of his own design he was able to achieve great precision in tracing the course of that force to which dowsers respond. In the course of his work he made the remarkable discovery that the entire geographical arrangement of prehistoric Britain coincides with the lines and centres of the subterranean influence. Every stone circle has at its centre a strong source of energy, referred to by Underwood as a blind spring, and the individual standing stones mark the paths and spirals of underground streams, cracks or other features associated with intensified magnetism. Underwood distinguishes between three different types of current, one emanating from underground flowing water and two others, aquastats and track lines, whose nature is not altogether certain, but which frequently follow the course of old tracks, linear earthworks, ancient banks and boundaries. The current that runs along these lines is everywhere related to the traces of prehistoric engineering, to lines of standing stones and earth ridges. Its course, therefore, has evidently remained constant for thousands of years although, according to Underwood, the direction of its flow varies with the phases of the moon.

The practice of locating sacred centres in accordance with the flow of terrestrial magnetic current was not confined to prehistoric times, for it appears that every Christian church was similarly sited. The orientation of a church, even its dimensions and architectural plan, was determined by the lines of current, of which the strongest spring is frequently located directly beneath the tower. At this spot the celestial influences, attracted by the spire, combine with the terrestrial force to produce the fusion.

It becomes apparent that the prehistoric leys and dragon paths of Britain are indeed lines of the earth current. And the most remarkable feature of the whole system is that the paths of underground streams or of magnetic flow are not naturally straight; they spiral and undulate like surface rivers or currents of air; yet the currents that follow prehistoric alignments are as direct and regular below ground as are the leys on the surface. The magnetic centres lie in straight rows across the country with a precision that characterizes human construction rather than the work of nature. In other words, the present pattern of the earth currents in Britain must be of artificial origin.

There is, of course, no principle openly recognized today which can explain for what purpose this great work was undertaken. We neither understand the exact nature of the terrestrial magnetic current, nor do we know of any way in which its flow can be regulated. Yet we can be certain that this force, formerly identified with the earth spirit and the mystic serpent, provided the power and inspiration by which the ancient civilization was sustained. The mysteries and divinations of the Druids were founded upon the secret of the spiritual paths. Certain trees and plants were held sacred; mistletoe, the yew tree and the thorn for example; and these, Underwood finds, are invariably to be found growing over a blind spring or at a centre of magnetic influence. Such places are chosen by birds for building their nests, by animals for giving birth. Cows standing on an old mound or barrow are attracted by the emanating current, the centre of which coincides with the monument. Farmers, noticing their cattle gathering round a prehistoric stone, suppose it originally to have been put up for their convenience as a rubbing post. Yet it is not the stone itself that appeals to the animals, but the hidden spring over which it was erected. Migrating birds, whose flights were closely observed, by the natural magicians of antiquity, follow lines of magnetic current; so do animals and insects. The signs and portents by which the auspicious sites for churches and tombs were once located, were those that indicate the spots of inherent sanctity, discernible through observation of nature, the interpretation of growth and movement.

The arts of divination, by which the natural centres and lines of the sacred current may be discerned, were formerly practised in connection with the universal science of spiritual engineering. In the first place the lines were straightened to conform to a system of regular geometry. Underwood discovered that the forms of prehistoric structures are repeated underground in the rings, spirals and straight channels of the magnetic current. He concludes that stones and earthworks were placed to mark the subterranean flow. Yet it is evident from his examples that the monumental achievements of the prehistoric builders were not intended merely to mark the natural channels. For where, as at Stonehenge, stones have fallen or moved from their original position, the current has shifted with them. Moreover, Underwood finds that the present outlines of the White Horse, cut into the chalk face of the Berkshire Downs, also follow the lines of influences discernable by dowsers. It has been shown by aerial photographs, however, that the White Horse no longer occupies its original position, erosion of the turf over the centuries having caused it to move some distance down the hill. It can therefore be inferred that in some way the pattern of structures on the surface of the earth affects the course of the subterranean flow. The massive works of the prehistoric landscape architects may have determined rather than marked the paths of current.

The nature of this current, subtle, omnipresent, yet ever indefinable in terms of the dimensions apparent to our senses, is at least as puzzling for modern physicists as it was for their predecessors, the magicians. The phenomenon, described by Victorian scientists as the Ether, now considered rather as a manifestation of the relationship between space and time, has the same identity as that force through which magicians attempted to produce physical effects by means of mental and specific ritual processes.